THE BIG BOOK OF HOME LEARNING
Volume Two: Preschool & Elementary

Also by Mary Pride:

The Way Home
All the Way Home
Schoolproof
The Child Abuse Industry
Baby Doe
The Better Butter Battle
The Greenie
Too Many Chickens

With Paul deParrie:

Unholy Sacrifices of the New Age
Ancient Empires of the New Age

THE
BIG
BOOK
OF
HOME
LEARNING

Volume Two: Preschool & Elementary

Mary Pride

Crossway Books • Wheaton, Illinois
A Division of Good News Publishers

The Big Book of Home Learning: Volume 2.

Copyright © 1991 by Mary Pride.
Published by Crossway Books, a division of
Good News Publishers, 1300 Crescent Street, Wheaton, Illinois 60187.

Cover Design by Mark Schramm.
Interior Design by Mark Schramm and Mary Pride, based on the
original concept by Karen L. Mulder.
Layout by Bill Pride and Mary Pride.
Cover illustration by Guy Wolek.

First printing, 1990.

Printed in the United States of America

Library of Congress Cataloging-in-Publication Data
Pride, Mary
    Big book of home learning / Mary Pride
        v.   cm.
    Includes bibliographic references.
    Contents: v. 1. Getting started — v. 2. Preschool and elementary —
v. 3. Teen and adult — v. 4. Afterschooling and extras.
    1. Home schooling—United States. 2. Home schooling—United
States—Curricula. 3. Education—United States—Parent
participation. 4. Child rearing—United States I. Title.
LC40.P75 1990   649'.68 ' 0973—dc20   89-81254
ISBN 0-89107-549-6 (v. 2)

99	98	97	96	95	94	93	92	91
15	14	13	12	11	10	9	8	7	6	5	4	3	2

TABLE OF CONTENTS

INTRODUCTION

"Mommy, please read to me!" "Daddy, show me how to do that!" From the beginning of time, children have wheedled their parents into teaching them things the children wanted to know.

Then someone invented school . . . and suddenly kids discovered that they didn't really want to learn anything any more!

Well, that's not *exactly* how it happened. Still, it's smart for us parents nowadays not to rely solely on the public (or even private) school system to teach our children everything they need to know. For one thing, God never gave schools that job. For another thing (and I know you already know all about this), public schools today are failing rather spectacularly to fulfill these enormous expectations. I'm not going to dwell on the reasons for that, other than to merely hint that giving more money to the same people who caused the mess is *not* terribly bright. We don't need more of the same; we need quite a bit less of it. On the other hand, you and I didn't cause the mess—we're clean. (This is also true of the kind of teacher who is willing to read this book!) So we're the logical people to clean things up.

Does that mean becoming a full-time educational revolutionary? Heavens no. It just means cleaning up the mess in front of our own front doors and in our own classrooms.

The good news is that you don't need to move to the country's best school district, get elected to your local school board, or buy stock in a textbook company in order to positively influence American education. You can positively influence *your own children's* education, starting right now, and without waiting for permission from the state textbook approval committee. It's fun, it's easy, and your kids will love you for it. All you need is access to some good resources, and you're holding that in your hands. There's some mighty fine programs out there; with the teensiest little bit of effort you can buy or put together a preschool and elementary program that will beat anything your local school can scrape together.

In the three other volumes of this series you will find resources for getting started with home education, resources for teens and adults, and "fun stuff" for after-schooling. This volume is dedicated to the little kids, from the wide-eyed newborn to the rough 'n ready preteen turning cartwheels on the lawn!

Since this is the Preschool and Elementary volume, I have limited it to resources at the typical skill level of that age group in modern American public schools. However, be prepared for the fact that home-taught children tend to be ready for teen and adult resources years before they are actually teenagers. My six-year-old has read *Robinson Crusoe,* and my 10-year-old has read *David Copperfield*—totally without pressure from me, I might add. The books were on our shelves, and they decided on their own that they wanted to read them. Similarly, Ted has been doing algebra since he was nine years old, and both he and eight-year-old Joseph are learning to type. I'm not saying that our young children interact with great literature on the same level as an adult would, or that they mature by the age of seven if they are taught at home, but that we must be careful not to dumb down our expectations to what is currently expected of children. Children are capable of learning a lot more than we give them credit for. This is not a brief for superbabies—just a gentle hint that you might find some items of interest in the *Teen & Adult* volume of this series, even before your children are technically teens!

Our nation may be educationally at risk, as the experts inform us, but our kids still can be winners. All they need are the right resources and a little loving teaching.

Go for it!

HOW TO USE THIS BOOK

You know how to read a resource book. Just turn to the section that interests you and browse through the reviews.

Well, guess what?

You can do the same thing with this book!

The editors and I have, however, incorporated a few innovative features that, we hope, will make each volume of *The Big Book of Home Learning* more useful than the average resource book.

If you'll flip to the Index of Suppliers you can see that it is more than just names with addresses attached. We're added all sorts of helpful information: toll-free telephone numbers for ordering, fax numbers, best times of day to call, methods of payment allowed, refund policy, whether or not the supplier has a free brochure or catalog and what it costs if it *isn't* free, plus a brief description of the supplier's product line.

It is easy to find the address of any given company. Instead of searching through a chapter to find the company, as you have to when full addresses are given in the text, just flip to the index.

What all this means is that you can relax and enjoy *The Big Book of Home Learning* without having to write down reams of information about every product that interests you. Just jot down the name of the supplier, the name of the item, and its price on a handy index card or Post-It™. When you get your whole list together, then you can turn to the index and highlight or underline the companies you intend to contact. Stick the card you were taking notes on in the index and go your merry way. When you are ready to sit down and send away for catalogs, or to call up and order, all the addresses are in one convenient location and you have all the item names and prices handy, too. And you can always find any item whose review you want to reread by turning to the General Index.

The information in *The Big Book of Home Learning* is as current and up to date as we could possibly make it. After the reviews were written, both they and the index information were sent back to the suppliers for verification. Even so, *it is always wise to write or call the supplier to check on prices before ordering.* The prices in this book are included to help you compare different products for value and are not permanently guaranteed. Prices go up and down. Both you and the supplier will feel better if the supplier does not have to return your order because the check you enclosed was not for the right amount.

The four volumes of this third edition of *The Big Book of Home Learning* are not only bigger than the two volumes of the previous edition; we hope they are better as well. Over some product reviews you will see the heading, "**NEW****." This means you are looking at a new review, not necessarily a new product. We decided to highlight the new reviews in this way, so that readers of previous editions can immediately turn to the new items. Products that have undergone significant revision are also highlighted as "updated" or "improved." Product reviews that are essentially the same, except for new prices, have no special headings. All prices and reviews have been updated, and the Suppliers' Index now includes fax numbers and foreign suppliers. We have several hundred new suppliers and over a thousand new products reviewed. All this is laid out in a way that should make it easy for you to instantly find the resources you need in any school or afterschool subject area.

And the best news of all—the products themselves are better! I keep telling you, people, that education suppliers are listening to you! This edition includes products that are better, more colorful, more educationally sound, simpler to use, and even (sometimes) cheaper than ever before.

So if you need to learn more about education, to set up a home education program (whether home school or afterschool), or to find out what's happening in packaged home-schooling curriculum—turn to Volume One.

If you are looking for resources for a preschooler or elementary-level child in the basic school subjects—you're in the right place right now.

If you need more advanced resources at the junior high, high school, or adult level—turn to Volume Three. (Most home-taught children are ready for this in their preteens.)

And if you are looking for the resources to round out your family's education, and want to have some fun—check out Volume Four.

All four volumes have been designed for the everyday, normal reader. I'm assuming that you are no more interested in boring textbooks and tedious worksheets than I am. I do review quite a few fine books and workbooks, but only a relatively few (generally non-public school) textbooks. The reason is that the textbook approval process has been captured by special interest factions, and the resulting books are not only inaccurate but dull, dull, dull. Happily, there are lots of alternatives. You'll find lots of posters, videos, and make-it-yourself kits throughout each volume, along with the better traditional resources, including some revived classics from yesteryear. How about learning history through historical biographies, songs, and time lines, for instance? Simply reading about what's available in all these areas is an education in itself.

One last note. This book would not have been possible without the active cooperation of many of the companies listed. Those who supplied me with samples and free catalogs bravely ran the risks of review, and I have not hesitated to point out their products' warts. I would like them to feel they gained more than a critical going-over by their generosity. Both the publisher and I would be grateful if you would mention *The Big Book of Home Learning* when you contact a supplier whose product is mentioned here.

PRESCHOOL
& KINDERGARTEN

CHAPTER ONE

PRESCHOOL AT HOME

S ee Dick run! Happy, happy Dick. Dick is at home. *See Dick play. See Dick do things with Mom. Dick can do his ABC! Dick can count . . . one, two, three! See Dad bounce Dick on his knee! Glad Dad! Glad Mom! Glad Dick!*

See Dick sit! Dick is at preschool. Work, Dick, work! No Mom. No Dad. Just Dick and Teacher and twenty other kids. No free time for Dick. No time to think and think. No tastes of cookie batter. No time for lots of questions. Keep it up for 14 years, Dick!

Have you read those articles about the lengths to which yuppy parents go in order to get their child into the "right" preschool? Parents fight and claw to get Junior into Ye Snobbe Childe Academy, and are devastated if Junior doesn't pass the stiff admission test (at age three, yet!) Yet the only reason Ye Snobbe enjoys such a good reputation is that they are careful to take only children who would succeed no matter *where* they are taught. It takes no talent to teach Mozart music, or Rembrandt painting. The test of a good preschool program is its ability to succeed with kids who *aren't* in the 99th percentile already.

It just so happens that I know of a dynamite preschool with a one-to-one teacher/student ratio. The teachers truly love the students, and even spend their own money on classroom supplies. What is even more rare, the students truly love the teachers and were

born wanting to please them! Better yet, this school accepts *any* child, even the most severely handicapped, and charges nothing whatsoever for its 24-hour services! Naturally, this marvelous school is your own home.

Am I saying that your home can be as good a learning environment as a good preschool? No. Your home is a *better* teaching environment than any preschool! Learning to speak is harder than learning to read, and you've already taught your child to speak. Potty training is harder than learning to write, and I've never heard of a child whose parents didn't manage somehow to potty train him. Even without any help, you'd probably do a good job of teaching your children if you just put your native ingenuity to work. But add in access to the best tools and books and techniques, and watch out! Your child's natural cleverness and curiosity will explode!

It turns out, you see, that the greatest predictor of genius, the factor that shows up most often in case studies of geniuses, is the *large* amount of time they spent with adults and the *small* amount they spent with agemates. Of course, this refers to adults who actively spend time with their children. Plopping in front of the TV with your baby in your lap may be cozy, but it's not very instructive. But when children spend a lot of time helping adults, watching adults, talking to adults, going where they go and seeing what they see, those children grow intellectually by leaps and bounds. One would expect this to be so, since by an early immersion in the adult world, including the world of adult thoughts and language, these fortunate children are getting the raw data that will prepare them for *real* thinking about the things grown-up people really think and talk about. Children isolated in a special little peer group of their own, on the other hand, are deprived of this exposure to adult thinking and ideas. They are being encouraged to remain childish and to function only in the artificial setting of the age-segregated group, a setting they will never again encounter outside of school.

PRESCHOOL OR HOME SCHOOL?

The one big reason that out-of-home preschool is so fashionable at the moment is careerism. If it weren't bad enough that the men of America have been persuaded that their destiny lies in becoming corporation employees, rather than in striving to build up their own businesses, this same line has been handed to the women. If neither Dad nor Mom will stay home with Junior, then Junior gets zooped off to daycare or preschool.

To facilitate this process of providing cheap female labor for Big Business, miles of forest are being felled to produce propaganda asserting that children can only fulfill their potential if they are snatched from the very breast and plunked down behind a desk somewhere. This plan is very convenient for the hordes of eager young would-be teachers who have been lured into selecting Early Childhood Education as their major, but in my view it is disastrous to children. Why? Because, for very young children, playing is learning, or at least the essential precursor of learning. Without raw data to chew over and digest—without a chance to become familiar with ideas and objects before being taught rules—learning difficulties multiply. This

doesn't mean that formal instruction has absolutely no place in our children's lives; rather, that for formal instruction to succeed, it must be preceded by a period of getting familiar with the new materials and ideas in a completely non-threatening, take-all-the-time-you-want, non-graded way.

The earlier the champions of early childhood education get their hands on our children, the better the chances that your son or daughter will be labeled "dyslexic" or "learning disabled" or, for heaven's sake, "hyperactive." *All* young children are dyslexic when first learning to read, and no normal three-year-old wants to sit for hours gazing at an adult's face. Ram schooling down younger and younger children's throats, and soon they *all* will be labeled "learning disabled"!

Mom and Dad are well aware of the pitfalls awaiting Junior in the halls of academe. That is why, if they can afford it, they do their best to sign Junior up for a "quality" preschool, and maybe even a private school. But why should we knock ourselves out paying for the best preschool, at stiff rates, to be followed perhaps by years of expensive private school and years of outrageously expensive college, when we could be providing a far better education, without guilt, if only one or both parents would consider working at home?

When you teach your own, the more you have, the more you save! It takes $3 earned to equal $1 not spent, counting in taxes, donations, extra cars, office clothes, and other business expenses. So if you give one child a $5,000/year education, it's like earning $15,000 a year. If you have two, you're making $30,000. Think about it!

THERE'S NO PLACE LIKE HOME

When we look into it, we discover that the home, in contrast to institutional settings, is an ideal environment for preschool learning. It's quite humorous to leaf through the catalogs of preschool and Montessori materials and see how many of them are copies of items found in any house. Play stoves, play pots and pans, little squares of different textures, trays for sorting little objects (remember Mama's button box?), dress-up clothes (what happened to raiding Mom and Dad's closet?) are just some of the products schools buy in an attempt to copy the home environment. Many more of the products you can easily make yourself, like beanbags and sandpaper letters. Any you *can't* easily make or copy are now available to you from suppliers listed right here in this section. So what's Ye Snobbe

Academy got that you haven't got—besides high price, the risk of handing your baby over to strangers, and a fertile breeding ground for serious childhood diseases?

You are your child's best teacher. Kids are born wanting to please their parents, and nobody knows a kid better than his own mother and father. Your job is far easier than the challenge faced by a 22-year-old with an education degree facing a room of 20 preschoolers who would all rather be home anyway. The "experts" can't do a single thing for your child that you can't do—and half the time, they aren't all that "expert" anyway. If all you ever do with your preschooler is read to him, admire his crayoning, play with him, and answer his questions, you will *already* be providing a richer educational environment than the harried preschool teacher of 20. Remember, it's one-on-one time that counts the most!

Good resources do help, of course. There's plenty in the next four chapters—more than any one family could ever realistically use. (I know. We've tried!) But remember, Suzy can learn a whole lot just by stacking soup cans and sorting socks.

You don't have to spend a fortune to give your child a rich education. Just give her yourself!

CHAPTER TWO

BABY AND TODDLER EDUCATION

Welcome, brave pioneer! First, congratulations on the birth or adoption of your baby. Babies are *wonderful*, and so are people who are willing to welcome these little gifts of God into their homes (that means you!). But you're going to do even more than provide clothes and hugs. You're going to *spend time* with your baby (which Baby will love), doing all kinds of fun things together. I know this is true 'cause you're reading this chapter!

Lots of us are willing to spend time with our little ones, but haven't the faintest idea of how to play with, entertain, or teach a baby. Let's face it: high school and college are usually baby-free environments. So are the Office, the Truck, the Warehouse, the Married-With-out-Children Apartment, and all those other adults-only places where we spend our lives before Baby arrives.

So here it is. You're alone with the baby. First you try "This Little Piggy Went to Market." That's always good for a few laughs, if Baby is old enough to appreciate it. Kisses and hugs are also fun. You change a diaper and wipe up some spitup. Another hug and kiss. Now you're stuck! You rack your brains for the games your own folks played with you when you were that age. If you didn't have little brothers and sisters, or nephews and nieces, you are likely to come up blank. Time to reach for the expensive Johnson & Johnson toys you bought at Child World. These hold Baby's at-

tention, all right—for five minutes or so. You are starting to discover an important truth; store-bought toys *do* provide "hours of fun," but not all at once. It's more like "minutes of fun," with constant breaks to switch toys.

Here's right where most parents wimp out. They switch on the TV, or the electric lullaby-gizmo, or wind up the baby swing, and leave, figuring they have spent "quality time" with Baby. If this is their first baby, they are thinking, "I've never felt so exhausted so fast in all my life!" Already they are on their way to the Yellow Pages to check out prices at the local day-care center, because, as all the articles in "parenting" magazines tell us, "you gotta have a break away from the baby."

Take courage! If you don't give up and hand your baby over to other people (like those terribly well-trained high-school-dropout girls at the local Kiddie Heaven Day Care Zoo), you will learn to keep Baby happy *and* learning without even thinking about it. But first, you have to put in your apprenticeship. This means taking time to maybe make a few baby toys yourself, reading some books about baby games, and not forgetting the hugging and kissing! In an incredibly short time, you will learn how to amuse a baby for an entire half-hour armed with nothing more than a diaper that happened to be hanging over the arm of your sofa. What's more, you will be able to do all this while simultaneously catching up on your reading (in snatches, since Baby gets jealous if you don't give him enough attention). You will learn all this in record time, since mothering hormones make every woman a genius when it comes to keeping her baby happy, if she can keep away from those silly females in print and on TV who keep urging us to "have it all" (meaning large paychecks, emaciated bodies, fancy hairdos, STDs, guilt, and heart attacks). Fathers don't have special father hormones, but babies are naturally inclined to love Daddy to pieces, and this translates to a willingness to be happy when cradled on Daddy's arm or shoulder.

Now comes the amazing secret that you never learned in Home Ec class; babies are *fun!* You've just got to learn their language and culture. Once you do, you will find yourself enjoying activities that the gang at the office would never have believed, such as rolling tomato paste cans back and forth on the floor with your toddler. You will learn to lighten up, stop being so overdignified, and take pleasure in little things, like an unexpected wildflower growing by your mailbox.

Children have a gift of joy and gratefulness that can nurture our morose adult spirits. They are not perfect little angels from Over the Rainbow, of course, any more than *you* are a perfect little angel from Over the Rainbow. But children are born trusting and willing to appreciate the good life brings. This great gift of childlike faith is why Jesus said we must change and become like little children before we can enter the Kingdom of Heaven—and there's no better way to soak up all the good qualities of a little child than showing him how to use his God-given abilities constructively and introducing him to the best parts of this beautiful world of ours.

READINESS FOR BABIES

Bear Creek Publications
No Bored Babies, $6.50 postpaid.

No Bored Babies is the ultimate readiness book. Take one bored baby wailing in his crib. Add one creative mom or dad who, using this book, makes delightful toys for the bored baby. Result: one eager learner having a whole lot of fun.

Follow the simple directions in this graphically appealing, not at all overwhelming book and you will be zapping out dozens of toys in next to no time. Sections include: Why Make Your Own Toys; Setting Up Your Toy Workshop (materials to save or collect); Safe-

ty; The Visual Crib (birth to six weeks); Batting Practice Time (six weeks to three months); Reaching Grasping, Chewing and Kicking (three months to six months); The Mover and Shaker (six to nine months); The Explorer (nine to 14 months); Challenge (14 to 24 months); and Household Objects as Playthings. A sampling of the fantastic ideas (all illustrated with line drawings): Make a Feelie Mural of different fabric pieces glued to cardboard to hang on the wall next to the changing table. Make soft blocks (your choice of hidden jingles tucked in a plastic film canister or straight polyester fiber stuffing). Chewable books! Caterpillar pull toy! Shape sorter! Sponge puzzle! The directions are absurdly simple and easy to follow. In fact, a wide-awake six-year-old could make many of these toys. And thus, an idea: why not get double duty from *No Bored Babies* by letting your other children make them? Eureka! No bored older children, either!

NEW**
Bio-Alpha, Inc.
Slow and Steady, Get Me Ready, $19.95 plus $2.00 shipping.

Slow and Steady, Get Me Ready: A Parents' Handbook might be the answer for home-schooling parents who ask, "What can I do with the little ones while the older ones are having home school?" This one book, written by a retired kindergarten teacher for her grandchildren, is a complete readiness curriculum for children from birth to age 5. *Slow and Steady, Get Me Ready* gives you one new activity for every week of your child's first five years of life—260 activities in all.

These are really good activities, using materials found around your house and taking only 10 minutes or so a day.

Under each activity you'll find a list of the skills it develops. A sample activity for age 0, week 35: blowing bubbles. The author tells you how to use soap and a wet thread spool to blow bubbles and how to use this time to stimulate verbal communication. That week she also encourages you to draw baby's attention to water sounds during tub time, using various objects like sponges, washcloths, and measuring cups. As you can see, she takes a simple activity, tells you when Baby is ready for you to introduce it, and gives you all kinds of interesting twists on it.

Half the time reading this book you'll be saying to yourself, "I should have thought of that!" The other half you'll be saying, "I never would have thought of that!" and chuckling in amazement at the cleverness of the suggested activities.

Lavish art is not included, nor is necessary at all in this book, as the activities are so clearly explained. A few simple drawings illustrate the more spatial activities.

Life will definitely be more fun for kids whose parents use this book. It also will be less stressful for time-poor parents, since the activities are already organized into just one per week. You won't have to figure out which activity to do when, or feel guilty because you aren't doing them all at once. If you have a baby, a lot to do, and not enough time to do it, this is your book.

NEW★★
Bright Baby Books
Toy gym, $18. *Homegrown Babies*, $3. *Homegrown Infants*, $3. *Moving Right Along*, $6. Shipping extra. Other toys, books available.

Bright Baby Books, a company founded by occupational therapist Barbara Sher, a lady with a lot of experience in movement and exercise training for children, publishes a whole series of physical development books with easy activities and games for different age groups. *Homegrown Infants*, for babies 0-8 months, has a slightly risqué cover (crude pen sketch of undressed mom holding baby in such a way that he covers her torso). Its interior graphics are also on the amateurish side. The text contents, however, have good suggestions for stimulating and developing each muscle area, as well as general balance and mental stimulation. *Homegrown Babies*, for ages 8-12 months, has better

graphics. Like the first book, this is nicely arranged in logical topics, such as Movement, Self Care, Exploring and Experimenting, and Social Awareness. *Caution:* Suggested toys for baby in both these books include some that are *not* safe for him to be left alone with, since he might choke on them. The author intends for you to be there with your child as he plays with these items. Finally, you might be interested in the Bright Babies Toy Gym, a versatile device for hanging toys over baby's head when he's at the age to play but not to roll and crawl.

Children's Small Press Collection
Look at Me, $9.95.

Large, thick paperback—about 2/3 as thick as this book you are now reading—crammed with activities for babies and toddlers. Well-organized pages have: large, clear print; large, clear graphics; and short, clear directions. Sections include: lists of things to buy and save; The First Wondrous Year; toys to make (including classic toys of yesteryear); learning games; indoor/outdoor fun; books and reading; positive self-image; imaginative play; poems, songs, and fingerplays; arts and crafts using all sorts of media; nature and science fun; party fun (games, treats, and decorations children can make); easy, nutritious recipes; and a small section labeled "'Expert' Advice." Some of the activities, chosen at random from the hundreds in this book: cotton ball art, a toddler obstacle course, paint brush cookies, make-your-own board books, and movement games for babies. Really good ideas charmingly presented at an inexpensive price.

EDC Publishing
Parents' Guides to Entertaining and Educating Young Children, Babies & Toddlers, $6.95 each. Library binding 13.96. Shipping extra.

Entertaining and Educating Babies & Toddlers has an introductory advice and how-to-use-this-book section; three toys-you-can-make sections—Things to Look At, Things to Listen To, Things to Feel and Hold; Learning to Talk; Books, Pictures, and Stories; Energetic Play; Messy Play; Imitating and Pretending; Things to Fit Together and Take Apart; Walks and Trips; Going Swimming; Music, Songs, and Rhymes; Guide to Stages of Development; and a handy index. All sections include make-it-yourself suggestions, in keeping with the strained financial situation of young British couples.

Entertaining and Educating Young Children also has a wealth of clever suggestions. Notice the book's philosophy—

Children will play, provided they are not actually prevented from doing so, whether or not they have help from adults but there is no doubt that the learning quality of their play can be greatly influenced by the adults around them. Adults can provide materials, suggest directions, give advice and encouragement and open the door to new activities.

The emphasis in this book is on activities for adults and children to share together.

Those activities include Drawing and Coloring; Painting and Printing; Cutting and Sticking; Modelling and Building; Books, Pictures, and Stories; Fun with Words and Letters; Fun with Numbers; Listening to and Making Music; Playing with Sand and Water; Dressing Up and Pretending; In the Kitchen; Growing Things; Learning About Animals; Collecting Things; Getting Exercise; Going Swimming; Outings and Journeys; Parties. There also are sections on wet afternoons and other difficult times and the study of play, as well as an index.

READINESS ACTIVITIES FOR TODDLERS

NEW★★
Bio-Alpha, Inc.
Slow and Steady, Get Me Ready, $19.95 plus $2.00 shipping, VA residents 90¢ tax.

This complete readiness curriculum for children from birth to age 5 is written up above under Readiness for Babies. Even if your little one is past the baby stage, you've still got four years or so of readiness activities in this one oversized book. The book provides one readiness activity per week: just enough to keep your little roamer busy and interested. Recommended.

NEW★★
Bright Baby Books
Moving Right Along, $6. *Easy Going Games*, $8. Shipping extra. Other toys, books available.

If you're looking for phys-ed-in-a-book, I may have something here for you. *Moving Right Along*, for ages 1-7, is a collection of easy movement games organized according to specific motor skills. *Easy Going Games*, for kids 5-12, shows you how to turn mateless

socks, hula hoops, and carpet squares into instant games. These are really good, doable activities that don't involve a lot of fuss. Just reading these books awakens you to new possibilities for physical development.

Children's Small Press Collection

See review of *Look at Me: Activities for Babies and Toddlers* in the Readiness for Babies section above.

NEW★★
Innovation Station
Creative Play Areas, $9.95 plus $2 shipping.

Creative Play Areas is a fantastic treasure trove of over 185 easy-to-make, inexpensive projects that families can make together to expand the children's imagination and ingenuity in a creative play environment. Everything from using scarves and hats as props for dramatic play to making your own floor "Road City Map." Find out the creative possibilities lurking in your card table, pillows, and stacks of old tires! Show your children how to make their own bows and arrows, obstacle courses, and instruments. Tons more, plus over 200 charming drawings, photos, and illustrations that show exactly how to do it. Great for kids from preschool to preteen (and even older, if they aren't too busy pretending to be cool).

The author pleads strongly for children to be allowed to be "their own engineers and custom designers," as in the days when kids made their own dolls and treehouses. As she says, "Children need an environment where they help build, where they can change and reconstruct and be responsible." Right on!

NEW★★
Parenting Press
Baby and I Can Play and *Fun with Toddlers*, one combined volume, $6.95 (paperback) or $16.95 (library binding).

"Go play nicely with the baby, dear." Good idea, Mom! But *how* can a little kid play with the baby or toddler without causing pain, sorrow, distress, or even boredom?

Now, here in one book, are activities that older kids can pursue with the babies or toddlers in their families, plus developmental information presented on a preschooler's level so older brother or sister can understand what to expect from a baby or toddler and what they are *not* ready to tackle. The author, a social worker, unfortunately believes the popular myth that older kids naturally have times of longing for the baby to disappear. This is strictly a matter of how your kids are trained in the virtues of affection and sharing. I was the oldest of seven and I *never* wanted to "send back" any of my little brothers and sisters!

HOW TO TEACH PRESCHOOLERS

Do all of the writers reviewed below agree on how best to teach preschoolers? They do not! Then why include all of them? Won't it just confuse you? Perhaps it may, although I hope not. I feel that each of these writers has something valid to share, from Doreen Claggett's insistence on discipline and structure to Raymond Moore's belief in developing character through chores and service projects. These authors all agree that home is the best school, and that early compulsory public schooling harms more than it helps. Beyond that, I suspect we are seeing some differences of temperament, as well as differences in religious background. Dr. Moore is a Seventh-day Adventist: Doreen Claggett is a fundamentalist Christian.

We will all do well to realize that while Jack Sprat could eat no fat, his wife could also eat no lean; in other words, well-organized parents are going to approach preschool education differently than artistic, Bohemian types. One of us might drop everything and rush the kids to the window to see a spectacular sunset, while another one of us will keep her head down and steadily work through the dishes. Both are right in their own way, and undoubtedly right for their own children, who (unless adopted) share their organized or artistic genes. Either taken to an extreme is wrong; both all work and all play make Jack a dull boy.

As long as we're spending time with our children, and not using our educational philosophy, whatever it is, to justify ignoring them, we're doing OK. I happen to believe that learning to read early is good, but I believe that having a childhood like Heidi's, playing with the goats in Alpine meadows and watching Grandfather make cheese, is also good. What would the advocates of total structure say about Heidi, I wonder? And what would the advocates of delayed formal education

say about my own kids, who all have learned to read before the age of six, and some before the age of four?

Good parents are going to do what they think is best for the kids. If the world seems a threatening place, we are going to want them to be independent and educationally equipped as soon as possible. If we believe we will be able to protect them from the evils of the world, we will feel free to let them be Heidi a little bit longer. In the meantime, let's all settle in our own minds what we'd like to teach our children when, and try to be charitable to each other.

NEW**
Dove Christian Books
Never Too Early, $7.95.

In *Never Too Early,* Christian author Doreen Claggett, a early childhood educator with many years' experience, makes a strong case for early childhood instruction. Quoting the Bible, history, and her own experience and that of others who have taught youngsters in church-run early education programs, she does her best to demonstrate that kids benefit at an early age from discipline and structure, including academics. This does not necessarily mean *out-of-home* instruction, as Mrs. Claggett, the author of a preschool program widely used by home schoolers, readily acknowledges. Her quarrel is with those who don't want children subjected to any methodical form of academic instruction in their early years. Lots of how-to tips included. Thought-provoking reading.

NEW**
Education Services
Teaching Preschoolers: It's Not Exactly Easy But Here Is How to Do It and *Teaching Kindergartners: How to Understand and Instruct Fours and Fives,* $6.45 each.

Ruth Beechick is a lady who knows a tremendous amount about teaching. Her books on teaching preschoolers and kindergartners, though written for Sunday school teachers, are loaded with insights and practical tips useful in general home schooling as well. Dr. Beechick brings up *and deals with* topics you may never have thought of, such as "How do children think? Do they learn differently at different ages? What is the best way to teach memorization? Are behavioral objectives in Christian curriculums good or bad?"

Dr. Beechick takes a middle of the road position on when preschool teaching should start. She believes in a developmental approach, based on when children are ready, but does not strongly urge putting off formal academics to age 8, as some do. Beyond her Christian view of child development, you also get explicit instruction in how to teach each age group about Christ, sin, salvation, and essential doctrines. She also deals with the mundane how-tos such as how to present flannelboard and puppet lessons, the uses of singing games, and so on.

Hewitt Child Development Center
Better Late Than Early, $6. *Home-Style Teaching*, $10. Add 12% shipping.

From the other side of the tracks, here are some books by Dr. Raymond Moore that have convinced many parents to home school simply in order to protect their little one from being hurried into early academics! Although a book has been recently written questioning some of Dr. Moore's research (particularly his claims that early reading causes eye problems), a lot of what's written here still draws legitimate attention to the problems that arise when young children, especially boys, are thrust into a formal, female-run, institutional setting in which physical energy is a minus and docile compliance a plus. As Dr. Moore points out, none of our compulsory attendance laws were ever based on research, and there are definite minuses to increasingly early compulsory attendance.

The Moores' approach to early childhood education stresses chores, nature, and acts of kindness to others over reading, writing, and 'rithmetic. This is all described in detail in *Home-Style Teaching*, their "how-to" book.

NEW**
Teaching Home
February/March 1987 back issue, $3.75. Complete six-issue set of 1987 back issues, $17.50, includes free set of 6 plastic magazine holders for your ring binder.

If you want some cutting-edge thinking on Biblical methods and philosophy for early childhood education, it's all lurking there within the covers of *Teaching Home*'s February/March 1987 back issue. *Teaching Home* keeps its back issues in print forever, and when you get this one, you will see why. Doreen Claggett's article on the history of early childhood education philosophy is alone worth the price of the back issue. Plus you get teaching tips, inspiration, and a whole lot more!

UPDATED**
Warren Publishing House, Inc./Totline Books
Totline, one year (6 issues) $24, sample issue $1. *Teaching Tips*, $3.95 plus $2 shipping.

Totline is an activity newsletter for teachers of preschoolers. No long philosophy articles or interviews: just lots and lots of things to do! Each issue now includes patterns and flannelboard cutouts. These used to come in a separate publication, *Preschool Patterns*, which has now been merged with *Totline*.

Teaching Tips is an attractive little booklet with over 300 helpful hints from *Totline* subscribers, geared to preschool and early elementary classes. Classroom tips: equipment, decorations. Curriculum tips: art, music, and general learning. Special times tips: transition times, quiet times, outdoor times, snack times, group times, clean-up times. Sample hint: old plastic shower and window curtains make great table or floor coverings for messy play! Or how about using a pizza pan as a magnet board for learning games? And did you know that glossy magazines, such as *Time* and *Newsweek*, make better paper chains than ordinary construction paper? If you love this kind of lore (and what mother doesn't?), send for a copy.

CHAPTER THREE

READINESS PROGRAMS

What is a readiness curriculum? It's meeting the numbers and letters. It's lots of arts and crafts activities. It's learning "concept" words, like *up* and *down* and *more* and *less*. It's everything short of reading 'n writing 'n seatwork—short, zingy activities geared to a preschooler's interest span. If it has workbooks, they are big and splashy and each page takes little time to complete. No writing required: just tracing, cutting, and pasting! All this helps children get ready for their academic studies while having a whole bunch of fun.

So now you want to enrich your home with exciting stuff? The place to start is the School Supply people. Teacher's stores and school supply catalogs carry a huge variety of fun and clever learning tools. You can craft homemade versions of many of these products and this is well to keep in mind when flipping through such a catalog. We have, for example, made our own jumbo-size flannelboard and our own beanbags. I collected the tops of gallon milk jugs to use for arithmetic counters and game markers, and the styrofoam trays meat comes packed in serve as collage trays. Large disposable diaper boxes make excellent puppet theaters. Ingenious woodworkers can make jigsaw puzzles, beanbag targets, and building blocks (well sanded, of course!). Ingenious seamstresses can save fabric scraps to make their own doll clothes, stuffed puppets, and felt figures. Virtually any arithmetic manipulative can

be made at home with the right tools. You can make a bug house out of an empty peanut butter jar with holes drilled in the lid. You can make your own play dough and other crafts mixtures (see the Crafts chapter in Volume 4 for several great books of crafts recipes). If fingerpaint you must, you can even make your own fingerpaint.

I am not suggesting that you should get a school supply catalog or two merely to give you ideas for home-made learning tools, though. These catalogs also contain an array of items you can't make at home, and that you probably won't want to do without. (For a list of the best school supply catalogs, see Volume 1.) We're going to look at some of that good preschool stuff later in this chapter . . . but first, let's see what's available in readiness curriculum.

READINESS CURRICULUM

Following is a list of home school curriculum providers that offer readiness programs, whether their readiness program is called *nursery, preschool,* or *kindergarten.* Academic (non-readiness) kindergarten programs are listed separately, in the Kindergarten chapter.

What's the difference? Well, academic early learning programs are like a mini first grade. These normally include phonics, simple math, and often art, music, simple history lessons, and other activities as well. Readiness, on the other hand, is more like what we've traditionally thought of as preschool and kindergarten. It involves a lot of creative play, exploring various art media, doing simple dramatics, becoming familiar with colors and shapes, listening to stories and nursery rhymes, and becoming acquainted with seasonal activities. Towards the end of the school year, counting and letters are usually introduced in a very low-key way.

Trying to separate "readiness" from "academic" programs can be quite confusing when reading companies' brochures. That's why I've separated them out for you! Full reviews of these programs, plus addresses and ordering information, are contained in the Curriculum Buyer's Guide in Volume 1 (there simply wasn't room to repeat it all in this volume).

So, which should you start with, readiness or kindergarten? Assuming that Johnny is young enough for this to be a serious decision, I recommend always starting with a readiness program, for three reasons. (1) Readiness programs give kids a really positive attitude towards school, because they are so much fun. (2) Readiness is also a gentle way for you to ease into your new teaching responsibilities—a whole lot less pressure than starting right out trying to teach Johnny to read. (3) Readiness helps kids get *ready!* You don't want Suzy to be struggling with her kindergarten studies because she has never learned how to handle crayons and scissors, or doesn't know the concepts "before" and "after." Readiness programs make sure any such gaps in school readiness are eliminated before they can cause any serious trouble.

You can purchase a prepackaged readiness or academic curriculum from the suppliers below, or make up your own from the great resources in these chapters. If you lack teaching confidence, and especially if this is your first encounter with home schooling, a prepackaged readiness curriculum is your best bet. Of the list below, I am partial to Calvert. It is fun, complete, easy to use, and does a fine job of helping a mother (or father) learn to teach. You can't go wrong with Calvert! However, other programs are less expensive and have features Calvert lacks, such as Bible content (A Beka, Bob Jones, etc.), a particular doctrinal emphasis (e.g., Catholic or Mennonite), or a greater emphasis on history and geography (Smiling Heart Press). If you're willing to spend a lot of time at the library and want to give your child the richest possible Christian preschool education, the Smiling Heart Press curriculum is hard to beat. If you have hardly any time

and are willing to settle for a one-workbook readiness program, then ESP Publications has what you're looking for. Other providers have their strong points, too. As you can see, you have plenty of options.

- A Beka Books (nursery for two- and three-year olds).
- Advanced Training Institute (preschoolers have activities in Parent's Guide, but no separate program available for preschoolers)
- Bob Jones University Press (K4 readiness).
- Calvert School (kindergarten is a readiness program).
- Carden Educational Foundation (readiness preschool)
- Clonlara School (any age, whatever kind of program you want).
- Educational Products (preschool readiness kit or Home Kit phonics program)
- Hewitt Child Development Center (readiness program for children aged five to seven).
- Home Study International (preschool readiness).
- International Institute (kindergarten covers readiness and reading).
- Oak Meadow School (kindergarten—readiness with Waldorf storytelling and artistic approach).
- Our Lady of the Rosary (kindergarten course is a readiness program)
- Seton Home Study School (kindergarten—readiness and phonics).
- Smiling Heart Press (preschool is combined with kindergarten in one-volume curriculum).
- Sycamore Tree (readiness and phonics both available).

READINESS MATERIALS

UPDATED**
Alpha Omega Publications
Readiness, Set, Go! $77.95. *Introduction to . . . Alphabet and Handwriting,* $38.95; *Numbers,* $62.95; *Telling Time,* $29.95; *Christian Character Development,* $29.95. Shipping extra.

What is *Readiness, Set, Go!?* It's the readiness portion of Alpha Omega's kindergarten program *Little Patriots in Action,* redesigned and enriched into an informal, hands-on approach that you can use to help your children learn the foundational skills of color, shape, size, coordination, matching, directions, and categories. *Readiness, Set, Go!* includes:

- *Little Patriots in Action* reading readiness program (includes Teacher's Manual and student book)
- Wipe-off crayons
- *Colors & Shapes Lotto* (a matching game)
- *Colors & Shapes* wipe-off book
- *Shapes in God's World* book
- A "Growing Tree" chart for measuring your child's height
- *Sizes in God's World* book
- "Go Together Matchmates" mini-puzzles for matching a number of sets of two related objects
- *Same or Different* wipe-off board sets
- *See It, Make It* wipe-off boards (early art activities with simple shapes; your child imitates the drawings on the left of the boards)
- *Play and Learn Rooms Lotto*—a matching game that also teaches children to notice things about their house
- *My Animal Friends* book
- A Preschool Guide.

Also available: packages similarly designed to introduce the alphabet, handwriting, numbers, timetelling, Bible, and character development. Like *Readiness: Set: Go!* these include a selection of products from different vendors.

The *Christian Character* set includes four preschool Bible activities books, one *Growing God's Way* book, four board books (*God Made My Family, God Made Friends, Hello God,* and *Goodnight God*), and a preschool guide. Activities include mostly coloring, cutting, and folding.

The *Learning with Numbers* kit includes a boxed set of *Let's Count* wipe-off boards from TREND Enterprises, a *Numbers Lotto* game (also from TREND), *Numbers in God's World,* an Ideal School Supply counting frame (ten rows of colored beads on wires inside a frame), a Peg-It Numbers Board (kids stick the proper number of colored pegs into each counting board), wipe-off crayons, and a preschool guide.

Let's Tell Time includes a genuine "Judy Clock" (movable hands and an elapsed-time bezel), *Telling Time Match Me* cards from TREND, *Time in God's World,* a *Telling Time* activity book from TREND, wipe-off crayons, and a preschool guide. Your little one will learn both digital and dial time telling with this set.

Finally, the *Alphabet and Handwriting* kit comes with *Alphabet Match Me* flash cards, an *Alphabet Lotto*

matching game, *Alphabet & Numbers Fun* (another great TREND Enterprises wipe-off book), *God Made My World* (student book and teacher edition), alphabet flash cards, *A to Z God Loves Me* book, an alphabet wall chart, wipe-off crayons, and a preschool guide.

Alpha Omega's big, beautiful *Horizons* catalog also includes scads of other items for preschoolers. The items listed above in these kits can be purchased separately through the catalog. The advantage of purchasing a kit is that kit prices are discounted. Everything is pictured in large, full-color photo illustrations and very completely described. A fabulous resource!

NEW**
Bio-Alpha, Inc.
Slow and Steady, Get Me Ready, $19.95 plus $2.00 shipping, VA residents 90¢ tax.

I've mentioned this book twice before, once under Baby Readiness and once under Toddler Readiness. Here we go for the third time! Why so many mentions? Because this is a complete readiness curriculum for children from birth to age 5. Most readiness programs start only at age three or four: *Slow and Steady, Get Me Ready* starts in the crib, providing one new activity for every week of your child's first five years of life—260 activities in all. These are really good activities, using materials found around your house and taking only 10 minutes or so a day.

We're looking at older kids now, so let's look at a sample activity for age 3, chosen totally at random. Judge for yourself if your child will find this interesting:

Suspend a nerf ball, sock ball, yarn ball or a stuffed paper bag from an open doorway by attaching a piece of yarn or string at the top of the door frame and tying it to one of the balls or the bag. The yarn or string should be long enough so that the ball hangs at the child's eye level.

The author continues with instructions on how to teach your child to successfully hit the hanging object using a bat or yardstick, and suggests extending the activity by having the child count how often she can hit the ball.

Every single activity in this book has solid educational value *and* entertainment value for the child as well. Many can be done without supervision, or with only minimal supervision. All use simple everyday objects. The author goes out of her way to suggest alternative materials for doing the activities. In the example above, for instance, you have your choice of a nerf ball, sock ball (*everyone* has socks!), yarn ball, or stuffed paper bag for the ball, and a yardstick or bat for the bat. Many activities promote family values and affection. Author June Oberlander's years of experience with young children come through in the ways she anticipates possible misunderstandings and problems in carrying out the activities and deals with them before they arise. She doesn't just tell you to have your child try to hit the ball; she mentions various ways kids might mess up, and how to teach them to hit it correctly. A good resource.

UPDATED★★
Educational Products
Preschool Kit, $29.95. *On Your Mark, Get Set* preschool workbooks, $9.75 each separately. Shipping extra.

From the people who brought you the delightful *Sing, Spell, Read and Write* reading program comes a preschool kit. It includes a Teacher's Manual, short vowel cards, a music tape, a learning game, and a pair of preschool readiness workbooks with a Raceway theme: *On Your Mark* and *Get Set*.

On Your Mark has a pair of shoes pictured on its back cover, with punched-out holes and real shoelaces for practicing lacing. This workbook covers colors, shapes, visual discrimination, matching, opposites, classification, sequencing, and seasons. *Get Set* has a giant clock with turnable handles on the back cover, and includes letter shapes and sounds and recognizing beginning letters. The accompanying Teacher's Guide

is friendly and helpful, and includes readiness activities to go along with the workbook exercises.

Fearon Teacher Aids
Get Ready, Set, Grow!, $10.95. *Learning Things*, $10.95.

Fearon's *Get Ready, Set, Grow!* is the least expensive one-year preschool curriculum I have seen. You have to supply all the materials, but many of them are items you already have around the house—pots and pans, catalogs, rice and measuring cups, crayons, and so on. You get weekly (not daily) lesson plans, each with three Activity Units. These include such things as indoor play, art, music, kid-made snacks, Learning Times that get into science and drama, outdoor play, and storytime. The book is very attractive and easy to follow, and since the lesson plans are weekly you can easily flex them to fit your energy level, instead of getting the guilts for not doing everything on a given day.

Get Ready, Set, Grow! includes secular holiday activities (bunny for Easter, "let's hide the matzoh" for Passover). At the end of the books you will find words but not music to the classic children's songs used in the program, as well as nursery rhymes, finger plays, circle dances, and a fine index to all activities, for those who want to look up the playdough recipe or try the shopping mall trip on a week where it was not planned. The book is punched like a calendar so you can hang it on the wall. And it was designed for use not only by teachers, play groups, and day-care centers, but parents too! It makes a neat gift and can be used to supplement any other program you may be using.

In the same vein, Fearon Teacher Aids has another book titled *Learning Things: Games that Make Learning Fun for Children 3-8 Years Old*. The Fearon Teacher Aids catalog has all sorts of interesting arts and crafts for children of all ages. Look for these at your friendly neighborhood bookstore, or order directly from the publisher.

NEW**
Frank Schaffer, Inc.
Reproducible workbooks, $3.98 to $7.95 each. Flash cards, $6.95/box. Many other items available.

Mothers often write to me asking, "What do you use with your *own* children?" To save time, here's part of the answer. We always buy Frank Schaffer workbooks for our preschool children. Nobody can beat Frank Schaffer for cuddly cut-'n-paste activities, not to mention dot-to-dot, matching, simple mazes, tracing, and all the other preschool readiness activities little kids love so much.

Frank Schaffer has a complete line of workbooks for children in preschool, kindergarten, and early grades, all available (most likely) down at your local teacher's supply store. The ones we always get are the *Getting Ready for Kindergarten* series (a series of 10 workbooks, each $3.98) and *Preschool Workbooks* (a set of two), plus whatever else we happen to pick up on the fly.

Learning at Home
Short and Sweet, $10. Shipping extra.

Like the other Learning at Home guides, *Short and Sweet* is simple and direct. You get a list of goals and some hints about helping young children discover the world. More: this readiness guide provides oodles of activities under the headings Ourselves (outside your body, inside your body, "a book about me," using a tape recorder), Inside (kitchen, bathroom, bedroom, rest of the house), Outside (yard, park, sky, garden), Anywhere (stuff to do while you're waiting in the dentist's office), and Creative Expression ("crayons and big fat markers," watercolor, tempera, finger paint, collage . . .

all sorts of gooey creative projects). You have to pick which activity to do when. Think of this as an idea-sparker more than a planned curriculum. Lots of teaching tips interspersed with the activities are an extra.

NEW**
Rod and Staff Publishers
Adventures with Books, Counting with Numbers, Bible Pictures to Color, $2.25 each. *Bible Stories to Read,* $4.60. Other book prices TBA. Shipping free if order $10 or more; otherwise add small order fee of $1.

Just out from the good plain folks at Rod and Staff Publishers is this new series, their "answer for preschool children who are eager to go to school" or reluctant kids who could use a little pre-academic preparation. As the publishers say,

> These workbooks are intended to help children learn to take good care of books, do work neatly, follow directions carefully, grow in vocabulary usage, appreciate and increase [their] interest in the world around them, show courtesy and helpfulness to others, and so forth. . . . While children should enjoy using these books, this work is not intended to help children feel overconfident in their abilities. The highest aim for children is to show an excellent, cooperative spirit.

Adventures with Books teaches basic preschool skills such as tracking from left to right and top to bottom, following simple directions, learning the colors, cutting and pasting, drawing with lines and circles, recognizing simple shapes, and learning important preschool concepts such as *up–down* and *big–small*. Similarly, *Counting with Numbers* is a pre-math book designed to teach children about the numbers 1–10, including how to write them, what quantity each represents, what number comes before or after, and simple numerical concepts like *more–less* and *empty–full*.

Bible Pictures to Color encourages children to color neatly and with realistic colors, and even includes color-by-number pictures. The companion book, *Bible Stories to Read,* has 60 Biblically-accurate stories written on the preschool level: 36 from the Old Testament and 24 from the New. Each comes with a few discussion questions and a memory verse.

Do It Carefully, a book teaching how to write the letters and recognize letter sounds, is just out. Not yet out at the time I write this, but coming soon, are *Everywhere We Go* (colors, shapes, numbers, letters, and sounds) and *Finding the Answers* (thinking skills).

These readiness books look like a good choice for those who appreciate Rod and Staff's sober, unworldly, Mennonite approach to education.

Shekinah Curriculum Cellar

Potter's Press Preschool Curriculum: 32 10-page learning units, $29.95, with binder $34.95. Correlated learning aids, $5.95. Add 10% shipping ($2.95 minimum). Add 6% sales tax in California.

Cute-as-a-button intro to letters, numbers, colors, shapes, and Bible stories (Adam-Zaccheus). You get 32 ten-page workbooks plus a *very* brief teacher's brochure. The latter gives teaching hints, suggests a follow-up phonics method, and outlines a simple approach to science and history that you can easily add in to your preschool program. Starting with *How Hermie the Glow Wormie Got His Name*, every booklet has a little story (Bible stories start in book 3) and simple exercises built into the booklet's basic theme. Example: count the food items on the Ark and color in the rainbow. Time required: only a few minutes a day.

Correlated learning aids include black-and-white Alphabet Flash Cards (short A is for Adam, long A is for Abel), 17 Practice Printing sheets, and Reading with Vowels, a minicourse in combining letter sounds to form words.

If you're not really excited about baking pretzels with your kids or planting rose bushes together (and all the other creative activities in regular readiness programs), or if you'd like some Bible-based prereading and premath to supplement one of those activity-laden programs, you won't find anything simpler or cuter than Potter's Press.

Smiling Heart Press

Pre-K and K, one book, $50. Grade 1, $50. Grade 2, $50. Add 10% shipping.

Not to be confused with the Learning at Home company's teaching guide, *Learning at Home: A Christian Parent's Guide Using the Library as a Resource* is a complete preschool and kindergarten curriculum in one spiral-bound, nicely typeset volume dressed up with rubber stamp graphics. For preschool you get a really rich program of learning activities, including: Bible concepts (four times a week), reading readiness (four times), arithmetic readiness (four times), God's world (social studies—twice), character building (once), health, safety, manners (once), art (twice), music (twice), physical education skills (four times), Bible memory verses (four times), and stories (four times). This schedule should take you an hour and a half four days a week. Friday is set aside just for field trips.

As is typical with rich curricula, *Learning at Home* requires considerably more work than just opening a manual and turning to the proper page. You have to collect materials for the activities, find books at the library, schedule field trips if desired, and so on. Author Ann Ward has made this somewhat easier by providing card catalog numbers for the books she recommends. This means you can find another book on the same topic easily if the one you're looking for isn't there, and you won't have to spend hours flipping through cards or microfiche.

The kindergarten program in the back of the manual is considerably different. This includes a kindergarten arithmetic section and a phonics section based on a popular phonogram-based approach. (Smiling Heart's phonics section is written up in more depth in chapter 7). To this you can add the preschool activities, but that means you will be flipping back and forth between three sections of the manual. However, this may be worth the effort to you, especially if you are teaching both a preschooler and kindergartner together.

How useful this program is for you depends on how well stocked your local library is with the recommended books, or at least other good books in their card catalog number categories. If you can find the right books, it's as good as correspondence programs I've seen that cost six times as much.

NEW**
TREND Enterprises, Inc.

Each bulletin board set, $5.95, includes free Discovery Guide. Requires 4 x 6' bulletin board. Wipe-off workbooks,

TREND has quite an assortment of bulletin board sets for preschoolers. Each presents a basic concept. *Color Cats* shows cats of assorted colors, plus how primary colors combine to make other colors. *Shapes* is six super-size basic shapes, labeled by name, plus a reproducible activity page. *Mother Goose* is 10 illustrated nursery rhymes. *Beginning Consonants* includes 21 punch-out consonant letters, each with illustrations of items that begin with that letter.

TREND also makes a dazzling array of stickers, scented and unscented, for those of you who are into this form of approval.

But the best thing TREND makes are their write-on, wipe-off workbooks. These are colorful, lots of fun, and can be passed down through a dozen kids if properly cared for. The price is minimal, under $3 as of this writing, and they are great practice motivators. Of all the wipe-off workbooks I have seen, TREND® makes the best ones. We have used all of theirs, but especially recommend the pre-handwriting, manuscript, cursive, and numeral books. Of these, the pre-handwriting book, which helps kids practice their loops, curves, and angles in a fun way, is for us practically indispensable.

CHAPTER FOUR

KINDERGARTEN PROGRAMS

Kindergarten is a German word. It means literally "child garden." The German educator who invented it back in 1837, Friedrich Wilhelm August Froebel, believed that certain basic readiness activities such as paper cutting, clay modeling, and weaving were the building blocks of later vocational skills, and that children should be exposed to them in a happy, child-centered environment guided by an ever-understanding and loving teacher—a veritable garden of children.

The kindergartens you and I attended when we were kids more or less fit this mold. We cut and pasted. We fingerpainted. We pretended we were little flowers raising our tiny faces to the sun. We listened to stories about Mr. Busy Bee and Mrs. Robin Redbreast. We ate cookies and milk. We napped. We learned which hand was the right hand, which color was orange, and that God was great and good and we should thank Him for our food.

But somewhere during the years we were in college or going out into the world, the bright boys who are responsible for the current illiteracy fiasco in the public schools came up with a theory that has, in effect, eliminated old-fashioned kindergarten. They reasoned that, since they weren't able to teach kids to read in grades 1–12, they should start one grade earlier, and that would make all the difference.

So today, "kindergarten" is often really a mini-first grade. Kids are expected to learn reading, addition and subtraction, handwriting, and other skills traditionally reserved for the six-year-olds. This leads to all kinds of parental and child distress, as the pressure mounts to keep Junior from "falling behind."

Now, I happen to think that kids of that age *are* capable of learning these things—but not necessarily in a formal, lockstep, institutional setting. Kids learn in fits and starts, especially little kids. You can show a little kid how to make the numeral "2" dozens of times, to absolutely no effect, and then all of a sudden one day he will "get it." The same goes for blending letters to make words, or understanding the concept of "same" and "different." You can't pick a day and say, "On this day all five-year-olds across America will be ready to learn to write the lowercase alphabet." This would not matter terribly much, except that in school you are labeled *stupid* if you fail to learn what the schedule book says you should learn on a given date. Oh, pardon me, not *stupid*—"learning disabled," or "minimal brain dysfunction," or "attention deficit disorder," etc. This last one is particularly interesting. Being translated it means, "Johnny is bored with his lessons and would rather run around the room or sit staring blankly at the clock." Just think—after all these years, I finally discovered that I suffered grievously from attention deficit disorder—just like a million other perfectly normal kids with boring teachers!

As the schools become more inflexible about what kids should learn at what age, parents at home, and especially home-schooling parents, have a golden opportunity to both recapture a little of the fun of our crayon-lovin' childhoods and ease our little ones more gradually into the academic mainstream. The secret is to give our kids readiness training before launching into academics, and to take the academics at whatever pace is comfortable for the kids.

All that said, it's now time to take a look at some kindergarten programs designed especially for you to use at home. These are *not* readiness programs; those are covered in the last chapter. In fact, these aren't kindergarten at all, in the classic, Froebelian sense of the word. Think of these as the transition from babyhood to student, for kids who are ready for more formal instruction than a readiness program.

KINDERGARTEN CURRICULUM

The following suppliers offer complete academic kindergarten programs. For more information, see the complete reviews, addresses, and ordering information in Volume 1.

- A Beka Books (K4, K5—accelerated phonics/academic approach).

- Advanced Training Institute (academic kindergarten *without* math and phonics, which must be purchased elsewhere).
- A Beka Video School (academic kindergarten).
- Alpha Omega Publications (kindergarten—LITTLE PATRIOTS phonics program).
- Alta Vista Homeschool Curriculum (K–1 two-year integrated program: need separate phonics and math curriculum).
- Associated Christian Schools (kindergarten, *Right Start* phonics program).
- Basic Education (choice of two academic learning-to-read programs).
- Bob Jones University Press (K5 phonics).
- Carden Educational Foundation (academic kindergarten curriculum).
- Christ Centered Publications (preschool program is actually more like kindergarten).
- Christian Liberty Academy (junior and senior kindergarten—academic programs).
- Christian Light Education (academic kindergarten, a Learning to Read worktext program).
- Clonlara School (any age, whatever kind of program you want).
- Community Learning Center (K–3 curriculum objectives only).
- ESP Publications (kindergarten—*My Yearbook* huge supplemental workbook—both readiness and phonics).
- Home Study International (academic kindergarten).
- International Institute (kindergarten covers readiness and reading).
- KONOS (K–6 integrated manual: choose your activities: need separate phonics and math curriculum).
- Living Heritage Academy (kindergarten—*Basic Reading* program).
- Our Lady of Victory (kindergarten called "grade 1A"—highly structured and academic).
- Rod and Staff (kindergarten—phonics).
- Seton Home Study School (kindergarten—readiness and phonics).
- Smiling Heart Press (preschool is combined with kindergarten in one-volume curriculum).
- Summit Christian Academy (kindergarten—phonics using *The Writing Road to Reading*).
- Sycamore Tree (readiness and phonics both available).
- The Weaver (K–6 integrated curriculum).

KINDERGARTEN MATERIALS

Alpha Omega Publications

LITTLE PATRIOTS Complete Kindergarten Program: $117.45 Parent's Kit, $154/child for student materials. Little Patriots Series Overview, $3.95.

Mile-Hi Publishers' THE LITTLE PATRIOTS, which Alpha Omega distributes, is based upon three principles:

A. *God's Principle of Individuality.* Each subject is important and needs to have its individual place in the curriculum. Each letter in our language has its own name, its own shape, and its own sound.

B. *God's Principle of Order.* Each child, made in the image of the God of order, will learn more successfully when order prevails in the content and methodology of the curriculum.

C. *God's Wholistic Principle* . . . Viewing the whole of the particular subject to add meaning and unity to its parts. We view the whole structure of our language to understand its parts.

Subjects covered are "the American Language" (Brits and Aussies beware!), with subheadings of phonics, reading, writing, spelling, and vocabulary; Bible (basic Bible doctrines, with Bible stories and catechism questions); Math (number line and number families); Readiness (*Little Patriots in Action*, a nine-week program to prepare children for LITTLE PATRIOTS).

The LITTLE PATRIOTS phonics program covers everything that can be done with one-syllable words. For more info see the separate writeup of this program in Chapter 7.

LITTLE PATRIOTS math is fairly similar to other Christian programs. Covered are number recognition and formation, simple addition and subtraction, multiple counting by 2, 3, 4, 5, 6, 7, and 10, measurement; calendar; time-telling; money.

The curriculum includes a lot more: Teacher's Guides for every subject, penmanship books, phonics workbook and cassette tape, introductory reading book, comprehensive phonics/spelling manual, and Bible curriculum.

NEW**
Bookstuff

Alphabetiks, $19.95, includes manual and both tablets. Shipping extra.

Delightful, very gentle introduction to typical kindergarten skills—letter names and sounds, writing, drawing—and some quite untypical kindergarten skills like research and basic science experiments.

Alphabetiks is subtitled "Alphabet Activities for Young Children, ages 5–7," and that's what it is, plus some. You get three spiral-bound books: the curriculum manual, a manuscript writing tablet, and a dictionary tablet. The curriculum manual includes the following alphabet activities for each alphabet letter: a small rectangle containing information and the shape of the ancient letterform from which our modern letter is derived; a dictionary word beginning with that letter; a list of tools whose names begin with that letter; a suggested drawing subject whose name begins with that letter; an "ideas" list from which you can build your own mini-unit study (again, each idea name begins with that letter); a thought question for discussion around the dinner table; a short list of recommended picture books whose names begin with the letter; one or two extremely clever art or science projects; and a list of snacks whose names begin with the letter.

The Manuscript Handwriting Tablet has one page for each letter. In the illustrated border of the page you will find one or more objects whose names begin with that letter. At the top of the page are illustrated letterforms showing you how to construct the letter using a precursive approach. Underneath that are uppercase and lowercase copies of the letter to trace. Below that are a few lines for the child to write copies of the words beginning with that letter that are listed on the left side of the page.

Remember the dictionary word I mentioned in the curriculum manual? These are "big" words like *aqueduct* and *fabricate*. Parents look up the word for the child, thereby teaching an important research skill while increasing the child's vocabulary. The child then traces the word in the Dictionary Word Tablet and writes the word on the line provided. He also makes up a sentence using the word, which the parent copies down in the space provided for this. Finally, the child makes a drawing about the word, using the suggested sentence in the curriculum manual. For example, he might draw an ant pulling a piece of apple across an aqueduct. The parent is supposed to explain what the objects he is trying to draw look like before he starts drawing. If the child is not ready to produce a drawing that complicated, *Alphabetiks'* authors urge you to simplify the task.

Let me share just one letter's worth with you, to give you the flavor of this excellent program. The letter is B and the dictionary word is *burrow*. Tools are "simple balancing scale, binoculars, balloons." If you have these around the house, introduce your child to them and show him how to use them. Then have your child draw a bear balancing on a barge, crossing under a bridge. The "Ideas" are balloons (hot air or helium), balance, bones, building, bridges. Using a blackboard or a large sheet of paper, list what your child "knows or wants to know about each of these topics, branching down and out." For example, the progression might be, "BONES --> Rover has bones --> I have bones --> Are my bones different from Rover's?" Pick one of these topics to explore in depth, using the library or any resources you might have around the house. (You keep the results in a journal.) The recommended picture books are *Blueberries for Sal* and *Benjamin and Tulip*. Letter B has two projects: BUILD strong bridges and make a BOOK about one of the B ideas. The bridge project includes experimenting with different shapes for the bridge (which is made out of plasticene clay) and seeing how long a bridge your child can make (measure it!) and how many objects such as paper clips it will hold (count or weight them!). The book project instructions tell you how to construct and reinforce a simple book. Finally, you get a list of simple snacks: banana bread, bagels and butter, etc.

This curriculum is easier to use than any other kindergarten program. You just do one letter a week. The authors recommend that you teach a few consonants first, then a vowel or two, so you can start teaching your child to read simple three-letter words. Along the way the child will learn to use a variety of useful household tools, be prodded to think more creatively and scientifically, have a variety of excellent children's classics read to him, do some fantastic art projects and science experiments, pick up any readiness concepts he might be missing, and have a whole lot of fun.

For families with little time to spare for teaching, but who still want to give the kindergartner an unpressured, yet rich learning experience, *Alphabetiks* is a great choice. Just add a kindergarten math program (such as Cube-It's *Counting House* or Bob Jones kindergarten math) and you've got it made!

Christ Centered Publications
Teacher materials: Basic Program $149.95 (usable ages 3–7). Student/teacher workbooks and readers: K4 $35.95, K5 $43.95, first grade $43.95. Components available separately. Add 10% shipping.

This may be the most serious attempt yet at a truly Christ-centered kindergarten and early grades program. Author Doreen Claggett, a schoolteacher of many years and a firm believer in early childhood as the time to begin scholarly studies, has assembled a workbook curriculum focusing mainly on phonics and math, with some art and other activities built in. The basic home-school version Teacher's Manual ($25) outlines the full early childhood education program and explains how to do seatwork with young children. Included is an article entitled "Detecting Learning Disabilities." The Basic Program also contains Bible, phonics, and math lesson plans in separate binders plus related visual aids. The program's philosophy appears in Mrs. Claggett's book *Never Too Early: Rearing Godly Children Who Love to Learn*.

OK, OK. Now where does the "Christ-centered" part come in? Well, would you believe math starting with the days of creation? Each day's work begins with a Bible verse and ties in as many Biblical examples as possible. Drawing upon the traditional Biblical numerology (seven as the number of perfection, three as the number of Trinity), numbers are presented as they relate to their occurrences in the Bible. Colors also have their own (slightly more strained) typology: purple for royalty, blue for heaven, orange for "the completeness of Christ's crosswork" and so on. Along with this you get flash cards reminiscent of Thoburn Press's *Animal Families* curriculum, with Mr. One Penguin and his chick 1+0, and so on. The math flash cards come with stories derived from Bill Gothard's Institute of Basic Youth Conflicts animal character sketches.

Similarly, CCP's phonics program uses Bible names and words as key words for the phonics sounds. The full program includes phonics workbooks, a *Phonics*

Drill Reader, three little readers, phonics flash cards, alphabet wall cards, and other teaching devices. See the separate writeup of the phonics program in Chapter 7.

CCP's math program teaches the addition and subtraction facts in a somewhat roundabout way based on amounts less than or greater than 10. According to the author, this has caused no problems for the more than 1,000 students who have used CCP math in her school's classrooms over the last 14 years. The children have achieved very well on standardized achievement tests. Still, for the higher levels of math I personally would substitute Bob Jones University Press.

Spiritually, most people get excited by the program's intense concentration on spiritual application—some so much so that the author has to warn against the temptation to use too much time preaching the lesson's spiritual theme at the expense of academics! CCP certainly is a far cry from the stray-Bible-verse-here-and-there or add-one-missionary-plus-one-missionary approach of much Christian curriculum. Send for the free information and you will see what I mean.

NEW**
Dale Seymour Publications
Kindergarten: A Sourcebook for School and Home, $8.95.

Supplementary kindergarten activities for parents. The first part introduces you to kindergarten, just in case your dear old memories of cutting and pasting are wearing thin. Chapter 2 explains how to make the best educational use of time with your child. Chapter 3 provides an array of activities arrayed by subject area. Scads of activities: more than 120 in all! A great resource for unschoolers or anyone unfamiliar with kindergarten teaching techniques.

NEW**
Family Learning Center
Commonsense Kindergarten Program, $77 complete. Program without Beechick books, $59.40. All items available separately: *Teaching Kindergartners*, $5.95. *Home Start, Easy Start*, $3.50 each. *Primary Thinking Skills*, $10.95 each. Box Full of Numbers kit, $14.95. *Language and Thinking*, $6.95. Workbooks, $2.95 each. Handbook, $5.95. Add 5% shipping.

The main goal of the Family Learning Center is "to provide low-cost easy to use curriculum that follows the educational approach of Ruth Beechick." This means treating each child as an individual made in the image of God, yet imperfect and needing much training. It also means taking a developmental approach, taking it fairly slow and easy and making sure the child is ready for each new learning experience.

The program includes several of Dr. Beechick's books, for those not familiar with her teaching tips and philosophy, but can be purchased without them if you already own these books. Designed for four- and five-year-olds who are ready for kindergarten, the Commonsense Kindergarten Program includes readiness exercises and a book (by Ruth Beechick) on how to teach your child to read. Subjects covered are Bible, reading, writing, math, thinking skills (unusual for a kindergarten program), art, and ideas for role play and physical education. Program contents include:

- *Teaching Kindergartners: How to Understand and Instruct Fours and Fives* by Dr. Ruth Beechick.

- *A Home Start in Reading* by Dr. Beechick. Small book includes complete, logical instructions for how to teach phonics, plus prereading activities. Usable up to third grade level.

- *An Easy Start in Arithmetic* by Dr. Beechick. Pre-math activities, math instruction tips, games, and guidelines. K–3. (All three of these books are reviewed elsewhere in this series.)

- *Language and Thinking* by Dr. Ruth Beechick and Jeannie Nelson (Mott Media). A wonderful book! Includes units of how to get the most out of telling and reading stories (plus six complete classic children's stories to read), activities to improve vocabulary and language skills (nutrition vocabulary, traffic vocabulary, numbers, measurement, classifying and organizing), language games (these are excellent!), items to memorize (personal info, letters, numbers, prayers, Bible verses, poems, hymns, patriotic songs, the calendar), telephone use and manners (including emergency phoning skills), poems (from baby poems to one-liners, funny poems, and rope jumping rhymes), manners (a very important unit that teaches polite words, how to accept and give compliments, how to meet and greet people, special manners for boys and girls, and public manners for church, library, store, and restaurant), and how to get the most educational value out of field trips (including suggested field trips).

• *Primary Thinking Skills A-1* (Midwest Publications). Over 47 hands-on activities in the areas of language, drama, and thinking skills. These were written for the classroom, so some activities require adaptation. You also will not be able to do all the suggested extra activities; don't burn out trying it! Each lesson takes about an hour, including some preparation time for finding materials, etc. You are expected to do one lesson a week.

• *Primary Thinking Skills A-2* (Midwest Publications). Another 42 hands-on thinking skills tasks, this time concentrating on numbers, problem solving, and science experiments. This volume is "programmed"; that is, every word the teacher needs to say is spelled out for you. This makes it easier to use than the first volume, in my opinion.

• *A Box Full of Numbers: Math Games for Kindergartners.* This is an absolutely super set, not available in stores, with all the ingredients you need for over 35 math games. Included are 12 Bingo cards, two memory decks, 12 sequencing strips, two dice game boards, four Tic Tac Toe boards, a Just Ten number deck, 14 sandpaper cards (numerals 0–9 and simple shapes), one 100 Chart, 12 wooden blocks (two dice and ten various colored blocks with numbers, dots, and shapes on various sides), and five each of green, red, blue, and purple counters. A Box Full of Numbers comes with a list of all math skills needed in kindergarten and early first grade. Games to teach each skill are listed immediately after the skill itself. Directions for all games are included.

• *The First Learning Workbook* series from EDC Publications: five colorful activity books covering counting to ten, same and different, time telling, opposites, and prewriting skills. These are not reusable workbooks, unfortunately—once your child writes in the EDC workbooks the first time, that's it for them.

• *The Commonsense Kindergarten Program Handbook* by Susan Simpson. Written for the new home-schooling parent, it includes an excellent sequence of Bible lessons concentrating on the difference between wisdom and foolishness, weekly and monthly planning suggestions, planning sheets, attendance records, evaluation forms, and enrichment suggestions for all subjects. The handbook is now being rewritten in a weekly lesson plan format, based on the Language and Thinking book, and should be available in the new format by the time you read this. Each week will contain activities for all subject areas, including music, art, and phys ed.

CHAPTER FIVE

PRESCHOOL HELPS

The stuff in this chapter isn't exactly *curriculum*, but it's definitely educational—and even fun!

I had originally intended to call this chapter "Preschool Widgets" or "Preschool Accessories," but the first one sounded like a kiddie hardware store and the second sounded like we would be talking about designer handbags for moppets. Too bad I couldn't think of one word to encompass floor puzzles, shape and color sorters, clean-up gear for kiddies, wipe-off books, preschool learning games, and all the other neat extras you'll find in this chapter! Kids can learn many of the basic preschool and kindergarten concepts just as well with these goodies as with a packaged curriculum, even if the process is somewhat less formal and methodical. Some of these resources teach skills not found in any regular packaged program, such as geometric logic (otherwise known as *puzzling*) and practical life skills (otherwise known as *mopping the floor*). If you're like me, your birthday shopping buck might stop right here!

FLOOR PUZZLES

NEW**
Frank Schaffer, Inc.
Floor puzzles, $12.95 each.

When the alphabet floor puzzle from Frank Schaffer arrived, I was not terribly excited. As an all-wise, all-knowing adult, I was sure that (a) my children wouldn't enjoy trying to put together such a big puzzle, and (b) they wouldn't learn any letters from it. After all (so I reasoned), the letters were intermingled so extensively with illustrations that their eyes couldn't differentiate between the two.

Well, (a) the alphabet floor puzzle became their favorite toy almost immediately, and (b) I noticed that my son Franklin, age two at the time, was figuring out how to put the pieces together by learning where the letters went.

So here I am, eating my words. Go ahead and get Frank Schaffer's alphabet floor puzzle. Collect *all* his floor puzzles!

All the following Frank Schaffer floor puzzles are for ages 2-7, except for the U.S. Map floor puzzle, which is for ages 4 and up: *Alphabet, Colors, Numbers 1-10, Dinosaurs Set 1, Dinosaurs Set 2, Animals, United States Map, Ocean Life, Nursery Rhymes, Body Parts, Food Groups, Transportation, Circus Time, Animals and*

Their Babies, Shapes, Farm, City, and *Children Around the World.*

The kids will play with these for hours, and—who knows?—they might even learn something.

OTHER WONDERFUL PRESCHOOL PUZZLES

NEW**
Lauri, Inc.

Shape and Color Sorter, $11.95. Crepe Foam Rubber Picture Puzzles, $5.95 each. Perception Puzzles, $5.95 each. Large Pattern Puzzles, $12.95 each. Lace-a-Puppet, $9.95. Lace-a-Saurus, Lace-a-Pet Puppet, $6.50 each. Needles for Lacing, 36/$3.95. Laces for Lacing, 24 36" laces, assorted colors, $3.95. Beads 'n Baubles, $4.95. Feel & Match Textures, $4.95. Fit-a-Space, $9.95. A-Z Panels, $6.95 each for uppercase or lowercase. 1-10 Panel, $4.50. Lauri's Build-a-Skill, $5.95 each. Tons more available!

This is one catalog you *really* ought to get. Lauri produces their own crepe rubber preschool learning goodies, which cover just about every important preschool skill, all at extremely good prices. Let's run through just a few of their hundreds of wonderful, colorful, fun-to-use products.

(1) Fit-a-Space. This was Lauri's first product, and it's still a winner. You get 16 round crepe foam rubber disks, each with small colored shape cutouts that fit inside—52 fit-in shapes in all. This one set provides enough mini-puzzles for a flock of preschoolers, or a real challenge for one lucky kid.

(2) Crepe Foam Rubber Puzzles. I should have put these first, since after all these puzzles are what Lauri is most famous for. Brightly colored, washable, imper-

vious to curling or tearing, quiet, and, most of all, beautiful puzzles that can be put together and taken apart again and again for years and years. Lauri has puzzles in all difficulty categories, from very easy puzzles like their Fit-a-Space to the Large Pattern Puzzles with up to 76 pieces. You might also want to try one or more of Lauri's Perception Puzzles. These are readiness aids, designed to help kids learn to discriminate between similar shapes. One puzzle has butterflies, each with a slightly different shape; another has fish, another cars 'n trucks, and yet another cookie-cutter-style kids engaged in a variety of activities.

(3) The A-Z panels and 1–10 Panel. I consider these essential learning aids. These are inexpensive foam rubber panels into which you fit alphabet letters (uppercase or lowercase) or numbers. You can take the letters and numbers out and use them separately to practice alphabetic or numeric sequencing. You can use the nubbly letters or numbers for kids to rub their fingers over, thereby learning how to form the letters. Or you can simply use them as puzzles, while your kids become unconsciously familiar with the basic letter and number shapes. Very highly recommended.

NEW**
Pacific Puzzle Company

Alphabet Puzzle (choice of uppercase or lowercase), 12 x 16", $25 each. Number puzzle, 9 x 12", $12. Geometric shapes, 9 x 12" knobbed, $18. Puzzles for younger children, 8 x 8", $12.50 each (can add knobs). Nineteen Dinosaurs puzzle, $18, can have knobs. Optional knobs are 20¢ apiece, $3 minimum per puzzle. Knobs not possible on the following puzzles: Creepers and Crawlers puzzle, 31 pieces, $20. Whales & Fishes, 40 pieces, $24. Birds of a Feather, 45 pieces, $24. Add $3 shipping for first puzzle, $1 each additional. Canada, AK, HI, add an additional 50% of the shipping rate. Foreign orders, inquire for foreign shipping rates.

Puzzling is a basic preschool skill. In fact, the makers of a rather famous Japanese math drill program always start their preschool students off with puzzles, because, as the sales rep told me, "Puzzles develop pre-math skills." This is not as far-fetched as it might sound. Fitting puzzles together requires recognizing shapes (pre-geometry), some trial and error, and a lot of logical elimination of possibilities (math thinking skills).

So you're going to run right down to the local Kiddie World and pick up some of those 99¢ cardboard puzzles for your preschooler, right? I hope not! There's nothing like warped, bent, soggy, chewed cardboard to turn a kid *and* his parents off puzzling for life! We have seven kids, and believe me, we pitched dozens of those tacky cardboard puzzles in the trash (when they had descended to the gross and ratty stage) before we figured out that we should go for quality when buying puzzles.

I've already told you about Lauri puzzles. These are one good quality choice. Now let me tell you about some absolutely fabulous hardwood puzzles for little kids and adults from Pacific Puzzle Company. These are colorful, too, since Pacific Puzzle Company stains the pieces different colors, while the hardwood frame remains its beautiful natural wood color. Yes, I said "hardwood frame," since these, unlike regular jigsaw puzzles, come with a back and surrounding frame into which the puzzle itself fits. A finger hole is provided for pushing the pieces out. We're talking family heirlooms here; the sort of puzzles the Rich and Famous, if they had/have good taste, could/can leave lying around their living rooms without worrying that the puzzles will clash with their $100,000 furniture. Class. Elegance. Savoir-faire. *That* sort of puzzle.

First, for strictly education-minded parents, consider Pacific Puzzle Company's hardwood Alphabet, Numbers, and Shapes puzzles. These come with either dark wood pieces on a natural wood background, or natural wood pieces on a dark wood background— your choice. Any of these can be purchased with knobs for an additional cost, but I recommend against it. The Geometric Shapes puzzle comes pre-knobbed. Although I have never actually seen any of these puzzles, they look really good in the catalog picture, and judging from the quality of the PPC puzzles I *have* seen (including those I am about to describe for you), you ought to be proud to give them to your children.

For beauty, fun, and the love of puzzling, PPC's Intertwining Animal Puzzles are really great. We have several of these that we bought as birthday presents for our younger children. Younger children's intertwining animal puzzles are 8 x 8" and include Four Horses, Five Rabbits, Six Dinosaurs, Seven Cats, and Eight Elephants. Each comes with the number of pieces mentioned in its name—e.g., Four Horses has four pieces. Nonetheless, thanks to the unique design of these puzzles, they will not be "too easy" for the kids. The puzzles with fewer pieces can be tackled by kids ages 3–5, but as an adult, I've found them absorbing! The pieces interlock in interesting ways, and if you don't request knobs on the pieces, the pieces are reversible. This means that your little guy or gal has to figure out not only where the piece goes, but

which side faces up! Add on the knobs, and a younger child can handle it.

Puzzles with more pieces are 9 x 12", and can pose quite a challenge to all family members. These are not impossible puzzles, though, like those 2,000-piece wonders that you left five years ago on the table in the basement intending to finish it "someday." It just takes perseverance and logic to put them together. Those with more pieces are *not* suitable for preschoolers until they are beyond the stick-it-in-the-mouth stage, since they do have small pieces. Once your children pass this stage, though, the smaller intertwining animal puzzles get my nod for your little ones' first "grown-up" puzzles.

PLAY CRAFTS

NEW**
EDC Publishing
Each book, $5.95 paperback or $13.96 with library binding. Shipping extra.

The new "You & Your Child" series from EDC Publishing is terrific! Each book has 32 pages loaded with instructions and step-by-step full-color illustrations of fresh and original projects for 3–6 year olds. The *Paperplay* book, for instance, gives directions for mobiles, paper plate masks, a trapeze-artist paper doll, standup critters, shadow boxes, puppets, costumes, paper jewelry, greeting cards, and lots more. The *Playdough* book shows you have to make pigs (and a pen to house them), sheep (and a field with shrubs and flowers for them to lie in), hedgehogs, the ever-popular "snakes in a basket," a Christmas nativity scene, play food of all sorts, playdough jewelry, and more. The *Odds & Ends* book shows how to turn sponges, bottle tops, paper cups, toilet paper rolls, cardboard boxes, old pillowcases, carpet scraps, and the like into great projects like a fully furnished dollhouse, a play cookstove, a pull-along train, and a moon rocket! Due out in fall 1991, the *Kitchen Fun* book will add food experiences to the list.

These are really doable projects, with great suggestions for project variations. Text accompanies each illustrated step, making it super-simple to follow. The book itself, with its cheerful, colorful illustrations, is bound to inspire young children (and their older siblings), and the text is easy enough for older children to read by themselves. The activities gently promote basic readiness skills, while helping children see the creative possibilities all around them.

PRACTICAL LIFE SKILLS PLUS MONTESSORI

NEW★★
Montessori Services

Toddler apron, $8, choice of vinyl with elastic, vinyl with velcro, or cloth with velcro. Set of five brooms and mops, $27.50. *Small World Cookbook*, $9. Booklet rings, various sizes, from $2 for a bag of 50. *Red Letter Alphabet Book*, $14. *Blue Number Counting Book*, $12. Sundial and booklet, $8.

Montessori Services' free catalog lists over 400 items, and you're going to want to buy them all. For the younger child (ages 2–7), they provide child-sized household tools. These include tools for polishing, food preparation, washing, clean-up, and all those other chore activities so dear to parental hearts. The selection includes aprons for all sized kids, right down to the toddler; scrub boards (a future collector's item!); child-sized clothespins; child-sized brooms and mops; and lots of other items you just can't find at K-Mart. Maria Montessori was a big believer in these "practical life" experiences, and I'm 100 percent on her side in this!

Now on to movement education. You can get lesson plans, gravel-filled bean bags (the selling point here is that wet gravel, unlike real beans, doesn't rot and sprout), and even parachutes in three different sizes! How about art appreciation books and creative art materials, from extra-sharp scissors to child-sized rolling pins for rolling out clay? Booklet rings also look good, as they provide a super-easy way for kids to turn a few sheets of paper into a "real book." The catalog has several pages of language materials, including the perennial best-seller *The Red Letter Alphabet Book*, with touch-sensitive letters for children to trace as they learn the sounds. They also carry the *Bob Books* (see Primers chapter); a large section of containers, baskets, and trays so children can organize their own materials and collections; cross-cultural resources, such as the *Small World Cookbook* with recipes from every continent and lots of cultural info besides; and materials for what other people call "unit studies" (e.g., a sundial and accompanying booklet for teaching numbers, timetelling, history, astronomy, reading, and various research projects). Just a few examples: a leaf and flower press for nature activities, carved wooden animals from Kenya, soapstone box from India, rawhide box from Mali (all for cross-cultural appreciation).

LANGUAGE ACTIVITIES

NEW★★
Children's Small Press Collection
Language Games, $7.95 plus $1 shipping.

Jean Warren. Talented lady. Wrote this book eight years ago. What is it? "A collection of over 100 concrete and practical ideas that encourage language development in young children." Like other Jean Warren materials, what you have here is tons of clever, doable ideas, lavishly illustrated. Seven sections to this book: Props, Stories, Listening, Rhyme & Rhythm, Words, Letters, Guessing. All ideas are fun to do and use everyday objects. A quick browse through this book will really get your creative juices flowing!

PERCEPTION TRAINING

UPDATED★★
Bookstuff
Alphabet Attributes, *Doing Dinosaurs Attribute Book*, *Toy Chest Attributes*, *Math Attributes*, *Attributes Activities*, $6.95 each. *Patterns*, $13.95. Shipping extra.

The *Attributes* series from Bookstuff is utterly unique. What you get are spiral-bound books full of perception-training riddles. You open the book. Staring at you are a bunch of matrices. I mean, 2 x 2 or 3 x 3 squares. On the top and left side of each box of squares are items arranged to show differences. For example, in *Alphabet Attributes* you might find a tiger standing up and a tiger lying down on the left side, while on the top you see blades of grass leaning left, standing up straight, and learning right. The idea is to cut out the page of accompanying pictures and paste each picture into the correct spot. Thus, the picture of a tiger standing up near a clump of left-leaning grass goes in the row with the tiger standing up and in the column with the left-leaning grass. This exercise promotes visual discrimination, fine motor skills (cutting and pasting), pre-math readiness (graphing, counting, coordinates, etc.), and logic (the Midwest Publications thinking-skills series uses a similar user interface, for example).

Alphabet Attributes has animals corresponding to alphabet sounds—a total of 26 2 x 2 matrices. For ages 4-6.

Doing Dinosaurs has (naturally) dinosaurs. Twelve 2 x 2 and 3 x 3 matrices altogether. Ages 4-8.

Toy Chest Attributes is more challenging. Designed for ages 5-8, it features toy chest objects such as roller skates, teddy bears, and toy ships, in 12 matrices up to 4 x 5 in size.

Math Attributes, for ages 4-6, is 12 matrices with simple geometric shapes. Children develop a math vocabulary while making comparisons based on size, position, etc.

Attributes Activities, for ages 4-7, is 15 matrices ranging in size from 2 x 2 to 4 x 4. Most have a whimsical animal motif—e.g., a mama kangaroo with a pig or a turtle in her pouch.

Bookstuff's *Patterns* is 26 worksheets containing a total of 130 patterns. Each page represents a letter of the alphabet. For example, the letter "p" page has a pig, panda, and penguin. Cut out the answer and paste it in. It can be used for enrichment with a phonics program.

Alphabetiks, Bookstuff's wonderful one-book kindergarten curriculum, is reviewed in Chapter 4.

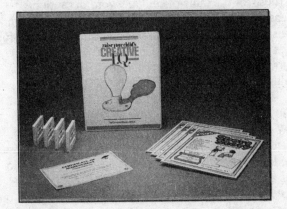

UPDATED★★
Perception Publications
Package containing *IQ Booster Kit* cassettes, *Developing the Early Learner* workbook series, and *151 Fun Activities*, $69 plus $4 shipping. *Developing the Early Learner* series alone, $24.95 for all 4 workbooks plus $4 shipping. Individual workbooks available separately. *151 Fun Activities* purchased separately, $25.

The *IQ Booster Kit* from Perception Publications is a perception-training program I really like. Drawing on her ten years as a classroom teacher, author Simone Bibeau, M.Ed., produced a four-workbook series that exercises your child in these four areas: Motor (left-right tracking, mazes, eye movements, hand-eye coordination), Visual (similarities, memory, figure ground, space orientation), Auditory (similarities, memory,

rhyming), and Comprehension (categories, sequence, language, awareness).

This all sounds very complicated, but really it's not. The exercises are laid out in a carefully graduated sequence of fun activities. None of these require strain on your or your child's part. He practices drawing lines from here to there without running his lines into the "obstacles," he solves mazes, he colors the happy face if the birdies look alike and the sad face if they don't. For the auditory exercises, you might need to ding a spoon on a cup or thunk a book on the table while Junior listens with his eyes shut. Even this small effort can be removed by buying the accompanying cassette with the auditory exercises on it.

We bought this series for our oldest son when he was four, and he absolutely loved it. "When do I get to play 'Same and Different?'" Ted would ask. We could almost visibly see his mind sharpening up as he did the exercises. Let me mention that when the *IQ Booster Kit* has been tested, 95 percent of all children tested significantly increased their learning abilities by using the program.

The art is engaging, and since the books are all black and white your child can have the added fun of coloring them in. If your son or daughter is old enough to hold a crayon, he or she is ready to start on the first book of the series. By the time a child gets to book four, he is solving complicated mazes and figuring out the answers to questions like "House is to tent like glass is to—?"

Each book contains a diagnostic Progress Chart and suggested exercises for testing and remedying perceptual handicaps.

You get four cassettes with the complete *IQ Booster Kit*. The first two share the program's educational philosophy and train you to use the kit effectively. On the last two are the auditory exercises.

151 Fun Activities for Children is a two-tape set with accompanying manual and binder. Down-to-earth explanations of how and why to train your child's thinking and motor skills, plus 151 easy-to-do activities that develop those skills. Since the last time I revised this book, Simone has thrown it in along with the *IQ Booster Kit*—and lowered the price as well! She reduced the price of the kit to include the *151 Fun Activities* book "because we believe so strongly in educating our parents. Too many parents just give the books to their children—they are used as busy work and so much of the valuable skill development is missed. All learning does not take place in a workbook—thus the need for games and activities to enhance the child's perceptual growth." In other words, she believes you will get much more out of her program if you get the $69 package including the workbooks, *IQ Booster* cassettes, and *151 Fun Activities* book, rather than just purchasing the workbooks. If you do not have much of a background in child development and perception training, I believe she is right; however, if you can't afford the entire program, even just the workbooks, used according to directions, can make a significant difference in your child's mental sharpness.

PRESCHOOL SKILL DRILL

NEW★★
Educational Insights
Professor Purple, $17.95. Kitty Kat Bingo games, $14.95 each. Counters (box of 100), $14.95 each style. Letter Perfect, $14.95. Tub O'Letters (86 extra tiles), $8.95 each for uppercase and lowercase. Picture Perfect, $17.95. Tub O'Colors (86 extra tiles), $8.95. Beginning Skills FunThinker, $7.95. Decoder Box and Tiles for Fun-Thinkers, $7.95.

As often happens with Educational Insights, I am amazed at the price of this whimsical drill device. For $17.95 you get Professor Purple, a large purple widget with eyes that move up and down, a mouth area in which questions are displayed, a tie that points to the answer your child selects, and a tummy area on which you mount a dial from which your child chooses his answer. Here's how it works. You pick a question wheel and mount it on Professor Purple's back. (Takes about five seconds.) Now a question is showing in Professor Purple's mouth. You also mount the appropriate answer wheel on his tummy. (Another five seconds.) Your child then moves the answer wheel until Professor Purple's tie is pointing to what she considers the right answer. Push down on Professor Purple's eyes and nose to reveal the correct answer lower in his mouth. Your child then pushes Professor Purple's eyes and nose back up to advance to the next question.

This inexpensive widget comes with enough question dials to let your child practice matching colors, learn color words, match sets of objects to the appropriate numeral, drill number words, match lowercase letters, match capital and lowercase letters, and match beginning sounds to the appropriate letter, and practice simple addition and subtraction—eight double-sided plastic-coated question wheels in all. You also get three double-sided answer dials—colors, numeral,

and alphabet—plus a short teacher's guide.

You will need to explain what to do with each of the dials, but once this is accomplished, a child can play with Professor Purple without adult supervision. This is a really fun, self-checking way for preschool kids to drill their basic facts.

Another neat basic skill 'n drill resource from Educational Insights is their lineup of Kitty Kat Bingo games. These include *Color and Shape Bingo, Number Bingo, Alphabet Bingo, Sight Word Bingo,* and *Telling Time Bingo.* Each bingo game comes with eight full-color bingo cards with three rows and columns each, spinner, instructions, and 65 precious little colored plastic Kitty Kat counters, molded to look like teeny-weeny kittens. You can also use the Kitty Kat counters for counting, sorting, matching, and lots of other preschool skill drill, by the way, and they *are* available separately. Or if you prefer tyrannosaurus, stegosaurus, or brontosaurus counters, in the same colors and about the same size as the Kitty Kats, you can get 100 of those for the same price. One word of caution: please do *not* give Kitty Kat counters to little ones who are still sticking things into their mouths! These are for kids ages 3–7, who are old enough to learn colors, numbers, and the alphabet, and to make a stab at telling time.

Letter Perfect is another nifty drill resource, this time for alphabet learning. You put the see-through tray over any of the eight colorful activity cards, and then snap the included 1" letter tiles in place to match the letters on the cards. Includes a game card with no letters, for use in a word-making game. A similar device called Picture Perfect can be used as a variation on that old favorite, parquetry, by placing the see-through plastic grid over one of the 16 colorful picture patterns and then snapping the correct design tile into place. Graduated difficulty of designs for increasing drill in shape and color recognition, matching, and pattern recognition.

OK, this is the last self-checking goodie from Educational Insights that I'm going to plug in this chapter. It's the *Beginning Skills FunThinker.* FunThinkers are a bit complicated for young preschoolers to use, but are really fun for kindergarten-age kids. These motivational *and* self-checking widgets work as follows. First, you open the book (three are included in each Fun-Thinkers kit) to the lesson you want to do. Next, you open the FunThinkers Decoder Box. (You have to buy this, and the tiles, separately, by the way, but it works with *every* FunThinkers kit.) Place the Decoder Box, which is like a large grid with four rows and four columns, over both pages of the lesson, so the picture squares fit inside the grid squares. Next, place tiles 1–16 in order, number side up, in the grid squares on the left page. (Ed Insights makes this task easier for young children by including the appropriate number on each picture square.) Then, read the directions at the top of the left-hand page. Pick up tile 1 and look at the picture square. Find the matching picture or answer on the other side and place tile 1 there. Continue in this way until all of the tiles are now on the right-hand grid. Then close the Decoder Box tightly and turn it over. You will see that the tiles are colored on the back and form a pattern. Check this pattern against the answer in the back of the book to see if you did the lesson right. (This last step may be too hard for a younger student; let 'em call Mom in at this point!)

The *Beginning Skills FunThinker* kit comes with three books: *All Around Fun* (matching shapes, big and little, matching colors, matching animal parts, opposite directions, matching hats to the workers, putting objects in alphabetical order), *Sounds and Letters* (matching uppercase letters, matching lowercase letters, matching uppercase to lowercase, matching letters to objects, finding beginning letters), and *Numbers to 10* (matching sets of objects, matching sets and numerals, matching sets with the missing number in a sequence, finding the number of colored shapes in each picture and matching it to a shape and number on the other page). Plenty here to keep your kindergartner happily busy! And don't forget the FunThinkers for older children: *Sounds and Words* and *Math Magic* (for grades 1–3) and *Reading Workout* and *Thinking Skills* (grades 3–6).

NEW**
Timberdoodle
Wrap-Ups, $7.25 each, or three or more for $6.25 each. Add 10% shipping (minimum $4, maximum $15).

These gizmos won my Widget-of-the-Year prize for 1990. They are something entirely new: self-correcting drill sticks, about double the size of a butter knife blade and about as thick. You get 10 in a small cardboard can, each with different problems on it, plus 10 colorful strings. Pull the string to pop the top off the cardboard tube. Step one now   is to attach a string to each Wrap-Up (this only has to be done once, thankfully). From now on, Marvin and Sally can use them by themselves. Simply wrap the string from the problem on the left to the answer on the right, going from top to bottom. Then turn the Wrap-Up

around and see whether the string covers the embossed lines on the back of the Wrap-Up. If you did all the problems right, the string and the lines match up. If not, unwind the string and try, try again! This activity builds the left-right concept, hand-eye coordination, and visual tracking skills, while providing a really fun way to drill simple skills that does not require constant adult problem checking.

Many of you will eventually want to get the math Wrap-Ups: separate sets for addition, subtraction, multiplication, division, and fractions. For your preschooler, Timberdoodle has Wrap-Ups sets to drill numbers (matching, counting in sequence, etc.), the alphabet (e.g., matching upper- and lowercase letters), and shapes and logic.

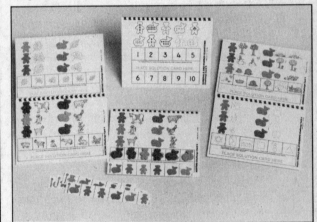

HANDS-ON PART 1:
LACE, SORT, STRING, FEEL, MATCH

NEW**
Lauri, Inc.
Shape and Color Sorter, $11.95. Lace-a-Puppet, $9.95. Lace-a-Saurus, Lace-a-Pet Puppet, $6.50 each. Needles for Lacing, 36/$3.95. Laces for Lacing, 24 36" laces, assorted colors, $3.95. Beads 'n Baubles, $4.95. Feel & Match Textures, $4.95. Lauri's Build-a-Skill, $5.95 each. Tons more available!

You remember Lauri. They're the people I mentioned above who make those wonderful crepe foam rubber puzzles. Lauri also makes an enormous array of wonderful hands-on learning stuff for pre-first grade (and older) kids. Here are some of their best:

(1) Shape and Color Sorter. Every kid age 2 and up could use one of these! You get a foam rubber base, five colored pegs, and 25 pieces of double-thick colored crepe foam rubber cut into squares, circles, triangles, stars, and hearts. Your little one can sort them ei-

ther by shape or by color: red, yellow, blue, green, and orange. This is the closest I have seen to a toy that really *does* provide "hours of fun," and it teaches colors, shapes, and hand-eye coordination as well!

(2) Lacing goodies. Lacing is a pre-needlework skill that also develops fine motor skills, and is a wonderfully soothing activity to pull out when the kids are frazzling your nerves. I got a review sample of the Lace-a-Puppet, and had to beat off our girls long enough to look it over myself! The Lace-a-Puppet has six "people" to lace up, while the Lace-a-Saurus and Lace-a-Pet Puppet each have three lacing critters. Each kit includes precut felt body shapes, plastic needles, yarn, and lots of remnant felt pieces so your kids can decorate their finished hand puppets. And for those of you who are always losing your lacing needles, Lauri has those, and lacing laces for regular lacing projects, too.

(3) Beads 'n Baubles. Stringing is a slightly different skill than lacing, but is just as quiet and satisfying. Your little ones will enjoy stringing the 100+ variously-sized and colored crepe foam rubber pieces in the three tipped laces. If they are like mine, they will also quickly catch on to the idea of stringing the rubber pieces on in pretty patterns—by color, shape, or both—another readiness skill!

(4) Feel 'n Match Textures. I first ran across this idea in a special education brochure. You stick objects of different textures into a bag, and ask kids to pick out two that feel the same. The kit includes 12 3½" disks, six different textures in all: plastic, felt, rubber, chipboard, a really nice squeezable foam, and another fun furry piece. Good for strengthening tactile skills.

(5) We'll close this tour of the Lauri line with their newest product: the Build-a-Skill series. It's a self-checking educational system that's a bit hard to explain but not at all hard to use. Here's how it works. Each Build-a-Skill has nine spiral-bound, plastic-coated Challenge Cards. A kid reads the challenge, or has it read to him. He then places the included rubber shapes in the proper answer spaces on the card, and checks to see if he did it right with the enclosed Solution Card. One challenge, for instance, asks kids, "Which animal belongs in which family?" On the Challenge Card, a red teddy bear is next to the lion and tiger, so your child puts the red teddy bear under the cat at the bottom of the card. A yellow whale is next to the two fish, so he puts the yellow whale marker under the fish at the bottom of the card. As you can see, the challenges require kids to mark answers with the proper rubber shape, which takes a bit of thinking.

It's more fun than marking answers with crayon or pencil in a workbook, and also means that these kits are almost infinitely reusable. The series includes *Beginning Sorting and Classifying, Advanced Classification and Sequencing, Number Recognition and Counting, Beginning Addition, Addition with Numbers to 99, Beginning Subtraction, Subtraction with Numbers to 99, Beginning Multiplication, Beginning Division, Learning the Alphabet—CAPITALS, Learning the Alphabet—Lower Case,* and *Beginning Spelling.*

HANDS-ON PART 2: FLIP, FLASH, AND WIPE

NEW**
Frank Schaffer Publications
Easy Alphabet, Colors, Numbers, and Shapes set, $6.95 for all, boxed.

Flash cards are flash cards, right? Well, this is a really cute set of flash cards covering basic preschool concepts, all packed in a small, sturdy, reusable box. WHAT YOU GET: 100 flash cards with full-color illustrations on one side and a letter, word, or numeral on the other. The Alphabet set has a picture of an object beginning with that letter, and the name of that object, on the front, with the large lowercase letter on the back. You get two color words sets. One has an object colored that color on the front, and the name of the color on the front and the (in larger letters) back. The other, for skill checking, has only the color on the front, and its name on the back. Shape flash cards have the shape on the front and the name on the back. You also get two sets of number words flash cards. The first has the numeral (in color) on the front and its name on the back. The second has a number of colored objects on the front and the numeral on the back. Learning suggestions are included; I'd disregard the suggestion to teach "sight words," though. A really good price for a lot of colorful, basic, flash cards.

NEW**
TREND Enterprises, Inc.

Fun-to-Know™ series, $3.99 each except for *Presidents* and *States & Capitals*, $4.99 each. Match Me® Flash Cards, $3.99/set. Spin 'n Learn Flash Cards, $3.99/set. Wipe-Off® Cards, $6.95/set. Flip Books, $1.99 each, except for *Alphabet*, which is $2.99. Reusable activity books, $1.99 each. Wipe-Off® Books, $2.95 each. Wipe-Off® crayons, 79¢/box. Bull's Eye® Activity Cards, $3.49/set.

You don't know what I've gone through trying to protect these review samples from the kids long enough to write them up! These are really *fun* products!

(1) The Fun-to-Know series. (I trust we can dispense with trademark signs for the rest of this writeup, since they are all displayed above.) Here's a new twist on flash cards: full-color 4 x 6" card sets, each in a sturdy, colorful storage box. Some real thought went into putting these sets together. You get your standard Alphabet set of 26 cards with upper- and lowercase letter and picture on one side and letters only on the other, and your set of *Numbers 0–25* with colorful items to count and the numeral on one side and the numeral only on the other. So far, nothing new. But how about these other card sets:

- Famous Places (basic cultural literacy, from the Leaning Tower of Pisa to the White House)

- Personal Safety (excellent coverage of everything from water safety to the safe use of tools)

- Smart Choices (role-play of childhood dilemmas with three choices on back *and* comments on how good or bad each choice is)

- Community Helpers (job requirements, personal qualities, duties, discussion questions; unrealistic feminist portrayal of job roles, unfortunately, with female mechanic, plumber, dentist, fire fighter, and construction worker, among others; no housewives/mothers or businesspeople)

- Dinosaurs & Prehistorics (from *anchisaurus* to *wooly mammoth*; evolutionary)

- Animals (food, size, color, where found, habitat, characteristics, fascinating fact, discussion questions—from *alligator* to *turtle*)

- Transportation (descriptions of 26 vehicles from *airplane* to *tanker*, plus fascinating facts and discussion questions)

- Signs and Symbols (safety and survival signs plus drill questions)

- Presidents of the United States, and

- States and Capitals

Some of these are written up in more detail in other chapters. For now, let's just say that each of these sets has fascinating facts and/or "Think About It" questions on the back, plus full-color pictures on the front. Really good early learning resources, except for *Famous Places*, *Presidents*, and *States*, which are designed for preteens.

(2) Whew! We're just getting started! Now on to Match Me Flash Cards. This is another really neat idea; double-sided flash card sets you can match up four ways! They come in pairs, loosely connected. In the Match Me Money set, for example, two matching cards have the same amount of money pictured on the front—but with different coin combinations. On the back, one card has the price in numeric notation (e.g., "35¢") while the other has it written out (e.g., "thirty-five cents"). You can match coin combinations to the price in numerals or words or to a matching (but different) coin combination. Series includes *Alphabet* (two different pictures starting with the letter, upper- and lowercase letters), *Numbers 0–25* (numerals, words, and two different illustrations of that quantity of items), *Telling Time* (clock dial, digital clock face, time in words, and time in notation), and *Money*.

(3) Spin 'n Learn Flash Cards. These are really neat—self-checking flash cards! Turn the wheel to pick the answer. Then turn over the card to see if you got it right! Series includes *Long Vowels*, *Short vowels*, *Beginning Consonants*, *Addition*, *Subtraction*, *Multiplication*, *Fractions*, and *Telling Time*. Oh, one more thing: each Spin 'n Learn card is shaped like some kid-pleasing, colorful object, such as a robot, video screen, camera, or rocket. Several cards per durable storage box.

(4) Now we come to some *real* preschool essentials—TREND's Wipe-Off Card sets. These are double-sided, oversized, plastic-coated cards that you can write on again and again, preferably with TREND's plastic wipe-off crayons. These are the exact same exercises you get in the better preschool readiness workbooks, except they are full-color and can be repeated

again and again! Series includes *Let's Count* (writing numerals, circling the correct number of objects, etc.), *Follow the Path* (great pre-handwriting practice), *Finish the Picture* (great pre-art practice), *I Can Print* (now we're getting into real manuscript writing), *See It, Make It* (simple designs to copy using basic geometric figures), *Match the Letters* (capital to capital, lowercase to lowercase, capital to lowercase), *Colors and Shapes* (tracing and matching), and the wonderful perception-training set, *Same or Different*.

(5) Flip Books. Another self-checking exercise, this time without loose pages that can get scattered around! Youngsters flip top and bottom halves of the pages in these small spiral-bound books. When the top and bottom half match, a proper picture emerges on the facing pages. Now, let's be honest—at first the kids will *not* match things up properly, because it's more fun to see a kangaroo with elephant legs than to see a proper kangaroo. After a while of this, though, they'll use the books as intended, providing a lot of simple drill practice that requires no adult supervision. Series includes *Colors, Alphabet* (matching uppercase and lowercase letters), *Shapes* (find matching shapes), and *Numbers* (match numerals to sets of that quantity).

(6) Reusable Activity Books. Sixteen full-color, plastic-coated Wipe-Off pages in each small book. Center pages cut out to make flash cards or other activities. Very inexpensive and fun. Series includes *Colors and Shapes, Number Fun* (matching and writing), *Alphabet Fun* (matching and writing), *Simple Mazes* (good pre-handwriting and logic practice), *Great Games* (Tic-Tac-Toe, Hangman, etc.), *Dot to Dot* (upper- and lowercase letters, numbers 0–36, counting by twos, all with the adorable Dot family), *Finish the Picture, Good Thinking* (same and different), *Telling Time, Money Fun, Vowel Parade,* and *Go-Togethers* (match-ups and concentration activities).

(7) Tired yet? I hope not, because here come TREND's famous Wipe-Off books! Of these, we have been using *Before I Print!* (pre-handwriting with lines, circles, and wavy lines), *Let's Print!,* and *Let's Write Numbers!* for years and years. These are *great* reusable, colorful books your kids will *want* to use. Series also includes other useful drill and skill reusable books: *Colors & Color Words!, Colors & Shapes!, Let's Write!, Alphabet & Number Fun!, Count to 10!, I Can Add!, I Can Subtract!* and *I Can Multiply!* These are also very good books; we just personally tend to drill these concepts orally more than with written exercises.

(8) Finally, yet another unique self-checking drill series: Bull's Eye Activity Cards. Here's how they work.

The question is on the front. Underneath are three possible answers, each with a hole punched beneath. Poke your finger through the hole of the answer you think is correct. Then turn the card around and see if your finger is through the hole with the gray ring around it. If so, you answered the problem correctly. *Very* easy to use. Kids don't need to read to use these cards, since questions consist entirely of matching illustrations to answers. E.g., in the *Beginning Consonants* set the child is shown a picture of a goat and asked to choose between *b, h,* and *g* as the beginning consonant. Series includes *Short Vowels, Beginning Consonants, Long Vowels,* and *Counting 1–10.*

HANDS-ON PART 3: GIFTS PRESCHOOLERS CAN MAKE

NEW*
Fearon Teacher Aids
From Kids with Love, $8.95

More than 60 gifts preschoolers can put together with very little help from you. Some are items adults and other kids might actually want, such as the sock puppets and handmade soap balls, while others fall into the timeless category of "collectibles"—"It's a good thing Grandma has so much shelf space in her condo." Sections include paper gifts and cards, cloth gifts, gifts from nature, gifts from odds and ends, mix and measure gifts, holiday gifts and decorations, and creative wrapping papers. That last section is alone worth the price of the book, since every kid needs wrapping paper for Christmas and birthday presents, even if he doesn't make the present himself. Each project comes with an illustration, materials list, and detailed instructions, plus helpful hints for project variations. A short appendix tells you how to make your own stamp pads, colored sand, and colored pasta, and how to dry flowers. Lots and lots of fun projects that will never have to clutter up your house (it truly *is* better to give than to receive!)

ELECTRONIC PRESCHOOL

NEW**
Educational Insights
Charlie battery model, $49 (batteries not included). Charlie A/C model (comes with earphone jack), $79.95. Headphones for A/C model, $19.95. Learning packets, $12.95 each. Reading Readiness I set of 4 packets, $49.95. Reading Readiness II set of 4 packets, $49.95. Alphabet Skills set of 4 packets, $49.95. Math Readiness set of 4 packets, $49.95. Charlie Listening Sets, $17.95 each or $99.95 for all 6.

What costs bunches less than a computer and is much easier to use, but is just as exciting to kindergartners? Introducing Charlie, the "teaching robot" from Educational Insights. The clever folks at this company have designed a complete program of K–5 drill lessons on colorful, durable cards. Each card presents between three and five multiple-choice questions on each side, with 20 cards in each pack. At the lowest level, these involve matching shapes, choosing colors, and recognizing differences (no reading required). Your child inserts the card on the top of Charlie (any two-year-old can do this), then presses with the attached stylus on the answer he thinks correct. If he's right, Charlie lights up and makes a happy sound.

You can buy Charlie learning packets separately, or save a smidgin by buying them in sets of four. Reading Readiness I includes one packet each for *Visual Discrimination*, *Spatial Relationship*, *Identifying Objects*, and one called *Who, What, When, Where, Why*. Reading Readiness II includes *Basic Reading Skills: Animals*, *What's Wrong?*, *Big and Little*, and *Picture Sequencing*. The Alphabet Skills set includes *Lowercase Letters: Visual Discrimination*, *Uppercase Letters: Visual Discrimination*, *Alphabet Sequence*, and *Alphabet: Upper- and Lowercase*. The Math Readiness set includes *What Shape?*, *Classification Skills*, *How Many?* and *Basic Number and Color Words*. This is only the tip of the iceberg, as you can get all sorts of more advanced packs for phonics skills, reading skills, math skills, language skills, and vocabulary skills. For math skill drill, for example, there's Math Skills I (grades 1–2), Math Skills II (grades 2–4), Math Skills III (grades 3–5), and Everyday Math (grades 2–4). Each of these includes four learning packets.

And that's not all! Charlie Listening Sets are also available. Each comes with a cassette tape, 10 full-color Charlie cards, a teaching guide, and a storage box. Kids listen to stories and poems and answer the narrator's questions by picking the right answer on the appropriate Charlie program card. The series includes *Beginning Consonants I, Beginning Consonants II, Short Vowels, Long Vowels, Beginning Blends,* and *Learning to Count.*

Unless Charlie's space-age sounds bother you, or you expect your kids to use Charlie for hours every day, there's no reason not to get the inexpensive battery-powered model. The battery model has a built-in, volume control. Once the kids understand how to use Charlie, and you've run through what is expected on each card, they can use Charlie pretty much on their own. You'll want to be nearby, of course, to answer questions and admire their progress!

Charlie is really fun to use, and children easily learn how to use him on their own. Children get instant feedback on their choices—very important for young learners. And the program really does cover all important preschool skills. You'd want to add art and crafts activities, and of course a good preschool program also requires lots of reading aloud to your children. With this in mind, you could honestly use Charlie as the nucleus of a super-simple, highly motivational preschool program—*and* for drill practice in the early grades as well!

ALL-IN-ONE PRESCHOOL LEARNING GAME

NEW**
Shekinah Curriculum Cellar
Fast Progress, retail $24.95, Shekinah's price $22.95 plus 10% shipping $3 minimum, CA residents add 6¼% sales tax.

Michele Robinson of Shekinah Curriculum Cellar sent me a review sample of the *Fast Progress: The Game of Communication Skills.* Designed for four to seven year olds, this nifty game is the only one I've ever seen that teaches communication skills needed for success in school.

First, what you get. The game comes with a colorful game board of the move-along-the-straight-path variety, 180 game cards, die, timer, six player pieces, 10 blank cards, and complete instructions. Someone who knows how to read needs to read the cards to the young players. Average playing time ranges from 20 minutes to an hour.

Each small blue card has two questions on it, directed to different readiness levels. This simple device means children of different ages can play competitively. Simply have the younger children answer Level I questions while the older ones answer Level II. Cards with one right answer are answered on the Answer List. Some questions, such as, "What is your name?" are not answered on the answer list. You only use the one-minute timer if necessary to keep the game moving along.

To play, pick as many cards as you think your child is up to answering. Each player rolls a die, and the highest number goes first. When it's his turn, each player takes a card and tries to answer that question. If he can answer it correctly, he rolls the die and moves that number of spaces. If the card he draws gives a direction (e.g., "If you are on red, move to the next nearest blue") he follows the directions first and then rolls the die to move again. The object is to arrive exactly at the "Finish" space.

Questions are an intriguing mix. Some require kids to think out the answers, while others test what kids know. All use the typical communication skills required in school. Topics cover those kids need to be familiar with before entering first grade: body parts, personal data, time concepts, directionality (right/left, up/down), classifying, making analogies, antonyms (words that are opposites), rhyming, describing, vocabulary, math concepts, and general practical knowledge. The game author encourages you to have the children answer each question in a complete sentence, if they are old enough to make this feasible.

Here are a few sample questions:

- (Level I) How many sides does a triangle have? (Level II) Which is more money, a quarter or a nickel?

- After you touch a green box on the board, touch a white one.

- (Level I) What do you wear that comes in a pair? (Level II) What number is at the bottom of a clock?

- (Level I) Name three things that could be below you. (Level II) Name the months of the year.

- (Level I) How does a mother cat clean her babies? (Level II) What is hail?

I really admire the questions in this game. They really cover an amazingly broad range of stuff kids need to know and be thinking about.

Now, is *Fast Progress* fun to play? You betcha! It really moves fast. And is it really educational? For sure. This is not another boring educational game—it's more like Preschool Student's Educational and Thinking Trivia. Any kid whose parents play this game with him before he starts his school studies (whether at school or in home school) will have a definite edge on most kids who don't.

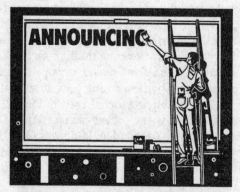

BULLETIN BOARD LEARNING

NEW**
TREND Enterprises, Inc.
Each bulletin board set, $5.95, includes free Discovery Guide. Requires 4 x 6' bulletin board.

TREND's Challenge Charts bulletin board sets present basic skills plus a progress chart with enough spaces for even the *biggest* family! The idea is to stick incentive stickers on the chart (stickers are included) when each child learns the skills on the accompanying skills charts. The *Good Beginnings* Challenge Chart set teaches the alphabet, colors, and numbers. *Dino Skills* includes famous dinosaurs, punctuation marks, and the famous 12 x 12 multiplication chart we all loved so much as children. I can't believe the low-low price of these sets!

MAKE A BOOK, TAKE A THEME

NEW★★
Warren Publishing House, Inc.
1•2•3 Art, $12.95. *1•2•3 Games*, $7.95. *Piggyback Songs*, $6.95 or $7.95 each volume. *Cut & Tell* series, $6.95 each. *Theme-A-Saurus* and *Theme-A-Saurus II*, $19.95 each. *Alphabet & Number Rhymes*, $12.95. *Color, Shape & Season Rhymes*, $12.95. Shipping extra.

Warren Publishing House has a whole line of cut-and-tell scissor stories (you've never seen anything like them!) and *Piggyback Songs* (new words to familiar tunes teach concepts or are just fun). Not to mention their preschool art curriculum, or preschool games book, or sugar-free kid-made snacks book. Etc.

New from Warren Publishing House are "Take-Home" Books. This is a new twist on the old idea of preschool kiddies making their own simple books. *Alphabet & Number Rhymes* includes an Alphabet Book, a Farm Counting Book, and a Sea Life Counting Book. *Color, Shape & Season Rhymes* includes Color Books, Shape Books, and Season Books. Each book of books is an oversized paperback. Preschool teachers are urged to photocopy the reproducible pages, cut each page into a top half and a bottom half (each has its own rhyme and illustration), and let the kids collate them, make their own covers, bind the books themselves, and take them home to Mom and Dad. Hence the name, "Take-Home." At home you don't need to bother with the photocopying or cutting; just tear out a bunch of pages at a time and let your little ones make their own preschool learning books!

Another new item from Warren Publishing House worth mentioning: *Theme-A-Saurus: The Great Big Book of Mini Teaching Themes,* and its sequel, *Theme-A-Saurus II.* For the benefit of those who, like me, hadn't the faintest idea what a "teaching theme" is, here's the scoop. Take an ice cube. Stare intently at that cube for two hours. Tell me every clever idea you came up with for teaching preschool concepts using ice cubes or activities themed around ice cubes. Now collect all those ideas from all the thousands of preschool teachers who subscribe to Jean Warren's publications. Now you have an ice cube teaching theme.

Ice actually is one of the themes in *Theme-A-Saurus II,* and here's what you get: Ice sculpture. Ice painting (use tempera powder and rub ice cubes over it). Ice cube magic (how to lift an ice cube out of a glass of water without touching the cube—a simple science demonstration). Melting ice experiments. A game involving passing ice cubes in a circle. Color combining using colored ice cubes (food coloring plus water). Ice cube counting. Pretending to be icicles while reciting a poem. Imaginary ice skating. Ice cube snacks.

I tend to find the themes centered around everyday objects more useful than those that take, say, "Zebra" as the theme. These latter try to both teach something about (in this case) zebras and use zebra shapes and other zebra characteristics to teach other subjects. So this is what you end up with: Zebra masks. Pretending to be zebras. Stripe matching activities? Zebra poems. These activities aren't *bad;* it's just that they are stretching things a bit to stick to the theme. Each oversized, amply illustrated Warren book is loaded with so many themes (over 50 in the first and over 60 in the second) and so many activities (over 600 in each) that you'll have more to choose from than you could possibly ever use with one child. Even the most experienced parent or teacher will find something to wow him or her in these theme books!

Every single thing Warren Publishing House puts out is intelligently organized, dressed up with beautiful graphics, and super-simple to use. Did I forget to mention the low prices?

PUT A BOOK AWAY

NEW★★
Northstar Learning Systems
Lookshelf™, $20.99 postpaid.

Anyone who has lived with small children any amount of time knows what bookshelves are for in a small child's mind. They are for pulling books *out of*, but not for putting books *back*. That's because it is physically too difficult for a young child to push the heavy line of books already in the shelf aside in order to put a book away. The child also often feels that he must pull out every book on the shelf in order to find the one he is searching for, because he can't see the cover. Result: mess.

There is a solution to this problem: a special children's bookshelf with ledges constructed so books can be placed with their covers facing you. Such convenience has its price, unfortunately. Wood models of this kind of children's bookshelf cost upwards of $100 apiece.

You, however, can have all this convenience for far less cost, because the inventive folks at Northstar Learning Systems have figured out how to design a children's bookshelf made out of heavy-duty cardboard. It comes all flattened out, and you let your 10-year-old put it together. (At least I did. He enjoyed it!) When constructed, the Lookshelf is a very attractive, sturdy place for your toddler's books that actually can make a difference in how easy it is to keep your house neat. It's made a difference in *our* house, for which I am suitably grateful. Now our little ones can both take out and put away their books without any help from me; the floor is no longer carpeted with Dr. Seuss; and my books are no longer dragged out of their shelves.

The people at Northstar think of the Lookshelf as an educational accessory, prompting children to spend more time with books. Since our kids were practically born with books in their hands, it's hard for me to say. But if you've had to put the kids' books up high so they won't mess up the house, this is the answer.

SONGS 'N STUFF

Kimbo Educational

Huge assortment of music, filmstrips, and books for little people. From Raffi's *Singable Songs for the Very Young* to read-along cassette/book packs to all sorts of children's music and movement albums, Kimbo's got it. The catalog is attractive and easy to use. If you're looking for secular educational audiovisual materials for your preschooler, here's one place to start.

Plough Publishing House
Songs books, $16 each. Hardbound. *Shepherd's Pipe* cassette $7, choral book $3. All cassettes and records, a very reasonable $7 each, all choral books $3 each. Many other booklets and books. Prices include U.S. shipping.

Here's something different—poems and songs for young children from the Hutterian Brethren. Formed as a Christian commune generations ago in Germany, the Bruderhof share Mennonite values and practice pacifism.

Popular offerings: *Sing Through the Seasons* and *Sing Through the Day* are gorgeous songbooks splashed freely with pictures that, as Lois Lenski remarked, reflect both "the beauty and guilelessness of childhood." These *large* books (10¼ x 11") are just the size that little ones love—so big and important! Others books are available—poems and Christmas celebrations, theology, and thoughts on education.

The Bruderhof also have records and cassettes to accompany their songbooks, as well as an original Christmas cantata called *The Shepherd's Pipe*. The singing is simple, direct, clear, and unforced. I realize that your preschooler is probably not into cantatas (though you never know!), but I did want to mention the Brethren's music somewhere in this book.

ALL-IN-ONE PRESCHOOL LEARNING LIBRARY

NEW★★
World Book, Inc.
Childcraft is sold by World Book sales representatives. Prices vary, and are always lower if you buy other World Book products at the same time.

For years World Book has been producing the very fancy *Childcraft* How and Why Library for parents and schools to use with kids from preschool through the elementary years. This is a fairly complete educational resource for kids to dip into and learn on their own or as parents read to them, rather like you use the encyclopedia. No lesson plans, no discussion questions.

The latest version of *Childcraft* now includes:

- *Once Upon a Time,* a read-to-me book for preschoolers, with stories, poems, and illustrations by some of the best and most famous children's writers and artists, such as Beatrix Potter, Ezra Jack Keats, Ernest Shepard, and others. These are mostly classic stories and nursery rhymes you have seen before. The book has 34 stories and 202 nursery rhymes and poems.

- *Times to Read* is a collection of 21 stories and 129 poems and rhymes that can be read to preschoolers and that children six to eight years old can read on their own.

- *Stories and Poems* is for kids who are starting to read well. It includes 27 stories and 91 poems, including excerpts from three Newberry Award winners.

Stop here for a minute, because these are the three volumes your kids are likely to use the most. I have looked these over quite carefully, since as time goes on mainstream publishers are introducing more occult

and anti-family stuff into their collections. *Childcraft* is pretty free of this so far (I'm writing in mid-1990), but personally there are a few stories and poems in there we always skip.

- *World and Space* tells about over 300 interesting phenomena.

- *About Animals* presents hundreds of critters, from alligators to zebras, with more than 400 illustrations.

- *The Green Kingdom* is a favorite with us. This volume, besides giving lots of fun facts about plants, has some really neat learning activities built in.

- *Story of the Sea* uses "photographs, illustrations, poetry, factual articles, legends, and adventure stories" to present the sea and its many facets.

- *About Us* explores the characteristics of different nations and ethnic groups, with a "we are all just as good as each other" emphasis.

- *Holidays and Birthdays* is another multi-cultural presentation, this time of some pretty obscure holidays and famous people's birthdays, along with info on how popular holidays are celebrated in different places.

- *Places to Know* continues the multi-cultural theme, introducing more than 140 famous places around the world and providing more "cultural heritage" info.

- *Make and Do,* another favorite, includes more than 300 make-it projects for kids from preschool through preteen.

- *How Things Work* introduces basic physical science, explaining how familiar machines work and the nature of sound, light, heat, etc.

- *Mathemagic* is supposed to "stimulate interest in mathematics through the fun of puzzles, games, and stories." It's a gallant try, but this book won't "take" unless Mom and Dad make sure Junior spends some time with it. Making stuff or reading books is *always* more attractive to kids than mental effort, math geniuses excepted.

- *About Me* is a fairly skippable introduction to what modern experts think about kids as physical, emotional, rational, and social beings, presented as absolute fact.

- *Guide to Childcraft* is even more skippable—in fact, I would strongly suggest not spending any time with it, even if you buy the set. It's "designed to help parents meet many of the typical problems of parenthood," so right off the bat you know that this is *not* going to be a warm guide to loving your kids. Modern American culture is presented as a given—e.g., your kid is supposed to be peer-dependent, sassy, and all those other fun things. The "solutions" read like they were written by childless clinicians. Nowhere is religion, let alone Christianity, even mentioned as a possible solution to any childhood problems. I suppose World Book feels they have to present the blandest, most mainstream message to reach the largest number, but they sure ain't reachin' *me* with this last volume!

Childcraft still is an excellent educational resource and a pretty good buy, when you consider how many pages of solid info you're getting, in spite of the hard things I've said about a few of its features. We've had our set for four years now, and the kids still take one or more of the volumes out to read almost every day.

Oh, yeah: if you buy *Childcraft,* you'll get a chance every so often to update your set with a new volume. *Story of the Sea,* for example, didn't come in the set we bought several years back, but we picked it up through one of these special offers.

PART II

LEARNING
TO
READ

CHAPTER SIX

HOW TO TEACH YOUR CHILD TO READ

Reading is like toilet training; until your little one does it, you're afraid he never will. Unlike toilet training, however, there seems to be a good choice that your fears are justified. And this is odd, because of the 24 million functional illiterates the Department of Education estimates live in the USA, virtually all have had between eight and 12 years of compulsory public schooling. This is more than enough time to teach kids to read, one would think!

Once the public schools actually did teach kids to read. As educational historian Sam Blumenfeld documents in his book *NEA: Trojan Horse in American Education*, statistics compiled by the Bureau of Education showed, "Of children from 10 to 14 years of age there were in 1910 only 22 out of every 1,000 who could neither read nor write." In 1910, nine states and the District of Columbia actually reported only *one* child in 1,000 between the ages of 10 and 14 as illiterate. And let me point out that when they said in those days that Johnny could read and write, they meant he could handle literature that's now beyond most Harvard freshmen.

As Mr. Blumenfeld notes, "Apparently they knew how to teach children to read in 1910. Also, there was no such thing as 'functional illiteracy,' that is, a kind of low, inadequate reading ability. . . . The illiteracy of 1910 was the result of some children having *no* schooling" (Emphasis mine).

How did those old-time schoolteachers work this miracle? With longer school years? No way! In rural districts school often was only in session from six weeks to a few months at a time several times a year. With more years of reading instruction? Nope. Kids frequently dropped out at early ages to help out on the farm. How about Head Start and other get-'em-early programs? Didn't exist. Johnny and Janie often didn't start school until age 7 or 8. Higher pay for teachers? Dream on! Schoolteachers were paid in room and board and very little more. Teachers were also often required to be single, for the very good reason that a married man couldn't possibly support a family on a teacher's pay.

People keep saying that we can't turn back the clock. Maybe not. But we can get it fixed and wind it up again! So first let's find out what went wrong, and then we can see what we should do about it.

WHY JOHNNY CAN'T READ

So why can't so many kids read today? Johnny can't read, quite simply, because Johnny was never taught properly how to read. We can forget all the piffle about learning disabilities, underfunded schools (when they get an average $5,000-plus per pupil per year!), nutritional deficiencies, etc. We can also see through and reject the subtle racism of those who try to blame illiteracy on increased immigration and the larger numbers of "inner-city" (they mean minority) kids in the public schools. Black and Hispanic kids can learn to read English just as well as the Hungarian and Polish immigrant kids of the 1910s.

What I really want to do is to get the resources into your hands to make your kids literate. But first, you need to know what's going on. For the past 40 years, the teacher-training colleges have been indoctrinating eager young teachers in the doctrine of whole-word memorization. This approach, sometimes called "look-say," but more recently rechristened "Whole Language," consists of having children *memorize* words by their *shapes*. Typically, kids are "taught" to read this way by seeing large labels on objects around the classroom, having the same sentences in the same books read to them again and again until the child can "read" the sentence (I put "read" in quotes, because he's actually *memorized* the sentence), having flash cards flashed at them hundreds of times, guessing at the word from "context clues" and "picture clues" in books (unbelievably, this kind of guessing is actually taught separately as an essential "reading skill"!), and literally hundreds of stupid, trivial, and irrelevant activities only dimly related to reading, such as making a collage of objects that begin with the letter R. (The latter is a perfect example of the "phony phonics" activities that always accompany look-say programs. More on phony phonics in a minute.)

If you wonder whether your child is being taught to "read" by look-say, do what one mother did. Take the book your child is "reading" from in school, write some of the words on flash cards, and see if he can read the words *without* picture and context clues. If he can do that, then make up some similar *nonsense* words and see if he can read *them*! For example, if he can "read" the sentence, "John looked at the fish," he should be able to read the nonsense words *mooked* and *bish*. If he can't do this, you'd better keep reading this chapter.

Interestingly, look-say was not invented to teach normal American kids to read. It was invented for the benefit of *deaf* kids! Here's how it happened. Once there was a good man, a reformer, named Thomas Gallaudet. Mr. Gallaudet was concerned about deaf children. He wanted to help them learn to read. Deaf children could not sound out words like hearing children, so to get around that difficulty Mr. Gallaudet devised a method of picture-word association. The child would be shown a picture of a cat and the word *cat*. By memorizing the

configuration of the word the child could build up a very limited reading vocabulary. The reason his vocabulary would of necessity be limited is that so many words look like each other: *bag* and *bay*, *ball* and *bell*, *play* and *ploy*. As the child tried to memorize more and more words *by their appearance alone*, sooner or later his memory would give out. This method was, however, useful in its limited way and for its original audience.

As Kathryn Diehl, the author (with G. K. Hodenfield) of *Johnny STILL Can't Read—But You Can Teach Him at Home*, says, "Why it was ever decided that this would be an effective way to teach children who *can* hear and speak remains a mystery to this day." But that is exactly what happened! Since good readers read whole words, someone decided it was time to skip those silly phonics lessons and get right into "real" reading—sort of like skipping the swimming lessons and trying to swim the English Channel.

At this point, entire publishing empires have been built on supplying the hundreds of little vocabulary-controlled readers and millions of consumable workbooks that look-say requires. More than a few inflated reputations in those teacher-training colleges are at stake, not to mention big bucks in remedial education programs and years and years of employment for reading teachers, as reading instruction now continues beyond the elementary level, yea even unto college itself. These entrenched interests aren't about to let the look-say goose that is laying them such big fat golden eggs get killed without a struggle. These are big bucks. Over $3 billion dollars a year goes to the illiteracy mafia just in ECIA Chapter I funds alone. That is the real reason for our reading crisis.

Under the present setup, the more kids fail to read, the better life is for their school districts, as the federal money showers money on school districts for "remedial" programs and "special education." This may explain why New Hampshire, with the highest SAT scores in the nation (35 points above the national average), has the lowest per-pupil spending—$3,400 per pupil as opposed to New York's $11,000 per pupil. New York kids manage to score a whopping 105 points lower on the SAT than Granite Staters, so naturally those "teaching" them get almost three times as much per kid! If New Hampshire teachers would quit teaching the kids to read, they too could get more federal money.

Now, we Americans aren't totally stupid. We know something is wrong with what we fondly call "our" public schools, and we demand reforms. So every few years a "new" reading method is unveiled in the government school system. This time around it's the "Whole Language" method. When you boil them down, though, the supposed "reforms" *always* turn out to be sight-word reading, "phony phonics" (e.g., a few phonics principles introduced here and there in no systematic sequence), and tons and tons of expensive non-reading-related classroom materials. What's missing in this picture is always some *systematic* method of instructing the child in the sounds of the letters and combinations of letters that make the words of his country's language. Instead, we get "creative teaching methods" that jump around from one thing to another like a dog that just stepped on a porcupine. We get literally *millions* of kids labeled "learning disabled," when it's really the reading methods that are "teaching disabled"!

The currently fashionable Whole Language method, for example, believes in "immersing the child in print." The child is supposed to "do lots of reading and writing," but somehow he is never really *taught* to read and write. It is believed that kids will learn to become superb readers if they just have enough comic books, newspapers, play scripts, and can wrappers thrust before their noses. Coming to school dressed as Little Red Riding Hood is supposed to help, as is putting on a play circus and taking the parts of various animals. (I'm not making this up—these are actual Whole Language activities I've seen written up in teacher's magazines and supplier's catalogs!) The reading problem is theorized, by Whole Learning advocates, to be merely a lack of motivation—those stupid kids don't *want* to learn to read—and of access—their equally stupid parents are depriving them of a rich print environment. Kids are told to write their own books and plays when they haven't learned to decode words yet. Any activity involving letters is sacred, yet they are never systematically taught the letters' *sounds*. Maybe that's why one school using this method had *double* the usual number of "learning disabled" kids in the very first class taught by Whole Language methods.

Now, some of the Whole Language objectives are noble, such as the objective of getting kids reading real literature instead of crummy Dick-and-Jane vocabulary-controlled basal readers. But noble *goals* and noble *results* are two different stories, unfortunately. Without a systematic method for teaching kids to decode new words *without* having to memorize them, reading success is limited to those who are able to guess the rules on their own.

HOW JOHNNY CAN LEARN TO READ

So what does work? Phonics. Since 1910, 124 studies have compared the look-say approach with phonics programs. *Not one study showed the look-say approach to be superior.* The reason is simple. Phonics is a logical approach that helps kids organize their way of attacking new words. Once children have learned a few rules, the exceptions won't knock them for a loop. In fact, even the "exceptions" have some phonetic elements. The three common "sight" words *do*, *the*, and *said*, for example, are at least 50 percent phonetic, and the irregular sounds can be easily figured out from the sense of the sentence. In fact, even *do* is 100 percent phonetic in some phonics methods I have seen, where more than one sound of the letter O is taught! The look-say approach, in contrast, is *all* exceptions. Each and every word has to be memorized on its own, and there is no end to this task. No wonder children give up in despair!

One of the most exciting things about teaching phonics is the way it brings back hope to children who have been taught by the schools to consider themselves stupid. You need no gimmicks or frills to accomplish this miracle—just time-tested phonics.

I am delighted to announce that there are literally dozens of home phonics programs that really work just as well as the public schools used to work in 1910. If you have "teaching blood," some excellent books can give you the whys and hows of teaching reading. If you haven't a teaching bone in your body, several methods have the teacher on the record, or provide programmed instructions that tell you everything you have to say. Prices range from a few measly shekels to over $200 for a complete language arts program that includes all your child could ever hope to learn in this area from the best private school in the country.

HOW TO TEACH PHONICS

So here you are. You want to teach your child, or the neighborhood children, or the kids in your class, to read. The first thing you need to do is to *honestly* assess your teaching ability. If you have never taught children, or have had little success with your teaching efforts in the past, you might run into the Rule of Three. This rule states that whatever program you use first won't work. The second one might not either. But the *third* phonics program will work wonderfully well!

I discovered this rule when I started getting letters from some people complaining that Phonics Program A didn't work, but that the problem disappeared when they bought Phonics Program B, while others wrote that Phonics Program B was no good and *their* child had learned to read in no time with Phonics Program A. Yet others complained that neither A nor B was any good, but that C had solved all their problems. And so on.

After a while I began to catch on to what was really happening. Little kids always learn in spurts. So, when Johnny started on Program A, he did fine for a while, until he hit his next learning plateau. At that point his parents despaired and bought Program B. Faced with a fresh new approach to phonics, Johnny again picked up speed for a while, but then hit another plateau. Enter Program C. By now Johnny had seen phonics presented in lots of different ways, one of which was bound to make sense to him eventually. So

when his next learning spurt came along, he spurted all the way to real reading.

Sometimes it also happens that Program A stresses auditory skills more than Program B, which stresses hands-on learning, while Program C is more visual in its approach. Under these circumstances, parents who are unaware of their child's learning style will stumble along until they happen on a program that fits that style, and then conclude the other programs are "no good."

I might point out that parents also have different *teaching* styles. A very organized, time-consuming method might not work for a mother who refuses to be organized and systematic about how she teaches, whereas with a program that only requires using a few flash cards once a day she might have great success. Typically, it's not so much that the first one or two phonics programs failed, but that the parents didn't understand the directions or follow them consistently.

Teaching phonics is not terribly difficult. It's just that the average parent has a learning curve to follow before becoming a phonics expert. One way to accelerate up the learning curve is to use several phonics programs in succession. This makes you familiar with a number of teaching approaches, and also helps tamp down in *your* mind just how phonics works. Once you start comparing phonics methods in your mind, and figuring out which one you consider superior, you are a teacher!

Now let me ask you again—how good a teacher are you? If you have any doubts on this score at all, the number-one thing you should be looking for in a phonics program is *good, clear instructions,* especially instructions in how to recognize and overcome the typical trouble spots. It doesn't matter how thorough or clever a program is if you can't figure out how to use it, or if you're lost every time Johnny doesn't "get it" right away. Parents with teaching experience or talent can be successful with just about any program, but the rest of us need to stick with something safe, no matter how tempting the glitzy games in another program might be. Keep this in mind as you look through the programs reviewed in this book.

Since the biggest hurdle in phonics instruction is just getting clear in your mind what you're trying to teach, here, free to the readers of this book, is a sequential list of what your child needs to know, along with some bare-bones teaching suggestions. This alone might be enough to teach your Johnny to read! And if not, since many of us have to foul up with at least one phonics program before we get good at teaching phonics, at least I've making it easy for you to foul up for free!

READ TO ME

The first step in successful phonics instruction is to forget all about phonics instruction. Read, read, read to your kids! Kids need to be read to and to see lots of different sorts of print to build up a picture of reading in their minds, which the phonics method can then tie together. You may think you have no skill whatsoever as a teacher. If you read to your children, though, you are giving them the foundation without which even skilled teachers have difficulty succeeding.

To paraphrase the old rock 'n roll song, "You gotta scribble, babble, and hear" before you can write, talk, and read. Children need to be read to in order to build up an understanding of what reading is. When Suzy snuggles up to you and begs for *The Cat in the Hat* for the hundredth time, she is not being a nuisance; she is requesting pre-reading instruction. Children who are read to learn that the little black squiggles on the page always say the same words. They discover the different book forms—adventure, mystery, fairy tale, poetry, Bible—and become aware of rhythm and rhyme.

You can start reading to a baby. Pick books with interesting pictures and just a few words per page. When Baby gets just a little bit bigger, you can start pointing out interesting happenings and characters in the pictures. A little bit bigger than that, and you can ask him to point them out to you! Flap books, pop-up books, poke-the-finger-through-the-hole books, furry books, and gloriously illustrated board books are excellent first books. The Ladybird and EDC Publishing lines are particularly good. Use your sense of drama. Let the lions ROAR and the field mice squeak! Make lazy characters yawn and type-A characters talk fast and choppy. Hush your voice for dramatic buildups. Make sound effects: a zooming noise for a race car, bubble-blowing noises for a fish. This helps your child (1) learn how to get involved in a story plot—to see it in his mind's eye, and (2) develop his dramatic abilities. More on the latter in the Speech and Drama chapter!

So read, read, read to Johnny. Leave all kinds of reading material around for Johnny to pick up and pretend that he's reading to himself. And let him see you reading for pleasure and enjoying it. That's all we Prides do, and every single one of our kids has preferred books to any other toys from the age of one on up.

The more print of all sorts a child gets to see, the better his chances of understanding what's happening when the grown-ups decide it's time to teach him to read. (This is *not* the same thing as substituting "print immersion" for phonics, as the Whole Languagers do!)

Or, in the case of those laid-back folks who insist that children should initiate their own education, the more likely it is that Johnny will someday ask you to teach him to read. He will have imbibed the necessary data. When you give him the framework, it will not strain his little brain, but will fill in the answers to his own unspoken questions.

One more point that reading methods rarely mention, but that has a major effect on your child's reading potential—if you are *really* committed to your children's educational success, try junking your TV, or at least substituting a TV-free video player for it. Print just can't compete with the moving image, and, even worse, TV *teaches* kids to have low attention spans. There is also some evidence that it can prevent the ability to imagine stories in your own head from fully developing in some children. This ability, of course, is absolutely essential to successful reading. So control the TV, and if you can't (be honest now!—nine out of 10 people are TV addicts), get rid of it.

WRITE ON!

It is important for children, if at all possible, to learn to write at the same time they learn to read. Because of a muscle weakness our oldest son was not able to write when he learned to read. Teddy, being a very visually-oriented little chap, learned nonetheless. Joseph, on the other hand, kept switching his *b*'s and *d*'s around until he learned to write them himself. By feeling and manipulating letters, and ultimately writing them, children with the dreaded "dyslexic" tendency can learn to read as well as anyone else.

Kids don't have to write *before* they can learn to read, though. The two skills reinforce each other, but are not interdependent. Reading is for pleasure; writing is for communication. Few kids love to write for its own sake. If you force your child to write every blessed thing he is learning to read (as a few methods would have it), he may never learn to love to read.

NOW I KNOW MY ABC'S . . .

The next chapter lists resources for alphabet-learning practice. Let's move on now, to actually teaching phonics itself. Here's the alphabet sounds a child must know:

a as in *at*
b as in *bag*
c as in *cat*
d as in *dog* (make sure he's not confusing lowercase *b* and *d*)
e as in *egg*
f as in *fan*
g as in *gas* (handwritten *g* and *q* are identical except for the direction of the tail)
h as in *ham*
i as in *in* (watch out for *i* getting confused with *j*, and *I* getting mixed up with *l*)
j as in *jam*
k as in *kid*
l as in *lap*
m as in *man* (kids also confuse capital *w* and *m*)
n as in *nap*
o as in *ox*
p as in *pass* (lowercase *p* sometimes gets confused with lowercase *q*)
qu (pronounced together as "kw") as in *queen*
r as in *rat*
s as in *sat*
t as in *tap*
u as in *up*
v as in *van*
w as in *wax*
x as in the ending sound of *ax*, *fox*, and *wax*
y as in *yell* (we'll save the ending sounds of *y* for later)
z as in *zoom!*

If you prefer to teach all the sounds of each letter at once, add the following:

a as in *late* and *pa* (teach at the same time as the first A sound, if you are using this method)
e as in *Eve*
i as in *I*
o as in *oh* and *do*
u as in *cute*
y as in *baby* and *by*
c as in *cent*
g as in *gym*
s as in *bags* (a *z* sound)

This more or less covers it. Some people manage to come up with one or two more sounds for the vowels, but they are so close to the sounds above that you don't really need to bother to try to teach them. All kids need is enough information to sound out a word, after all—they're not applying for a Ph.D. in linguistics!

It's important to isolate the pure sound of the letter: say the sound *b* with just a little puff of sound, instead of saying "buh." If this is difficult for you, try isolating the consonant sounds at the *ends* of words—e.g., *b* as in *cab*. Vowel sounds can be dragged out until Johnny can hear and repeat them clearly.

I always teach this stage with flash cards with no pictures, so our little ones won't end up "reading" the pictures instead of the letters! I made my own set years ago with a few chopped-out sheets of heavy white cardboard and a Magic Marker. They have the capital letters on one side and the lowercase letters on the other. Now, you can teach the alphabet sounds lots of ways, but this is how we do it. We simply flash the cards several times in alphabetical sequence, showing the letter and making its sound at the same time. I ask my child to repeat the sound after me. I also go through the deck once and have him trace each letter with his finger (make sure he does it right!). There's no testing at all until we've done this for several days. Then I let him try to "get" the cards without me saying the sound first. Those he "gets," he holds, while we run through the remaining cards several times with me making the alphabet sounds and him repeating. Throughout the day, I also ask him to find, say, all the *y*s on the Cheerios box, or all the *b*s on one page of a book I am reading to him. Do this enough days in a row and your children will know the alphabet sounds.

Of course, this is not the only way to begin. Some programs teach *all* the sounds of each letter at once. Some teach only uppercase or lowercase letters, or teach the letters in a particular order. All are good approaches, based on good reasons, and all of them work. Don't worry about this! I'm just trying to give you an overview of what you're going to accomplish, not telling you exactly how to do it. I haven't even discussed other ways you can help children learn the letters, such as tracing them, writing them on the blackboard, air writing, sand writing, sandpaper letters, writing them in pudding, walking around a letter outlined on the floor, and so on. All this detailed information is in the books at the end of this chapter or in the programs in the next chapters. Remember, we're just looking at the *steps* of phonics instruction here!

SAM SAT ON A RAT

After your learner has mastered the basic alphabet sounds, it's time for the next big step: blending them into words. A typical first word is *at*. The child makes the "aaa" sound, then makes the "t" sound. You show him how to blend the two together: "aaaaat—at." You show him some other words (on a chalkboard, paper, or flash cards, if you're doing this all by yourself without a phonics program) and let him try them: *Sam, sat, rat, pat, fat, man*. You will notice I only included words using short vowel *a* in that first reading list. There's a reason for that: the short *a* sound is the easiest for kids to distinguish. Most phonics programs initiate blending practice, therefore, with short *a* words of three letters. This step can take anywhere from 10 minutes to 10 weeks, depending on how ready your child is to learn to read. If he doesn't get it, no matter how often you explain it, give it a rest and come back to it in a couple of days or weeks.

Try to stay cheerful and relaxed, but don't beat yourself over the head if you catch yourself pushing too much. Almost everybody pushes too hard the first time he or she teaches phonics. Just apologize and go do something fun together!

Once your child has blending under control, you move on to words with short *o* (the next easiest short vowel), then words with short *e, i,* and *u*. Ideally, Johnny is reading sentences and even whole stories in a simple phonics primer by now.

Phonics readers are a great help at the early stages, but please don't feel you must slavishly stick to them alone. The "you can't go on to the next step until you do this one perfectly" approach (otherwise known as Mastery Learning) does not really fit the way human beings learn. Based on the Pavlovian model of behavior manipulation, it puts the learner in the position of *only* being allowed to learn what the teacher is ready to dole out at the moment. This is great for producing compliant drones, but not so good if you want your students to become intellectually mature. Also, since human beings can both organize data and take in new data at the same time, kids benefit from occasionally struggling with books or ideas above their present learning level. In our own family, we combine phonics readers with short sessions picking out as many words as possible in good children's books (books they really *want* to read, as opposed to the rather boring cat-rat-mat stories in the phonics readers). Dr. Seuss's early books are great for this. Thus encouraged, our children have all become avid readers at quite young ages.

DON'T STOP NOW!

At the point when a child is able to read his first books a lot of parents figure their child is reading and they don't need to teach him any more. Not so! He still has to learn about long vowels—the silent *e* that turns *man* into *mane*—and blends, diphthongs, and digraphs. These latter three imposing terms have fancy technical definitions which only make life more confusing for people who don't already know what they mean. For our purposes, blends are two-or-more consonant combinations like *br, bl, st,* and *spr,* where the individual sounds of the letters are heard. Diphthongs are two-vowel combinations like *ai* and *ou* that actually combine two sounds (*ai* sounds like *ah-ee* if you say it slowly enough). Digraphs are two letters that make a single sound, like *th, ch, sh,* and *wh* and *oa, ee,* and *ui.* And then there are the *tions, ighs, oulds,* and other weirdo combinations. Finally, a few words really ought to be taught as sight words: *the* and *come,* for example.

What happens in real life is that you don't actually end up teaching all this. At some point, the child starts to figure out new combinations on his own. You'd better oversee the process, though, or you'll end up with a child who thinks, like I used to, that pigs eat out of something pronounced a "trow"!

To practice blends, just run your kid systematically through words using them, and some nonsense words too: *brat, drat, frat, blat, flat, slat,* etc. The phonics drill books listed at the end of Chapter 9 make this task much easier, if by this time you still don't have a complete program that includes this kind of drill. Diphthongs, some of which have more than one sound, are considerably trickier. Kids have to puzzle over questions like, "Is the *ai* in 'bait' pronounced as BAYT or BITE?" Digraphs can be tricky too. Consider the two sounds of *th* in *think* and *that,* and the word *read,* which can be pronounced either "reed" or "red." Just to make life more complicated, that same *ea* diphthong can also be pronounced "ay," as in *bear*. If you're very smart, you can figure all this out and how to teach it. If you're too busy for this, then at this point you're definitely ready for an official phonics program.

Now, should we teach phonics and spelling *rules*, or just expose kids to the *patterns*? I personally think we should do both. Knowing the rules gives kids a sense of confidence, and running through the word-family patterns turns those words into words the kids can read on sight. Knowing the rules *alone* is not enough. Picture a kid sitting there with the world *child*. According to one method, he would have memorized a little four-line jingle that shows all the ways long *i* is used in words. Can we realistically expect him to hum through this entire jingle, sorting it out from all the other jingles, every time he sees a new word? The "phonogram" method, where *ild* is memorized as a sound unit, and then the child is drilled in words using the two sounds of *ild* (e.g., *child* and *gild*), works a lot better for instantaneous recall.

Learning the phonics rules does fit very neatly into learning the *spelling* rules, since they are often one and the same. You might also have noticed that once a child knows the basic alphabet sounds and can sound out *at*, he immediately is able to read *bat, cat, fat, hat, mat, Nat, pat, rat, sat, tat,* and *vat*. Twelve words for the price of one! In the look-say method, he would have had to learn each of these words by its "configuration"—in other words, its outline. This gives you a clue as to why intensive phonics is such a powerful learning method.

The most important thing for your child to learn is what Frank Rogers, the author of the TATRAS phonics program, calls the "phonics habit." This means the habit of *decoding*, or *sounding out*, words rather than guessing at them. I would urge you to beware of "phonics" programs that present an excessive number of words for kids to memorize as sight words. Once a child gets into the habit of guessing at a word, rather than trying to decode *all* words, it's awfully hard to break. The worst part is that often parents don't suspect this has happened until the child hits third or fourth grade, when he moves out of the strictly vocabulary-controlled readers of the early grades. This delayed reaction makes it possible for people to claim great results for their sight-word-larded programs, since *at first* it looks like the kids are really learning to read.

The true test of a phonics program is not how quickly a child can learn to parrot vocabulary-controlled readers, but whether he has learned the phon-

ics habit and has enough tools when he finishes the program to decode *any* word. Properly taught, a six-year-old child should be able to decode the words in a college text with reasonable accuracy. He won't *understand* the college text, but that's because comprehension is not the same thing as reading. I can *read* Einstein's writings on relativity, but I won't promise you I'll *comprehend* them!

A sure sign that a reading method is tainted with look-say is that the author will try to pit comprehension against reading. It's like pitting digestion against eating. Although it's possible to eat something too inedible to digest, there's no way to digest without eating. A child who reads, "See the nice pony," when the words on the page actually say, "Look! A nice horse!" is neither comprehending nor reading, and the minute he hits third grade, the whole world will know it.

Now that you have a general idea of what you want to accomplish, I hope you see that you *can* teach phonics. There are a finite number of steps, and only a few really big "new" things to teach. The main learning plateaus seem to occur at the alphabet-learning stage (learning to tell *b* from *d* and *l* from capital *I*, for example), at the word-blending stage, and at the point of adding that elusive silent *e* to the end of words. Aside from that, with a good intensive phonics program, it's all smooth sailing. And the better phonics programs will even tell you how to get past those learning plateaus. It's just a matter of time and practice. Results guaranteed!

RECOMMENDED BOOKS

There isn't space in this book to list all the diphthongs, digraphs, etc. (often known by the simpler names of "phoneme" or "phonogram," meaning "bunch of letters frequently used together in words"), or to provide teaching help for the plateaus. This would bother me a lot if I were the only person in the world who knew how to teach kids to read; but happily, I am not. Others have written helpful books on this subject, and here they are!

NEW**
Eagle's Wings Educational Materials

Eagle's Wings Comprehensive Handbook of Phonics for Spelling, Reading and Writing, $25. Add $4 shipping.

The Eagle's Wings Letterland program, reviewed in Chapters 7 and 8, is a rule-based phonics program with a lot of unique features. Rules are in poem form and tell you when each sound has each spelling. The number of rules is far less than in other programs, and each rule is more complete.

I wished, when I first saw it, that the clever features of Letterland were available separately, without all the workbooks, games, etc. The authors have such a unique, useful way of breaking down English spelling and decoding into just a few rules that it would be really worthwhile for anyone seriously involved in teaching reading to learn this approach. Now Eagle's Wings has made it possible for you to inexpensively master their approach with their new *Handbook of Phonics & Spelling*. It contains "the essence of the program without workbooks or reference manuals," and can be used as a phonics and spelling program from grades K–8, or as a supplement to any other phonics program. As they say,

> When a rule is taught, it is important to know if it holds true for five words or 500. No longer do you have to take the word of the "experts," because complete word charts allow you to see the patterns for yourself and to judge the validity of any rule.

Rules are often made memorable by giving them "personality." For example, the "boy" vowels are *a, o*, and *u*, while *e* and *i* are "girl" vowels. Thus it's possible to clue kids into the two pronunciations of *c* by pointing out that Clever C sounds like *k* when he's playing with the other boys, but makes a silly *s* sound whenever he's around the "girls." Other rules that don't easily fit around the letter personalities are cram-jammed into as little space as possible. Here's an example, just one of many: the different ways to spell the long sound *i*.

What makes a long 'i'?	Example
To make a long 'i', use 'i' with silent 'e',	mine
But at ends of words, a 'y' will usually be.	sky
And then 'i' is long with 'igh' or 'ind',	high/find
And again with 'ign' or 'ild'.	sign/child

This covers all the options in just four rhyming lines. Then the program expands on the poem. For example, the *igh* phonogram is found in only 16 common words. So you get a story poem using all 16 words, along with a picture illustrating the poem and labeled with the words.

To find a particular word or topic, you can either locate it in the Table of Contents or in the comprehensive charts of consonants and vowels. Each chart deals with a particular pattern or concept, and an explanation is usually given on the page across from the chart.

Although the *Handbook*'s primary emphasis is on phonics for spelling, the authors also address phonics for reading. A set of phonogram flashcards ("Tell-a-phone" cards) is included with the handbook, and larger cards are available upon request. Teaching directions are given in the "Teaching Supplement" (also included with the handbook). The *Handbook* includes many more extras: lists of prefixes, suffixes, and roots; lists of synonyms, antonyms, and homonyms; specific instructions in poem form on how to form the lowercase manuscript letters; pages of phonics games; and an assortment of stories and "fun forms" from the Eagle's Wings *Letterland Phonics* program.

The *Handbook* will provide you with many insights into the generally unrecognized regularities of the English language, or if you have a little teaching ability you can use it as an inexpensive phonics program all by itself.

Education Services

A Home Start in Reading, part of a "3 R's" set including also *A Strong Start in Language* and *An Easy Start in Arithmetic*. $12 for the set.

Is $4 too much to spend for understanding the five steps of teaching reading? *A Home Start in Reading*, written by Dr. Ruth Beechick, gives the outline of how to teach reading and allows you to use *any* readers you choose, from cereal boxes to easy books from the library. Step 1, "Prereading," answers the questions of how to prepare your child for reading and when is the right time to start. The next three steps, "Beginning," "Blending," and "Decoding," provide the simplest possible way for a child to move from learning his first letter to sounding out any word on sight. Dr. Beechick provides a chart of all the basic sounds you need to teach. Finally, Step 5, "Fluency," shows how to stretch your child toward total fluency without frustrating him with too-hard reading. This chapter also deals with comprehension.

The essence of the Beechick approach is (1) streamlining—decluttering the educational process and (2) freeing the child from the stranglehold of a strict inch-by-inch approach. Dr. Beechick recognizes that children can leap ahead and learn on their own, and that what she calls "the messiness of phonics" make some words or syllables easier to learn on their own rather than according to an abstract rule. As she says,

> You don't have to continue until every last phonics rule and obscure sound is mastered. You can start off systematically teaching a list of sounds. But at some point your child will take off and fly with her reading skills. She forms her own rules and doesn't need the rest that you planned to teach. Let her fly.

If you want to avoid the effort of making up flash cards and would like some tangible evidence of your youngster's progress, the *Easy Reading Kit* (see next chapter) makes an excellent companion for *Home Start.*

Elijah Company
How to Tutor by Samuel Blumenfeld. $11.95 plus $2.50 shipping.

Sam Blumenfeld's excellent *How to Tutor* presents far more than advice on the basics of tutoring. In just one book you find out how to successfully teach Readin', Ritin', and 'Rithmetic in one-on-one situations. Stripped-down, no-frills, easy to read and easy to do. Step-by-step instructions, with explanations of why Mr. Blumenfeld has such success with his approach. This last feature, the reasoned explanations of why you should follow classic methods of instruction, sets *How to Tutor* apart. It would be quite possible to take your child from zero to grade 6 in the three R's armed with this book alone.

Mott Media
The ABC's and All Their Tricks: The Complete Reference Book of PHONICS and SPELLING by Margaret M. Bishop. Hardbound. $22.95. Add 10% shipping ($3 minimum).

A basic reference work designed to help the teacher help his students understand all the rules and exceptions of phonics and spelling. The main body of *The ABC's and All Their Tricks* is laid out in alphabetical order (e.g., *Z* as in zebra followed by *Z* as in waltz, *ZE* as in sneeze, *Z* as in azure, and *ZZ* as in buzz). This makes the book very simple to use. Plus it contains all you need to know about root words, syllables, vowels, consonants, suffixes, and much more. A truly useful encyclopedia of phonics information that will make you an expert.

NEW**
Paradigm Co.
Audio tapes to accompany *Alpha-Phonics*, $15 postpaid.

If you liked Sam Blumenfeld's *How to Tutor*, you ought to love his new audio tapes designed to accompany his *Alpha-Phonics* phonics program. On these two audiocassettes Sam explains

- The history of the alphabetic system

- How to teach reading to anyone, using *Alpha-Phonics*

- He walks you through all 128 lessons

- He clearly reproduces the 44 speech sounds taught in *Alpha-Phonics.*

If you are planning on using *Alpha-Phonics,* this tape set would be a wise investment.

Elijah Company distributes *Alpha-Phonics* to the home market. See the writeup of this program in Chapter 8.

Parent-Child Press
Tutoring Is Caring, $19.95 plus $2 shipping.

Extremely complete manual meant to teach you how to tutor in reading. *Tutoring Is Caring: you can help someone learn to read* is not just a page-by-page list of activities and reading lists (although *Tutoring Is Caring* does include those). Much instruction in teaching techniques is scattered throughout, and the large (over

200 pages), spiral-bound, hardcovered book ends with an entire section of "Suggestions for Specific Situations," several resource lists, and an index.

Author Aline D. Wolf applies her Montessori philosophy to teaching throughout. This program includes many games and activities, lots of writing and letter manipulation, and even color-coded word lists that emphasize the phonogram being studied!

You will have to make a number of items: Movable Alphabet cards, Consonant Sound cards, and so on. Since the manual, as far as possible, covers *all* learning situations and problems, you may end up putting more effort into learning to follow the program than is necessary for teaching only one bright child to read. If, however, you plan to teach many children (or adults), or truly love learning about teaching, *Tutoring Is Caring* is a treasure chest.

Pecci Educational Publishers
At Last! A Reading Method for Every Child, $24.95. Add 10% shipping.

One of the first books I would really urge you to buy, if you are interested in understanding how to teach reading, is Mary Pecci's *At Last! A Reading Method for EVERY Child!* This book's strong points are: (1) the discussion of *all* known methods of teaching reading, and (2) Mary Pecci's method itself. She has trimmed the teaching of reading down to seven steps only (compare this with the so-called "Mastery Learning" method of over one hundred steps!).

Mary Pecci begins by teaching the alphabet *in order*, so children by looking at an alphabet strip can help themselves find the letter they need. She then teaches the consonants, divided into "good guys" who make a sound like their name and "tough guys" who change their sounds or don't sound like their name. Next the blends (*bl, br, scr,* . . .) and digraphs (*ch, sh, th, wh*). Now, vowels, both short and long, followed by some "sight" phonemes (*ay, oo, er, tion,* . . .). That's it!

The rest of the book shows how to teach this information by getting children to ask, "What's the family?" (at, cat, sat) and "What's the clue?" (teaching them to approach weird words like *do* and *friend* by connecting with the regular sounds in the word).

Children using Mary Pecci's method can use *any* written material, not just phonics readers, from early on. It is just a wonderfully-organized, teacher-pleasing approach with which every reading teacher should be familiar.

NEW**
Teach America to Read and Spell
Penny Primer and TATRAS #1 60-minute audiocassette, $8.75 postpaid.

Here's a great introduction to "vertical" phonics for the average parent. "Vertical" phonics means teaching all the sounds of each phonogram at the same time. Author Frank Rogers explains on cassette tape exactly how to use the *Penny Primer* to teach kids the sounds of the first eight phonograms (*a, t, s, l, e, m, i,* and *n*) and to impart the "phonics habit," which is to decode words systematically rather than wildly guessing at the words. Also on cassette is a no-nonsense analysis of what is wrong about the way reading is taught in the schools, plus a penetrating discussion of how best to teach phonics. For more info, see the writeup of the entire program in Chapter 8.

The *Penny Primer* is a lot of information packed into a small, brown 12-page tract. It includes information on how to use the enclosed "finger clock" card to print the eight letters, and sample words to decode, all from the MOO list of Most Often Occurring words.

You won't learn everything you need to know to teach phonics from just this cassette and tract, of course. However, the minimal time and money investment will be amply repaid if it gives you the confidence and basic skills needed to start teaching reading at home.

Frank Rogers suggests that you get the *Penny Primer* and cassette first and then, once familiar with these, send for his complete program. Recommended.

Thoburn Press

An Acorn in My Hand, $7.95. Add $2 shipping.

Unusual book written by a Christian schoolteacher, Ethel Bouldin, whose great success in teaching all her first-graders to read and cipher, even after she lost the use of her voice, has inspired many people. The teaching method itself properly starts on page 23, the sections preceding being given up to testimonials and some of Mrs. Bouldin's educational philosophy. Since Mrs. Bouldin's strategy is interspersed with teaching tips, you will have to read and reread—slowly!—to get at the meat of what she is saying.

An Acorn in My Hand more resembles a long in-service lecture by a master teacher on which you must take notes than a step-by-step plan for teaching reading. Many parents have reported being really helped by this book, and you *could* use it to develop a home reading program. I personally found the book hard to follow. If you're looking for a program, rather than instruction in how to teach, many sources in the next chapter are easier to work with.

CHAPTER SEVEN

PHONICS FOR PRESCHOOLERS

Phonics instruction starts with recognizing the alphabet letters and learning to write them. Some methods teach both the names and sounds of the letters; others teach only the sounds. The reason for teaching the letter names is that this makes it easier for the teacher to give directions to the students—e.g., "Johnny, write an *A* on the blackboard." Those who prefer to teach only the sounds also have a valid point, namely that one less thing to learn means one less chance of confusing young kids. Resolving this issue, it seems clear that bright kids can be taught sounds and letters simultaneously, while slower (though not necessarily less intelligent) learners should be taught alphabet sounds first, and the letter names later, once they are reading successfully.

Learning to write the letters also has a practical advantage, especially for kinesthetic learners, who memorize letter shapes much better when writing than when just looking at them. The downside is that some kids are ready to read before they are ready to write. It is possible to be mentally more advanced than you are physically. This was true in the case of our first son. However, whether reading is taught first or together with writing, learning to write can't help but improve reading skills, just from the extra opportunity to practice spelling and letter shapes.

Here, first, are some simple, fun, and not-terribly-expensive resources to help you help your children

learn to recognize and write the alphabet letters. After these I have provided a complete listing, with reviews, of major preschool phonics programs designed for parents to use with their pre-school age children. The difference between these programs and programs for school-age children is that preschool phonics programs generally are more hands-on, require little or no writing, and include at least some readiness activities. These are low-pressure programs, moving at a fairly slow pace, and often not covering as much ground as phonics programs for older children. Although many "regular" phonics programs can be used with preschool children and vice versa, the programs in this chapter are specifically designed for use with your younger children.

LEARN THE ALPHABET

NEW**
A Beka Books
Basic Phonics Charts, $7.40. Basic Phonics Flashcards, $15.85. Clue Word Cards, $7.40. Basic Phonics Sounds Cassette, $7.95. Alphabet Charts and Games, $15.85. Letter Picture Flashcards, $11.95. Large Alphabet Flashcards, $9.50. Felt House Boardgame, $4.95. Felt Upper-

Case Alphabet, $7.95. Felt Lower-Case Alphabet, $6.95. Miniature Alphabet Flashcards, $2. Full phonics programs for nursery–grade 2, many other related materials available.

As you can see, A Beka has tons of how-to-learn-the-alphabet accessories. See description below under Preschool Phonics Programs.

Alphagator Al
Teacher's manual $9.98, letter book $3.98, writing tablet $3.98, letter songs cassette $6.98, flash cards $7.98, hand puppet $18.98. Add $2 shipping.

Phonics with animal fantasies. Your little ones will learn to recognize, sound, and write consonant and short vowels. Every lesson includes flash cards, a goofy letter song, a really silly story starring some alliterative animal and the sound-of-the-week, drawing practice, and letter games. Designed for preschools, Alphagator Al takes only a few minutes three days a week.

Now, how about a sample song?

Bubble gum, bubble gum,
What a bubble blower I've become!
When a big bubble blows,
I get B-B-Bubbles on my nose.

A sample story would take up too much space here, so let me just say that Alphagator Al's own story centers on his allergy to words beginning with short A . . . the poor critter sneezes, "A-a-a-CHOO!" whenever he hears one. An apple a day sends the allergy away, and your kids get to sit there yelling, "A-a-a-CHOO!" every time you read a short A word from the list of words following the lesson. Get the picture?

All Alphagator Al materials are professional, produced by the same people who do the Praise Hymn music program for Christian schools (see Volume 4). With no pretensions to molding future leaders or producing Einsteins, this simple, wacky program appeals to young kids and does teach the letters.

NEW★★
Children's Small Press Collection
Icky Bug Alphabet Book, Bird Alphabet Book, Flower Alphabet Book, $5.95 each.
Also available but not seen by me, *Ocean ABC, Yucky Reptile, Furry Animals,* and *Frog and Amphibians,* also $5.95 each.

Few kids learn the alphabet from alphabet books, but they are a fun way to expose littlest kids to the idea that there is such a thing as the alphabet. Our kids love *Dr. Seuss's ABC,* but most other alphabet books leave me cold.

If you, like me, are tired of typical alphabet books, here's something really different. These three alphabet books, like other alphabet books, have one letter per page and an object beginning with that letter. There the resemblance stops. The gorgeous artwork in these three books is large, colorful pictures of, respectively, icky bugs, birds, and flowers. Accompanying text gives simple nature information about the bug, bird, or flower-of-the-page. Some of the icky bugs really are icky, by the way. Tarantulas and scorpions—ugh! Others, like my friends the Monarch butterfly and lady-bug, are really rather beautiful. The text is really cute in spots. An example from the Icky Bug book: "U is for Unfinished Painting. On this page the illustrator forgot to finish painting the picture. [Next page] U is for Unicorn Beetle. O.K., that's better. Now the illustrator has finished the painting." Another example (in the Birds book): "B is for Bat. Hey, wait a second! Bats are not birds. Bats are mammals. Even though they have wings and they can fly, they do not have feathers. Get out of this book, you Bats!" From the Flowers book: "M is for Marigold. Believe it or not, chicken farmers feed Marigolds to their chickens so that the chickens will have healthy looking yellow skin." A fine introduction to nature lore and the alphabet, all at once!

IMPROVED★★
Christ Centered Publications
Colored phonics flash cards, $24.95. Colored Alphabet Wall Cards, $7.95. Colored Math Flashcards, $14.95. Add $3 shipping.

If you want a set of Bible-based flash cards, here's one source. Sample for the letter A: "To remain in *Adam* all shall die/But in Christ, eternal life is nigh." These flash cards are now printed in color, as are CCP's other flashcard sets. This is a terrific improvement, since color is an important part of the "message" of each card, and it used to take a full workweek to color the former cards in! See writeup below under Preschool Phonics Programs.

DIDAX

DIDAX is the place for all sorts of nifty hands-on reading aids. Sandpaper letters, stencils, alphabet stamps, phonics activity cards, word-building puzzle cards, flip books, and reading games are all there in the pages of this fascinating color catalog. If your child learns by grabbing things and making lovely messes this catalog has what you need to teach him.

NEW**
The Letter-Match Co.
The Letter-Match Cards, $5. Extra deck, $3, when purchased at same time. Add $2 shipping. Coloring book and set of cards for lowercase letters, price TBA.

This unusual set of flash cards is designed to help kids learn both the sounds and the shapes of the uppercase letters. Typically, letter-picture flash cards either (1) simply show a picture of an object starting with the letter, (2) show an object onto which the letter is superimposed, or (3) show an object twisted into the shape of the letter. The Letter-Match Cards are different. The objects (which are a different color than the letters, to aid in visual perception) are presented in such a way that they help kids remember the shape of the letters. For example, "B is a bunk bed for Balls." The picture shows a B with a ball nestled in each of the two curves of the B. Both the long and short sounds of the vowels are presented—e.g., "A has a place to Act like an Ape." The picture shows an ape hanging by his legs from the bar of the A. Accompanying instructions explain the system's rationale and explain how to use it to maximum effect.

You can either use one deck of cards for flash cards, or get a second deck for a Concentration-style game. One neat feature of the game directions: little kids are allowed to turn over three (or even more) cards looking for a match. This gives them a bigger chance to succeed.

Now in development: a coloring book using the Letter-Match approach, with large letters to color in and room at the bottom of each page for the student to write several rows of letters himself. Also under development: a set of Letter-Match style flash cards for the lowercase letters. These sound good. Write the folks at Letter-Match for info.

PRESCHOOL PHONICS PROGRAMS

Designed especially for younger children, these phonics programs can also be used with first-graders. Similarly, regular phonics programs can often be used with younger children. For your convenience, below are reviews of both separate phonics programs and the phonics components of the most popular complete kindergarten programs. I have not included suppliers who use phonics programs published by others, just the publishers of the programs themselves, as what you really need to know is, "How good is program XYZ?," not "How many people are selling it?" The only exception to this rule is when a supplier designs his own phonics course around someone else's program, thereby substantially adding value to the original material.

Was all that technical enough for you? Well, forget the introduction then, and let's get into the programs!

NEW**
A Beka Books
Nursery Correspondence School, $300. K4 Readiness Correspondence School, $300. Kindergarten Correspondence School, $400. Basic Phonics Charts, $7.40. Basic Phonics Flashcards, $15.85. Clue Word Cards, $7.40. Basic Phonics Sounds Cassette, $7.95. Blend Practice Cards A, $6.30. Blends Practice Cards B, $7.40. Phonics Manual, $21.15. Alphabet Charts and Games, $15.85. Blend Ladders, $15.85. Letter Picture Flashcards, $11.95. Large Alphabet Flashcards, $9.50. Felt House Boardgame, $4.95. Felt Upper-Case Alphabet, $7.95. Felt Lower-Case Alphabet, $6.95. Nursery school phonics materials: Learn About Numbers and Phonics I and II, $4.50 each. K4 phonics materials: Little Books 1–10, $4; Little Owl Books, $4.20; ABC-123, $7.40; My Blend and Word Sheets, $2.50; Miniature Alphabet Flashcards, $2. K5 phonics materials: Basic phonics reading program (10 little books), $4.95. Reading for Fun Enrichment Library, $19.95; four Big Owl Books, 55¢ each; *Sound and Count A*, $8.50; Phonics/Reading/Writing Curriculum, $60. Many other related materials available.

A Beka Books is a major Christian publisher of school materials for all subjects and ages, including phonics materials for all ages from age 2 on up. They publish oodles of supplementary phonics aids: flash cards, charts, games, readers, workbooks, writing pads, etc. Or you can sign up for their complete correspondence courses or video correspondence school (as reviewed in Volume 1). Each correspondence option includes all the phonics goodies for that grade.

So, where to start if you are not signing up for a complete A Beka correspondence program? Probably with the A Beka Phonics Manual, "a complete phonics program for an entire year" that can be used in any grade. (You don't need this if you already have the kindergarten, first, second, or third grade A Beka curriculum guide.) Once you get the Manual, you'll see which of the supplementary aids you will need for the lessons.

A Beka uses the "ladder letters" approach rather than the "word families" approach. This means teaching the blends *ba, be, bi, bo, bu* rather than teaching, say, *at* and then *bat, cat, fat,* and *mat.* They also use "key words" for not only the basic letter sounds, but for other phonograms. This very aggressive phonics program, which starts in nursery school, works well for some kids but not for others.

BEST FEATURES: Very complete line of supplemental aids. Many can be used with other programs. Lots of adorable little readers. Integrated supplies for handwriting, Bible, etc. Quality production.

WORST FEATURES: Pace of learning and early acceleration may be too much for some children. Not as easy to use as some other programs. Classroom-oriented. The "ladder letters" approach doesn't work for all children.

Alpha Omega Publications
LITTLE PATRIOTS Complete Kindergarten Program, $239.95. Little Patriots Series Overview, $3.95.

LITTLE PATRIOTS is a complete kindergarten program, including readiness, phonics, reading, writing, spelling, vocabulary, basic Bible doctrines, and math. See Chapter 4 for more details.

The LITTLE PATRIOTS phonics program covers everything that can be done with one-syllable words. From *I Can Spell Cat* to *I Can Spell Crown,* there are six spiral-bound spellers in all, each with lots and lots of pages with spelling words on the left and spaces to copy them on the right. These are not "spelling words" in the usual sense of words that are exceptions to the phonics rules. Rather, as each phonics rule is introduced, the child writes out hundreds of words that use the rule. Along with each speller comes a reader, with vocabulary limited to the one-syllable words studied so far.

BEST FEATURES: Complete. Systematic. Teaches self-discipline.

WORST FEATURE: Many of the stories have unhappy endings.

NEW**
Bob Jones University Press
Beginnings Master Teacher's Manual (3 vols.), $110. Beginnings Worktext set (3 vols), $11.95. Beginnings Reader Set (8 books), $5.50. Up the Ladder Reader Set (10 books), $3.50. Practi-Slate with Inserts, $4.50. PreCursive Handwriting Charts, $6.50. Phonics Charts, $15.95. English Skills K5 Charts, $4.50. Response Cards, $1.80. Songs Cassette, $6.30. Sound Effects and Stories Cassette, $6.30. Word Cards Set 1 (400 cards), $19.50. Other optional materials available.

As I have noted elsewhere, Bob Jones University Press is publishing the best-quality Christian textbooks available today. Their Beginnings for Christian Schools® series has the usual excellent production qualities and common-sense educational approach that characterizes other BJUP materials.

Beginnings is not a high-pressure program. It combines readiness with alphabet-learning, basic phonics, handwriting, composition, grammar, and spelling. The 10 units combine language arts with lessons for art, music, motor development, science, and Heritage Studies, BJUP's answer to social studies. As their catalog says, "Children who are not ready for mastery of these skills still enjoy the rich and varied experiences in the lessons and gain background for future learning." Personally, I prefer this to the do-or-die approach of more highly-pressured programs.

You will need the Beginnings Master Teacher's Manual (without which the Beginnings Worktext set makes no sense), the readers, the Response Card set (44 laminated cards, one for each phonogram BJUP introduces), the set of 44 laminated Phonics Charts, the Beginnings Word Cards, and the cassettes. You might also want to get the handwriting paper and some of the other optional materials.

BJUP says you need their Practi-Slate, a sort of magic slate into which you slip sheets with models of the BJUP precursive letters and spelling lists, for pre-handwriting practice, but I have found these do not hold up well in our home environment. I suggest you substitute a lap chalkboard (such as those sold by Educational Insights) and the PreCursive Handwriting Charts, which hold up much better than the inserts for the Practi-Slate.

Somehow BJUP always does an excellent job of inculcating a sense of wonder and excitement for learning. Maybe this is because they are such good-natured people. Our family really enjoyed our brief visit to their Home Education Leadership Program convention in the summer of '90, and were especially impressed by the cheerful, straightforward attitude of all the BJUP staffers we met on their campus.

For a complete kindergarten program, just add in their excellent Bible and math materials and (if you are so inclined) their music program.

BEST FEATURES: Complete. Systematic. Kid-appealing. Highest-quality materials (with the exception of the not-very-durable Practi-Slate).

WORST FEATURES: Expensive if you just want a phonics program, since this is a full kindergarten program with the addition of a few inexpensive resources. The three large ring-bound teacher's manuals are clunky to carry around, and you have to flip back and forth between volumes since some sections in Volume A are used with Volumes B and C.

NEW★★
Carden Educational Foundation
Basic Carden Course, 15 hours of on-site instruction to groups of 10 or more, $120/person attending. Teacher instruction cassettes, around $13 apiece. Purchasers requested to take Carden Basic Course if at all possible. This requirement may be waived; however, you would be very wise to read Miss Carden's books and listen to the teacher instruction cassettes before beginning this program. Cassette: Basic Sounds and Carden Controls, $9. *Fundamental Sounds of the Carden Reading Method*, $10.95. Reader 1, $9.55. Manual for Reader 1, $12.55. Home Workbook for Reader 1, $4.95. Mae Carden, Inc. Chart 1 (consonants), $6.80. Carden Language Method Vowel Chart, $6.80. Mae Carden, Inc. Chart 2 (advanced vowel charts), $8.40. K4 phonics materials: *Learning to Listen*, $5.65, teacher's manual, $8.65; *Learning the Letters*, $5.15, teacher's manual (includes copy of child's book), $7.65. Other books available. Add 10% shipping.

Miss Mae Carden was a brilliant educator with a sense of humor and respect for children coupled with high academic and moral standards. Before her death she helped establish 75 successful schools all over the United States. Due to the high teacher-training standards required of all Carden School staff members, and the Carden Foundation trustees' reluctance to use Madison Avenue techniques to promote their materials, you've probably never heard of the Carden Schools before. That's OK. You're hearing about them now.

I have written up the Carden program as a whole in Volume 1. It includes art, music, French (even for little kids), classic literature, plays, poetry, and other goodies, along with the normal basics. For the moment, we're looking at phonics. Carden phonics materials are available for all grades in nursery school through grade 1. After grade 1, Carden students are expected to know how to read well.

Carden materials stress the importance of understanding over memorizing, beauty over expediency, learning for its own sake rather than artificial rewards, and structured learning over letting children drift as their whims take them. The curriculum is designed "incrementally"; that is, children are given a chance to digest new material before being pressured to use it, and are given sufficient opportunity to practice with it until it becomes second nature. Teachers are encouraged to show children the meaning of their lessons in terms of "the needs of life," which to Miss Carden did not mean "how to get a better job" so much as "how to find out who you are and what you can contribute to the world."

The Carden phonics materials place an emphasis from the first on *thinking* about what you read. Carden readers stress traditional values. The readers are not illustrated, as Miss Carden did not believe in letting children get distracted by pictures when they were trying to learn to read.

I gave you a few sample prices for Carden phonics materials above. Many more readers and instructional materials are available. You don't need to spend too much money, though, since only a subset of them are required for any one grade. Your best bet is to get the Cost List and see for yourself which materials seem appropriate for your child.

Carden materials were all designed for classroom use, meaning that the teacher's manuals are not the simplest books to zip through. If you can't attend Carden Basic Training, you will be well-advised to obtain the teacher instruction cassettes for subjects and grades you want to teach, as these will greatly enhance your ability to get the most out of Carden materials.

BEST FEATURES: Incremental learning takes pressure off kids, ensures success sooner or later. Traditional, wholesome values in both course materials and educational approach. Kids are treated with both respect and firmness. Systematic. Thorough.

WORST FEATURES: Teacher's manuals are quite complex. Much teacher preparation time is required to become familiar with the Carden approach. (This time is not wasted, though, if you really want to improve your teaching philosophy and methods.)

NEW★★
Cheryl Morris
Teach America to Read, $25 postpaid.

Teach America to Read: Your Basic Reading Skills Handbook is a complete K–2 phonics program in one fairly slim spiral-bound manual, with the kindergarten portion lasting only eight weeks. In kindergarten, the student learns the letters in order, blending (with word families), writing, reading simple words, writing the letters, and a few sight words. Color and number words are taught as sight words. In first grade, the word family approach continues, with "core words" and rhyming, "consonant clusters" (e.g., blends), "consonant phonograms" (e.g., digraphs), silent *e*, soft *c* and *g*, *r*-controlled vowels (*ar, er, ir, ur*), common endings, compound words, and so on. The second grade section starts with a review of the phonograms learned so far (28 of them, not including the alphabet letters), the calendar, contractions, more compound words, syllabication, prefixes and suffixes, and other advanced stuff.

Lessons are designed to take one hour a day, but not necessarily all at the same time. You might, for example, play "Inviting Mr. R" at suppertime, in which you all try to think of as many words as possible that start with *r*.

The appendices include useful word lists (in order by phonogram) and a separate second grade word list in alphabetical order of words your child ought to be able to read by then. Alphabet and phonogram sounds are also listed, and you also get a few phonetic stories for reading practice.

BEST FEATURES: Simple. Inexpensive. Understandable—no special teacher training required, no confusing technical vocabulary. Everything in one book. Multisensory. Systematic. Complete. Clever games. Includes teaching tips. Useful appendices.

WORST FEATURES: Instructions in tiny print (words that the student will read are in larger print). No tunes supplied for suggested letter-learning jingles. You have to either make your own flash cards or buy them separately.

NEW★★
Christ Centered Publications
Teacher materials: Basic package $149.95 (usable ages 3–7). Student/teacher workbooks and readers: K4 $34.95, K5 $42.95, first grade $49.95. Components available separately. *Phonics Drill Reader*, $15 for Teacher Edition, $10 for Student Edition. Add 8% shipping.

I wrote this Christ-centered kindergarten and early grades program up in some detail in Chapter 4. Let's look at its phonics component now. You can buy all the phonics materials separately, by the way.

CCP's phonics program uses Bible names and words as key words for the phonics sounds. For short A the rhyme goes, "To remain in *Adam* all shall die/But in Christ, eternal life is nigh." The flash cards illustrate this rhyme with beautiful color pictures. The phonics material is quite similar to the Creation's Child beginning phonics program, right down to a visualized *Noah's Vowel Song*. However, CCP's phonics program goes farther, right through second grade.

CCP's phonics workbooks are more than Bible verses and letters. For every new phonogram, you get a page of "phonics art"—pictures for you to draw piece by piece while your children copy, until one of them is able to guess what the picture is. (Hint: each of the four pictures per lesson begins with the letter or sound you are studying.) Our kids love this! You also get a page of tracing/writing practice for every new sound, as well as lots of vowel practice. The latter is particularly helpful, since preschoolers often confuse their vowels.

CCP also offers a *Phonics Drill Reader* very similar to Victory Drill Book, timed drills and all. Nice laminated color cover, pages very light card stock. More: little readers (Creation: *God Made Me*, Fall: *God Loves Me*, Flood: *God Saves Me*) contain the same principles, but fewer words for younger children. Along with this you can purchase phonics flash cards, alphabet wall cards, and other teaching devices. No matter how many add-ons you get, the program is easy to use, thanks to the basically logical workbook format.

BEST FEATURES: Bible-centered. Systematic. Thorough.

WORST FEATURES: Key word verses often don't start with the key word.

Creation's Child

Teacher's Manual, $13.50—over 120 pages in the second edition. $2.50 shipping. Cassette tape, $4.50. Add 10% shipping, plus additional $1 for orders under $15.

Beginning phonics based on Bible words. You get Bible verses, rhymes, sound jingles, definitions, and Bible memory verses. Children learn the letters A-Z and how to decode simple three-letter words. The program also includes alphabetical lists for Bible animals, foods, plants, alphabet songs, and an alphabetical Bible word list.

Purchasers may reproduce notebook pages, large-print flash cards, alphabet picture cards, awards, book-marks, and other pages. The program may be used with manuscript or slant-style (precursive) print. Bible verses are from the King James Version.

The Creation's Child program is quite similar to Christ-Centered Phonics, right down to a Noah's Ark vowel song (each program has different words). Creation's Child was developed first, but does not go as far. It is more of a beginning phonics program—very easy to handle, good for young children. You can also use it as an inexpensive Biblically-based supplement to a secular phonics program.

BEST FEATURES: Bible-based. Simple. Clever.

WORST FEATURES: Inexpensive production quality.

IMPROVED★★
Eagle's Wings Educational Materials

Letterland Phonics program (kindergarten version), $65. Letterland Kindergarten (includes Letterland Phonics and Kinder-Math), $85. Add $4 per program.

"We're off to see the letters . . . the wonderful letters of Oz!" No, Letterland Phonics (a production of Eagle's Wings Educational Materials) does not include this song, but it does have a little of the flavor of Oz. Here we have a fantasy land populated by people with letters on their bodies. From Baby "A" to Zany "Z," each letter person's personality corresponds to phonetic rules. Baby "A," for example, says, "W-a-a-a-ah" (the short *a* sound is the drawn-out "a-a-a-ah"), and can only be baby-sat by Shy "I" and Yours Truly "Y" (*ai* and *ay* are the only two diphthongs beginning with *a*).

Each letter also has his or her own poem to introduce its formation as a lowercase letter. Example:

Baby 'A' needs his stomach nice and round.
Close it up and come back down.

You have to admit this is cute and clever. But of course, the program consists of more than little people and little poems. The authors, two home-schooling sisters, have a definite educational philosophy. They introduce letter formation through writing letters in the air following the poem's directions. Lowercase letters are taught first. Vowels are introduced before consonants, which are then taught alphabetically. The "word family" approach is used rather than the "ladder letter" approach. In other words, *at-cat-fat-hat* are introduced together, rather than teaching children to say "ba-be-bi-bo-bu" and then add a consonant at the end. Complete word lists are given for every rule, including the exceptions. Where a limited number of words share a common element, such as the tricky *ough*, they are made into a poem or little story.

The kindergarten course includes three parts: *Getting to Know Letterland*, in which children learn to recognize the alphabet characters by sight and sound and write them in lowercase; *Learning to Read in Letterland,* where uppercase letters, alphabetizing, and rhyming are introduced, as well as three-letter words; and an attractive three-ring organizer with cassette tape, flash cards, and games. A kindergarten math course is also available (see Chapter 21).

You get the workbooks and teacher's manuals for all three parts, a cassette tape of songs and stories, Letterland Alphabet Cards for yourself and your student, a game board and cards, and sheets of cut-'em-out flash cards. All of this material is tucked into a printed vinyl organizer.

As the brochure warns, the workbooks make no sense without the teacher's manuals. After you have spent several hours coloring, laminating, and cutting out the Letterland Phonics cards (different cards go together by color), you will get to use the very nice manuals. These have a definite desktop-publishing look: crisp, clear, and easy to follow. The lesson sequences have also been improved since I first reviewed this program for *Teaching Home*. The letters A–Z are introduced in order, with no funny business about teaching *ph* at the same time as *f*. Another improvement: a previous edition of this program featured Quivering "Q." Although Q is still missing a leg, and needs his friend Studious "U" to help him get around, he is now Qualified "Q," a much superior characterization. Some of the phonics activities still are too complicated, though. For example, a child might be required to cross out the consonants and connect the dots in numerical order when he is not really competent in distinguishing consonants and vowels and has not even learned the numerals yet! Letter names and sounds are introduced together, another potential stumbling-block for the slower student. And I still can't figure out why such emphasis was placed on introducing the lowercase letters via Letterland people, while the uppercase letters are just introduced as letters. The characters are cute, but the letters in the middle of their bodies don't stand out as much as they should. Rolling "O" looks almost like an upside-down "U." Quibbles like these make the program unsuitable for children with perceptual problems or difficulty in learning.

The average child can learn to read with Letterland. He (or especially, she) will enjoy it very much.

BEST FEATURES: Poems for letter and numeral formation. Characterization of phonics rules (very well done and unique). Cuddly approach works well with little children, especially girls. Alphabetizing emphasis. Less rules than other rules-based program; rules are more complete. Rules are rhymed and sung for added memorability. Uses all learning styles. Spelling emphasis. Kid-appealing.

WORST FEATURES: Vowel dot-to-dot exercises are too complicated for many preschoolers. Introduces uppercase letters and new word families at the same time, causing potential difficulties for slower learners.

UPDATED★★
Educational Products
Sing, Spell, Read & Write Home Kit in Treasure chest w/cassettes, $110; w/records, $119. *Off We Go, Raceway* workbooks, $8.75 each. *Raceway* book with car, $9.30. Shipping extra.

The entire Sing, Spell, Read & Write program is wonderful with preschool children. You may want to skip readiness and go straight to the Level I workbooks. *Off We Go* starts right in with the letters. Each giant letter has a page to itself, and children also cut and paste, match letters, do dot to dot, and learn to write both capital and small letters in pre-cursive. The book is simple, clean, and fun. The *Raceway Book* follows this up with words to write that correspond to each of the SSR&W storybooks, activities, and vocabulary and comprehension tests. The book is intended

for first-graders, but once your preschool child finishes *Off We Go* (see the Readiness section) I see no reason why he shouldn't tackle the *Raceway Book*.

I almost forgot to mention that directions for doing the workbook exercises are printed on each page of the workbooks. They're supereasy to use!

NEW★★
Individualized Education Systems
Beginning Reading at Home, $25 postpaid.

This really cute little program is just enough to get you started without overburdening you with bunches of teacher's directions. You get 10 take-apart kits, a short Reading Readiness Measurement test, and a parent's guidebook. The take-apart kits are hole-punched 5½ x 8½" colored cards tied together with orange yarn. Kits have four parts. Blue cards have letter names and sound cards. Green cards are letter-touch cards, with tactile letters for your learner to trace. Orange cards are for practicing sounding out words, and yellow cards have stories on them. You take apart a kit and work through the concepts on each card. Each kit is about 15 cards or less, making it easy to master one kit in a short time. This is highly motivational stuff—your kids will beg for lessons! The entire program covers most introductory phonics, stopping short of diphthongs and some digraphs, and is an excellent choice for the three- to six-year-old set, for whom it was designed.

BEST FEATURES: Simple. Fun. Clever. Takes little time to do and no preparation time at all. Inexpensive.

WORST FEATURES: None.

NEW★★
Landmark's Freedom Baptist Curriculum

This curriculum was originally published by Associated Christian Schools, and is now administered by Landmark Baptist Church, a church with a day school, college, and AM/FM radio station. Associated Christian Schools was founded by well-known Baptist author Dr. Donald Boys to provide an "educationally sound and biblically true" curriculum for Christian schools. With the help of 54 writers (almost all of whom hold Masters or Doctorates), he produced a complete K-12 program.

The LFBC program is mainly a worktext series. Their *Right Start* program for kindergartners uses a strong phonics approach.

LFBC curriculum is designed to be as easy as possible for the teacher to use. All the lessons for one week appear in one chapter of the subject's large worktext. This eliminates the need for setting goals or drawing up lesson plans. Also, LFBC is "the only publisher of school material that provides weekly quizzes."

BEST FEATURE: Very easy to use. Everything is right in the book. Systematic, step by step. Christian emphasis.

WORST FEATURE: Cheap repro quality.

NEW★★
Living Heritage Academy
$135 Learning-to-Read Kit, $27.50 second student. $250 ABC's of A.C.E., $75 second student. 5% prepayment discount. Services: *Home Study Handbook* for parents, diagnostic testing, record-keeping. To enroll you must send a copy of the student's birth certificate and a recent picture with the appropriate fees and a completed application form for each child.

Living Heritage Academy is the correspondence-school provider for Basic Education materials. Basic Education, previously known as A.C.E. (Accelerated Christian Education), is famous for inventing the low-cost Christian school in which children of all ages sit at study carrels, studying individually at their own pace, with a few adults hovering nearby to help answer questions and grade tests.

The Basic Reading program teaches 35 phonetic sounds through "visuals, coordination exercises, music, phonetic drills, writing of the letters, and stories" using an animal motif. Originally written for classroom teaching, Basic Reading is both a reading and readiness program, and requires a substantial amount of parent involvement.

Basic Education moves more slowly through material in the first two grades than other programs. There is a reason for this; the curriculum writers felt that the reason so many children were failing in school was in-

adequate time spent on "the basics" before jumping into more advanced studies. Research seems to bear them out, since students taught using Basic Education test *lower* in the first two grades than children using other programs, but *higher* by grade 9 than children following the regular public-school schedule.

The other phonics program offered, *ABC's of A.C.E.*, is an integrated program using (I believe) the self-pronouncing alphabet approach, where letters having different sounds are differentiated by special marks. The two sounds of *c*, for example, are marked so you can tell when to pronounce *c* as *k* and when to pronounce it as *s*. The program is an integrated curriculum including phonics, memory, coordination, math, and Christian character. It comes with two ring-bound volumes of the *Daily Instructional Manual*, Alphabet Display Cards, a music tape, and 60 full-color workbooks.

BEST FEATURE: Lesson plans are comprehensive and easy to follow. You also get the services of a correspondence school, e.g., someone to call when you need help.

WORST FEATURE: The Basic Ed program requires lots of teacher preparation. Phonics is mixed with all sorts of other activities. The ABC's program requires kids to switch from a self-pronouncing alphabet to reading words without the special marks.

NEW★★
Smiling Heart Press
Pre-K and K, one book, $50. Add 10% shipping.

This one-book manual covers both readiness (for three- and four-year-olds) and a kindergarten phonics and math program for five-year-olds. The very complete readiness program is written up in Chapter 3. The phonics program is set up as daily lesson plans. Here's a sample lesson plan:

Week 7, Wednesday
Review first 54 phonograms by method shown in Week 2, Monday.
Review yesterday's spelling list; practice any missed words.
Write the following spelling words by method shown in Week 5, Tuesday: boy, book, by, have, are, had, over.

Not too complicated, is it? The book also includes the Morrison-McCall Spelling Scale, recommended by Romalda Spalding in her book *The Writing Road to Reading*.

BEST FEATURES: Includes an entire readiness and kindergarten program, along with the Spalding reading lesson plans. Simple, clear directions. Spelling Scale is included.

WORST FEATURES: Reading itself doesn't start until week 19! Until then the child is just learning phonograms and practicing spelling.

NEW✱✱
Teach America to Read and Spell
Penny Primer , TATRAS #1 audiocassette, finger-clock card, and pencil gripper, $8.75 postpaid. The Great Saltmine and Hifwip Reading Package, $35.50 postpaid.

The TATRAS phonics program works well for all ages. See the writeup of their Penny Primer introductory sample lesson that teaches eight phonograms in Chapter 6, and the writeup of the entire program in Chapter 8.

BEST FEATURES: Elegant phonetic approach uses a minimum of phonograms and rules. Multisensory. Teacher-training emphasis directed at parents, with a complete explanation of why phonics works and look-say doesn't, as well as how to use the program. Free phone consultations. No burdensome overemphasis on writing, although writing is taught. Timings make it easy to record progress, motivate student. Only phonics program to concentrate on the MOO (Most Often Occurring) words that comprise more than 50 percent of both children's and adult's literature.

WORST FEATURE: Disorganized (but pretty) manual. TATRAS #2 cassette, "Introduction to the S&H Manual," distributed with the complete Saltmine and Hifwip program since mid-June 1990, makes the manual much easier to use.

NEW✱✱
Timberdoodle
Teach Your Child to Read in 100 Easy Lessons, $14.25. Shipping extra.

Here's the program I've been using to teach my five-year-old and three-year-old to read this year. While writing this book I haven't had time for elaborate lessons, so *Teach Your Child to Read in 100 Easy Lessons* has been a lifesaver. It's a 100-day program for home use, adapted from the Distar Fast Cycle Reading Program used in public schools. Distar has been shown again and again to be the most successful public-school reading method of the 70s. This home program is an absolutely fail-safe method. All you need is

this book, a chalkboard, and 15 minutes a day.

Teach Your Child to Read couldn't be easier to use. It uses a "programmed" approach, in which everything the teacher says and does is spelled out for him literally word by word. The method introduces letter sounds before letter names. It also uses special orthography—e.g., "funny print,"—in which the letters are printed different ways depending on how they are pronounced. This orthography, used only in the beginning stages of reading, makes the English words used in those stages totally phonetically regular, so they can be read with very little effort. Silent letters are shown much smaller than voiced letters. This way the child sees that the silent letters are in the word, but isn't distracted by complex phonograms. Simple reading comprehension exercises are introduced right along with the decoding skills.

Every day's lesson should take around 15 minutes. Your job is to follow your script (printed in red), and reinforce or correct the child as explained in the book. This is outrageously simple. You don't need flash cards, pre-primers, or anything else. All the reading and drill material is provided right in the book. This includes huge lowercase letters with balls and arrows underneath them, so your child can follow your finger moving from right to left with exactly the right tempo (as explained in the book), and (in the later lessons) multitudes of silly stories featuring bugs, ants, ducks, girls, and eagles.

Teach Your Child to Read in 100 Easy Lessons makes sure your child knows *every* necessary reading skill, including those skipped by virtually every other program. For example, some time is spent in every early lesson on having your child practice *slowly* saying the letter sounds he has learned. You say words using long, drawn-out sounds—e.g., *mmmmaaaannnn*. He first repeats the word slowly, then says it fast. Since when a child is first learning to blend he will be saying the sounds very slowly, these exercises help him learn to "hear" a slowly-spoken word. He also traces and writes two letters per day on the chalkboard (you can substitute paper and pencil). In the early lesson, he does simple rhyming exercises. Once he starts reading simple sentences, he is asked to identify individual words in the sentences. This prevents "guessing" at words. You then ask him several questions about the story and the picture that goes with the story (questions are provided in the text). No other program covers this ground so systematically.

You literally don't have to know a thing about phonics to use *Teach Your Child.* Simple instructions to the parent in the front of the book explain how to use the program. Also in the front of the book are a chart of how to write the letters the Distar way and another chart telling you how to make the individual letter sounds. You don't need to prepare a thing or collect any flash cards, readers, etc. All you have to do each day is get the book, sit down, and tell your child, "It's time for your reading lesson!" Because each lesson is broken up into small segments, each lasting only a few minutes or even less, your child's interest remains high.

The book is designed to teach reading skills up to the second grade level. From then on, you'll need to invest in some phonogram cards or follow up with a more advanced program. Since the book does *not* teach phonics rules, most children will need this kind of help to bridge the gap between sounding out words and knowing *which* sounds to use in every word. For example, the "magic E" rule tells kids that *mad* is pronounced with the short sound of A, while *made* has the long sound of A ("the A says its own name"). This rule is not taught in the book.

If you're tired, busy, insecure about your teaching ability, or just unwilling to spend a lot of time and money on teaching reading, this is your book—as long as you are willing to eventually learn and teach the phonics rules separately.

BEST FEATURES: Easiest to use program around. Inexpensive. Everything in one book. Reusable. No strain on the child or the teacher.

WORST FEATURE: Silly stories. If you fail to teach your child the phonics rules (which are not included in the book), he may develop into a "phonogram guesser," unable to immediately recognize which vowel sound to use in a word.

CHAPTER EIGHT

PHONICS FOR SCHOOL-AGE CHILDREN

Once upon a time, there were three kinds of phonics programs: Papa Phonics (complete language arts programs covering all phonics and spelling rules), Mama Phonics (basic phonics courses that start a child reading but lack some heavy-duty extras), and Baby Phonics (introductory phonics).

Goldilocks, speaking for students everywhere, always preferred Baby Phonics, claiming the others were "too hard" or "too much." But Goldilocks, an impatient porridge-pincher, might have changed her tune if she could have seen the whole family of phonics programs at once. Each of the three program types has its place, depending on each student's and teacher's needs.

Some of us prefer to save money and do a lot of teaching ourselves. Others wouldn't even consider teaching reading without the help of explicit instructions or a recorded teacher. Some need only a bare description of how to teach phonics; others are looking for devices to motivate a child who has already failed with other methods. Some demand workbooks; others hate them. Some love smiley-face stickers and gold stars; others think those kind of rewards are demeaning. Some programs are designed for children; some work best for adults.

Add to these differences the wide variety in price among the better reading programs, and you'll see that it's up to you to carefully decide what you want to pay for. Do you want music and games to reinforce learning? Are you looking for a complete language arts program or just a little help over a tough spot? Whatever you are looking for, it's out there waiting for you.

INTRODUCTORY PHONICS COURSES (BABY PHONICS)

Below is a list of *introductory* phonics courses—courses that teach the alphabet, writing, short vowel sounds, and blending, but stop short of complicating stuff like polysyllabic words. These all may be found in the previous chapter.

- Alphagator Al
- Alpha Omega—Little Patriots
- Christ-Centered Publications—first workbooks
- Creation's Child—*Beginning Phonics with Bible Words*
- Eagle's Wings Educational Materials—*Letterland Phonics*
- Educational Products—Sing, Spell, Read & Write's preschool kit featuring *Off We Go* and *Raceway Book*
- Individualized Education Systems—*Beginning Reading at Home*
- Teach America to Read and Spell (TATRAS)—*Penny Primer*

- Smiling Heart Press—*Learning at Home* (kindergarten course)

BASIC PHONICS COURSES (MAMA PHONICS)

These courses go somewhat further, covering simple blending and so on. They are not *comprehensive*—that is, they do not cover every rule and combination of letters—but they do bring a child along far enough to read easy books on his own.

Alpha Omega—Little Patriots

See the Preschool section for a review of this course based on a decoding strategy for all one-syllable words.

NEW**
Cheryl Morris
Teach America to Read, $25 postpaid.

K–2 phonics program written up in Chapter 7.

Easy Reading Kit
Kit, $19.75 plus $2 shipping. CA residents add $1.20 tax.

This very simple, inexpensive phonics method is designed for teaching young children of ages five to eight how to read. It can, however, be used for all ages, since there are no cutesy instructions or adorable animal manipulatives, etc.

You get easy instructions on how to use the Kit, four packets of nicely-done flash cards (94 in all), an Achievement Chart, and sheets of shiny stars. Children first learn the sounds of the consonants, including the "soft" sounds of *c* and *g*, then the vowels (both long and short), vowel and vowel-consonant blends such as *ar*, *ea*, and *oy*, and consonant blends (including digraphs). There are flash cards for each grouping, printed on colored card stock with professional *large* type and drawings. Examples of words using the phoneme in question are included on the cards, as are irregular sounds of that phoneme. As the child learns a sound, he gets to place a star on the chart in the appropriate space.

The Kit also includes lists of irregular sounds such as *tion* and *ould* and *pn*, a list of silent letters (like the *b* in "lamb" and the *t* in "hasten"), plus a list of the more common prefixes *with* their meanings and sounds.

Intended as an introduction to reading and spelling, Leora Stanfield's Kit certainly gives you value for the money. The flash cards are appealing, the instructions are clear and uncomplicated, and the Achievement Chart is motivating. A good buy.

BEST FEATURES: Easiest program to use. No preparation time required. Achievement Chart motivates, records progress. No clutter.

WORST FEATURES: None.

Educational Insights
Course with choice of records or cassettes, and one workbook, $29.95. Extra workbooks, $4.95 each. Course with choice of records or cassettes, and 10 workbooks, $59.95. *Apprendiendo a Leer* for ESL Classes, cassettes and one workbook, $29.95.

I really like just about everything Educational Insights produces, and their *Hear-See-Say Phonics Course* is no exception. Designed for classroom or home use, the *Course* comes with three records or cassettes and a pupil workbook. Classroom teachers can buy the *Course* with a set of ten workbooks, or buy extra workbooks individually. The *Course* is also available in a version called *Apprendiendo a Leer* for ESL classes, with introduction in Spanish and the sounds in English.

Here is how it works: Instructions for the entire program are on the record (or cassette). A young female teacher gives the instructions, and your learner answers along with the recorded "alpha kids." Once you have gone through the record with him, the learner can follow the program in his workbook all by himself. Beginning with the sounds of the alphabet, the *Course* progresses to digraphs, the common endings *ck* and *ing*, short and long vowels, diphthongs and blends. The alpha kids answer very rapidly, so Junior might be hard pressed to keep up with them at first. However, the alpha kids' obvious competence acts as a spur—if they can do it, so can he! Periodic quizzes are integrated into the easy-to-use 33-page workbook.

Hear-See-Say is not a complete phonics course. It does have charm and is very easy to use, since the teacher is on the record. Literally millions of kids have used the *Course* in schools and homes. It is recommended for beginning readers age five to seven, or as remedial practice for ages 8 to 11.

BEST FEATURES: Easy to use. Motivational effect of repeating along with kids on recording. Systematic. Nice layout.

WORST FEATURE: Rapid speech of kids on recording.

UPDATED★★
Mott Media
Mrs. Silver's Phonics Workbook, $5.95. Teacher edition, $5.95. *Phonics Made Plain,* $19.95. Add 10% shipping ($3 minimum).

Phonics Made Plain is essentially a large set of phonogram flash cards, a wall chart listing all the phonics rules in this program and the phonograms to be learned, and two sides of one card giving *very* streamlined instructions on how to use the program. The writer assumes you know how to teach, and thus throws out teaching hints rather than giving programmed teaching directions. You can teach the phonograms in whatever order you think best, although the wall chart does present a particular order for those who want some guidance. Designed to be used with any set of readers, this is a very flexible approach to phonics.

Mrs. Silver's Phonics Workbook is a very attractive 80-page workbook with no copyright information and no instructions on any of the pages. Every page has a variety of writing, drawing, and picture recognition activities centered around the phonogram for that page, and many pages have Bible verses at the bottom. This preprimer/workbook helps students learn beginning and ending consonant sounds, middle short vowel sounds, and the digraphs *ch, sh,* and *th.* The teacher's edition explains what to do with each workbook page and provides oodles of readiness and enrichment activities. The method presented in the teacher's edition relies heavily on you providing numerous pictures or real-life items shown in the workbook: e.g., apple, ax, ant, anchor, alligator, anteater, ambulance. There is also an attempt to integrate the phonics lessons with Bible, social studies, science, health, math, art, and music. This can be pretty forced. For example, when learning the letter W, the social studies activity is "Find pictures and read stories about *work* of men, women, and children in families and communities." I really doubt that kids are going to keep the letter W in mind when listening to *Mike Mulligan and His Steam Shovel.*

BEST FEATURES: Clever activities I haven't seen elsewhere, such as filling in a letter outline with gummed circles. Easy-to-follow, step-by-step lessons.

WORST FEATURES: Lots of teacher preparation required to make the program accessories, laminate pictures on file folders, prepare sentence strips, etc. "Integrated curriculum" approach can divert attention from phonics study. Activities are designed for large groups of children; some are too much trouble for just one or two children.

NEW★★
Timberdoodle
Teach Your Child to Read in 100 Easy Lessons, $14.25. Shipping extra.

This is a terrific, easy-to-use reading program that covers reading skills up to the second grade level. See review in Chapter 7.

COMPLETE PHONICS COURSES (PAPA PHONICS)

Now we're in the big time! These are the heavy-duty phonics programs prepared to teach your child *everything* he needs to know about reading. Some of these cost serious money, so you'll want to look the selection over carefully to find the best match for your child's learning style(s) and your family's budget.

Ball-Stick-Bird
Set #1, Books 1-5 with Instructor's Manual, $74.95. Set #2, Books 6-10 with Instructor's Manual, $74.95. Free shipping.

Ball-Stick-Bird, a phonics program invented by research psychologist Dr. Renée Fuller, differs tremendously from every other phonics system. For one thing, it was designed to teach certified, institutionalized retardates to read (people with an IQ of 60 or less). For another thing, it works. No other phonics program, not one, has ever made its debut under such difficult circumstances.

Dr. Fuller's breakthrough, at first sight, might seem to be her system for breaking down the capital letters into three strokes: the Ball (a circle), the Stick (a line), and the Bird (two lines joined at an angle, like the cartoon of a bird in flight). Color-coding these basic forms to make the difference between the strokes even more dramatic, beginning with capital letters presented in a carefully planned sequence, and requiring the student to "build" each letter out of its forms (thus involving all four sense modalities), Ball-Stick-Bird goes out of its way to make basic phonics mastery painless.

But—and here comes the rub—other phonics programs also feature simplified approaches to reading. Yet nobody dares take them inside institutions for the mentally handicapped and expect success.

Ball-Stick-Bird gets its punch from, of all things, a really different story approach. Dressed up in the cutting-edge formula of a science-fiction story, Dr. Fuller's stories present some heavy-duty moral applications. Her Good Guys and Bad Guys star in fables about human nature: the lust for power, the foolishness of sloganeering, how experts use their authority to stifle criticism of their actions, and so on.

It is easy to see why labeled people—like the "mentally retarded" and "special education" children—lap up these stories. Dr. Fuller tells it like it is. She literally gives them the words that explain their experience as the powerless victims of experts.

I should mention that Ball-Stick-Bird can be used with any person or child mentally old enough to follow a story. Dr. Fuller's contention is that Story Readiness, not some mystical amount of Motor Skill Readiness, is the real preparation for reading, and that successful reading itself grows out of the basic human desire to understand one's own life as a story.

From a Christian perspective, this makes great sense. If the spirit of a man is truly independent of his physical brain, there is no reason why any human being, however "mentally deficient," should not be reachable through the basically spiritual medium of stories—especially stories that help him make sense of his own life. Like, for example, the original, unbowdlerized Bible stories. Let's start thinking about it . . .

BEST FEATURES: Stories use extremely simple vocabulary, but treat readers with respect. Unusual emphasis on right versus wrong. Supersimple approach to letter recognition and printing the capital letters. Extremely easy to use. Only program to achieve spectacular results with severely retarded learners.

WORST FEATURES: Some people don't approve of science fiction starring superheroes as a child's first reading material. This extremely non-traditional approach would not suit someone who prefers old-fashioned primers.

NEW**
Carden Educational Foundation

Phonics programs for kids from K4 through first grade. The first grade course does the whole job. See writeup in Chapter 7.

NEW**
Chalen Edu-Systems
Reading Step-by-Step: A Winning Formula, complete program, $89.95. Add $4.50 shipping. Sampler, $4.95 postpaid.

Developed by a classroom teacher with 25 years of experience, the *Reading Step-by-Step* program is systematic phonics mixed with the memorizing of 310 sight words. Some of the "sight" words, like *if* and *off*, are 100 percent phonetic; others, like *do* and *to*, are phonetic in systems that teach multiple sounds for each phonogram.

Reading Step-by-Step follows the "horizontal" phonics method. You teach consonant sounds and use picture cards cut out from sheets in the back of the manual to practice matching beginning consonants to pictures of objects beginning with that name. Following the typical horizontal phonics approach, short vowels are taught next. Next come some consonant digraphs and blends, then the "two-vowel rule,": "If there are two vowels together, the first one says its name and the second one is silent," followed by silent *e* words, *r*-controlled vowels, more blends, digraphs, and vowel combinations. After all this, your child learns about contractions and root changes, syllables, and prefixes and suffixes.

Everything is in one attractive, printed ring binder, with your teaching instructions on two cassettes that snap inside the front cover. You don't have to sweat over flash cards with this program; they're on pages right inside the binder. Just cut 'em out as you come to them! The few worksheets you will need are also right next to their lesson. So are the "sticker" pages, with words on stickers next to the "rules" for each word. Your child gets to stick each sticker on a grid on the next page after sounding out the word.

Each lesson is designed to take 30 minutes, including 15 minutes or more spent reviewing previously-covered material. Author Charlotte Lenzen, an energetic lady, does her best to inspire you to make this quality time with your child. Her cassette instructions are excellent, walking you through every page of the course. She also includes many worthwhile teaching tips, including some that can prevent learning problems, such as reversals.

This program is *very* easy to use. You won't even have to rewind and replay the cassette, since Charlotte tells you when to pause (and go do something) or stop the tape (so you can start at that spot for the next lesson).

The sheets of sight words are set up so that words that look alike are often on the same sheet, as are some words containing phonograms taught in the lesson. Often, a "sight" word for one lesson has its parts taught in a future lesson. Example: the word *my* is introduced before the sounds of final *y* are introduced.

It's good sense to make kids practice distinguishing between words that look alike, and to drill them on rapidly reading words they have *already decoded*. Make sure to follow the manual directions when teaching the sight words! I suggest you the time to look through the manual and separating out the words whose parts will be taught later. Save those to be drilled at that lesson. One more tip not included in this system: Have the kids every so often separate the flash cards into piles of cards of similar words (e.g., all

the short words ending in *y*, like *by, my,* and *shy*). This is a good hands-on exercise for letting kids discover, or reinforce, the patterns of English phonics, as well as detecting the occasional exception.

Kids really do need to develop a "sight" vocabulary, meaning an increasing group of words they recognize instantly without having to stop and sound them out. The 310 sight words included in this program occur frequently in all children's literature, and it's a good idea to drill your children on them. Just make sure that your child sounds out *every* word he encounters. It's better to say, "Yes, the word *very* should sound like *vurry* if it followed the rules—remember, when you read 'vurry' it's really 'very'!" than to ignore the three-out-of-four phonetically perfect elements in this word (*v, r,* and *y*) and risk your child becoming a word-guesser. If you follow this advice, then you'll have an excellent, thorough program here.

BEST FEATURES: Everything is in one book, including the flash cards. Hand-lettered text is friendly and nonthreatening. Wonderful instructions designed for home-schooling parents make using it a breeze. Easy-to-understand program starts right at the beginning with letter recognition and deals with typical learning difficulties, such as seeing the difference between *b* and *d*. Clever games and teaching tips. Very little writing required. Handy format with laminated index tabs is easy to use, stands up to abuse. Trouble areas are explained. Teaches you how to teach, so you'll understand what you're doing. Thorough: goes right through third grade material such as prefixes and suffixes. Reusable. Two-month money-back guarantee. Sampler available so you can try before you buy.

WORST FEATURE: The "two vowels together" rule has too many exceptions. Be careful how you teach the sight words.

NEW★★
Char-L Inc.
Discover Intensive Phonics for Yourself kit, home schooler price $99. Mini Reverse Listening Card Set for home schoolers, $10. Manual only, $69. Posters, $10. Video (VHS or Beta), $59. Shipping extra.

"Discover Intensive Phonics for Yourself" from CHAR-L is a completely non-consumable, reasonably-priced, and absolutely clutter-free program. The only supplies you need are a blackboard or markerboard and something to write on it with. (We made our own lined blackboard, from instructions in the manual.)

Charlotte F. Lockhart ("Char-L, the Biphonic Woman"), the program's author, sounds like an interesting person. Her program has been tested and proven effective all over the country—as well it might, being written by a lady with years of experience as a teacher and principal.

You don't have to know a thing about phonics to use Char-L's system, and your child doesn't have to know a single thing about it either. *Discover Intensive Phonics for Yourself* starts right at the beginning, with letter recognition. Children learn to write letters at the blackboard. (Char-L even tells you how to make a blackboard, if you don't have one!) Lesson one starts with consonant *b*. Next comes *f*, then *d*, *g*, and *a*. Your children then learn the "slide," blending a consonant and vowel together. After that they learn the rest of the letters . . . and then the real fun begins!

Char-L has broken down the entire decoding process into 42 sounds. Your child will also learn spelling rules, contractions, and stuff like suffixes and synonyms. The big orange manual tells you what to do every step of the way. An enclosed cassette teaches you the sounds and explains the program. Two big orange posters (you assemble them out of six included pieces of cardboard) show the 42 sounds, blends, and special vowel combinations your student will be learning.

Unique to this program are the included Reverse Listening Cards. These are 324 cards printed on cheerful colored card stock. Every card is different. You are supposed to laminate the cards or cover them with contact paper, then cut them out.

What is "reverse listening"? Char-L explains it like this:

> Even before I had written my material, a teacher once complained that her students could write and spell anything that she dictated, but when they saw the same words in print, they could not read them. This gave me the idea of *reversing* the process—to use cards with words on them so the students would *see* the letters and words (instead of *hearing* them all of the time).

> With the Reverse Listening cards, they *see* the words in print, they copy the words on the chalkboard, following the instructions, then *read the words aloud* to the teacher, who checks to see if they have mastered the skills involved.

"Nonsense words" are included to see if the student is really reading and understanding or just memorizing word shapes.

Char-L's new set of Mini Reverse Listening Cards was designed just for home schoolers. Its 18 8½ x 11" sheets for a total of 176 Reverse Listening cards are also (I *think*) included in the basic kit price.

Char-L's program can be used with a whole school class at once, without any need for segregating the kids into ability groups, by the way. Teachers who hate making little slow Johnny feel bad definitely should look into this program which includes him right along with everyone else, with no extra effort for them! Her new 70-minute teacher training videotape entitled *You Can Teach Anyone to Read and Spell* (which I have not seen) might be of special interest to classroom teachers.

Every component of this program looks really professional and sharp. Char-L doesn't miss a trick. And she'll even answer your questions once you are using her program. If you can't live without games and activities, this isn't the program for you. But if you just want your children to *read* . . . and you want to enjoy teaching them . . . this is a great little program.

BEST FEATURES: Step-by-step lessons start at the beginning and assume nothing. No clutter. Active learning at the blackboard. "Nonsense" words make sure your student really understands. No need for separate reading groups when used in a classroom. Whole program is completely reusable. All components available separately.

WORST FEATURES: Instructions could be more systematic and easy to follow.

NEW★★
Christian Light Education
Option 1: Basic Information Teacher Training Kit—$20, and, if you have a first-grader, *Basics for Beginners,* the training program for teaching the Learning to Read program—$7.50 and the Teacher Handbook for that program—$4.95. Option 2: *Basics for Beginners* (if needed), one-week parent-training program, available by mail or at CLE's regular late spring and summer training sessions—$75. Option 3: *Basics for Beginners* (if needed), parent training program, record-keeping, telephone counseling (you call and describe problem and they get back to you)—$100. Curriculum extra for all options.

Christian Light Education is a part of the ministry of Christian Light Publications, a provider of school materials to the conservative wing of the Mennonite community. Mennonites are followers of Menno Simons, a sixteenth-century religious leader who practiced believers' baptism, pacifism, and unworldliness. The Pennsylvania "Dutch," or Amish, are one well-known Mennonite group.

Designed for use in first grade, Christian Light's intensive phonics *Learning to Read* program is easy to teach and inexpensive. It's not anything earthshaking; just typical phonics instruction as it used to be taught in public schools forty years ago. Pictures reflect Mennonite community values: women have uncut, covered hair, dress is very modest, we see nice large families.

BEST FEATURES: Wholesome values, straightforward approach, teacher-training built in.

WORST FEATURES: Fairly complex teacher's instructions written for classroom use.

Eagle Forum Education Fund
Headstart Reading Course #1, $26 (includes Phonics Workbook A, teacher's edition of same, and *McGuffey First Reader*). *Headstart Reading Course #2* includes Phonics Workbooks B and C plus teacher's editions and *McGuffey's Second Reader:* $46.

Phyllis Schlafly taught her children to read at home and thinks you can do it too! Eagle Forum, the pro-family volunteer group Phyllis founded, made this its first educational project. Workbooks are the time-tested *Hay-Wingo-Hletko Lippincott Phonics Workbooks* and are the same intensive phonics system Phyllis used with her own children. Phyllis's method was to teach reading to five- or six-year-old Schlaflys at home, and then enroll them at age six directly in second grade. All have gone on to do outstanding academic work. Says Phyllis, "Any child who can't read anything he or she wants by midyear of the first grade has been cheated and should transfer to an intensive phonics-first system such as this one."

BEST FEATURE: Workbook format is simple to use. Time-tested materials.

WORST FEATURE: Can't say, since I haven't used this one personally.

NEW**
Eagle's Wings Educational Materials
Letterland Phonics (kindergarten), $65. Letterland Phonics (advanced), $85. Both for $130. Add $4 shipping per program.

I told you about the kindergarten program from Eagle's Wings in Chapter 7. Now let's look at the advanced program.

First, what do you get? *Phonics Fun in Letterland,* a teacher's manual and workbook that introduces all the phonics rules and activities, plus 15–20 daily spelling words. After reviewing the basics covered in kindergarten, *Phonics Fun* teaches blends, digraphs, silent *e,* and consonants that change their spelling. *Spelling in Letterland,* another teacher's manual and workbook combo, gives poems and mini-stories to teach the rules students can use to spell over 3,000 spelling words without memorizing the words directly. The *Eagle's Wings Handbook of Phonics & Spelling* (written up in Chapter 6), is also included, as are a cassette tape, flash cards, games, and organizer.

As I mentioned elsewhere, Letterland is a fantasy land populated by people with letters on their bodies. From Baby "A" to Zany "Z," each letter person's personality corresponds to phonetic rules. Baby "A," for example, says, "W-a-a-a-ah" (the short *a* sound is the drawn-out "a-a-a-ah"), and can only be babysat by Shy "I" and Yours Truly "Y" (*ai* and *ay* are the only two diphthongs beginning with *a*). Each letter also has his or her own poem to introduce its formation as a lower-case letter. Example:

Baby 'A' needs his stomach nice and round.
Close it up and come back down.

Letter formation is introduced through writing letters in the air following the poem's directions. Lowercase letters are taught first. Vowels are introduced before consonants, which are then taught alphabetically. The "word family" approach is used rather than the "ladder letter" approach. In other words, *at-cat-fat-hat* are introduced together, rather than teaching children to say "ba-be-bi-bo-bu" and then add a consonant at the end. Complete word lists are given for every rule, including the exceptions. Where a limited number of words share a common element, such as the tricky *ough,* they are made into a poem or little story.

BEST FEATURES: Poems for letter and numeral formation. Characterization of phonics rules (very well done and unique). Cuddly approach works well with little children, especially girls. Alphabetizing emphasis. Less rules than other rules-based program; rules are more complete. Rules are rhymed and sung for added memorability. Uses all learning styles. Spelling emphasis. Kid-appealing.

WORST FEATURES: Hard to distinguish visually between letters and their characters' bodies. Complicated activities may require some skills not yet taught.

Moves too slowly once you get to blending. Introduces uppercase letters and new word families at the same time, causing potential difficulties for slower learners.

UPDATED★★
Educational Products
Complete Home Kit including *Off We Go* and *Raceway* workbooks, $110 with cassettes, $119 with records. Preschool *On Your Mark, Get Set* student books, $9.75 each. Level II workbooks, *Down the Track, To the Finish*, $8.75 each. Level III workbooks, *Trophy Book 1* and *Trophy Book 2*, $7.75 each. Extra set of 17 Storybook Readers, $75. Sing-along videotapes, $29.95. Shipping extra.

Sing, Spell, Read & Write is a total language arts program for grades K-3 including—what else?—singing, spelling, reading, and writing! It has recently been repackaged and repriced, and as old readers of the *Big Books* will note, the company name has been changed. It's still the same publishing company, though, and the same basic content.

SSR&W comes in the most exciting package I have seen. Upon opening the outer box, your child finds a Teacher's Manual, two student workbooks, and a treasure-chest made of sturdy cardboard. Opening the chest he finds: six color-coded song cassettes; 17 colorful phonics readers; several reading and spelling games, including Bingo chips and colored cards; a bag of nifty little prizes; a tiny magnetic car; and, a large, colorful raceway chart that you can stick on your refrigerator. The little car is placed on the step your child has just completed. After two laps he has learned it all!

The impact of unwrapping all that is immense. It's like Christmas in July! (Hint to grandparents: *SSR&W* makes an impressive and useful gift!) It made *me* wish I could learn to read all over again!

SSR&W teaches pre-cursive script (one point in its favor) and acquaints children with *both* the printed and type alphabet symbols (another good point). I am not aware of any other program that does both these things. The workbooks are delightful—just enough exercises, not overdone, and a lot of fun reinforcement. The games are likewise delightful. And what kid could resist a chance to win lots of prizes?

The songs, which are intended to teach such things as the alphabet, short and long vowel sounds, and digraphs and diphthongs, have catchy lyrics and nice tunes. They are sung by children with professional orchestration. The little phonics readers are cute stories about various children, pets, talking bears and bugs, and so on. I liked their strong family emphasis.

You have to do a lot of teaching with *SSR&W*. But the teaching is fun. And there are only 36 steps!

To make *SSR&W* more self-instructional, purchase the VHS videotapes. These include 12 songs and activities for your children to do along with the children on the tape.

You can get a preschool workbook for younger children. More advanced workbooks are also available. Level III workbooks cover English language and grammar up to grade 8. These workbooks are not included in the basic Home Kit; order separately.

As enticing as the brochure is, it doesn't do the program justice. In real life the contents are much more colorful and exciting than they appear on the brochure picture. (It's better this way than the other way around!)

SSR&W is the *ideal* supplementary reading program. The activities, games, and songs reinforce phonics lessons learned elsewhere. *SSR&W* is also a good program on its own, although it is not self-instructional like *Play 'N Talk*. It does take a lot of work, though, and some kids have trouble with its "ladder letters" approach (e.g., teaching *ba - be - bi - bo - bu* rather than "word families" like *bat - cat - fat - mat - sat*).

BEST FEATURES: Tons of games and fun activities. Song cassettes make phonics rules easy to memorize. Super motivating. Includes its own fine set of phonics primers. Completely reusable except for the workbooks.

WORST FEATURES: Lessons take some teacher preparation. You might get stuck at some learning plateaus, as the teacher materials do not address the question of how to "unstick" kids who just don't get the new concepts. "Ladder letters" don't work as well as word families.

NEW**
Educators Publishing Service, Inc.
Reading: The Right Start, $8.50 postpaid.

What you see is what you get. Mrs. Gould, a reading consultant in New York City for 35 years, has put together a book that is one part educational philosophy, one part a "How-To" section on how to teach reading and reading readiness with games and activities, and part an ad for her Structured Reading Program (not available, unfortunately, from EPS).

Here's the program philosophy, straight from the horse's mouth:

> *Reading* is intended for those parents who want to encourage their children . . . challenge their minds without pressuring them to perform . . . not for those who want to produce super children.

If you are willing to take the time to cut out magazines for pictures of objects whose names start with *m* or *b*, if you are able to take the time to make dotted letters for your children to trace, if you'd like to hunt for objects to place on a tray so your child can figure out which one you remove, then you really only need this book, and you've got yourself a complete readiness and phonics course for $8.50 (plus the cost of a bottle or two of Elmer's Glue).

Don't get me wrong. I'm not putting down this book. In fact, for children with learning problems, Mrs. Gould's approach is the best. She starts with the problem areas: audio perception, visual perception, memory, concentration, and eye-hand coordination. Based on her years of experience in tutoring children with these problems, and flavored with anecdotes from those tutoring sessions, she lays out before you a step-by-step sequence for making sure children are able to follow the directions and instructions they get in a reading program. These kids are often hard to deal with, but Mrs. Gould gets around that by making games out of the exercises they need to perform. She follows this up with her Structural Reading Program approach, in which the *structure* of the English language is made clear by step-by-step phonics and by strictly limiting the vocabulary read to only words that follow the structure. Again, this may not be necessary with average kids, but can make all the difference in the world to kids with reading difficulties.

Regardless of whether you decide to use the Structured Reading approach or not, you will find this book interesting. Mrs. Gould is strongly against teaching the alphabet letter names to young children, believing that children only gain insight into the structure of English through knowing the sounds of the letters. She also passionately pleads for teaching children to read *before* they start school. Her argument is that "natural readers" will tend to teach themselves some mistakes that could cause problems later, and slow children need the extra early intervention to keep them from failing in first grade and consequently giving up on learning. She undermines her point somewhat by calling for schools to provide this early intervention, since as her own examples point out, it is the experience of being compared to other children in school that causes slower children to feel inferior. Otherwise, her discussion of why in her estimation there is a "critical period" for learning to read provides much food for thought, especially for followers of the better-late-than-early and unschooling philosophies.

I wonder if EPS could be persuaded to carry the Structured Reading materials that go along with this book: the Learn-to-Read books, Early Reading Activities kits (so you don't have to spend your family vacation putting together readiness games), and pupil and teacher books. It would be handy to have all of them in one place. EPS is in process of publishing a series of readiness books by Toni Gould. In the meantime, the Keys to Excellence readiness series covers similar ground.

BEST FEATURES: Inexpensive. Intelligent discussion of reading issues. Sequenced activities and games to win over hyper and listless young children. Structured approach is virtually failure-proof.

WORST FEATURES: Requires lots of teacher preparation, lots of time practicing readiness skills. This might be overkill for average or bright children with no perceptual problems. All the same, the book is a good education for parents concerned about their abilities to teach reading to their children.

Elijah Company
Alpha-Phonics, $21.95 plus $2.50 shipping.

Sam Blumenfeld's great *Alpha-Phonics: A Primer for Beginning Readers* is a one-book, step-by-step phonics program that has both instructions and reading practice matter in the same oversized 169-page book. It couldn't be easier to use. The print is so large you can use *Alpha-Phonics* with a two-year-old, if you are so inclined. I taught one of my children to read with this book.

Now, what is *Alpha-Phonics?* It's step-by-step lessons in decoding words, generally one or two lessons per page, using a phonogram approach. This means one vowel or phonetic sound is presented at a time, and then the learner gets to practice reading all the possible word families of that sound. Very systematic and thorough.

The words are hand-printed by a calligrapher in a very large size. Some lessons include word lists only (set up to show the natural phonetic patterns), and others have practice sentences, some delightfully goofy. The amount of reading required at any lesson is not overlarge, and the book is paced so children can move right along. Mr. Blumenfeld starts blending right at the beginning, and adds letters as he goes. Everything you need is right in the (reusable) book, including some very brief pre-reading exercises and suggestions for introducing cursive handwriting.

BEST FEATURES: Price. Ultra-simple format. Practice exercises built in. Takes kids seriously (no dippy activities or patronizing silliness). Sequential. Thorough. An excellent value.

WORST FEATURES: Very few teaching tips or instructions; how to overcome common trouble areas is *not* explained. Overcome this problem by purchasing Sam Blumenfeld's step-by-step audiocassettes from Paradigm Company—reviewed in Chapter 6.

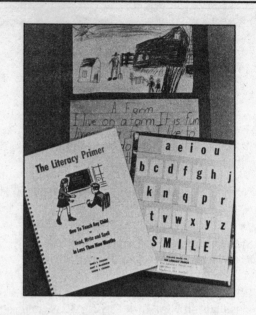

The Literacy Press, Inc.
The Literary Press's phonics program, complete package $38.50 plus $1.75 postage. Extra Spelling Board for second child, $2.75.

This small mail-order firm has an offer that's hard to beat: if, after trying their reading program with your most difficult pupil, you aren't satisfied that it's the best method you've seen, "return the USED BOOK with the shipping label for a full refund." The kit is designed, in the publisher's words, to "Teach Any Child to Read, Write, and Spell in Less Than Nine Months." Used as directed, children will read independently in eight to ten weeks, and be writing well-spelled compositions at the end of nine months.

How does it work? You get a *Literacy Primer,* which contains the lessons (in large type) and teacher's notes (in small type). The *Primer* is reusable, since children finger trace and say the letters in the book, writing them on separate paper (provided in the Spelling Kit) or a chalkboard. The trace-and-say method is supplemented with a Spelling Board Kit, consisting of a sturdy cardboard frame with accordion pockets into which single letters are placed to spell out words. The many kinesthetic drills using tracing and the Spelling Board reinforce reading concepts, and are a great help for those children who the schools like to label "learning disabled." Moreover, using the Spelling Board Kit, children can spell all the words they can read even *before* they learn to write. This is a feature not found elsewhere. (You can buy the Spelling Board separately.)

The Teacher's Supplement, also provided, is a minicourse in how to teach reading, spelling, and composition skills. Classroom teachers will find the teaching tips absolutely invaluable. These include time-tested motivational ideas and helps for getting problem pupils over the "humps."

And then there are the accompanying *Homestead Readers*. These delightful little books (*Jon and Jim on the Homestead, Homestead School,* and *Jon and Jim Discover Alternate Energy*) include drawing activities and questions for the children to show their comprehension of the story. Very thoughtfully, the writers have provided an appendix of simplified line drawings for this purpose. These drawings, like the rest of the art, are rather amateurish: not gorgeous, but acceptable.

In *Homestead School*, each story describes how to do some pioneer activity, like making soap. In *Alternate Energy*, you guessed it, the stories tell about alternate energy sources. Stories contain some Christian emphasis.

The people at Literacy Press have a lovely attitude, as this quote shows: "We do not feel that others who are promoting LITERACY are our competitors. The need is wide." Amen!

BEST FEATURES: Great guarantee. Systematic approach, easy to use. Spelling Board allows kids who aren't ready to write to spell out words. Cute readers include clever comprehension exercises.

WORST FEATURES: Amateurish production quality. They hope to remedy this in their next printing which will be a hardback *Literacy Primer*.

UPDATED**
Play 'N Talk

Complete program, $250 postpaid. Components not available separately except as replacements. Optional budget plan: pay total sum with one check or a series of postdated checks, include credit card info. Sample kit, $5, refundable on purchase of complete program. New teacher's kit including *Amplified Instructor's Manual* and flash card patterns, plus free 2-hour VHS Teacher Training Workshop video, $40, only available to previous Play 'N Talk owners.

Play 'N Talk™, a complete and expensive phonics program that has been around for over 25 years, still gives you more teaching aids than any other phonics program. These are:

- A Reading Readiness kit, consisting of a 12" LP *Sing 'N Sound* album with the alphabet song, big flash cards, 10 singing lessons on phonics sounds, a musical score for the songs for both piano and guitar, a giant phonics chart, and a colorful manuscript handwriting chart with directional arrows.

- The *Play 'N Talk* Basic Course. Series I is an 80-page large print text and two 12" LP records with "the teacher on the record." (More on that in a minute.) Series II is a 66-page text and three 12" LPs. Between them, these cover all the basic phonics skills taught in most courses. 92 recorded lessons in all.

- The *Play 'N Talk* Advanced Course. Series III is a 56-page book and three 12" LPs. Series IV is a 76-page book and three 12" LPs. Between them, these include 125 recorded phonics and spelling lessons, including all the rules your child needs to become an advanced speller.

- *Slide 'N Sound,* a clever word-making kit for practicing phonics skills. You get a plastic-coated picture of a bay, including dock and lighthouse. Using two plastic-coated slide rules that fit into slits in the picture, young learners are able to construct a large variety of words. Example: using the beginning consonants and the family "at," how many words can you construct? *At, bat, cat, fat* . . . The maximum totals for each combination are given in the accompanying book. You can build over 1,800 one-syllable words twiddling those little slides! *Slide 'N Sound* is good manipulative practice and helps cure reversals and other spelling problems.

- *Spell Lingo,* a set of 24 Bingo spelling games. By using the game cards, you can pinpoint your learner's spelling problems as well as provide practice in overcoming them. The game cards are designed to diagnose whether skills are being learned as expected. *Spell Lingo* is an easy and fun way to help you stop spelling problems before they start, and the best phonics Bingo games I've seen.

- *Ring 'N Key,* also included in the *Play 'N Talk* program, is a simple touch-typing course. You get three sets of color-coded rings (small, medium, and large) and two sets of color-coded dots with the keyboard letters printed on them. The finger with red belongs on the red row, and so on. The accompanying lesson book begins immediately with simple short-vowel-family words. A very motivational method, especially good for older learners and those with dyslexic tendencies.

• *Riddles 'N Rhyme*, a set of phonics riddles on three 7" LP records with three accompanying 28-page booklets. Cute but not essential—you can skip these when you get the program, with my blessing.

• NEW: Think you might have a hard time figuring out when to use the accessory learning aids listed above? The new *Amplified Instructor's Manual* is an attempt to solve this problem. Watch out for occasional patches of ghastly prose that interrupt the day-by-day lesson plans! The manual itself is broken into 12 units and exactly enough lessons to fill up a school year, with plenty of review and break time built in. Unit 1 starts with basic readiness and alphabet learning, including lots of suggested activities you may not have thought of unless you have taught phonics before. Units 2–12 go through the entire course on the records and tell you exactly when to use each Spell Lingo, Riddles 'n Rhyme, Slide 'n Sound, and Ring 'n Key component. Most lessons use only the items that are included with *Play 'N Talk,* so if you keep them all handy it won't take you too long to get everything out that you need for the day's lesson. You really should take it easy with the "Reinforcement Activities" after each lesson, though, unless your child really needs extra help in an area or you just feel like spending more time together with phonics that day. The manual insists strongly that *all* the activities are wonderfully beneficial, which of course in some cases they are. If you do all the activities, though, the lessons evolve from 10 minutes to 30 minutes or even an hour or more, which is not practical with little kids. Better to stop while the kids are begging for more!

• NEW: *Flash Card Patterns* book. You get 96 pages with 790 patterns for phonics sounds and words, plus a reproducible Score Pad page for use with *Slide 'N Sound.* These flash cards make it easy to drill and practice the new sounds—once you make them. You will have to photocopy all 96 pages, instead of just cutting out the patterns, since the patterns are printed on both sides of each page. If you also follow the directions about laminating the cards and/or mounting them on index cards for extra sturdiness, you will be spending a fair amount of time at this. The publisher's theory is that thrifty parents will prefer to photocopy new sets of cards, or new replacement cards, as needed, rather than purchase a new set of cards. Personally, I have never worn out a set of phonics flash cards—I wish the publisher had seen fit to just print the cards themselves on single-sided sturdy paper.

• NEW: Also included as a free gift is a new item I haven't seen yet: the video. This two-hour video is said to cover "how to detect potential learning difficulties, including mixed dominance, dyslexia, and speech disorders," plus the history of *Play 'N Talk,* how to use each item properly, how to form the phonics sounds properly, and other "teacher-training techniques not easily explained on paper."

What do you get when you put this all together? A total language arts program, containing every phonics rule and exception in the English language, plus instruction in manuscript writing, spelling, and even diction (thanks to the fine quality of the recordings).

How does *Play 'N Talk* work? You put the record on and turn to the correct place in the accompanying book. (Four-record series, each with its own book, come with the program, as noted above—12 LP records in all.) The teacher on the record takes it from there. All instructions are on the record (except for instructions on when to use the accessory items, which you'll now find in the manual). A group of children do all the exercises right on the record. For some reason that kids' chorus proves irresistible, and your child will want to join in with them. A perfectly delightful young lady with just a slight upper-class English accent did the narration of the first records, and Mrs. LeDoux, the producer of *Play 'N Talk,* did the rest. Mood music sets the stage at the beginning of each lesson, and each lesson comes to a definite musical close.

A storyline moves the program along. Your children meet the alphabet family and different word families. All the phonics groups are portrayed as people. For example: "Here are Mr. and Mrs. Digraph, and their children. WH is a fat one. He puffs out his name!" "Long Vowels wear straight hats. Short Vowels wear laughing hats. They turn up like the corners of our mouths do when we laugh." Little kids love it.

Play 'N Talk is a classy program. Harpo Marx's son did the very genteel mood music. A Disney artist did the illustrations. The program itself comes from that used by the Isabelle Buckley School in Southern California, one of the top private schools in the nation. In over fifty years of operation, they have never had a reading failure for any child who enrolled before third grade.

The entire program is nonconsumable. That means that if you are careful with the records, not only your children but your grandchildren can all learn to read without spending a dime more than the initial investment. If you should lose or break any of the items, replacements are available.

Mrs. LeDoux is extremely anxious to help you in any way she can, and thus she encloses all sorts of literature about nutrition, vitamins, learning disabilities, etc. in your *Play 'N Talk* packet. Don't let all this loose paper confuse you—it has nothing to do with the basic program.

Play 'N Talk has been used in tens of thousands of homes and thousands of schools over the last 25 years. All *Play 'N Talk* items are approved under all Federal Fund Titles NESEA.

BEST FEATURES: Most complete program—covers everything. Very motivational. Games are lots of fun, involve all learning styles. Teacher on the record. Warm, cuddly storyline. Classy music. Nonconsumable program can be used again and again without needing to purchase anything more. Flash cards for increasing reading speed. Systematic lesson plans, lots of instruction in *how* to teach phonics and overcome trouble spots. Typing course included. Mrs. LeDoux offers free telephone consultations and will answer your questions about the program before you buy it.

WORST FEATURES: Some people find records cumbersome to use. Components not available separately, except as replacement items for sets already purchased. Flash card *patterns* (printed on two sides of the paper) should have been flash card *book* (printed on one side only), as it will take you hours to make the patterns into flash cards.

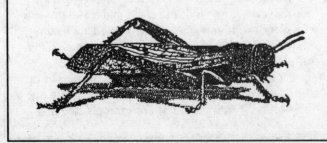

NEW**
Rod & Staff Publishers

Grade 1 material: Reader Unit 1, $4.30. Reader Units 2 & 3 (one book), $7.60. Reader Units 4 & 5, $9.45. Reading Workbook, 5 units in 3 books, around $3 each. Phonics workbook, all 5 units covered in 3 workbooks, around $3 each. Worksheets Unit 1, $2.40. Worksheets Units 2–4 (one set), $5.50. Worksheets Unit 5, $2.55. Teacher's manuals, 3 for the grade, around $9.50 each. Vocabulary word flash cards, 250 cards, $11.10. Phrase flash cards, 223 cards, $13.50. Phonics flash cards, 186 cards, $11.95. Grade 2 materials: Reader Units 1–3 (one book), $9.30. Reader Units 4 & 5, $8.70. Reading workbooks, one for each of 5 units, between $3 and $5 each. Phonics workbooks, 5 units in 3 workbooks, around $3 each. Teachers manual for reading, $8.35. Teacher's manual for phonics, $6.85. Grade 3 materials: Readers (2 books), around $10 each. Reading workbooks, one for each of 5 units, around $3 each. Teacher's manual, $6.95. Grade 4 materials: Reader, $9.50. Reading workbooks, one for each of 3 units, around $3 each. Teacher's manual, $5.20 Journeys of Paul Map, $3.40. U.S. orders, all prices postpaid ($1 small order fee on orders less than $10). Canadian and foreign, add 10% shipping.

Rod & Staff, a publisher of Mennonite textbooks, has come out with a revised edition of their popular *Bible Nurture and Reader Series*. In grades 1 and 2 of this series, an eclectic phonics/sight word approach is integrated with readers featuring simplified Bible stories.

Unlike other phonics programs, this utilizes the diacritical marks extensively. Diacritical marks are those fancy symbols used in dictionaries to indicate the exact pronunciation of letters.

Previous editions of this program were, to put it mildly, difficult for young children. We used them with our own first two children, and I can remember Joseph crying in frustration because he couldn't handle the extensive writing and difficult questions. The revised edition has kept the biblical content while simplifying the texts and exercises. Another difference: the major phonics review now is in grade 2 rather than in grade 3, as previously.

Grade 1 of the *Bible Nurture and Reader Series* is broken into five units with 30 lessons in each unit. Each lesson has five divisions: reading from the Reader, working in the Reading Workbook, working in the Phonics Workbook, doing a worksheet, and optional printing practice. Grade 2 also has 5 units of 30 lessons each, but just three divisions in each lesson: reading from the Reader, working in the Reading Workbook, and working in the Phonics Workbook. Together, these books cover reading, phonics, language skills, spelling, and penmanship. Grades 3 and 4 do not include separate phonics workbooks.

In grade 1, the first unit, "We Learn About God," covers the Creation and the Fall. The second unit, "We Learn More About God," reviews Creation and goes on to Cain, Abel, and Noah, with some practical applications. The third unit, "Poems About God," is poems about history from the Creation until after the Flood. The fourth unit is stories about Abraham, Isaac, and Jacob. The fifth unit contains stories about Joseph, the son of Jacob, and stories about Jesus from the Gospel of Matthew.

Unit 1 of grade 2 reviews Genesis. Unit 2 is "Moses Leads God's People," while unit 3 covers "More About Moses," "Balaam," and "Israel in Canaan." Unit 4 is "Stories from Ruth and 1 Samuel." Unit 5 goes through the Gospel of Mark.

Grade 3 leads off with "Stories About David and Solomon," followed by "Stories of the Kings—Rehoboam to Jeroboam" and "Stories of the Last Kings and Prophets." Unit 4, "God's People During and After the Captivity," includes parts of Ezekiel, Daniel, Ezra, Nehemiah, Esther, and Jonah. The fifth unit works through the Gospel of Luke.

Grade 4 has only one reader, with noticeably smaller print than that of the earlier grades. It includes three units: "The Gospel of John," "The Book of Acts," and "Job, Psalms, Proverbs."

Plans are in the works to provide a new chronological Bible curriculum for grades 5–7, which will then fill in any Bible books not covered by the *Bible Nurture and Reader Series.*

As you can see, the books are God-oriented rather than man-oriented. This makes a welcome change from the too-typical "God Love Me . . . I Learn About Me . . . Wonderful Me" emphasis of other publishers. The stories also are very carefully kept close to Scripture, without any flights of fancy.

The teacher's manuals for grade 1 include instructions in both phonics and reading, unit by unit. In grade 2, there are separate manuals for phonics and reading, and each covers the entire year. Teacher's manuals for all grades include answers for the workbook exercises, plus teaching tips, oral drill exercises, and lesson plans.

Flash cards are used with the program. The Vocabulary Word Cards cover each reading word introduced in the first two units of grade 1. Phrase Cards include phrases from those same two units. The Phonics Cards are divided into 10 sets as follows: 26 alphabet cards, 21 consonant sounds, 17 vowel sounds, six combina-

tion sounds, 23 digraphs, 39 consonant blends, four diphthongs, eight letters with more than one sound, 27 letter sounds with certain letters, and 15 silent letters (e.g., *kn* and *gn*, in which *k* and *g* are respectively silent).

BEST FEATURES: Solid biblical emphasis. The only complete phonics program whose readers consist of solid Bible stories without added flights of fancy. Systematic approach, with the same basic lesson plan every day. Phonics systematically taught (only irregular words are considered "sight words"). Deep concern for children's moral fiber. Thorough. Character-building.

WORST FEATURES: Diacritical marks are more difficult to understand than the simple first sound/second sound phonogram method. Complete program still requires quite a bit of writing at an early age. Classroom-oriented teacher's manuals.

UPDATED★★
St. Ursula Academy, S.U.A. Phonics Department
Professor Phonics 4-part Primary Kit, $16.20. Five-part Master Kit, $22. Components available separately. New 2½ hour training videotape, $60.

Professor Phonics is an inexpensive program that works well for children six years of age or older, for whom it was designed.

The Primary Kit includes a combined practice book/reader that contains a total intensive phonics program. The accompanying manual gives page-by-page instructions. Alphabet picture flash cards and a spelling and reading word list round out the package. For a few extra dollars, the Master Kit also includes *A Sound Track to Reading* and its built-in manual. This is a more advanced book that can be used with teens and adults, as well as with kids who have finished the *Professor Phonics* book.

Marva Collins, a woman who has had phenomenal success in teaching inner-city, minority children, recommends *Professor Phonics* highly as being "one of the simplest methods of teaching children to read." That it certainly is. What it lacks in tinsel and pizzazz *Professor Phonics* provides in simplicity.

Reading begins on the very first lesson page, as children learn the sounds of *m*, *s*, *t*, and *a* and immediately blend them into words. This immediate reading, and the association of pictures with the sounds, differentiates *Professor Phonics* from the other systems.

Professor Phonics has a really simple method of presenting vowel sounds. They are either short, long, the "third sound," or diphthongs. For example, the first (short) sound of *a* is found in *apple.* Its second (long) sound is found in *ate.* Its third sound is heard in the word *all.* The three diphthongs are the *ow* sound as in *owl,* the *oi* sound, and the *ur* sound. Vowel digraphs, i.e., two vowels that together make a single sound, like *oa* in *boat,* are taught separately, along with the other advanced phonograms.

Sister Monica Foltzer, the program author, really knows her stuff, and I was anxious to view her new videotape. Unhappily the soundtrack on the new *Professor Phonics* videotape is very murky. We had real trouble hearing what Sister Monica had to say. (It was possible to make most of it out, with intense concentration and a bit of lip-reading!) The video explains how to teach intensive phonics with the *Professor Phonics* Master Kit system. Sister Monica, a Roman Catholic nun, has been teaching others how to teach intensive phonics for years and years. Her experience is that many first-graders can learn to read (and she means *really* read) in one semester, using her method.

BEST FEATURES: Least-expensive total phonics program around. Time-tested. Explains *what* you are doing; you'll learn how to teach phonics, instead of just using a program without understanding it. Anticipates and solves learning problems. Best suited for parents with "teaching instinct."

WORST FEATURES: Teacher's instructions are not the easiest to follow. Repro quality of both books and tape is not the best.

NEW**
Teach America to Read and Spell
Penny Primer and TATRAS #1 audiocassette, $8.75 postpaid. The Great Saltmine and Hifwip Reading Package, $32 plus $3.50 shipping, includes manual and following items: PAT Flash Cards, Flash Card Rack, dictation notebook, academic countdown timer.

Here's an inexpensive, phonogram-based program quite different from the famous phonogram-based

Spalding Method. Author Frank Rogers believes that "reading is the road to writing," rather than that writing is the road to reading, as Spalding says. His set of phonograms also differs markedly from Spalding's. It is based on computer analysis of the English language, and makes it possible to decode most of the MOO (Most Often Occurring) words, unlike other programs in which many of these words are taught as "sight" words. Also unlike Spalding and other methods, the phonics rules in this program are not mixed with spelling rules.

Frankly, I was really impressed with all the program components, from the *Penny Primer* kit to the *Great Saltmine and Hifwip Reading Package.* (S A L T M I N and E are the first eight phonograms taught in this system, in case you're curious. *Hifwip* stands for High Frequency Words in Print.) The Penny Primer kit is written up in Chapter 6. It serves as an inexpensive introduction to this phonics system, *and* the first eight lessons of the program! (These are also repeated in the program manual.)

WHAT YOU GET: Comb-bound instruction manual complete with word lists, step-by-step program outline, daily lesson format, and a separate "Fast Track" sequence with special "Confidence Builder" word lists for remedial students of all ages, and an audiocassette "Introduction to the S&H Manual" that explains various features of the manual and how to use them. An electronic countdown timer, fully adjustable for anywhere from one second to 99 minutes, with a handy feature that allows you to restart the timer with the same count it had the last time you used it. Phonogram flash cards and flash card rack (you use the rack for spelling words with the cards). A blue and red-lined dictation notebook. Laminated "finger clock" card for teaching students proper letter formation (e.g., *a* starts at two o'clock . . .). Pencils and pencil gripper, to teach proper finger position while writing.

Saltmine and Hifwip is a "vertical phonics" program. That means you teach all the sounds of each phonogram at once. The three sounds of *a,* for example, are presented as "/A/t /AY//AW/." This means that the first sound is the *a* in *at,* the second sound (called the "long a" by other systems) sounds like *ay,* and the third sound is pronounced like *aw.* The *Penny Primer* and teaching cassette explain exactly how to present the material, right down to suggested wording for the teacher to use with the student. Possible obstacles are acknowledged and you are told how to overcome them.

The bottom line of *The Great Saltmine and Hifwip Reading Package* is to get kids reading *for pleasure* as soon as possible. That's why so much attention is focused on those MOO words. Typical phonics programs ignore those words, or teach many of them by whole-word memorization. But TATRAS deliberately attacks these words—*and* lets you know which still remain irregular in this phonetic system! (Less than 3 percent.)

The flash cards are rather unusual. Phonograms in black are on one side, phonograms in red are on the other. The black phonograms are those that occur most often, while the red ones occur less often but must be taught for spelling purposes. Sounds and teacher instructions are on the opposite side of the card from the corresponding phonogram. This means the teacher can see the answer but the student can't. Phonograms are printed in the upper left corner, so the flash cards can easily be staggered to spell out words (a good feature for kids whose motor skills are not yet up to writing).

This is about the best-thought-out phonics program I have seen. I just wish the author had provided more structure in the manual. You *can* figure out how to use the manual, but I know I'm not the only one who initially found the format confusing. Word lists, rules, phonogram charts, irregular words, abbreviations, etc. are all clustered together, while the lesson format and program outline is in the front of the books. The word lists themselves are littered with (admittedly useful) sub-scripts and icons. These indicate such things as "spoken word has two spellings" or "first word to use newly introduced phonogram." All this technical stuff is perfectly clear to veteran phonics teachers, but a bit unnerving for the novice. The new "Introduction to the S&H Manual" cassette walks you through it all, which helps; be sure to take notes in your manual as you listen!

If you're interested in this program, be sure to start with the Penny Primer kit. Play that cassette a couple of times and *take notes!*

BEST FEATURES: Elegant phonetic approach uses a minimum of phonograms and rules. Multisensory. Inexpensive. Teacher-training emphasis directed at parents, with a complete explanation of why phonics works and look-say doesn't, as well as how to use the program. Free phone consultations. No burdensome overemphasis on writing, although writing is taught. Timings make it easy to record progress, motivate student. Only phonics program to concentrate on the MOO (Most Often Occurring) words that comprise more than 50 percent of both children's and adult's literature. Lessons are short.

WORST FEATURE: Manual *looks* disorganized (though it's not) and makes you have to work harder

than you should. The new TATRAS #2 cassette, "Introduction to the S&H Manual," helps—if you purchased the program before June 15, 1990, you might want to sent $2.50 to TATRAS for this cassette.

NEW★★
Total Reading
Primary Manual, $42. Read Aloud Comprehension, $22. Games & Puzzles, $22. Dictation cassette, $6.50. Sound Cards, $7.50. Word Cards, $9. Primary Teaching set, includes all above plus *Guide for Basal*, $100. 2nd/3rd Review Manual, $22. Student materials (Level I worksheets, Level II cards, Level II reading, Level III workbook, Level IVa workbook, Level IVb workbook, Level IVc workbook), $3.75 each. *I Can Read by Myself*, $6.50. *I Can Read More Stories*, $5.50. Total Writing set, $110. Reading Comprehension set: Level II, III, & IVa (all together), $50; Level IVb for 2nd and 3rd grade, $66; Level IVc for 3rd and 4th grade, $40; Content Area Reading, $30. Some items discounted 50% on order of $200 or more after discount. Shipping extra. Free scope & sequence chart, free 7-day loan of presentation video.

As you listen to the Total Reading promotional video, you are immediately struck by the absence of one word: phonics. This is intentional. Total Reading is indeed a phonics system, but its promoters know that public educators have been trained to disdain phonics as "mere word-calling." So the video, while outlining the terrific results obtained with Total Reading (*every* child in the district using Total Reading scoring in the 90th percentile on reading tests, ghetto kids outdistancing non-Total Reading suburbanites, "dyslexics" reading like normal kids, etc.), does its best to avoid red flags that will prevent school administrators and teachers from purchasing this system. So far, wise as serpents—and that's OK. (It didn't work, though; California didn't adopt Total Reading, *or any other phonics-based program*, as a basic reading program, *in spite of state guidelines* that seem to prefer phonics!)

The program itself combines listening, decoding skills (phonics), spelling rules, writing, and How-To-Do-Well-on-Reading-Comprehension-Tests. The teacher starts by reading to the children and asking them questions about the story. This is absolutely correct and essential in teaching children to read. As the course progresses and the children learn to read on their own, they are taught to "read with a question in mind." Again, this is essential to becoming a real reader. But I'm getting ahead of myself. Let's quickly flash over the other distinctive features of this program:

- The use of diacritical marks to speed-up beginning reading (diacritical marks are the line, curve, and dots used to tell vowel sounds apart).

- Writing as a accompaniment to reading.

- Phonics used not only for decoding but for spelling (e.g., the hard *k* sound at the beginning of a word is spelled K before *i* and *e*).

- Phonics taught through dictation. Students learn to say and write words dictated by the teacher.

- Emphasis on creativity and awareness of the world through all five senses.

- Library books used as readers. This is a very unusual feature for a school-based program.

- Comprehension questions correlated with every popular basal reader series in the country. This feature is not so important for home schoolers.

- In the higher levels, creative writing, proofreading, and vocabulary training.

- Student independence and self-reliance is promoted. Children are allowed to proceed at their own pace. The goal is for each student to become "independent of the teacher as early as is compatible with their ability."

- Comprehension taught through literal (who, what, when, where, why?), evaluative (what is the main idea?), and interpretive (relating it to other experiences) questions. Give Total Read-

ing credit for going beyond fill-in-the-blanks to more important "thinking" questions.

Some of these features are found in other programs. Distar® reading programs use coded letterforms. Romalda Spalding's *Writing Road to Reading* stresses phonograms and teaching writing along with reading. Play 'N Talk teaches all the spelling rules as well as the decoding rules. Total Reading stands out mainly for its *scope* (it encompasses several grades' worth of material in all language arts areas), its *emphasis on comprehension,* and its use of *library books.*

Here's how it works. In Level I the child learns to "write and say the sounds of the single letters, memorize a vowel code, blend sounds into words orally, answer content questions about and retell stories that the teacher reads aloud, use vocabulary words in sentences, and participate in group storytelling." In Level II, he continues "learning the sounds of the phonograms, writing words from simple dictation, unlocking words for reading through the vowel code, reading sentences and simple stories, answering evaluative and interpretative questions about stories read aloud, and participating in group oral creativity." Level III gets into advanced dictation, spelling rules, writing and proofreading "complete, creative sentences," answering factual questions and finding the main idea, and reading easy library books. Level IV includes mastery of the spelling rules, grammar and punctuation, increasing vocabulary, writing creatively and proofreading the result, and increasing "speed, comprehension, and oral fluency in reading."

Total Reading also has a remedial reading program, *Six Steps to Literacy,* and an Intermediate language arts program for upper elementary and middle grades. Bilingual materials are also available.

Other features (none necessary for the basic phonics instruction): Integrated curriculum—two books of science and social studies. Poster Charts. Reading comprehension questions for 1100 library books, by reading level, are available separately. (See writeup in Chapter 19.)

You can request the Total Reading presentation video free of charge. Don't expect to be exhilarated by it. In keeping with its attempt to sound professional and scientific, the presentation is downright chilly. Each sample of classroom teaching sounded like a drill sergeant rehearsing the troops. Is this what government schools have come to? If not, Total Reading staff would be wise to add in some shots of delighted children and some cheerier-sounding teachers before promoting this video to parents.

Total Reading now has a nice letter and order form just for homeschool parents, explaining which items you will find most useful in their program. First, *the nonconsumable Total Reading Primary Manual is all you need to teach the first four levels.* We're talking about a $42 total investment here. You can make the cards and games and write comprehension questions for whatever literature you choose to use. (You probably will want to get the inexpensive Word Cards and Sound Cards, as the manual frequently asks you to use these.) If you prefer to use the Total Reading materials, they recommend you purchase the Primary Teaching Set (which includes the Primary Manual plus a Read Aloud Comprehension book, games and puzzles, a dictation cassette, sound cards, word cards, and a basal reading guide), all the student materials (Level I–IVc workbooks plus *I Can Read By Myself* and *I Can Read More Stories*), the Creativity manual, and Reading Comprehension levels II, III, IVa, and IVb, plus the Booklists. That total comes to $286.25, if I added it up correctly, plus you get a $58 discount on the Reading Comprehension materials (since your order is over $200), making a grand total of $228.25 plus shipping. This is less than the cost of Play 'n Talk, placing it within the range of upper-crust phonics/language arts programs.

Here's what reader Debbie Mangini has to say about her experience using Total Reading:

> I submit to you that Total Reading is an ideal home school curriculum that has been adapted to the classroom setting. It was compiled by an experienced teacher trying to meet the needs of her dyslexic son. Total Reading is a multi-sensory curriculum with special instruction for your child's areas of difficulty and/or strengths.

> Total Reading is very efficient as I do not need to prepare lesson plans and I have one manual in which phonics, reading, spelling, grammar, penmanship creative writing, literature, and speech are taught in an integrated manner. Other optional teacher supplements are available, but they are only extras and the student workbooks are only necessary in a classroom setting.

> As mother of five, I find it a curriculum of little clutter (busy work or gimmicks), with complete and comprehensive lesson plans. After one year of use, my children have come up 2–3 grade levels in all areas of language arts. However, my most important objective that has been met is their ability to express themselves through correct and creative writing—going beyond teaching reading.

You're right that other curriculums have covered some of these areas, but not in such a clear, concise, and unified manner. This systematic and yet flexible curriculum supplies all the components necessary for personalized application. It is also the only curriculum that I know of that offers a review manual to enable an older student to get through the first three levels in just one month.

Language Arts has never been my area, and I'm having a ball teaching Total Reading.

Total Reading also has "contracts and comprehension questions" for the major basal reading series (books for beginning readers) from a large variety of publishers, including A Beka Books. For a $5 postage charge, they will let you borrow and photocopy the contracts and comprehension questions for each publisher of your choice. Publishers presently covered include Harcourt Brace Jovanovitch, Houghton-Mifflin (1982, 1987, and 1989 series), Holt, Scott-Foresman, Ginn 720, Ginn Reading, Macmillan-R, Lippincott, Scribner Reading Series (1987), Economy, and (as mentioned) A Beka. They particularly recommend the Houghton Mifflin 1989 readers, if you're looking for a secular series to purchase.

The bottom line: this is a wonderful program for schools. It has all the deskwork and tests that schools live on. It really covers the material. It lets children read real literature—good stuff like *Sam and the Firefly* and *Caddie Woodlawn* and *Rikki Tikki Tavi*. The reading comprehension portion actually works.

BEST FEATURES: Very thorough, complete, easy to use, and even inexpensive if you skip the extras. Covers all language arts in one book. Lesson plans tell you everything you need to do each day. Children read from library books or your choice of basal readers, including A Beka's Christian readers. Multisensory approach works with all learning styles. Spelling rules taught as well as decoding rules. Emphasis on reading comprehension. Emphasis on narrating stories back and oral creativity exercises. Uses dictation instead of just multiple-choice (students can't fake dictation exercises!) Promotes student independence. Students taught to proofread their own papers. Review manual allows older student to quickly zoom through the early phonics material. Phenomenal results when tested in schools. They have a special letter and order form set up just for home schoolers.

WORST FEATURES: More deskwork than necessary for home schools (but not if you skip the extra workbooks and accessories and stick with the Manual).

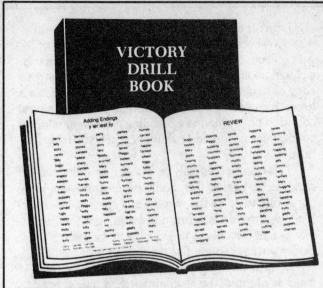

Victory Drill Book

VDB, $11.25. Teacher's Guide, $8.95. Cassette tape, $5.75. Worksheets and learning activities, $15.95. Predrill Book, $3.75. Shipping, $5 on orders under $30. Total program, $45.65 postpaid. Quantity discounts.

Phonics program based on step-by-step learning and timed drills. You get the *Victory Drill Book*, a Teacher's Guide, a cassette tape of the phonetic sounds, along with teaching tips, worksheets, and a predrill book that teaches short vowels and consonants and how to write a ball-and-stick alphabet. The heart of the program is the *Victory Drill Book* itself. This very attractive hardbound book consists of word lists and sentences. There are no stories or pictures, except for the initial alphabet pictures at the beginning of the *VDB*. Students learn the phonetic sounds and then practice their skills with *timed drills* on the word pages. After achieving the speed considered necessary for his age level, the student goes on to the next phonetic combinations and the next page. After finishing the *VDB* the first time, he can freely read anything he wants. The publishers recommend that students go through the *VDB* a total of three times to ensure that total mastery has taken place.

The *VDB* was developed for Christian schools and includes prayers to God and references to preachers and church.

What do I think of the total *VDB* program? It's definitely meant for serious students, lacking the frills of other systems. Well-disciplined children with a yen to read can certainly succeed with this method. Also, if you are looking for phonics worksheets, the *VDB* worksheets beat any others, in my opinion. The type is

large enough for very young learners, there are just enough exercises to practice the concepts, and you do *not* get endless pages of pictures to "color if the object pictured begins with the letter *p*." The focus is on words, not illustrations, as it should be.

The *VDB* emphasis on *timed* drill keeps you alert to where your learner actually is. At home, you can time drills just for the fun of it and avoid the invidious comparisons of the classroom.

VDB also makes sure the *teacher* is able to teach phonics. Get the cassette tape if you are at all unsure of yourself in this area.

To sum up: The *VDB* program is functional but not exciting. The Worksheet packet, cassette tape, and *VDB* are valuable adjuncts to *any* phonics program. The approach is equally useful for older and younger students, not being the least bit cutesy. *VDB* does not include as much tactile input as some other programs, and this is a factor to consider if your child is a late bloomer or shows signs of learning difficulties.

VDB students have achieved outstanding scores on standardized tests. *VDB* is used all over the USA and in other countries.

BEST FEATURES: Everything in one book. The learner knows exactly what he is supposed to do and how he's doing at all times.

WORST FEATURES: Short on teacher instructions. Not a good choice for kinesthetic (or just not well-disciplined) kids. Best for visual learners.

SPALDING PHONICS

I have a problem here. I originally intended to tell you about the phonics method invented by Romalda Spalding and presented in her book *The Writing Road to Reading* ($17.95, published by William Morrow and Co.). This phonogram-based method teaches phonics, spelling, and handwriting all at once. Children learn to keep their own personalized spelling notebooks, and 29 basic rules of English spelling. The very thorough, disciplined approach develops listening skills, logic, and self-discipline. The method is multisensory; kids of all learning styles can learn from it. When children finish learning the 70 basic phonograms of the English language (as defined by Spalding), they will be able to read any word they see.

It sounds good so far, doesn't it? A lot of other people have thought so, too. Unfortunately, Mrs. Spalding's book is not organized in any way that resembles a series of lesson plans. Her teaching philosophy is all there, but it's virtually impossible for a home-schooling parent to apply it using just that book. Yes, certified Spalding instructors exist (about 70 of them, I'm told), but their training is geared towards a classroom situation. The "pure" Spalding method also requires about three hours of teaching time per day, which is more than most of us can afford at home.

Realizing this dilemma, a number of creative individuals developed lesson plans, phonogram flash cards, drill material, and other wonderful teaching aids to help simplify and apply the Spalding Method. I obtained review samples of a number of these programs and went to all the trouble of writing them up. Then I discovered at the last minute, through a phone call to the president of the Spalding Educational Foundation, that lawsuits were being launched against a number of these suppliers. Apparently any attempt to simplify Spalding's basic approach was not being looked upon with favor, and neither was the use of the word "Spalding" when referring to a supplier's teaching method.

I can't speak to the legal ins and outs of this situation. However, what seems clear is that, because of legal problems, for the moment the Spalding method is a closed book to home schoolers. You can always get a copy of *Writing Road to Reading* and try to puzzle out a lesson plan yourself. Aside from that, or from taking a course to be certified as a Spalding teacher, or taking a course *from* a certified Spalding teacher, you're out of luck.

This is not necessarily an disaster. Spalding has her critics as well as her fans. Some people think that forcing a child to do all that writing and spelling before he is allowed to read is a turn-off to reading. Other deny that a child even needs to write before he can read. I personally have taught five children to read (actually, one of them was taught by an older brother) without using any form of the Spalding method. Life goes on. But this just reinforces my feeling that copyright should only last for five years instead of effectively forever, so people can be allowed to improve on other people's ideas without getting dragged into court.

CHAPTER NINE

PHONICS HELPS

Here is the place to shop for phonics flash cards, primers, and accessories to your reading program. Some, like sandpaper letters and stencils, aren't strictly necessary with most children, although they are fun. So are phonics games. Here also you'll find the more traditional workbooks and supplementary readers.

Don't forget to also check out the Preschool section for other prereading accessories, if that's what you're interested in.

Happy browsing!

WHERE ARE WE?

NEW★★
Academic Therapy Publications
Quick Phonics Survey, $8.50. *Quick Cognitive Inventory* specimen set (manual and 1 test booklet), $12. *QCI* Test Kit (manual and 10 test booklets), $30. Add $2.50 shipping.

Feel you know little about phonics, but want to find out how well your child is doing in phonics? The *Quick Phonics Survey* is a short, 13-step skills inventory that can do the job. Designed for classroom use, it comes with a pad of 50 Recording Forms, plus a Direction Card and a Sound/Symbol card, both 8½ x 11" and laminated. Using the Response Form and the

Sound/Symbol card, you follow the directions to test your child on his knowledge of how to read, write, and hear letters and blends. Save the extra 49 forms to use with your younger children and the neighborhood kids.

Academic Therapy Publications also sells a much more complete (and more interesting) *Quick Cognitive Inventory.* This language-free, culture-free assessment checks whether kids have "developed the cognitive abilities prerequisite to academic instruction presented in English." Through the use of spontaneous drawing, copying, figural analogies, and visual arithmetic, this 45-minute test is specially designed for language-delayed or ESL kids aged K–3. The *QCI* is *only* available to legitimate schools, and *must* be ordered on official purchase order forms or professional letterhead. They don't mean "home schools," either. I'm only mentioning it here for the sake of you schoolteachers who might be interested in this unique screening tool.

PHONOGRAM CARDS

NEW★★
Bob Jones University Press
Phonics Charts, $15.95. Response Cards, $1.80. Songs Cassette, $6.30. Sound Effects and Stories Cassette, $6.30. Word Cards Set 1 (400 cards), $19.50. Other optional materials available.

BJUP's Response Card set is 44 laminated cards, one for each phonogram BJUP introduces. Other alphabet- and phonogram-learning items: the set of 44 laminated Phonics Charts, the Beginnings Word Cards, and the cassettes. You might also want to get the handwriting paper and some of the other optional materials. See complete writeup in Chapter 7.

NEW★★
Homeschool Instructional Services
Gift of Reading Phonogram Cards, $15.95. Phonogram Tape, $6.95. Handbook, price TBA. Add 10% shipping (minimum $2).

Trudy Palmer, a lady with years of experience as a classroom teacher and tutor, was having such success with her phonogram-based phonics method that other people started asking her to teach them how to use the method with their children. Out of these requests was born her home business, which publishes her excellent phonogram cards and tape, soon to be followed by a handbook detailing her phonics method.

Trudy's phonogram cards look like they could have been produced by a million-dollar company. The set of 73 8½ x 4¾" cards can almost be used to teach reading by itself! Each card has a phonogram in lowercase letters on the front. Remember, a phonogram is a set of letters that makes a single sound. Sometimes one phonogram can have two or more separate sounds, like the phonogram *oo* which can either say *ew* as in *moo* or *euh* as in *book*. Teaching these is no joke. So on the back of each card you'll find a list of example words that use the phonogram . . . instructions for the teacher to say to the student . . . teaching tips, spelling rules, and explanations of the phonogram's peculiar features for the teacher . . . and a list of "exception" words that include the phonogram but are *not* pronounced according to the usual rules. The accompanying tape includes both teaching tips and the sounds of each phonogram, so you'll know exactly how to teach your student the sounds. Unique feature: the tape is recorded in such as way as to mimic

one of Trudy's tutoring sessions—in other words, it sounds as though she is speaking directly to your child. This provides you with a model for your own home teaching.

NEW★★
Small Ventures
Phonics Fun game, $12.95. Basic Phonograms cassette tape, $3.95. Add $2 shipping per product.

Phonics Fun is two decks of phonogram cards without any special directions on the back. These cards can be used with any phonics programs. One deck has a pink square pattern on the back, while the other is blue. Each deck is divided into sections by a symbol which appears in the top right corner of each card. The circle represents single letter phonograms. The square and triangle are for multi-letter phonograms. The star is for the most advanced phonograms, e.g., *gn*. Cards are laminated, jelly-proof, business-card size. Complete directions for four games are included. Three are similar to the well-known card games of Concentration, Old Maid, and Fish. In the last game, players combine cards to form words within a time limit.

For parents and teachers who have difficulty figuring out the sounds of the phonograms from written instructions only, Small Ventures also provides a *Basic Phonograms Tape*. This is an audiocassette with the sounds of the phonograms and their rules narrated for you.

PRIMERS

NEW★★
Bob Books® for Beginning Readers
Bob Books®, More Bob Books®, Even More Bob Books®, $12.95 each per set in a special book bag. Add $1.50 shipping for one set, $2.50 for two sets. Free shipping if you order 3 or more sets at once.

Ruth Beechick recommends them. Two different suppliers sent me samples of them. A friend gave me a set. What are these little phonics readers, and why do so many people love them so much?

The Bob books are the product of schoolteacher Bobby Lynn Maslen. She wrote them for her own students, to make learning to read simple and fun. Each book is sized for little hands, printed on heavyweight paper, and illustrated with charmingly naive drawings using shapes even little children can draw. Book covers are different colors, just to be pretty.

The first series of 12 books, *Bob Books®*, starts off easily. Book 1 teaches only four sounds—*m, a, t, s*—and the word "on." Each of the books in this first series has only eight pages of actual reading material, for instant reading success, and is written using only three-letter words with short-vowel sounds. By the end of the series, kids have learned all the letters of the alphabet except Q and all the numerals. The enclosed instruction sheet explains the series philosophy, summarizes the plots of the books, and gives some wonderful pre-reading and reading teaching techniques.

Series 2, *More Bob Books®*, continues the short vowels taught in series 1, and adds more letter combinations and longer words. Silent *e* words are introduced, as well as easy consonant blends such as *nd* in *land* and *mp* in *bump*. Color words are introduced as sight words in book 7 of this series. This series has eight books, but more total reading pages than series 1.

Series 3, *Even More Bob Books®*, is another set of eight books. Here silent *e* words are introduced, and so are vowel digraphs and compound words.

The Bob stories are all warm and friendly. The characters sometimes get into trouble, or even quarrel, but everything always turn out all right in the end. There's quite a strong emphasis on kindness, sharing, and forgiveness. Recommended.

Bookstuff
My First Bookstuff, My Second Bookstuff, $5.95 each or $10.95 for both. *Thinking Things*, $5.95. *Attributes Activity Package*, $6.95. Shipping extra. Free poster with each order.

This is the most unusual set of primers you will see in a long, long time. You go through and fill in the blanks in each 8½ x 11" booklet with your child's name and the names of family, friends, and pets where appropriate. While doing so, you notice the large number of *rebuses* (pictures of things instead of words). This allows the authors to include words like "camel" and "monster" in the very first book. The primer/workbook also includes space for the neophyte reader to copy some of the simple words in *Bookstuff*. A yellow instruction sheet is tucked in to help anxious parents understand what we are doing. Book 2 has room in the back for the child to write his own story, or for a mom or dad to write a dictated story.

Each page has a separate little sequence of sentences. Rather than stories, in *My First Bookstuff* these sentence sequences ask the reader questions, like, "Can a [picture of lion] make a [picture of kite] go? Can a [picture of mouse] stop a [picture of boat]? Can you make a [picture of kite] go? Can you stop a [picture of boat]?" *My Second Bookstuff* has some little real-life stories.

The art, and artistic hand-printing of words, are very nice. Content is modern and secular.

Also available from the curriculum specialist and art-and-science teacher who invented Bookstuff are *Attributes Activity Book* (cut and paste format of increasing difficulty to help children learn colors, shapes, etc.) and *Thinking Things* (a set of pages featuring one question of the "How is a caterpillar like a butterfly?" variety per page. Other Bookstuff products, including their great kindergarten program *Alphabetiks*, are reviewed in the Preschool section.

NEW**
Christian Liberty Press
Eclectic Reader Book A, $1.95. Book B, $2.50. Nine other readers available for higher grades. Add 10% shipping (minimum $1.50).

Christian Liberty Academy is busily producing its own readers, spellers, nature books, and so on. The *Christian Liberty Eclectic Reading Series*, in keeping with Christian Liberty Academy's traditional, patriotic, evangelical style, is made up of selections from old-time readers used by American schoolkids long ago, such as the McGuffey, Franklin, and Union readers.

Christian Liberty Eclectic Reader Book A starts with the alphabet and then moves on to three-letter words. Short and long vowels are both introduced.

Book B starts off with three- and four-word sentences. Eventually it moves on to longer sentences and entire paragraphs. Some silent-letter words are introduced.

These two books, designed for advanced kindergarten and first grade students respectively, are the only two books in the series that could accurately be called "primers." The series progresses, at one book per grade, right up to the sophomore year of high school.

Cumberland Missionary Society
Pictorial Tract Primer, $6.50. *Pictorial Alphabet Flash Cards*, $2. Accompaniment cassette of readings from *Primer*, $5. Workbook to accompany *Primer*, $3. Shipping extra.

Very lovely reprint of classic primer from the olden days. Embossed, gold-stamped, slim green hardback uses the "ladder-letter" approach: e.g., *ba, be, bi, bo, bu*. The big attraction here, besides looks and tradition, is the Bible-saturated content. This primer contains not only phonics instruction and old-timey teaching tips, but Dr. Isaac Watt's *First Catechism, The Children's Scripture Catechism, Easy Questions for Little Children*, and an alphabet of Scripture texts in short words. Examples: the text for A is "A new heart will I give you." B's text is "Be thou in the fear of the Lord all the day long." C is "Choose you this day whom you will serve." Period engravings throughout.

UPDATED**
Educational Products
Set of 17 Storybook Readers, $75. Shipping extra.

Correlated to the *Sing, Spell, Read & Write* program, these readers cover every phonics rule in the book. Each book concentrates on a particular phonogram: the short vowel *a* or the digraph *ch*, for example. Many, many words containing the phonogram are used in the story, plus phonograms taught in previous lessons. The stories are all good-humored but not distinctively Christian.

These readers are more durable than others I have seen. The art in the original edition was amateurish. I haven't seen the newest edition, but the people at Educational Products tell me it has been upgraded from two color to four color. (Adult quibble: our children never minded.)

NEW**
Merrill Publishers

Sister Monica Foltzer, author of the popular *Professor Phonics* program, recommends the Merrill Linguistic Readers (first eight books only) for use with her program. That's all I know about 'em, as I didn't have time to write for info.

Reading Reform Foundation
MAC and TAB readers, 5 sets of 10 booklets each, $15.95/set. Add 10% shipping ($1.50 minimum).

Popular set of phonics readers with some strange plot twists and morals. In the very first volume, *Mac and Tab*, Mac the rat steals some of his friend Tab the cat's food, so Tab eats him. Happily, Mac gets removed from Tab's stomach safe and sound in a later booklet, but this first little story was quite a shock! In *The Tin Man*, a pig bites and gets hit in return. *Al* is the story of an alligator who steals and gets hit, but then the kids give him *more* food (as a reward for stealing?). In *The Jet*, a kid's jet dive-bombs various people and upsets them. Moral: "His big, tin jet is a lot of fun." When Tag and Kit steal a wig (in *The Wig*), we find that "It is fun to rob a wig." *Every* one of the first ten readers has some such hitting/stealing theme.

Series II brings us the glad news that *Mac Is Safe*, removed as previously mentioned from the innards of his short-tempered friend. The characters from the first series reappear throughout this series, which also features better art than the first series.

Continuing this upward trend, Series III through V have even better art and much more logical (and morally intelligent) stories.

All the books in this series follow the usual phonics order of short vowel words first (Mac and Tab), then long vowels, then other diphthongs and digraphs.

Thoburn Press
Short Vowel Reading Series (set of 10 books), $12.50. Long Vowel Reading Series (10 books), also $12.50.

Naive art and excellent morals adorn this set of short vowel readers. Every little booklet has a Scripture verse on the inside back cover explaining the moral of the story. As mentioned, the vocabulary in the first series consists solely of short vowel words; in the second, long vowels are introduced.

MCGUFFEY PRIMERS

The various versions of Rev. McGuffey's readers are in a class by themselves. Loaded with moralistic tales, but little explicitly Christian (as opposed to theistic) content, McGuffeys are making a serious comeback. Many home-school programs offer one version or another of these readers *as* readers, rather than as literature or ethics.

I have written up all three major McGuffey versions in Chapter 16. These all have their varying strengths as readers. As phonics primers, however, the version from Thoburn Press is clearly superior. See Chapter 16 for more details.

PHONICS DRILL

UPDATED★★
Educational Products
Sing, Spell, Read & Write Home Kit, $110 with cassettes, $119 with records. Shipping extra.

This is as good a place as any to remind you that *Sing, Spell, Read & Write's* home kit is the one single best source of jazzy phonics supplementation around. Although designed as a stand-alone phonics program, the tremendous amount of supplementary material—17 storybook readers (available separately), six phonics song cassettes, Raceway Chart with magnetic car, five games, and Treasure-Chest full of prizes—just begs to be added to whatever phonics program you choose. You don't *need* all this stuff, let me hasten to add. It's just so much *fun!*

Elijah Company
Alpha-Phonics, $21.95 plus $2.50 shipping.

As I mentioned in a previous section, *Alpha-Phonics* is a page-by-page phonics program based on word lists and practice sentences. You can also use it for a phonics drill book.

NEW★★
Hayes School Publishing Co., Inc.
Hayes Phonics Series, books 1A–1C, 2A, 2B, $4.95 each (specify blackline masters). Books 3A and 3B only available in form to be run on duplicating machine. Add $1.50 shipping for first item, 35¢ each additional.

The Hayes Phonics Series, *not* to be confused with their look-say *Sounds We Use* series (misleadingly labeled "Phonics" in the catalog), is a nice, simple, inexpensive series of phonics drill workbooks. Starting in Book 1A with the standard public-school skills of writing letters and matching letters with pictures of objects beginning with that sound, the series progresses to digraphs, compound words, contractions, roots and endings, syllables, and more by Book 2B. A complete teacher's guide with excellent instructions covering both how to teach phonics and how to use each worksheet is included in each book. Classroom teachers photocopy the worksheet pages and thus have all the materials needed for a whole class all in one place.

You could conceivably use these "drill" materials as an actual phonics course.

Learning Systems Corporation

I am adamantly opposed to almost all phonics workbooks, as they are unhelpful, drawn-out exercises in tedium. Not so with Learning Systems Corporation's material. For one thing, the workbooks cost a measly 79 cents. Yes, you read that right! Eight thin dimes will get you one of a wide selection of 16-page miniworkbooks. The workbooks are approximately 5 x 8 inches, in two colors, professional in appearance, and clever in execution.

Not only does LSC have workbooks for learning the alphabet and for practicing basic phonics skills, but also vocabulary-builders, books on syllabication, using the dictionary, punctuation, and a host of other necessary skills. Since the workbooks are so small, these skills are not overtaught.

LSC also has math materials, reviewed in the "Math" section.

Pecci Publications
Phonics Grab Bag (grades 1-3), 138 pages, $9.95. *Linguistic Exercises* (grades 1-6), 106 pages, $9.95. *Word Skills* (grades 1-6), 238 pages, $16.95. Add 10% shipping.

Mary Pecci's friendly Super Seatwork series contains several volumes of supplemental phonics exercises that I really like. Correlated with her reading method (reviewed in the "Reading" section), the *Phonics Grab Bag* has 12 different fun types of exercises. Some are cut-and-paste, some involve drawing, some require writing. There are Phonic Picture Puzzles, Phonics Crossword Puzzles, Word Wheels, Let's Play Categories, and lots more! As with all Mary Pecci's seatwork, the book is big and the pictures are simple and entertaining.

Linguistic Exercises consists mainly of valuable word-family exercises. A page, for example, may feature repetitions of *ore, ote, ove,* and *oze.* Some the student just reads. Towards the end of the book he does some writing and drawing. This pattern-building is the way our brains construct frameworks for storing the data we feed them, unlike short-term "rote" memory which quickly fades away unless refreshed.

Word Skills is a handy compendium of all the ways we build onto words. Standard textbooks usually drag this out over years. Included are roots and endings, plus all the rules for irregular endings (change *y* to *i* before adding *es*, etc.), compound words, possessives, contractions, prefixes, suffixes, syllabication, and dictionary skills, including practice in unraveling those weird little dictionary pronunciation symbols. The exercises are simple and nonthreatening, gradually pro-gressing without beating the student to death with overdone repetition. After going through this book, children who have had a basic phonics course should have no spelling or reading problems.

NEW
You Can Read
Read and Spell with Phono-Bear, $45. Teacher's Guide included. *Index of the 1700 Most Frequently Used English Words,* $4.50 non-bound, $7.50 with binding and cover.

Phonics drill and practice material correlated with *The Writing Road to Reading,* but that can be used with other programs as well. The worksheets are appropriate for grades 1-6. The following types of worksheets are represented:

- "Phono-Review": practice with individual phonograms, including using them in reading passages.

- "Phono-Lesson": English usage skill drill.

- "Phono-Bear Says": exercises related to one of the 29 basic spelling rules.

- "Phono-Challenge": advanced exercises.

- "Phono-Fun": phonics game.

- "Phono-Practice": general skill drill.

There are 185 different sheets and 63 pages in the Teacher's Guide. The sheets are numbered and catagorized by subject area. The subject areas are: Phonogram Review, Spelling Rules Review, Parts of Speech, Capitalization, Syllabication, Word Affixes, Handwriting Practice: Manuscript, Handwriting Practice: Cursive or Connected Writing, How to Write a Sentence, How to Write a Paragraph, How to Write a Composition, Alphabetization, Word Usage, Dictionary Skills, Reading Comprehension, Using Reference Manuals, Writing in Our World, and Just for Fun and Challenge. Grade levels are left to the teacher's discretion. Sheets are arranged within each subject area in order of increasing difficulty.

These are well-designed drill sheets. Many sheets provide instruction in the skills they are exercising. Instructions are clear and easy to follow. The sheets drill worthwhile skills. An answer key, plus teaching instructions, and a simplified sequence for learning the phonograms, is included in the teacher's guide.

Victory Drill Book

VDB, $11.50. Other phonics items available. Shipping, $5 on orders under $30. Quantity discounts.

Every household should have a copy of the *Victory Drill Book*, or some similar phonics drill book. The *VDB*, a very attractive hardbound book, consists of word lists and sentences. There are no stories or pictures except for the initial alphabet pictures at the beginning of the *VDB*. Students learn the phonetic sounds and then practice their skills with *timed drills* on the word pages. After achieving the speed considered necessary for his age level, the student goes on to the next phonetic combinations and the next page. After finishing the *VDB* the first time, he can freely read anything he wants. The publishers recommend that students go through the *VDB* a total of three times to ensure that total mastery has taken place.

If your youngsters run through the *VDB* once or twice, you'll catch any weaknesses in their reading before they develop into serious problems. The hardbound book is durable enough to hand on to your great-grandchildren, should God so bless you.

The *VDB* was developed for Christian schools and includes prayers to God and references to preachers and church.

PHONICS GAMES

NEW★★
E-Z Grader Co.

1st and 2nd Phonics Slide Rule (one combined two-sided rule), $3.50. 3rd & 4th Phonics Slide Rule (2-sided), $3.50. 5th Phonics Slide Rule, $3.50. Add 10% shipping ($1 minimum).

These exciting, inexpensive phonics tools provide a marvelously simple way for children to practice building—and reading—words that exercise their newly-acquired phonics skills.

The First and Second Phonic Slide Rules are actually two sides of a single device. It's made of durable white cardboard die-cut, printed in two colors, and securely fastened together with small metal studs. In between is another piece of heavy coated cardboard that slides back and forth. On the sliding part are series of beginning consonants. On the outer part are word ends, such as *ack* and *ake*. Each time the child slides the rule to a new position, he gets a new batch of words to decode—240 words in all!

The First Phonic Slide Rule drills short vowel words. Since the word endings in any row are not all the same, the child can't just mindlessly tack on the beginning sounds to make new words. For example, row 1 word ends are *ad, ag, an,* and *at.* The Second Phonic Slide Rule lets the child practice short and long *a,* short and long *i,* short and long *o,* and short and long *u.* The long-vowel words are all silent *e* words.

The Third and Fourth Phonic Slide Rules are, again, two sides of a single device. Both sides drill consonant blends, digraphs, and short vowel sounds, but in different ways. The Third Phonic Slide Rule has lists of short vowel endings on the slider, and blends and digraphs on the outer rule. When the slider is in its first position, you see short *a* endings. In its second position, all the beginning sounds line up with short *e* endings. And so on. Words made with this rule range from *brand* to *whopper.* The Fourth Phonic Slide Rule has vowel combinations on the slider. In first position you get *ai, a-e* (this means "a long *a* word with silent *e* at the end"), and *ay.* In second position, it's *ea, ee,* and *e-e.* In third position, it's *i-e* and *y.* In fourth position, it's *oa, o-e,* and the long sound of *ow.* In fifth position, it's *ue, ui, u-e,* the long sound of *oo,* and *ew.* The outer rule has 20 blends, from *br* and *bl* to *spr,* plus *qu, ch, sh,* and *wh.* This rule makes another 216 words.

Enclosed with my Third and Fourth Phonic Slide Rule was a slider with columns similar to the regular slider, but with the word spaces left blank so you can fill in more word endings of your own choosing.

The Fifth Phonic Slide Rule is one ruler with two sides. Both sides drill word endings—both suffixes and compound words, in totally random order, so you never know what's coming next. Side 1 has words with the *al, aw, au, or, ou,* short *ow, oi,* and *oy* vowel combinations. Side 2 drills words with *a* as in *care, ar* as in *car,* and the three r-controlled vowels that all say "er": *er, ir, or,* and *ur.* Another 216 words in all!

These inexpensive aids are super-simple to use, stand up to rough classroom handling, and are a fun way to practice word building, especially for kids whose fine motor skills are not yet advanced for a lot of pencil-and-paper work. Recommended.

NEW★★
Family Learning Center

The Letterlearning Games, $14.95 plus 5% shipping.

The *Letterlearning Games* has that warm and friendly feeling I have come to expect from home schooler-produced products. You get a set of 42

8½ x 11" colored cards, plus all the Bingo chips, colored paper clips, and so on that you need to play more than 20 phonics games. Many of those oversized cards hold several game pieces—e.g., four Bingo cards or five Sentence Strips—so you'll have to spend some time with the scissors getting the games ready. Once the snipping is done, though, these are very easy games to play.

Games cover the gamut of phonics skills, from letter recognition to reading simple sentences. They include Pencil Poke (picture side faces child, parent asks him to find a picture that begins or ends with a particular sound and poke a pencil through that hole), Rhyming Cards (match rhyming picture cards in a Concentration game, or in an Old Maid game), Sentence Strips (child reads sentence and places paper clip on correct ending word; checks against mark on back of strip), Dominoes (you know how to play this one!), six different card games with upper- and lower-case letters, five Bingo games (letters, blends, digraphs, word families, and sight words), and Which Word? (played like Sentence Strips, only the child is matching a picture to a word).

Can you keep all this organized? Yes, if you follow the authors' suggestions and keep each game and its playing pieces in a jumbo ziploc bag. All games are really easy to set up and play. Just take the pieces, including directions, out of the bag and go!

NEW★★
Kanos Enterprises
Phonics Adventure game, $24.95 plus $3 shipping.

Phonics Adventure, "The Game That Helps You Learn to Read," is a really nifty game with many levels for helping you practice and recognize decoding principles. You will have to teach your child the ABC's and

their basic sounds before you can really use this game. However, once they have mastered this first step, you can practice beginning through advanced phonics painlessly with this easy-to-use game.

You get a colorful game board with the usual tokens, dice, and trek from Start to Finish interspersed with squares that let you jump ahead and others that make you gain or lose a turn. You also get three color-coded sets of cards. Level A (yellow) lets your child practice matching sounds to letters, telling sounds, reading simple sight words, and describing vowels and consonants. Level B (green) goes on to consonant blends, more vowel sounds and sight words, contractions, and a very good section of phonics rule questions that make the child *think*. Level C (orange) continues with advanced vowel/consonant combinations (such as *tion* and *sion*), more sight words and advanced phonics rules, prefixes and suffixes. These two latter levels can be used to teach the phonics as well as to review it.

The cards explain themselves—you need no professional phonics knowledge to use *Phonics Adventure,* although at least one experienced reader needs to play to help the others. The game is very complete, and can be used as a card game (if you answer correctly you keep the card) or as flash cards, if you prefer a change from the board-game format. Some fancy dictionary marks are used—circumflex, dot, dieresis, and so on—but you can easily ignore these if your phonics program doesn't use them. It takes about two minutes to figure the whole game out, and there is no clutter of hundreds of strange little pieces to sort out. A nice, professionally-presented, quality game that will make phonics drill and advanced phonics much more simple and fun.

NEW★★
Success House
Wordo™, $6.95. Shipping $1.

Five simple card games that provide reading practice and vocabulary development. You get one set each of 27 orange and 27 blue cards, plus a yellow instruction booklet. Blue cards have word beginnings like *w* and *pl* on their top left and bottom right corners, while orange cards have word endings like *ay* and *ill*. If this sounds like you are going to play word-building dominoes, you're right. You also can play variations on Tic-Tac-Toe, Concentration, Rummy, and Solitaire. The Wordo™ Word Checking Chart in the middle of the instruction booklet tells you which word combinations are licit, of the possible 1,054.

PHONICS ORGANIZATIONS

Who out there can help you with reading problems? Forget the "experts" whose august advice has *caused* our current illiteracy problem. Unlike those whose main activities seem to be discouraging the use of phonics and patting themselves on the back, the following two groups can really help parents of kids with reading problems—and teachers who want to make sure the kids in *their* classes don't develop reading problems!

The Orton Dyslexia Society
$3 donation requested if you write for information.

Years ago, Samuel T. Orton, M.D., and his associates worked out an approach to teaching dyslexics that appears to have real sense. Using phonics, multisensory input, and an individualized teaching method, the Orton Dyslexic Society believes that

> every undamaged person (and even many less fortunate) can learn • to understand and speak the language he/she hears • to read with skill and comprehension to the level of his/her inborn intelligence • to write legibly • to spell passably well • to put his/her thoughts into clear, understandable, spoken or written words.

The Orton Society does not teach or tutor. It functions as an information clearinghouse to help you find the help you need.

Educators Publishing Service of Cambridge, Massachusetts carries materials based on this method.

Reading Reform Foundation
Membership, $25/year. Information packet, including book list, $2.

Ta da! Here come the folks in the white hats, galloping up to save the day! Formed in 1961 to combat illiteracy in America the Reading Reform Foundation exists to "encourage the correct teaching of systematic, multisensory phonics."

RRF is interested in crusading for a cause, not in pumping up their leaders' and members' reputations. Consequently, they are a very busy group, offering workshops, speakers, courses, referral services, and consulting services. The folks at RRF are truly helpful, and if they can't help you in person, they're in touch with the people who can.

Now, let me tell you about their mail-order bookstore. Containing both documentation of reading research and the history of American reading instruction, and books and programs for actually teaching intensive phonics, the RRF order form is a great resource for any teacher of reading. Many books recommended in this book of mine are offered for sale: Romalda Spalding's *Writing Road to Reading*, with phonogram flash cards and tutoring outline; *Professor Phonics* and *A Sound Track to Reading*; Char-L's *Discover Intensive Phonics for Yourself*; Richard Mitchell's books; Sam Blumenfeld's books; plus a number of programs and books that I have had no time to review, but that look excellent. All materials RRF offers are very reasonably priced.

SOUL FOOD

CHAPTER TEN

GETTING STARTED WITH BIBLE

"The B-I-B-L-E . . . yes, that's the book we see . . . it sits alone covered up with dust while we all watch the TV!" Well, that might change. TV shows are getting worse all the time. And Bible-learning resources are getting better!

Since the last edition of this book, in which I just about despaired of ever seeing a really good selection of Bible programs for home use, a lot of people have sent me brand new, innovative, and actually *useful* Bible resources. We have enough good new stuff now, in fact, to justify breaking up the old Bible chapter into four new chapters, each one of which has more good products showcased in it than I could find in the whole last edition.

First, we're going to look at specially useful Bibles and storybooks, aids for learning the books of the Bible, and other elementary pre-Bible helps. Second, we're going to look at Bible memory programs. Third, we're going to look at complete Bible courses. Last, we'll consider visual aids, games, puzzles, music and other Bible-based material. That ought to about cover it, don't you think?

DISCOUNT CHRISTIAN BOOK CLUBS

Before we go any further, let me tell you where to get a lot of your Bible study material at BIG discounts. Although you'll want to visit the Christian bookstore to see what's new and just for the fun of shopping in person, often a bookstore won't have a big stock of in-depth Bible programs and other specialized helps. Or, if you live on Rural Route 2 in Outer Limits, Iowa, chances are you don't get in to the bookstore all that often. So here are not one but *two* sources for thousands of topflight Christian materials at up to 90 percent off!

Christian Book Distributors

CBD offers a wide range of Christian books written from various theological perspectives, including evangelical, Arminian, conservative, and liberal works. You can get discounts of 20 to 90 percent on over 4,000 titles from 60 publishers, including major sets necessary for the library of every serious Bible student, plus Christian records and cassettes. Wide selection of Bibles, Christian bestsellers, youth ministry, and counseling books, all also at discount. First quality books. Annual membership of $3 entitles you to six bimonthly catalogs and six Members' Newsletters offering additional savings off the catalog prices. "Speedy shipping and helpful service." You don't need to be a member to order.

Great Christian Books
$5 for one-year membership (U.S.), $8 (Canada/Mexico), $12 (overseas). Every time you buy, it's automatically extended one year from that date.

GCB changed my life. Bill and I were new Christians, unsteady on our feet, and unable to find a bookstore that had anything but frothy testimonies and Christian cookbooks. (There are many fine Christian bookstores, but we were living in a spiritually deprived neighborhood.) Enter GCB. All of a sudden we had a selection of thousands of the finest Christian books, both classic and modern, at greatly discounted prices. We joined, we read, we learned.

GCB also has a wide selection of Christian music on CD's and cassettes. More, they also have hundreds of children's books. Even more, you can get commentaries and books on Hebrew and Greek, plus Bible study aids. Plus the new line of home schooling books and workbooks—name brands like A Beka and Christian Life Workshops, most at discount. This is a great book service to join if you buy any of the above on a regular basis.

Superfast delivery, 5,000 titles, and great prices.

BIBLE STORY BOOKS

Lots of people like to start their little ones off with Bible storybooks. These are not actual translations, but trimmed-down versions of the Bible stories, usually adorned with lots of colorful pictures. Sometimes the vocabulary is simple enough to serve as a young child's first primer. Other times the stories are narrated with the same depth of vocabulary as other children's storybooks.

You have to be careful when selecting a Bible storybook. Some authors embellish or even misrepresent the original stories, in an effort to explain them or make them more entertaining. Morals often don't fit the story. Misleading illustrations are common. So far every Bible storybook illustration I have seen of Moses before the burning bush had Moses with his sandals *on*. Jesus is often portrayed as a sissy Aryan instead of a tough, manual-laboring Jew. The Ark is drawn like a bathtub boat instead of the long box it actually was. Worse yet are the anachronisms. One children's Bible story series I was sent, for example, had David shooting *tin cans* with his sling, and Jonah taking a suitcase covered with airline labels on his trip to Nineveh! These may have been intended to be cute, but little kids who haven't yet been told that tin cans and airlines didn't exist back then can get some pretty strange mental pictures of Bible times from storybooks like those.

I've written up some popular Bible storybooks below, all of which follow the Bible stories more closely than most, and one set of Bible board books for very young children.

NEW**
Kregel Publications
My Bible Storybook, $8.95.

My Bible Storybook from Kregel Publications by Dena Korfker is a reprint of a book that has almost a quarter million copies in print. It includes "270 easy-to-read stories written on the level of the child's understanding," as the publisher says. I checked out these stories, and found that indeed they were well told and the right length for a bedtime or devotional reading. Each selection has three questions at the end to test your child's understanding. Personally, I would rather have the listener narrate the whole story back, as Charlotte Mason recommends, than test him or her with questions, but as questions go, these aren't bad.

The stories truly are told in a way that will hold a child's interest. As with all Bible storybooks, the author has injected some of her own explanations and end-of-story morals. Still, this is the most accurate Bible storybook I have seen, and the first that I would consider using with my own children.

NEW**
Ladybird Books, Inc.
Square Bible Books, $3.95 each. Other books, $2.95 each. Wall chart, $1.95.

Here's something different! Ladybird's Square Books Bible Stories series for very young children includes, besides the usual books on the likes of Moses and David, a book on the Lord's Prayer and one on Psalm 23. This focus on worship continues in Ladybird's Prayers & Hymns series for early-elementary children, which includes *The Lord's Prayer and Other Prayers, Book of Prayers,* and *Hymns and Songs.* For this age group Ladybird also has a series of easy-reading Bible stories (including four books of parables and two of miracles), and a Bible Stories series for preteens. You can even get a "Lord's Prayer" illustrated 24½ x 15¾" wall chart!

NEW★★
Multnomah Press
Advanced Theology for Very Tiny Persons, Volume 1, $12.95 for slipcased set of four books.

This absolutely delightful set of four enameled, hardcovered, board books for tiny children is a great introduction to basic Bible teachings. With colorful pictures and only a few words on each page, your child is introduced to the *Names of God, The World of God* (the story of Creation in 32 words!), *The Child of God* (the fruit of the Spirit from Galatians 5:22, 23), and *The Friends of God* (nine Bible characters, plus a mirror at the end so he can see himself as a friend of God). The set is cleverly designed to resemble a tiny theology collection, and is just the right size to be prized by babies and toddlers. I hope that Multnomah really means the "Volume 1," and that this will be the first of a series. Recommended.

NEW★★
Questar Publishers, Inc.
The Beginner's Bible, $14.95.

The Beginner's Bible is a charming, and very popular, thick little book with a Bible-style format, includ-

ing listing of books and mini-"concordance" in the back. Each page only has a few sentences of very simple text, with a colorful, simple illustration above. The text is more-or-less true to the Bible, and the whole 530-page package is quite appealing. So appealing, in fact, that 200,000 copies were sold in the first eight months it was out.

Does it cover the whole Bible? Yes and no. The story choices are nonthreatening to the extreme. Daniel's lions never eat anybody. Jacob's extra wives are never mentioned. The minor prophets are all left out (as usual). You do get a lot of coverage of the popular Bible stories and the life of Christ, though.

One thing I found troublesome in this series was the inaccurate women's dress. No head coverings. Tight T-shirt-styled dresses. Grandmas with short white hair. According to another reviewer, this is supposed to be a "careful bridging of history with experience" that allows kids to identify with the characters. To me, it's just tampering with the historical truth. I wish they hadn't done that, because otherwise this is the most delightful beginner's Bible storybook I've seen.

NEW★★
Reformed Free Publishing Association
Come, Ye Children Bible storybook, hardcover and illustrated, $22.95. Shipping extra.

Solid Dutch Calvinistic Bible storybook. Author is the well-known Bible curriculum author Gertrude Hoeksema. 200 Bible stories, each ending with a thought to remember, accompanied by realistic drawings. Durable binding, convenient 7 x 10" size.

NEW★★
Rod & Staff Publishers
Grade 1: Reader Unit 1, $4.30. Reader Units 2 & 3 (one book), $7.60. Reader Units 4 & 5 (one book), $9.45. Grade 2: Reader Units 1–3 (one book), $9.30. Reader Units 4 & 5 (one book), $8.70. Grade 3: Readers Units 1–3 (one book), $10.40. Reader Units 4 & 5 (one book), $9.30. Grade 4: Reader, $9.50. U.S. orders, all prices postpaid ($1 small order fee on orders less than $10). Canadian and foreign, add 10% shipping.

Rod and Staff has a complete phonics and language arts program based on its unique Bible storybooks. It's called *The Bible Nurture and Reader Series,* and is written up in Chapter 8.

If you don't want the workbooks, teacher's manuals, and phonics instruction, you might still be interested in the Bible storybooks. The stories are very carefully kept close to Scripture, without any flights of fancy.

Each grade's material includes portions of both the Old and New Testament. In grade 1, the first unit, "We Learn About God," covers the Creation and the Fall. The second unit, "We Learn More About God," reviews Creation and goes on to Cain, Abel, and Noah, with some practical applications. The third unit, "Poems About God," is poems about history from the Creation until after the Flood. The fourth unit is stories about Abraham, Isaac, and Jacob. The fifth unit contains stories about Joseph, the son of Jacob, and stories about Jesus from the Gospel of Matthew.

Unit 1 of grade 2 reviews Genesis. Unit 2 is "Moses Leads God's People," while unit 3 covers "More About Moses," "Balaam," and "Israel in Canaan." Unit 4 is "Stories from Ruth and 1 Samuel." Unit 5 goes through the Gospel of Mark.

Grade 3 leads off with "Stories About David and Solomon," followed by "Stories of the Kings—Rehoboam to Jeroboam" and "Stories of the Last Kings and Prophets." Unit 4, "God's People During and After the Captivity," includes parts of Ezekiel, Daniel, Ezra, Nehemiah, Esther, and Jonah. The fifth unit works through the Gospel of Luke.

Grade 4 has only one reader, with noticeably smaller print than that of the earlier grades. It includes three units: "The Gospel of John," "The Book of Acts," and "Job, Psalms, Proverbs."

These make excellent Bible storybooks for children to read themselves, without any of the grownup twaddle and dubious preaching that infests most read-aloud storybooks. Recommended.

NEW★★
Triangle Press
Bible Truths for Little Children, five volumes, set $32.50, $7.50 each.

This set of five Bible storybooks is a revision of a classic set written a hundred years ago. The revision retains the McGuffeyesque character of the original, now translated into "proper English and children's language." Highly moralistic, it includes comments on the stories along with an interactive style in which children are asked questions during the telling of the story. Example:

> You have heard how the Israelites came into the land of Canaan. I shall tell you what happened to them in Canaan after Joshua died. Do you know who was

their king? God was their king. Joshua was not their king, though he used to tell them what God wanted them to do. . . .

An example of the moralizing style:

> Among the worshipers at the tabernacle, was a man who had two wives. Men long ago could have more than one wife, though they must not now.

> One of these wives was a very Godly woman named Hannah. She had no child. The other wife was unkind, and she acted very wicked. The unkind wife laughed at Hannah. She told Hannah that God gave her no child because He did not love her. This was not true, for God loved Hannah very much. Poor Hannah used to cry when the other wife spoke so unkindly to her. . . .

As you can see this type of storytelling is very lively and involving, since the author isn't afraid to ask the readers to identify with the good guys and hiss the bad guys.

Volume 1 covers Creation through the story of Joseph, son of Jacob. Volume 2 is the story of Moses and the Israelites. Volume 3 is the stories of Samuel and David. Volume 4 carries on with Solomon and the other prophets and kings of Israel and Judah. Volume 5 is the life of Christ. All are written on a third grade reading level, so children can read them to themselves.

WHY YOU DON'T NEED A KIDDIE BIBLE

One of the things I had to learn as a new Christian was how to find my way around the alphabet soup of Bible translations. In the beginning was the KJV (King James Version, named after King James of England, who authorized its translation). Actually, that wasn't the first English Bible, but since Wycliffe's translations and the other versions that informed the KJV went out of print around 1600 A.D., the KJV is the oldest version available today. Next was the ASV (American Standard Version), the NASB (New American Standard Bible), and the RSV (Revised Standard Version). Shortly after I got saved, out came the NIV (New International Version), and then the NKJV (New King James Version). And of course there are the various paraphrases, such as *The Living Bible* and *Good News for Modern Man*. Time fails me to speak of the study Bibles, color-coded Bibles, chronological Bibles . . .

Since the Bible is still the world's bestselling book, there are swarms of Bibles competing for your dollars, and particularly swarms of *children's* Bibles. Why? Because they have pretty color pictures. Because they have nice large print and easy words. Because, as one article I read on the subject said, "justification" and "sanctification" are terms too hard even for modern adults, and expecting some innocent child to understand them is asking too much.

Husband Bill decided to test this theory out. Enter eight-year-old son.

"Son, would you understand what I meant if I said that justification is God declaring you not guilty?"

Son looks at his father as if wondering if Dad has flipped his lid. "Sure, Daddy! Justification means God says you are not guilty."

Here come six-year-old son and four-year-old daughter. "Kids, I'm going to say something and I want you to pay attention. Sanctification is God making you holy. What did I just say?"

"Sanctification is God making you holy."

"Do you know what that means?"

Two more kids are looking at Daddy as if he is slightly nuts. "Of course we know what it means! God wants Christians to be holy."

So much for the case for theological illiteracy . . .

There is, however, a need for a special children's Bible. Let me describe this unique, and presently nonexistent, item. It has a binding that just won't quit. Peanut butter and jelly wipe right off. The print is large and open and the pages are tear-resistant. I was describing this gem among Bibles to Bill, and he pointed out that Bible publishers *have* to use thin paper in order to fit the whole Bible into a reasonable size book. I, in turn, suggested to him that perhaps someone could find a way to print the Bible on extra-thin Tyvek® paper. (Tyvek is that stuff used in the large, tear-proof envelopes businesses use to mail their important documents.) If I were smart, I'd patent the idea. Since I'm not, I offer it here to any Bible publisher who might be interested.

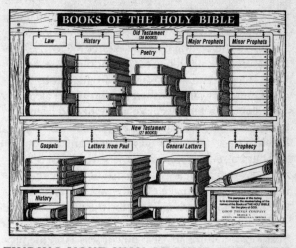

FINDING YOUR WAY AROUND THE BOOK

Good Things Company
Books of the Holy Bible: small chart (8 x 10"), full-color and laminated, $6; small chart in black-and-white outline without book titles, $2; large full-color laminated chart (20 x 24"), $12; large in black-and-white outline without book titles, $4. Shipping included.

Good Things Company's *Books of the Holy Bible* poster is a very useful visual tool that shows the books of the Bible stacked on two shelves, one for the Old Testament and one for the New. Above each stack of books is a label, like Law or History or Minor Prophets. The books are in the order of the Bible. We started off our little ones with this chart by reading it, and letting the ones who can talk repeat each name after us. "Genesis." "Gen'sith." "Exodus." "Ex'dith." "Leviticus." "Cus." Great stuff! In no time at all, they are getting the idea. You can also get plain paper outlines of this same chart with the book titles left out, for your youngsters to fill in. Very simple, well-organized way to understand how the whole Bible fits together and get used to the names of Bible books.

HEARING THE WORD

NEW**
The World's Greatest Stories
Each tape $8.95 plus $1 shipping, specify NIV or KJV..

These are the best Bible-narration tapes I have ever heard. *The World's Greatest Stories from the World's Greatest Book* series so far includes two tapes: *The Prophets* and *The Life of Christ*, both narrated word by word from the New International Version and King

James Version translations of the Bible. What makes these tapes different is the terrific interpretation of the characters and setting by actor George W. Sarris. Nebuchadnezzar *sounds* like a tough Middle-Eastern emperor. His descendant Belshazzar, frightened by the writing on the wall, mumbles his fears in an alcohol-slurred voice (totally accurate, since he had been drinking heavily all day). The Bible characters cry, or threaten, or do whatever they do with amazing realism. But more than this, even the strictly descriptive portions are read in a way that makes them come to life. Mr. Sarris can make even the words, "Nebuchadnezzar, king of Babylon," describe the man's personality. Plus the well-chosen special effects and music do a great job of helping us "see" how it was. And the production quality and packaging are first-class.

You probably realize by now that I'm really tough on Bible resources when it comes to accuracy. So tough, in fact, that I haven't even bothered to include several series of Bible tapes that I went to the trouble of listening to, since they consistently made obvious mistakes. These tapes are different. They're really great. And I'm not the only one who thinks so. Bill Gothard's Institute in Basic Youth Conflicts has ordered 14,000 of these tapes in the past two years!

The *Prophets* tape has these stories: The Burning Fiery Furnace, The Handwriting on the Wall, Daniel in the Lions' Den, Elijah and the Prophets of Baal, and The Prophecy of Jonah. The *Life of Christ* tape includes The Real Story of Christmas, The Baptism and Temptation of Jesus, The Healing of the Blind Man, Things Jesus Said and Did, and The Real Story of Easter.

Storyteller George Sarris has a Bachelor of Science degree in Speech from Northwestern University and the Master of Divinity from Gordon-Conwell Theological Seminary. He has a background in acting and broadcasting, and if he ever comes to your area to do his Bible dramatizing, don't miss it!

If you're not a Christian, or have always thought of the Bible as a boring book, these tapes will revolutionize your thinking. If you just want to turn your children on to Bible study, or want to learn how to read the Bible in a way that makes the text jump up and turn cartwheels, these tapes will do it for you. Get them today!

BIBLE TIME LINES AND CHARTS

NEW**
Donald and Mary Baker
Bible Study Guide for All Ages, four volumes, $19.95/volume. Add 15% shipping for orders under $50, 10% for orders over $50.

This really terrific Bible study program includes directions for making your own time lines out of styrofoam sheets, fabric, and the included cutouts in the back of each volume. Of all the Bible time lines I've used, this one is the most educationally useful. You can drill the kids with it, too, since it's designed to have all the pieces *pinned* on instead of permanently stapled. Just take off some of the patriarchs, for example, and see if the kids can put them up on the time line where they belong. All this and a full year's Bible lessons in every volume, too!

Good Things Company
Adam and Eve Family Tree: cassette tapes, $9.50; paper chart, $14.50; laminated chart, $19.50. Shipping included.

The Adam and Eve Family Tree is a colorful wall poster that shows who was related to whom and what they were up to for all of Bible history until Christ, plus giving selected Scripture references for further study. Talk about genealogical research! The Chart is accurate and easy to use, and will provide hours of educational browsing for any Bible lover. And it's so handy to have a *laminated* chart which the little folks can't shred before they're old enough to appreciate it!

The Chart comes in both laminated and plain paper styles, both colorful and very beautiful. You can also get a tape that explains how to use it.

NEW**
Heritage Products, Inc.
The Bible Overview Chart, $4.95.

Reader Mrs. Paul Steigerwald from La Pryor, Texas wrote, "I thought you might like to know about a laminated Bible time line that I purchased for $4.95." Yes, indeed, I was interested!

The *Bible Overview Chart* is full-color, 25½ x 11", printed on card stock and laminated on both sides. It folds to 8½ x 11" so you can carry it with your Bible for ready reference. It provides a bird's-eye view of the entire Bible, with a ton of information in an easy-to-follow format. For each book, the chart has a mini-map above the time line, color-keyed to the time line itself. The name of the Bible book is on the time line, with its general content, chapter numbers, chapter content, special map references, significant events highlighted, book's author, place of writing, and more! This is not all jumbled together, but presented visually in a way that a seven-year-old can understand. At this price, almost everyone can afford this wonderful resource.

KONOS
Bible characters time line figures $59.95. Shipping 10%.

KONOS takes a different approach, focusing on Bible characters rather than Bible books. Lots and lots of colorful laminated Bible figures to cut out and staple to a wall time line, each labeled with name and date and carrying a symbol of his or her historical role. Ancestors of Jesus wear a gold cross; kings have crowns; shepherds have sheep; Jonah has his big fish (looks suspiciously like a whale!). Lots of fun if you like to cut things out. Requires a long wall.

CHAPTER ELEVEN

BIBLE MEMORY PROGRAMS

Numerous authorities remind us that the elementary-school years are the best time for children to start memorizing. Memory work just comes naturally to little kids, and why not? *Their* minds aren't cluttered with trying to remember monthly bills, the phone numbers of 100 friends and relatives, house maintenance task schedules, and the names and supposed qualifications of the fifty or so candidates running for political offices in your area at any given time!

Today's little tykes certainly are able to remember hundreds of Bible verses. In the 1800s, it was not uncommon for children to memorize entire Bible chapters, and even whole Bible books, before they turned ten. The point, of course, is not that we prod our children to become memory whizzes, but that they understand and remember God's eternal truths.

What to memorize? You could just go through the Bible, picking key verses from each book. Or you could follow the topical approach and select key Scriptures that illuminate important truths of the Christian life, like most of the programs below. Some combination of the two is probably most helpful. You don't want your children to grow up quoting verses out of context, but you also want them to quickly remember verses related to essential topics.

Now, here is my personal Bible memory study tip: Ignore the verse number! It takes four times as much effort to remember both chapter and verse as it does to just remember the chapter—but if you know the chapter, you can quickly find the verse.

NEW**
Bible Memory Association
Enrollments received by November 15, March 15, or July 15, cost $8 per person or $25 per family. After these dates, fees increase as follows: $10 per person and $30 per family until December 1, April 1, and August 1; $15 per person and $45 per family until December 15, April 15, and August 15.

I know some of you out there have used BMA materials since you were that high—with over 700,000 users since 1944, BMA is not exactly the new kid on the block. But judging by the number of churches who have *no* systematic memory program for either adults or children, the good word could be spread a mite further.

The list of BMA features goes on and on:

- A Bible memory plan for each age. Littlest kids start with *Bible ABC's*, one verse for each letter of the alphabet, followed by *Bible Bees*. Each memory book is divided into fifteen assignments, each with its own introduction and explanatory notes. Elementary ages have up to two verses per week; preteens learn three verses per week; teens and weakminded adults like you and me get four. Those who want to tackle an entire book of the New Testament (James, 1 John, 1 Peter, Philippians, and Ephesians are available) learn 7–11 verses per week.

• Specific requirements and accountability. Which verses to memorize, when they must be learned, who will check you on your recitation, and how many errors are allowed are all spelled out in advance. Unlike other disciplines, where it makes sense to "go at your own pace," memorization works best when it is systematic and structured. You will know exactly what to do when, *and* when you have done enough.

• Family memory plans for families that like to study together. Everyone memorizes the same verses; adults and older children get longer portions. There are three family series, each with a book for children 6–12, a book for youth, and a book for adults. The three series are: Wisdom for Daily Living, Life of Christ, and Our Wonderful God.

• You can earn a large discount off the price of BMA camp at one of seven North American locations by completing your memory course inside of the twelve months preceding May 31 of any year! This means that a week of camp in 1990 cost as little as $59 per person. Campers must be nine years old or accompanied by parents (yes, BMA has family camp).

• Prizes for completing memory work. BMA's *Reward Catalog* lists hundreds of Bibles, coloring books, puzzles, Christian books, posters, and so on. You can pay for these with Reward Certificates (one certificate is earned per completed assignment) or with cash. *Caution:* some of the newer books feature "slice of life" situations that home-schooled kids don't really need.

• The BMA Memory Plans cover all the basics of salvation, Christian living, and doctrine, without getting into denominational sticky wickets.

• Each memory booklet explains and applies the verses. You go beyond memory to understanding.

• BMA's carefully-chosen topics and verses, spelled-out requirements, and incentives to complete each course in a definite time period combine to increase your chances of success.

HOW IT WORKS: You sign up yourself and/or the kids for a memory course. You select a Supervisor who will hear Bible verse recitations (this can be you, in the case of a home-schooling family). Deadline to sign up for the January course is November 15; for the May course, March 15; for the September course, July 15. For the January course, enrollments can be entered up until a month after the deadline date, but fees are increased for late enrollment. You choose which Plan you will work on (preschool, beginner, intermediate, youth, adult, family, basic book . . .). Enclose your check, and BMA will send you the Memory Books, Reward Certificates, and Reward Catalog. If you go at a normal pace, you do fifteen assignments in 30 weeks, with six more weeks for review, making up a typical 36-week school year.

All BMA memory verses are in the King James Version.

NEW★★
Bob Jones University Press
Two-Edged Sword Memory Program, $15.25/all four volumes or $4 each. Shipping extra.

This Bible memory plan, developed by Evangelist Jerry Sivnksty, comes in four topical booklets, each with 130 Bible verses. The booklets are completely independent of each other. Booklet 1 has verses for daily living, booklet 2 has verses about character traits, booklet 3 is for Bible doctrine, and booklet 4 has verses about Christian family life. Each booklet has 26 subjects, with five verses in each subject. If you are using the plan at home, the author suggests that you memorize verses during 26 weeks of the year and review or meditate upon them for the remaining 26.

Naturally, he means that you would learn verses one week and review them the next, not that you would take half a year off from Bible memory!

Verses are well chosen, and the booklets include little boxes where you can check off your reviewing. Verses are supposed to be reviewed daily for five days, then monthly thereafter. All verses are from the King James Version.

NEW★★
Church Resource Ministries
Memlok Bible Memory System, $39.95 plus $4.30 shipping. Shipping for additionals, $2 each. Pocket cardholder, $3. Available versions: NASB, NIV, KJV.

Memlok™ is an exciting new approach to topical Bible memorization, based on flash cards with pictures symbolizing the first words of each verse. For example, the front of the card might say, "SOVEREIGNTY. John 1:22." Under this is a picture of an outline "F" with an eye in it. When you turn over the card, you find the verse is, "If I want him to remain until I come, what is that to you? You follow Me!"

As opposed to other "visual" systems, Memlok does not try to present an entire verse in pictures. This means less strain on your brain (in my opinion), and avoids the problem of associating Bible teaching with silly mental images. You are asked to spend only five minutes a day, five days a week, learning one new verse a week. The author calls this a "long range — low pressure" system. By the end, you will have memorized verses from every New Testament chapter, Old Testament book, and every chapter of the book of Proverbs. Memlok is the only topical system I know about that has such complete Bible coverage.

You select your own verses from 48 topics totalling 700 verses. Each topic has an illustrated summary card, with a kooky sentence made up of the beginning illus-

trations from each of the memory verses. All the cards and summary cards are included in the binder, in pre-perfed pages of 12 cards per page. Also included are instructions in how to use Memlok, a sample Contract of Accountability to use with a memory partner, a completion record, memory tips, a complete alphabetical and topical index of all the verses, a plastic Weekly Cardholder with pockets for the cards you are currently learning, five plastic Monthly Cardholders for cards you are reviewing, and of course the cards themselves! The cards are printed on sturdy ivory cardstock, professionally illustrated, and look really sharp.

I am really impressed with Memlok. The packaging is really great, and the cards are kid-appealing. Available in KJV, NIV, and NASB versions. Recommended.

NEW★★
Hear An' Tell Adventures
Big *Word Maps* book volume 1, $6. Book and tape, $12. Smaller book, $3. Add $1 shipping to order.

Patricia Al-Attas, owner of Hear An' Tell Adventures, is preparing visualized materials to aid in learning the Hide the Word in Your Heart verses (see write-up below). She sent me a sample of her first big *Word Maps* book. This is a very large book, sized so a teacher can hold it before a class and everyone can see it at once. A smaller version (8½ x 11") is also available. On each page a verse is spelled out with a combination of words and rebuses (pictures that stand for words). This was imaginatively done; even the graphic layout of the words on the page helps explain the verse and make it more memorable! Contact Patricia for info on what additional Bible memory materials she now has available.

NEW★★
Hide the Word in Your Heart Club
How to Start a "Hide the Word in Your Heart" Club, $3. Six one-hour videos, $15 each. Shipping extra.

This Bible memory program was designed for churches, but individuals can use its methods too. Reader Donna Young says, "Our church has Hide the Word in Your Heart Clubs for different age groups. The oldest group not only works on Scripture, the members make up their own tracts and, along with the adult leaders, go street witnessing. People who would snub an adult are much more open to children. Plus, the group uses the railroad as their club theme and earn railroad hats and scarves along with their badges—making adults and other children curious as to why they are dressed as they are. The children really are enthusiastic about the witnessing and it's terrific to see them wanting to learn Scripture." According to the *Hide the Word in Your Heart Banner* newsletter she enclosed, the club is prepared to offer material in English, Spanish, Chinese, French, and Bulgarian.

The approach is topical. Kids are given verses to memorize for each topic, and you are supposed to give them a badge when they successfully recite them. Verses include both longish Scripture passages (e.g., Psalm 23) and single verses (e.g., John 3:16).

I was able to talk our church leaders into letting us use this approach in Sunday school, and while it lasted, the kids loved it. (The program was eventually canceled only because some people feared our age-integrated Sunday school was "too different" from other churches. Personally, I considered that a plus!)

"Hide the Word in Your Heart Club" videos are also available—six of them, in fact. All feature the Star Family, who founded the club. On each video, the Stars' nine home-schooled children recite entire chapters of Scripture. Their in-person appearances have inspired families and churches worldwide to get serious about Scripture memory.

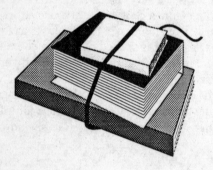

NEW★★
The Home Educator
Book by Book, $5 postpaid.

I had planned on coming up with a product like this, but now I don't have to! Brent Allan Winters, a home-schooling dad, has put together a spiral-bound, desktop-published book with themes and key verses from every book of the Bible. By systematically working through this book, your children will have a bird's-eye view of the entire Bible.

How does it work? Here's an example: the theme and key verse from the book of 2 Samuel.

Theme: The Reason for David's Success
II Samuel 23:3
"The God of Israel said, the Rock of Israel spake to me, He that ruleth over men must be just, ruling in the fear of God."

This isn't too complicated, is it?

Looking through this book, I see that Brent has done a really good job of choosing themes and key verses. I recognize several that my Old Testament prof in seminary used for key verses, proving that great minds think alike. Most verses are from the KJV; three are from the NIV. You, of course, can substitute key verses of your own choosing here and there, as he points out.

Brent has both the M.Div. and Th.M. from Biola University, among other degrees. His majors were Old and New Testament Exegesis. (Just in case you're impressed by such things!)

It's so important to make sure the kids have an overall view of the Bible before we start narrowly focusing on individual topical verses. Before starting any of the fancier programs in this section, why not try this one? Recommended.

NEW★★
HoneyWord
Old Testament, Parables & Miracles, and *Gospels*, $13 each postpaid. Promotional video (20 minutes), $29.95. Teaching video (1 hour), $39.95. Videos only available in VHS. Add 20% shipping to price of videos. Quantity discounts available.

The HoneyWord System is *not* a Bible memory program. So why did I put it in the Bible memory section? Because, although this is supposed to be a Bible study program, it's built around a unique visual-memory system that enables students to remember what chapter and book each major Bible event occurs in.

Here's how it works. Animals represent the books of the Bible. A mouse stands for the gospel of Matthew and a lion for the gospel of Luke, for instance. Special cartoon symbols represent chapter numbers. An ark stands for the number 2, because the animals entered into the ark two by two. Toes represent the number 10, because people have ten toes. Kids first memorize the symbols and what they represent. Then you start the program.

For each lesson, first the students learn the Bible story, including one main lesson from the story. Next, they learn the cartoon story and what it represents. For example, consider the cartoon of a lion sunning himself on the beach. He want to get a "good summer tan." Unfortunately for him, a crab is about to pinch his toes. The HoneyWord Lion represents the Gospel of Luke, since they both begin with the *L* sound. Since most of us have ten toes, the big HoneyWord toes always represent chapter 10. So now you know that the story of the Good Samaritan (good summer tan—get it?) is in Luke chapter 10.

Next, the teacher is supposed to lead the students in discussion stimulated by both the Bible story and the cartoon story. The fourth step is drill and review, checking the kids on which Bible story is found where. These are the basic steps of the program. You can add extras, as explained in the front of each oversized book: making a lifetime notebook, "glueing on" additional points to each Bible story by using file folders, creatively marking your Bible, and many other ideas. Perhaps the most provocative idea of all is the use of everyday objects, as used in the cartoons, for "trigger points" to bring Bible lessons to mind. For example, a cane is used in the cartoon story of Cain and Abel. The lesson for that story is, "I am my brother's keeper." So every time you see a cane, you can remind yourself that you are your brother's keeper.

Every two pages of a HoneyWord book is one lesson. You get a brief summary of the Bible passage, the Bible reference, the cartoon story, a For the Parents section that helps explain the cartoon, a Pick/Point/Put section explaining the main new symbols used in the cartoon, a "worms" cartoon, an application section asking, "What lesson is in the Bible story for me today?," and a space to write down "what God is telling me about Himself in this story." About those worms: Some little worms and their friend, a turtle, appear in a humorous cartoon at the bottom of each lesson. Sometimes the cartoon has something to do with the lesson topic, sometimes it doesn't, but it's always funny and kid-appealing.

You can get a promotional video loaded with testimonies of kids and teachers who have used this system. After you've heard the testimonies for about 10 minutes or so, the video explains the program and shows how it works. The video is called (I'm not making this up) *The Eyes of a Child That Sparkle for Jesus!* I haven't seen the teacher-training video yet.

The HoneyWord series so far includes *The Old Testament: Creation to King Saul, The Gospels: Parables and Miracles of Jesus,* and *The Gospels: Other Events of Jesus' Life.* These are all very professionally produced, with excellent quality cartoons and layout, and bristling with endorsements from Mr. and Mrs. Josh McDowell, Tim LaHaye, Paul Meier, Frank Minirth, Bill and Vonette Bright, and Gary Smalley.

NEW**
NavPress
Well-Versed Kids, $10.95.

NavPress, the publishing arm of the Navigators parachurch ministry, recently came out with a very snazzy Bible memory resource for kids called *Well-Versed Kids.* This is a big step for Navigators, which until this time has concentrated on adult Bible memory and discipleship.

I spotted *Well-Versed Kids* on the shelf at my local Christian bookstore and immediately snapped it up, intrigued by the package design and promises. Inside, the small but thick parent-teacher manual informed me that *Well-Versed Kids* is "more than a memory course—it's a course on Christian living specifically designed for elementary children."

That's a big claim. How do they try to carry it out?

You get 108 verse cards with verses in both the KJV and NKJV versions, one "verse pack," a little yellow vinyl folder for carrying around cards you are memorizing, one verse box, otherwise known as the package in which this program comes, and one parent-teacher manual, already mentioned. *Well-Versed Kids* covers six color-coded main topics: understanding salvation, knowing God, growing as a Christian, enjoying God, building character, and Great Bible Truths. These are in turn divided up into subtopics, which are intended to move from the simple to the more complex, providing three levels for different age groups.

This is carried out rather well in the Understanding Salvation topic, as the same six questions are answered with different Bible verses on each level. On topics such as Knowing God there is no apparent rhyme or reason to the division of subtopics. Level 1 covers Jesus the Son and Jesus my Savior, level 2 introduces God the Father and God, My Creator, and level 3 has God the Holy Spirit and The Spirit in Me. Clearly, it makes no sense to spread the Trinity over three levels like this, especially when each level is intended as a year of Bible memory work. It would have been far better to use the same "question" approach as in the Understanding Salvation topic, with the same questions (or subtopics) on each level, but with increasingly deep answers to each question.

The parent-teacher manual takes *Well-Versed Kids* beyond a mere pack of Scripture cards. Along with helpful general teaching tips and a program overview, it explains the concept taught in each verse, with mini-word studies of key words in the verse and ideas on how to communicate the verse concept.

Aside from the problem of splitting important doctrines into separate levels, the one other weakness of what is otherwise an extremely creative and useful program is one I find endemic in modern evangelicalism. It involves the difference between *sinfulness* and *sins*.

The manual states, "A Christian has admitted his sinfulness, has recognized that Jesus paid the penalty for his sin by dying on the cross, and has asked Jesus to come into his life." What is wrong with that? Nothing, except it's not biblical. According to the Bible, a Christian has *repented of* (not just admitted) his *specific sins* (not just his general lack of perfection), has recognized that Jesus paid the penalty for his *sins* (not his "sin," a totally nebulous concept), and has *begged* (not asked) Jesus to *take over* (not come into) his life. This is such an earth-shaking event that the Bible calls it being "born again." I therefore worry that question 6, "How can I be sure I am a Christian?" in the Understanding Salvation topic is answered too glibly (as in fact most of the questions in that section are). What about checking the fruit to see if there is any root? Isn't

the heart "desperately wicked and deceitful above all things?" Is getting saved nothing more than making some kind of mental assent to the doctrine of the substitutionary atonement? Is this all the Bible means when it talks about "believing in Christ"?

Also, I may have missed it, but I sure have had trouble finding the word "Hell" or any teaching on that subject in this program. The manual talks about "spiritual and physical death," but Jesus had a bit more than that to say about the eternal fate of the unsaved. Considering that Jesus said more about Heaven and Hell when on earth than any other single topic, we could have reasonably expected *both* to be covered in this program.

Having said all that, authors Bill and Sue Tell have invented a marvelous user interface for children's memory programs. Their educational approach is very sound and inviting. Just be aware that with this, as with all topical memory systems, you are limited to the topics the authors choose, which may or may not be a Scriptural balance.

NEW**
Rapids Christian Press
Set of 10 assorted text cards, 89¢. Shipping extra.

Rapids Christian Press has tons of useful Bible tools, including simple Bible courses and Vivian Gunderson's Scripture Catechism (see writeup below). Also available from this company, and useful for simple Bible memory work: Text Cards to Color. Each 8½ x 11" card has a picture and a Bible verse to color. You color both the picture *and* the verse, since the letters of the verse are large and outlined. Cards come in sets of 10. For classroom use, you can buy quantities of each card at a very good price. The Bird Text Cards each have a verse about speaking like a Christian. The Farm Animal Text Cards each has a salvation topic. The Flower Text Cards have commandments. The Wild Animal Text Cards are all about sin. The Wildflower Text Cards are about obedience to the Lord. The new Australian Animal Text Cards has verses about the Bible, plus info on the card's envelope about the animals!

NEW

The Ten Commandments

Ten Commandments packet, contribution appreciated but not required.

Quick! Name five of the Ten Commandments! They can be in any order. I'll wait . . .

If you're like most people, you had trouble with this assignment. Since the late Fifties, when the Supreme Court decided free speech rights didn't apply to God, most American children have grown up never knowing God's simplest rules for people. Now these life-changing rules can be at your fingertips, *without* tedious memorizing! You'll know them in any order, and you'll remember which Commandment is which!

WHAT YOU GET: A set of 10 Ten Commandment sheets plus one for your personal use. Each lists an abbreviated version of the Commandments on the front, with the unique visualized memory helps on the back. These use pictures associated with numerals to help you remember the Commandments. The pack comes with an introductory page explaining how to use the sheets, and a set of pledge forms people can sign if they get serious about learning and passing on the Ten Commandments.

The publisher hopes to persuade you to share God's laws with 10 other people. Considering that the Ten Commandments used to be the basis of American society and laws back when people didn't need to lock their doors at night, even a confirmed atheist ought to think twice before passing them over in favor of the ten zillion conflicting commandments continually gushing forth from Washington, D.C.

CATECHISMS

I realize this section is scanty, but that's because I only decided to throw it in it at the last minute. So if your denomination's catechism isn't included here, don't get mad, just send me a sample copy so I can review it for the next edition!

For centuries Christians used catechisms to train their children. What is a catechism? It is a series of questions and answers that children or adults memorize. The questions are designed to cover what the catechism designer considers the most important areas of Christian life. Catechisms are written as memory devices, to help kids know by heart the basic teachings of the church. Some object to this as "head knowledge," but it sure beats *no* knowledge, which is where a lot of our kids are today.

Don't be afraid to teach your children the catechism. Little kids adore this kind of memory work and are surprisingly good at it. Just a simple chart with squares for the questions, plus some gold stars to put in the blocks when the questions were learned was sufficient to motivate our kids to learn them.

NEW

Rapids Christian Press

Bible Answer Cards, set of all 44, $2.50. Certificate for learning one card, $1/dozen, $6 per 100. Set of 10 assorted text cards, 89¢. Shipping extra.

Vivian Gunderson, noted Sunday school material author, has prepared what she calls a "Scripture Catechism." Consisting of two cards for preschoolers, four for kindergartners, and 38 more for primary-aged and older children, covering a total of 30 topics, her *Bible Answer Cards* series is a graduated, topical Scripture-memory program that runs from preschool through high school, using Bible verses for the answers to its questions.

This idea is not new: such types of catechisms were used long ago. What is new is the correlated storybooks, color-it-in texts, and memory work certificates for successful learners.

The Bible Answer Cards may not be packaged as fancily as *Well-Versed Kids* (see above), but the entire set is only $2.50, making this a terrific bargain.

Each card has either five or 10 questions on it. Each question is answered by a complete Bible verse. An example from card 41, "Our Words":

1. What should we always speak?

Each card has either five or 10 questions on it. Each question is answered by a complete Bible verse. An example from card 41, "Our Words":

1. What should we always speak?
"Speak every man truth with his neighbor." Ephesians 4:25

2. What kind of lips does the Lord hate?
"Lying lips are abomination to the Lord: but they that deal truly are His delight." Proverbs 12:22

3. Should we say unkind things about others?
"Speak not evil one of another." James 4:11

The two Nursery Class cards, "Verses About God" and "Verses I Can Learn," each have five questions. The four Beginner Cards, "The Greatness of God," "God Saves Sinners," "Clean Hearts," and "Bible Verses for Me," each also have five questions. All the rest of the cards in the series each have 10 questions. This includes the Primary Cards and the Topical Cards. Primary cards are "Learning About God," "About the Lord Jesus," "Good Behavior," "Learning About Sin," "Learning About Heaven," "Learning to Serve God," "Learning to Pray," and "Learning Right Words." Topics cards cover the Bible, creation, man's responsibility to God, conduct toward God, God's gifts, giving to God, God the Son, the work of Christ, the Resurrection, Satan, sin, salvation, conduct toward others, God the Holy Spirit, the Christian life, the Christian and the Law, Bible study, faith, prayer, eating and drinking, love, joy, peace, angels, our works, our words, our thoughts, Heaven and Hell, and soul-winning.

Also available from this company, and useful for simple Bible memory work: Text Cards to Color. Each 8½ x 11" card has a picture and a Bible verse to color. You color both the picture *and* the verse, since the letters of the verse are large and outlined. Cards come in sets of 10. For classroom use, you can buy quantities of each card at a very good price. The Bird Text Cards each have a verse about speaking like a Christian. The Farm Animal Text Cards each have a salvation topic. The Flower Text Cards have commandments. The Wild Animal Text Cards are all about sin. The Wildflower Text Cards are about obedience to the Lord. The new Australian Animal Text Cards has verses about the Bible, plus info on the card's envelope about the animals!

NEW**
Vic Lockman
The Catechism for Young Children with Cartoons, two volumes, $1.50 each. Add $1.00 shipping.

The Westminster Confession of Faith is the one followed for the past 300 years by many Presbyterian and Congregational churches. Now this classic catechism has been illustrated in cartoons that make the questions and answers meaningful to young children. Talented cartoonist Vic Lockman has put together the two booklets in this series with bright, cheery drawings showing children applying the teachings in their everyday lives. Excellent quality, kid-appealing. Recommended.

CHAPTER TWELVE

BIBLE COURSES

Sometimes someone else says what you wanted to say so well that you don't have to say it. Here's Clifford E. Miller, editor of the Rapids Christian Press catalog, with some words on the best way to teach kids the Bible:

Children's voices were heard, seriously singing, "Jesus, help me to remember some sweet lessons from Thy word. . ." It was a fitting ending for a three-hour session of Vacation Bible School. The time had been spent on two Bible lessons (the main emphasis for the day), memory work, singing, a 15-minute recess, some notebook work for older children and handwork for the little ones, and perhaps a brief object lesson. Children loved it! There were no puppets, no cassettes, no skits, no imaginative adventures. Just Bible. And kids found it delightful! The program was not designed to make them laugh, but they said it was fun!

"But that was 50 years ago," you say. "They're smarter, so they wouldn't be able to stand two Bible lessons in a forenoon. They're used to being entertained, so we have to amuse them."

Granted, today's children are different. They are much more knowledgeable about sin, sad to say. But their hearts are the same. They are all sinners who need, not more hilarity and excitement, but the living Word of God. Is there someone among our readers who would dare to conduct a new kind of Vacation Bible

School this year, the kind that used to be common but has been all but forgotten? Hebrew 4:12 is still true. Let's make it a BIBLE school this year!

With that in mind, and at the risk of sounding old-fashioned, I would like to mention that great old standby for teaching Bible. It's called, "The Bible."

What with all the puppet lessons, flannelgraphs, Bible stories, Bible videos, Bible dolls, and so on, sometimes our Bible programs end up missing the mark. For some reason, Bible curriculum designers have been really heaping on the fun 'n games lately. They load us up with "easy activities," like finding the puppet figures, dragging out flannel pieces 22A-24F, or correcting a Friends of Jesus Crossword Puzzle. That's OK for fun on Sunday afternoon, but it does get rather old after a few school weeks.

So how about just *reading the Bible to your children* instead? They are going to pay attention because, after reading, you will have each one *tell you the passage in his own words*. Alternatively, the children can act out the passage (with or without costumes), draw pictures that explain the passage, model it in clay (quick, and you don't have to save the results forever unless you want to), or write it out.

With a little creative imagination, your children can be actively listening and retelling all of Scripture to you in their own words. And that even includes the "tough" passages like the genealogies in Chronicles. Try making name tags for the important characters and have the children sort them in order as to who begat whom. Or you can make a time line! You can even use the Bible as your basic language arts exercise book—see the Grammar chapter for details.

HOW TO TEACH BIBLE

The above approach works for all ages and levels of Bible literacy—and it's free. But some of us feel like we need more of a helping hand. That's OK, provided the Bible curriculum we choose actually helps!

Here are some questions to ask when shopping for Bible resources.

- **Is it complete?** In too many programs, well-worn stories appear again year after year, while major events like the downfall of Jerusalem in 586 B.C. are either passed over quickly or completely ignored. (As one curriculum author complains, "A lot of these programs never get out of the wilderness"—referring to the tendency to start again and again at Genesis and poop out at Exodus, with only a few brief excursions into the rest of the Bible.) If your only contact with the Bible was through some of these programs, you would never guess that Leviticus, Deuteronomy, large sections of Judges, the two books of Chronicles, most of the message of the major prophets, or any of the minor prophets even existed. Since these are just the areas in which most Christian parents are weak, it makes sense to keep looking until you find a program that shores up your own weak areas instead of tiptoeing around them.

- **Is it easy to understand?** I'm not asking, "Does it use easy words?" but "Is the teaching systematic?" Does one thing follow another in logical sequence, or does the curriculum hop-skip-and-jump all over the place? Is the program designed to help the child remember his lessons . . . or do the authors simply throw a lot of unorganized data at the children?

- **Does it have depth and thoroughness?** Don't assume that because it's a Bible curriculum the authors necessarily know what they are talking about. Surrounding material may be frivolous, irrelevant, or downright wrong. One Bible program I know cites Goliath as an "example of courage." Sure. A nine-foot bully would have to be pretty brave to face a young unarmored Israelite! Another turns the story of Moses in the bulrushes into a sermonette on Miriam's courage, in which Miriam is made to constantly state that she trusts in the Lord and will not be afraid. Good sentiments, except they appear nowhere in this passage. Still another shows young David zapping tin cans off a fence with his slingshot. Only problem is, tin cans weren't invented until this century. Why these silly treatments of important passages? Because the authors are trying too hard to jam every lesson into one shoebox—a moral of the week. A really good curriculum, rather than grasping for a "moral of the week," will teach students to get deeper and deeper into every passage, finding dozens of applications.

- **Does the program challenge children to grow spiritually?** Or does it assume they are only interested in fun and games? Even when the lesson claims to teach the story's basic message, often so much time is given to side activities, like making puppets of David and Goliath, that the actual message vanishes in the creative swirl.

- **Is preaching substituted for teaching?** Do the curriculum designers prefer to sermonize about, say, the need to avoid drugs rather than tell us what the difficult words in the Bible passage mean? Are children taught how to handle Scripture study tools like concordances and given a systematic outline of Bible history? Are they given an understanding of Bible cultures (Hebrew, Egyptian, Assyrian, Canaanite, Philistine, Babylonian, Greek, Roman, New Testament Jewish . . .), and a workable Bible memory program? Or does an unbalanced appeal solely to the emotions replace solid teaching for the intellect?

• **Does it trivialize the sacred?** A crossword puzzle is a crossword puzzle. And Jesus Christ did not die on the cross to get His name into a crossword puzzle. Often Bible curriculum, in an attempt to be clever or relevant, focuses more interest on an activity than on the person or doctrine supposedly being taught. I think, for example, of the cutesy idea of having children write modern-day news reports about Jesus' birth or other Biblical events. Game-show formats, "interviews" with Biblical characters, and other such activities all tend to trivialize the Bible's message. Should prophets of God, before whom kings trembled, be reduced to interview subjects for snide eight-year-olds? (I seem to recall that a gang of irreverent youth once got into serious trouble for taking a prophet—Elisha—lightly.) Right in line with this is the practice of "dumbing down" Scripture into a small, easily-memorized list of clichés and slogans. Should children be taught to be satisfied with pigeonholing Jeremiah as "the weeping prophet" without ever really hearing his message?

The main purpose of Bible teaching is to provide us with enough *understanding* of the Word of God so that the Holy Spirit, through His appointed means of preaching and meditation, can apply it to our hearts.

At home, we parents don't need a load of sermons-in-workbook-form as much as we need resources for sharing the vast amount of *information* in the Bible with our children. Before we go flying off into the air with all kinds of great applications of Scripture, we have to know what the Bible *says*. Seminaries today are forced to provide remedial Bible classes for men who have graduated from Bible college and attended Sunday school all their lives—all because of this overeagerness to get to the preaching and the application before children even know Hosea from Joshua. You don't want this to happen to your family!

What we really need in a Bible curriculum is:

• **Chronological knowledge of Bible events.** This includes some understanding of the cultural framework of these events, which the Bible itself readily supplies.

• **Book-by-book knowledge of what is in the Bible,** so you can find your way around it.

These first two types of biblical knowledge provide the framework for what is to follow:

• **Knowledge of how to understand the Bible** (exegesis), **how to apply its teachings, and which teaching applies to which situation.** The Bible calls this "wisdom" and says only those who belong to God and practice what they already know of His commandments ever achieve it.

• **Knowledge of the basic Bible teachings** about God, man, sin, redemption, creation, eternity, the meaning of life, etc. We all know what the world teaches about such things. Trust me, the Bible says something different.

Now, here's one quickie resource to help you struggle with these issues.

NEW**
Teaching Home
December 1987, $3.75. Complete six-issue set of 1987 back issues, $17.50, includes free set of 6 plastic magazine holders for your ring binder.

As I've said before, each *Teaching Home* magazine back issue on a given topic is like a minicourse in teaching that topic. December 1987 the topic was "Bible." It was a "wow" issue, too, with articles on teaching toddlers, Bible memory for little ones, Bible storytelling, Bible study, Bible learning software, two excellent articles by Ruth Beechick and Jon Lindvall on how and why to memorize Scripture, children's devotions, increasing your spiritual life, using the Bible as a reader (they did this for 200 years in America), and the Bible and academics. Name authors, lively discussion!

BIBLE PROGRAMS

Here are your day-in, day-out Bible study programs for preschool through grade 6. This section does not include programs that require long set-up times or lots of visuals, as you are unlikely to want to spend so much time every day just getting ready to teach. Those kinds of resources, found in the next chapter, are more useful for family worship and Sunday use (Saturday, for you seventh-day Baptists and Adventists).

NEW★★
A Beka Books

Flash-a-Card series: Salvation Series, $13.95. Mini Salvation Series 1 and 2, $1.85 each (personal-size for student). Other series cost between $9.70 and $14.95 each. Bible Curriculum Materials Kits: nursery, $140; K4, $183; K5, $186; Advanced K5, $160; grade 1, $195; grade 2, $185; grade 3, $166; grade 4, $161; grade 5, $192; grade 6, $197. Daily Bible curriculum plans (included in Bible Curriculum Materials Kits), $14 each grade. Add 10% shipping (minimum $2.75).

A Beka Books' unique Flash-a-Card® approach to Bible study for grades K–6 is based on large full-color cards and does not require the use of notebooks. Starting in Genesis with the story of Creation, the series includes

- Salvation Series: five stories illustrated on 35 cards.

- Genesis 21-lesson series: Creation/Adam/Cain, Enoch/Noah/Babel, Abraham and Isaac, Jacob, and Joseph

- Life of Moses 20-lesson series: Moses in Egypt, Journey to Sinai, and Journey through the Wilderness.

- Joshua: 7 lessons on 35 cards.

- Judges: 6 lessons on 34 cards.

- The Tabernacle: three lessons on nine cards.

- Elisha: eight lessons on 42 cards.

- Elijah: six lessons on 38 cards.

- Daniel: six lessons on 32 cards.

- Samuel: four lessons on 18 cards.

- Ruth: three lessons on seven cards.

- Life of Christ includes five series, with 35 lessons in all: The First Christmas, Boyhood and Early Ministry, Jesus Heals and Helps, Later Ministry of Jesus, and Crucifixion and Resurrection.

- Paul 1 series has five lessons on 26 cards.

- Paul 2 series has nine lessons on 34 cards.

Helpful lesson guides are provided with each set. The illustrations are outstanding.

If you prefer, you can also obtain a Bible Curriculum Materials Kit for each grade level. Each includes several Flash-a-Card series, a songbook for hymns and choruses, a daily curriculum guide, planning tips, and Bible Doctrinal Drills. The nursery kit includes flannelgraphs instead of Flash-a-Cards.

NEW★★
Accent Publications
$11 per quarter per level.

More from Mrs. Paul Steigerwald of Texas:

I would like to tell you about Accent Bible Curriculum, which is the cornerstone of our home study. My 3½ year old son began with the Preschool (ages 2 and 3) materials when he was just learning to talk. That quarter's lesson was about how God made the sun, moon, and stars. It is one of my most precious memories of how, after reading the lesson, I took my little one out to the back porch, and pointed to the moon and stars. He learned the words that night. The preschool curriculum includes storybooks, fingerplays, pictures to color, drawing and crafts ideas, songs, and music cassettes. Peter has cut out pieces from construction paper and glued them to an outline of Noah's ark about 20 times; I would never have thought of these things on my own. The teacher's manual helps me by explaining an aim for the lesson that is appropriate for a preschooler. For example, Noah obeyed God and we should too. God said it would rain, and it did. Now, whenever it rains, our little one remarks that God sent the rain.

My fourth-grader uses the Junior program, which is an Old and New Testament survey for three years. The aim of the lesson is especially chosen to be appropriate for his age. In fact, what interested me in Accent curriculum initially was that I read a copy of their teacher-training book which indicated that the material is written with intense appreciation for the stages of child development, both mentally and spiritually. My fourth-grader writes a summary of each lesson, ending with a sentence which states what the lesson means to him. We use these aims of the lesson in our prayer time. Of course, the summary our son writes is good practice for all the language arts. He also gives an oral summary of his lesson to his father. . . .

The readers are vocabulary-controlled and new word cards are a part of the younger child's curriculum.

Well, I haven't seen that program personally, but you just heard from one happy user!

UPDATED✶✶
Alpha Omega Publications
Bible LIFEPACS, 10 per grade, levels 100-300 (grades 1-3) $2.25 each, $19.95 for set of 10; levels 400-600 (grades 4-6) $2.45 each, $21.95 for set of 10; levels 700-900 (grades 7-9) $2.75 each, $24.95 for set of 10; and levels 1000-1200 (grades 10-12) $2.95 each, $26.95 for set of 10. Bible Teacher Handbooks, $4.95 per grade. *Bible-Based Math*, $2.95 each, 2 per grade. *B-B M Teacher Handbooks*, $4.95.

Alpha Omega's Bible course for grades 2 to 12 contains seven major themes: Christian growth, theology themes, attributes of God, Christian evidences, Bible literature, Bible geography and archaeology, and a special theme for each level. Each one-year course includes nine workbooks, with full instructions built in, plus one workbook that reviews the entire course. The teacher handbooks include additional tests, enrichment activities, and discussion questions. In the early grades, the Bible course is integrated with language arts instruction, which means you get word exercises, phonics drills, and so forth. You will still need a separate grammar, spelling, and phonics program to use along with the Bible course.

Let's go through this curriculum grade by grade. In grade 1, the LIFEPAC titles are: God Created All Things, God Loves His Children, We Can Pray, God Wants You to Be Good, Old Testament Stories (men, women, and children of the Old Testament), God's Promise to Men, Jesus Our Savior, God Calls You to Be a Missionary, and New Testament Stories (men, women, and children of the New Testament). Grade 2: Who Am I? (subtopics: God Made Use, God Loves Me, God Helps Me, and God Helped Daniel), The Story of Moses, God and You (subtopics: God is Great, God is Dependable, You Should Obey God, and God Rewards His People), How Your Bible Came to You, Z-Z-Z-Zing! Went David's Sling (I didn't make that up!), God is Everywhere, The Story of Joseph, God and the Family,

and God Made the Nations. Grade 3: Why Am I Here? (answers: to love, obey, praise, and worship God), The Life of Jesus Christ, O Joseph! What Was God's Plan for You? (Joseph, the son of Jacob, not Joseph the husband of Mary), You Can Use the Bible (how to study and memorize Scripture), God Takes Care of His People, How Do I Know the Bible is the World of God?, Archaeology and the Bible, God Gave Us the Need for Friends (teaching about Christian love and personal needs), and God Wants Man to Hep Man. Grade 4: How Can I Live for God?, God's Knowledge (how to become wise), Saul Begins to Live for God (Saul the Apostle Paul, not Saul the king of Israel), The Bible and Me (studying, memorizing, and living out the Bible), God Cares for Use (Jesus, David, and Daniel), How Can I Know God Exists?, Geography of the Old Testament, God-Given Worth (self-esteem), and Witnessing for Jesus. Grade 5: How Others Lived for God, Angels, The Presence of God, Bible Methods and Structure (parts of the Bible), The Christian in the world (behavior at home, school, and work), Proving What We Believe, Missionary Journeys of Paul, God Created Man for Eternity (the final judgment and rewards), and Authority and Law. Grade 6, the basic Bible survey, is broken up into: From Creation to Moses, From Joshua to Samuel, the Kingdoms of Israel, The Divided Kingdom, Captivity and Restoration, The Life of Jesus, The Followers of Jesus, The Apostle Paul, Hebrews and General Epistles, and Revelation and Review.

As a whole, I do not think the "seven-themes" approach is the best, since it doesn't stick with a subject long enough to build a really good framework. Grade 6 is the exception, covering the entire Bible without any special units on apologetics and self-esteem.

On the positive side, you can hardly find a more inexpensive or easy to use set of Bible worktexts. All Alpha Omega's products encourage thought—there is little rote fill-in-the-blanks, and students write an increasing number of sentence and essay answers as they go up the grade levels. On the negative side, the first few grades are rather rinky-dink, in my estimation, and the constant emphasis on "I am a very special person" and "I must love myself" wears thin. Things pick up in grades 3–5, with the exception of the unfortunate unit on self-esteem in grade 4. The grade 6 chronological Bible Survey course is quite good, including maps, timelines, and detailed explanations of Bible times practices. It covers *all* the Old Testament prophets (rare in an elementary Bible curriculum) and includes a mid-course review of the Old Testament, before getting into the New Testament.

Alpha Omega also has a math enrichment program, *Bible-Based Mathematics*. This series not only provides valuable practice for the math concepts at each level for grades 2 to 7, but directs the student to worship God as the Creator of our regular, mathematical universe and to use math to obey Him. This is not as strained as it sounds—honesty in business revolves around honest weights, measures, and prices, for example. The *Bible-Based Math* series costs more than other LIFEPACS because it is two-color and the worktexts are thicker. Alpha Omega suggests that it could be used at home devotionally, as well as for math enrichment.

Bob Jones University Press
Student worktexts: K4 children's packet, $7.95; K5 and grades 1-4, $5.95 each; grades 5 and 6, $6.95 each. Teacher's Edition, $29.50 each grade 1–6. Cassettes, storybooks, and so on are extra.

The first two grades of the Bob Jones University Press Bible Truths series provide a chronological overview of the entire Bible. These books impart some solid knowledge along with the salvation emphasis, covering the Children's Catechism along with the Bible and emphasizing simple "Bible Action Truths." Both K and 1 include enjoyable memory and handwork activities. Grades 2 through 4 systematically study the fundamental doctrines of the Christian faith. Grade 5 is a New Testament survey, while grade 6 surveys the Old Testament.

Like all other Bob Jones products, the art, layout, and general quality of these books is impeccable. The content is clean, clear, educationally excellent, and contains nothing "iffy." Eschatology is handled separately from other subjects, making it possible for families with diverse eschatological views to use these books.

In the lower grades, the teacher's manuals make a big difference. You get teaching tips, explanations of the activities, and supplemental activities.

The series was designed for use in daily Christian schools, making it deeper than Sunday school-style materials.

NEW★★
Christian Liberty Academy
The Child's Own Book of Bible Stories (kindergarten), $3.95. *Boys and Girls of the Bible* (grade 1), *Bible Steps for Little Pilgrims* (grade 2), and *The Child's Life of Christ* (grade 3), $2.95 each. *Studying God's Word Book E* (grade 4) and *Book F* (grade 5), $4.25 each. *Bible History for Christian Schools* (grade 6), $2.50. Add 10% shipping, minimum $1.50.

Christian Liberty Academy is one of the most popular curriculum providers in the home school market. Starting years ago with an eclectic curriculum made up of materials from many publishers, they have gradually begun to publish more of their own materials.

The Christian Liberty Bible Series starts with three softbound texts, each about 300 pages long, covering all the major events in the New and Old Testaments. These are illustrated with etchings and black-and-white photographs. *A Child's Life of Christ,* the book for third grade, has the same format but covers only the life of Christ. I haven't seen any of these.

Studying God's Word Book E, for fourth-graders, covers Genesis through Ruth. *Book F* covers the rest of the Old Testament. Each of these workbooks is organized chronologically, so students can follow the flow of Bible history. Each lesson includes time line information, lesson goals, optional memory verse, background information about the Bible passage, fact and thought questions, lesson review, and supplemental exercises like Bible crosswords. In addition, the workbooks provide historical backgrounds and outlines of each Bible book studied. I have seen Books "E" and "F," and must say that they do a fine job of leading children through both the facts and meaning of these Bible books.

Finally, in sixth grade *Bible History for Christian Schools* is a comprehensive overview of the Old and New Testaments in nonconsumable textbooks form, with comprehension questions built into the text.

All families who purchase Books "E" or "F" receive a teacher's manual at no extra cost. These manuals include both teaching instructions and answer keys for the workbooks.

For more information about the Christian Liberty Academy home-study programs, see the Curriculum Buyer's Guide in Volume 1.

NEW✶✶
Christian Schools International

Teacher guides, $34.99 each grade. Student texts, $7.24 each grade except grades 6–8 students texts, which are $14.50 hardcover or $9.36 softcover. Add 12% shipping on orders over $15, $3 on orders from $5–$15.

The people at Christian Schools International are very excited about their new preschool–grade 8 Bible curriculum, _The Story of God and His People._ Organized chronologically, rather than by Bible themes, and using a historical-literary approach rather than a topical "preaching" approach, it covers the Bible as a whole five times, and dips into every book in the Bible at least once. Over 1,600 classroom Bible teachers provided input to this project, which has a strong "covenantal" emphasis.

The Story of God and His People uses the same lesson format from grade to grade, but changes the type of lesson activities as students grow older. Each lesson includes a short title, summarizing the theme of the Bible passage, a Bible reference, lesson objectives, and list of preparation and materials required. In addition, some lessons have memory work, songs, or background information.

The body of the lesson itself is called "Lesson Steps." These may include review, telling or reading the story, discussion questions, and related activities. To increase the teacher's storytelling abilities, in the early grades a step-by-step Bible story outline is provided for each lesson. This hits the high points of the Bible story, but does not leave you just reading other people's words.

The preschool curriculum, _God's Family,_ is all included in the teacher's guide. The 32 full-color story cards (included in the K–2 courses only) are intended to be used by the parents at home, to review the story and help children understand the sequence of events. Each card has a watercolor illustration on one side and a Bible story summary on the other side, plus suggestions for what you can ask your child to tell you about the story. The curriculum is designed for 35 weeks of instruction, two days a week. Each of the nine units has a rather scanty one or two Bible memory verses. An introductory "background" to each unit summarizes the Bible portion being studied. A helpful Lesson Overview Chart lets you see at a glance the title, focus, teaching method, and follow-up activity for each lesson. You'll find lots of hands-on and full-body involvement in this course, from making and playing rubberband harps in the "David's Songs" lesson to the teacher

taking the part of Hannah or using a handmade "creation wheel" to visualize the days of creation. The lesson presentation method is constantly varied to keep up student interest and involvement. Extra reproducible activity pages are in the back of the book.

The kindergarten course, _God's Wonders,_ includes a set of 32 story cards, as does the first grade course, _God's Plan,_ and the second grade course, _God's Promises._ These three grades have a hands-on emphasis, with more writing-oriented activities progressively added. Children make a Ten Plagues booklet, for example.

Grade 3, _The Calling of God's Tribe,_ focuses on understanding Bible times. Grade 4, _The Record of God's Nation,_ focuses on the books of the Bible. Grade 5, _Witnesses to the Gospel,_ looks at the writers and different types of writing in the Bible. In these grades students have an activity book which includes activities, memory work cards, and a brief illustrated Bible dictionary.

The grades 6–8 courses are quite advanced, covering such things as archaeology (grade 6), intertestamentary times (grade 7), and early church history (grade 8). This gets quite graphic, as in the Babylonian account of creation and the flood included in the grade 6 book, and the Albrecht Durer engraving of a naked Adam and Eve with only their genital areas (and not even all their genital hair) covered by two convenient leaves. Although the tone of these books is clearly addressed to teens, the content is right up there with seminary courses I have taken. The format changes for these grades, as students now have their own textbooks and optional student workbook, while the teacher book is now an expanded edition of the student text.

This curriculum, like most, has its mistakes. The Ethiopian eunuch is shown driving his own _totally empty_ chariot (I wonder how he was planning on surviving his journey through the desert) while sitting _sideways_ (a totally unique position for driving a chariot!) and _reading_ (ever try to drive a chariot and read at the same time?). (Undoubtedly the eunuch had a chariot driver, and the "chariot" was more like a carriage, with room for Philip to come up and sit with him, as befitted a man of his importance.) In the pre-K David and Goliath activity, David is supposed to be four feet high (no way) to Goliath's nine. The lessons themselves are generally free of these embarrassing errors, which crop up mostly in the activities.

God's judgments and hatred of sin, though mentioned in passing, are not really emphasized, while lesson after lesson emphasizes God's love. Sometimes this leads to actual errors, as in the pre-K lesson description of Peter's Pentecost sermon as Peter telling the people, "Jesus is alive and Jesus loves you." (Look up Acts 3 to see what's missing from that description.)

You have to have the teacher books to use this program. The student workbooks (which are very good, by the way) make no sense without them.

As far as user format goes, this is an excellent program. The spiral-bound teacher books are well-organized, graphically clear, and easy to use.

The overall tone is relaxed and bland; you won't find a lot of heart-searing fiery applications or salvation appeals. Children are more likely to be soothed than awed by the Bible as it is presented here.

NEW★★
Donald and Mary Baker
Bible Study Guide for All Ages, four volumes, $19.95/volume. Add 15% shipping if order is under $50, 10% if over $50.

This program literally does work for "all ages," from preschool on up. Each volume of this four-volume program provides a full year of Bible study material for the entire family, if you have two lessons a week. Together, the four volumes cover the entire Bible.

Each lesson includes drill work (e.g., practicing saying the 10 Commandments), review of important questions from previous lessons, seven questions on the Bible chapter for this lesson (you read the chapter aloud), a song, an applicable Bible verse for meditation

or memorization, prayer time, and a visual. Some lessons also have an "additional Scriptures" section, with a few verses to read from other sections of the Bible that help explain the passage of the day, and/or an "According to the Dictionary" section that explains unusual words or customs occurring in the passage. Map work is also included where appropriate. All this is on *just one page for each lesson*, making it super easy to use.

Already this program towers head and shoulders above all others for sheer usefulness. Find me another program that the whole family, from preschooler to Grandpa, can study together at once, let alone one where the entire lesson is so well organized it fits on one page! But there's more. Each volume of *Bible Study Guide for All Ages* also includes all sorts of visual-aid cutouts, flap pages, and drawings in the back, plus literally dozens of suggested Bible games to help pep up your lessons, and (this is what excites me the most) complete plans for an incredibly useful Bible time line and wall map that your kids can both put together and test themselves with. Plus you even get the cutouts to put on the time line! All for (hold your breath) $19.95 per volume!

The program moves back and forth between sections of the Old and New Testaments, with review lessons providing natural transitions. This means you don't have to wait forever to teach your children about Jesus, and since the segments are organized logically—e.g., "Divided and Conquered Kingdoms"—your children won't get confused.

There's no written work required at all for this program—another plus in the eyes of many of us. Designed originally for use in family study times, it is infinitely adaptable to any number of individual or group situations for Bible students of all ages. On a scale of 1 to 100, I give this one a 100.

NEW★★
Judah Bible Curriculum
Bible Curriculum Pack, includes teacher training audiocassettes in binder and Curriculum Document, $49.95 plus 10% shipping.

The Principle Approach is popping up everywhere these days. This is the first Bible curriculum for school-age children I have seen to use it.

For the benefit of the uninitiated, the Principle Approach is a method of study applicable to any subject, based on what some modern researchers consider the way Americans used to study in the early days of the colonies and Republic. It emphasizes a providential view of history (God as the agent making things happen), a "dominion" emphasis (God's purposes shall prevail on this earth), and the development of student character, especially self-discipline, through a rigorous program of study and creating notebooks.

As this applies to Bible study, Judah Bible Curriculum students are supposed to record in a notebook all the findings they have researched. This finished notebook is supposed to be a model of neatness and organization, not to mention deep thinking. Students are given questions to answer and a way of recording information that forces them to think through Bible principles for themselves.

The curriculum is now in process of revision, but I haven't seen the final version, so let's look at the original edition. It consisted of the "Curriculum Document" and a set of eight "Teacher Training Audio Cassettes" in a cassette binder. The cassettes included a curriculum overview (pretty much the same thing said in the Document), a cassette on "How God Changes Nations," another on "Internal Government: Creation–Flood," one on "Internal Government: Abraham–Malachi," one on "Internal Government: Matthew–Revelation," one on "Internal Government: Pentecost–Present," a cassette on the unique methods used in the curriculum, and one entitled "Personal Destiny—Studying the Life of Joseph."

The tapes featured an Arminian, as opposed to Calvinist, outlook. The speaker stressed that God has "overall superintendency" over what happens rather than actually causing everything directly to happen. The author tells me that the revised material will take a a stronger approach to God's sovereignty.

I was not able to make it through all the tapes before getting out this book, mainly because all the material is covered so *slowly*. The speaker repeats a lot of the material in the Document, speaks slowly, has long pauses, and spends a lot of time retelling Bible history, often quoting great chunks straight out of the Bible. Since I sincerely wanted to get to the heart of the program, I found all this quite frustrating. Happily, the author told me he plans to write up the material in the tapes along with suggestions on what to teach so that you won't need to listen to the tapes, which will then become optional. I hope he will have finished that project by the time you read this.

Bill Burtness, the curriculum's author, believes that *liberty* is the main theme of the Bible. He put it in the title of his curriculum—"Judah Bible Curriculum: Education for Liberty." Heaven is shown as a situation in which everyone is perfectly self-governed under God.

Hell is just the opposite; everyone is totally governed from the outside. Here on earth, society wavers between self-government and outside government, depending strictly on how well we govern ourselves. People and nations who refuse to exercise self-control succumb to tyranny. The history of the Jews and the church is seen to be one of moving towards or away from liberty, depending on whether they (we) were (are) following God or not. All the character emphasis of the course is directed towards helping the student become a self-governing individual who then will be empowered to expand his sphere of influence as a godly servant, like Joseph, the curriculum's hero, who ended up ruling the largest empire of his age.

Now, the Curriculum Document. These three-hole-punched, photocopied pages break the Bible down into five historical periods, called "themes." Each theme is broken down into "Biblical Keys." Bible portions are studied in terms of key individuals, key events, key institutions, and key documents. Each of these keys has a different "Key Sheet" on which the student writes all that he could find about that person, place, or thing. For example, the Key Sheet for Key Institutions has three sections: Doctrinal Base, Character of the People, and Government. Under Doctrinal Base are the words *foundations, truths taught as foundational,* and *controlling ideas.* Under Character of the People you find *physical, moral disposition,* and *mental disposition.* Under Government are the phrases *manner of controlling men (internal/external), form of civil government, constitution/laws, how men are directed/controlled,* and *conduct.* Using these topics and subtopics as a guideline, the student researches and fills out his Key Sheet. If the institution was "Egypt" for example, he might write down, "Idolatry and the worship of Pharaoh as God" as a controlling idea in the Doctrinal Basis column.

Each week of study is grouped around a Weekly Theme Focus. Students read the Scripture passage themselves and analyze the Weekly Theme Focus using the appropriate Key Sheets. It's up to the teacher to explain how the key people, places, and things fit into God's plan. It's also up to him to come up with assignments like map-making, time lines, art and craft projects, and so on that can further bring out the weekly theme. The student puts one or two of these projects in his notebook each week

A course overview (scope and sequence) and Suggested Weekly Themes Guide for all seven years of the course and suggested weekly themes guide for the first year are included.

The course contents are repeated twice between kindergarten and twelfth grade. All five major "themes" (Bible periods) are covered each year, but different individuals and events are studied each time. Sample blank key sheets are also included that you can photocopy in quantity for your students' use. The Appendix includes visuals illustrating the concepts outlined on the teacher tapes, plus samples of filled-out Key Sheets and a Bible time line. The author says he will also be coming out with a Curriculum Idea Book of ideas and resources this year.

The Judah Bible Curriculum is a teacher-directed program. You *will* be using the Bible as your textbook, as the ads say. It requires a scholarly mindset and a lot of commitment on the part of both student and teacher. If you are good at teaching and enjoy coming up with creative ways to present things, and creative assignments for your students, you might very well find this a fascinating program.

LifeWay Christian School Curriculum

Preschool course, $79.95 complete. K-8, student workbook for each grade $4.50, Teacher's Guide for each grade $16.95. Resource packet: K and 1, $9.95 each; grade 2, $7.95. Suedegraphs, $4.95 each. Many other optional resources correlated with the curriculum. Shipping, add 95¢/item, $2.95 maximum.

LifeWay Christian School Curriculum now provides a Home School Manual to accompany their K-8 Christian school Bible program. Good for them! This very handy manual gives teaching philosophy and tips, as well as sections on adapting each grade's curriculum to home schooling.

LifeWay's preschool Bible course, featuring Peter Panda and his pals, comes with a lot of materials. You get a 304-page teacher's guide, Peter Panda puppet, 52 flannelgraph Peter Panda stories, *Fun with Peter Panda* and *Adventures with Peter Panda* storybooks, three suedegraphs (Creation, Noah, birth of Jesus), song cassette, and 26 full-color captioned Bible teaching pictures, all in an attractive, durable, colorful large cardboard box. Peter, a normally naughty little panda, never needs a spanking because his sins always have immediately tangible negative consequences. Some stories are inconsistent: e.g., in one story Lucy Leaf is chosen as the Queen of the Garden, in spite of her lack of outward beauty, because she is so unselfish. A few stories later, we find Lucy unkindly deceiving her friends to make them jump in the water. The Peter Panda stories deal with common themes in secular material for this age: jealousy of little siblings, fighting

among friends, running away from home, and so on. You also, as is common with preschool programs, get Bible stories to read in place of the Bible itself.

In the upper grades, LifeWay has a much stronger Biblical emphasis. The courses originally designed by Dr. Phyllis Roberts are excellent. You get lots of information about Biblical culture, history, laws, and so on, and lots of look-it-up exercises to build budding Bible study skills. Some grade levels, cleaving closely to Dr. Roberts' design, concentrate on teaching objective truths. These are the best. And the third grade course, which focuses on Bible background and research skills, is the best of the best.

At all levels, the Teacher's Guides are excellent. Each lesson is carefully outlined, with Bible basis, Bible truth, lesson aim, suggested and additional memory verses, a lesson-at-a-glance outline that provides a suggested daily schedule, materials needed, and enrichment activities. You also get a Bible story to tell if the lesson contains one, discussion questions, and all sorts of extra information, all neatly presented in easy-to-use form.

The LifeWay catalog tells you just what items you need or might want for teaching each grade. Cost of the essential student workbook and teacher's guide together comes to less than $20 per year—and the teacher's guide is reusable.

Junior high literature electives, teacher supplements, teaching aids, flannelgraphs, story cassettes, children's books, and reference materials round out this curriculum.

NEW**
Rapids Christian Press

Bible Learn and Do lessons: teacher's manuals, $2.95 each. Pupil's book, $1.75 each. Landmarks silhouette picture sets, 8 pictures each, $1 each. Bible Learn and Do series available: Genesis Part 1, Genesis Part 2, Exodus, Numbers, Gospel of Mark, What's the Bible Like?—Old Testament (pupil book only), What's the Bible Like?—New Testament (pupil book only), and The Bible is the Best Book (pupil book only). Things to Learn series: teacher's manuals, $1.75 each. Beginner pupil and primary pupil books, 85¢ each. Landmarks, $1 each. Handwork, 85¢ each. *Isaac* course, $7.75 for all materials except Bible Story-Cards, which are $5.95. Similar pricing on other courses. Shipping extra.

Bible materials author Vivian D. Gunderson, a prolific writer, has three series. *Things to Learn* are for children ages 4 to 8. *Bible Learn and Do* is for ages 8 to 12. And the *Scripture Catechism* (also known as *Bible*

Answer Cards) is a graduated Scripture-memory series that runs from preschool through high school (see above, under "Bible Memory").

Each *Things to Learn* ten-lesson course contains a teacher's manual, separate books for primary pupils and beginner (non-reading) pupils, and a handwork packet. You can purchase each separately. This is really a Bible readiness course. Each primary pupil book contains memory verses (listed in the front), questions and answers (e.g., "What is the first verse in the Bible . . . Who was safe during the flood . . . Tell one fine thing about Isaac"), very simple Bible stories, pictures to color, and a simple pencil-and-paper activity to fill in at the bottom of the lesson. The beginner pupil books have memory verses, questions and answers (by the way, answers are in the back of the book in both versions), and 10 pictures to color, each facing a short text in giant outline letters that can be colored in. Each Handwork Packet has ten simple items to color, cut out, and suchlike. Landmarks are sets of eight silhouette pictures to use for review. The accompanying teacher manual contains lesson aims, words and music for songs correlated with the lesson, Bible stories, teaching tips, and lesson applications.

Things to Learn series available: Genesis, Exodus, Numbers, Joshua, I Samuel/Judges, Matthew, Mark, Luke, John, Acts Part I, Acts Part II.

These manuals are designed for class use, and are not really necessary for home use, unless you yourself are weak in the Scriptures and need a helping hand. You will do fine just reading the appropriate Scripture passage or a Bible story and going through the primary pupil book with your child. Preschool children will enjoy following along in the beginner's book. The handwork is simple, uncluttered, has directions right on the package, and requires no fancy supplies. Unlike most Sunday school crafts, it readily suits itself to supplementing a home lesson.

The *Bible Learn and Do* series, which by the way I have not seen, features, according to the product literature, lessons from consecutive Bible passages. Each book has varied puzzles and other activities. The program design appears similar to the *Things to Learn* series for younger children: teacher's manual, silhouette pictures, Bible questions, and so forth. A new feature here: each Old Testament lesson book concludes with Bible Question tickets to cut out and use as flash cards or as pieces in a Bible memory game.

The entire series is remarkably inexpensive. At the moment it only covers part of the Bible—I hope Vivian (a lady with a truly impressive teaching resumé) will *quickly* finish these series, as her books are the best-suited to home use of any Sunday school program I have seen.

Also available from Rapids Christian Press are some rather unique courses by Carol E. Miller. The *Isaac Bible Course for Children and Adults*, for example, is available either in a sample package with the materials for all ages, or as individual sets of youth/adult material, junior high material (teacher book, junior high workbook, junior workbook), beginner-primary material (teacher book and workbook), nursery workbook, accessory packet needed for beginner/primary/nursery. Available separately for this five-lesson series are Bible Story Cards with 52 oversized stick-figure illustrations in all. Other five-lesson courses written in this format (materials for all ages) are *Under the Sun* and *In the Heavenlies* (a course on Ecclesiastes), *The Good News by Mark, Disciples of Jesus*. Ten-lesson courses for all ages are *The Ten Commandments, Lessons from Leviticus,* and *The Book of Jeremiah*.

Rapids Christian Press also carries the complete "Krata-Kraft" line of inexpensive visualized lessons (see review under Message of Life Publications below), and lots of other straight-arrow fundamentalist teaching materials, all at wonderful prices.

NEW**
Reformed Free Publishing Association
Suffer Little Children: Book 1, $11.95; Books 2 and 3, $8.95 each; workbooks for book 2 and 3, $3.95 each; complete set of all five books, $29.95. *Show Me Thy Ways* (book 4), textbook $15.95, workbook $4.95. Fifth-grade book, price TBA. *Peaceable Fruit*, $9.95. Shipping extra.

Yes, Virginia, there really is a Bible study series named *Suffer Little Children*. Those of us with little Bible study in their backgrounds might naturally wonder at such a title. "Struggle, little children? Hurt, little children? Make your Bible study an ordeal, little children? What in the world does that title mean?" In reality, it is based on Christ's words in the King James Version, "Suffer the little children to come unto me and hinder them not, for of such is the kingdom of Heaven."

As so often happens with denominational literature, we have to get by the title and get by the author's assumption that every reader has been raised from the cradle as a member of the denomination (in this case, Dutch Reformed). Once we do so, we find that Gertrude Hoeksema, the author of this series, has put together a really decent three-year curriculum that goes through the entire Bible, with the exception of some of the minor prophets.

Let me digress here for a minute. I am unusual in that the first thing I do when I get a new Bible curriculum is run to check if it covers the minor prophets: Joel, Amos, Obadiah, Jonah, Micah, Nahum, Habakkuk, Zephaniah, Haggai, Zechariah, and Malachi. Jonah, although he is a minor prophet, is always covered. The others never are. One publisher explained it was because "People aren't interested in these prophets. I'd lose a barrel of money if I put them in my curriculum." Leaving his reprehensible attitude on the side, is he right? Are we really unwilling to share anything but "Bible stories" with our children?

Back to *Suffer Little Children*. Ignore the unfortunate title. Your children will not suffer with this curriculum. This is not your average cut-and-paste-and-color bunch of Bible stories and crafts. Thanks to solid Dutch Calvinism, your children are expected to *learn* something.

You get a large teacher's manual for first grade (Book 1), with the program's philosophy and teaching instructions built right in. Since the children are supposedly not readers at this stage, there is no workbook. For second and third grade, workbooks are supplied.

Once you get by the overwhelmingly intellectual introduction to Book 1, you find a well-thought-out series of lessons that carries you from Creation to Saul's last battle. Each lesson lists a Scripture passage (covered in chronological order), gives a background/introduction for you to read, outlines the lesson, provides low-key lesson applications, gives one or at most two simple suggested activities, and a Bible verse to memorize. To keep memory work simple, the verses are all listed in chart form in the back with a box for you to check off when the verse is mastered. You may photocopy that page for use with all your students.

Books 2 and 3 proceed in the same fashion. Book 2 covers the rest of the Old Testament; Book 3, all of the New.

One remarkable feature of this curriculum is the extensive amount of map work. Outline maps are provided throughout, with instructions on how to fill in the place names, peoples, and other important items, so the student can "make" the map himself. The section of review questions and true/false questions is also very helpful. The whole program is delightfully easy to use: no shades of *Suffer, Old Teacher* here!

The author's father-in-law was a theologian of some renown, and his daughter-in-law appears to be a bit of a theologian herself. Each lesson could be viewed as a child-sized commentary on the Bible passage. It all is very solid—no hype or tinsel, and definitely none of this wretched pandering to self-esteem with which so many newer Bible programs are loaded.

A new fourth-grade book, *Show Me Thy Ways*, follows the same historical divisions as *Suffer Little Children*, but with more historical, cultural, and geographical detail. You'll need the workbook in order to follow all the geographical references in the text. The text has 102 lessons, and the workbook has one lesson for each three text lessons. A fifth grade text also should be out by the time you read this, and maybe even a sixth grade text, both by the same author.

NEW**
Rod & Staff Publishers

Grade 1 material: Reader Unit 1, $4.30. Reader Units 2 & 3 (one book), $7.60. Reader Units 4 & 5, $9.45. Reading Workbook, 5 units in 3 books, around $3 each. Phonics workbook, all 5 units covered in 3 workbooks, around $3 each. Worksheets Unit 1, $2.40. Worksheets Units 2–4 (one set), $5.50. Worksheets Unit 5, $2.55. Teacher's manuals, 3 for the grade, around $9.50 each. Vocabulary word flash cards, 250 cards, $11.10. Phrase flash cards, 223 cards, $13.50. Phonics flash cards, 186 cards, $11.95. Grade 2 materials: Reader Units 1–3 (one book), $9.30. Reader Units 4 & 5, $8.70. Reading workbooks, one for each of 5 units, between $3 and $5 each. Phonics workbooks, 5 units in 3 workbooks, around $3 each. Teachers manual for reading, $8.35. Teacher's manual for phonics, $6.85. Grade 3 materials: Readers (2 books), around $10 each. Reading workbooks, one for each of 5 units, around $3 each. Teacher's manual, $6.95. Grade 4 materials: Reader, $9.50. Reading workbooks, one for each of 3 units, around $3 each. Teacher's manual, $5.20 Journeys of Paul Map, $3.40. U.S. orders, all prices postpaid ($1 small order fee on orders less than $10). Canadian and foreign, add 10% shipping.

Rod and Staff's revised *Bible Nurture and Reader* series is a unique combined Bible study and phonics program. In grades 1 and 2 of this series, an eclectic phonics/sight word approach is integrated with readers featuring simplified Bible stories, while the grades 3 and 4 materials concentrate simply on the Bible and reading skills.

I have written up the phonics aspects of this program in Chapter 8. Now, let's look at its Bible coverage.

In grade 1, the first unit, "We Learn About God," covers the Creation and the Fall. The second unit, "We Learn More About God," reviews Creation and goes on to Cain, Abel, and Noah, with some practical applications. The third unit, "Poems About God," is poems about history from the Creation until after the Flood. The fourth unit is stories about Abraham, Isaac, and Jacob. The fifth unit contains stories about Joseph, the son of Jacob, and stories about Jesus from the Gospel of Matthew.

Unit 1 of grade 2 reviews Genesis. Unit 2 is "Moses Leads God's People," while unit 3 covers "More About Moses," "Balaam," and "Israel in Canaan." Unit 4 is "Stories from Ruth and 1 Samuel." Unit 5 goes through the Gospel of Mark.

Grade 3 leads off with "Stories About David and Solomon," followed by "Stories of the Kings—Rehoboam to Jeroboam" and "Stories of the Last Kings and Prophets." Unit 4, "God's People During and After the Captivity," includes parts of Ezekiel, Daniel, Ezra, Nehemiah, Esther, and Jonah. The fifth unit works through the Gospel of Luke.

Grade 4 has only one reader, with noticeably smaller print than that of the earlier grades. It includes three units: "The Gospel of John," "The Book of Acts," and "Job, Psalms, Proverbs."

Plans are in the works to provide a new chronological Bible curriculum for grades 5–7, which will then fill in any Bible books not covered by the *Bible Nurture and Reader Series*.

As you can see, the books are God-oriented rather than man-oriented. This makes a welcome change from the too-typical "God Love Me . . . I Learn About Me . . . Wonderful Me" emphasis of other publishers. The stories also are very carefully kept close to Scripture, without any flights of fancy.

The teacher's manuals for grade 1 include instructions in both phonics and reading, unit by unit. In grade 2, there are separate manuals for phonics and reading, and each covers the entire year. Teacher's manuals for all grades include answers for the workbook exercises, plus teaching tips, oral drill exercises, and lesson plans.

This is the only complete phonics program whose readers consist of solid Bible stories without added

flights of fancy. Considered simply as Bible story books, the Rod and Staff readers are the best on the market. If you want to integrate your Bible study with language arts, this series certainly deserves a look.

NEW**
The Weaver
Pre-K (includes manipulatives, visuals, manuscript pages, and music tape), $95. Volume 1 K-6, $115. Volume II K-6, $115. Volume III, $115. *Teaching Tips* manual, $30. *Skills Evaluation for the Home School*, $15. Sample 10-day lesson, $4 (Pre-K), $5 (Vol. I). Add 8% postage ($1.25 minimum). Supportive resource materials for each volume available at discounts.

The Weaver is a complete multilevel academic program for K–6, expandable to grades 7–12 with the new 1990 supplements, based on a series of unit studies chronologically going through the first books of the Bible. The preschool-kindergarten manual starts at Genesis 1 and continues through Genesis 10. Volume 1 covers Genesis 11–50, Volume 2 does the same for Exodus and the Books of Law, and Volume III covers Joshua, Judges, and Ruth. All these are cross-referenced to other Bible verses, so you cover more of the Bible than you initially expect.

Volume I includes these topics: City, Architecture, Language, History, Transportation, Famine—Water, Plants, Animals, Stewardship of Money, Solar System and Stars, Covenant/Character Sketch, Family (life cycle and reproduction), Character Sketch of Isaac and Rebekah, Character Sketch of Jacob (focusing on deceit and its consequences), Character Sketch of Joseph (including a study of slavery). By Volume III you are getting into topics like Exploration, Espionage and Communications, How History Is Recorded, Fortifications, Music, Thinking Skills, Time, Conquest of the

Land (correlated with U.S. history 1790-1861), Idolatry, and Judicial Systems. Each volume also covers some aspect of world history.

You can get a complete resource set for each volume. These books are drawn from a wide range of publishers, are multilevel, and are completely evolution-free. A Resource Catalog describing these comes with the free Weaver catalog.

The Weaver also has a very attractive Bible-based unit study program called Interlock for the preschool and kindergarten set. The price includes a copy of Kathy Diehl's *Johnny STILL Can't Read . . . But You Can Teach Him at Home,* a music tape, and a manuscript writing program. You can also get an optional Resource Set that includes a lot of colorful beginning nature books, a Sesame Street paper dolls book with seasonal outfits, and a Bible flannelgraph set.

Much "integrated" material stumbles over its choice of integration point. The Interlock program, based on Genesis 1–10 and with heavy emphasis on the days of creation, is blessed with a natural sequence of items to study: first God as Father, Son, Holy Spirit, and Trinity, then light, air, sun, moon, stars, animals, vegetables, man, and so on. Your preschool or kindergarten child is literally (and systematically) introduced to everything in creation through the course of this program. I was impressed!

For more information, see the complete writeup in the Curriculum Buyer's Guide in Volume 1.

BIBLE EXPERIENCES

This is a whole new category, created especially for the program that follows. It's the difference between *studying* the Bible and *reenacting* it. Sound interesting? Read on!

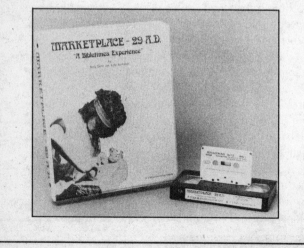

NEW**
Marketplace 29 A.D.

Revised '89 edition manual of *Marketplace 29 A.D.* with binder and cassette, $59.95. Video, $29.95. Advent program, $32.95. Advent audiocassette only, $4. Shipping extra.

Take a trip back in time. The year: 29 A.D. The place: Judea. The setting: A marketplace. The characters: Potters, beggars, stone cutters, shepherds, storytellers, brick makers . . . and even the the obnoxious Roman soldiers and the tax collector.

Designed as the ultimate Vacation Bible School (VBS), Marketplace 29 A.D. is a hands-on event, a "happening" in the jargon of my youth. Your congregation makes simple Judean costumes out of bed sheets, sets up craft booths, scrounges up some tents and a piece of land, and recreates a marketplace as it more-or-less was at the time of Jesus. Children are grouped in tribal "families" under the leadership of an adult. They work as apprentices under a craftsman, learning to make ropes or sandals, for example. They hear Bible stories from the storyteller. They reenact Jewish ceremonies and learn to dance the *hora* and *dabka* and sing "Shalom Chaverim." As much as possible, they get to touch, feel, and smell the past. At odd moments, the Roman soldier or tax collector may barge in, hassling the merchants and teaching the children in the process something of what it felt like to be a Jew under Roman oppression.

For your $54.95, obviously you don't get all the tents, candles, banners, and so on. What you do get is a very complete manual in a nice three-ring binder, plus a cassette with music for the *hora* and *dabka* and the song "Shalom Chaverim." The manual provides patterns for all the costumes and crafts, background information on Bible times, and complete instructions on how to schedule, delegate, and arrange the setup of the entire Marketplace VBS. The manual instructions are very complete, including even ordering information for any hard-to-find items you will need for a given marketplace shop. The Pre-Schooler Supplement gives instructions for setting up a separate pre-school Marketplace for the little kids. The accompanying video, only available separately, is visual snippets from actual Marketplaces put on by different churches. It will give you an idea of what it all looks like, and is mainly useful for selling the idea to your church.

Here's the list of marketplace shops, characters, and events: athletic events of Bible times, beggar, baker, basket weaver, brickmaker, candymaker, carpenter, kite maker (very little historical justification for this shop in Judea), money maker, jeweler, magician (another dubious character—I can't see this guy plying his trade openly in the Judean marketplace), metal worker, musical instrument maker, potter, rope maker, Roman soldier, sandal maker, scribe, seal maker/glyptic artist, shepherd, stonecutter/sculptor, storyteller, synagogue school, tax collector, and weaver. On top of this, there are "tent mothers" who lead their "families" through Jewish rituals like the blessing of the bread and shepherd the children to the various shops and events. The program includes a daily drama in which Jesus visits the marketplace and performs a miracle or tells a parable. The manual has actual scripts for the daily dramas, however you are free to invent your own, or even skip them altogether. Storytelling is from the Old Testament.

Marketplace A.D. 29 is usable by people of all religions and denominations with an interest in biblical Judea. Home schoolers are also potential users of this program. If you are a home schooler with either (a) lots of kids or (b) lots of home-schooling friends, Marketplace A.D. 29 would make a great unit study curriculum, and an even greater co-op project. You don't have to do all the booths and events at once—you could try some new ones each year. Anyone with abundant energy who likes crafts and hands-on learning will enjoy this program.

New from this company, the Marketplace Advent program provides eight scripted Bibletimes experiences based on the Nativity account in the Gospel of Luke. You hear Isaiah propesy, see Gabriel announce the birth of Jesus to Mary, witness Mary's meeting with Elizabeth, encounter a census taker and innkeeper in Bethlehem, visit the Bethlehem marketplace, and with the shepherds have a short worship experience while visiting the stable where Baby Jesus lies. Again, you'll need a large group to put this on. Scripts and costume patterns are provided (Roman soldier, shepherds, women, etc.), as well as fairly detailed information on how to construct the scenes and marketplace booths and occupations to highlight in the booths. The manual even provides sources for buying hard-to-find items like Bibletimes spices and non-tearing paper for making scrolls. All finishes with (I kid you not) a recipe for a roast camel feast. "First, catch your camel." . . . I don't think the author actually expects you to eat a camel (even if stuffed with lamb and chickens), but it's an authentic, if non-kosher, Palestinian recipe.

I'm going to try to talk my church into doing one or both of these programs. It occurs to me that preparing for these events is a far better use of Sunday school crafts time than the usual throwaway projects concocted during that time. (You know: gluing bits of cotton to paper plates in the shape of the little lost lamb, or painting switchplates with verses about Jesus being the light of the world.) I can just see our kids sewing away on their costumes, hammering together booths, and learning about the lives of ancient Roman centuarians and Jewish rabbis. Having the *kids* involved in preparing for the events is not even suggested in the manuals—I give you the suggestion freely, and can't wait for us to get started.

CHAPTER THIRTEEN

BIBLE EXTRAS

The materials in this chapter are not primary teaching material, but Bible activities . . . flannelgraphs . . . visuals . . . Bible games . . . and devotional helps.

VISUALIZED BIBLE LESSONS

BCM Publications (a ministry of BCM International, Inc.)
Search magazine, $4/year for U.S.A. and foreign single subscription. $3/year each for U.S.A. and foreign bulk subscriptions—10 or more subscriptions to the same address.

Bible-centered lesson materials for all ages, preschool through adult. For the mentally impaired, BCM publishes *Steps of Faith for Special Children*. Their *Tiny Steps of Faith* materials are for preschoolers. Included in each kit are plastic figures to use as visuals, plus a teacher's text and other teaching aids. For ages 8 to 14, there is *Footsteps of Faith* (available also in French and Spanish), a chronological three-year Bible program that covers the whole Bible from Genesis to Revelation. For teens through adults, *Steps to Maturity* is a three-volume teaching series accompanied by a student manual. All materials are ungraded and undated. Other materials available: Five-Day Bible Club kits, missionary lessons, Christian life lessons, Come Alive Series (includes stories), visualized songs, tracts, backgrounds, and other resources for teaching children.

BCM's *Search* magazine for kids includes a Bible contest with prizes, action stories, a puzzle page, fun food recipes, and subscriber feedback. The few pages are nicely done, and considering the price it's worth it.

BCM International has also developed a plan whereby you can conduct a Bible Club from your own home using Bible correspondence courses. Mailbox Bible Club is for all ages, kindergarten through adult. Club leaders send Bible lessons through the mail. Contact BCM for more information.

Betty Lukens
Large Bible Story Set, $129.95. Large Bible File System, $54.95. Large Mounted Scenes, $27.95 each. Large backgrounds (fit on 32 x 48" board), between $11.95 and $15.95 each. Small Bible Story Set, $59.95. Small Bible File System, $24.95. Small Mounted Scenes, $12.95 each. Small backgrounds (fit on 16 x 24" board), between $4.25 and $6.95 each. Shipping extra.

Let me rave for a bit about the most gorgeous set of Bible-teaching visuals I have ever seen. Not flocked pictures, but actual air-brushed felt! *Through the Bible in Felt* comes in two sizes: the expensive large size (12-inch figures) and the affordable regular size (6½-inch figures). Background scenes of the same superb quality are also available. A Teacher's Manual to help you present the Bible in a three-year sequence (once a week) is also included. The manual could be more helpful; it merely shows two felt scenes, lists the items needed, gives the Scripture, and leaves you to figure out how to tell it.

Although some of the later history of Israel and Judah is not covered in the manual, there are more than enough figures to tell any story you choose.

If you order all the backgrounds for the small set, and the indispensable storage case (which organizes the whole kit and caboodle onto outlined velour sheets), you'll spend just over $100. If you include the mounted boards, which make teaching the lessons a lot easier, since you can switch back and forth between two scenes without changing backgrounds, it comes to about $130 retail. (If you don't get the mounted scenes, you will have to mount at least one scene yourself—i.e., cut out a large piece of masonite or extra-heavy cardboard and attach the scene, in order to have a firm surface on which to place the felts.) That sounds like a lot, but what you're getting is a lifetime invest-

ment in Bible teaching that you can use even with the smallest children in your family, and perhaps pass on to your grandchildren. The price is really low for all you are getting—because *you* are going to cut the figures out! I look upon this as a fun family project, and it was for us, with even our five-year-old cutting out some "easy" pieces.

A number of home school suppliers sell the individual Betty Lukens pieces: Timberdoodle, Sycamore Tree, etc. Of these, at this moment of writing Timberdoodle has the best discounts. Or if you want an entire set of all the backgrounds, figures, and storage case, Home Life has the best prices: $99 for the family set or $199 for the large set (add 10% shipping for each), including two mounted background scenes. These are better than the prices you'd get buying directly from Betty Lukens. Home Life is the only supplier I know of to offer mounted backgrounds, but we only offer complete sets. Otherwise, if all you want is the figures and/or filing system, Timberdoodle is your best bet.

Bible Visuals, Inc.
Visualized Bible volumes, $4.95 each. Available for less in sets. 29 for Old Testament so far, 46 for New Testament. *Mini Visualized Bible* volumes, 75¢ each. Twenty-nine New Testament titles, twelve Old Testament. Grades 1–6.

Bible Visuals, a supplier of children's church and child evangelism materials, celebrated its 31st anniversary in 1990. For the home, BV's *Visualized Bible* series is one of the simplest to use. Each volume is a large 10 x 14" book with teaching hints on the inside covers and lesson plans in the middle. Each book contains four lessons. The rest of the book is given over to sixteen large illustrations of the lessons. No flocked paper to cut out, no gimmicks. I have not seen the whole series, but the art in the one sample volume I did see was just right—not too much detail, but not oversimplified either. And what a relief to see drawings of Jesus that makes him look *Jewish* and *strong* instead of Aryan and weak!

Bible Visuals also carries visualized missionary stories, visualized songs, mini-Bible stories, five- and ten-day packets, and Spanish materials, plus other supporting items. The minibooks are exceedingly inexpensive and contain the same illustrations as the large volumes, but without lesson text.

Bible Visuals takes care to assure us that they teach "*Bible* doctrine (not *church* doctrine)." The one volume I saw was remarkably free of flights of fancy and irrelevant sermonizing.

Child Evangelism Fellowship

Teach Me Now, 4 volumes, $24.99 each. Biblegrams, Missiongrams, $5–$10 range. *Salvation Songs*, $2.99/volume. Videos, $14.95 each. Five-part video courses, $56 each course.

Child Evangelism Fellowship has been around for a good long time. As the name indicates, CEF focuses on child evangelism, and produces many highly visual materials for the same.

CEF's visuals are mostly colored, flocked pictures that you cut out, and large flash cards (usually spirally bound into a book with the teaching text). All art is of acceptable, professional quality. Their selection is larger than BCM's, and includes more individual units (BCM materials are mostly in course form).

Of special interest: *Teach Me Now* preschool lessons come with musical cassette, songbook, games, finger plays, visuals—both flocked and unflocked— and complete instructions. Personally, I would only use the instructions as suggestions. The series comes in four volumes. If you can only get one, make it Volume 1, as this presents God as Creator, tells about the Fall, introduces Jesus, and presents the gospel.

Biblegrams and *Missiongrams* each contain five or six lessons on their respective subjects. *Growgrams* are single lessons with activities on Christian growth. *Salvation Songs* is four volumes of the best. Plus videos, visualized Bible songs and verses, and more!

Good News Clubs™ and 5-Day Clubs™ are other CEF projects, in case you are looking for a neighborhood evangelism ministry that you and your children can share together. CEF has materials for these clubs and can provide training for those who would like to start such a club. CEF missionaries give seminars and workshops on how to evangelize and disciple children. (Some are now available on video.) We attended one of those in our area and found it to be an excellent presentation.

Global Visuals

Visualized Christian materials, $3.50–$8.70 each. Quantity discounts available.

Cute little visualized stories and visualized songs. Some are illustrations of Bible verses, others are doctrinal lessons in fictional story form. Get a feel for Global's offerings from these catalog descriptions, chosen at random from among hundreds:

> SG107-PRIZE CAKE
> Forgiving was hard for Ruby, especially since Warren had cut the cake she had ready to enter in the baking contest!

> SG108-WHICH ONE ARE YOU?
> The proud peacock, strutting giraffe, and lowly camel help us learn a lesson in humbling ourselves.

Global's artwork is professional and the storyline sounds like it has kid appeal in a corny, innocent sort of way.

Janzen Specialties

Object lessons and games, 30¢ each. Send SASE for brochure.

Unlike BCM, Child Evangelism Fellowship doesn't produce their own flannel backgrounds for Bible stories. The Janzens sell Smith Backgrounds, which are uncolored, functional backgrounds used by CEF people (also popular with Sunday school teachers, and Awanas). Each basic background has an outline drawing of a Bible on it to show that the story illustrated comes from the Bible. Colors are available by special request. Inexpensive, but more useful for Sunday school work than at home.

Janzen also now carries Edith Mackay Tabernacle Backgrounds.

Their 30¢ object lessons and games are popular, inexpensive teaching aids that work well in home schools.

Message of Life Publications

Each "Krata-Kraft" lesson costs around $2. The good folks at Message of Life offer a 25 percent discount for Christian schools (including home schools) when you prepay and tell them you're a school. Shipping 15%. All ages.

"Krata-Kraft" Bible lessons are printed in bright colors on durable stock, either in book form or on ovals and circles for use on flannelgraph boards. Some have pictures that pop off for an element of surprise. Pictures are prepunched, but you have to peel off and adhere felt circles on the backs (these come with the package). Simple and straightforward, not tedious or "talky." Gospel emphasis throughout.

Now available: 31 English Bible lessons, 28 Spanish lessons. Also in Spanish: 12 five-day DVBS courses (songs, maps, workbooks, etc.). Plus nine 15-week illustrated Bible studies with workbooks and take-home papers.

Here are some titles in the "Krata-Kraft" lineup:

- *The Gospel in a Nutshell,* an 18-inch tagboard nutshell with the nine parts of John 3:16, each with words and a colored picture.

- *The Lamb of God.* Illustrates the meaning of the burnt offering in the O.T., plus pictures the transfer of Christ's righteousness to all who trust in Him.

- *Five Little Men.* Ho, So, No, Go, and Lo tell the message from Isaiah 55:1, John 3:16, Romans 8:1, Mark 16:15, and Matthew 28:20. Clever!

- *Esther,* a spiral-bound story with elements of surprise. $2.50.

- *Halloween,* a strong visual contrast between the black cats, ghosts, and other underworld characters and the angels.

These are the most economical visual lessons around.

Standard Publishing

This catalog is a "must" for anyone interested in low-cost, high-interest Bible visuals and activities for children.

Standard's Bible visuals come in several sizes. Large size *Pict-O-Graphs* have eight to eleven stories, forty or more pre-cut figures (just punch out to use) up to 11 inches tall. Artwork is superior and colorful. More than 50 Bible stories are covered in these packs. Also available are patterns for making large-size background objects, supplementary objects (altars, wineskins, etc). Standard also has many how-to books for teachers.

Standard's *Visual Talks* series includes many object talks centering around such items as a football, salt, a telephone, and other common household items. They're ridiculously inexpensive.

We have used a number of Standard products, and are well-pleased with the quality. You get more for your money here than anywhere else.

BIBLE GAMES AND PUZZLES

UPDATED**
Baker Book House

Easy-to-Use Bible Activity Sheets, $7.95. *101 Bible Activity Sheets, Bible Activity Sheets for Special Days,* $8.95 each.

Baker Book House's retail catalog division has a nice large catalog brimful of helpful items for Christians of all ages. Coloring books, videos, books, and Bible accessories are just a few of the items that decorate the pages of the catalog. Plus the catalog also includes Bibles for all ages (including large print), Bible story books, fiction, youth books, and children's books such as the best-selling *Precious Moments Stories from the Bible, Precious Moments Bedtime Stories,* and *Precious Moments Through the Year Stories.*

Another example of Baker's own books for kids is *Easy-to-Use Bible Activity Sheets.* The four sections of this book teach children about the Old and New Testament as they search for words, unscramble letters, and find their way through mazes. Every kid in the family can find something to do, unlike other activity books designed for a narrow range of ages. Walter Kerr's illustrations are charmingly innocent. New in this series: *Easy -to-Use Bible Activity Sheets* and *Bible Activity Sheets for Special Days. Easy-to-Use Bible Activity Sheets* is divided into Old Testament, New Testament, and Miscellaneous (fruits of the Spirit, Bible birds, etc.). Pages 97–122 has A-Z Bible memory verses. *Bible Activities for Special Days* has activities for Valentine's Day, Easter, Bible Sunday, Ascension Day, Pentecost, Trinity Sunday, Mother's Day, Father's Day, Reformation Day, Thanksgiving Day, Advent, and oodles of sheets for Christmas. Each special day has at least two or three activity sheets, and most have more. Each activity sheet in all three books is designed to teach you something about the activity topic. For example, sheet 47 in the *Special Days* book is a set of drawings made up of letters. Unscramble the letters in each drawing to find the name of something to be thankful for. (The topic is Thanksgiving Day.)

Rainfall Inc.
Bible Challenge, $19.99

Bible Challenge is the best Bible board game I've seen. The concept is simple and effective; the game is elegant. Each player tries to collect seven different-colored rings, each representing a different question category, while moving around a board whose squares represent books of the Bible. The game includes 2,100 well-chosen questions on 300 cards.

All members of the family can play the Family Edition. Our small fry can answer some of the questions, but even Bill gets stumped occasionally—so adults won't necessarily always win.

You can register your game and thus replace any lost or broken pieces. It comes in a beautiful, durable box that can be stored like a book on a shelf. Every-

thing about this game is professional and high quality. It's the nicest way I've seen of testing our children on their Bible knowledge, and giving them the incentive to gain more.

NEW**
Shining Star Publications
Shining Star magazine, one year (4 issues), $16.95. Sample copy $4. Bible Baffler series, 10 books, $5.95 each. Bible Story Hidden Pictures series, $5.95 each.

Shining Star is a Christian education magazine loaded with 80 pages of reproducible puzzles, games, and work sheets, plus teacher tips, family worship suggestions, stories, and a three-month Activity Calendar. *Shining Star* work sheets are divided into units including New Testament Heroes, Christian Values, and Memory Verses. Mainstream evangelical flavor (self-esteem, some trivializing, etc.). Answer key in the back.

The Shining Star Publications catalog includes "over 100 reproducible resource books for teaching Christian principles." Some of these are OK, such as the Bible Baffler series. These reproducible books test kids on their Bible knowledge in various creative ways, such as crosswords, rebus puzzles, codes, and trivia. Another OK set is their Bible Story Hidden Pictures series for ages 5–11. These include Bible stories on the left page and hidden-pictures illustrations on the right. Others are busywork designed to fill up Sunday school and Christian school hours that will take too much of a parent's time at home. This is true of most of their activity books. The activities in these books are fun for kids, but time-consuming and not all that educational for the time you have to put into each one. You'll burn out pretty fast if you try to fit all the activities in even one of these activity books into your home-school program. Stick with the workbooks designed for kids to do on their own.

Standard Publishing

Besides their Bible visuals and object lessons (mentioned above), Standard also has puppet packs; quiz books; game books; Bible study charts (fantastic for kid's room), maps and charts; craft ideas; seals and stickers (some with a Christian message); complete Bible activity programs; classroom Bible activity books; teacher training resources; songbooks; and much more!

NEW★★
Timberdoodle

Bible Lands Puzzles, $75/set of four. Add 10% shipping ($4 minimum, $15 maximum).

The good folks at Timberdoodle, bless their hearts, are now distributors of Pacific Puzzle Company's Bible Land Puzzles. They've dropped the price down from its original $96, too! These heirloom quality puzzles are made of the highest quality imported birch plywood, overlaid with full-color maps like you find in the back of your Bible. The set of these 11 x 14" puzzles includes:

• Early Bible Times Puzzle (Middle Eastern kingdoms)

• Old Testament Palestine Puzzle

• New Testament Palestine Puzzle

• Roman Empire Puzzle (this shows Paul's journeys).

These are great in the home, as a wonderful Sunday activity for energetic kids. Or how about a set for your church's Sunday school?

EASY DEVOTIONAL MATERIAL FOR KIDS

NEW★★
Bible Talk Times

$7.50/four issues. All subscriptions begin with Genesis. *Proverbs for Children,* $6.95 plus $1.50 shipping.

Bible Talk Times is "an idea-packed guide to high-interest devotionals." Each 20-page tabloid-sized paper includes thirteen weeks' worth of thru-the-Bible devotional talks . . . follow up puzzles, games and crafts . . . a kid's-eye view of Bible times . . . and teaching tips for classroom teachers and parents. The format includes many short articles, quizzes, activities, puzzles, and illustrations. Strong conservative emphasis. Ages 5-12.

Proverbs for Children presents 26 Biblical proverbs in the categories of learning about God, listening to God, growing in God's way, and getting along with others in God's way. Each two-page section starts with the proverb, definitions of important words in the proverb, and explanation of the proverb, an illustration, and a few simple questions related to the proverb. On the next page is a prayer, space for the child to write a paraphrase of the proverb in his own words, and an art activity. An "Activities" appendix with additional games and study activities is included, along with a section on bulletin boards and door banners. Ages 4-9.

NEW★★
Christian Life Workshops

Listen, Color, and Learn, $5.95 each coloring book. Add 10% shipping ($2 minimum, $5 maximum).

Coloring books for family devotions? Now you've heard everything! These reproducible books are meant to help active little kids keep their hands from being bored and their minds on the Bible passage while it's being read. The complete series will illustrate all the Psalms.

Here's how it works: You get the book and photocopy enough copies of each page for all your coloring-age kiddies. (Or you just buy extra copies of the book, which I personally recommend.) You get each kid a set of crayons. You read the excellent introduction with suggestions for successful family devotions, written by Gregg Harris. You then read a Psalm and discuss it while your children color. For older children there's a Bible verse word puzzle at the bottom of each page—

either fill in the blanks, rearrange the words, or unscramble the letters. Finally, finish with prayer.

Each volume covers 30 Psalms. Each picture illustrates the Psalm's message very well, helping your children focus on the main point of the Psalm. Modern people are shown in situations your child can relate to.

As with all CLW products, these books are beautifully produced, with durable illustrated covers and quality paper. And Gregg Harris's family devotion tips are alone worth the price of the book!

NEW**
Harvest House Publishers
Seekers in Sneakers, 3 volumes, $5.95 each.

Sometimes we teach our kids. Other times we just give them something fun to fool with and let them alone. Here's some fun fluff for those fooling-around times for kids in grades 2–5: *Seekers in Sneakers* from Harvest House Publishers.

Subtitled "A Creative Devotional for Young People," *Seekers* follows nerdish Templeton and his dog, Furlock, as they romp through an assortment of guessing games, word searches, crossword puzzles, creative writing exercises, and all the other time-fillers so beloved of classroom teachers. The activities in these books, however, are actually doable! At the rate of one activity a day, each book will last you four weeks.

This program includes a minimal amount of Bible memory (four cards in the back of each book), with of course a sprinkling of other verses throughout the book. Templeton has silly conversations with his friends about trying to drive to Heaven in a Ferrari (you can't) or waiting at the mailbox to get a letter from God (Templeton's Sunday school teacher really meant he should read the Bible).

Topics covered in volume 1 of this series: Searching God's Treasure Book, Exploring God's Handiwork, Entering God's Kingdom, Keeping in Step (first steps of Christian growth), Exercising Right Attitudes (becoming like Jesus), Realizing God's Majesty (the attributes of God), Springing into Action (the daily walk with God). Volume 2, *Learning to Follow Jesus,* presents the people and places of the Bible. Volume 3, *Becoming Kingdom Kids,* introduces character lessons for virtues such as grace, forgiveness, prayer, working cheerfully, making right choices, telling the truth, and fleeing temptation.

Give Harvest House credit for tackling some "unfluffy" subjects like the attributes of God and how to be holy in a temptation-filled world. Unlike some oth-

er "fun-filled" devotionals I have seen, the teaching itself never gets silly, even if some lesson introductions are silly! Great graphics, wonderful layout, easy and clever activities, and (believe it or not) a more realistic attitude about sin and salvation than other programs I have seen.

NEW**
Lynn's Bookshelf
A Coloring Book of Bible Proverbs, $2.50.

The Coloring Book of Bible Proverbs is just that—32 pages of adequate art to color, each illustrating a particular proverb listed at the bottom.

UNUSUAL BIBLE MUSIC RESOURCES

NEW**
JTG of Nashville
Each Play a Tune book, $14.95–$17.95. Add $2.50 shipping.

JTG's Play a Tune books are spiral-bound books with color-coded electronic mini-keyboards attached. Kids can play the songs themselves, following the color-coded notes written in simplified musical notation. You have to know how long each note should be held, since all notes are simply portrayed as colored circles with numbers inside them. Unlike other electronic keyboard books, these have slightly raised keys "for a more realistic effect." I couldn't say this made a great difference to me, but I did notice that the batteries lasted a lot longer than in another model I tried, and that the whole package held together very well in spite of rough handling by the littlest children in our family.

The series includes a really great cross-section of our cultural heritage, including American Songs (famous folk tunes like "This Land is Your Land"), Jewish Songs (I don't know about you, but I love Jewish music), Bible Songs, Christmas Songs, Children's Songs, More Children's Songs, All-Time Disney Classics, and even (coming out just after I write this) The Berenstain Family Favorites, starring your old pals, the Berenstain

Bears. Each song page is faced with a full-color illustration, and notes are provided where helpful.

The Bible Songs Play a Tune book includes *Praise Him, Praise Him; The B-I-B-L-E; God Is So Good; Kum Ba Yah; Jesus Loves Me; Rise and Shine (Arky, Arky); This Little Light of Mine; Jesus in the Morning; Zacchaeus; Oh, How I Love Jesus; Do, Lord;* and *All Night, All Day.* And now I can finally stop chasing the kids around begging them to leave it near my desk long enough for me to write it up!

NEW**
Judy Rogers
Why Can't I See God? cassette, *Go to the Ant* cassette, $8 each. Music track without words for *Go to the Ant,* $10. Add $1.50 shipping for each order.

Judy Rogers has done the impossible. She put the Westminster Children's Catechism and Shorter Catechism to music and it is *good.* What you get are 20 songs that cover the great themes of Scripture: Creation, the nature of God, the Fall, sin, salvation, and the Christian life. Selections include "How Can I Glorify God?," "God Is a Spirit," "The Lord Our God Is One," "Jesus Our Prophet, Priest, and King," "The Ten Commandments Song," "What Is a Sacrament," and "The Lord's Prayer." Quality music that is respectful of children, professionally performed and recorded, and not the least cutesy.

Since the time I heard her first tape, Judy has produced several more. Of these, the most useful for young kids is *Go to the Ant,* a collection of songs based on teachings from the book of Proverbs. Topics include controlling your tongue, laziness, indifference towards learning, pouting and crying, and other common childhood sins. Lively lyrics, no screamin' demon tunes.

Reformed Presbyterian Board of Publications
Book of Psalms for Singing. Hardbound $12.95 plus $2 shipping. Bulk prices available.

The Book of Psalms for Singing is a wonderful tool for reviving godly worship in your home. The Bible says we should sing "psalms, hymns, and spiritual songs" (Colossians 3:16). Unhappily, so much time has been spent justifying the use of hymns *in addition* to psalms that nowadays most churches sing hymns *instead* of psalms! The few psalms in the modern hymnbook by no means reflect the Psalms' actual richness. What are we missing? Psalms for times of despair. Psalms for the repentant sinner. Psalms that promise victory in the battle with God's enemies. Psalms about the Messiah. Psalms on every topic of the *real* spiritual life, not the trimmed-down, always-grinning version.

Many of the tunes are familiar to hymn-singers, and most of those that aren't are easy to learn. For the convenience of those who don't know how to read music, the RP Board of Publications also offers cassettes of some of the most popular Psalms.

Can little kids learn to sing and enjoy Psalms? Start 'em out with Psalm 127 and see what happens!

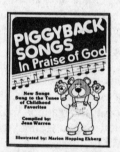

Warren Publishing House, Inc./Totline Books
Piggyback Songs, Piggyback Songs for Infants and Toddlers, Piggyback Songs in Praise of God, $6.95 each. *More Piggyback Songs, Piggyback Songs in Praise of Jesus, Holiday Piggyback Songs,* $7.95 each. *Animal Piggyback Songs,* $8.95 each. Add $3 shipping.

Music for every child. No notes to read, no tunes to forget. What you get are new songs to sing to familiar old tunes. Each song has chord names above it (F, C, C7, and so on), so you can play along with an autoharp, guitar, or other chorded instrument. All books are a large 8½ x 11 inches and contain between 64 and 96 pages.

BIBLE VIDEO

I had absolutely nothing good to say about kiddie Bible videos in the last edition. Still don't about most of them. Smarmy. Inaccurate. Stupid. Here's an exception.

NEW★★
Vision Video
Children's Heroes of the Bible, $99.95/13-video set. Add $5 shipping.

First, this is an incredible value. Who has ever heard of *thirteen* videos for $99.95? Second, it's way more accurate than any other children's Bible video I've seen. No mutant teenage 20th-century kids plopped into the plot. No cartoon critters, no fictitious Israelite children, no smarmy preachments about self-esteem. Instead you get animated, realistic cartoons of the actual Bible stories.

Of course, with a price like this, something's gotta give. This is not Disney-quality animation. However, it will still hold a child's interest—or the interest of a group of children in a church or other group setting.

The series covers the stories of Joseph, Elijah, Moses, David, Jeremiah, Esther, Jesus, and the acts of the apostles. Created by a Lutheran church body, it very seldom lapses from the straight scriptural text. The clothing, terrain, and so on is all quite accurate. An excellent Sunday school purchase, and even affordable for support groups or well-off families.

CHAPTER FOURTEEN

CHARACTER EDUCATION

There are two ways of representing and recommending true religion and virtue to the world; the one, by doctrine and precept; the other, instance and example.
                    —Jonathan Edwards

True character means never having to say you're sorry—and if you *do* have to say you're sorry, saying it. It means doing what's right when it hurts, even when Mom and Dad aren't watching and nobody's going to pat you on the back for it. It means keeping your promises, telling the truth, and looking out for other people, not just for Number One.

Are human beings born with this kind of character? That's an interesting question. No question about it, some of us naturally find it easier to be truthful. Others, who struggle against a constant temptation to embellish the truth, may have a natural extra dose of courage, or kindness, or something. The bottom line is that all of us need help, and some of us need a *lot* of help!

So how can we help our children develop good character? First, we have to quit expecting the schools to do this for us. Until the Republican and Democratic parties vanish from the face of the earth, never to be replaced by other political factions, everything that happens in school will continue to be hostage to partisan politics. Character education is no exception. Since the two parties that between them run our country can't agree on basic moral issues (we'll know we're in *real* trouble when they start agreeing!), character education in the schools will continue to be a hodgepodge of:

- "What do *you* want to do, Johnny? Have you clarified your own personal values for yourself?"

- "Obey the teacher. Why? Because she says so!"

- "If it feels right, it must be right."

- "Just say no."

- "Smart kids don't do drugs."

See what's missing in this list? It's three little letters that have been banned from all public school classrooms since the fifties. Those letters are G-O-D.

Every "character-building" program in the schools can only appeal to two authorities: *force* (your teacher can *make* you do things, the judge can *make* you go to reform school) and *self* (do it to be successful, because you want to, because you're so special, etc.). True character, though, is based on doing what is *right,* even *in the face of* external force and your own less-worthy desires..

We already have a nice short list of righteous character traits supplied to us in the Ten Commandments and the Golden Rule. "Thou shalt not steal. . . . Thou shalt not murder. . . . Thou shalt not commit adultery.

. . . Thou shalt not bear false testimony against thy neighbor. . . . Thou shalt not covet anything that is thy neighbor's. . . . Honor thy father and mother." Almost everyone can see the sense in these. The first three commandments, to have no gods before God, to honor His name, and to keep the Sabbath, might only make sense to Bible believers, but that doesn't make the other seven irrelevant. Try running a society without them, as we have been doing for about forty years now, and you'll see the results. Try keeping the last seven, though, and the first three might suddenly start making a lot more sense!

GOD'S LAWS AND EARTH'S HEROES

Most Americans still profess some kind of belief in God. It's not too late to revive character education that passes down His laws *as* laws! Johnny should not steal because God says, "Thou shalt not steal." He should learn to share because Jesus said, "Do unto others as you would have them do unto you." As long as the child understands that his parents are also under God's laws and are not merely using the Bible to tyrannize him, he will readily accept these rules.

Once you have given your child a framework of *where* the rules of life come from and *why* they should be followed, the next step is showing him *how* to do this and making sure he does it. Teaching a child *what* he should do is not the same thing as training him to do it. The latter involves giving him opportunities to build his character and following up those opportunities with meaningful feedback that lets him know how well he did. That's why our grandparents used to call character education "child training."

One real help in this area is providing good role models— "heroes"—for your child to follow. You have to be careful about this, though. People who don't believe in God have always followed human "gods" (or as we call them today, "stars"), accepting everything their idol does as right. This is just as true today as it was 3,000 years ago. Curriculum publishers are well aware of this. So today, entertainment and sports stars are fre-

quently showcased in school curriculum just like they are in regular commercials. The product being sold is "what the grownups want you to learn in school," and the sellers hope to persuade kids to buy it because their favorite stars endorse it or appear in it.

The problem with the role-model approach is not only that the lifestyle of many modern stars isn't worth copying. Hero worship can be overdone even when you've found a *real* hero. George Washington and Davy Crockett weren't perfect either (although I would spot them quite a few points against Madonna and Prince!). The danger here is that, "Do it because your hero does or endorses it," will take the place of, "Do it because it's *right*." The hero's conduct is not the rule for your child's life, just (ideally) a pretty good example of how a human being can follow God's rules. Grownups and children alike can admire our heroes' character and achievements, but we need to also be alert to their flaws.

There is, of course, more to character building than laying down rules and providing role models. We lack space here to get into the whole question of child-training and how to raise happy, self-disciplined children. I commend to your attention the Charlotte Mason Home Education series from Tyndale House Publishers and H. Clay Trumbull's *Hints on Child Training* from Wolgemuth & Hyatt Publishers (both written over 100 years ago and now available through your Christian bookstore) for good answers to these questions.

CURRICULUM BASED ON CHARACTER TRAITS

The following two character-based curricula present academic subjects in a different way—as they relate to developing a child's character. This approach, odd as it may seem at first, has the advantage of immediately relating all learned material to the child—and not to the child as he is (the fatal mistake of typical affective training), but the child as he can and should be. For detailed information about these and other home education programs, see Volume 1.

Advanced Training Institute of America

Bill Gothard's Advanced Training Institute curriculum is based on character traits and strongly emphasizes the father's leadership role in home education. A pilot program available only to alumni of Bill Gothard's Advanced Basic Education Seminar, the ATIA curriculum is highly praised by its users.

Konos Character Curriculum

Integrated academic curriculum in three volumes that covers all subjects for K-6 except phonics, upper level language arts, and math and that stresses Christian character development. Each volume good for one or two years of study for an entire family. Units based on character themes (example: Attentiveness).

CHARACTER-BUILDING CHILDREN'S MAGAZINES

One reason you never see my books advertised in those newsletters put out by huge pro-family organizations is that, as much as I admire the work some of these groups are doing, I just can't bring myself to endorse their kiddie materials. Typically, when such a group wants to put out a children's magazine, they go straight to Madison Avenue for the user interface. We're talking sassy styling, ultra-fashionable models, "hip" text, the whole bag. Then they expect the kids to pick up from this that they're supposed to be chaste, honest, humble, hard-working, and non-materialistic? Get real!

My feeling is that if you have to search for a saved biker or rock musician to be your kids' role model, and if every article has to be aimed at mallflowers, you've already lost it. So now you know where I'm coming from—Leave it to Beaverland, right? Well, pretty close. I just happen to think that character building means holding up ideals and leaders somewhat *different* from what the MTV Generation might pick "on their own," that is, different from the ones the folks with big bucks are selling to them.

Speaking of big bucks—if you want one simple reason for why the kids of today exhibit so many negative character traits, from dress faddishness right up to drug abuse, the answer is just these five letters: M-O-N-E-Y. Kids today are a $13 *billion* dollar market, a fact which has not escaped the *Advertising Age* crowd. Since kids are generally more gullible than adults, the more the "kid market" can be segregated from the "adult market," i.e. from the influence of Mom and Dad, the better for the people who want to sell them useless, high-status junk. Conversely, if every kid in the country has his allowance suddenly cut to zero, and all the advertisers knew about it, much of the social pressure on kids would vanish overnight.

I'm all for reduced social pressure. So are the following excellent magazines for children.

UPDATED**
"Children's Bible Hour"

News & Notes, CBH's bimonthly magazine, features poems, a story, a song, and letters from listeners. *Search the Scriptures* is CBH's correspondence course of 10 lessons from the New Testament. *Grow, Grow, Grow* is a new 13-lesson course designed as a follow-up to *Search the Scriptures*. *Keys For Kids*, their family devotional booklet, is free, but you'll send $1 to pay for it if you're nice folks! *Keys* contains stories and Bible activities for kids. Old-timey tone, modern settings. Full catalog available upon request.

God's World Publications

God's Big World (K), *Sharing God's World* (grade 1), *Exploring God's World* (grades 2-3), *It's God's World* (grades 4-6), *God's World Today* (junior high), $15.95 single edition, or $9.95 each for any two editions. Higher quantity discounts available. *World* (senior high and adult), $27.95, *World* student rate (28 issues), $16.95. Bulk orders receive discount. Each paper 28 issues, September to May, except *World* (40 issues).

Q: What's black and white and read all over?
A: *God's World* weekly newspapers for Christian
   schools!

What an intriguing idea—the news for kids from a Christian viewpoint! GWP has papers for all different reading levels from kindergarten to adult. The papers for children are carefully matched to their interests and abilities. Following a newspaper format, you get feature stories, reports on hot news items, editorials, cartoons, and letters to the editor. Papers for the kindergarten through junior high set also include activities for kids. A teacher's guide is included with each edition. No fuzzy-wuzzy copouts here either; the editors of the children's editions know what the Bible says and aren't ashamed of it. The adult magazine tries to be more intellectual, and thus sometimes sounds a more uncertain trumpet (especially in the Arts section).

Young Companion
$6/year (11 issues). Ages 9–18.

Our home school group took a field trip to Amish country not long ago. While we were there visiting the harness shop, buying cheese, and so on, I ran across a copy of this magazine for Amish young people. The publishers are anxious to preserve virtue in their community, and concerned about such things as young Amish marrying "outside" or picking up worldly habits like playing pool. Ah, lost innocence! It looked charming and certainly represents a different point of view than "Dallas".

BOOKS AND COURSES

Character-training material from a lecture or decision-making approach—that's what you'll find in this section. These materials are less emotive and more intellectual, but not necessarily less valuable, than the story-based materials in the next section. Scripture shows

God using both methods: spelling out what is right or wrong with the Ten Commandments and other parts of the Law, and involving us in true stories that show the consequences of good or bad behavior.

NEW✶✶
Bluestocking Press
The Impossible Child, $10.95 plus $2 shipping. Age: adult reader. Applies to: children of all ages.

"There is a subset of children who appear to learn well and easily on one day, but not on another. They seem unable to function consistently well in school. They often act appropriately but suddenly, for no apparent reason, their behavior can exasperate the most patient teacher or parent. Other children appear unable to learn or behave most of the time. Some are too active; others are too tired. . . . Many have recurrent headaches, leg aches, or digestive complaints."

Any of this sound familiar? Then *The Impossible Child* might hold some answers for you. The purpose of this book is to show you how to detect if your youngster is experiencing an unsuspected allergic reaction, and what to do if he or she is. The book does not lay the blame for all bad behavior at the feet of allergies. It does, however, point out that some kids get high on some foods, or bummed out by molds and pollens, and that we all have a much harder time functioning properly under such circumstances.

This is not a superficial book, in spite of its easy-reading style. You are given specific facial or body clues to tip you off to a possible allergic reaction—e.g., red earlobes. The book also includes numerous before-and-after examples of children's work and considerable detail about specific allergies and how to spot and treat them.

Is behavior modification therapy the solution to non-allergy-caused behavior problems? Author Doris Rapp says yes. I say no. This fairly major disagreement aside, I think this is a good book. We do owe it to our kids to find out if they suffer when exposed to chemicals, pollen, pets, or dairy products. However, in no way can the vast increase in kids' rotten behavior today be blamed on allergies. Allergies may indeed provide extra pressure, but even a splitting migraine does not have the power to force any of us to bite, spit, and swear unless we let it. All this granted, before you give up on a child who is not responding normally to character training, it's worthwhile checking out whether he is suffering extra pressure from undetected allergies—and this book can help with that.

NEW**
Christian Life Workshops

21 House Rules Preschooler's Training Kit, Rules for Friends, $10.95 each. *Uncommon Courtesy for Kids,* $12.95. All three kits, including coloring books, posters, and instructions, $29.95. *Child Training God's Way* video rental $25 plus $50 refundable deposit, video purchase $49, cassette tapes $11.95. Add 10% shipping ($2.50 minimum, $7.50 maximum). Ages 2–16.

Want to teach your kids basic rules of Christian behavior without a lot of fuss? Gregg Harris's *21 House Rules Preschooler's Training Kit* is for you! This wonderful kit provides a framework of totally reasonable rules for behavior that children themselves will agree with! Rules like, "We obey our Lord Jesus Christ. . . . We do not hurt one another with unkind words or deeds. . . . When someone is sorry, we forgive him. . . . When we have work to do, we do it without complaining. . . . When we take something out, we put it away." Following these simple rules will eliminate 80 percent of the parent-child strife around your house. Of course, *you will have to obey the rules too!* The kit comes with a reproducible training manual/coloring book that illustrates all 21 rules (some great drawings by Gregg's son Joshua), a laminated (jelly-proof) 21 House Rules Master Sheet to post on your fridge or bulletin board, 21 individual rule posters, and complete instructions. Over 3,000 satisfied families have used it. Very highly recommended.

Rules for Friends is just exactly what every family needs to keep "socialization" from becoming a social disease! Following the same format as CLW's *21 House Rules Preschool Training Kit, Rules for Friends* trains your children how to treat their friends and lets the children's friends know what is expected of them when they visit your home. This one is designed for somewhat older children.

Just out is the brand-new *Uncommon Courtesy for Kids,* co-authored by Gregg and Joshua. This "training manual for everyone" introduces the concept of courtesy to both kid and adult readers, then gives Six Manners of Speech, Four Words to the Wise, Five Rules for Public Transportation, Six Ways to Be Considerate to Adults, Six Table Manners, Phone Manners, How to Take a Phone Message, Seven Rules for Going to Church, Eight Rules for Traveling in the Car, Four Awkward Things That Happen to Everybody, and more! Each set of rules is illustrated with examples of people of all ages following (or not following!) the rules. Parents are also told how to train kids gently in

these rules. Knowing what a wicked world this is, Gregg also includes instructions in when *not* to obey or follow adults. You'll get a lot more out of *Uncommon Courtesy* if you get the complete kit, which includes not only the basic coloring book manual but also a laminated poster summarizing all the rules and individual "rules" posters, plus instructions in how to use these materials to help your kids actually learn to be courteous. *Very* highly recommended!

Finally, Gregg's *Child Training God's Way* workshop is available both in video and audiocassette formats. In 90 minutes you'll learn how to *train* your child to be "faithful in small things" rather than just reacting to his bad behavior. Extremely highly recommended.

NEW**
Doorposts

"If-Then" Chart, $4. Blessing chart and booklet, $4.50. Patterns for "Blessing Chart" rewards, $4. "Service Opportunities" chart, $4. "Armor of God" pattern, $4. Proverbs calendar, $6.50. Add $2 shipping. Ages 2–14.

The very day I was planning to finish writing the last reviews for this chapter, this character education material arrived in the mail. Normally I would have said, "Too bad—I'm behind deadline and can't include any more new products." But once I started looking through it, I started getting enthusiastic and wanted to tell you about it.

As you know, child training takes a carrot and a stick. This course provides guidance for both.

The "If-Then" chart is the stick. This large (16 x 22") wall chart lists common kid misbehaviors on the left, along with a cute cartoon of each problem area. Next to each misbehavior is a Scripture verse commenting on that misbehavior. For example, next to "Arguing, Complaining, Whining" is the verse, "Do all things without murmurings and disputings" (Phil.

2:14). A blank column on the right is where you will fill in the agreed-on consequences of each misbehavior. The "If-Then" chart comes with a list of suggested consequences for each sin. These include additional work, loss of a privilege, fines, double restitution, asking forgiveness, and a specified number of swats with a spanking spoon. The authors make it clear that these are only their suggestions; each family is free to choose its own disciplinary measures. You can cut out the pre-lettered and illustrated "consequences" and glue them onto your chart or write in your own.

The "Blessing" chart is the carrot. It's the same size and format as the "If-Then" chart, except that *good* character qualities are listed and illustrated down the left-hand side. The Blessing chart comes with a little booklet, *How to Use the Blessing Chart,* that has some really clever ideas for Scriptural methods of rewarding your children. For example, one of the two verses for the character trait of "Truthfulness" is, "Righteous lips are the delight of kings, and they love him who speaks what is right" (Prov. 16:13). So here are some of the ideas they associate with that verse: Prince-for-a-Day (with crown, robe, and servants); go to work with Daddy; a family parade in honor of the truthful child; special clothing; special privilege; and a blank space for you to write in your own ideas. Patterns for some of the recurring reward ideas are also available. These include a flag to fly from your front porch with the child's name on it, felt banner and patches, certificates, medals of honor, and a cloth crown.

Also from the same prolific family is the Proverbs calendar. The 1992 calendar will be available in September 1991. This has a cartoon illustrating one proverb for each month of the year. You have to figure out what the proverb is for yourself. This is pretty obvious to anyone who knows the Bible. The pig with the ring in his snout reclining on the couch next to the shady lady was a dead giveaway, for example. If you don't know the book of Proverbs very well, though, these illustrations will inspire some digging! Fun for the whole family.

More products from Doorposts: a "Service Opportunities" chart for organizing chore assignments and a set of "Armor of God" patterns, with instructions, so you can make a set of armor for your children like that mentioned in Ephesians 6:10–17.

These materials all look really friendly and professional. Excellent lettering, illustrations in the style of Joshua Harris. Combine these with the Christian Life Workshops "courtesy" materials for a really great jump start on your character training program.

NEW**
Human Resource Development Press
Peer Pressure Reversal, Positive Peer Groups, $9.95 each. *How to Say No and Keep Your Friends, How to Say Yes and Make Friends,* $7.95 each. Package price for all four books, $29.95. Add $1.50 shipping per book (maximum $3). Ages 9 and up. Quantity discounts available.

Back in the Jimmy Stewart days, good kids used to know what to say when someone tried to talk them into bad behavior. Responses varied from flat refusals, to cutting the offender dead socially, to telling him to take a jump in the lake. There was peer pressure, all right: *positive* peer pressure. The good kids were on top, socially, and the bad kids felt ashamed of being bad. All of respectable child and adult society stood against bad behavior. If you misbehaved (stealing, drinking, lying, or fornicating), you had to face socially serious consequences. There still was such a thing as getting a "bad reputation"; "bad" had not come to mean "cool." About the only peer pressure weapon the bad kids had was to accuse you of being a "goody two-shoes" or a "chicken."

Today, things have flip-flopped. Kids who do well in school are not admired, but persecuted. Kids who obey their parents are considered weird. Kids who are still virgins by the ripe old age of 16 are afraid to let it be known, as if they were hiding some bizarre perversion. Thanks to the total abdication of adult responsibility that started when the Supreme Court yanked the Ten Commandments out of the classroom, kids today face *negative* peer pressure like never before. And it's pressure to do serious stuff, too. Drugs. Sex. Robbery. Assault. Kids get the pressure from all directions: from their friends, their TV sets, their music, their adult role models. Madonna alone has made $125,000,000 selling aggressive promiscuous sex to teens and pre-teens. Nice for her, but not so nice for the souls, health, or future hopes of the little girls who follow her advice.

You say your kids don't listen to U-2 or Madonna, don't wear designer jeans, and don't watch *Dallas*? (Let me guess: they're home schooled!) Even those of us who have done our best to avoid the consumer culture can't avoid the kids who are soaked in it. Your daughter may never have seen Madonna in concert, but 90% of the girls she meets listen to Madonna.

Your kids are up against billions of bucks dedicated to promoting hedonistic, mindless consumerism. Everyone loves an impulsive buyer with huge wants and no self-control. Media make their money from advertising, and the advertising industry is bent on encouraging this kind of character among our kids. Even if your kids don't fall for the live-for-today-and-use-your-credit-card culture, they are surrounded by millions of kids who will beg, threaten, and cajole them to become one of the scofflaw herd.

Sharon Scott, author of the books above, spent seven years with the Dallas Police Department as director of the First Offender Program. She "began seeing that the number-one reason why kids were making bad decisions, including breaking laws, was because they did not know what to say to their friends when begged, bribed, dared, or challenged." It's easy to "Just Say No!" to some creepy guy hanging around the schoolyard, but not so easy to say no to your boyfriend, girlfriend, best friend, or the popular kids in school.

Sharon took this as a challenge to train teens in *positive* peer group techniques and peer pressure *reversal* techniques. So far she has trained over 100,000 kids and adults in these techniques, and written several books, which have garnered endorsements from such sources as the Boy Scouts of America, the U.S. Department of Education, and the National Federation of Parents.

Mrs. Scott's *Positive Peer Groups* book gives instructions in how to set up a positive peer group program in your school. This book doesn't really apply to the home situation, but may be of interest to those of you with school connections. *When to Say Yes and Make More Friends* likewise is advice for kids on how to reach out and make good friends in school. The kids who most need this advice tend to be from broken or otherwise messed-up homes, as is evident by the case histories given.

Of interest to just about everyone are *Peer Pressure Reversal: An Adult Guide to Developing a Responsible Child* and *How to Say No and Keep Your Friends,* a book with the same message, but directed to teen readers. Mrs. Scott's philosophy is, "You can say no to trouble *and* be liked." She gives specific steps: Check Out the Scene (look and listen, ask yourself "Is this trouble?"), Make a Good Decision (think of the consequences on both sides and take action), and Act to Avoid Trouble (what to say and how to say it). This gets really specific. I'll list her 10 peer pressure reversal responses:

1. Just say no
2. Leave
3. Ignore
4. Make an excuse
5. Change the subject
6. Make a joke
7. Act shocked
8. Flattery
9. A better idea
10. Return the challenge

Each one of these responses is presented in detail, with illustrations, examples, and suggestions. Example (under Return the Challenge):

When a peer accuses you with "I thought you were my friend!" several possible comebacks are:

"Yes, I am your best friend; and that's why I'm not going to do this with you."

"If you were my friend, then you wouldn't be trying to talk me into doing something that I don't want to do."

"With friends like you, who needs enemies? If you were really my friend, you'd stop trying to push me around."

"If you were my friend, you wouldn't be so bossy."

And of course, a more stinging comeback could always be: "Who said you were my friend?"

Learn other valuable techniques, such as the Thirty Second Rule (start trying to get out of the situation within thirty seconds or less) and the Two No Rule (never say no more than twice before leaving or changing the subject). This all takes practice, so the book provides numerous role-playing situations for kids to exercise their new skills.

Peer Pressure Reversal, a larger book, explains the Peer Pressure Reversal philosophy to parents and explains how to teach it to the kids (again with role-playing a number of situations). This takes 90-odd pages of the book. Section Four of the book has reinforcement suggestions ranging from the usual behavior modification techniques (positive reinforcement for encouragement and, for discipline, deprivation of privileges) to organized family activities and influencing the child's circle of friends.

NEW**
Plain Path Publishers
Christian Manhood, $12 for 259-page student text, $6 for 148-page teacher's guide. *Christian Character,* $10, answer key $1. Add 10% shipping (minimum $2.50). Ages 10–14.

> *Christian Character* is a book that provides an intensive examination of the character that should be found in the lives of our young people. *Christian Character* is Scriptural, practical, and convicting; clearly examining the lives of young people who use the book, and then guiding them in setting short-term, specific goals.

That's what the flyer says. Can any book live up to it? This one sure comes close! Designed for kids aged 10–14, *Christian Character: A Guide for Training Young People to Have the Habits That Will Lead to Godly Character* is a series of lessons, in alphabetical order, on 28 major character traits. Each lesson includes a brief introduction defining the character trait in everyday language, with supporting Scripture citations, one or more student exercises, a personal evaluation, and a goal-setting section. One type of student exercise requires the student to answer questions about Bible verses pertaining to the character trait. Another type asks the student to apply what he knows about that character trait to a number of hypothetical situations. The personal evaluation usually is a pretty comprehensive checklist whereby the student can evaluate how well he is doing as far as that character trait is concerned. The questions are quite discerning and interesting to work through. In the goal-setting section, the student is exhorted to set a specific short-term goal for improvement in that area.

The author's point of view is best expressed in his own words:

> After Salvation, the constant indoctrination by example of the "live as you please" philosophy (through TV, music, adults in the world, etc.) produces young people who lack standards, and therefore are also weak in character. . . . So that provision is not made to fulfil the lusts of the flesh, a young person must be busily engaged in putting into practice principles from God's Word by forming habits of behavior—these behaviors in total forming the various areas of character development. . . . We must teach the Word of God faithfully (Deut. 6:6, 7) and then train young people (Prov. 22:6) by expecting habitual conformity to God's Word as it has been taught. It is a mistake to only teach and then leave the "doing" entirely to the discretion of the child. We . . . cannot produce children with strong character through the philosophy of the world—teach, and then leave them alone to allow them a free choice. . . . Setting goals should become a life-long habit whenever they learn about something that God requires of them and make a decision to do it. A decision without further action is worthless.

Although originally designed by a teacher for classroom use, *Christian Character* works beautifully in the home. The answer key gives the answers to all the exercises that aren't open-ended, and the whole program couldn't be easier to use.

Author Gary Maldaner's point of view is staunchly fundamentalist. He is opposed to rock and contemporary Christian music and is for treating girls and women with special honor (if this be male chauvinism, make the most of it!). He believes in modest dress and the rightness of fighting in a just war. None of these points is beaten to death in *Christian Character;* you could presumably disagree with him on every one of them and still use it by skipping over the questions when they crop up.

Also by the same author, *Christian Manhood: A Guide for Training Boys to be Spiritually Strong Young Men* is for boys ages 10–14. This 45-lesson text doesn't flinch from any of the "tough" areas, from homosexuality and sexual identity to a kid's choice of entertainment. Good biblical common sense, along with a fair amount of insight into spiritual warfare. The author's fundamentalist beliefs are much more basic to this course. The student text has a similar format to the *Christian Character* text, except that lessons are arranged topically rather than alphabetically. You'll also need the teacher's guide, which includes lesson objectives, suggested memory verses, vocabulary from those verses, explanation of the lesson goal, introduction, pointers on leading the classroom discussion, additional activities, discussion questions, and answers to the student exercises.

Sycamore Tree

Character Foundation Curriculum, $4.95 for student's edition each grade, $8.95 for teacher's manual each grade, ages 6–11. *Ladder of Life* series, $18.95, accompanying tapes $26.95, ages 3–6. *Let's Talk About* series, each book $4.95, ages 4–11. Shipping extra.

Sycamore Tree, a full-service home school supplier, devoted three letter-sized pages to character development in their most recent catalog. Notable among these are the Christian Charm and Man in Demand courses reviewed in Volume 3 (see the Harvest House listing), Christian family activity books, a series of family devotionals, the *Character Foundation Curriculum* workbook series, the *Ladder of Life* series, and Jo Wilt Berry's *Let's Talk About It* series.

The *Christian Foundation Curriculum* is, as noted, a workbook curriculum. Children write Bible verses, fill in the blanks, and perform a variety of activities designed to reinforce Biblical character traits. I found the workbook format to be overfussy for a home school situation—too much seatwork. If you use this at home, you might want to pick and choose activities rather than faithfully following the format. I'd also recommend skipping the self-disclosure questions—you know, the kind of exercises where the student has to write down some pledge of future goodness or some confession of past misbehavior. That sort of thing always makes me squirm with embarrassment for the poor child asked to reveal to a fellow human what is really nobody's business but his own and God's.

The *Ladder of Life* series, designed for ages three through six, is eight books with a teacher's guide. This lovely, gentle series was produced by the Seventh Day Adventists, but to my untutored eyes seems free of denominational distinctives. Titles include *Faith, Virtue, Knowledge, Temperance, Patience, Goodness, Brotherly Kindness,* and *Love.*

Definitely the zippiest offering from Sycamore Tree is the *Let's Talk About It* series. Colorful, cartooned books present common childhood experiences and explain the difference between the right and wrong way to handle them. Presently numbering 26 books, the series covers such common problems as being destructive, being lazy, cheating, complaining, disobeying, fighting, showing off, being bossy, and overdoing it.

Preachiness is at a minimum, and bad behavior is shown as not only wrong, but foolish.

CHARACTER BUILDING WITH STORIES

Character training through stories is as old as stories themselves. Æsop's *Fables,* Homer's *Iliad* and *Odyssey,* and even the Bible itself are all examples of how a story can be used to involve and motivate the listener.

"Character-building" fiction has changed a lot in recent years, though. Good and evil never struggle in most modern stories. In fact, evil scarcely exists; the "bad" characters are only poor lonely souls with unmet needs who immediately blossom into sanctified goodness the first time someone smiles at them. This trivial view of temptation and sin also extends to a trivial view of faith and perseverance. The "character-building" hero immediately succeeds once he learns his "lesson," rather than having to struggle on in faith, believing that in time his faith will be rewarded.

The animals in Æsop bear scant resemblance to the cuddly coons and gushy giraffes in today's animal fables. These latter smarmy creatures never come to grips with real evil or even the unpredictableness of real life. They never work for a living or manifest any genuine human or animal characteristics. All-important is the search for friends and self-esteem. Perhaps the most damning thing that can be said about them is that the stories are written as if the peer-group-based life of grade school is the real world.

This is not to say that fiction can't be used to build character. Those who want to exclude fiction from the Christian's reading table fail to remember that everything human beings produce has an element of fiction in it, except possibly for instruction manuals! "True" stories, to be readable, must contain fictional elements. Rare is the person who can remember the weather and everything he said on a given day; thus, historical biographies contain "reconstructed" dialogs and "best guesses" at weather conditions, the appearance of characters and their surroundings, and the like.

Good true stories are as faithful as possible to the historical details. Good fiction is "true to life." And, as Gregg Harris notes, all good literature (including fantasy, which is neither true to history nor true to life) is "true to principle." Are good and evil portrayed realistically? Do the characters make realistic choices? Are their behavior and surroundings consistent with what we know about the time period and culture? If the author does a good job in all these areas, he has, *whether he wanted to or not,* created a powerful vehicle for teaching character lessons. If there is a "good" character or "hero," the reader will naturally identify with him or her. If there are no good characters, or the hero is an anti-hero, the reader will find that consuming sizeable amounts of that kind of literature for pleasure will exert a draining effect on his own character.

A parent's response to the stories his child reads and hears also has a powerful teaching effect. If Mom thinks Scarlett O'Hara was a bimbo who got what she deserved, Suzy Q will look at Scarlett in an entirely different way than Janie, whose mom secretly wishes she could have *been* Scarlett!

You can still find lots of good character-building children's books at the library, but they are being edged out by the increasing horde of books with later copyright dates. In general, most books written for children before 1960 are relatively safe, while the more modern the copyright, the more carefully you have to read the story.

"Children's Bible Hour"

For decades CBH has been on the air with Christian stories aimed at the young. Some stories have an evangelistic emphasis; some concern Christian growth; all are interesting and available on cassettes as well! CBH tapes and records are available for $5.50 each. Also cartooned filmstrip stories ($12 each) and a video containing three of the film strip stories ($15). The program is aired on over 700 stations—check yours.

CBH, unlike some other Christian groups, isn't afraid to share the *whole* truth—including the reality of hell. All material is of professional quality. Stories are sweet but not sugary. I'd avoid the occasional tale that features Christian kids' misbehavior, because although they always repent, it can be a poor example. Otherwise, recommended.

UPDATED**
Donut Records
Cassettes, $7.95 each. Accompanying picture books, $3.95 each. Add $1.50 shipping. Ages 2 to adult.

Everybody's gotta have a hook . . . Robert Evans, a Christian folksinger, one morning stuffed a pastry doughnut hole back into the middle of a doughnut as a joke for his kids. Suddenly realizing what a great object lesson the doughnut hole motif was for how the Word of God fills the emptiness in our lives, he

rechristened himself the Donut Man. This smart move immediately made him more memorable, and furthermore prepared audiences for his parable-laden songs and stories.

Let me tell you about these tapes. As we listened to them the first time, we began to notice that every song was done in a different musical style. "All that's missing is some Messianic Jewish music," Bill said jokingly, and sure enough the next song was Messianic Jewish! Irish, Pop, March, Dixie, County & Western, Ragtime, you name it, the Donut Man sings it.

Ah, yes, but what about content? *Bible Tails, Bible Friends, Shout Hosanna,* and *Look to the Ant* are collections of parables and Bible stories set to music. *Bible Parables* is for ages 2-12 and features parables of Jesus. Each has an accompanying coloring book with all the words of the songs and with comic-strip pictures drawn by a Marvel Comics artist.

Like most Bible stories, these songs are not exact transcriptions of the Biblical text. You may have to point out to your children that all these details are not found in the original stories. Thus these belong more in the category of Character Education than Bible Study. All the same, I've been told that Donut Records music has more direct Biblical content than any other similar music on the market. Fun and exciting? Yes. Talented? Definitely.

NEW**
High Noon Books
9–5 Series, $15 postpaid for all five books. Add $2.50 shipping. Grades 3 to adult.

The 9–5 Series are small books with easy-reading vocabulary and sentence lengths. Each is the story of a young man or woman with a summer job who has to solve a mystery concerning his job. The books are intended to teach preteens and teens how to solve problems that might arise in applying for and keeping their first blue-collar job. Some of the problems—like learning to not "talk silly" around the boss—are part of everyday life, and others—like trying to catch the person who is poisoning food at the supermarket—are thrown in to make the books more interesting. The main characters model good character traits like diligence and honesty.

In *Box Girl,* Patty Walker learns to overcome her impetuousness while working as a supermarket box girl. Troy Martin learns he likes nursery work in *A New Leaf,* but are those really mushrooms Pete is growing in his greenhouse with the windows painted black? In *A Nugget of Gold,* Lucy goes to work at the animal shelter, where the dog she likes the best is "adopted" under suspicious circumstances. Jake gets his friend Lee a job at City Auto in *The Set-Up*, only to wonder if Lee is the person ripping cars off from the lot. In my personal favorite, *The Secret Solution,* Jim gets accused of robbing the houses his crew has been painting.

Like the other High Noon books, these are absorbing reading. Kids can painlessly discover which work attitudes lead to rewards and which will get you fired by reading these books.

NEW**
Home Life
Baby Doe, The Better Butter Battle, Too Many Chickens, The Greenie, $8.95 each. Add 10% shipping ($2 minimum).

The Old Wise Tales™ series, published by Wolgemuth & Hyatt Publishers, is my attempt to revive the character-building fable, á là Æsop. I don't want to sound braggy, so let me praise the cartooning. It's really great!

In *Baby Doe,* a baby deer is born lame. Her parents abandon her, but she is providentially saved by a kind old woodsman. When he takes her with him to his city job at the circus, she saves the day in a surprising way The book makes many subtle prolife points.

The Better Butter Battle is a more accurate allegory of the Cold War than Dr. Seuss's *Big Butter Battle,* which inspired it. Here the Yikks really are bad and the Yooks really are good, although influenced by negative media propaganda in their own country. The Cold War ends with the Yooks deciding to promote liberty and the Wall being torn down. (I wrote this two years before the Berlin Wall came down!)

In *Too Many Chickens,* the pigs decide to increase their corn supply by convincing the hens to only lay two or less eggs. Mrs. Pinfeather and her large family are exiled from the farm, but in the end the barnyard animals discover that large families are indeed a blessing.

The Greenie is a cute little guy who wants to clean up the environment. He goes overboard, though, and is eventually brought back to reality. Along the way kids discover Biblical answers to some of the most urgent environmental issues.

If these books do well, Wolgemuth & Hyatt hope to eventually have a series of 24 or so titles dealing with just about every modern social dilemma. We'll see how it goes.

NEW**
The Landmark Company
The Lighthouse Adventures 12-cassette series, $39.95 plus $3.50 shipping.

I never encourage people to send me their cassette programs, since it takes so long to listen through even a few cassettes. Happily, the staff at The Landmark Company didn't know this. They sent me the best dramatized Christian cassette series I have ever heard.

It's called *The Lighthouse Adventures,* and briefly, it's the story of Pete and Tim and how they both come to know the Lord, all on twelve cassettes neatly packed into a binder with a fancy little sheet of questions for discussion. Along the way you meet Tony, the tough guy who's into some serious stuff, ever-glib and ever-unreliable Skip and his bonehead pal Danny, old Nathaniel Bolt the lighthouse keeper, sweet-sixteen Christy, bombshell Missy—in short a whole raft of unforgettable characters.

Unlike most Christian fiction, this series doesn't miss a beat. The acting is wonderful, as are the sound effects. The story is so gripping you might well hear the whole series through in one sitting. Our kids kept begging for "one more cassette" and we wanted to keep on going, too! The discussion questions and Bible verses are just right: short, sweet, and pointed. Topics covered are important to every child: obedience, trust in God, honesty, standing against peer pressure, the dangers of showing off, true versus false friendship, and so on. Never does the story become cloying. In fact, the characterizations are so realistic that even what I regarded as faults in designing the characters (e.g., the mother's weak failure to control her sons) led to the results you would expect—all without one iota of preaching. There are more lessons in this series than the writers themselves may realize! Even the price is right: it works out to just over $3 per tape.

The big question, "Will the kids listen to this more than once?" was answered immediately in my own family by them requesting it a second time the moment the last cassette was over. I enjoyed it as much the second time—in fact, more, since now I saw more nuances in the plot. I am sure we will play this series again and again.

UPDATED★★
Majesty Music
All Patch the Pirate super long-play recordings, $9.98 each. Accompaniment cassette tapes, $45. Music books: Captain's Copy (for choir director), $5.95 each; Sailor's Copy (lyrics and melody line only), $3.95. Patch Club curriculum: leader's book, $5.95 each; children's book, $4.95 each. Shipping extra. Ages 3–12.

You're probably going to think I don't like the Patch the Pirate series because it features cartoon characters and fantasy situations. Well, you're wrong. For every rule there is an exception, and this happens to be the exception.

First, let me describe the series. Patch the Pirate is the invention of one Ron Hamilton. After losing an eye to cancer, Ron was forced to wear an eyepatch. Hence the moniker "Patch the Pirate." Making the most of this unhappy situation, Ron decided to dress up as a pirate and tell Christian stories. One thing led to another, and that's how we got the Patch the Pirate series.

Patch is a very straight-arrow pirate. In fact, he does nothing piratical at all except sail the sea and use sailor talk.

Instead of a crowd of squirmingly cute stuffed animals or unbelievably adorable children whose adventures resemble nothing on this earth or the next, the Patch adventures are parables of the Christian life. They feature really bad villains who do not roll over and play dead if you just smile sweetly at them. Hence their interest for our family.

Patch, a Real Man, leads the crew—a welcome change from all those series of Worlds Without Adults, Amen.

Kidnapped on I-Land is an action-packed excursion into the kingdom of the nasty King Me-First. Silas Sailor, found floating on a raft by Patch and his crew,

succumbs to the blandishments of King Me-First, who promises him a marvelous life on his own if Silas will just determine to always put himself first. With Silas firmly chained to him, King Me-First flies off to I-Land and flings Silas into Pity-Party Pit, a particularly dark corner of the Prison of No Sing-Sing. Patch and friends set out to rescue Silas, who is slated to become a barbecued sailor steak, courtesy of King Me-First's pet, Torch the Dragon. Silas finally decides to put Jesus first, at which point the castle disappears, Me-First shrinks into nothingness, and all is well. The whole adventure resembles John Bunyan's *Pilgrim's Progress* (on a somewhat lower literary level) and is characterized by frequent clever jokes and lots of bright, happy music.

The Great American Time Machine has Patch and his crew escorting a delegation of two from Bonkinland back through American history to discover the secret of America's greatness. The Bonkers only understand coercive power (in Bonkinland every higher Bonker gets to bonk everyone lower than him to keep them in line), and the sight of George Washington kneeling in the snow at Valley Forge and Dwight L. Moody preaching in Chicago, among other peeks into American roots, amaze them. Lots of good songs and nice effects, like the Statue of Liberty speaking with a Bronx accent.

The Patch lineup also includes *Patch the Pirate Goes to the Jungle*, *Patch the Pirate Goes West*, *Patch the Pirate Goes to Space*, *The Misterslippi River Race*, *The Calliope Caper*, *Camp Kookawackawoods*, *The Custard's Last Stand*, and *Sing Along with Patch the Pirate*. Musical accompaniment and music books for choir directors and members are also available, in case your church wants to put one of these adventures on. And apparently, lots of them do!

New from Majesty Music: a Patch Club curriculum that teaches music theory and has a daily children's devotion. Leaders and children each need a new book every three months during the school year. Each quarterly contains "an exciting, four-part story illustrating the specific godly character trait for that month."

NEW**
Vision Video
Dangerous Journey, $59.95 for set of 2 videos, color story book, teacher's guide, and Scripture guide, all in gift pack. Add $3.95 shipping.

John Bunyan's all-time bestseller *Pilgrim's Progress* has got to be the greatest character-building book of all time. Based on Bunyan's book, *Dangerous Journey* features the truly excellent, detailed illustrations of Alan Parry and excellent narration besides. The art fits the old-fashioned flavor of Bunyan's book, and the length of the series give the narrator plenty of time to cover much of Bunyan's best ground. Instead of animation, the producers used camera angles and special effects to move the story along. I had worried that our children would be bored because of the lack of animation, but what we lost in animation was more than made up for by the vividness of the illustrations. This is one of our children's favorite videos. Warning: the monsters in this series do look monstrous. (Not that it bothers our crowd!)

The new version of *Dangerous Journey* includes nine programs on two full-color VHS videotapes, plus a *Dangerous Journey* 128-page color story book, a teacher's guide, and a Scripture guide, all in a gift pack. Tape 1 includes the Slough of Despond, the Interpreter's House, the Hill Difficulty, the fight with Apollyon, and the Valley of the Shadow of Death. Tape 2 takes you to Vanity Fair, Doubting Castle, the Dark River, and the story of Christiana. A good deal, especially since they've dropped the price $20 (it used to be $79.95).

GAMES THAT TEACH CHARACTER

NEW**
Ornament Publications
The Richest Christian, $23 postpaid. Ages 6 to adult (one player needs to be good at addition and subtraction).

The Richest Christian is my children's favorite board game, superior in their opinion to *Generosity*. Like *Generosity*, the aim is to learn biblical principles of money; but *The Richest Christian* emphasizes how money is earned as well as how it is spent. The game is for two to six players, who need to know how to read. One player, the cashier, needs to know how to add and subtract large whole numbers.

The large, illustrated gameboard is easy to read and use. Most spaces have a topic and Bible verse at the top, a picture applying the verse in the middle, and a game action at the bottom. Example:

TOO MUCH TALK
" . . . The talk of the lips tendeth only to poverty."
Proverbs 14:23

[Picture of a man in business clothes, feet up on desk, chatting with a friend holding a cup of coffee]

You are a salesman who wastes too much time talking with other salesmen. Lose $400.

Other spaces tell you to draw a Disaster card or give you a chance to earn game rewards if you have performed a prescribed pious action recently, e.g., if you can quote a Bible verse you learned this month. Opportunity cards may be chosen once you have passed the first round, assuming you aren't in debt at this point. These give you the opportunity to do a good deed with some or all of your game money, thereby earning Eternal Treasures. The game is over when all Eternal Treasures (pretty gold-foil cards with their value printed on them in blue) have been passed out. The player with the most Eternal Treasures wins.

Watch out for the ominous green paths on both sides of the board. If you land on a shady transaction space, you make some money on the deal, but then have to suffer through a series of disasters, some brought on by your own evil character (you make unwise investments and lose most of your money, for example) and some visited on you directly by the Lord.

Three of the game cards I could do without. One Disaster card informs you, "If you have $1,000 or more, you are spending too much time trying to make money. Lose your next turn." This comes perilously close to the philosophy of envy, which says having money is a sin. I also would in real life pass up two of the "opportunities": one, to give all my money to help a missionary in poor health and two, to sell some of my jewelry and give $500 to a radio preacher. For one thing, I don't have any jewelry! For another, only in exceptional circumstances and under a direct conviction from the Lord should any of us impoverish himself for another. The goal, as the Apostle Paul points out, is not that we who give should be hard pressed while others live in plenty, but that all who deserve it should have enough. (The game publisher tells me these cards will be changed in the next edition.)

The Richest Christian admirably teaches principles of diligence, inventiveness, thrift, and generosity, while exposing the pitfalls of get-rich-quick thinking, laziness, dishonesty, show-off giving, and selfishness. It's also easy to learn and fun to play. Can't ask one board game to do much more than that!

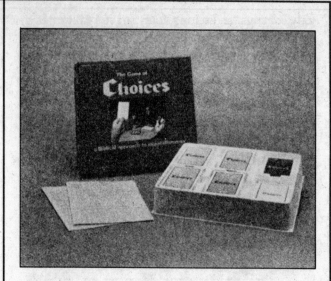

UPDATED✶✶
Rainfall Inc.
Kids' Choices (ages 6–12), *Teen Choices* (ages 13–18), *Adult Choices* (ages 19 and up), $14.99 each.

The *Choices* series of games helps you explore ethical decision-making with your children, teens, or other adults. Each game includes 170 real-life dilemmas spelled out on sturdy cards, 20 Answer Cards, 10 Principle Cards, a reference booklet, an instruction sheet (natch), and a plastic storage tray. Families, Sunday school classes, and youth or adult groups will find these games illuminating and challenging, as they come face to face with life and sometimes nose to nose with opposing views of it.

Three to ten players can play each *Choices* game (four to eight players are best). Each game is suitable for team play.

Example of a dilemma from the adult game: "You get home from the supermarket only to notice that the check-out clerk charged you less than she should have. Do you go back to the store and correct the error?" You place either a "Yes" or "No" Answer Card face-down in front of you. Other players guess how you will respond, playing their own Answer Cards, and you try to justify your answer with various Scriptural principles.

Each game includes Biblical principle cards, as well as a reference booklet which shows what Bible verses the principles are based on and gives recommended principles for resolving every dilemma. Right and wrong answers are not spelled out. This can make for some lively discussions, especially in games played with more players.

Some of the dilemma cards put you in the position of having already committed a sin. Example, from the Teen game: "You lied to your parents about where you were going and now you have been in a car accident. Will you tell them the truth?" Others falsely assume that kids are just bound to get into compromising situations. Another example from the Teen game: "If you (your girlfriend) became pregnant would you marry the father (mother)?" This is like the old question, "When's the last time you beat your wife?" It doesn't allow for the possibility that any teen playing the game might *not* be sexually involved, since the only allowable answers are, "Yes, I would marry him (her)," and "No, I would not." One way to overcome this problem is to allow a third answer, "I wouldn't get in the situation in the first place."

School and home problems appear frequently in the Kids' and Teen games, and many Teen dilemmas also focus on dating and boyfriend/girlfriend dilemmas. Example of a family problem, again from the Teen deck: "While cleaning out the garage you found some pornographic magazines on your father's shelf. Will you tell anyone?" This somewhat reduces the games' usefulness for those who homeschool and have good family lives. I can also see these questions leading to some rather embarrassing moments in the youth group. (Simple solution: pull and toss those cards.)

I like the basic idea of the *Choices* games, and the new format is much more playable than the old "figure out a Bible verse that applies and look it up" format. With 170 dilemma cards to choose from, you can get rid of any that don't apply and still have plenty left to play with. It is a fascinating way to gain insight into the thought processes of family members, and to bring up questions in a family format that might be a lot tougher to face for the first time in real life.

NEW★★
TREND Enterprises, Inc.
Smart Choices Fun-To-Know Flash Cards, $3.99. Ages 6 and up. Add $2 shipping. Minimum order: $10.

Smart Choices is another unique set of fact cards from TREND. Each card features a typical kid dilemma (illustrated on the front) and gives three possible ways of handling it on the back. Three cheers for TREND for *not* leaving it at this—they go one step farther and show why two out of the three suggested responses are not the best, and why the third is better. Example:

Your Dad says you must clean your messy room before going outside. You:
1. ask your brother/sister to clean the room.
2. begin to clean your room right away.
3. stomp your feet and yell, "It isn't fair! I like my room messy. Why can't I leave it that way?"
About your answer:
A. No. You are avoiding your responsibility for the mess.
B. Right. By starting right away, you'll have more time for going outside. You also show you can take care of your own things.
C. No. Anger won't solve your problem.

This particular box of cards focuses on everyday problems, such as people talking when you are trying to have a conversation or getting the wrong amount of change at the store, not life-threatening problems like storms or evil strangers. The answers are right on and the makers thoughtfully provide several clever ways to use these cards to cement problem-solving skills. Caveat: Self-sacrifice is not really promoted as the best option. Rather, assertiveness and mutual sharing are given top marks. You might want to make up some scenarios of your own where self-sacrifice is the correct response.

REWARDS

Some people like to make charts and on those charts mark their children's spiritual progress.

Others don't.

Some people like to buy stickers and rewards and hand them out to deserving young lads and lasses.

Others don't.

Some people, who are looking for rewards and incentives for their children and character-building games, will want to read this section.

Others won't (but go ahead, sneak a peek anyway!).

Jonson Specialties

Jonson Specialties has it all: stick-ons, balloons, lollipops, giveaway toys, games, rings, flag picks, pens, pencils, pencil tops, toy animals, treasure chests, and even vending machines and capsules. Any oddball item a teacher might be tempted to buy to hand out to her little flock, they have. Need a dozen yo-yos, or a package of twist balloons? How about the Success Mix—a bag of 500 (count 'em!) assorted charms, gimmicks, and rings for $9.95? Relive your fond memories of your childhood eraser collection with animal erasers or fruit erasers (36 for $5.50), book-shaped erasers (48 for $7.95), pencil top erasers (72 for $7.95), and on and on.

Not unexpectedly, the lifetime of these toys is short. After a while, they break or disappear. But then, you didn't really want 500 charms and gimmicks around permanently, did you?

Sycamore Tree

Sycamore Tree Incentive Charts, set of 52 (13 each of 4 designs, a 3-months' supply), $4.95. Motivational Stamp Kits, $6.95. Achievement Awards, package of 32, $2.95. Seals, stickers, stars, 98¢ apiece except for the stick-n-sniffers.

If you believe in rewards, Sycamore Tree has pages and pages of what you want.

Sycamore Tree's exclusive Incentive Charts cover lessons, chores, manners, and personal habits, with squares sized for mini-stickers or stars.

Motivational Stamp Kits are sets of six goofy stamps that run the gamut from gentle prodding ("Try Again!" says the Apple) to ecstatic ("Wow" exclaims the Cutie Bug). No, I am not making this up. You have your choice of bunnies, robots, kittens, puppies, Cutie Bugs, happy faces, apples, teddy bears, coin tails, and coin heads.

Now, let's talk about stickers. Sycamore Tree has large and small gold stars and stars in assorted colors. Wild Animal seals. Life of Christ seals. Seasonal mini-stickers. Religious mini-stickers. Stars. More!

NEW**
Timberdoodle

Sticker Bonanza, $3.95, or two sets for $3.50 each. Critters Stickers, $6 or two sets for $5 each. Shipping extra.

Stickers for people with artistic tastes. These are not your common stars and smiley faces, but designer stickers that are works of art. The "Mrs. Grossman's" line they carry are virtually acid-free, so they can be used in photo albums as well as on letters, envelopes, school assignments, lunch boxes, etc.

The Critters Stickers include 250 stickers—32 different animals in varying amounts from four normal size to 16 tiny ones. Timberdoodle price is 50% off retail. Beautiful, multi-colored creatures, from panda bears to birds.

Sticker Bonanza is a grab bag of discontinued or end-of-roll stickers. Again, you get oodles of designer stickers at a bargain price. Selection changes constantly. The set I recently ordered included animals, party items (hats, horns, balloons, etc.), toys (sailboats, fans, balls . . .), rainbows, and snowflakes—dozens of different items. Use them for art projects or rewards—it's your choice!

PART IV

LANGUAGE ARTS

CHAPTER FIFTEEN

CHILDREN'S CLASSICS

Your daughter knows how to read. Wonderful! Now . . . *what* is she going to read?

In all the concern about teaching our children to read, it is well to remember that the purpose of learning to read is to read *something*. If the only printed matter in the world were the backs of cereal boxes, the need to read would be far less urgent. If our children are only going to read popular magazines and the instructions on government forms, it's hard to see why we don't just switch over to phonetic spelling, which is much easier to learn. (Example: "Inflayshun Down, Prezident Sez.")

The only legitimate reason our kids struggle through the odd English orthography is so they can read books written before today—preferably, the better of these books, otherwise known as The Classics.

Please note, gentle reader: school "basal reading series" are *not* The Classics. Often they *include* snippets from a classic or two. When they do, the snippets are often edited or abridged, sometimes totally contrary to the tone of the original writing. But the bulk of virtually every modern series of "readers" is made up of modern works, often written expressly for the series.

To put it as bluntly as possible, "readers" are *not* literature. They may *include* some literature, just as a soft drink may include fruit juice. But they also include a lot of *other* stuff. When parents object to the offensive items included in a public school reader, such as stories promoting witchcraft or suicide, the publishers can then point to the "classics" and paint the parents as people who "want to censor *The Wizard of Oz*." Never mind that the publishers have already censored most of the Western classics out of their books in the first place!

Now, when we talk about "the classics of Western civilization," I don't mean *Amelia Bedelia* or *Frog and Toad are Friends*. Such books may be several decades old—kids may love them—they may be bestsellers or good literature—but they are not *classics*. *David Copperfield* by Charles Dickens, on the other hand, *is* a classic. It has been regarded as such for generations. It has affected our culture. It deals with significant issues with stylistic excellence.

Sadly, your child is likely to emerge from his school experience having read *Amelia Bedelia*, but not having read *David Copperfield*. "So what?" someone asks. Well, among other things, it is a grave loss to our cultural vocabulary. Time was when everyone knew what you meant when you say, "Mr. X is a Uriah Heep," or "Mrs. Y is a regular Betsy Trotwood." It's also a grave loss to our combined wisdom and discernment, as it is very handy to know about the Uriah Heep character type and to be able to recognize him when he tries to oil his way into power. The Dickens novels are almost a complete course in character traits, presented as memorable stories.

And that's just *Dickens*.

IN FAVOR OF OLD BOOKS

Ah, those good old books! This is what a child gets when he spends hours, weeks, and months immersed in classic literature:

(1) Grammar. This subject can be "caught" as well as "taught." Correct usage was considered essential in previous generations, and the sentence structure of their books reflects this.

(2) Vocabulary. This almost goes without saying. Children can vastly increase their passive vocabulary by reading old books (though they may need to consult a dictionary in order to pronounce the words correctly). Today the trend is towards dumbing-down literature, in hopes an increasingly illiterate population will be able to read it. Not so then. Even barefoot boys of the Huck Finn variety read the King Arthur and Robin Hood legends, archaic language and all. Give kids a good plot, and they'll make the effort to pick up the extra vocabulary needed to understand it.

(3) Spelling. This varies from child to child, but in my experience visual learners can pick up correct spelling simply by reading a lot of books containing correct spelling

(4) Creative writing. In the past, youngsters learned the techniques of good writing by copying extracts from great writers. Without going to the effort of actually writing paragraphs out, those who read a lot of great writing still unconsciously imbibe its forms.

(5) History. Even if the old book in question isn't a historical book *per se*, it is historical by virtue of being old. A book written in 1920 can't help presenting us with 1920s ideas, architecture, fashions, and so on.

(6) Worldview. Another benefit of reading old books is that they do not all fit into the increasingly homogeneous 1990s mindset. Old books are windows into different ways of thinking as well as doors into different time periods.

Keep in mind that I'm only listing benefits kids pick up *without* extra study. Children who read lots of old books will come by improved grammar, vocabulary, spelling, creative writing, historical understanding, and a more thoughtful worldview whether or not they ever write book reports or take tests. I would, in fact, argue against book reports and tests, except possibly for an occasional one thrown in just for practice. Literature has power because is it so enjoyable. Turn it into an assignment and most of its appeal disappears.

In any case, effortful assignments based on kids' reading aren't necessary. Good books spark interest in further study all by themselves. Kids who read Jules Verne novels are almost guaranteed to develop an interest in science, geography, and engineering, just like kids who read James Fenimore Cooper's books want to make their own bows and arrows. Any "book" place that can be located on the map teaches geography in a way not easily forgotten. Any "book" event can spark further historical study. Your job will be just to find the resources to satisfy your child's new interests.

HOW TO TEACH CHILDREN'S LITERATURE

NEW**
Family Learning Center
Learning Language Arts through Literature, Red Book (grade 2), $17.95. Yellow book (grade 3), $17.95. Tan book (grade 4–6), $12.95. Grey book (grades 7–8), $12.95. Add 10% shipping ($2 minimum).

Based on Ruth Beechick's methods, as outlined in her book *You Can Teach Your Child Successfully*, *Learning Language Arts through Literature* is a dictation-based program centering on excerpts from great children's literature. The original (tan) book was written for ages 10–13, and is now joined by books for children down to age 6 and up to beginning high-school level.

I wrote this program up in detail in the Creative Writing chapter, although really it belongs in a half-dozen chapters, since it includes *all* the following—spelling, grammar, vocabulary, writing mechanics, literature, penmanship, and thinking skills—all broken down into sensible daily and weekly lessons. Speaking just about its literary side, the literature selections are wonderful! In the Tan Book, starting with Psalm 1, you proceed to *Bambi*, *The Wheel on the School*, a poem by Tennyson (famous poets are that week's special feature!), *Little House on the Prairie*, *The Bronze Bow*, *Caddie Woodlawn*, *King of the Wind* by Marguerite Henry, *Lassie Come Home*, *The Hiding Place*, *Kidnapped*, the Gettysburg Address, *Swallows and Amazons*, *Anne of Green Gables*, *Prince Caspian*, *Rascal*, *Robinson Crusoe*, *Star of Light* by Patricia St. John, *The Railway Children*, *David Copperfield*, *The Wind in the Willows*, *Little Women*, and *Big Red* by Jim Kjelgaard. In fact, this list would make an excellent reading list, if you are looking for library books to use with your children!

NEW**
Teacher Created Materials
Literature and Critical Thinking series volume TCM315, $9.95. Grades 2–6.

Each book in the Literature and Critical Thinking series from Teacher Created Materials uses six or more famous children's books as a starting point. You get plot summaries and a few, generally well-chosen, art and thinking activities based on each story. I can't recommend most of the volumes for home use, because the activities are so time-consuming and the art activities are printed on *both* sides of the paper (making it impossible to cut them out without photocopying first). The "Poetry" volume (Volume 16) is a worthwhile exception.

Let's look at how *Casey at the Bat* is handled in the "Poetry" volume. First you get a plot summary—a mini-review of the poem, including info about how old it is and why it is famous. Next is a matching exercise designed to make sure kids know the vocabulary words used in the poem. Then the reader is asked to rewrite the poem in prose form; find the line in the poem that corresponds to each of a number of prose sentences; do a comprehension activity, predicting what will happen before Casey takes his final swing (this should have been the first activity—it was poor planning to put it after the others); a page of Baseball Math problems; some questions about how Casey would react if he were (a) a veteran player in his last game or (b) a little league player in the playoffs; and a dramatic-reading exercise, matching words and lines from the poem to a list of emotions.

Exercises like these teach more than you'd see on the surface. After trying to recast Casey in prose, and comparing the book's prose sentences to the poem's lilting lines, any student is bound to see the power of poetry to add punch to ideas. Similarly, time spent matching lines of poetry to the emotions with which

one should read them cannot fail to develop a child's dramatic abilities.

Please note that the book does *not* include the text of the stories you will be studying. You will have to go to the library and take out those books. This should be easy, since the series authors have only chosen to work with extremely popular children's books.

Since most of you will be using this book at home, I'd suggest simply asking your children the questions, rather than requiring written answers, unless the activity is a writing activity (e.g., rewriting *Casey at the Bat* in prose). More children can participate together this way.

NEW**
Teaching Home
June/July 1988 issue, $3.75. Complete six-issue set for 1988, $17.50, includes free set of 6 plastic magazine holders for your ring binder.

As I've said before, each *Teaching Home* magazine back issue on a given topic is like a minicourse in teaching that topic. June/July 1988 was the issue on teaching literature. There were several articles on how to teach literature, motivating children to love books, using literature to influence your children's values, lives of great men and women, how to choose and use good books for all ages, and the Bible and literature. This all is a lot livelier than it sounds—these are hands-on ideas and principles from people actually involved in home teaching!

FIRST BOOKS FOR LITTLEST KIDS

The books we are going to be talking about in this section are *not* primers. Primers are (at least in *The Big Book* !) books designed to help children practice their phonics. Rather, this section is for "first books." Some first books are books you read to your child. Others are books you look at and talk about together. These are essential pre-reading steps.

NEW**
Ladybird Books, Inc.
Each book, $2.95. Flap books, $6.95 each. Ages 1–7.

Ladybird has an incredible assortment of books for littlest kids. Starting with their cloth books, we move on to the Flap books (lift up flaps to see what's underneath!), activity books, bath books, board books, facts books, fairy tales, ready-to-read books (see the pictures and figure out the plot), action rhymes, Ladybird rhymes, storytime books (one each for children ages 1–7), Mother Goose, "Talkabouts" picture books, and more! You can even get a set of "Square Books Bible Stories." "Square" refers to the books' shape; Ladybird does not think Bible stories are square!

Of all these, my personal favorites are the flap books, starring lovable Baby Bear. In *Baby Bear's Noisy Farm*, for example, your little one will find farm animals hiding behind barn doors, hedges, and other likely places. These are great first books, as children get so involved with the simple storyline, which they assist by opening the flaps. The series includes *Baby Bear's Noisy Farm*, *Baby Bear's Shopping Day*, *Baby Bear's Hide and Seek*, and *Baby Bear's Best Friends*.

CLASSICS MADE SIMPLE

NEW★★
Ladybird Books, Inc.
Each book, $3.50. Ages 6–10.

If you're looking for classics recast in Dick-and-Jane vocabulary, Ladybird has the stuff! To British readers, the Ladybird series of children's books needs no introduction. Tremendously popular in the British Isles, Ladybird's inexpensive, stunning children's books run the gamut from early readers of the "Peter likes the dog" sort to colorful "facts" books for preteens.

These books are brightly colored and lavishly illustrated retellings of classics and fables. This grew, as you can guess, out of the "sight word" approach. Ladybird also sells a sight word reader series of 36 (count 'em) little books plus two picture dictionaries and workbooks, very aptly titled *The Key Words Reading Scheme*. (Not that they aren't cute and clever little books—it's just that any program which persuades teachers and parents that they must buy 36 readers deserves to be called a "scheme.") I've written the Ladybird readers up in Chapter 16.

But we digress. Right now, we're looking at Ladybird's children's classics. Reworded for children ages 8–10, the series now embraces 26 titles, all recognized classics. Each volume is illustrated throughout with pictures on every double-page spread. Better than Cliff Notes, your child's loss in literary beauty is made up for by his increase in cultural literacy.

Ladybird also has a set of horror classics (*Dracula*, *Frankenstein*, *The Mummy*, and *Dr. Jekyll and Mr. Hyde*), a set of legends (*Aladdin*, *Ali Baba*, *Robin Hood*, and *King Arthur*), and three books of fables (two of Æsop's and one of the French master La Fontaine's).

The Ladybird classics are inexpensive (singly) and will provide a diluted taste of the real thing for very young readers or those whose progress has been temporarily crippled by look-say.

UPDATED★★
EDC Publishing, Inc.
Greek Myths and Legends, $7.95. *Norse Myths and Legends*, $6.95. Ages 11–15.

You won't find a less expensive, more colorful, more sprightly intro to the classics anywhere than right here. Top-quality art combines with vibrant illustrations as is usual with EDC series. The legends series for younger children has unfortunately been discontinued, but we still have *Greek Myths and Legends* and *Norse Myths and Legends*. These feature grotesque fantasy art suitable to the actual gloomy myths themselves, and are definitely more suited to upper-elementary and teen readers.

Educational Insights
Each set of 12 cartoon books, 12 spirit masters, and teacher's guide, $39.95. Accompanying read-along cassettes for each set, $40. Thirty-six-booklet sets, $69.95. *Read-Along* cassettes, $110. Ages 9–15.

What do you get when you cross Spiderman with Edgar Allan Poe? Something I wouldn't want to meet in a dark alley—or the Educational Insights literature comics. Yes, you read that right! Educational Insights has compiled several boxes of four-page comics. Each comic tells, in compact form, one classic tale. And there's more! For the really hard-to-motivate literary dilettante, you can also purchase read-along cassettes to accompany the comics!

Each box also contains a number of spirit masters equal to the number of comics, and a teacher's guide. The spirit masters, one presumes, are for testing the carefree readers to see if they were really reading or just had a schoolbook propped open inside the comic.

Sets are: American Short Stories, which has 36 different comics by 35 different authors; Short Stories Around the World, which has 12 stories each at second, third, and fourth grade reading levels; three series of Adventure Stories (Ghost and Monsters, Adventures in Mystery, and Adventures in Science Fiction) each featuring 12 tales; and three series of Classic Tales (Tales of Robin Hood, Tales of King Arthur, and Tales from Shakespeare—the latter "in modern dialog"), each likewise containing twelve tales. Oh, yes, I almost forgot the set of Great Sports Stories, perhaps because it doesn't really count as literature in the finest, truest sense of the word.

Your learner will not discover great writing by reading comics, but he will at least become aware of the main plot of many masterpieces and perhaps become interested in the masterpieces themselves. I read several of these comics, or something like them, when I was in pigtails and it didn't cripple me for life. (What almost did turn me off to the classics was trying to read the agonizingly long *Lorna Doone* in an unabridged version at the age of eight.) We do not scoff, then, at Educational Insights' humble efforts to bring the classics to the people.

GAMES

Aristoplay
By Jove! $22. Add $4.75 shipping. Ages 10 to adult.

It can't be any simpler or more enjoyable than this. "What can't be simpler than what?" asks Bill.

"Learning Greek and Roman mythology, which happens to supply the background knowledge you need to understand all classical literature," I explain patiently, "is usually a bit of a chore. Jason, the Minotaur, Odysseus, Hera, Athena, and all the rest get jumbled up. What you really need," I continue, "is a fun way to remember all those stories." "So?" interjects Bill. "*By Jove!*" I exclaim. "Step on your foot?" Bill asks solicitously. "No, I mean *By Jove!*, the board game from Aristoplay. It's a beautiful board game simulation of one of the bigger and better myths—Jason and the Golden Fleece. You, a mere mortal, voyage about the board contending with oracles and the whimsical, ever-foolish gods and goddesses. It all comes with: the invaluable, award-winning *By Jove Stories*, eight hero cards with stands, one game board, one pair dice, 16 potluck cards, 12 minotaur/labyrinth awards, 50 VAP cards (I'll explain those later), 60 gold coins, and 40 oracle cards. Up to six players can play at a time . . . Hey! Where are you going?" I hear Bill hallooing in the next room, "Boys! Want to play one of the new games that came today!" Shucks. Didn't even get to explain the VAP cards . . .

READING LISTS

Crossway Books
Books Children Love, $12.95. *For the Children's Sake*, $6.95. Add $1 shipping.

You want more than reading lists? *For the Children's Sake* is a wonderful book about how children learn which, among other things, shares the idea of learning through "living books"—real masterpieces—rather than committee-written textbooks. Based on the writings of British educator Charlotte Mason, *For the Children's Sake* presents a natural, rich style of learning founded on Christian principles and suited to all times and cultures.

From the same publisher (Crossway Books), *Books Children Love: A Guide to the Best Children's Literature* goes far beyond a reading-list approach. Most reading lists deal exclusively with fiction, but *Books Children Love* lists hundreds of books from more than two dozen subject areas, with comments on each one. Author Elizabeth Wilson has selected "excellently written, interest-holding books on as wide a range of topics as possible—books that also embody ideas and ideals in harmony with traditional values and a Christian worldview." Susan Schaeffer Macaulay wrote the foreword to this lovely thick book.

Foundation for American Christian Education
A Family Program for Reading Aloud, second edition, $6.50.

A family reading program that reflects American patriotism, the Foundation for American Christian Education's *Family Program for Reading Aloud* contains discussions of more than 200 literary classics. In Part I, three chapters introduce reading aloud and the listening-learning skills. Three more suggest books to read to the youngest (FACE is pro-Mother Goose). Six chapters introduce American themes, including immigrants and ethnic groups, pioneers and Indians, and even American horses, and give a sample of how to teach the Principle Approach using historical biographies. The last two chapters help you evaluate your family reading program.

The new second edition now includes a Part II on reading in depth for high-school students. Some topics: the ocean, pioneers, teaching and learning, and the French Revolution. Some authors covered in depth: Charles Dickens, Sir Walter Scott, Washington Irving, and Nathaniel Hawthorne. A section on restoring heroes and heroines in literature includes Richard E. Byrd, Charles A. Lindbergh, Eddy Rickenbacker, Anne Bradstreet, Lydia Darrah, and Mercy Otis Warren. The last section highlights people who preserve our history and the Mount Vernon Ladies Association who pioneered historical preservation in America.

Zondervan Books
Honey for a Child's Heart, $5.95. At your Christian bookstore.

Have I got a book for you! Zondervan's *Honey for a Child's Heart*, subtitled *The Imaginative Use of Books in Family Life*, is the most fantastic, inspiring book about books that I have ever read. Gladys Hunt, the author, expertly deals with the questions of what makes a good book a good book and explains how to make family reading a rich part of your life, as well as providing 58 pages of suggested reading for different age levels. The book is illustrated with pictures from recommended books and is an absolute delight to read. Gladys Hunt says everything I wanted to say about literature, and says it better. I'd put this book in my own mail-order catalog in a minute if Zondervan would quit insisting that they sell "only to established bookstores." Your best bet is to hop down to the bookstore and hunt it up.

CHAPTER SIXTEEN

CREATIVE WRITING

Writing receives less attention in the public school curriculum than any other core subject. It takes time to teach children to write well, and teachers are overburdened. It takes attention to detail, and many teachers have been taught to believe that details are petty. It takes, most of all, an appreciation and understanding of good writing, and the present generation of teachers has itself been denied this instruction.

To give you an example of how ridiculous the teaching of creative writing has become: Have you ever heard of "topic sentences"? Here's how children are actually being taught to write a paragraph:

1) Write a topic sentence. This states the theme of the paragraph.

2) Add several "supporting" sentences. These give extra details and support the theme.

3) Write a concluding sentence to summarize the paragraph.

This approach leads to lively writing of the following sort:

Scott is a good dog. He comes when I call him. He never wets the rug. He doesn't bite the letter carrier. Yes, Scott is a good dog.

Workbooks are actually available, with titles like *How to Write a Paragraph*, that teach kids this is the right way to write.

Too bad nobody was around to teach these rules to Robert Louis Stevenson (I pick him almost by random). Take a look at the second paragraph of *Treasure Island*:

I remember him as if it were yesterday, as he came plodding to the inn door, his sea chest following behind him in a hand-barrow; a tall, strong, heavy, nut-brown man; his tarry pigtail falling over the shoulders of his soiled blue coat; his hands ragged and scarred, with black, broken nails; and the sabre cut across one cheek, a dirty, livid white. I remember him looking round the cove and whistling to himself as he did so, and then breaking out in that old sea-song that he sang so often afterward:—

Fifteen men on the dead man's chest—
Yo-ho-ho, and a bottle of rum!

in the high, old tottering voice that seemed to have been tuned and broken at the capstan bars. Then he rapped on the door with a bit of stick like a hand-spike that he carried, and when my father appeared, called roughly for a glass of rum. This, when it was brought to him, he drank slowly, like a connoisseur, lingering on the taste, and still looking about him at the cliffs and up at our sign-board.

We translate this now, according to the rules of topic sentences, supporting sentences, and summary sentences:

> I remember what a character the old seaman was. He was tall and strong. He was heavy and tanned. He had a tarry pigtail. His coat was blue and dirty. His hands were ragged and scarred. His fingernails were black and broken. He had a sabre cut across one cheek. Yes, he was a real character!

> The old seaman did strange things. He looked around the cove and whistled to himself. Then he sang a sea-song: "Fifteen men on the dead man's chest, Yo-ho-ho and a bottle of rum!" He sang it in a high, old voice. Then he rapped on the inn door with a stick. He called for a bottle of rum. He drank the rum slowly, enjoying the taste. All the time he was drinking he was looking about him at the cliffs and up at our sign-board. Yes, he was a strange person!

These are the kinds of sentences and paragraphs kids are learning to write in school. They are bad sentences. They are bad paragraphs. Yes, kids are learning to write badly in school!

You may be wondering why I chose the second paragraph of *Treasure Island* for an example of the great gulf fixed between real literature and topic-sentence writing. That's because the *first* paragraph of *Treasure Island* is a single sentence!

The first antidote to topic-sentence hack writing, then, is to write *real* literature. (See the last chapter for suggestions.) The second? See the resources below—especially *Any Child Can Write* (listed under Shekinah Curriculum Cellar).

HOW TO TEACH CREATIVE WRITING

NEW★★
Education Services
You CAN Teach Your Child Successfully. $13.70/softcover, $18.95 hardcover. For adults to use while teaching children in grades 4–8.

Ruth Beechick's new book, titled *You CAN Teach Your Child Successfully*, is (a) designed to help you teach children from fourth to eighth grade and is (b) absolutely wonderful! Like all Beechick books, this has gems on every page. Her comments about time lines and how best to use them are alone worth the price of the book. Considering how little advice on instruction is available for anyone whose children are past the learning-to-read stage, this book is a must-buy for home-schooling parents.

NEW★★
Hayes School Publishing Co., Inc.
Outlining, Note Taking and Report Writing Skills: A Step-by-Step Guide to Mastery, $4.95. For grade levels 4–8. Add $1.50 postage for first item, 35¢ each additional item.

This wonderful book starts with simple classifying exercises and takes your child right up through all the outlining and note-taking skills he will ever need.

Outlining promotes logical thinking, and helps us get so much more out of what we study and hear. It's absolutely fundamental to real progress in any intellectual endeavor. Knowing this, most textbook companies throw in a unit on Outlining somewhere in their English courses. However, almost universally they don't take it slowly enough, explain it enough, or provide enough practice for children to really master this essential skill. The solution: this book. It's a public-school workbook, so some of its text selections have that flavor, but even so, it's the best, easiest-to-use resource on this subject I have yet found. Recommended.

NEW★★
Shekinah Curriculum Cellar
Any Child Can Write, $9.95. Add $2.95 shipping. Adults read this book, then use the methods with their children ages 1–19.

Writing is easy to teach at home. All you have to do is (1) get a copy of *Any Child Can Write* by Harvey Weiner, and (2) put it into practice. *Any Child Can Write* is absolutely the best book ever written, and quite possibly the best that ever *will* be written, on teaching children to write. It's simple. It's inspiring. It's thorough. It's based on the author's own extensive experience teaching in schools, and on his experience teaching his own daughter at home. Melissa Weiner was writing and illustrating before she was four, and by the time she was five she was coming up with imagery like this:

> This is me. I like to dance and sing a song like a robin. I love to ice skate in red skates. I slip and slide and go *errrrr* on the freezing ice.

Thanks to Bantam Books, this fantastic book is finally back in print.

I can't tell you anything about writing that Dr. Weiner hasn't already put in his book. Here are some of the high points for beginning writers. Writing begins with speaking. Encourage complete sentences, and draw your children on to describe what they see and feel as crisply as possible. Once a child learns to write, *let* him write! Letters to Grandma and shopping lists make things really happen. Mom or Dad can act as secretary and write out Johnny's stories if handwriting is still a struggle. Then Dr. Weiner shows you how to help your kids make their ideas come alive by inserting adjectives and adverbs, choosing sparkling nouns and verbs, adding word pictures, and all the other gambits that separate the real writer from the topic-sentence hack.

Dr. Weiner's great contribution is in showing parents how to nourish the creative process. The vitality and joy that children pour into their poetry and prose when they have discovered how to see the world with an artist's eye make this book a delight to read. Very highly recommended.

NEW**
Shekinah Curriculum Cellar
If you're trying to teach kids to write, you've gotta have this book!, $12.95. Shipping $2.95. A book for teachers, moms, and dads.

Want to be a success in home schooling? Then realize that your job is to learn the subject you want to teach! Once you know a subject, and know how to teach it, you can use virtually any resource and teach it successfully.

So, if you want to teach kids creative writing, learn how to teach it first. To learn how to teach it, get Ruth Beechick's *You CAN Teach Your Child Successfully* (from Education Services) and get *If you're trying to teach kids to write, you've gotta have this book!* by Marjorie Frank. The title says it all. Packed into these 220 pages are more thoughts, tips, philosophy, examples, resources, and helps for teaching creative writing than you'll find in any other one spot except Mrs. Beechick's book. Sections like "100 Alternatives to *What I Did on My Summer Vacation*" take you beyond the typical loser writing lesson. Find out how to motivate the reluctant writer, the gifted writer, the very young writer. How to recover from floppo lessons. What to do with the finished writing. How to criticize writing constructively (wish all *my* critics would read that section!). How to start "word collections" of words like *smithereens* and *bamboozle* that are fun just to say. People-watching: an essential skill for writers of fiction and non-fiction alike. Tons more, all shared from the heart of a writer who evidently loves writing and cares about helping your children do likewise.

NEW**
Teaching Home
October/November 1987 issue, $3.75. Complete six-issue set for 1987, $17.50, includes free set of 6 plastic magazine holders for your ring binder.

Teaching Home magazine as its usual policy devotes each issue of the magazine to one educational theme. Articles treat the topic in depth, suggesting ideas and profiling methods and resources. It's like a minicourse in teaching that topic! October/November 1987 was the issue on creative writing. Articles covered using a word processor, writing readiness, using writing in other subjects, cultivating a lifelong writing habit, poetry, motivation, proofreading and editing, and a great article by Ruth Beechick on "The Road to Good Writing."

PROGRAMS FOR TEACHING CREATIVE WRITING

Alpha Omega Publications
Ten LIFEPACS/grade, $2.25–$2.95 each. Discount on each complete set of 10 LIFEPACS. Teacher's guides, answer keys extra. Grades K–12.

Alpha Omega's English LIFEPACS feature an excellent worktext approach to composition. All forms of writing are covered, including some secular tales, and analyzed from a Christian perspective. The series emphasizes creative thinking, and (unlike some others) actually gets the student writing a good number of compositions.

Students using Alpha Omega's English program have scored grade levels above students using conventional texts.

Bob Jones University Press
Clear and Lively Writing, $16.10. Shipping extra. A book for teachers.

BJUP decided to distribute this book, a volume of "simple, enjoyable games and exercises to develop listening, reading, speaking, and especially writing skills," as an aid to teachers of writing. A point in its favor is that the author actually knows how to write. Another is the emphasis on recognizing and overcoming communication problems, such as a child's inability to make analogies that really analogize.

Clear and Lively Writing is divided into three sections: Prescription, Practice, and Proficiency. Part 1, Prescription, includes many games and activities, as well as philosophy. Part 2 proceeds to more complicated activities, while Part 3 is a school-year calendar of writing activities.

The integration of games and activities into the philosophy sections means this is not a book to pick up and dip into. You will have to spend time with *Clear and Lively Writing* to become familiar with the author's philosophy and comfortable with the games.

Christian Schools International
Teacher's guides, $32.80 each for grades K–6; $52.50 each for grades 7 and 8 (these grades include blackline masters for student activities). Student Activity Set (folder and worksheets), $10. Packet of 5 Student Activity Sets on one grade level, $31.75. Grades K–8.

CSI's K-8 *Writing Rainbow* series looks exciting. Unlike other programs, *Writing Rainbow* recognizes that children need to be filled with experience before they can write. Prewriting experience, then, is built into the exercises. Next, CSI emphasizes writing-to-be-read, rather than wastebasket "for the teacher only" writing. Practice in all the different forms of writing is afforded by the logical layout of this program, which includes instruction in grammar and ethics as well as composition skills.

See these two units from the grade 4 workbooks:

Unit Nine **WISE WRITERS PLAY WITH POETRY**
Lesson 1 Words Sound Off!
Lesson 2 Cinquains Have Five Lines
Lesson 3 Poets Go Beyond the Senses
Lesson 4 Colors Are Alive with Feelings
Lesson 5 Poets Express Feelings
Lesson 6 We Can Express Feelings in Poems
Lesson 7 Know the Poets
Lesson 8 Rewrite the Classics
Lesson 9 Poetry Is for Sharing

Unit Ten **WISE WRITERS ADVERTISE RESPONSIBLY**
Lesson 1 Advertisers Want to Persuade You, Part I
Lesson 2 Advertisers Want to Persuade You, Part II
Lesson 3 How Should We Advertise
Lesson 4 Writing Truthful Advertising Scripts
Lesson 5 Lights! Camera! Action!

See how the authors introduce poetry and ideas about poetry before requiring actual poetry from the students. Note also the emphasis on ethics.

Or how about this unit from the kindergarten book:

Unit Four **WRITING COMES FROM WITHIN**
Lesson 1 Writing Requires Invented Spelling
Lesson 2 We Can Write Information on Charts
Lesson 3 We Can Write Conversation
Lesson 4 We Talk Together at Home
Lesson 5 Pictures Suggest Stories
Lesson 6 Stories are Embedded in Wordless Books
Lesson 7 A Puppet Makes a Good Story Character
Lesson 8 Greeting Cards Give Messages
Lesson 9 A Newsletter Reports Our News

Do you see how the kindergarten student is exposed to the idea of writing to build a foundation for writing of his own?

Teacher's guides contain background information, daily lesson plans, evaluation ideas, and follow-up activities. You also get 10–25 pages of tearout cards for supplemental writing activities. Students in grades 1–6 get two-pocket folders for storing their writing assignments and a complete set of activity pages.

Education Services
Basic Learning Packet includes *A Strong Start in Language* and two booklets about teaching reading and math, $10. Grades K–12.

Ruth Beechick does it again! *A Strong Start in Language* presents a powerful *natural* method that will help anyone become a good (maybe even great!) writer. Starting from the very beginning with a student who can physically write but has no understanding of sentence structure, Dr. Beechick's 13-step method can take you as far as you want to go. Ben Franklin used this method; so did Jack London. Included are grade-level guidelines, 14 sample lessons, instructions for spelling improvement, and some sample Bible sentences for writing practice. No supplies necessary except good library books, paper, and pencils.

NEW**
Family Learning Center
Learning Language Arts through Literature, Red Book (grade 2), $17.95. Yellow book (grade 3), $17.95. Tan book (grades 4–6), $12.95. Grey book (grades 7–8), $12.95. Add 10% shipping ($2 minimum).

Based on Ruth Beechick's methods, as outlined in her book *You Can Teach Your Child Successfully*, *Learning Language Arts through Literature* is a dictation-based program centered on excerpts from great children's literature. The original (tan) book was written for ages 10–13, and is now joined by books for children down to age 6 and up to beginning high-school level.

Each of the 25–45 weekly lessons includes a literary passage and five daily activities designed to help your student learn thinking and writing skills. You may use either copying (using the Student Editing Model) or dictation. The book itself contains Student Editing Models for all the literary passages. Each is in

large print. The student may use the Student Models to check his own work.

Every language art is included: spelling, grammar, vocabulary, writing mechanics, penmanship, and thinking skills. The authors follow Ruth Beechick's exceedingly sensible approach of only using misspelled words for the Spelling List. In fact, the entire series is based on Mrs. Beechick's wonderful teaching methods, as outlined in her book, *You Can Teach Your Child Successfully*. Grammar is taught in the context of writing, not as an isolated subject. For a grammar reference, the authors suggest *Learning Grammar through Writing* from Educators Publishing Service. (See writeup of this program in the Grammar chapter.) Vocabulary is developed through studying English classics and through the dictation/copying exercises. Penmanship is practiced in the same way.

Each dictation lesson also includes a writing activity designed to increase thinking skills. For example, the student might be asked to rewrite an entire passage in the past tense or change it from third to first person. Doing this with technical correctness and literary flair will take some thought!

Authors Diane Welch, Susan Simpson, and Debbie Strayer have also included instructions on how to use each level of *Learning Language Arts* with children of different ages, or with many children at once in a multi-level setting. They also provide instruction in how to dictate properly and a complete bibliography of every book used in the dictation lessons.

All you need is a separate notebook or notebook section for each child for the dictation exercises, and colored pencils to mark the completed lessons according to the program's special directions. You might also want to purchase additional copies of the Student Editing Models. These are the literary dictation selections in large print. Each child uses one to check his own work. One set of the Student Editing Models is provided in the back of the book.

The literature selections are wonderful! In the Tan Book, starting with Psalm 1 you proceed to *Bambi*, *The Wheel on the School*, a poem by Tennyson (famous poets are that week's special feature!), *Little House on the Prairie*, *The Bronze Bow*, *Caddie Woodlawn*, *King of the Wind* by Marguerite Henry, *Lassie Come Home*, *The Hiding Place*, *Kidnapped*, the Gettysburg Address, *Swallows and Amazons*, *Anne of Green Gables*, *Prince Caspian*, *Rascal*, *Robinson Crusoe*, *Star of Light* by Patricia St. John, *The Railway Children*, *David Copperfield*, *The Wind in the Willows*, *Little Women*, and *Big Red* by Jim Kjelgaard. In fact, this list would make an excellent reading list, if you are looking for library books to use with your children! Highly recommended.

NEW★★
Isha Enterprises
Easy Writing, $19.95. Ages 7–14.

Easy Writing, by Wanda Phillips, author of *Easy Grammar*, is a big, thick workbook full of carefully sequenced and graded exercises to help students spiff up their sentences by the use of more complex sentence structures. In other words, instead of "Bill ran. Ann ran, too. They were screaming. They ran to the house," the student will learn to write, "Screaming, Bill and Ann ran to the house." An improvement, no?

The book has several innovative features. For one thing, each unit comes in two levels. Level 1 is for lower and upper elementary students, while Level 2 is for upper elementary on up. Her book is also very logically laid out, with one unit each on writing items in a series, semicolons, appositives, participial phrases (both past and present participles), the use of "having" plus the past participle, and subordinate and relative clauses. If this all sounds rather gruesome, it really isn't so when you get into it. You get clear instructions, lots of examples, and doable exercises. Each exercise set fits on two pages and should take only about 15 minutes to complete. There's lots of repetition in both the instructions and the exercises. None of this here-today gone-tomorrow outlook about *Easy Writing*!

In the original edition, sentences transformed by this book's rules sometimes fell short of literary perfection. Example:

This book is a funny one. This book is from the library.

was an exercise in the Level 1—Appositives unit. The "right answer" is supposed to be,

This book, a funny one, is from the library.

How awkward! Try this instead:

This funny book is from the library.

The instructions also suffered from teacherese: passive sentence construction ("It is recommended" rather than "I recommend"), overuse of abstract nouns, etc. There's an occasional blooper in the answer keys, too. Consider this sentence: "Having learned to use a computer, John's work is much easier." John's work never learned to use a computer! A sensible sentence would have read something like, "Having learned to use a computer, John found his work much easier." Even better—skip the dreadful "having" altogether with a solution like, "John found his work to be much easier now that he had learned to use a computer." (Mrs. Phillips assures me these bad sentences and bloopers will be fixed in the spring 1991 reprinting.)

Having said all that (notice how I'm not taking my own creative-writing advice?), this book does have its merits. It's extremely simple to use. Everything is explained right in the lesson. No preparation time is needed. The exercises are easy to grade with the answer keys at the end of each section. You can use this one book with children of all ages—a whole *Cheaper by the Dozen* family, if they write the answers on separate paper! There's enough repetition to learn the concepts, without so much as to cause unutterable boredom. If you balance the one-size-fits-all suggested answers with a dash of William Zinsser's *On Writing Well*, your child will be scribbling better sentences than 97% of today's American high school graduates.

NEW★★
Midwest Publications
Each book, $9.95. Grades 4–7.

Critical Thinking Activities to Improve Writing Skills. Who comes up with titles like these? The subtitles are every bit as exciting and helpful: *Where-Abouts, Arguments,* and *Descriptive Mysteries.*

Since we're talking about creative writing, I'm going to untangle these mysteries for you in a minute; but first, let's talk about packaging. How many bottles do you think Coca-Cola would have sold if their drink had been named *Refreshing Beverage with Little Bubbles*? Or, as Gertrude Stein never said, a rose is not just an odiferous flower. Schoolbook publishers, take note!

Back to our subject. These books actually can improve writing skills. Take *Descriptive Mysteries,* for example. Each exercise in the book has an identical format: "Kid, describe this thingummy so folks can pick it out of a page of similar thingummies." Kids will get to practice observing, comparing, and describing items on the basis of size, colors and patterns, shape, expression, and direction. That is a fairly limited vocabulary, so the astute teacher will do well to drag in some real-life examples as well. In the book, for instance, one exercise involves describing a high-topped tennis shoe with a star on the heel. In real life, your tennies might be dirty or stained, smelly, worn, run-down at the heel, blue-red-orange-neon yellow-or-whatever, cotton-or-canvas-or-leather (etc.), size 8/19/10/etc., with frayed laces (or new white laces), and so on. Smell, texture, color, and condition are worth describing, among other things. And don't forget the use of simile and metaphor . . . Hey, I'm going to start talking you into buying *Any Child Can Write* again!

Arguments is really a logic book. Someone you know has a problem. You have to solve the problem by logical reasoning and write them a letter explaining your answer. Since most high school graduates nowadays can't write two consecutive logical paragraphs, I suppose this counts as creative writing.

Where-Abouts is exercises in telling people how to get from here to there. You, the writer, have a map with special information on it, e.g., "Walking on the grass is not permitted anywhere in the park except in the picnic area (GOAL)." Armed with this information, not available on the reader's map, you tell your reader how to wend his way successfully from start to finish, avoiding all migrating caterpillars and sinkholes not shown on his map. This is good practice in careful writing and reading of directions. Again, you have to be imaginative to make these into truly *creative* writing assignments. I'd rather have kids describe their journeys in Heroic Quest fashion ("I paused a moment at the statue, a granite lion with head thrown back to roar. What was that sound I heard . . . like millions of tiny trampling feet? It was the park caterpillars' annual migration! They swept by on the next path, a rippling wave of smooth green and fuzzy black . . .") This would be a lot more interesting than giving picnic directions.

UPDATED**
Perception Publications

Creative IQ Program now includes *Active Listening* tape, $69 plus $4 shipping. Grades 2–6.

The *Creative IQ Program* is a four-cassette set with four accompanying creative writing workbooks, certifi-

cate of achievement, and binder. Simone Bibeau, a schoolteacher with ten years' experience, explains on tape why creativity is vital to your child's success and the keys to developing a creative climate. She also discusses creative communications skills, creative writing and performing, and creative problem solving skills, and gives artistic activities for you to pursue.

I personally don't think it would be that much fun to fill out the workbook pages. Your student would end up doing an awful lot before he or she ever finished a story, since a lot of the work is pre-writing exercises to generate ideas. What *would* work is to ask the workbook questions and either (a) tape your child's answers, (b) let Mom or Dad act as secretary and write down any answers you agree are important, or (c) just ask the questions and forget about writing the answers. You can describe the main character's appearance and character verbally before beginning to write, for example. It is not necessary to write down all these details in advance. It *is* good to learn to think like a writer, though, and going through these workbooks will definitely help your child do this.

NEW**
Shekinah Curriculum Cellar

The Write Source handbook (grades 4–9), $8.50. *Basic Writing* workbook (grades 6–8), $5.95 for either student book or teacher's edition. *Mechanics of Writing* workbook (grades 6–9), $2.95 for either student book or teacher's edition. *Revising Process* workbook (grades 6–9), $2.95 for either student book or teacher's edition. Shipping extra.

The Write Source, published by the company of the same name, is an excellent English grammar, writing, and general information handbook. I am delighted that Shekinah is carrying it, because the publisher was not set up to handle individual orders and I thought I'd have to leave it out of my book!

The Write Source handbook includes a great deal of information useful to students in grades 4-9. Writing skills covered: the writing process, the classroom report, the book review, the short story, the poem, the letter, thinking and study skills, vocabulary and spelling skills, library skills, and speech skills . . . for a start! Other useful information includes: The United States Constitution, U.S. and world maps, computer terms, and more! It's a bit hard to describe such a compendium of everything-you-need-to-know-about-everything. Suffice it to say that this is a great source of information about writing, loaded with facts writers find useful. *The Write Source* has the write stuff, all right!

Shekinah is also making the rest of the *Write Source* line of workbooks available. These are designed to be used with the handbook. *Basic Writing* concentrates on creative writing skills activities. *Mechanics of Writing* includes lessons on punctuation, usage, capitalization, plurals, abbreviations, etc. *Revising Process* shows you how to spot subject-verb mismatches, fragments, run-on sentences, wordiness, and other bloopers; how to replace bland adjectives with zippy ones; how to add supporting details; how to kill off passive sentences; and so on.

NEW**
Teacher Created Materials
I Can series, $3.95 each.

If you don't mind delirious rabbits cluttering up the covers of your children's workbooks, you can quickly review or work through a number of language arts problem areas with the *I Can* series from Teacher Created Materials. Each 32-page workbook has an answer key in the back and is designed for grades 2–6. The workbooks include a mix of "teaching" exercises (e.g., this-is-the-heading-of-the-letter, this-is-the-body), creative exercises, and skills exercises. Ecstatic bunnies cavort about the pages—this is for the public-school kids, to fool them into believing schoolwork is fun. The exercises do have flashes of wit, both overt and tongue-in-cheek. An example of the latter is this sample sentence for an exercise in adding dependent clauses to a main sentence: "Because a substitute teacher was here today, we behaved perfectly so our teacher would be proud of us."

Don't expect miracles here. Like other public-school materials, the *I Can* series was written to teach kids minimal skills and drill them on the same. Consider this a starting point, a taste of each grammar and writing area, not the last word.

The *I Can* series includes: *I Can Write a Letter, I Can Punctuate, I Can Write a Poem, I Can Write a Paragraph* (your basic topic-sentence approach!), *I Can Write a Sentence, I Can Capitalize,* and *I Can Write a Re-*

search Paper. All the books are reproducible, meaning classroom teachers can order one and then copy it for the whole class.

INSPIRATION AND EXAMPLES

Gazelle Publications
Bubbles, $11.50 postpaid. Hardcover, 159 pages. Ages 5–12.

Bubbles is an unusual book designed to interest and involve children in poetry. Beyond the more than 100 poems (chosen out of more than two thousand submissions), *Bubbles* also has notes about each of the authors, questions to highlight thoughts in some of the poems, notes on what inspired them, and activities that use them as launching pads. You can quickly find notes about each poem and its author through handy cross-references beneath each poem.

NEW**
Pennsylvania Homeschoolers
A Baby Learns What is What, $3.50. *A Crayfish Abroad,* $3.50. Free shipping on prepaid orders. Ages 7–12.

Still more from the Richmans, a leading family in Pennsylvania homeschooling: *A Baby Learns What is What* is an absolutely delightful spiral-bound book written and illustrated by eight-year-old Jacob. Follow baby Hannah through her busy day, as seen through the eyes of a real live brother. Anyone who has ever had a baby or who has ever home educated a preteen boy will especially enjoy Jacob's tell-it-like-it-is approach!

Eleven-year-old Jesse also gets into the act with *A Crayfish Abroad,* the thrilling fiction tale of a crayfish captured from his stream and placed in a big glass tank, where . . . but I'd better not spoil the story by telling you what happens next! Spiral-bound with line illustrations, this book, like Jacob's, is bound to inspire your children to write "a real book" themselves.

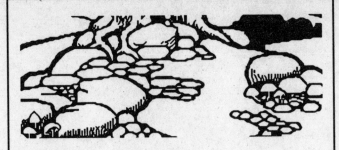

UPDATED**
Stone Soup: the magazine by children
$23 membership in Children's Art Foundation includes subscription. Ages 6–13.

Stone Soup is a production of the Children's Art Foundation. They look for stories and poems in which the writer does a good job of observing the world and telling us something about his or her life. *Stone Soup* includes work by children from all kinds of backgrounds. In the last two years they have published six stories by Navajo children writing about their lives on the reservation. They have also published stories by Southeast Asian refugee children and stories written in Black English.

Stone Soup is printed on quality paper and stapled into a hefty booklet. An activity guide correlated with the magazine is bound into each issue. Older children can use the activity guide on their own.

Stone Soup has the same cultural flavor as *Zoom!*—what PBS is to television, *Stone Soup* is to children's magazines.

Stone Soup contains upbeat and funny stories. It also includes a fair number of selections featuring fear, alienation, and despair. Some examples of the upbeat: in "Too Many Jennifers," a girl decides to change her name because there are three Jennifers in her class and even the new dog in the neighborhood is named Jennifer! Balance this against the tale of a girl who used to enjoy a close relationship with her teenage brother, but who now writes bemoaning how he has deleted her from his life. Upbeat: A country kid misses his old home until he wins a contest to design and name a new city park. Downbeat: Stories featuring divorce, sibling battles, pets dying, grandparents dying, disasters of all kinds, even war! Decide if your child is ready to look at life "from both sides now" (and without religious faith in time of crisis presented as a solution to human misery) before subscribing.

CHAPTER SEVENTEEN

GRAMMAR

Admit it—you used to hate grammar when you were a kid. You used to grouch about the grammar homework old Mrs. Pickle sent home with you. You failed to leap for joy when the class discussion topic was participial phrases. Way down deep, you figured you would *never, ever* learn or use all those rules, anyway, so what was the point?

Now, in that remorseless way life has of rolling on and over us, you have a child. A child who needs to learn grammar. Rules. Such as, that these last few sentences are all ungrammatical and *wrong, wrong, wrong*! I can just see old Mrs. Pickle getting out her red pen right now. "Mary is a bright girl but her grammar needs improvement . . ."

Here's a simple solution to your panic over teaching Junior his grammar. A *really* simple solution. First, *you* learn correct grammar. You're bigger and tougher than Junior—you make the sacrifice. Then, once you have learned the grammatical rules, you can easily teach them to Junior, using any program you like. In fact, you won't even need a program. Once you understand grammar, you can teach it from classic literature and/or the Bible, working in handwriting, spelling, vocabulary improvement, and every other language art skill at the same time.

Here's one way of doing this. Every day, have Junior read a chapter from the Bible and narrate the chapter back to you (Bible study, speech practice,

thinking skills, oral creativity). Then have him write out a paragraph from that chapter in his best handwriting (handwriting practice). Next, have Junior identify every word in that paragraph. He can write N over a noun, V over a verb, ADJ over an adjective, PREP over a preposition . . . you get the idea. If Junior is a little older, and you understand diagramming, he can diagram the sentences. The Bible is a fairly complicated book, so sooner or later Junior will run into every grammatical construction. This takes care of grammar. Now, dictate another paragraph (or sentence, or phrase, depending on Junior's age) to Junior from that chapter. Check for spelling mistakes. Have Junior rewrite every misspelled words five times and put the word in his personal spelling notebook. There's your spelling instruction. If you like, Junior can act out the visual scenes, if any, in the chapter (drama). Vocabulary improvement will take care of itself as long as you're available to tell Junior what the words mean that he doesn't yet understand, assuming you aren't using one of those dumbed-down pseudo-translations.

This same method can be used with classic literature. In both cases, Junior can also pick his favorite extracts and copy them in a creative writing notebook. He can then use the form of each extract to produce a creative sentence or paragraph of his own (creative writing). For example, take Shakespeare's "Parting is such sweet sorrow/Let us say goodnight, till it be morrow" as an example. A typical 10-year-old takeoff on that might be "Eating is such great delight/Let's eat all day, till it be night!" This may seem like a trivial exercise, but becoming familiar with the style and phraseology of the great authors is what learning to write creatively is all about.

This method can only succeed, of course, if you are absolutely certain of your own grammar, since you won't find an answer key anywhere that has the whole Bible diagrammed into sentences and the individual parts of speech all identified. However, the freedom to pick your own source material for language arts study is what makes this kind of teaching really fun. So, once again, I suggest that you pick your favorite grammar resource from the list below and whip through it yourself. You're a lot older and wiser than when you first struggled with the subject, and besides your earlier school experience will make it much easier for you to learn all this the second time around. Then you can either just use that same resource (with which you will be very familiar and comfortable) with your children, or add the best tips and ideas you gleaned from it to a literature-based method such as I outlined above.

Is it worth making this effort? Yes! Kids pick up their language patterns from listening to you, not from workbooks. Any improvement in your own grammar or vocabulary will have lasting beneficial effects for your children. And after reading thousands of magazines and newsletters, I can say with confidence that most people need to refresh their grammatical training. Our whole society is losing the ability to distinguish the proper uses of *its* and *it's,* for example. *Its* is the possessive pronoun, as in *The boat slipped from its moorings. It's* is short for *it is,* as in *It's raining outside.* Yet over just the past few years I have seen the two mixed up everywhere. I really wince when I see fancy curriculum products with *its* where *it's* should be, and vice versa. This common mistake, like many others, is easy to fix once the teachers learn the rule.

It's?
Its?

GRAMMAR PROGRAMS FOR ELEMENTARY GRADES

A Beka Book Publications
Oral Language Exercises, $10.05. Add $3.25 shipping.

Thanks-for-writing department: Sharon See of Santa Rosa, California recommends *Oral Language Exercises.* This language aid is based on the premise that people often use incorrect grammar because they ain't used to hearin' people who talk good. Rather like the Professor's idea in *My Fair Lady.* You, the teacher, are provided ten daily word usage sentences that will, according to the catalog, "help train students' ears and inculcate correct language skills." Words commonly misused, such as well/good and bad/badly, are explained and used correctly in sentences. Your students then repeat the sentences. All together, 1,750 sentences in a spiral-bound book, for use primarily in grades 1–8.

Because it took me five minutes to find it, let me tell you that the order blank for *Oral Language Exercises* is located under "Language Teaching Aids" near the beginning of the A Beka order form. I only found it in the catalog by trial-and-error searching. Wouldn't it be nice if next year's A Beka catalog had an index!

Alpha Omega Publications
Exploring Truths worktext $5.95, answer key $2.95, grades 6–12. *Exploring Truths Through Diagramming* student text with answer key, $3.95, grades 6–12. *Easy English* $9.95, grades 8–12. Shipping extra.

Did you know that Sunday school was invented to help poor children learn to read, and that their text was the Bible? For centuries the Bible was used as a text for reading, literature, grammar, and composition, and Sunday school is just one of the educational enterprises in this tradition.

Alpha Omega Publications has a series based on this old concept. *Exploring Truths* is subtitled "A systematic approach to learning English through the Bible." Designed to be used by individuals or groups who possess at least sixth grade skills, *Exploring Truths* is for anyone who wants to "learn grammar through studying God's Word." Alpha Omega suggests that the text can be used by individual students for review or enrichment, or by the whole family. *Exploring Truths Through Diagramming,* a companion book, revives the honored custom of learning grammar and parts of speech through diagramming sentences from the Bible book of Joshua.

UPDATED**
Educational Products
Trophy books I and II, $7.75 each. Shipping extra. Grades 3–8.

This two-workbook series for third-graders or bright second-graders isn't quite as inspired as the rest of the *Sing, Spell, Read and Write* program, but it still beats the standard public school texts. Book I covers alphabetical order, kinds of sentences, capital letters, and punctuation. Book II has Writing Letters, Writing Stories, Word Usage, Language Manners, a "Parts of Speech" song, Articles, Nouns, Adjectives, Pronouns, Verbs, Adverbs, Conjunctions, Prepositions, Interjections, and Practical Everyday Reading Skills. Both books have a spelling section in the back, with 10 words for each of 95 days, and accompanying puzzles, crosswords, word searches, and other games. Together they cover in one year what regular schoolbooks drag out over ten.

NEW**
Educators Publishing Service
Rules of the Game: Grammar through Discovery, Books 1 (grades 5–7), 2 (grades 6–8), and 3 (grades 7–9), $6 each; answer key for each book, $2 each. *Learning Grammar Through Writing*, $6.70. Shipping extra.

Educators Publishing Service now enters the fray with their brand-new series, *Rules of the Game: Grammar through Discovery*. Like all EPS materials, the books are inexpensive. Like most of them, they are easy to use. Using the inductive approach, *Rules of the Game* leads students to discover grammar rules and definitions. Example: "In the following sentences, underline any words that name people, animals, places, things, ideas, or feelings." When the student does this, he discovers those words are called *nouns*.

Workbook 1 has just enough exercises to carry you from parts of speech through punctuation, capital-ization, and sentence structure, to subject and verb agreement. Answer key is included—so they say, anyway. It didn't come with my copy. Book 2 teaches direct and indirect objects, linking verbs, predicate nouns and adjectives, and more. Book 3 includes work on dependent clauses, complex and compound-complex sentences, gerunds, participles, and infinitives.

For those who themselves have a reasonable command of grammar and wish to help others, whether children or adults, who are not so fortunately endowed, *Learning Grammar Through Writing* is a wonderful tool. "The central idea of *Learning Grammar Through Writing* is to teach grammar to students by having them write compositions regularly and then correct their own work, at a level which they can reasonably be expected to achieve." The book is divided into 13 categories—e.g., Verbs, The Sentence, Punctuation—and within each category you will find all the necessary rules and examples in *nice large print*. The book is inexpensive and reusable.

NEW**
Hayes School Publishing Co., Inc.
Learning English, grades 3–8, $3.95 each. Teacher's key for grade 8, 50¢. Add $1.50 postage for first item, 35¢ each additional item.

Learning English is a series of cleverly-designed, inexpensive 86–156 page workbooks. Books are divided into sections, each with its own diagnostic test, practice lessons to reinforce any skills found wanting on the diagnostic test, and a mastery test to check the student's work after finishing the unit. Diagnostic tests are at the end of the book. Mastery tests are in the middle of the book, pre-perfed for easy removal. All workbooks except that for grade 8 have a pull-to-remove answer key with answers for all tests and practice exercises.

The diagnostic tests are designed to help your child avoid any unnecessary drill work. Each question is linked with a lesson practice page. If the child misses the question, you can assign the exact page to drill that particular skill. This means only necessary practice gets assigned. Lesson practice pages do more than drill; they teach the skill with both rules and examples, as well as drill exercises, thus quickly bringing your child up to speed.

For further ease of use, each workbook is divided into 6–13 units, each dealing with one topic. For example, the grade 3 units are Sentence Sense, Capital

Letters, Correct Usage, Composition, Letter Writing, and Word Study. For grade 7, the units are Mastering the Sentence, Building Paragraphs, Nouns, Pronouns, Verbs and Their Uses, Classification of Modifiers, Adjective Modifiers, Adverbial Modifiers, Prepositional Phrase Modifiers, Classification of Sentences, Punctuation and Capitalization, General Review, and Letter Writing. Individual units can be studied in any order. An excellent, clutter-free series for learning or drilling grammar and usage.

Hayes also has an *Exercises in English* series, with a similar format to their *Reading Comprehension* series. *Exercises in English* is much less thought-provoking, more fill-in-the-blankish. I would definitely choose *Learning English* over Hayes' *Exercises in English* series.

UPDATED**
Hewitt Research Foundation
Winston Grammar, $29 (grades 3–8). *Advanced Winston Grammar*, $23 (grades 9–12). Shipping extra.

Here's a product that actually makes grammar *fun*, even for little kids who aren't neat and orderly types. It's called the Winston Grammar series, and it teaches grammatical constructions by pattern building with colored flash cards, rather than by diagramming.

HOW IT WORKS: Children identify the parts of speech in worksheet sentences by laying out their part-of-speech cards in the proper order. For example, in the first lesson, when children have just learned articles and nouns, they would lay out the sentence, "The boy and the girl saw a man eat an apple" as article-noun-blank-article-noun-blank-article-noun-blank-article-noun. Later on, they learn more parts of speech and eventually are able to lay out even complex sentences without using blank cards. (The cards, by the way, have "clues" on one side and the part-of-speech name on the other, for added learning value.) They also learn to identify parts of speech and constructions by underlining and writing abbreviations above the words in a sentence.

Each *Winston Grammar* program includes a set of worksheets bound with a pre- and post-test, a teacher's manual, quiz keys, and the color-coded noun function cards and parts-of-speech cards. *Winston Grammar* comes in a really fancy custom molded plastic binder, with space for adding the advanced kit later.

The basic course teaches parts of speech, noun functions, prepositional phrases, and the principles of modification. Parts of speech taught are: article, noun, personal pronoun, verb, adjective, adverb, preposition

(and object), coordinating conjunction, and interjection. Noun and pronoun functions are taught in the following sequence: object of preposition, subject, direct object, indirect object, predicate nominative, appositive, and noun of direct address. All in all, it's supposed to take you 50–75 sessions to complete this course, including the frequent review lessons.

The *Advanced Winston Grammar* has 55 worksheets, as opposed to the 30 worksheets in the basic course. After a review of the previous course, it goes on to possessive adjectives, pronouns, nouns, and adjectives; reflexives; interrogative pronouns; present and past participles; correlative conjunctions; simple infinitives and gerunds; subject-verb combinations; clause identification; adverb clauses; compound and complex sentences; relative pronouns; adjective clauses; ellipsed relative pronouns; embedded clauses; and noun clauses as direct objects, indirect objects, predicate nominatives, objects of prepositions, appositives, and subjects. The additional cards used in this course are: possessive adjective, possessive pronoun, pronoun/adjective, verbals, Tricky Words, and Tricky Word Clues.

Hewitt tells me the basic kit is good for three to four years of grammar instruction; then the advanced kit takes your student through high school.

NEW**
Maupin House Publishing
Caught'Ya!, grades 3–12, $14.95. Available from Shekinah Curriculum Cellar.

Bored middle-school kids. Hate grammar. Frustrated teacher. Wants kids to connect grammar skills taught in class to real life. Serendipitous synergy results in . . .

Caught'Ya: Grammar with a Giggle. Appalling (but memorable) title, this. (Endless possibilities: *Math with a Mumble. Science with a Sneer. History with a Hiss.*)

Enough of this tomfoolery. Back to real sentences. Believing that "frustration has to be the real mother of invention," teacher Jane Bell Kiester developed a simple, 10-minute-a-day technique that reconnects writing with grammar. *Caught'Ya!* outlines the technique, which has been classroom-tested in local (Florida) state schools and church schools for 10 years.

Her approach: soap opera. Every day the teacher writes a sentence in the ongoing saga on the blackboard. Each day's sentence contains five to ten mistakes that must be discovered and corrected. A mistake is only counted wrong if the student doesn't catch it during the self-grading time, when the teacher explains all the mistakes. This means everyone, even the dullest student, has the chance for a perfect score. Result: kids start concentrating on grammar, improving their writing, and enjoying English class!

The book both explains the technique and provides three 100-sentence sample soap opera sagas, complete with a new vocabulary word each day and the corrections needed for each sentence. These soap operas are pretty bad. Romeo and Juliet go to the mall. Students trip about the world with magic purple umbrellas. Hairy Beast suffers from a hopeless crush on a fickle female. Kids learn from these sagas that rudeness pays, revenge is fun, and that kids should keep secrets from their parents. Be glad you don't have to use the prewritten soaps to use the easy, fun, and effective techniques taught in *Caught'Ya!*

Mott Media
Harvey's Elementary Grammar and Composition, $10.95. *Harvey's Revised English Grammar*, $13.95. Both hardcover.

This duo of classic grammars widely used in the McGuffey era requires (and produces) far more intellectual vigor than any workbooks available today. The teacher is urged to question the student and guide him to discovering the correct answer, rather than either giving him the answer or leaving him to "creatively" thrash it out on his own. As the introduction to the *Elementary Grammar* says,

Great care has been taken never to define a term or to enunciate a principle without first preparing the mind of the pupil to grasp and comprehend the meaning and use of the term defined or the principle enumerated.

That will give you an idea of what you're in for. Students begin in the *Elementary Grammar* with the study of words, parts of speech, and sentences (figuring out principles concerning each along the way), and move on in the *Revised English Grammar* to complete sentence analysis and parsing (you may remember this as diagramming). Punctuation, orthography, etymology, syntax, and prosody are thoroughly covered in the latter; some composition is included.

The *Elementary Grammar* is not really "elementary" in the sense of "ridiculously easy." It is intended for grades 4–6, while the *Revised Grammar* goes through junior high and high school.

These are "programmed" texts; that is, everything the teacher is supposed to say and everything the student is supposed to answer is spelled out, albeit in somewhat outdated language. Example:

In the sentence, "Ellen and Mary study botany," what two words are used as the subject? "Ellen" and "Mary." Why? Because something is affirmed of them: both Ellen and Mary study botany.

Both volumes are notably short on review. Subjects are introduced one after another, and it is assumed that the student has sufficient strength of mind to hang on to each new rule or term while not forgetting the old.

The publisher says two companion volumes are on the way, as are teacher-edition answer keys and a corresponding composition book.

NEW**
Resource Publications
Understanding Grammar, $15 plus $1.60 shipping. All ages.

This slim easy-to-follow spiral-bound book chronicles the highly successful method designed by Mary Schwalm to teach her own four sons grammar at home. Starting with games, your whole family learns the three basic sentence types, the parts of speech, verb tenses, and on to more esoteric stuff. Step follows step in a very simple, clutter-free fashion that concentrates on explaining the *how* and *why* of our English language, often illustrated by sentence diagramming techniques. You will find this book a breeze to use and a wonderful introduction to/accompaniment for a formal grammar handbook such as *Harvey's* or *Warriner's*.

This is the neatest course in the hows and whys of grammar, including games and diagramming, that I have seen. Super easy to use.

NEW★★
Shekinah Curriculum Cellar

The Write Source handbook (grades 4–9), $8.50. *Basic Writing* workbook (grades 6–8), $5.95 for either student book or teacher's edition. *Mechanics of Writing* workbook (grades 6–9), $2.95 for either student book or teacher's edition. *Revising Process* workbook (grades 6–9), $2.95 for either student book or teacher's edition. Shipping extra.

The Write Source, published by the company of the same name, is an excellent English grammar, writing, and general information handbook. I described the handbook and creative-writing workbooks briefly in the Creative Writing chapter. The series also includes a grammar workbook, *Mechanics of Writing*, with lessons on punctuation, usage, capitalization, plurals, abbreviations, etc. If you would like a combined creative-writing and grammar program for your preteen children, the handbook and workbooks are worth a look.

GRAMMAR DRILL

NEW★★
Harlan Enterprises
Games, $3.50 each. Grades 3 and up.

Card games that drill grammar facts. In *Noun Fun* you match nouns to their description. "Books," for example, matches "common, plural" whereas "Len's" matches "proper, singular, possessive." With *Punctuation Fun* you match each sentence to its proper ending punctuation. Each game can be played as a memory game (turn over two cards and if they match you keep them and take another turn) or as a pick-from-the-stack style game. For more detailed description, see the Math Drill chapter.

UPDATED★★
Isha Enterprises
Easy Grammar text (includes all workbook exercises plus teaching instructions), 505 pages, $21. *Easy Grammar Workbook*, $8.95. *Daily GRAMS*, $14.50 each. *Daily GRAMS for Second and Third Grades*, price TBA. Add 15% shipping.

This might be *the* answer for busy home schoolers. *Easy Grammar* is the easiest complete grammar course around. Minimal effort, maximum results. Workbook for kids, teacher's manual with all the answers and teaching tips. Zero lesson preparation time, easy to teach, easy to understand, easy to correct.

Author Wanda Phillips, a schoolteacher for many years, had the bright idea of teaching children prepositions *first*. Her students crossed out the prepositional phrases in normal sentences, enabling them to easily find nouns, verbs, and so on.

Rather than diagramming, Mrs. Phillips employs a system of underlining and notation.

These big red workbooks really are doable—easy to use and easy to teach. The course is complete, covering everything from antecedent pronouns and appositives through how to write a business letter.

Following the "mastery" system of learning popularized by Madeline Hunter, grammar is introduced step by step. Each unit also contains material from the previous units, for a continuous review.

If you need grammar review more than grammar instruction, you can always get *Daily GRAMS: Guided Review Aiding Mastery Skills.* All *Daily GRAMS* books have the same format. Exercise 1 on each page is always capitalization review. Exercise 2 is always punctuation review, and 5 is always a sentence combining exercise. Numbers 3 and 4 are general reviews of grammar usage, sentence types, and (in the third and fourth grade levels) dictionary skills. Concepts are repeated every 20–25 days.

There are three *Daily GRAMS* workbooks: *Daily GRAMS for Third and Fourth Grades, Daily GRAMS for*

Fourth and Fifth Grades, and *Daily GRAMS for Sixth Grade and Up.* All levels of *Daily GRAMS* contain 180 daily reviews, one per teaching day. A GRAM a day only takes ten minutes or so, including correction time.

Last-minute news: a new *Daily GRAMS for Second and Third Grades* is due out in Spring 1991 (just a smidgin too late for me to see it!).

NEW★★
McDougal, Littell
Daily Oral Language program, $12 each teacher's manual. Grades 1–12 available. Add $4 shipping.

"We wanna use daily oral Language every day, dont you?"

Did you find all the usage errors in the question above? Like the *Caught'Ya!* program, *Oral Language Exercises* provides two sentences a day for you to write on the chalkboard. Your children "play detective" as they solve and recognize the usage and mechanics errors in these sentences. It all takes about five minutes a day, with no blanks to fill in.

Are you a bit rusty on such things as pronoun case and subject-verb agreement? No problem! Each teacher's manual contains the correct sentences for each exercise, plus a list of all the errors in each sentence, all right next to each other on the page.

Unlike *Caught'Ya!*, the *Daily Oral Language* program sentences have no "plot." Each sentence stands alone, totally unconnected to the others. This is a pity, since the anticipation of following an unfolding story does add a lot of interest to daily sentence drills. While I'm complaining, the total lack of capitalization in every single sentence in all 12 grades also gets a bit old. Also, the egregious usage errors the program hopes to correct are unlikely to be a problem outside of the most remote backwoods or derelict inner-city neighborhoods. I seriously doubt any of my children would ever come close to writing anything resembling, "He brang home the most pretty picture him could find" (an actual sentence from Day 3, Level 6).

In my judgment, you should either skip the sentences with usage totally foreign to the way your family normally writes and speaks or rephrase them, so you will be practicing grammar conventions rather than drilling the kids in bad usages they never would have thought of on their own. Example: "the burglar taked these items clothes jewelry and shoes" could become "the burglar took these items clothes jewelry and shoes." In both cases, the correct answer is, "The bur-

glar took these items: clothes, jewelry, and shoes," but in the revised example, you were practicing listing items in a series and how to use a colon instead of puzzling over a weird phrase like "the burglar taked."

Kids do learn a lot better by proofreading and editing sentences than by filling in the blanks in endless workbooks. If you're only teaching one child, he can correct the sentences right at the blackboard. If you have more than one budding grammarian, they will need to write the sentences correctly in their notebooks, so each of them has a chance to solve the sentences' problems. Very simple; you get results in five to ten minutes a day.

Though the sentences in this program may be a bit dull, and the plot element is lacking, the sentences do uphold traditional values and are very easy to use. With the addition of a few commonsense changes, as suggested above, this program could take most of the pain out of grammar drill.

GRAMMAR ACCESSORIES

Audio Memory Publishing
Grammar Songs kit (includes cassette, songbook/workbook, answers, progress chart, and teacher's guide), $16.95. *Grammar Songs* workbook without teacher's guide and answers, $4.50. Add $2 shipping. Grades K–12.

"I and You and He and She and We and It and They are all . . . pronouns. Koo koo ka choo." Just call it *Sergeant Pepper's Lonely Grammar Band.* This set of grammar songs does *not* include the aforementioned lyrics, but does have 16 musically professional pop/light rock grammar songs giving you the lowdown about nouns, verbs, adjectives, and so on—even Greek and Latin prefixes and suffixes! The lyrics really educate. For example, part of the first "Verb Song" goes:

I'm *running, jumping, singing*—that's because I am a verb.
I'm *hopping, dancing, ringing*—that's because I am a verb.
I'm *coming, going, hitting, throwing,*
Humming, rowing, sitting, blowing,
Riding, hiding, gliding, sliding—
Because I'm a verb.
I'm a verb, verb, verb—I'm an action word.
So put me where the action is 'cause I'm an action word.

Other verses list examples of helping verbs and linking verbs, and explain that verbs can describe what you're doing in your head—"The action isn't physical, it's in my mind instead."

The *Grammar Song* kit includes not only this cassette, but a workbook illustrated with sassy cartoons. This includes a teacher's guide and answers to the (fairly standard) exercises in the back. Also available are books without the teacher notes and answers.

You can do the workbook exercises if you must, but the real appeal of *Grammar Songs* is the idea of inculcating so many concepts effortlessly through song. If, that is, you like a pop beat.

NEW**
EDC Publishing
The Word Detective, $11.95. Shipping extra. Ages 5–12.

I love detective stories, and I love the Usborne books from EDC Publishing. Put them together, and what have you got? Inspector Noun and Sergeant Verb and the other goofy characters in *The Word Detective*. Laid out like a Richard Scarry book, each page of this oversized, fully illustrated, colorful book features a part of speech. Inspector Noun, for example, tracks down thieves in a supermarket by passing by displays of all the different fruits and vegetables—all nouns, of course. Or we see Sergeant Verb performing all the duties of a busy crook-chasing day—all verbs, of course. When I tell you this great book is available in French and German as well as English, you can see why Usborne has left other educational publishers in the dust.

NEW**
TREND Enterprises, Inc.
Each bulletin board set, $5.99, includes free Discovery Guide. Requires 4 x 6' bulletin board. Add $2 shipping (minimum order $10).

Kids who have trouble recognizing and remembering basic punctuation can find help with TREND's *Punctuation Pals* bulletin board set. These BIG punctuation marks come with pin-up captions and text describing how to use each of them. The *Punctuation Pointers* bulletin board set goes one step farther. In this set, each punctuation mark is given a personality that explains its use. For example, the hyphen is shown with a wrench, because he connects words together. Hyper kids and kids with poor eyesight who have trouble picking out itty-bitty punctuation marks can't help getting socked in the eye by these big, colorful visuals.

TREND also has bulletin board sets featuring capitalization and parts of speech, in case you wanted to know!

CHAPTER EIGHTEEN

HANDWRITING AND KEYBOARDING

In the wishful spirit of welcome mats that proclaim, "Dull women have spotless homes," it has been said, "Poor handwriting is a sign of genius." Granted, doctors and top executives are often guilty of illegible scrawling. But they usually develop this annoying incommunicability only after acquiring a secretary who is capable of deciphering their scribbles. You don't get to be a corporate president by, as a little boy, having all your school papers returned with points marked off for illegibility. No, the written hash produced by busy leaders is really the sad remains of what used to be decent handwriting.

It has also been said, in educational circles anyway, "Kids don't really need to learn to write any more. They can just learn to type on a computer keyboard. After all, everything's computerized nowadays." Sorry, but that won't work either. Human beings sometimes need to write down ideas when they are more than six feet away from a wall outlet. Henry David Thoreau would have had a pretty poor time trying to write *Walden* at a computer console.

So let's just give up and admit it; children should learn to write legibly. Now comes the crunch: *how* shall we teach them?

Today four major methods are contending in the handwriting field. They are:

- **Ball and stick.** One group favors manuscript writing ("ball and stick") for young children because it is so easy to teach (all strokes begin on a line) and it resembles print, thus making the teaching of reading less confusing. Unhappily, ball and stick degenerates into a hash of bouncing balls and chopped-up sticks when students are trying to write fast, and once a child has started with ball and stick he has to make the dreaded transition to cursive from scratch.

- **Precursive.** Recognizing the flaws of ball-and-stick manuscript, a number of companies are now vending a type of manuscript handwriting closely allied to cursive. Letters are formed with a single stroke rather than with several as in ball and stick, and generally they follow the cursive form. What's left out are the connectors. Precursive moves smoothly to cursive, with only a few letters changing (such as *b* and *f*). The goal here is to end up with legible cursive writing.

- **Starting with cursive.** It is possible to begin with a simplified cursive script and stick with it, thus making no transitions at all. Drawback: for beginning readers, the large difference between cursive and book print may confuse matters.

- **Italic.** Here the ultimate goal is to develop a beautiful and functional calligraphic hand based on calligraphic italic, rather than the standard cursive. The new italic hands do not require special pens, but can be written with anything from a ballpoint pen to a fine tip marker or even a pencil. Students begin with precursive and move towards italic mastery. A big difference in this system is that the capitals are the manuscript forms, rather than the fancy and hard to read cursive capitals. Furthermore, since calligraphy is an art form, children are encouraged to develop their own style rather than to adhere to a uniform model.

Personally, I much prefer the precursive-leading-to-italic approach. Why should handwriting merely be legible handwriting when it could be gorgeous? Also, I find cursive capitals frustrating, and cursive hands very easily get out of control and end up being illegible. Properly done, italic is much more legible than cursive and just as fast to write. Furthermore, since most cursive methods stress connecting all the letters all the time, this places a burden on creative students, who handwriting studies show are more inclined to want to leave letters unconnected.

However, in the final analysis, handwriting style is a matter of personal choice. If your daughter is learning at home and she just loves old-fashioned copperplate writing, indulge her. Similarly, if she likes to print everything, let her. The only reason schools struggle with standardized handwriting systems is that they don't have the resources to deal with students as individuals. As a parent, you do have these resources. As long as the results are legible, you and your children are free to choose any system at all—even ball and stick!

HANDWRITING PROGRAMS AND RESOURCES

Christian Liberty Press
$4.95 each handwriting workbook. Add 10% shipping, minimum $1.50. Grades K–8.

Christian Liberty Academy's new handwriting program, based on the traditional Palmer method (manuscript and cursive), takes 15 to 20 minutes a day, introduces cursive after a year's practice with manuscript, and combines patriotism with Scriptural themes and everyday life. Each slim book (60 to 76 pages) also includes teaching instructions, eliminating the need for separate teacher's manuals. The publishers include a free writing practice pad with each book.

For four- and five-year-olds, Book 1, *In the Beginning*, has 20 pages of fun readiness instructions before children are introduced to the manuscript alphabet (in alphabetical order) and the numerals. Book 2, *Writing with Diligence*, starts with just a few pages of readiness activities, then settles down to drilling the manuscript stroke groups (i.e., letters that use similar strokes). This book, intended for first- and second-graders, follows each group of stroke drills with a page of independent writing and an self-evaluation page—four in all. Book 3, *Writing with Prayer*, starts with manuscript review and finishes up with cursive, introduced in stroke groups. Also directed at first- and second-graders, Book 3 handwriting exercises include punctuation practice.

Writing with Grace is designed for third- and fourth-graders. It has four sections: Difficult Lowercase Cursive Letters, Manuscript Maintenance, Uppercase A-N Cursive, and Uppercase O-Z Cursive. Each section contains a varied mix of activities, such as unscrambling a poem, a crossword puzzle, making outlines, writing sentences to describe the action in a series of pictures, and so on. The mild emphasis on grammar continues, with some alphabetization work and the introduction of homonyms and quotations. Each section also draws attention to a "Home Education Model" such as Abraham Lincoln, Thomas Alva Edison, and Helen Keller. Toward the end of this book, creative writing begins to take the place of the previous copy-this-sentence and rewrite-that-sentence-according-to-this-grammatical-principle exercises.

Writing with Power, a new book, provides a review of the principles of advanced cursive for children in grades 4–8.

A unique feature are the "Home Education Models" in the advanced books. These are brief bios of famous people who were educated at home.

These books mix a few language arts activities in with the handwriting practice. Otherwise, the format is simple, logical, and concise.

UPDATED**
Concerned Communications
A Reason for Writing. Student books, $8.95 each. Instruction Guidebook, $9.95. Shipping extra. Quantity discounts available on student books. Grades K–6.

A Reason for Writing is the only K–6 handwriting curriculum using Scripture verses (from *The Living Bible*) as the total subject material. Children in grades K–2 learn manuscript, and in grades 4–6 practice cursive. Third grade is set aside for making the transition between these two handwriting styles.

Concerned Communications' suggested weekly schedule has students practicing strokes, letters, or words from the Verse of the Week from Monday through Wednesday. On Thursday, students practice the verse itself, finally writing it on a Scripture Border Sheet. On Friday, students color the design on the Scripture Border Sheet. These sheets are meant to be shared with others, such as relatives or nursing home residents, thus motivating the children to do their best work. The sheets have been made into incentives and rewards, classroom decorations, thank-you notes, birthday cards, and placemats. as well as used in witnessing projects or for memory verses. Sharing the verses provides the "Reason for Writing" mentioned in the program's title.

The handy new Instruction Guidebook covers the complete curriculum, giving stroke-by-stroke instructions in how the letters should be formed, information on how to teach the style of writing covered, and supplementary activities. A separate section of the Guidebook contains 26 large alphabet letter sheets. Very helpful.

Student books in the series include: *God Made My World* (kindergarten—Creation theme), *Words of Jesus* (grade 1—Gospels), *Words of Promise* (grade 2—Psalms and Proverbs), *Words to Live By* (grade 3—Epistles), *Words of Love* (grade 4—Gospels), *Words of Praise* (grade 5—Psalms), *Words of Wisdom* (grade 6—Proverbs).

NEW**
Essential Learning Products
Each practice book, $2.95. Buy five and get one free. Add $2.25 per order for shipping ($3 in Canada). California, Pennsylvania, Ohio residents add tax. Canadians add GST.

I really, really, really like these little practice 'n drill books put out by the people who publish *Highlights* magazine for children. First of all, the price is right, as you can see. Second, each book is just the right size (5¼ x 8½") for children to not feel threatened by the amount of work to do on a page. The one-step-up-from-newsprint paper is easy for children to write on with a pencil or crayon, and the illustrations (where applicable) have a nice, familiar, friendly feel. Print is nice and large. Drills have just the right amount of repetition and cover just the right questions. These books are professionally designed by people who obviously know what they are doing, and it shows.

The handwriting practice books for preschool through grade 4 begin with prehandwriting exercises in the preschool book. The grade 1 and 2 books cover manuscript handwriting in a virtually identical fashion. Children first practice each lowercase letter individually, and write it on the spaces provided in the middle of printed words, then handle uppercase letters and numbers in the same way. Grades 3, 4, and 5 cover cursive, again introducing a letter at a time. These three books provide not only letter and word models, but also greyed-out models to trace, before the student attempts to write a word or letter on his own. The letter size in the grade 4 book is noticeably smaller—that's the only major difference between the grade 3 and 4 books. Grade 5 leaves out the midline and can be considered an "adult" cursive book.

The series includes arithmetic practice books (Preschool Activities, Addition, Subtraction, Multiplication, Division, Fractions, Decimals, Metric, Word Problems, and Money), reading practice books (Preschool Activities and six reading activity books for grades K–5 and up), phonics skills practice books (Initial Consonants, Medial and Final Consonants, Short and Long Vowels, Vowel Combinations, and Blends

THE BIG BOOK OF HOME LEARNING — VOLUME II

197 ☐

and Digraphs), and spelling practice books for grades 1–6. New in August 1990: a grammar drill series, which I have not yet seen. New in March 1991: two new series in Study and Thinking Skills, with more to come in succeeding months. Things are hopping at Essential Learning Products!

Essential Learning Products books are the only practice books my kids have ever pestered me to let them use. At the price, you can afford to buy all the practice books you need for every child in your household! I would recommend this series to every family.

NEW**
Handwriting Without Tears
Handwriting Without Tears, $5. *My Printing Book,* $3. *Printing Teacher's Guide, Cursive Teacher's Guide,* $3 each. *Cursive Handwriting,* $4.50. Printing charts, $3. Cursive charts, $3. Add $2 shipping per order. Grades K–6 or remedial.

The Handwriting Without Tears system was invented by an occupational therapist whose son developed handwriting difficulties. Jan Olsen put her training in sensory-motor treatment to work and produced a method that drastically simplifies the teaching of handwriting.

The sequence Mrs. Olsen chose is (1) uppercase printing, (2) lowercase printing, taught in a special order, (3) lowercase cursive, and (4) uppercase cursive (she says it's OK to let kids continue with uppercase printed capitals as well). She uses a double-lined paper with a smiley face to indicate the starting point, rather than the typical school paper with a dotted or solid middle line, which she feels (and I have observed) causes kids confusion. This makes it easy to show kids which letters start "up in the sky" and which "go down to the water," i.e., which go above or below the area taken up by an "o." As she says,

When I first developed this paper for my own child to use, I thought I was the only one to use double lines. Only later did I find out that double lines are widely used in teaching French, English, Hebrew, and German. When my son's French teacher saw my paper her reaction was, "I like your paper, it's like the paper we use in France. You know, you Americans try to give your children so much help that you only confuse them."

Mrs. Olsen considers handwriting a separate skill that should be taught separately from reading. She begins with wood and vinyl letter parts (patterns are in the book). Children fit together letters by imitating the teacher, since Mrs. Olsen feels "imitation has been neglected and should be rediscovered with appreciation." Kids first imitate, then copy, then finally write independently.

Handwriting Without Tears explains the whole system. It includes reproducible pages of double-lined paper and patterns for the letter parts. The best part of this book is the way Mrs. Olsen discusses all the methods used for teaching handwriting at each stage, and explains why some popular approaches should be avoided. She does this without being autocratic or overly dogmatic; her interest is in helping kids (even those with "learning disabilities") learn to write. Mostly her book is just loaded with good common sense.

My Printing Book and *Cursive Handwriting* are exercise books. Unlike other exercise books, each model is copied just once, and there is no attempt to integrate handwriting with history, geography, math, careers, and skateboarding. The *Cursive Handwriting* book uses a simplified vertical (straight up-and-down) cursive. Accompanying teacher's guides for each book are now available.

The final result of all this will be legible (not gorgeous) handwriting, taught and learned with the least amount of struggle and backtracking. Perfect for busy home-school moms who can live without ornate Spencerian script or lovely calligraphy. The method also works well for kids who are already failing at other methods (Mrs. Olsen enclosed a number of testimonies from parents of such kids!). I've learned a lot from reading these books.

cat dog

NEW**
Hayes School Publishing Co., Inc.
Let's Write series, books 1–4, $4.95 each. (Specify blackline masters.) Add $1.50 postage for first item, 35¢ each additional item. Grades 1–6.

The *Let's Write* series from Hayes competently covers penmanship skills taught in grades 1–6. Originally written in 1967, it has a serene, Leave-it-to-Beaver flavor.

Book 1, *Let's Write Manuscript*, does just that. Step-by-step presentation of manuscript basics plus space allotted on each page for the student to copy the example letters, words, and sentences. Excellent teacher's notes in the front of the book explain just how to present each new skill. For grades 1–2.

The transition from manuscript to cursive is difficult for many children. Book 2, *Let's Write Cursive*, makes it as painless as possible. Again, exercise space and a teacher's guide are built in. For children making this transition, anywhere from grades 2–6.

Books 3 and 4, *Let's Drill Cursive* and *Advanced Cursive Writing*, follow a similar format. Book 4 is especially endearing. Written examples in this book include patriotic source material (portions of the Declaration of Independence, Bill of Rights, Gettysburg Address, etc.) and sage sayings and maxims from our own good ol' Western culture.

The presentation in these books is remarkably clutter-free. You cover a lot in just 44 pages!

Each book looks just like a regular workbook (which it is). Since these are considered "blackline masters," though, you have permission from the publisher to copy each page for use with all the children you are teaching. I personally would just get each of my children his own workbook, but if you want to penny-pinch, you can!

Macmillan Publishing Company

Palmer Method Handwriting is based on the so-true idea that handwriting practice should *be* handwriting practice, not poetry composing time or puzzle-solving time. If the learner has to concentrate on language arts at the same time as practicing his handwriting, obviously his task will be complicated. As they say, "Handwriting class should be to teach 'how' to write so the rest of the day may be used to teach 'what' to write." The method is over 100 years old, and is still the company's only product. The handwriting produced is a very lovely cursive hand. Workbooks are less than $4 in all grades, and teacher's editions are under $10.

Mott Media
Complete Spencerian set, including theory book and all five copy books, $13.95. Individual copy books $2.25, theory book $4.95.

Mott Media has resurrected ye olde Spencerian handwriting books from ye tombe of oblivion. These books were used for over 100 years, and are based on the method of Platt Rogers Spencer.

If John Henry was born with a hammer in his hand, young Spencer was born with a pen. As a child he first drew letters on birch bark, and soon he was scribbling everywhere. A born calligrapher, Spencer greatly admired John Hancock's elegant signature on the Declaration of Independence and desired to design a handwriting system that would produce that kind of grace, yet be easy to learn. The result, carried on by his disciples, was Spencerian writing, a complete system based on a few simple arm movements and seven basic strokes. Every letter is broken down into those strokes. The result is a gorgeous "copperplate" system of writing, quaint and elegant.

Spencer's theory book reads like a catechism, with its questions and answers. "Will you measure and analyze small *r*? . . . How should the small *r* be formed?" The five accompanying consumable copy books take the student from writing the "short" letters on graphed paper to penning such sentences as "Angels are guardian spirits," (this was before the ACLU, remember) and "Modesty always charms." Like all Mott's Classic Curriculum, the books can be used at all age levels and at any pace that fits the student.

Aa Bb Cc Dd Ee Ff Gg Hh Ii Jj Kk Ll Mm Nn Oo Pp
Aa Bb Cc Dd Ee Ff Gg Hh Ii Jj Kk Ll Mi
nan nbn ncn ndn nen nfn ngn nhn nin njn nkn nln nm
CURSIVE ITALIC ALPHABET NUMERAL DESK STRIP (INCLUDING BASIC ITALIC) NO. 202
q Rr Ss Tt Uu Vv Ww Xx Yy Zz 0 1 2 3 4 5 6 7 8 9
Vn Oo Pp Qq Rr Ss Tt Uu Vv Ww Xx Yy Zz
nn non npn nqn nrn nsn ntn nun nvn nwn nxn nyn nzi

Portland State University handwriting chart

UPDATED**
Portland State University/Continuing Education Press

Books A through G and Instructor's Manual, $4.25 each ($3.25), Specimen Set containing all the above, $32 ($25). Basic Blackline Master Practice Sheets for Home-schoolers (covers books A, B, C), Cursive Blackline Master Practice Sheets for Homeschoolers (covers books D, E, F), $10 each. Classroom Wall Charts, two sets: Basic Italic Alphabet and Numerals, Cursive Italic Alphabet and Numerals, $5.75/set ($4.50). Alphabet Desk Strips (specify Basic Italic or Cursive Italic), $5.75 set of 30 ($4.50), individual desk strip 50¢ each. New: Movable Alphabet, set of 415 2" high letters with storage box, $37. New videotape, $7 rental, copying permitted. Shipping and handling $4 up to 2 items, then add 25¢ per item. Second price in parentheses is school price. Use school price if your order totals $20 or more. Grades K–6.

Believe it or not, some public school systems are getting into teaching italic handwriting. The series they are using is published by Portland State University. It begins with prewriting exercises in Book A and goes all the way to a very professional italic hand. The series is spread out over seven grades, starting with kindergarten, like most public school courses; but you don't need to buy all the workbooks if you are using them at home.

Barbara Getty and Inga Dubay are the two ladies who invented this simple italic teaching method. Differences between the Getty-Dubay approach and other public-school handwriting programs:

- How many letters change shape when making the transition from manuscript to cursive? Only two capital letters and one manuscript letter change shape in the Getty-Dubay approach. Compare this to the 18 capital letter changes in the D'Nealian system and the 26 capital letter

changes in Palmer, Bowmar-Noble, and Zaner-Bloser, and to the 13 lowercase letter changes (D'Nealian) and 26 (Palmer, Bowmar-Noble, and Zaner-Bloser).

- Getty-Dubay is the only public-school method in which capital cursive forms are based on the manuscript forms.

- Getty-Dubay uses no loops, aiding both legibility and ease of teaching.

- Capital letters, ascenders, and descenders are in the same proportions as those found in book typefaces, allowing closer writing without tangling letters together. Other methods use ascenders and descenders which frequently become tangled. Example: try writing the word *fly* in cursive handwriting and then writing *fall* directly underneath. If you learned from one of the other methods, the loops of the *f*'s will be getting tangled, and so will the bottom loop of the *y* in *fly* and the top loops of the *l*'s. The same words, written in Getty-Dubay script, don't tangle at all.

- Letter slope can be a problem. In Palmer, Bowmar-Noble, and Zaner-Bloser, the slopes changes from 0° in the manuscript books to 27 degrees in the cursive books. The D'Nealian slope remains at 17 degrees for both manuscript and cursive. Getty-Dubay script slopes at only 5 degrees, which they feel is a more natural slope better suited to both manuscript and cursive.

My inclination would be to skip Book A, which is merely the italic alphabet with one letter per page. There are no review pages in the book—for these you need the blackline masters—so the student could easily forget all the early letters by the time he gets to the end of the book, unless he practices using the lined paper masters supplied in the instructor's manual. Joins are first introduced in Book C, and thereafter the letter size gets smaller and smaller. Books B through E seem the most valuable of the series, if you don't want to buy the entire set. Or, if you want only one book for yourself or an older student, Book G has a self-teaching approach to the whole system.

You can also get an instructor's manual, which includes teaching techniques, a scope and sequence, and the theory behind the course. Blackline masters contain follow-up practice exercises. Portland State University has recently put together two sets of blackline masters (which include permission to photocopy) just for home schoolers.

New: a training video for the parent or teacher explains how to teach handwriting the Getty-Dubay way. It only costs $7 plus shipping to rent, and you can copy it to keep it for your own permanent use.

NEW★★
Providence Project
ReadyWriter, $15.95. Add $2.50 shipping. Stylus skills and penmanship for ages 4–7.

Could Junior's horrible handwriting stem from a simple lack of stylus skills? Has he ever really learned how to make neat lines, zigzags, spirals, and circles? If not, why not take a couple of minutes a day to practice these skills with the fun, motivational *ReadyWriter* program from Providence Project?

Each *ReadyWriter* practice sheet features a scene on Farmer Brown's farm. You read the paragraph-long "story" of the day, and your student gets to work filling in the missing parts of the picture. Example:

> Mrs. Brown has just fixed a big batch of the Brown family's favorite dessert—brownies (naturally)! They've cooled off just a bit, so now let's help her cut them. Start at the top of the page, and with your pencil "cut" one panful at a time, first from top to bottom and then from left to right. Try to make nice square brownies of the same size, and try not to cut into the middle (shaded area) of the brownies. It might be a good idea to have some *real* brownies sometime, too!

What red-blooded kid could resist helping Mrs. Brown cut out her brownies? Your child repeats this sheet every day until he's making nice unjiggly lines. Then he moves on to helping Farmer Brown sharpen his saw blades (zigzags), helping the sheep wake up by coloring in their eyes, drawing spirals on the ends of Farmer Brown's logs, helping Farmer Brown fix his roof by tracing the lines that slant in different directions . . . you get the idea. Even when we had finished this program, our children were begging to do it again!

ReadyWriter comes with 12 sheets for each of the 16 exercises (enough for several children, if they learn quickly) and an instructor's guide with the stories and directions for use. Very highly recommended.

Thoburn Press
Set of three workbooks and teacher's guide, $20. Each workbook, $4.25. Teacher's guide $7.25.

Perhaps the ultimate resource for Christian teachers of ball-and-stick manuscript is Thoburn Press's very lovely *E-Z as A-B-C* penmanship series.

Book A begins with numbers, alphabet letters, and digraphs. Individual letters are then introduced according to their characteristics: "circle letters" like *c* and *o*, "candy cane" letters like *h* and *r*, "slant stick" letters, look-alikes, tall stick letters, straight line letters, and so on. Both the upper- and lowercase manuscript alphabet are handled in this book.

Book B goes on to handwriting practice with short vowel words, long vowel words, sight words, and *s* sounds like *z* words.

Finally, Book C has students copying the names of Bible people, books of the Old and New Testaments, the twelve disciples, some kings and women of the Bible, and so on.

Instead of blah black lines to write on, each workbook uses "stop light" (green, yellow, and red) color-coded lines. It's all in a clean, easy-on-the-eyes format and reinforces any good phonics program.

HANDWRITING AND PRE-HANDWRITING ACCESSORIES

NEW★★
Educational Insights
Tactile Letters, $7.95. Shipping extra.

This new handwriting manipulative solves the problem of other tactile letter-tracing tools, namely that when Johnny works with them by himself, he gets into the habit of tracing some letters in the wrong directions.

Tactile Letters are plastic letters with little triangles sticking up out of them. The triangles all point in the direction in which the letter should be written. When your child runs his fingers down the letter in the right direction, it slides right along. When he does it in the wrong direction, he feels the rounded triangle points and knows he is doing it wrong!

TREND, Inc.

All wipe-off® books, $2.95 each. Wipe-off® crayons, 79¢/pack of 6. Add $2 shipping (minimum order $10).

I wouldn't want to be without TREND's colorful write 'n wipe handwriting books. The pre-handwriting book lets children trace the different shapes and strokes they will use in writing. The numbers book gives practice in writing numerals and in counting. You can use the manuscript book as a precursive intro by just having your student start some letters differently and using one continuous stroke. TREND even has a cursive book, with a silly race car theme. The books are great for practice, lively and colorful, and can be used again and again by every kid in a family of twelve.

TREND'S wipe-off crayons for use with the books are super cheap and come in assorted zippy colors.

KEYBOARDING FOR CHILDREN

NEW★★
Educators Publishing Service
Type It, $8. Shipping extra. Grades K–12.

Type It is the best beginning course in touch typing for the money. This is real touch typing, starting with home row keys and covering the entire keyboard except for the special characters above the numbers. It's also *linguistically-oriented* touch typing. The words chosen for the exercises are phonetically regular, so you can use *Type It* for children as young as six.

Type It now has a bound-in standing easel, so you can simply prop the *Type It* manual open at the ideal height for typing. The manual is spiral-bound, with exercises set in large type. Eight lessons in all, with 16 exercise sets per lesson. Kids can check off completed exercises on the Progress Chart on the inside of the back cover.

There's no magic here—just do the exercises in order, according to the one page of directions at the beginning of the book. You'll need to hover around to make sure your child is using the right fingers, as bad typing habits are easier to prevent than to break. Aside from that, you have nothing to do except *ooh* and *aah* over Junior's newfound typing skills.

CHAPTER NINETEEN

READERS

When I say, "Readers," the world shouts, "McGuffey!" In previous editions of this book, I wondered out loud why people were so excited about a set of readers mostly made up of extracts of famous writing with a number of old-fashioned morality tales thrown in. Couldn't we just go to the library and take out the books from which McGuffey had extracted his reader selections? After all, as a child I had read most of the literature McGuffey quotes right off the library shelf.

What I had not taken into account was the increasing censorship of old books in the public library. I hate to use the word *censorship*, as it will sound unfair to some of you. Aren't librarians in the forefront of the crusade against censorship? Don't libraries promote "National Banned Books Week," a protest against any form of censorship of written material? Yes, all that's true. However, for whatever reason, librarians everywhere are busily tossing out the old library books and replacing them with Judy Blume paperbacks. When I go to the library in search of something as nonthreatening as Jerome K. Jerome's comedy classic *Three Men in a Boat,* chances are I will have to take it out on interlibrary loan, if I can even find it at all. The same goes for *Hans Brinker, or The Silver Skates.* This in a huge modern suburban library branch, with racks of teen gothic romances, all the latest high-tech equipment, and floor space equal to K-Mart!

Librarians complain, somewhat justly, that old books get moth-eaten and *have* to be thrown out. This is sometimes true, but I've seen a lot of old books on library book tables that were good for another 20 years of service, if the library had wanted to keep them. New bestsellers get ripped up, too, and the library just writes another check and replaces them. "But we *can't* replace the old books!" librarians cry. They're absolutely right, and here's the reason: the publishers won't publish them any more.

Let's talk about a character we'll call Paddy the Pig for a minute (not his real name). This classic children's series about a farm full of talking animals was my personal childhood favorite. As an adult with a family bookselling business, I was anxious to sell the Paddy series. So I tracked down the publisher and asked for terms, only to find out that most of the books were out of stock and they had no plans to reprint them. So I started asking about buying the rights. I thought I could persuade another publisher to revive the Paddy series, or, failing that, perhaps publish them myself.

At this point the publisher's rights-and-permissions lady became strangely evasive. No, they were not reprinting, and would not even reprint a special volume order for us. No, they were not interested in selling the rights. They "might" be reissuing Paddy in a couple of years. Could they give me any dates? No, they couldn't. And on it went.

Is this publisher suppressing Paddy? I don't know. But it really bothers me that the copyrights on so many great old books are owned today by publishing houses that have no interest in reprinting those books *or allowing anyone else to reprint them.* I don't believe copyright law ought to allow anyone to *prevent* books from being published, which is exactly what happens when the copyright owner refuses to print or to sell the rights to someone else who would print the book.

Copyright only used to last 20 years. After that a work was in the "public domain." This meant that anyone could publish it, quote it, excerpt it, or whatever without having to ask anyone for permission. Then a group of well-known authors started crusading for "intellectual property rights." Their view prevailed, and now books that, like Freddy, have been around since the 1930s and *should* have been public domain for years are suddenly the "intellectual property" of a publishing house somewhere who decided to take out a copyright on them under the new laws. Our cultural heritage is now owned by a bunch of New Yorkers, and we only get to see the parts they want us to see.

The sad truth is that just about every major publishing house is firmly in the grip of an ideological elite. These gals and guys want all their books to be feminist, socialist, anti-racist, etc. Just about every good old book fails one or more of these three tests—at least in the eyes of these people. Mark Twain is a good case in point. Some well-meaning, but not terribly astute, people have complained about Twain's "racism" because he printed racial slurs in his books, not recognizing that he did so only to knock racism in the first place! *Huckleberry Finn* is an anti-racist tract second only to *Uncle Tom's Cabin,* but because Twain chose to use satire rather than drama, now we get castrated versions of *Huckleberry Finn* on our library shelves. (The only reason we still have these books at all is that Twain is such a major American literary figure it's impossible at this point to bury him completely.) Similarly, Sophronia, the black cook in the classic children's book *Rabbit Hill,* has lost her race in the newer editions. So instead of a jolly black lady who happens to be a great cook, we don't get to meet any black people in the story at all. A real step forward for race relations!

I don't see why, if kids can be taught in school that slavery and negative racial attitudes were once a part of mainstream American life, it should be a big shock to read old books that reflect these attitudes. The past, after all, is the past.

In any case, racism isn't the real killer of old books, for the very good reason that most of them feature 100 percent lily-white characters. No black people there *at all,* though there might be a smattering of Italian organ grinders. It's just that those old books reflect attitudes and morals that are just too embarrassingly *different* from the way media people now conduct their lives. Virginity until marriage. Death before dishonor. Cowards and thieves shunned. Family togetherness. Mom at home. Kids who respected their parents. Government a non-factor in business operations. Christianity the national religion (which is quite different from having a state church). Self-sacrifice considered the highest virtue, rather than self-esteem. Thrift commended, debt condemned. Personal charity to the poor, rather than attending benefit rock concerts. People expected to achieve on their own, instead of banding together as a group and demanding preferential "victim" status. Patriotism. Loyalty. Trust in authority. Pride in coming from a "good family line" (ragamuffin heroes often turn out to be the long-lost kids of aristocrats) and the belief that "breeding will tell."

Now, I don't have to agree with every item on that list above (I have my problems with the last two) to see the importance of allowing the past to speak for itself, good or bad. This trend towards suppressing any voice from the past that does not reflect what the New York elite believes in the present alarms me. It all reminds me too much of the "memory hole" George Orwell warned us against in his classic *1984.* (If you've never read that book, get it out from the library and read it. Now. If your library has a copy!) Orwell envisioned a fascist/communist (they amount to the same thing) Superstate in which every fact that didn't fit what the leaders currently taught was dumped down the memory hole—a kind of shredder—never to be seen again. Since the leaders constantly changed their positions, the memory hole was always busy.

So, even when a big publisher reissues a classic, chances are 50/50 that the classic has been revised and edited until the result fits our current smarmy ideas of twentieth-century righteousness. This from the same people who regularly go to the wall for the right to publish books like *The Joy of Teenage Lesbian Sex*!

In a way, this shows that these people have a touching belief in the power of God. Just like the atheists who are convinced their kids will convert to Christianity on the spot if they hear one single prayer in their 13 years of public school, the same people who claim that porn never provokes anyone to acts of sexual assault are firmly convinced that the slightest exposure to McGuffeyesque morality will turn the children of America into Puritans.

Faith like that can move mountains. Unfortunately, the mountain it is currently moving is a mountain of *ignorance,* as hardly any modern kids have ever read anything that challenges the media elite's view of reality.

Now we have answered our question, "Why buy a set of readers?" Because the books McGuffey and company extract, which I used to suggest you just take out from your public library, probably aren't *in* your public library. Because, whatever you might think of Rev. McGuffey and his kin, at least they provide a picture of what Americans used to think their kids ought to know and believe. Because they make such a nice change from *Teenage Mutant Ninja Turtles* and those other great modern media molders of children's character.

OLD-FASHIONED READERS

NEW**
Christian Liberty Press
Eclectic Reader Series, from $1.95–$2.95 per book. 11 books in all. Shipping extra.

Time to strengthen our vocabularies! (Bill Buckley, call your office.) We are considering the word *eclectic.* What on earth does the thing mean? "Sounds communist, Martha!" Actually, *eclectic* means "we pick the best bits from here, there, and everywhere." So Christian Liberty's Eclectic Reading Series is made up of what they consider the best extracts from the McGuffey, Union, and Franklin readers of bygone days. Even the illustrations are from the original books, which explains their somewhat tattered appearance (ah, the vagaries of photocopying!).

Christian Liberty Eclectic Reader Book A is for kindergarten, while B is for first grade, and so on. The series progresses step by step, starting with the alphabet and simple words and moving on to sentences, paragraphs, and literary selections of increasing difficulty. All the selections are extremely pro-family, pro-God, pro-hard work, pro-science, and pro-America. Famous authors like Washington Irving, Lord Byron, Noah Webster, and Charles Dickens are highlighted, as well as authors who once were famous but now (thanks to their unwavering Christian testimony) are bypassed. The J and K readers are quite challenging—far beyond what the public schools expect of their junior high students nowadays.

This series is not beautiful to look at (no color, poor repro quality), but then it is a virtuously inexpen-

sive taste of a culture today's media moguls are busy pretending didn't exist. Your child will at least know people once had a different outlook on life if he works his way through these books.

Mott Media
McGuffey Boxed Set, hardback, with teacher's guide $89.95, without teacher's guide $79.95. Primer, $3.95. Pictorial Primer, $8.95. First Reader, $8.95. Second Reader, $13.95. Third Reader, $14.95. Fourth Reader, $23.95. Progressive Speller, $7.95. Parent/Teacher Guide by Ruth Beechick, $10.95. Add 10% shipping, $3 minimum.

Mott Media prides itself on offering the *original McGuffeys,* à la the 1836-37 version compiled by Rev. McGuffey himself. Their hardbound version is not an exact reproduction; words have been changed, the grammar has been amended, and the layout has been revised. The early volumes of "original" McGuffey do not follow the normal pattern of introducing short vowels first, long vowels second, and exceptions last. Furthermore, presenting your child with an archaic vocabulary at the same time as asking him to tackle reading is a bit much. These McGuffeys work much better as supplemental literature than as phonics readers.

NEW**
Pathway Publishers
Clothbound readers, $6–$8 each. $93/complete set of 13 books. Workbooks, $1.60 each. Free shipping, U.S. only, on prepaid orders over $20; $1 shipping on orders less than $20. Send for a price list if you need to determine which books are suitable for your child's grade level.

Pathway Publishers created their delightful series of readers for the Amish community. This series stresses "character building" with a capital C. Starting with easy readers for very little children, the series goes up through the eighth grade level. True stories, animal stories, fictionalized history, poems, and straight fiction are mixed artistically to create books my children couldn't put down. Every reading selection in these books has a character-building emphasis, too, from stories in which children learn not to make fun of classmates to accounts of Anabaptist martyrs. And, since the writers are Amish, the story settings manage to be both old-fashioned and modern at the same time. Your children will get to experience a different culture in which children milk cows by hand, boys go fishing (infrequently) *after* doing hours of chores (or "choring," as the Amish say it), girls feed the chickens and watch the baby, and Mom and Dad are strict disciplinarians. Life is not all dreary drudgery, though. Story characters have plenty of personality and face realistic dilemmas as their fallen sinful nature conflicts with what they know Mom and Dad want them to do!

Nothing smarmy or phony in this series. Animals are seen from a farmer's point of view, not as the almost-human (and Biblically incorrect) characters in *Bambi* and other Hollywood fantasies. Children in these stories love their dogs but sometimes get irritated with the family cows. This is real life, as Bill informs me. He spent a summer working with cows when he was a teen, and he tells me that such an experience does not breed romantic feelings!

The Amish are Anabaptists and pacifists—genuine pacifists, not like the folks who in the name of pacifism lionize leftist dictators. Historically, Catholics and some Protestant leaders did persecute the Anabaptists. The "persecution" stories in the books include both true and fictional accounts of courageous Anabaptists suffering for their beliefs. The emphasis in the stories is not on how awful the persecutors are, though—it's on how God protected His people, and the courage of the martyrs. You'll find very little doctrinal argumentation, as the writers assume that the reader is familiar with and agrees with the Anabaptist position.

I am not an Anabaptist. This doesn't stop me from heartily enjoying these innocent and straightforward stories, though. Amish honesty and concern for spiritual realness put these books far above any other modern reader series I have seen.

Pathway Publishers also has a complete line of workbooks to accompany this series, including some pre-reading and early phonics notebooks. Some require an accompanying teacher's manual. The workbooks are optional—I wouldn't personally consider getting them unless you are planning to make this series the heart of your language-arts curriculum. Kids will enjoy the readers much more if they are just storybooks, not curriculum. (It's only fair to mention here that Pathway tells me at least 75 percent of home schoolers who buy their readers get the workbooks as well, so maybe I'm not on target this time!)

Books are about 400 pages each, except for the "beginner" readers.

My experience is that older children enjoy the little kids' books, so you might just want to go ahead and get the series as a wonderful character-building treat for your children. As you can see, prices are very inexpensive for all Pathway Publishers materials.

Thoburn Press
Christian School Edition McGuffey set, $49.95 for seven hardbound readers or $29.95 for seven paperback readers in a slipcase.

Not as concerned with the quest for the primordial McGuffey as with recovering excellence in academics, Thoburn Press has published a very successful Christian School Edition of the revised edition of 1880. These readers, which McGuffey actually had nothing to do with, are much more useful for actually teaching reading than McGuffey's first edition, since they follow a more phonetic plan. Compared to the Mott Media version, they moralize more and evangelize less.

BRITISH READERS

NEW**
Ladybird Books, Inc.
Each book, $3.50. Flashcards, $4.75 each box. Each workbook, $1.95.

Years ago we were urged to buy the Ladybird Key Reading Scheme. Popular in Britain, this is three series of books. Each series contains 12 colorfully-illustrated books featuring Peter, Jane, and their dog.

Those familiar with the American "Dick and Jane" series will feel a sense of *déjà vu* when confronting these books. "Look, Peter!" "We like the dog." "Jane wants a toy." That's because the series is built around the concept of "key words," e.g., the words that occur most frequently in books we read. A preponderance of these words tend to be "sight" words, that is, words that are not 100 percent phonetic. Thus, the series is presented in sight-word fashion, with lots of repetition of the words. Vocabulary is introduced gradually.

As with the Dick and Jane readers, the lack of literary stimulation is atoned for by high-interest illustrations that include an element of suspense. Lots more is going on in the pictures than in the text, in other words. Series A and B are readers; series C has questions and writing exercises correlated to series A and B. You can also get a set of six workbooks (one for each two books of each of the series) and two boxes of flashcards that between them cover the entire vocabulary of books 1–6 in the Reading Scheme (228 words in all).

Not content with just *one* set of readers, Ladybird also offers the Read It Yourself series of supplemental readers. These are mostly classic fairy tales and fables (as opposed to the realism of Peter and Jane) told in the controlled vocabulary of the Key Words List. Coordinated with the Key Words Reading Scheme, the series covers the pre-reading stage (four books), Level 2 (eight books), Level 3 (eight books), Level 4 (six books), and Level 5 (six books).

And there's more! Ladybird's Well-Loved Tales, for slightly older children, is another series of classic fairy tales and fables. This series covers some of the same ground as the Read It Yourself series—for example, there is a version of *Town Mouse and Country Mouse* in each series. The three levels of Well-Loved Tales are *not* coordinated with the Key Words scheme, but are just intended to separate varying levels of reading difficulty. Forty-six books in all.

Ladybird's Puddle Lane Reading Program is a nifty new idea in readers with an unfortunate occult emphasis. Each fully-illustrated book is one complete story, with text for you to read to your children on the left-hand page, and a few words for the child to read printed in larger type on the right-hand page. As you go up through the levels of the series, the child's portion gets progressively larger and more advanced. An old sorcerer is the somewhat creepy father figure in this series, and every story resolves around magic spells the sorcerer casts. Ladybird probably isn't trying to push witchcraft, just attempting to cash in on the current fad for the stuff, but all the same the stories had a squirmy feel to them, if you know what I mean.

CHAPTER TWENTY

READING COMPREHENSION

I'll level with you. I don't believe in "reading comprehension" tests, workbooks, or courses. Typically these consist of reading extracts followed by a list of multiple-choice questions. It's often (in fact, *usually*) possible to answer the questions correctly without even having read the reading extract. Even kids who can hardly read *at all* can get good scores on these tests by looking in the possible answers for "clue words" that appear in the extract.

"Reading comprehension" is really a substitute for the book reports, oral reports, and essay questions teachers used to assign. As "look-say" phonics began to cripple kids' ability to read and write, "reading comprehension" was discovered. So what if kids couldn't sound out words properly? *Understanding* was what counted—and understanding would be measured by multiple-choice questions that required *no* writing.

At home, you can just ask your kids to narrate back what they read. If they can tell you what the book or story was about, obviously they read it.

For those of you who want to go farther than this, I have scratched up a few reading comprehension programs that take your child's reading ability more-or-less for granted, and concentrate on helping him get more out of what he reads.

FIND YOUR CHILD'S READING LEVEL

NEW**
Academic Therapy Publications
Word Identification Scale, $10. Add $2.50 shipping. Grades 2–6.

Quickly get a handle on your children's reading level with the *Word Identification Scale*. The one-page test takes just minutes, and consists of the child reading individual words on the plastic word card. When he mispronounces a specified number of words, as indicated on the directions sheet, you will have a good idea of what reading level to use with this youngster. Comes with pad of 50 recording forms for recording student responses. Test the whole neighborhood!

READING COMPREHENSION IMPROVEMENT

NEW★★
Hayes School Publishing Co., Inc.
Exercises in Reading Comprehension, levels A–H, $3.50 each. Add $1.50 postage for first item, 35¢ each additional item.

If you absolutely can't live without a reading comprehension series, the *Exercises in Reading Comprehension* series from Hayes looks like a good bet. This attractive, simple series was copyrighted in 1980, but has the small-town flavor of the workbooks we remember from our youth. The series comes in levels A–H, covering grades 1–8. The exercises are well-chosen, both for informational content and practice in using thinking skills. Children are asked to interpret characters' motivations and the results of their actions, not just to parrot the facts in the reading selection. English skills are also put into play, as children analyze different literary forms while puzzling out their meanings. The reading selections are appealing, not overly hard, and less sensationalistic than those in more faddish series.

Expect to find a small sprinkling of feminism (female pilots, repairmen, and poor old Susan B. Anthony) and Modern Social Progress (the more government, the better), as seems required for all public-school material these days. These are offset by such exercises as, "The new baby increased our blessings - - - fold" and fair treatment of both political parties and the Northern and Southern sides in the Civil War. No fawning stories about rock stars or sports heroes—the series sticks to educationally important topics such as historical snippets, interesting science experiments, Greek myths treated *as* myths, info on how to use the library and an encyclopedia, and lots of other useful reading selections. If nothing else, this series will prompt some lively discussions at your house!

NEW★★
Libraries Unlimited
Quizzes for 220 Great Children's Books, $24.50 US, $29.50 foreign. Free shipping on prepaid orders.

Hate book reports? I'm with you. Here's an alternative that can help you determine what, how much, and how well your children read.

Quizzes for 220 Great Children's Books is just what its name implies. The idea is that your child will read some or all of these books. Books are ranked by difficulty level, with more points granted for more difficult books. After reading a book, the student takes the quiz. (Hint: DO NOT let your child write on the quiz sheet, thus making it unusable for other students. The teacher's manual describes how to prepare and photocopy up standard answer sheets.) Various record-keeping forms let you track your child's progress and motivate him (hopefully) to read more. All together, these form the "Quest Motivational Reading Program" (I have no idea why it's not listed by that name in the catalog).

The quizzes themselves are your basic true-false and multiple-choice variety, designed for simplicity of grading in the classroom. You might want to let your child take the tests both before *and* after reading the book—the questions are great interest-sparkers!

Quizzes includes a teacher's manual, a Students' Catalog with thumbnail descriptions of the program books sorted by book topic, and the quizzes themselves, three-hole-punched and shrink-wrapped. You'll need to supply your own binder. The teacher's manual has student record sheets, answer keys for all the quizzes, and instructions for using this simple program.

The "220 great children's books" covered in this program include Newberry and Caldecott winners and runners-up, such as *The High King* and *Sounder;* some classics; and popular books, such as *Ramona and Her Father, The Black Cauldron,* and Judy Blume's *Superfudge.* "Pop" selections definitely outweigh the classics—I wouldn't agree that *all* of the books are "*great* children's books"—but it is quite a representative selection.

To author Polly Jeanne Wickstrom's credit, she includes multiple books by the same author, instead of unnecessarily hopscotching around. Laura Ingalls Wilder, Marguerite Henry, Mary "The Borrowers" Norton, and Beverly Cleary are all well represented, for instance.

Although I can't recommend every single book selection in this program, by and large it gives you the best of several worlds. You get a recommended reading list with just enough info to help you decide whether a book might be worth reading. You get a simple method to both spark interest in reading the book and find out how much of it your child actually understood. (There are no trick questions on the quizzes—any child who actually reads the book with interest should be able to answer the questions correctly.) You also get a way of keeping track of your child's reading—useful for your record-keeping. Your child can either pick books by topics (thus following up an interest and maybe launching a unit study) or simply by difficulty level. Looks good!

NEW
Total Reading

Reading comprehension program totally integrated with phonics instruction. Very complete, no phoney baloney. See review in Phonics section.

CHAPTER TWENTY-ONE

SPEECH AND DRAMA

What's Donald Trump afraid of? According to a number of studies, the number one fear reported by top executives, far outweighing the fear of death, is the fear of speaking in public. (OK, so Mr. Trump doesn't suffer from this problem. There are exceptions.)

Executives, of course, face tough audiences. Bored bosses. Mean stockholders. Back-stabbing colleagues. This still doesn't explain why a little boy who wants to talk to everyone in the supermarket grows up into a man who would rather die than speak to an audience.

School is where most kids learn to fear public speaking. The classroom atmosphere just isn't what you'd call supportive. Make a mistake and everyone laughs. Talk a lot and they tell you to shut up. Get excited and people think you're a geek (as in, "How uncool!") Your audience doesn't want you to succeed.

In real life, of course, it's exactly the opposite. People who know a lot about public speaking all tell us that the audience always wants the speaker to succeed. They want to enjoy your speech, learn something new, get inspired, or otherwise justify the effort they made to attend the event. All you have to do is keep the ball rolling and they'll love ya, kid.

Here's where modern American training lets your kids down. Cool is the opposite of exciting. Cool means looking like you just fell out of the morgue and are only partially defrosted. Cool means talking like you're bored to death, which by definition means sounding boring yourself. Cool means wooden or nonexistent body language, slack facial expressions, and a total lack of oomph in your voice.

Cool, in other words, is the opposite of how your kids were at birth.

Take a newborn baby. He's all eyes and ears and waving arms and legs. He yodels and screams and goos with utter abandon. He's willing to look the world right in the eye and drool on it. His fear of public speaking is nil—in fact, he'll speak loudly at times you really wish he wouldn't!

What I'm saying is that all kids are born with natural "dramatic ability," whatever that is. This is not the same thing as dramatic technique, however. Dramatic technique means developing a vocabulary of body language and vocal characterizations, and knowing which to use when. Kids aren't born knowing how to imitate a lion or Leontyne Price. This we can teach them—as long as they aren't in the throes of terminal peer pressure, trying to be cool. May God send us the power to help our kids keep their wonderful enthusiasm, and help us protect them from the social settings that suck it out of them!

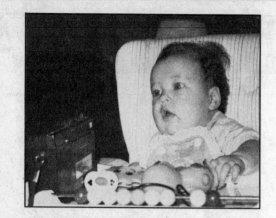

UNLOCKING SPEAKER'S BLOCK

NEW**
Achievement Basics
Speech Fun, $14 volume 1 alone, $21 for both volumes, grades K–3. *Beginning Drama,* $8.95, grades 3–6. *The Communication Commercials,* $12.50, grades 5–12. *Super Speech and Diction,* $8.95, grades 5–12. All prices postpaid.

Achievement Basics has a wide range of speech and listening-skill improvement materials. Taking them one by one:

• *Speech Fun* is for little kids, to help them improve their diction. It comes in two volumes, each on a separate audiocassette. Kids listen to the stories, each of which emphasizes a particular sound, and respond aloud to verbal cues. One teacher's guide covers both volumes. Music and sound effects.

• *Beginning Drama* helps kids learn how to talk like an actor. Dramatic inflection (how you raise or lower your voice), projection, pauses for effect, and other stage techniques are covered. One audiocassette with readalong script.

• *The Communications Commercials* teach communications skills through an ad format. They are a set of 23 commercials in printed form, each focused on a particular oral skill. Some of the commercials, plus speaking hints, are on the included audiocassette. Typical ad sound effects.

• *Super Speech and Diction* is the heavy-duty course on diction and speaking skills, from proper enunciation through volume and pitch. Lively

musical presentation, designed for upper-elementary through adult.

All courses are narrated by professional actors or announcers and designed for home use.

Achievement Basics also has remedial speech materials for special-needs children. Ask for their recommendations if you have a child in this category.

NEW**
Shekinah Curriculum Cellar
Talk with Your Child, $7.95. Add $2.95 shipping.

This pre-creative-writing book tells parents how to talk with our children in a way that will bring out their verbal, creative writing, and thinking abilities. Sounds trivial? No way! As author Harvey Weiner says,

> Modern-day parents may write with their children, may read with their children, may read *to* their children, but outside these highly structured and often anxious learning situations, parents leave children pretty much on their own to confront experience and to develop language that makes meaning from it. This is unfortunate . . .

> Simply using language in the child's presence earns no points in linguistic advancement. But talk directly with your child and he becomes a more competent user of language.

Talk with Your Child is about (surprise!) how to talk with your child: how to recognize opportunities for communication, how to "scaffold" onto your young child's imperfect utterances, how to not just read a book aloud but draw your child into discussing the book. ("Scaffolding," by the way, "is the technique of both drawing language out of your child and providing feedback on his observations.") The numerous real-life examples of parents and children talking in this book are both inspirational and humbling . . . who has the time to do all this? All of us, actually, since Mr. Wiener shows how we can use his techniques during the times we and the children are naturally together. We can even talk *while watching television.* (Sacrilege!) All it really takes is paying attention to our own children.

I can't endorse everything in this book. For one thing, Mr. Wiener stresses repeatedly that parents should not teach children to read. He's talking about overanxious parents pressuring their kids with superbaby books before starting school, though, not about home-schooling parents who take the time (and get the right resources) to do a professional job. I also occasionally get jarred by those New York City values of his. He makes onanism the subject of a simile about TV viewing, for example. Yuk! (Toto, when *will* you understand we're not in Kansas any more?) Not surprisingly, some of the 50 talk-about books he suggests for young kids are not the best choices for Christians (though the book descriptions are detailed enough so you can spot any you might want to skip).

After all these caveats, let me say that Harvey Wiener is terrific at enlightening everyday parents in how to share verbal and written skills with our children, and, as a good writer himself, his books are all fun to read. Whether Mr. Wiener intends it or not, parents who read his books *will* become good teachers, often better than professional teachers who don't read his books! (This is a hint to you professional teachers that *you* ought to read his books!)

Talk with Your Child is available through your local bookstore in paperback (Penguin Books) and hardbound (Viking Press), and mail-order shoppers can get it from Shekinah Curriculum Cellar.

UPDATED**
Teacher Created Materials
I Can Give a Speech, $4.95. Grades 3–6.

From the introduction to *I Can Give a Speech*—"The art of speaking has been too often neglected in the classroom as reading and writing take precedence." Boy, you can say that again! "Generally, we are evaluated first by how we speak, not by how we read or write." True again. So, what do you propose to do about it?

This reproducible workbook is a mixture of idea sparkers for speech activities and actual exercises designed to help you stand up in front of people and entertain or edify them. Some of the activities are actually creative-writing exercises disguised as speech exercises, and those I'd skip. Having to first write the story you read aloud is *not* really speech instruction! Better than those are the pantomime, improvisation, impromptu, and role play activities. As far as speeches (the workbook topic), the workbook doesn't provide much direct information on how to get the butterflies flying in formation, relying more on a discovery-learning approach.

This is an acceptable starting point for a home speech program, but you will want to follow it with more direct instruction on the fine points of public speaking.

ACTING UP

Everyone loves a story . . . especially a dramatized story. What is the difference between a ho-hum read-aloud session and one that keeps the audience on the edge of its seat? Dramatization! What is the difference between a boring after-dinner speaker and a Toastmaster award winner? Dramatization! What makes some people great actors, while others are more wooden than the backstage scenery? Dramatization!

We often make the mistake of talking about "dramatic ability" as if dramatization were one of those things that can't be taught. Nonsense! Anyone can learn to make his voice little for Baby Bear, sweet for Mama Bear, and big and gruff for Papa Bear. We all can learn to swoop like an eagle, climb an invisible rope hand-over-hand like a sailor, stand stiff and tall like Goliath and throw out our shoulders like Samson.

Kids love all this, of course, and will develop dramatic skills on their own given half a chance. I propose that we give them this half a chance by scattering dramatic equipment in their paths. Grandma's dress-up box will do just fine—but if you don't have an attic loaded with post-Victorian apparel, you might want to take a look at the costumes, face paints, etc. offered by the following companies, not to mention shadow theaters, puppet theaters, and so on!

NEW**
Childcraft

This toy catalog is another source for dress-up costumes, puppet theaters, and other props for young children's dramatic play. Costumes aren't too expensive: the police officer's outfit in the most recent catalog only cost $12.95 and included police vest, pocket ID, police cap, aviator sunglasses, working quartz digital police watch, safety flashlight, whistle, summons book, hand-cuffs, keys, police badge, and police wallet. The little bride's costume, on the other hand, rings the chimes at $34.95. Wear it with or without purple hair (odd-col-ored wigs sold separately).

NEW★★
Innovation Station
Creative Play Areas for Kids, $9.95 plus $2 shipping.

Absolutely fantastic book that tells you how to give your kids a childhood like you wish you'd had! Kids really love simple things they can use to create their own play worlds: boxes, boards, a hole to hide in, a sandbox, fabric to drape over a card table (thus turning it into a play house), old pillows, and so on. Many fantastic, classic play devices can be made fol-lowing the ultra-simple directions and charming illus-trations in this book. The section on dramatic play is alone worth the price of the book. Imagine, designs for almost two dozen character hats on one page! (As ev-ery child knows, all you need to pretend your way into a character is an appropriate hat.) No fancy supplies needed. Lots of loving advice on rediscovering the blessings of simple play.

NEW★★
Pleasant Company

These are the people who make those wonderful historical dolls and accessories written up in the histo-ry chapter. To go along with the books and dolls, they also offer historically-accurate dresses for your little girls. Now your daughter can pretend she is a Swedish pioneer girl, or a wealthy Victorian girl, or a snappy small-town girl during World War II. Each outfit is wearable not only as dress-up, but as daily party or play clothes. Accessories, such as boots, muffs, and Victorian hairbows, also available. Good quality items. Not cheap by a long shot, but oh, are they gorgeous!

NEW★★
Toys to Grow On

Toy catalog that includes, among other things, dress-up costumes, face paint, and other props for young children's dramatic play. Dress-up jewelry, Mas-ters of Disguise hat assortment, Sophisticated Ladies hat-gloves-boas assortment, medals of valor, crowns and scepters, doctor and teacher play kits, tutus, pink parasols, Wild West outfit, bridal outfit, etc.

They keep telling me not to put this in, but the fact is these outfits ain't cheap. The reason is that so many of them come packaged with lots of items, rather than as single items you can buy separately. The So-phisticated Ladies assortment, for example, which in-cludes two fancy hats, two pairs of fancy gloves, and two fun-fur boas, costs $36, and you can only get these items as part of that set. Not everything is in the $20–$55 price range, though: a simple gold crown and scepter is $9.95, and a set of three medals is $13.95, among other under-$20 items in this catalog.

NEW★★
The World's Greatest Stories
Each 1-hour tape, $8.95 plus $1 shipping. Specify KJV or NIV version. All ages.

George Sarris is the world's greatest Bible story reader. I didn't say "story *teller*," you'll notice, but "sto-ry *reader*." He can take a Bible story straight from the Good Book and make it snap, crackle, and pop with excitement, using nothing but his voice and a few au-thentic sound effects. Nebuchadnezzar *sounds* like a Middle Eastern emperor. The satraps, prefects, etc. *sound* like a bunch of scheming bozos. The way he makes passages with no dialog take on the personali-ties of the people mentioned in the passage simply has to be experienced.

At present, George has produced two tapes: "The Prophets" and "The Life of Christ." If your kids fall asleep when you read the Bible, get these tapes and learn from the master!

CHAPTER TWENTY-TWO

SPELLING

English is a lot of things,
But E-Z it is knot.
To lurn to spell, it wood be swell.
But then, there's words like "caught"—
And "through," and "new," and "blue," and
 "do,"
That sound just like each other, too.
Their spelling out of Latin grew
Or French, or German, or Hindu
And you are left without a clue—
Or so your teachers taught.

But wait! When phonics comes to play
Upon this lingo ours,
The sense it makes will quash mistakes,
Increase your spelling powers,
And you will gladly come to see
That English is no mystery.
It can be spelled consistently
E'en by the likes of you and me
And all the rules that set you free
Just take a couple hours.

Now you've endured my doggerel
And shown your patient side
Look down below, for it will show
How spelling gets untied
From all its knots and nots and naughts.
I've found you lots and lots and lots
Of ways to slip those words in slots
The finest money ever boughts!
(You see, a poet I am nots.)
The finest ever buyed!

As the poet says, "I think I'd better end this song." Don't let my poetic ineptitude stop you from getting the point, though, which is that *phonics cures spelling problems.* It does, that is, if the people who make up the program make sure to work on the translation of English to letters (spelling) as well as on letters to English (reading). A child may read *hill* and *well* and *doll* hundreds of times without ever stopping to think that short words ending in *l* following a short vowel generally have two *l*'s. Phonics programs are admirably suited to pointing these things out, and most of those reviewed in the chapter on Home Reading Programs do get into spelling at least a little.

The look-say or whole-word or sight-word method whereby children are forced to memorize words by their shape has been a disaster for spelling as it has for reading. Lacking systematic patterns, and loading short-term memory up with data fragments, look-say is the opposite of that logical order which English more or less follows.

In home school circles, the spelling debate is not between phonics and look-say, most home schoolers being firmly in favor of phonics. The new kid on the block is something called "invented spelling." "Let Johnny read and write and don't bother about his spelling," it is said. "In time, as Johnny becomes more acquainted with English in the course of his reading, his spelling will straighten out on its own."

Does this idea have merit? Empirically it has been shown to work in a number of instances. I suspect that the key ingredients to success with invented spelling are lots of reading and basic phonics instruction to begin with. In the cases I've heard of, children started out writing phonetically, and then progressed without adult aid to become good spellers. A mind logically trained to *decode* English—that is, any child taught to read phonetically—may very well in time discover the rules of *encoding* English.

Because most schoolchildren are *not* taught phonetically and are *not* allowed unpressured time to develop correct spelling on their own, the following spelling programs might be of help.

I'd like to end this section with three thoughts. The first, after John Holt, is that the only word lists worth practicing are lists of the words *you* have missed in *your* own writing. Why practice words you already know how to spell or that you never use? The second is that a good learning-to-read program, followed by enough *corrected* writing practice, will produce good spellers. It is not a good idea to make children rewrite whole papers for the sake of a few misspelled words. That cramps their writing and develops fear of using unusual words. Practicing misspelled words separately, in order to gain mastery, is very different from having your entire composition condemned for a spelling error. The third thought is that spelling is not worth stressing at all until the learner has had enough reading practice to form a framework of phonics rules and known words. More than one "creative" speller has developed into a model of spelling accuracy without any adult intervention at all. Older children should be expected to produce more professional work, but younger children can be allowed a certain time to develop their writing skills. Don't squash writing for the sake of spelling!

SPELLING PROGRAMS

NEW✶✶
Academic Therapy Publications
Quick Spelling Inventory, $10. Add $2.50 shipping.

Want to find out where your child, and 49 other children, stand in spelling competency? Give 'em this test. Pad of 50 sheets with numbered spaces for the spelling test plus laminated word list of 45 spelling words and easy directions. Read the word, a phrase using the word, and repeat the word. The child attempts

to write it correctly on his sheet. Example: "Number 26: kitchen . . . *kitchen* table . . . kitchen." This is obviously not an exhaustive test, but can quickly give you a general idea of a child's spelling level. For grades 2–6.

Arthur Bornstein School of Memory Training
Memory Techniques for Spelling, $39.95. Add 10% shipping.

Arthur Bornstein, famous memory training lecturer and educational consultant, has developed yet another flashy and entertaining memory program, this one for poor spellers. Based on Bornstein's memory techniques, *Memory Techniques for Spelling* provides 20 techniques for remembering odd and unusual spellings, as well as spelling rules, study tips, and memory devices for many commonly misspelled words. You get a set of 56 oversized, full-color flash cards, each illustrating a memory technique for recalling a specific word on the front and with teaching instructions on the back; an Instruction Manual/Spelling Guide; and an instructional cassette tape.

As an example of Bornstein's approach: the flash card for technique one, "Exaggeration of Letters," shows the word *separate*. *Separate* is in capital letters, with the troublesome *A* extending from floor to ceiling and flashing red. Your students will certainly pay attention to these flash cards! Spelling will become one of your most enjoyable subjects, instead of a tedious exercise in frustration. Bornstein has given us a program designed for success.

NEW✶✶
Bob Jones University Press
Spelling Home Education teacher's edition, $12.95 each grade (grades 1–6). Spelling worktext, $7.95 each grade (grades 2–6). Shipping extra.

Proving once again how committed they are to helping homeschoolers, BJUP has just come out with a special "Home Education" spelling program (they already had a spelling program series for Christian schools).

BJUP believes "spelling is a subject that must be taught, not just tested." Based on research into how children learn to spell, it groups words into common spelling patterns. Students also write a weekly journal, using their own choice of words, and entering any misspelled words in a personal spelling "Word Bank" at the back of the worktext.

Activities are specially designed for one-on-one work in a home setting. The teacher's instructions include not only the "how" but the "why" for each method and activity. A further bonus for BJUP curriculum users: the spelling lists in *Spelling 1* are coordinated with the word families taught in *First Grade English for Christian Schools Home Teacher's Edition*. Families using BJUP's first-grade English skills program will not encounter any spelling word family until at least three weeks after it has been taught in the phonics course (assuming you start both courses at the same time and teach them at the same rate of speed).

The worktexts are substantial in size (200-plus pages each), and illustrated in both color and black-and-white. The teacher's editions, besides all the teacher's instructions, contain scaled-down reproductions of all the pages in the student worktexts, with answers filled in.

The program includes many reinforcement activities, interesting word definitions (in sections entitled "The King's English"), frequent tests, and dictionary skills. Daily work does not take long to prepare or complete, and the program certainly is thorough!

NEW★★
Christian Liberty Press
Speller Book 1, $1.95. Books 2 and 3, $2.50 each. Books 4 and 5, $2.95 each. Add 10% shipping ($1.50 minimum).

A series of traditional, phonics-based spelling textbooks with an emphasis on building vocabulary. Words are presented in phonetic families, along with lots of oral and written drill exercises. Attention is paid to comprehension (using words in sentences) as well as correct pronunciation. Teaching suggestions and review lessons are a regular feature in all books of this series.

Christian Liberty Speller Book 1 is designed for first graders. You start with a review of the alphabet and lots of short word lists—that is, lists of short words! The book also includes exercises introducing prefixes, suffixes, double consonants, and word endings.

Christian Liberty Speller Book 2 covers the second and third grades. It begins with a review of short- and long-vowel words, and goes on to two- and three-syllable words. The second half of the book covers words with similar meanings, proper names, words with silent letters, abbreviations, and exercises in pronunciation and defining.

Christian Liberty Speller Book 3, for fourth- and fifth-graders, goes on to advanced phonetic spelling. Students learn Latin roots of our modern English words in this book.

Christian Liberty Speller Book 4 covers the sixth and seventh grades. Advanced exercises plus word lists in topical format, "so students will understand what vocabulary terms are used in certain vocations and spheres of society."

Christian Liberty Speller Book 5 is for eighth and ninth grade. This book continues the vocabulary-building emphasis introduced in the previous two books, plus lots of oral and written exercises applying advanced phonetic spelling rules.

Christian Schools International
Student workbook, $8.25 each grade. Teacher edition, $27.55 each grade. Grade 1 Teacher Guide includes whole course—no student workbook needed. Shipping extra.

CSI's *Spelling Spectrum* curriculum "helps students care about spelling as a way to love and serve God and others." Good thought. Now how do they propose to accomplish it? CSI begins at the beginning with an explanation of how our language developed, thus cluing students in to why our words look the way they do. Unique features include allowing the student to choose his favorite of three learning methods, spelling games, and a spelling progress chart. You get "varied, realistic, daily activities in 36 lessons."

NEW★★
E-Z Grader Co.
Homonym Slide Rule, $4.50 postpaid. Grades 3 and up.

Homonyms are words that sound alike but are spelled differently and have different meanings. So what's a "homonym slide rule"? It's 51 words written in cursive, with cutout windows beneath each row of three words. When the fingertip-pull slide is in all the way, a space appears in each window for the child to write the homonym. Pull out the slide, and the answers appear.

Like all the E-Z Grader slide rules products, the *Homonym Slide Rule* is made of strong, wipe-clean cardboard with durable, riveted construction. A fun, inexpensive way to cement the spelling and meaning of these words.

Educators Publishing Service
Spelling Dictionary for Beginning Writers, $2.70. Shipping extra. Ages 6–8.

Does this go under "Spelling," "Creative Writing," or "Vocabulary?" *A Spelling Dictionary for Beginning Writers,* as its author so aptly remarks, "contains a list of words that beginning writers use over and over in their writing. It is shorter and easier to use than a regular dictionary." So much for the first 34 pages, which are dedicated to ye olde A–Zs—about 1400 of them. Next comes the Mini-Thesaurus, with synonyms for the world's most overused words: *then, big, small/little, good/nice/great, went/ran, asked, answered,* and that all-time great dialog-killer, *said.* The Word Bank section lists theme words by subject. Some categories, like *home* and *sports,* are not likely to boast too many words kids need to learn. Others, such as *weather* and *geography,* could easily form the basis for a series of mini-studies. To do this, just go down the list asking for definitions and check off the words your child already knows. Then teach him the meanings of the rest.

Author Gregory Hurray has left plenty of room between the large printed words, so students can write in their own words. This can be very helpful, both in practicing alphabetizing skills and as a means of providing a personal dictionary of words your particular child often misspells.

EPS also offers more than a dozen different workbooks for students with spelling problems. *Power Over Words,* for fifth- through seventh-grade students, is a "discovery" workbook series. Students "develop a visual-phonetic-thinking method" for spelling words. You can also get a workbook of spelling exercises, a multi-sensory spelling program for students with reading difficulties, and so on.

Leonardo Press
Spelling Mastery Kit, $54.95. Additional materials for each student, $4. *1,001 Affixes,* $14.95. *Spelling Book of Verbs,* $9.95. All orders add 10% shipping.

Raymond E. Laurita is a man with a mission. Disgusted by the practice of teaching schoolchildren spelling by means of word lists, Professor Laurita set out to uncover the patterns of English spelling. English, Laurita believes, is essentially a regular language. While proving this thesis, Professor Laurita has assembled a number of useful tools for those who care about spelling and language.

In *1,001 Affixes and their Meanings: A Dictionary of Prefixes, Suffixes and Inflections,* Laurita divides those troublesome little morphs that make up English into their three categories: prefixes, suffixes, and inflections. He then defines each and every one, with examples of its use. E.g., "ptero- indicates feather, wing or winglike part: *pterodactyl* (ptero dact yl), *pterosaur* (ptero saur)." Reading through this book should improve both your spelling and your word power.

The Complete and Simplified Spelling Book of Verbs, another humdinger of a title, is another handy work. Laurita shows that 98.5 percent of all English verbs are regular. He also (and this is the truly useful part) includes a complete list of *all* irregular verb roots in the language, organized into 30 categories according to underlying vowel construction.

The Spelling Mastery Kit is a complete K–12 spelling program. You get a 5 x 8" plastic box with 200 color-coded cards containing over 12,000 words, all placed in categorical order; student lesson pad; student folder; the manual *Five Steps to Spelling Mastery;* and the booklet *Spelling as a Categorical Act.* The Spelling Mastery Kit is Laurita's vowel-centered approach to spelling. There are five levels of difficulty, all related. In level 1 the learner spells, for example, *ee* words: *deed, feed, heed, need . . .* In level 2 he spells *ee* words that use blends: *bleed, sleep, fleet, flee.* Level 3 brings in digraphs: *cheer, sheet, cheek.* Level 4 adds inflectional endings: *sleeting, cheekiest, cheered.* Level 5, the last, adds affixes (prefixes and suffixes): *uncheerful, sleety, cheekily.*

Laurita has produced a number of items specifically designed for home use which also work well in the classroom. Contact Leonardo Press for details.

NEW★★
Mott Media
McGuffey's Eclectic Progressive Speller, $7.95. Grades 1–12.

They knew how to make up titles in the old days! We're looking at *The Eclectic Progressive Spelling Book on an Improved Plan: Showing the Exact Sound of Each Syllable, According to the Most Approved Principles of English Orthoepy—Designed to Precede The Eclectic Readers,* by

Alexander H. McGuffey. (Don't bother looking up *orthoepy*—chances are your dictionary won't have it.)

Like most schoolbooks written back in the dear old mists of time, this book is heavy on logic. It starts with a brief analysis of the English alphabet: vowels and consonants, diphthongs and triphthongs, vowel sounds, consonant sounds, double consonants, and final syllables. This only takes a few pages and is well worth reading by any parent intent on assisting his children with their phonics and spelling.

The book then starts off slowly with some two-letter syllables, proceeding to three-letter words, and then on to bigger and better, longer and longer words. Words are listed by families: for example, four-letter words ending in silent *e* or words with the short sound of *ow*. Interspersed are short reading extracts.

By the end of the book, the student is reading (and presumably spelling) words such as *calumniation* and *areametry*. Some of these words have fallen out of use, but most make splendid vocabulary words, as well as practice in inductive spelling. You have to figure out what the rules are—no teacher's helps are provided in the body of the book, unfortunately.

NEW**
S. U. A. Phonics Department
Spelling and Reading Word List, $2.20 postpaid.

Intensive phonics is more than half the key to good spelling. The English language is rather more regular than otherwise; learn the rules and you learn to spell. Realizing this, Sister Monica Foltzer, author of the *Professor Phonics Gives Sound Advice* intensive phonics program (see chapter 8), has made her *Spelling and Reading Word List* available separately, for those who already know how to read but need extra help with spelling.

This short, 16-page booklet provides lists of words organized according to the phonics rule which governs them. Thus, after the rule, "In two or more syllable words, the sound of *k* is usually spelled *c*," you'll find words ranging from *antic* to *ecstatic* and *communistic*. You'll find lists of *dge* words, lists of *tch* words (these are frequently spelling problems), and lists of *tion* words. These lists are organized from simplest to most complicated, with the classic *at-bat-cat-fat* short-vowel words leading off the parade. A useful, inexpensive tool.

CHAPTER TWENTY-THREE

THINKING SKILLS

You don't have to teach kids to think. On this one Plato had it right—kids are *born* thinking.

So what's all the brouhaha about "thinking skills" in the school curriculum?

Some say it's shoddy sleight-of-hand designed to obscure the fact that kids aren't being taught *facts* anymore. E.g., "The world is changing so rapidly that all the facts we teach them will be out of date by the time they graduate, so let's teach them to think instead."

Granted that technology changes rapidly, *knowledge* doesn't change all that rapidly. Some knowledge, like 1 + 1 = 2, doesn't change at all. So the world-is-changing argument doesn't work.

Another, more convincing, argument goes like this. "Kids are born thinking, but they are *not* born thinking logically. They are able to understand and use logic when it is explained to them, however. Since logic is thinking organized according to certain rules, we need to teach our kids the rules."

Good enough. The fun thing is that logic is not just verbal logic (saying things logically and avoiding false arguments). It's also visual riddles, mathematical riddles, and story riddles. Preteens may not be ready for a formal course in verbal logic, but they love to solve riddles and mysteries. Genuine thinking-skills programs concentrate on these, as opposed to the open-ended malarkey in the Gifted and Talented programs (e.g., "Imagine the world of 2015 A.D. and write a paper about it"). People think in order to find *answers*, and he who finds the best answers wins.

VISUAL THINKING AND OBSERVATION SKILLS

NEW★★
Dale Seymour Publications
Visual Thinking, sets A and B, $29.95 per set. Grades 4–12.

So what, you ask, is visual thinking? Good question. In this case, it's the title of two boxes full of colorful task cards (100 per box) designed to teach visual thinking skills. And now, since I have not yet told you what visual thinking really *is*, and I don't want to leave you gnashing your teeth in frustration, here's a definition of visual thinking straight from the teacher's guide included with Set A:

Visual thinking is an integral part of our society. On any given day we might need to be able to interpret a graph, map, photograph, sculpture, graphic symbol, and/or body language. In order to understand a book or something told to us orally, we must be able to visualize characters, settings, and physical objects from the words that are given. And, in order to efficiently solve a problem, we need to be able to visualize possible approaches to solving it or to draw a picture of the elements of the problem.

So Dale Seymour's *Visual Thinking* series is designed to help fourth-graders and up acquire spatial perception skills. This is important because studies have shown that many students lack these skills. Success in geometry class, engineering, and even in art is based on the ability to interpret, remember, and mentally manipulate visual symbols.

So much for theory. What you get in each box is 100 task cards and a very short teacher's commentary with an answer key for the cards. The box itself, I might add, is very sturdy and attractive, looking as if it were designed by the people who do those upscale cheese popcorn bags. Each task card has a single assignment laid out on it, which should take between three and 15 minutes to complete. These are fun assignments, ranging in Set A from a set of five strings of colored circles with the instruction to "find the two designs that are exactly the same" to Card 100 which shows three different views of the same solid and asks how many triangular faces, edges, and vertices (corners) the solid has. (This is not as easy to figure out as you think, since you are looking at two-dimensional pictures of only part of a three-dimensional object!) In between you'll find problems asking you to draw spatial forms, count bricks in a stack (including the ones you *can't* see), find the missing puzzle piece, and all sorts of other ingenious ways to limber up your spatial sense. Problems become more difficult as you move through the cards. Set B is harder than Set A.

These sets are just excellent. The exercises really can improve your spatial skills, and they are lots of fun besides! The task card format means you can use the program just a little bit at a time, or do a whole lot at once—it's up to you. The durable cards should last for years; you can use them with every child in your family, and the grownups, too. Girls should especially benefit, as in general girls have weaker spatial skills than boys. Recommended.

NEW★★
Learn to Look Book
The Learn to Look Book, $3 postpaid.

Over 30 games and exercises designed to teach observation skills, all in one slim booklet. The author is a believer in the "right brain/left brain" doctrine, but this only pops up in the introduction. The games and exercises themselves follow a three step process:

• Learning to focus on a topic

• Learning to mentally "take a picture"

• Learning to recreate the picture by words, drawings, or gestures.

Some of the exercises teach other skills as well, such as discovering how colors combine to form new colors or increasing children's appreciation of God's creation. Other senses beyond sight are also exercised: you'll find several exercises for smell, hearing, taste, and touch.

NEW★★
Tin Man Press
Nifty Fifty, Brain Stations, $10.95 each. *Discover!* packs, $2.10. Series 1 or 2 (12 titles each), $25.50. Add 10% shipping ($2 minimum). Grades 2–6.

First, the Discover! series. These really neat little card packs each feature twenty observation and thinking activities centering on common household items. In *Discover Aluminum Foil,* for example, one card asks the child to look carefully at both sides of the foil and write about what he notices. Another card asks him to drop a square of foil and a ball of foil at the same time and see which falls faster.

Discover! Series 1 looks at a comb, paper bag, spoon, table knife, egg carton, handkerchief, paper clip, tape dispenser, pencil, crackers, scissors, and popcorn. Series 2 investigates buttons, a peanut, shoelace, key, toothbrush, crayon, paper plate, milk carton, envelope, notebook paper, aluminum foil, and your hand. Each card pack covers all learning styles (visual, conceptual, tactile, etc.) and is really *fun!*

Now, what's new from Tin Man Press? *Nifty Fifty* is "500 thinking challenges about 50 familiar things." I mean *really* familiar things, like bathtubs and telephones. Sample question: "Why can't you float in a bathtub?" (Answer: The water isn't deep enough.) Slightly tougher question: "Why is the bottom of a bathtub slanted slightly?" (Answer: So all of the water will run out when you open the drain.) Really fun little thinking activities you can pull out anytime. These do stimulate children to more precise and imaginative thinking; I've seen it with my own son.

Don't be misled by the title *Brain Stations: A Center Approach to Thinking Skills*. Harried classroom teachers might feel the need to actually set up centers with materials and copies of these activity sheets, but at home you can simply read the questions and instructions straight out of the book. They are fascinating, too. How about selecting 20 items to take with you to a deserted island—one out of each pair of choices? Would you take soap or toothpaste? A mirror or a compass? Why? Or how about the Down the Middle activity, in which you build a sentence around each given word. Example, for *hungry*— "The hungry shipwreck survivor turned head over heels in amazement when he saw the banana tree." (Teddy made that one up.) How about "stick stories," where you try to figure out which bent or straight line goes with which message. E.g., "Peek-a-boo!" goes with a short line "peeking" from the side of the picture frame. Some activities require cutting, drawing, and constructing items; others allow the student to draw or work with drawings. Fifty absorbing thinking activities in all.

LOGIC PUZZLES AND ACTIVITIES

NEW★★
Fearon Teacher Aids
Playing with Logic (grades 3–5), *Discovering Logic*, (grades 4–6), *Adventures with Logic*, (grades 5–7), $7.95 each. Add $3.50 shipping.

"The activities in this book are divided into five categories. The first is *relationships*, which involves classifying and comparing shapes and ideas. The next three are *sequencing, inference,* and *deduction*. The final section, *group activities*, is a collection of logical games for the entire class to play. These games use the skills developed in the previous sections."

That about sums it up for both books, but it's a bit dry. Let's try to give you a little flavor of the zany exercises and logic puzzles sequentially presented in *Playing with Logic*:

Can you identify these rare animals from the zoo on planet Woo? The zookeeper has identified the first one for you.

A *Scoo* is any animal that has more than two eyes. Put a circle around all Scoos.

A *Frooch* is any animal that has at least one horn. Put a triangle around all Frooches.

A *Ploom* is any animal that does *not* have a beard. Put a square around all Plooms.

[Following are pictures of eight nutty-looking animals. The first has a circle and a triangle about it.]

Just for fun, draw a Scoo Frooch Ploom on the back of this page!

We are only on page 5, and already we're into deep waters. A page or two farther on you get to do picture analogies: This is to that as this 'un is to that 'un. Little circle is to big circle as little square is to big square. Then on to verbal analogies: Herd is to cow as ___ is to ___.

In the Sequencing section, you get to put Captain Pepperoni's map of Pizza Island together in the right order and plan a tour of the Amusement Park that takes in all four public shows. Again, I'm just giving you a taste of the pages.

The Inference section includes goodies like lists of words with one letter missing. What could that missing letter be?

The Deduction section is your classic logic puzzles. If Violet is between Pinky and Little Red, and Pinky is not first, which duck is where? We work our way up to five-person matrix problems.

The games aren't all that hot, but since they were invented for classrooms, you don't have to feel guilty about not playing them. Better news is the answer key in the back of the book, the court of final resort for desperate beginning logicians. Not a bad start for your logic program.

Adventures with Logic is more of the same—same format and topics—but on a more advanced level. I especially liked the exercise where two newspaper stories were jumbled together and you had to separate the stories and place them in correct sequence. Also fun is the exercise where you find the secret word to replace the word in quotes. Consider these sentences:

1. Tom's mother was elected to the "Pickle" of Representatives.
2. Elaine's theater group played to a full "pickle."

"Pickle" stands for "house," of course, but I love it!. Maybe we *should* rename the House of Representatives the Pickle of Representatives. You and I always get in a pickle when those guys get together . . .

Adventures with Logic also includes word cartoons, Roman number riddles, and other goodies not found in the first book. And it, too, has an answer key at the end of its 59 pages. *Discovering Logic* is quite similar; I couldn't discern much difference between these two books.

NEW★★
Fearon Teacher Alds
Digging into Logic, $5.95, grades 5–8. *Logic in the Round*, $7.95, grades 5–8. *Logic, Anyone?*, $11.95, grades 5 and up. *Logic, Anyone?* Learning Workbook, $3.95. Add $3.50 shipping.

I've described matrix logic puzzles elsewhere. They are a son-of-a-gun to figure out if you've never run across one before. So someone thought of coming up with a book of logic problems for middle school that would actually explain *how to solve them*. Brilliant!

Digging into Logic has 30 matrix logic puzzles—with answer key—and excellent, simple instructions. A good first book of logic puzzles.

Logic in the Round, by the same authors, takes the same approach to circle logic puzzles. (These are puzzles in which you try to figure out who is in which position around a circle.) It contains 30 circle puzzles of increasing difficulty and instructions on how to solve this kind of puzzle.

Logic, Anyone? is a bigger book of 165 brain-stretching logic puzzles by the team who brought you *Digging into Logic* and *Logic in the Round*. The puzzles include analogies, matrix logic, table logic, circle logic, syllogisms, and Venn diagrams. Each section includes instructions on how to solve that kind of puzzle, and an answer key is mercifully provided. The book is reproducible, meaning you have permission to photocopy it for every child in your class or family. The *Logic, Anyone?* Learning Workbook, which is *non-* reproducible, has identical content but only three kinds of problems—matrix logic, syllogisms, and Venn diagrams—for 95 puzzles in all.

NEW★★
Harlan Enterprises
Games, $3.50 each. Grades 6–9.

Fact and Opinion Fun is a card-matching game that helps you move beyond grammar into the realm of thinking skills, discovering which sentences are factual and which are merely opinions. "Sunday is the first day of the week" matches "FACT," whereas "Basketball is the best sport" matches "OPINION." Each game can be played as a memory game (turn over two cards and if they match you keep them and take another turn) or as a pick-from-the-stack style game. For more detailed description, see the Math Drill chapter.

NEW★★
Timberdoodle
TOPS Beginning Problem Solving Series, $32.95. Shipping extra. Ages 5–7.

If you're the kind of person who likes to use words like *cute* and *precious*, you'll like this set of problem-solving experiences for young kids that does not require reading (on the kids' part, anyway). Each of these 64-page books includes 13 problem-solving activities with an animal motif, plus an introductory story that ties the book together. Frederika the Frog gets into muddles that require counting the bees or beavers. Sam the Baby Elephant hassles with addition. Maggie the Mouse saves the day with subtraction. Barney the Bear's life is full of addition and subtraction. To solve these problems, kids wind up making drawings, finding facts in pictures and tables, making tables to organize information, and recognizing clues in the stories. All the materials you need are right there in the book: cutout game cards, reproducible activity sheets, teacher's instructions. The series includes *Frederika and the Big Bad Biting Bee, Sam and the Storm at Willow Pond, Maggie the Mischievous Mouse, When Barney Stopped Laughing.*

The TOPS Beginning Problem Solving series includes all four Teacher's Resource Books. Published by Dale Seymour Publications.

MYSTERIES TO SOLVE

NEW**
EDC Publishing
Usborne Young Puzzle books, $5.95 each. Shipping extra. Ages 8 and up.

Get your thinker clicking with *Puzzle Island*! It's the first book in the Usborne Young Puzzle Books series. Plot: Sam, a young pirate, wants to become a real pirate. He needs to pick up the pieces of his pirate kit, solve the puzzles on every double-page spread, and outwit his sneaky enemy Horatio, while spotting the pink elephants on every page. Kids need keen observation to pick out Horatio, the elephants, and the pieces of pirate gear, while they use their noggins to find their way through mazes and decipher apparently contradictory clues.

The puzzles are easier than in the Usborne Puzzle Adventure series and the pages are bigger. Same bouncy, full-color, cartoon art, same wacky adventure themes, with no relationship to reality. (Sam is a pirate like Patch the Pirate is a pirate—i.e., not at all. His mom and dad see him off on his adventure, and he never threatens anyone with violence. Not to mention the pink elephants!) Fun reading.

Two future publications in this series expected in fall 1991: *Puzzle Town* and *Puzzle Farm*.

NEW**
EDC Publishing
Puzzle Adventure series, $4.50 each. Shipping extra. Ages 8–13.

Here's a new twist on puzzle solving: mystery cartoon books with clues to decipher on every page! All the Puzzle Adventures (18 now in print) feature young heroes, such as Agent Arthur. Arthur is the youngest member of the Action Agency, a worldwide network modeled after "The Man from U.N.C.L.E." He has to unscramble codes, notice strange happenings, follow maps, and solve riddles of all sorts in order to close his cases. Often he needs to remember information given earlier in the story—it pays to pay attention!

Bouncy, full-color art and the improbable plots beloved by fans of Nancy Drew and the Hardy Boys—preteens and teens, in other words—intrigue the readers of these books into wrestling with the puzzles. If you can't figure out a puzzle, you can always just go on to the next page and find out what happens next. If you're determined to get help, the solutions to each puzzle are in the back of the book.

The Agent Arthur series from Usborne in England is being remade into American editions. Fifteen volumes exist already for those in England and Europe, many with creepy titles like *Danger at Demon's Cover* or *The Curse of the Lost Idol*. (Some of these are straight spy stories, in spite of the spooky titles.) Other books in the Usborne Puzzle Adventure series are equally creepy (but fun) reading.

Only one book that I've seen treated the occult with any seriousness—*Journey to the Lost Temple*, where the plot partly hinges on an ancient idol having real powers. Yuk! The occult elements are usually campy (e.g., Aunt Martha's goofy ghost making a cameo appearance in Blood Castle). If they worry you, you can easily stick with the spy and mystery stories.

CHAPTER TWENTY-FOUR

VOCABULARY

"Hey, you! Kid! Ya wanna stay ignorant all your life? Wanna low-level job? Wanna be embarrassed to mingle in fancy social circles? Then just don't ever learn any of those big words, see? Big words impress people. They make it sound like you know something. Take that Buckley fellow. Nobody knows what he's sayin', but they all think he's smart. Got it, kid? Then quit hangin' around this pool hall and go do your vocabulary exercises . . ."

NEW★★
E-Z Grader Co.
Word Building Slide Rule, $4.50 postpaid. Grades 3–12.

You gotta find your roots. Also your prefixes and suffixes. Yes, friends and neighbors, it's time once again for playing Let's Take Apart (or Build) the Word!

I really admire the folks at E-Z Grader Co. for the effortless way they make the complex simple. Take their *Word Building Slide Rule*, for example. On one side of this rule you find (1) a whole slew of prefixes (defined), along with two roots to tack on to each of them; (2) 26 suffixes (not defined), each with another two roots. You can make 78 words with this side of the rule alone, not counting all the extra words children can put together once they learn the meanings of the prefixes and suffixes. Flip the *Word Building Slide Rule* over, and you find something even more clever. On

this side, you have a top row of nine defined prefixes. On the bottom, nine suffixes. As you move the slide so each prefix and its matching suffix appear in the windows, you find six roots in between the two. You can add the prefix and/or suffix to all the roots appearing between them, for a total of up to 18 words in each of the nine slide positions. Fun and clever!

UPDATED★★
Educators Publishing Service
Wordly Wise: Books A–C (grades 2–4), $4 each, keys $1 each. Books 1-5 (grades 4–8), $5.35 each; Books 6-9 (grades 9–12), $5.35 each; Teacher's Keys, $3 each. Shipping extra.

Unlike other alleged vocabulary-building series that I've seen, Educators Publishing Service's *Wordly Wise* is interesting, entertaining, and useful. Several major home school correspondence programs include it in their materials.

Wordly Wise A, B, and *C* are the first books in the series. Each introduces about 100 vocabulary words. Books A and B have 10 lessons each; Book C has 12.

Books 1–5, for grades 4–8, introduce about 375 words each. Each lesson includes about 12 new words, studied in a variety of ways. For each lesson, exercises A–C present words in context, show their multiple meanings (if any), and allow students to practice using the words in sentences. Exercise D reviews the lesson and earlier lessons. Exercise E is self-checking—when completed correctly, the student discovers part of a quotation, poem, or riddle. The Wordly Wise section in each lesson discusses words with interesting histories and distinguishes between commonly-confused words. Each third lesson has a crossword puzzle to fill in, using words studied in those three lessons.

Books 1–3 each have word glossaries. Beginning in Book 4, the student needs a separate dictionary, and each lesson has an extra exercise focused on roots, prefixes, and suffixes.

So much for dry, cribbed-from-the-catalog copy. Here's a sample of part of one lesson:

Wordly Wise 4
ABYSS is pronounced *a-BISS.*
NAIVE is pronounced *ny-EVE.*
TUMBREL may also be spelled *tumbril.* The rolling of the *tumbrel* brought fear into the hearts of noblemen during the French Revolution, for this was the cart that carried prisoners to their execution. Its destination was the guillotine (pronounced *GEE-yo-teen* in French, *GIL-a-teen* in English), a machine for chopping off the heads of those sentenced to death.

As you can see, words are not introduced according to common roots, or other methods of organization, but they *are* introduced memorably.

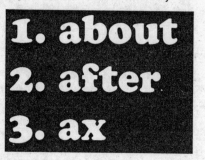

NEW★★
Providence Project
AlphaBetter, $15.95. Add $2.50 shipping. Grades 3–8.

"To improve your vocabulary, look up all new words in the dictionary." But how's a kid going to look anything up if he's not comfortable with the alphabet, in order, both forwards and backwards? Good questions. And here's the good answer.

You see, you can learn how to alphabetize without being really *good* at it. Children who have to struggle to remember which letter follows which are not likely to ever become heavy users of dictionaries, library card catalogs, encyclopedias, phone books, indexes, or any of the other myriad of reference tools indispensable to successful modern life. You don't really want to run through the "Alphabet Song" mentally every time you have to look something up!

Like the other modules of the Character and Competence Series from Providence Project, *AlphaBetter* is designed to "bridge the gap between learning what-and-how-to-do and doing it well. It takes students over the hump of alphabetizing with simple four-minute timed exercises, each on a single sheet. The first exercises begin by dividing the alphabet into eight overlapping groups of five letters each and drilling these combinations. The next exercises drill rapid recall of every letter's position in the alphabet relative to every other letter. Carefully planned alphabetizing drills come next, followed by exercises that translate these skills into actual use with reference book formats. Students try to "beat the clock" each day, doing the same sheet over and over until they are able to beat the time limit. The excitement of trying to beat the clock provides motivation sadly lacking in typical textbook alphabetizing drills, and the extra time spent on making this skill as effortless for the child as walking or talking pays rich dividends in confidence with all reference and alphabetized materials. Twelve sheets each of 16 drill exercises, printed on colorful bond paper.

NEW★★
Sign Talk
Sign Talk program, $29.95. Add $3 shipping. Grades 3–12.

Teachers know that the best way to increase vocabulary is to learn important prefixes and suffixes of words. But learning these vital parts of speech is Snore City for most kids. Here's a brand-new program designed to overcome the snore barrier!

Picture this. "Suzy, how'd you like to learn Indian sign language? Look, the program comes in a folded leatherette pouch with Indian decorations!"

Suzy: Ooh! Let me see! (Opening the pouch.) Ooh, look, lots of little colored cards! What are they all for?

You: First we're going to learn a lot of Indian hand signals, using the big tan and salmon cards. Then we're going to learn what they mean. Try this one—move your right hand in a flat, counterclockwise circle at chest height. What do you think that one means?

Suzy: Um . . . I don't know.

You: Well, we'll find out soon. Here, try some more of these signs. . . .

Time passes. Suzy and little brother Jamie have tried all the signs. Now you get out the blue Prefix Cards. These are the group stored in the left-hand back pocket of the pouch. They have the English meaning on top, and the hand sign below. On the back is the Latin prefix, upside down and backwards. To read it, an Indian Sign Decoder is included. This is really just a little sheet of reflective material in a paper holder.

You: OK, Suzy and Jamie. We're going to find out what some of those signs mean. Let's learn this one . . . (You make the hand motion.) It means *everywhere* or *present*. Why don't you say it and make it at the same time? . . . Now, this sign has a Latin name used in many English words. The name is hidden on the back. Want to use this special decoder to find out what it is? (General chorus of acclaim as kids grab for the decoder.)

Suzy: It says *omni*.

You: That's right! *Omni* means *everywhere* or *present,* and we say it in Indian language like this. (Demonstrate hand motion.) Now, hidden in this next batch of blue cards is the card that says *omni*. Can you find it for me? (Children find the card.) Good. Let's put these two blue cards at the bottom of the salmon sign card. Now there's one last blue card to find. It is an Example Word Card, and it has examples of words made with *omni*. Who can find it first? (Kids scramble through cards, triumphantly display the right one.) Let's staple all four of these together like the example in the booklet. This will be our sign for the day.

The Sign Talk program comes with 213 cards: salmon and blue Prefix Cards (as in the example above), grey and yellow Roots Cards, and white Suffix Cards. The Suffix Cards do not have corresponding Indian signs. They are learned separately in a little game. Kids cut out the Suffix Cards along the dotted lines and practice fitting them together like mini puzzles.

The Indian Sign Language gestures taught in this program are not merely interest-arousing gimmicks. Kids, of course, love anything and everything to do with Indians, but Indian Sign Language is not a toy. It is the foremost gesture language of the world, universally understood wherever people use signs. In fact, modern sign language is built on Indian signs!

In the included instruction booklet, you will find lists of prefixes, roots, and suffixes, and their corresponding English meanings. You will also find an Essential Word List. These are the words most frequently found on standardized tests. The booklet suggests you have your student look up five of these 164 words a day. I suggest you take it at a much easier pace, only tackling these words once the student has learned his prefixes, roots, and suffixes. One word a day is plenty.

Taking it at an easy pace, you can go through this kit in a little over a year. When you have finished, your child will have learned 54 Indian signs representing 29 prefixes and 25 roots of the English language, plus many essential words like *edible* and *courier.* Taken all together, by using this highly motivational program you will have given your student the key to the meaning of over 125,000 words.

MATH

CHAPTER TWENTY-FIVE

MATH MANIPULATIVES

I t's time . . . for Junk Food Math. We're going to talk about M&Ms in a minute. Yes, this is the chapter on math manipulatives. Most people think math manipulatives are those colorful, pricey little sticks, blocks, and cubes sold to schools. That's partly true. But, if I may borrow a term from the New Math, those blocks 'n cubes 'n so forth are merely a *subset* of all math manipulatives. Math manipulatives are *any* solid objects used by a teacher or student to demonstrate or discover math concepts.

Manipulatives are supposed to spark "discovery" learning. By handling the objects, children theoretically figure out arithmetic patterns for themselves. Let's see how that works with a "beans" program based on M&Ms.

What can a kid do with M&Ms? He can: (1) Count them. (2) Divide them into equal piles. (3) Divide them into piles by colors (classification). (4) Do subtraction and addition problems ("If you have two M&Ms and I give you two more, how many do you have?"). (5) Do multiplication problems ("Let's make three rows, each with three M&Ms in it. How many are there in all?") (6) Set up the Battle of Gettysburg, using M&Ms to represent the troops (social studies). (7) Make pictures using M&Ms as oversized color dots (impressionism, art). (8) Letting different colored M&Ms represent ones, tens, hundreds, and thousands, do complex addition and subtraction problems.

(9) Make the outline of a nation, state, or continent using M&Ms (geography). (10) Shoot them at each other on a frictionless surface (spray your table with PAM) for physics experimentation. (11) Eat them and observe how hyper everyone gets (nutrition). (12) Measure the time it takes for an M&M to melt in your palm (testing advertising claims, science). I could go on like this forever!

The dazzling array of manipulatives settles out into just a few categories. First, the "beans" programs. Lots and lots of similar items that kids count, arrange, or string together. Snap cubes. Links. Kitty-cat counters. Abacuses fit into this category, since they are basically beans on wires. Next, the "cubes" programs— rods and cubes used to teach base-10 concepts. Third, the "pies" programs. These are your classic fractions manipulatives—a circle cut into wedges. Fourth, dominoes. Fifth, time-telling manipulatives (clocks and calendars). Sixth, geometric and pre-geometric manipulatives (pattern blocks, geoboards, etc.). Seventh, weighing and measuring devices. Eighth, the Hundred Board and its cousins. Tenth, everything that doesn't fit into the first nine categories!

I wish life were really this simple. Actually, math manipulatives are like computers. It's what you *do* with them that counts. Thus, you might have two "beans" programs, one of which simply introduces kids to counting and the other which presents all of basic math. The curriculum that accompanies the manipulatives is like the software bundled with a computer. You have to compare manipulatives according to what they teach, not according to their type. This often means comparing "beans," "cubes," and Hundred Boards all at once.

The toughest thing to learn when first checking out math manipulatives is *which manipulative type is best suited to which topic.* Although you can, in theory, teach just about any math concept with just about any math manipulative, it's a lot easier to teach place value with cubes and rods or an abacus than with snap cubes. It's easier to teach perimeter with a geoboard than with links. It's easier to teach fractions with fraction manipulatives than with pattern blocks. Keep this in mind. Crazed math teachers have spent months concocting curriculum encouraging the hapless novice to use the wrong manipulative to teach basic school topics. Enamored with their set of links or tangrams, they want to ensnare you in hours of pointless struggling, forcing the manipulative to fit the topic. The results are like substituting a radial arm saw for a screwdriver and vice versa. Much better to get the right tool for the job in the first place.

Now, some basic math. A large bag of M&Ms costs around $2. "Beans" programs start at around $15 and top in the hundreds of dollars. So do you really need the beans? The question here is whether children learn just as rapidly working with numerals or real-world objects (such as M&Ms). In my own experience, children who have been exposed to counting, adding, etc. as real-world processes have no trouble understanding the more abstract ideas when the time comes. Families who learn at home can present fractions effectively with an actual blueberry pie that needs to be cut into quarters (or sixths, or eighths) than with felt "pie segments." Decimals, a specialized form of fraction, can be understood by anyone who understands fractions.

Manipulatives do have certain advantages, though. It's easier to stash fraction circles in your closet than to keep a constant supply of uncut blueberry pies in the fridge. Some of the more elaborate manipulatives programs (e.g. Cube-It and Mortensen Math) allow kids to "see" concepts, like quadratic equations, which are impossible to model with beans or pies. Kinesthetic learners, who often have difficulty following blackboard math, especially benefit from manipulatives. And remember, *"beans" programs are only ONE type of manipulative.* It's easy to substitute M&Ms or even real beans for the fancy counters in school "beans" programs, or to make your own geoboard (pound some

nails into a slab of scrap wood), but not as simple to make the other kinds of manipulatives. You *can* make your own base-10 rods and cubes from wood or cardboard, but they won't be as pretty and uniform or hold up as well as the classroom brands. The same goes for manipulative clocks and calendars and other complex manipulatives.

Here's the bottom line on manipulatives:

(1) Math manipulatives are a lot of fun to play with.

(2) Good math manipulatives can make math more real for kids and their parents.

(3) Good manipulatives often cost a lot. Sometimes you can reduce this cost by making your own; sometimes it's better to buy.

(4) Most kids can learn math without manipulatives. It just will take longer (in most cases) and they just won't enjoy it as much!

ALL-PURPOSE MATH MANIPULATIVES

Here's your Package Deals: manipulative sets that cover *all* the basic operations. Counting. Addition. Subtraction. Multiplication. Division. Fractions. Decimals (sometimes). Algebra (sometimes). Probability and statistics (sometimes). Not all these sets cover exactly the same territory, so you should read the reviews carefully when comparing.

NEW**
Activities for Learning
A-L Abacus, $15.95. *Abacus Activities*, $16.95. *Worksheets for Abacus*, $24.95. Math Card Games, $16.95. Six decks of math cards for games, $16.95. Corners colored plastic tiles, set of 50, $5.95. Place Value Cards, $4.95. Base 10 Picture Cards, $1.95. Suffix Flow Charts, $4.95. Shipping 10%, minimum $1.50.

Complete abacus-based elementary math calculations curriculum developed for her son by Joan A. Cotter, a lady with an impressive list of credentials. In 1980 she formed a company, Activities for Learning, and started publishing some of them. We're talking about doing math with an abacus and at the same time learning how all the math operations work.

The Activities for Learning abacus is a very nice-looking piece of work, with its wooden frame, ten strong wires, and 100 beads. The beads come in your choice of four color combinations: purple and pink, purple and yellow, blue and yellow, or green and yellow. The price is definitely right, and you can also purchase both an activities book with pre-K through grade 6 activities and a volume of worksheets designed for use with the abacus and book.

More about *Activities for the Abacus*. This is the second edition (a good sign, since loser books never have second editions!). Like the worksheet books, it has an oversized spiral-bound format. This book is *very* complete. For example, in Unit Five, Introducing Subtraction, you get Simple Subtraction (oral subtraction, written subtraction, subtracting from 10, subtracting 1), Subtractions < 10 (subtracting tens, subtracting single-digit numbers, subtracting double-digit numbers), Subtraction Results (greater than, equal to, or less than; remainders and differences; subtraction twins; equations; checking), and Special Effects (minuend decreased by 1, subtrahend decreased by 1, counting up, and the complement method). This is just one of the 11 units, which cover everything from how to read the abacus and basic math concepts to fancy stuff like squares and percentages, millions on the abacus, and how to use both the Japanese and Chinese abacus. The associated worksheet volumes contain correlated exercises on both paper and the abacus.

Math Card Games is an oversized spiral-bound book with games for every math concept from numeration (we know this as "counting"!) through all four basic arithmetic operations, clocks, money, and fractions. You will need to get the six decks of special cards from Activities for Learning to play the games outlined in the book. All six decks are only $16.95. These include Basic cards (12 of each number from 0 to 10), Product cards (numbers for products from 1 x 1 to 10 x 10), Money cards (50 cards using 5 coins), Corner cards, Clock cards (24 cards with numbers from 1 to 12 and :00 to :55), and Fraction cards (72 fraction cards and 20 percent cards).

Corners are also available in a set of 50 plastic titles in four colors, along with instructions for play. These are cards with numbers in different colors in the middle of each side. You can play over a dozen absorbing math games with these tiles. The basic Corners game involves matching colors of numbers *and* putting only numbers touching that add up to a multiple of five. Sort of like Dominoes.

Joan also has Place Value Cards (36 plastic cards for composing numbers from 1 to 9999 by overlapping) and Base 10 Picture Cards (87 pictures of the base 10 blocks, including 26 each of ones, tens, hundreds, and nine of the thousands).

All the Activities for Learning materials I've seen (and I've seen most of them) were *very* professionally done, nice to look at, durable, easy to follow, and even fun! Another great resource for kinesthetic learners.

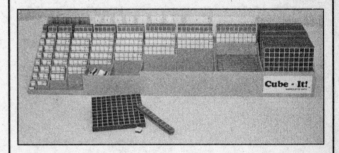

NEW**
Cube-It! Manipulative Math
SERIES 1 (grades K–4), $339.80, includes Cube-It! manipulative set. SERIES 2 (grades 5–8), $119.80, is an add-on to SERIES 1. SERIES 3 (grades 9–12), $119.80, is an add-on to SERIES 2.

A math manipulatives program for preschool through grade 12? "Sounds interesting," I told the man on the other end of the telephone line. "Send it along and I'll take a look at it."

I found that Cube-It™ is the best-organized, most complete set of math manipulatives available anywhere. With this one set you can demonstrate *all* the basic arithmetic operations, place value, fractions, measurement, algebra, calculus, and even negative numbers! The 213 pieces, made of an extra-tough, special grade of plastic that wears like iron and handles like wood, are organized in their own durable 7 x 24" blue organizing tray, which is so set up that you can find any piece you need at a glance. Pieces are metric in size, gridded into units, *and labeled*. The last is a very important feature, as it means you can instantly tell the 5 x 5" flat from the 5 x 6" flat or the 4 x 4" flat. Pieces are 1 cm in thickness, meaning you can do 3-D volume work with them as well.

Let's describe this setup. On the far left back of the tray are two sets of clear gridded plastic squares used in fractions work, from the one-ninths through the one-halfs. Along the back of the tray are labeled yellow fraction strips, ranging from nine ⅑ strips on the far left to two unit squares on the right. Everything neat and in its place so far. Now, let's talk about the actual positive and negative number flats. On the far left are labeled gridded rectangles of yellow plastic with a layer of black sandwiched in the middle, ranging from 1 x 1 to 1 x 9. At that top of that row are two red, gridded, 1 x 10s. The next row goes from 2 x 2 (on the bottom) to 2 x 9 (at the top), with two 2 x 10s at the very top. Similarly, we have rectangles for every value from 3 x 3 to 3 x 10; from 4 x 4 to 4 x 10; and so on, up to 9 x 9 and the two 9 x 10s in that row. Each rectangle has a clear plastic grid of the same size in front of it—these are used to signify negative numbers of that size. Each rectangle fits into its own individual storage spot, on its end so you can see its label.

Nine extra 1 x 1s are stored in a bin in the front, as are nine extra 1 x 10s. On the right-hand side of the organizing tray are fifteen 10 x 10 flats. These will come in handy when demonstrating operations like 24 x 28 or (2x + 2)(2x + 5).

I've often said that the Mortensen Math method is just turning everything into rectangles. Cube-It uses a very similar approach. Addition becomes "pushing together." Multiplication and division are performed as "area" operations, making or dividing up rectangles. This "area" approach allows you to go from simple counting to "algebra" (really, only binomials) with breathtaking speed.

Just as with Mortensen, it's not practical to *do* all your math problems with these manipulatives. There aren't enough hundred flats, for example, to do 64 x 58. You can, however, *demonstrate* every arithmetic and algebraic operation with Cube-It.

Compared to Mortensen, or indeed any other set of manipulatives, Cube-It is wondrously easy to use because of its size and organization. Mortensen's larger ½" grid means the pieces, while more colorful and fun for young children, take up more space on your table—and the Mortensen packaging makes individual pieces harder to find and put away. Neatness counts for home-school moms, as I can testify! If you have a co-op school situation, Cube-It is definitely a more attractive choice just because of its organizational features.

Cube-It! has recently upgraded both its "Cubes 'n Crows" blackline masters to include teaching explanations and added a teacher's manual that gives strategies for each concept. This is a welcome change, since the first edition of the blackline masters lacked explanations of what you were supposed to be doing on each page. A teacher's video is also included with each series and explains how to use the Cube-It Concept Cards for that series.

NEW**
Culsenaire Company of America
Jumbo Rods Set of 154 with self-sorting tray, $49.50. Jumbo Rods Teacher Set of 56 rods, $18.50. Cuisenaire® Rods Intro Set (74 rods with wall poster and 36-page booklet in plastic tray), $7.95/plastic, $8.95/wood. Starter Set (155 rods with self-sorting tray and 36-page booklet), $29.50/plastic, $31.95/wood. Supplementary Trays of 155 rods, $14.50/plastic, $17.50/wood. 100-cm Rod Track, $4.50. 50-cm Rod Track, $2.50.

Cuisenaire rods are my favorite all-purpose math manipulative for basic arithmetic operations. Their metric size (1 centimeter per side for the unit cube) and weight make them ideal for measuring and weighing activities. Their patented color-coding lets you tell a 4 from a 5 at a glance (not true of snap-together cubes, which you must count every time). Their shape and balance are wonderful for free play. Many of the best programs require the use of these blocks: *Miquon Math* and the Learning at Home math guides, to name just two.

Let me pause for just a moment to tell you what on earth we're talking about. Picture a unit cube. Color: natural (if wood) or white (if plastic). The 2 rod is red and twice as long. The 3 rod is light green and three times as long as the unit cube. And so on up to the orange 10 rod. None of the rods are marked in any way, save for their color, so you can call them ones, tens, *X*s, or whatever.

Now perceive the beauty of this system. To show 5 + 5 = 10, I need merely take two yellow rods and show that their combined length is the same as an orange rod. If I were doing this with counters, unit cubes, color tiles, or snap-together cubes, I would first have to count out five items and then either group or snap them together. After repeating this process, I would then have to count the total number of items. That's about 19 steps more than the Cuisenaire rod approach requires—just for that one problem!

To make life even easier, use the 50 or 100 cm Rod Tracks. Here, to work the problem 6 x 7 = ?, simply take either six black rods or seven dark green rods. Lay them end-to-end on the Rod Track and read off the answer: 42. Without a rod track, you would have to build a parallel rod of four orange 10 rods plus one red 2 rod to find that the answer was 42.

Since Cuisenaire rods come in one-centimeter multiples, and since that means the shorter rods are rather small, Cuisenaire Company has developed Jumbo Rods—and hidden them in a completely different section of the catalog than the section featuring regular

Cuisenaire rods, which is why I'm going out of my way to tell you about them. Jumbo Rods are exactly double the length of Cuisenaire rods in each dimension, making the volume of a Jumbo Rod eight times the volume of its corresponding regular Cuisenaire rod. While the smaller Jumbo Rods are still too small to be safe around babies, they are just perfect for preschool and the early grades. Not too many accessories are available for Jumbo Rods, but it doesn't matter, since you'll mainly be using them to introduce the rods and do some simple math (and a *lot* of building!).

You can get by with just the Teacher Set of Jumbo Rods (a mere 56 rods packed loose in a box). For the regular-sized rods, you should get at least a dozen of each size. This means at least two Supplementary Trays. If you want the booklet *Idea Book for Cuisenaire Rods at the Primary Level* you need one Starter Set and one Supplementary Tray. If you can live without a self-sorting tray but you still want the *Idea Book*, three of the Introductory Sets will do you (this is the least expensive option). Rods are actually more accessible, though not as neat, in the unsorted trays.

Reader Edith Best of Detroit, Michigan pointed out to me that Cuisenaire rods and Cuisenaire's Base Ten blocks "work just fine with Mortensen books and methods." I had come to the same conclusion independently, and feel it's worth repeating here, since the Cuisenaire materials cost far less than Mortensen.

All sorts of books and accessories are available for Cuisenaire rods, from sets of logic games and puzzles to pads of one-centimeter graph paper. My very favorite is still *Miquon Math* (see review under Key Curriculum Press heading in Elementary Math Programs).

NEW * *
Cuisenaire Company of America
Invicta Math Balance, $22. *The Balance Book*, $6.95.
Grades K–8.

This fascinating new math tool shows kids how equations literally "balance out." It's a scale with pegs numbered 1–10 sticking out on the arms, and a base with more pegs for storing the included weights. Place a weight on 3 and a weight on 1 on one side; see that one weight on 4 on the other side balances it, proving 3 + 1 = 4. Feel more sophisticated? Try 32 divided by 5. After placing six weights on the pegs numbered five, you discover that the sixth weight is too much. Experimenting, you find that one extra 2 balances the scale—so 32 = 5 x 6 + 2.

You can hang a maximum of eight weights both fore and aft on the pegs for a number, thus proving combinations up to 80, or even more if you are creative. 99, for example, could be 8 tens plus one nine plus two fives. You can also label the included stickers any way you like and place them on the provided spots on the backside of the scale, thus adding even more educational value. The little eight-page booklet suggests labeling the back side as fractions ($\frac{1}{4}$, $\frac{1}{2}$, $\frac{3}{4}$, etc.).

The Invicta Math Balance is durable, easy to set up and balance (just slide the little thingamajigs back and forth until the arms are horizontal), and made of excellent European plastic. It's self-checking, open-ended, and can be used to demonstrate every arithmetic operation in a very satisfying way.

The Balance Book (not included with the balance) is 94 pages of balance activities, presented as 5 x 8 tear-out task cards. These range from simple discoveries of what plus what equals what to more sophisticated problems like discovering which numbers can be balanced with exactly four weights. The book covers addition, multiplication, division, place value, problem solving, logic, and factoring. You need this book if you get the Invicta Math Balance. With both the book and the balance, you have an elementary math manipulative program that only lacks geometry.

UPDATED * *
Literacy Press
Early Math Literacy Packet: manual, 30 blackline masters, 100 printed but uncut tags, 100 brass cup hooks, 3 math workbooks, and Hundred Board kit instructions, all for $38.50 postpaid. Custom handcrafted 20 x 25" Plywood Hundred Board, $33.50. Add $1.75 shipping per packet.

Years ago Eunice Coleman, author of the Literacy Press's fine literary program, designed a math manipulative that is also a lovely room decoration and furthermore can be used to teach *every* arithmetic operation, even clocks, money, and fractions. No kidding.

The Hundred Board, Mrs. Coleman's invention, is a ten-by-ten grid with little color-coded sequentially numbered tags hanging off brass cup hooks. Starting with skip counting (e.g., counting by 2s, 5s, 6s, 10s), the *Early Math Literacy Packet* leads the student through addition, subtraction, multiplication, division, and even fractions, all using the Hundred Board. All no sweat, all high-interest. In Mrs. Coleman's classroom the children never lost a Hundred Board tag in eleven years and showed remarkable math gains in less time than you'd imagine. (I recently saw one of her Hundred Boards hanging on the wall behind a math teacher whose picture was in an *Insight* magazine article, by the way!)

If you want to make the Hundred Board yourself, you *can* color-code the included cardboard model and sort of use it as a Hundred Board. But if you want the real thing you need to follow the included plans and

- cut

- paint or rout

- sand

- stain

- and varnish a nice piece of wood

- drill 100 holes (for the provided 100 brass cup hooks)

- cut out the 100 tags

- and hang the handsome thing on the wall (too good-looking for the closet). Alternatively, you can now buy a handcrafted Hundred Board direct from Literacy Press. We have one of these on our wall, and it is a work of art! Even columns are dark-stained; odd columns are natural; a diagonal line runs through the 9s; the whole thing got five coats of varnish; and there it sits, with its little brass hooks and specially color-coded tags.

Along with the manual and Hundred Board plans and ingredients you get three Continental Press workbooks (grades 1–3) and 30 blackline masters for Hundred Board seatwork. You have to provide the training to keep your littler ones from flinging the tags madly about the room. They are endlessly fascinating to children; our little ones' first math lessons include putting the tags back on the board in the right place!

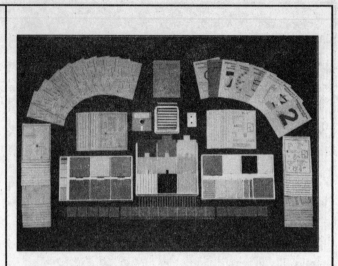

NEW**
Mortensen Math

Addition/Subtraction Tray, $25. Addition, subtraction, or multiplication facts cards only, $5. Multiplication Facts Tray, $50. All About Fractions Kit, $99. Very Basic Basic Operations Kit, $50. Basic Operations Kit, $350. Combo Kit, $139. Workbooks, $50/level (10 books each in Algebra, Arithmetic, Calculus, Problem Solving, and Measurement). Teachers Manual, $10/level. Home School Kit, includes Combo Kit (with skip-count underlays), Home Fractions Kit, Multiple Tens Kit, pieces from Very Basic Basic Operations kit, Level 1 workbooks and teachers manual, Apple II or IBM-compatible multiplication software, Multiplication Facts Mastery workbooks, set of Series A (how-to) teaching manuals, and audio tape with coloring book, $249. (The regular retail price of the items in the Home School Kit is over $500, but schools, including home schools, receive a reduced rate.) Add 10% shipping.

More Mortensen manipulatives—this time for the elementary-school-and-up crowd.

The real problem with Mortensen is that it doesn't come organized into one easy-to-use-and-put-away set. The Home Kit does come in one shipping box, but includes dozens of kits and books. There's so much to choose from! I imagine I'm not the first would-be buyer who has been paralyzed by all the choices. The thing to do is, first, forget for a minute about which basic rods set you are going to buy, and second, concentrate first on the specialty kits. We're going to look at them one by one.

The Addition/Subtraction Tray comes with a set of problem cards. You get the usual molded plastic tray, with indentations where you store the problem cards and bars, and two sets of unit bars (two each for the numbers 1–9). As in all the Mortensen materials, the

1 bars are all green, the 2 bars are orange, the 3 bars are pink, and so on, for easy recognition. At the bottom of the tray are two long grooves, in which you solve the problems using the unit bars. Say the problem is "8 + 4." You join the 8 bar to the 4 bar in one of the grooves. In the next groove is a 10 bar. You see that you need to add a 2 bar to the 10 bar to make a rod of equal length to 8 + 4. The answer, then, is 10 + 2, which is 12. For subtraction problems, you reverse the process. As straightforward as it can be. Another good point is that, unlike straight "beans" manipulatives, this manipulative method emphasizes 10s, which are so important when it comes to carrying and borrowing later on. If you like this, then get the Addition Tray and a set of subtraction cards to round it out.

The Multiplication Facts Tray is another really neat resource. It's a molded plastic tray in which reside nine each of the colorful multiple unit bars, skip count cards to place underneath the unit bars, and multiplication fact cards with the answers on the reverse side. On the bottom of this tray are four long grooves. In two of them are stored, end to end, ten 10 bars. You can solve a given problem, say 4 x 9, either by removing that number of bars from its storage area (thus revealing the answer underneath), or check it out physically by placing the bars end to end and checking the answer against the number of 10 bars. For example, 4 x 9 is as long as 3 of the 10 bars plus a 6 bar, so the answer is 36. This kit is great for teaching what multiplication is (adding multiples of a number) and cementing its base-10 nature (all answers are seen in terms of how many 10s fit into them). You can always use the cards for regular flash card drills, while the student can check every answer for himself.

These kits are pretty—really pretty. The Addition and Multiplication Trays are easy to keep neat, since everything has its own storage spot. Although the pieces are all compatible, you do not want to start mixing and matching between these sets. It's not necessary, since each contains all the pieces needed for its own operations. You also don't want to have more than one of these kits out at a time, since each takes up quite a bit of space.

The Mortensen Math workbooks and teacher's guides are described in the Math Programs chapter. With the addition of a Combo Kit, Very Basic Basic Operations Kit, and Fractions Kit (all written up separately elsewhere in this present chapter), you have a complete, impressive math manipulatives program.

NEW*
Success House
The Magic Multiplier™, $4.95. Whole Number Path to Math™ Kit, $19.95. Fraction Path to Math™ Kit (addition, subtraction, multiplication, and division of fractions), $24.95. Tic Tac Frac™, $4.95. Add $2.75 shipping per order.

Success House's Whole Number Path to Math and Magic Multiplier kits give you the "square" view of math at a fraction of the price of other manipulative kits. The downside is that the materials aren't as thick or easy to handle, and they won't come back with a smile if you spill your coffee all over them.

The Magic Multiplier is one colorful, preprinted square piece of heavy cardstock and one L-shaped "framer" to use in framing any multiplication problem from 1 x 1 to 10 x 10. To use the Magic Multiplier, your child must know how to count money using quarters, nickels, and pennies, since it works the same way. Clear as mud? Really, it's quite simple. By using a 5 x 5 gridded rectangle, 1 x 5 rectangles, and a red square (value 25) on the printed card, your child can figure out the answers to multiplication problems by adding. It's really a cute, unusual little visual device.

Whole Number Path to Math comes in a couple of ziplock bags. You will appreciate this, because the little pieces could easily get lost otherwise. You get

- 29 yellow "ones." These are ½" yellow matboard squares.

- 11 orange fives—matboard rods as long as five ones.

- 15 red tens—rods of length ten.

- one green twenty-five (a 5 x 5 square)

• two purple fifties (a 5 x 10 rectangle)

• one blue hundred (10 x 10 square)

• two Place Value Boards (heavy cardstock, with tens and ones marked)

• a multiplication mat with a square grid

• a division board

• three colored, numbered dice (two 10-sided, one regular)

• a 16-page instruction book describing 19 activities and 14 games of addition, subtraction, multiplication, and division. These are not solitaire games; you will need to play them with your child, or teach the children to play them together. All games have an element of chance. Alternatively, you can use the manipulatives simply as teaching devices.

Success House also sells a Fraction Path to Math Kit (addition, subtraction, multiplication, and division of fractions) and Tic Tac Frac, a two-player game which "gives meaning and practice in reducing fractions and in changing improper fractions to mixed numerals.

NEW★★
Sycamore Tree
Fun at the Beach complete set, including file box or flannelboard, $27.95. Without box, $17.95. Felt counting set, $10.95. Shipping extra.

Some of you have written wondering what happened to Grandma's Garden Felt Math (reviewed in an earlier edition). This very lovely, simple math felt set is no longer available, my spies tell me, because the people making it got buried by success. Too many orders, no procedure for having it manufactured outside. However, all is not lost. Sycamore Tree, one of the companies that used to supply Grandma's Garden, asked Little Folk Felts to put together a kit that would cover the same areas Grandma's Garden used to. So now we have Fun At the Beach and you can get it from Sycamore Tree.

Like Grandma's Garden, Fun At the Beach is fuzzy and wonderful. You get a felt beach scene, five felt children of various races, ten each of beach buckets,

toy boats, fish, starfish, shells, beach balls, and seals; symbols and numbers; three different sizes of the five basic shapes; nine nests with baby birds; twenty-five coconuts and two bunches of ten coconuts each for teaching place value. Oh, I forgot the five fraction circles. Along with this gloriously colorful stuff comes a short-and-sweet manual that explains how to teach counting, adding, subtracting, fractions, place value, multiplying, and dividing using the felt manipulatives. All very warm and cuddly and easy for little children to understand, not to mention marvelous *fun* for them to try! Unlike Grandma's Garden, *you* will have to cut out the pieces; but to make up for your extra effort, a file box is included in the basic set, and along with the box you get flocked sheets with outlines of each shape, for easy storage. The felts are airbrushed and gorgeous, rather like the Betty Lukens Bible felts, although produced by a different company. You will need a flannelboard to use with this set.

LEARNING ABOUT NUMBERS

Beans. Links. Snap cubes. Counters. Poker chips. You can demonstrate numbers, counting, adding, subtracting, and other introductory math concepts with all or any of these.

To avoid stuffing this book with hundreds of pages of beans programs, I have confined myself below to the best, most innovative, and most unusual basic number-learning manipulatives. Don't forget the all-purpose manipulatives reviewed in the last section, either!

NEW★★
Cube-It! Manipulative Math
Counting House, $39.95. *Build A Rectangle Addendum Kit*, $19.95. Grades K–4.

We are really enthusiastic about this super set of manipulatives for teaching basic arithmetic to preschool and elementary kids! First of all, the manipulatives are works of art. The 17 x 22" folding board on which the Counting House appears is made of bright yellow plastic. When I say "plastic" I know you're thinking "smooth, thin, cheap." Well, this plastic is an extra-tough, special grade that wears like iron and handles like wood. You've probably never seen anything like it before! On this background are glued more pieces of that plastic in different colors. Together they make up the shape of a house with a basement, first floor, and second floor. Outside the house, colorful stickers of balloons and children playing add eye-appeal. Inside the house, each floor is divided into two rooms, plus a narrow "closet" on the right in which you will place all your "one" cubes. Along with this you get a gorgeous set of bright, colorful manipulatives: three hundreds squares, 18 tens bars, and 18 units. These are gridded into units on one side, with the other side left blank for use representing abstract quantities in pre-algebra work. All the manipulatives come in a durable and attractive organizational box, along with a teacher's manual and student Cubes 'n Crows blackline masters.

Let's see how this works by running through a simple problem that your preschoolers will be able to do in a few days after getting this program: 231 + 129. First, you put two hundred blocks in the left second-story room, three ten-rods in the right second-storey room, and one unit block in the closet. Below, on the first floor, you put one hundred block in the left room, two ten-rods in the right room, and nine units in the closet. Now, push everything together in the basement! You wind up with three hundred blocks, five ten blocks, and 10 unit blocks. But only nine unit blocks will fit in the basement closet! So your child measures the 10 unit blocks against a 10 rod, finds they are the same, and substitutes a 10 rod. Now she reads the answer: "It's 360, Mommy!" Not bad for a four-year-old! (If you prefer, you can use the attic for "carrying," making it even more like a written math problem.)

To do algebra problems, simply turn the manipulatives over. Now the 10 rod stands for x and the hundred block stands for x^2. Piece of cake.

You can't do *all* the basic arithmetic operations with this set, which is why its makers now offer an Addendum Kit called Build a Rectangle for multiplication and division. Whether or not you get the extra kit, this is about the most fascinating introduction to math your children can get. The only requirement is that they be old enough to not put little pieces in their mouths.

NEW★★
Cuisenaire Company of America
Two-Color Counters, $9.95/set of 200. Grades K–12.

Sometimes the simplest ideas can be powerful. Whoever thought of making these counters with one side red and one side yellow stumbled onto something.

Counters, as you know, are sets of uniform objects used in schools for counting practice. They can be cute little plastic kitty cats, clear poker chips, beans, raisins, forks, spoons, or even children. The Two-Color Counters happen to be thickish plastic circles, a sandwich of yellow and red plastic. "So what?" you ask. So did I. I wasn't even going to review them until Maggie Holler of Cuisenaire Company pressed them on me.

They arrived. I opened the ziplock bag, noting the included instruction booklet. I grabbed a handful. They smell a little funny—like the Monsanto plastic factory I once worked in—but feel *good*. Satisfying. Chunky. They don't slip around like the poker chips. That's one for Anna. Next, I started doing problems with them. 3 + 3 = 6 becomes three red counters plus three yellow counters equals six counters in all. Hmm. That's a lot easier to see when the counters are different colors, and it's a lot easier to do when you can simply flip over a counter to get a different color. How about showing the fraction ⅘? Easy—four counters yellow-side-up and one red-side up. Five counters in all, of which four are yellow. Obviously ⅘ + ⅕ = 1. When presented this way any child can see it. Hmm again. Now how about some simple probability experiments? How often in 20 tosses will six counters come up with three yellow and three red? Try it! Keep records! Along the way your kids will pick up graphing and notetaking, plus experimental techniques.

As you can see, Two-Color Counters do a lot more than poker chips and kitty cats. They are especially useful for finding combinations (e.g., "What are all the pairs of numbers that add up to 10?"), single-operator math problems, working with fractions, and simple probability experiments. Simple is beautiful.

NEW**
Cuisenaire Company of America
Snap™ Cubes, $10.95/set of 100 (10 each of 10 colors). Set of 500, $44.50. Set of 1000, $81. 1–100 Operational Board, $15.75. 100 Track, $29.95. 1–10 Stair, $6.95. Grades K–6.

Cuisenaire Company's new Snap Cubes are ¾" on all six sides. One side of each cube has a jutting circular peg; the other five sides have circular indentations into which a peg can fit. Thus, when the catalog tells you the cubes "connect on all six sides," know that it takes a certain amount of ingenuity to design solid constructions using these cubes.

Snap Cubes are the same size as Unifix cubes, and can be used in all the same ways. Snap them together end-to-end for counting and arithmetic manipulations. Additionally, you can snap them together into solids, which is useful for demonstrating squaring and cubing and for 3-D work. All sets, no matter how large or small, come with equal numbers of cubes in each of 10 colors. This is handy for demonstrating that 2 + 5 = 7, since your set of 2 snapped-together cubes and your set of 5 snapped-together cubes can be different colors.

Snap Cubes have brighter colors than Unifix cubes. They fit together (and stay together) beautifully. Since any two rows only connect at one point, these irresistible little building blocks are great for showing rotations, flips, and transformations of solid objects.

Cuisenaire Company has a group of accessories just for use with Snap Cubes. Of these, the products that look like they'd be of most interest in the home are:

• The 1–100 Operational Board. This is our old friend the Hundred Board, gridded so that a single Snap Cube (or Unifix cube, etc.) can fit over each numeral.

• The 1–10 Stair appears to be a series of connected shallow trays, each topped with a numeral. The 1 stair only can hold one Snap Cube; the 2 tray can hold two; etc. Your child practices counting and numeral recognition by building the stair.

• The 100 Track is ingeniously designed so each ten-number section is a separate piece. Slide them together to form the track. Use the track to demonstrate that 17 + 8 = 25, or 4 x 9 = 36, or whatever your little heart desires. (I still feel that

Cuisenaire rods and the Cuisenaire Rod Track are better suited to this work, since you don't have to count up and snap together cubes every time you want a 5 or a 9.)

NEW**
Cuisenaire Company of America
Links, $4.25/set of 100, grades K–2. Link-Its™, $3.95 set of 100, grades K–8.

Links are the traditional plastic ovals first used for classroom linking activities. They come in four colors and stay together nicely. With them you can make great necklaces and demonstrate all the basic arithmetic operations, if you already know how. For example, one link plus one link equals a new chain of two links. Three chains of four links each, when linked together, make one new chain of 12 links. No instruction book included.

Link-Its are another new linking product that I think has more promise for home use. It's a set of one-inch square links in four colors. First, chains made of Link-Its do hold together (very important). Second, your set comes with an excellent, brief instructional booklet explaining how to use Link-Its for counting, patterning, arithmetic operations, fractions . . . *and* measurement, logic, graphing, and probability! Link-Its' uniform size offers all sorts of unusual uses, from measuring the perimeters of objects to creating basic geometric shapes. (Of course, links are *not* the natural tool to use for these topics—they're better suited to basic numbers work—but it might be fun to just do a few of these clever exercises.) Link-Its fit on the squares of Cuisenaire's Hundred Board and place value boards, but in real life you'll spend too much time putting them back onto the spaces off which they have slid to make this feature really worthwhile.

NEW**
Mortensen Math
Number/Picture Fun Kit, $30. Number Discovery Kit, $40. Numeral ID Kit, $10. Skip Count Tape and Coloring Books, $20. Add 10% shipping. Ages 3–6.

To make life easier, I'm reviewing Mortensen Math manipulatives by age level. Right now we're looking at manipulatives for the preschool set.

Yes, they are pricey. But boy, are they nifty! Let's start with the inexpensive Numeral ID Kit. Your child can learn the numbers and numerals 1–10 with this kit. You get a molded plastic tray, into which the colorful rods fit in ascending order. The idea is to place the card with the right number under the rod to which it corresponds. The backs of the cards are color-coded to the rods, so the child can check his own work. When not in use, the rods and cards store neatly in their own pockets on the tray.

Next comes the Number/Picture Fun Kit. This really fun set has five molded plastic puzzles. Children fit the colorful plastic rods into the indentations on the puzzle trays in order to "fill in" the pictures (a palm tree, a camel, etc.). This familiarizes them with the rods and develops thinking skills and hand-eye coordination (puzzling is the ultimate pre-math activity). As a bonus, it turns out that the tray for each puzzle into which the loose pieces are stacked has a width corresponding to a different number. Puzzle 1 has units: puzzle 2 uses both units and twos; puzzle 3 uses units, twos, and threes; and so on. As children put away their puzzle pieces after a session, they discover that a "one" and a "one" fit into the same space as a "two."

For more obvious discovery learning play, the Number Discovery Kit provides similar molded plastic puzzle trays. Here the puzzles are the numerals 1–9. Kids fit the rods for each puzzle into the indentations in order to form the outline of the numeral. The storage tray for the "1" puzzle is one unit wide; the storage tray for the "2" puzzle is two units wide; and so on.

Both the Number Discovery Kit and the Number/Picture Fun Kit come with outer plastic trays, in which you can store both the puzzles and all the number rods.

The Skip Count Tape is just what its name implies: a cassette of silly skip-count songs, sung by Mr. Mortensen himself. Although the tape recording quality is unfortunately rather "dusty" and muffled (I hear this will be fixed in the next release), the songs are catchy—the best skip-counting songs I've heard. Kids can't help relating to lyrics like,

> I saw a b-b-bug crawling up the wall
> He was orange and green
> He was nine feet tall.
> L-l-lucky for m-m-e, the bug was friendly
> Who needs nine feet of enemy?
> [The bug is joined by another, then another. This is the skip-count song for 9s.]

The accompanying coloring books are supposed to reinforce the tape.

With the exception of the skip count material, all these items are so colorful and exciting for little kids that you could give them as birthday gifts, no ques-

tions asked. They are designed for children between the ages of 3 and 5—toddlers under the age of 3 might be inclined to munch the smaller counting rods.

TEMPERATURE

NEW**
Cuisenaire Company of America
Demonstration Thermometer, $8.95. Grades 1–3.

The nice lady at Cuisenaire Company thought I was nuts when I asked for a sample of their Demonstration Thermometer. But I had my reasons. For one thing, it's the ideal tool for teaching children to read temperatures. One side shows a Fahrenheit scale marked off in two-degree increments. The other side shows -40 to +100 degrees centigrade in one-degree increments. For another thing, if you plan on using the *Mastering Mathematics* curriculum, you can either spend five hours making the demonstration thermometer recommended in that program or you can just buy this handy gadget. It's a strip of red fabric connected to a strip of white fabric on a two-foot thermometer background. Simply slide the fabric strip wherever you want it, and read the temperature indicated by the red.

TIME

Educational Insights
Clock-O-Dial, $14.95. Grades 1–3.

Teaching time to little kids just got a whole lot easier. Educational Insights, one of the world's most innovative school supply producers, has invented the *Clock-O-Dial*. This amazing gizmo provides a very durable large clockface with movable hands mounted in a green plastic rectangle. At the top of the rectangle is a little window. You place one of the four included snap-in discs behind the window to reveal a time problem: say, "3:15" or "half past eight." Set the hands on the large clockface to what you think is the right time, then check this answer by opening the little window to see a small, but identical, clock with the hands in the correct position. When you close the door, it sets the next problem for you. *Clock-O-Dial* covers *all* of time-telling, starting with telling time to the hour and ending with telling it to the minute. Six disc sides show number problems, two show words. The entire process is automatic and self-checking.

NEW★★
Klutz Press
The Time Book, $10.95. Shipping extra. Grades 1–adult (the book is a fun read even if you already know how to tell time).

Klutz looks like it has another winner in *The Time Book,* the only book on the subject that comes with a working electronic watch with an old-fashioned "real" watchface (you know, numbers around the edges, long and short hands, sweep second hand). Not that any other book on the subject comes with any kind of watch (as far as I know), and not that there *is* any other book on the subject (as far as I know). But it just goes to show that Klutz is serious about teaching those little guys and gals out there how to tell time like real men and women, not just reading it off a digital display like wimps.

Due to the humorous vagaries of publishing, although *The Time Book* is out and in the stores by the time you read this, it wasn't possible for me to get a final copy at the time of finishing *Big Book.* I did manage to snag a few sample pages, and let me tell you, it looks like a scream. Educationally sound, too. The best and simplest instructions on the subject I've ever seen. And I quote:

> Every time the short hand points exactly at a number, it is exactly that hour.
>
> If it points exactly at 3, it is exactly 3 o'clock.
>
> But MOST of the time, it is NOT pointing exactly at a number. It's pointing BETWEEN the numbers.
>
> That's OK. Here's how to deal with that.
>
> If it's a little past the 3, say, "It's a little past 3."
>
> If it's a lot past the 3, say, "It's a lot past 3." Or, you could say, "It's almost 4." Means the same thing.
>
> But what if it's right in the MIDDLE? Right between the 3 and the 4. Then what?

Gotcha! I just know you're dying to turn the page and find out what to say when it's right in the middle.

All this is illustrated with the goofy full-color drawings of watch faces, little kids, gorillas, dinosaurs, and others curious to tell the time that you can expect from the gang at Klutz. The catalog tells us *The Time Book* will also include, as a bonus, "A Complete Collection of Time Facts, including: The Truth about Bedtime, Why Commercials Always Take So Long, and What to Get Ready For When Your Parents Say, 'I'll only be a minute.'"

Did I mention that *The Time Book* is printed on sturdy cardboard with spiral binding, and the accompanying watch and band are in screaming two-tone neon? I loved my first Timex, but I would have loved it better in two-tone neon!

MONEY

NEW★★
Creative Teaching Associates
Allowance Game, $15.95. Add 10% shipping, $3 minimum. Grades 3–8.

Creative Teaching Associates manufactures a wide variety of educational consumer math games. I asked which would be most suitable for home use, and of the two they sent, *Allowance* is the clear winner.

The skills practiced in *Allowance* are counting and money math. Kids get an allowance each time they circle the board, which they either augment by extra chores or spend on movies, clothes, and other kid stuff. Take-A-Chance cards add some unpredictability to the mix. In the process, kids find out that savers and workers always beat spenders—a worthwhile lesson, for sure!

At every turn in this game someone has to make change. One person is supposed to act as the Cashier, but if this is Mom or Dad the kids will miss out on a lot of math practice. Game includes play money and small cards labeled with coin amounts.

NEW★★
TREND Enterprises, Inc.
Match Me Flash Cards, $3.99/set. *Money* bulletin board set, $5.99, includes free Discovery Guide. Requires 4 x 6' bulletin board. Add $2 shipping. Minimum order $10. Ages 4 and up.

TREND's *Money Match Me Flash Cards* provide a unique way to drill money recognition and counting. Each card has a different combination of coins pictured on the front, with its value on the back in either decimal notation (e.g., *35¢*) or spelled out (*thirty-five cents*). They come in 26 sets of two, so you can play the matching games described on the inside box cover. A little work with these cards will make your child a money expert! Four mix-and-match game instructions included, plus instructions for a game that gives practice counting large amounts of change.

The Match Me series also includes *Telling Time*, *Numbers 0–25*, and *Alphabet*.

Money is a fascinating bulletin board set. Here you get everything from the history of money to plastic-coated coins and bills from 1¢ to $20, plus checks, credit cards, and money counting wheels. The coin and paper currency cutouts were specifically designed to be used as manipulatives, as well as bulletin board decorations. The Discovery Guide starts children off with practice in bartering, then introduces money as a more convenient way to handle financial transactions. The background history of money in this guide is fascinating, and you also get 11 suggested activities ranging from setting up a play store to visiting a bank.

WEIGHING & MEASURING

NEW★★
Creative Teaching Associates
Gramstackers™, $16.75. Add 10% shipping, $3 minimum. Grades K–12.

All I've seen is the catalog picture, but I thought I'd mention this anyway. Gramstackers is a set of 49 highly-accurate, color-coded, stacking gram masses in hexagon shapes. Each set includes six 50-gram units, six 20-gram units, seven 10-gram units, ten 5-gram units, and twenty 1-gram units. Look useful for measurement activities.

NEW★★
EDC Publishing
Weighing and Measuring, $3.95. *Weighing and Measuring Workbook*, $1.95.

I know these are supposed to be part of the Usborne First Math series, but really they belong under science more than under math. Genial, warty monsters introduce every topic imaginable dealing with measurement. The book is full-color and includes activities such as constructing your own balance scale or figuring out what clothes to pack for which monster resort. The workbook is black-and-white, with spaces to write in the answers to all sorts of clever measurement puzzles. Lots of fun facts included, too, such as the weight of the world's heaviest man and the world's lightest woman of normal height.

Both books include both English and metric measures of temperature, weight, length, and area. Puzzle answers are in the back of the books. Educational fun for a rainy day.

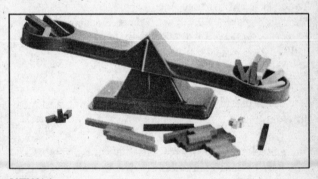

NEW★★
Learning at Home
Primary Balance with 2-pint containers, $15. Shipping extra. Grades K–6.

It Dropped on Me out of the Blue Department: I didn't ask for it, but the Learning at Home people sent me one of their Primary Balances to test. It's a sturdy blue-plastic gizmo in two pieces. Set the balance arms on the triangular base. Add the containers (two pints, with lids). Stick something in the containers (how about some Cuisenaire rods?). See what you can use to balance it with (more Cuisenaire rods?). The Learning at Home folks hope your children will use the Primary Balance for simple science experiences and free play, finding out what weighs the same as what just to satisfy their curiosity.

Make sure you place objects *carefully* in the balance pans, or you may find that unequal objects "weigh" the same! This can provoke some interesting discussions and experiments with placing objects nearer to or farther from the center of the balance. A neat educational tool you can just set out and watch the kids use to teach themselves.

NEW★★
Teachers' Laboratory
Basic Measurement Kit, $18.75. Add $2 shipping. Ages 6–13.

What is a Basic Measurement Kit? You get three plastic 150 cm tapes marked in centimeters and millimeters, three triangular plastic meter sticks with each side graduated differently (meters on one side, centimeters on another, and both cm and meters on the third), and a set of Notes to Teachers with clever measuring activities, some more doable at home than others. Share with your friends.

NEW★★
Teacher's Laboratory, Inc.
Stacking Weights, $8.50/set. Primer Balance with *Notes to Teachers*, $19.95, grades K–8. School Balance with Notes, $51, grades 4 and up. Add 10% shipping, $2 minimum.

Some useful items for studying weighing and measurement:

- Stacking Weights cost less than brass weights, are easier to use. Color-coded squares come in a set of 20 five-gram weights, 10 ten-gram weights, and five 20-gram weights (300 grams of weight in all). Weight is marked on each stacking square.

- Primer Balance includes two detachable, 500 ml. plastic buckets that allow you to weigh liquids or solids. Comes with *Notes to Teachers*.

- School Balance looks nice in the catalog picture. Accurate to 0.5 grams, with a 2,000 gram capacity, it has removable colored pans, a damping mechanism, and a zero-adjustment wheel. (The

damping mechanism saves time, as you don't have to wait so long for the balance to quit oscillating up and down after you load a weight into one side.) Beam and base are die-cast aluminum. Includes *Notes to Teachers*. Too pricey for the average home, but just the thing for you schoolteachers reading this, especially with a set or two of Stacking Weights. For grades 4 and above.

NEW★★
TREND Enterprises, Inc.
Each bulletin board set, $5.99, includes free Discovery Guide. Requires 4 x 6' bulletin board. Add $2 shipping. Minimum order $10.

TREND's *Measure-Up!* bulletin board set presents length, weight, and capacity with easy-to-follow visuals. Cups, pints, quarts, and gallons, for example, are shown as milk containers of those sizes. The set comes with an actual-size yardstick for on-the-spot measuring practice. Nice for your weights-'n-measures unit.

FRACTIONS

NEW★★
Cuisenaire Company of America
Everything's Coming Up Fractions with Cuisenaire® Rods, $7.95, does not include rods. Fraction Circles, $6.50. Circular Fraction Set, $6.95. Square Fraction Set, $7.95. Grades 3–6.

Fractions are easy to teach with Cuisenaire rods. I haven't seen the book *Everything's Coming Up Fractions with Cuisenaire Rods,* but can assume its 64 pages manage to explain how to do it.

Fraction Circles are notched on the back to fit onto a ring, making them easy to organize and use. Each pie-shaped section is marked—e.g., ½, ¼—and color-coded. The set includes halves, thirds, fourths, sixths, and eighths. No instruction booklet, but the wily parent can readily remove two ⅛ sections and substitute one ¼, thus proving that 2 x ⅛ = ¼. Other manipulation possibilities will occur, besides the obvious use of this set for demonstrating what ¾ and ⅚ look like (and which is larger).

Avoid the Circular and Square Fraction sets. Although you get more unmarked pieces for your money, they don't snap together in any way, making them an absolute bear to put back into the case and not as easy to use.

NEW★★
Mortensen Math
 All About Fractions Kit, $99. Home Fractions Kit, $99.
Multiple Tens Set, $49. Add 10% shipping.

The All About Fractions Kit introduces new types
of manipulatives. Until now we have been looking at
Mortensen kits with multiple-units bars. These bars
are all the same width—one unit wide—but different
lengths, depending on the numeral with which each is
associated. Now we are going to meet "multiple-ten
bars." These are all 10 units wide, but different
lengths, again depending on the numeral with which
each is associated.

This kit contains two multiple-ten bars for each
number from 1–9. It also includes fraction units, fraction strips, and clear plastic fraction overlays.

Fraction units are thin, square pieces of colored
plastic, each divided by white lines into a number of
equal pieces. The green fraction unit represents one
unit (no white lines dividing it). The orange fraction
unit has a white line down the middle, indicating it
comprises two halves. (Note that orange is the color
for 2 in the Mortensen system). The pink fraction unit
is divided into thirds (pink being the color for 3), and
so on.

Fraction bars are slices of colored plastic that fit
into the divisions on the fraction units. Two orange
fraction bars, each with an individual value of ½, fit
side by side to make one whole square. Three pink
fraction bars, each with a value of ⅓, make one
square.

The kit includes two of the orange bars, three pink
bars, and so on to nine of the light green bars (value:
⅑ each). It also includes clear plastic squares divided
into all the unit fractions from ½ to ⅑. Using this kit,
you can visually perform all the fraction operations—
addition, subtraction, multiplication, and division—
even of fractions with unlike denominators. Fraction
units, bars, and overlays all are stored in a ziplock bag
that fits into one of the indentations in the molded
plastic storage base.

The Home Fractions Kit includes two colored and
two clear of each quantity plus one set of strips for
each quantity. These are the same items included in
the All About Fractions Kit, just packaged in a different tray.

The Multiple Tens Set, very useful in multiplication and division work, includes one of each tens multiple from 10 to 100, plus a tray, but no fractions units
or strips.

NEW★★
TREND Enterprises, Inc.
Each bulletin board set, $5.99, includes free Discovery
Guide. Requires 4 x 6' bulletin board. Add $2 shipping.
Minimum order $10.

Fractions are a highly visual subject that works
well as a bulletin board visual. TREND's colorful *Fractions Adventure* bulletin board gives you lots of fractions instruction and activities (besides brightening
your home) for a fairly low price. Fractions are presented via a camping theme. You get bunches of fractions displayed as pieces of a pie, partly-filled bags, hot
dogs divided in two pieces, and so on. The fractional-
ly-divided apples can be matched to the fraction cards
for a hands-on activity. The Discovery Guide includes
two reproducible fractions quizzes.

PLACE VALUE/DECIMALS/POWERS OF TEN

NEW★★
Cuisenaire Company of America
Squared Materials, $18/five sets. Cardboard Thousands
Cubes, $7.50/set of 10. Starter Set for Powers of Ten,
$37. Base Ten Starter Set (the all-wood version), $27.
Thousands Cube, $5.50, has etched lines. *Base Ten
Mathematics*, $6.95 (included with Starter Set and Base
Ten set). Grades 2–6.

First, the Squared Materials. Each set of these inexpensive materials comes packed in a ziplock bag and
includes 20 units, 16 longs, and two flats that reverse
to a mini Hundred Board. Materials are plastic, not
cardboard, for added durability. Since they come as a
package of five sets, you end up with 100 units
(enough to cover every numeral on the Hundred
Board), 80 longs, and 10 flats. With these you can do
all the regular Hundred Board activities, plus work
with place value and powers of ten. Since the plastic is
thin, not chunky, you can't do volume work; ten flats

stacked on top of each other don't resemble a cube. Aware of this, Cuisenaire Company offers Cardboard Thousand Cubes, little hollow gridded boxes you build from folded cardboard. No instructions included with the Squared Materials or Thousand Cubes.

In contrast, Cuisenaire's powers-of-ten block sets match the metric size and volume of regular Cuisenaire rods. These are available in either a Starter Set for Powers of Ten (50 natural wood unit cubes, 20 etched orange plastic tens rods, 10 etched orange plastic hundreds squares, *Base Ten Mathematics* book, and 50 Place Value Mats) or the Base Ten Starter Set (identical materials except that the rods and squares are also natural wood).

Personally, I prefer the regular Starter Set. The orange 10 rods match the color coding of my Cuisenaire rods, and the orange flats and rods are more cheerful.

Neither set comes with a Thousand Cube. You can either construct a thousand cube by stacking 10 hundreds squares, or (my preferred option) you can buy a Thousand Cube separately.

The *Base Ten Mathematics* book included with Cuisenaire's powers-of-ten material is excellent. It introduces all the natural uses of the material. Learning to build numbers. Adding and subtracting, with and without carrying and borrowing. Multiplying. Primes. Division. Decimals (to the thousands and thousandths). Metric length, area, volume, and mass. Squares and square roots. Basic algebra. Everything you do with Mortensen and Cube-It, except fractions and pre-calculus, is covered in this one 60-page book. It even includes a Hundred Board printed inside the back cover, with some simple Hundred Board activities included in the book. I'd suggest you get *Base Ten Mathematics* if you are using either of these other programs, as neither of them explains how to use powers-of-ten material as well as this book.

It's not easy to compare the Cuisenaire powers-of-ten blocks with Mortensen and Cube-It. Both Mortensen and Cube-It make problems easier to set up by adding rods for 2–9 and 20–90. To represent 99 with Cube-It blocks only takes two blocks, while it takes 18 Cuisenaire powers-of-ten pieces. This Cube-It advantage becomes even more significant when doing problems like 24 x 36. Cube-It is metric like Cuisenaire, extremely well-organized, and includes material for negative numbers and fractions. Mortensen blocks are larger, making them easier to use and harder to store, and more colorful, which is fun. The specialized Mortensen kits are either an advantage or a disadvantage, depending on whether you like to present topics separately or whether you prefer one integrated system.

The larger sets of Cuisenaire powers-of-ten blocks are less expensive than either Mortensen or Cube-It and come with divided storage boxes, but still with only unit cubes. Who wants to solve a problem using 300 unit cubes? On the other hand, the Cuisenaire instructions are easier to follow and require less teacher training.

Bottom line: If all you want to do is *show* kids how the math works, the Cuisenaire Starter Set for Powers of Ten is a great value, covering everything from number recognition to early algebra. Add a set of regular and jumbo Cuisenaire rods to it for more extensive one-digit addition, subtraction, multiplication, division, and fractions work. If you want the kids to work a lot of complicated problems using your math manipulatives, or just enjoy math manipulatives that are works of art, take a good hard look at Cube-It and Mortensen as well.

NEW★★
Mortensen Math
Very Basic Basic Operations Kit, $50. Basic Operations Kit, $350. Combo Kit, $139. Multiple Kit, $200. Decimal Kit Half Tray, $29. Add 10% shipping. Grades 2–8.

The Combo Kit contains 10 hundred squares, 40 ten bars, 12 unit bars each of values 1 to 6, and nine unit bars each of values 7 to 9. These come packaged in two self-sorting molded trays. You'll have to study the setup for awhile, but after you do, it's easy to find the right place for every item.

Like other powers-of-ten material, the Combo Kit doesn't include enough material to demonstrate problems like 52 x 46. For that you would need 20 hundred squares. To solve a problem like 96 x 99 you'd need 81 hundred squares, or more than eight Combo Kits' worth of hundred squares! That's why the Mortensen workbooks tend to use 10, 11, 12, and 21 as the second multiplier. You also have to use a large number of 10 rods for each problem, since unlike the Cube-It system the Combo Kit does not include multiple ten bars. Those are available separately in the Multiple Kit, which contains a total of two red hundred squares, 10 green hundred squares, nine each of the various unit bars from 1–9, and two each of the multiple-ten bars from 2–9. Try not to faint when you see the price!

If you merely want to *demonstrate* decimals, multiplication, algebra, and basic operations, the Combo Kit works very well. The multiple unit bars make life easier than the single unit cubes in most other companies' powers-of-ten material. They do not work as well, however, for simple place value operations like 79 + 86 + 95, where it is beneficial to actually see 79 as seven tens and nine units. For these basic powers-of-ten operations, Mortensen has the Decimal Half Tray. I haven't seen this particular kit, but from the catalog picture it appears to include two whole units (also usable as hundreds), 20 tenths rods (also usable as tens), and 50 hundredths cubes (also usable as units), which is less than you get in the similar set from Cuisenaire Company.

Mortensen's Very Basic Basic Operations Kit helps you take powers of ten concepts up to the ten thousands. The Very Basic Basic Operations Kit contains 10 thousand bars, 10 hundred strips, 10 hundred squares, 20 ten bars, and 20 units. These items are all much smaller in scale than regular Mortensen manipulatives and made out of thin plastic rather than rodlike in shape. The units are almost impossible to handle, meaning you won't want to use this set for much basic multiplying. Its main virtue is the ability to show 100 as both a square and a strip, and 1000 as 10 hundred squares end-to-end. The set can be used for numbers up to the ten thousands and decimals to the ten thousandth. It can also be used to introduce algebra formulas including x^3 and x^4. The kit comes with a molded plastic tray for storing the units, squares, strips, and bars.

For really big-time operations, and big-time spenders, the Basic Operations Kit has multiple hundred bars, gazillions of hundred squares, and (if I can believe the catalog picture) some 5000 bars as well as multiple ten bars and units. With this set you ought to be able to solve just about any decent-sized problem, if you can keep track of the teeny-weeny unit pieces.

Both the Combo Kit and the Very Basic Basic Operations Kit are included in the Home Special.

CHAPTER TWENTY-SIX

GEOMETRY MANIPULATIVES

When I say, "Geometry manipulatives," the first thing most people think of is a geoboard. So now I'm going to tell you how to make your own geoboard.

Obtain a thick piece of non-warping wood, 20 cm x 20 cm. Paint one side black (the better to see the rubber bands, my dear). Pound in 25 roundheaded nails in a 5 x 5 array, each 4 cm from the next, and the outside rows 2 cm from the edges. Take care that the nails don't go all the way through! Now, while you're at it, make four more just like that one. Stick velcro on the sides, so when you connect the geoboards in a 2 x 2 square, they all stay together nicely. Now you can do percentage and decimal problems, since you have 100 pins to work with. Alternatively, make a 10-pin x 10-pin geoboard (a fairly hefty size). Draw lines with Magic Marker separating it into four 5-pin x 5-pin sections. Either way, you have 100 pins.

Got your rubber bands? Good! Now that you have your geoboard, you can slip rubber bands over those nails to make triangles, rectangles, squares, and all sorts of odd-shaped polygons. You can move your rubber bands around and watch how the shapes change. You can calculate areas and perimeters. It's instant geometry.

Later on we'll look at some commercial geoboards, compasses, and 3-D geometry materials that lead kids naturally into drafting and pre-engineering. First, though, let's start with pre-geometry manipulatives: pattern blocks, tangrams, and spatial puzzles.

PATTERN BLOCKS, TANGRAMS, AND OTHER SPATIAL PUZZLES

Everything that glitters ain't gold, and everything with little geometric pieces ain't the same, either. I have spent untold hours sorting out the difference between tangrams, pattern blocks, attribute blocks, and genuine geometric manipulatives. Here's the scoop.

Tangrams are a set of seven geometric pieces—six triangles of various sizes and shapes and one square—used in an ancient form of puzzling. The puzzler is given an outline, which he must fill in exactly using the seven pieces. The number of potential puzzles is enormous, and the similarity of the pieces can make any given puzzle quite tricky. Tangrams, like other sophisticated puzzles, aren't just for kids. As one book on the subject explains, Napoleon Bonaparte, Lewis Carroll, Edgar Allan Poe, and John Quincy Adams all enjoyed tangrams. Educational value of tangrams: like other puzzles, they develop your problem-solving and spatial skills.

Pattern blocks are similar to what we used to call "parquetry" when we were children. The sets of colorful hexagons, trapezoids, parallelograms, and triangles are used to fill in outline shapes, just like tangrams. Since more shapes are included, often the same outline can be filled in a variety of ways. Because the blocks fit together geometrically, children can pick up geometric relationships by working with them. Educational value of pattern blocks: problem solving, spatial skills, pre-geometry.

Attribute blocks also often come in geometric shapes. The shapes may or may not relate geometrically, depending on brand. The same shape will come in a variety of colors, sizes, and thicknesses. Attribute blocks are mainly used for logic puzzles, not geometry. Example: "Find all the blocks that are red *and* thick. Now find all the blocks that are small, not blue, not thick." Educational value of attribute blocks: logic, problem solving, occasionally pre-geometry and fractions (depending on brand).

Regular puzzles, the kind you buy at the store, teach much the same skills as tangrams and pattern blocks. At least one highly successful Japanese program uses puzzles as its pre-geometry curriculum.

An enterprising teacher can beat pattern blocks to death as educational tools, forcing children (for instance) to graph how many blocks they think will be needed to solve a problem and how many they actually used. I've seen a number of these workbooks. Avoid them. Tangrams can be similarly forced to tell children about symmetry, area, perimeter, and other concepts best introduced with mirrors, geoboards, and rulers. Attribute blocks, which lend themselves well to dominoes-like games, are fun to sort and classify—their basic use.

It's not fair to give a child what looks like a set of colorful toys and demand that he fill out endless workbook pages with exercises that incidentally use these toys. By puzzling with tangrams and pattern blocks, kids will squeeze out the legitimate educational value of these materials. By playing logic games, kids will get the best use of their attribute blocks. Let fun be fun and work be work.

NEW**
Creative Teaching Associates
Unifix Problem Solving Cards, Kits A–E $7.95 each. Unifix cubes, $11/set of 100 cubes (10 each of 10 colors). Add 10% shipping, $3 minimum.

For use with Unifix or compatible snap cubes, this series of kits each includes 12 full-size, full-color, laminated task cards, plus 12 blackline masters and complete instructions.

Kit A presents two-color patterns. Kit B presents three-color patterns, including all permutations and combinations of a particular color set. In Kit C, students are given several patterns of connected cubes and a set number of cubes to work with. They must determine which patterns can be made and which can't. Kit D introduces addition facts with sums to 10. Kids snap together the given number of cubes, read the sum against the answer bar at the top of the card. Kit E uses the same format to introduce subtraction facts to 10.

NEW**
Creative Teaching Associates
Primary Pattern Blocks Task Cards, sets A and B, $12.95 each. Primary Patterns for Creative Primary People, sets A–D, $12.95 each. Pattern blocks, $19.95/set of 250 plastic pattern blocks. Add 10% shipping, $3 minimum.

Creative Teaching Associates has several series of pattern block task cards. Primary Pattern Blocks Task Cards are sets of 22 durable full-color 8½ x 11" cards. Each card indicates the number and shape of pattern block required to fill in the pattern. Bonus questions open up each card for imaginative extras. For example: Card 14 in set A tells the child to take five orange square blocks, one green triangle, and five red rhombi to fill in the pattern, which happens to be the numeral 5. Since the set is designed for young children, needed pattern pieces are indicated by a picture of the piece with a number inside it. At the bottom the bonus question asks, "Which number is this? Make other numbers."

Picture Patterns for Creative Primary People are sets of 24 cards of the same size as those above. The "picture patterns" show pattern outlines against a full-color illustrated background. Sets A and C show exactly where each pattern block should go, outlining the individual blocks: sets B and D correspond to these, but with the pattern block outlines removed to provide more difficult exercises.

The pattern blocks from Creative Teaching Associates are the same colors and dimensions as those from other suppliers.

NEW**
Cuisenaire Company of America
Alphagrams, $8.95. Ages 4–10.

Alphagrams is the best easygoing book of tangram puzzles I have seen. See review under Attributes Manipulatives for more information.

NEW**
Cuisenaire Company of America
Pattern Animals Kit, $19.95 including set of 64 plastic pattern blocks, $12.95 for cards alone. *Pattern Animals Book*, $7.50. Student set of wood pattern blocks, $6.50. Grades 1–4.

Cuisenaire's set of wood pattern blocks includes 5 yellow hexagons, 5 orange squares, 10 green triangles, 10 red trapezoids, 10 blue parallelograms, and 10 tan rhombuses. This is my favorite set of pattern blocks—much nicer looking and more satisfying to use than plastic.

The Pattern Animals Kit includes 26 colorful animal outlines, from Arthur Alligator through Zachary Zebra, on 13 double-sided laminated sheets. These provide just about the right amount of work with these blocks, especially when you add in the sixteen color-coded task cards for use with these pictures. Example of a task card assignment:

> Cover Wanda Walrus with Pattern Blocks. How many different colors did you use? What are the fewest colors you can use?

The Pattern Animals Kit comes with a set of (yuk) plastic pattern blocks. You can buy just the cards and get a set of wood blocks instead, if you like, but the solutions to the task cards will not necessarily come out exactly the same.

By the same author, the *Pattern Animals Book* includes the same 26 animal puzzles (this time in black and white), plus pages and pages of fussy exercises only minimally related to patterning. Examples: "Make another animal that begins with the same letter [as the animal you just made]. . . . Make believe you are selling one of the animals and write an advertisement for the *Pattern Block News*. . . ." Yeesh!

ATTRIBUTES MANIPULATIVES

NEW**
Cuisenaire Company of America
Cuisenaire Attribute Shapes, $18.95. Attribute Logic Blocks Desk Set, $19.95 (group set $49, pocket set $11.95). RelationShapes™, $59. *Patches*, $7.95 (included with RelationShapes). *Alphagrams*, $8.95 (included with RelationShapes). Attrilinks™, $6.95/set of 40. Ages 4–10.

Cuisenaire Company is an excellent source for both attribute shapes and materials explaining how to use them. Let's look at the attribute shapes and blocks themselves first.

Attrilinks is a brand-new 40-piece set of attribute links: five different shapes in two sizes and four colors. The shapes are triangle, rectangle, square, hexagon, and circle. They come packed in a ziplock bag, along with a brief instructional guide. They work OK as an inexpensive attributes set, but not so well as linking material, since the openings in the links are so wide that chains of these links frequently come apart in use.

We now turn to Cuisenaire Attribute Shapes and the Attribute Logic Blocks from Invicta. These two sets look similar in the catalog pictures, and are featured on the same page, but are quite different. For one thing, the Cuisenaire set's pieces are geometrically related to each other. Two right triangles fit exactly over one square. Four small equilateral triangles fit exactly over one large equilateral triangle. A triangle fits inside a circle fits inside a larger triangle. This feature makes them suitable for exploring many geometric concepts and introducing simple fractions. The included booklet is excellent, providing just enough activities to demonstrate the concepts without beating them to death.

The Attribute Logic Blocks set, in contrast, is really only usable for logic exercises. You get hexagons, squares, rectangles, circles, and equilateral triangles. Like the Cuisenaire set, pieces come in three colors, two sizes, and two thicknesses. However, the Attribute Logic Blocks merely happen to be geometric shapes; they don't relate to each other geometrically. You can't put the rectangles together to form squares, or the triangles together to form other included shapes. The booklet included with the Attribute Logic Blocks naturally stresses logic problems only, including several forms with which most parents will not be familiar. All these logic puzzles could be presented equally well with the People Pieces set (people who are thin or fat, male or female, young or old, wearing red or blue), or with any other type of attributes material.

Since you can do logic problems with the Cuisenaire Attribute Shapes, but can't do geometry problems with the Attribute Logic Blocks, the Cuisenaire Attribute Shapes are the better choice of these two for home use. I can't recommend any of the attribute logic block card sets or workbooks included in the catalog (too fussy for home use), but it doesn't matter, since the booklet that comes with the Cuisenaire Attribute Shapes gives you plenty to do.

For some reason known only to themselves, the people designing the Cuisenaire catalog stuck their deluxe set of attribute blocks on page 52, while the other sets are all on page 18. So you don't miss it while browsing their catalog, let me describe it right now. RelationShapes is a beautifully-organized set of 266 plastic shapes in metric sizes. The set includes six shapes, each in four colors, three sizes, and two thicknesses. The shapes are circles, ellipse, square, rectangle, right triangle, equilateral triangle, and irregular triangle. The pieces are smooth and heavy in the hand, and fit neatly into the molded plastic form included. In fact, the children's first activity will be taking the pieces out of the plastic bags in which they arrive and neatly placing them in their proper slots. (Hint: the rectangles are easier to use, and don't move around as much, if you stack them on their sides.) Along with all this you get a copy of Cuisenaire's *Patches* workbook and the tangram-like puzzle book *Alphagrams* (to be described in a minute). Although the catalog never promised a spinner, one was also included with my set. (You'll need it to play some games in the *Patches* book.)

Patches is an open-ended workbook that can be used with anyone from grade K and up. Each page uses the shapes from RelationShapes to build creatures, letters, sequences, logic puzzles, area and geometry puzzles, and lots of other fun things. Along the way kids learn shape recognition, sorting, spatial skills, fractions, and graphing and notetaking. Engaging "Patch People" set the theme for many activities, e.g., building Patchville according to a set of logic rules.

Alphagrams (also included with RelationShapes), is a book of Shangrams. "Thanks a lot! Now I don't know any more about this book than before!" OK, simmer down. Shangrams are oversized tangram-like puzzles you fill in with a specified number of geometric pieces. In this case, you can either use eight triangles from the RelationShapes set, or the eight punch-out shiny blue

cardboard triangles included with *Alphagrams*. Choose from the baby puzzles in the back, with lines indicating which puzzle piece goes where, or the he-man puzzles in the front, with outer outlines only. My seven-year-old daughter is more of a he-man than I am; I got frankly stumped on the letter *A* puzzle and had to hand it over to Sarah to untangle! Puzzles are alphabet letters and objects beginning with each letter. Strictly kid stuff, accessible to all ages of kids (thanks to the two styles of puzzles). Cute and simple, good for hours of spatial-skills fun for a rainy day.

GEOBOARDS

NEW**
Cuisenaire Company of America
Plastic geoboard, $2.95, grades K–8. Wood geoboard, $3.95, grades K–8. *Introducing Geoboards*, $9.95, grades K–3. *Dot Paper Geometry*, $7.95, grades 4–8.

First, an answer to the question everyone asks: *which* geoboard should you get? My friend Pam Lancaster and I spent a happy hour fiddling around with Cuisenaire's plastic and wood geoboards, and we both preferred the wood model. The rounded nailheads hold the rubber bands more securely on the board, and the patterns show up better against the black wood background than the blue plastic background. The wood geoboard is also sturdier. True, the plastic model has a circular lattice on its back, but we must learn to do without some things in life. So there you have it: two out of two home-school mothers prefer wood.

Now that we've settled that question, what do you do with a geoboard? Not too much, probably, unless you're smart enough to get some teacher materials along with it. (Each geoboard comes with a set of colored rubber bands of the correct length and strength, but no instructions.) One good place to start, if you have young children in grades K–3, is *Introducing Geoboards,* an activity card set of 56 cards. *Introducing Geoboards* introduces common geometric figures, edges, vertices, tiling and mirror games, symmetry, area, and even telling time. You'll need the *plastic* geoboard, because it has a circle lattice on the back, which is necessary for some exercises. Each wipe-clean card is illustrated and easy to use. Cuisenaire also has activity card sets of higher-level geometry using the geoboard, none of which I've seen.

Dot Paper Geometry—With or Without a Geoboard takes a more traditional workbook form. Exercises are shown on small illustrations of geoboards. Covered are polygons and their properties, coordinate geometry, fractions, decimals, percent, area, metric length, perimeter, and measuring angles. This is all straight math. The geoboard, if used, simply makes the operations easier to see. All exercises use a standard 25-pin square lattice geoboard. You'll need *four* geoboards for some exercises (constructing larger figures or figuring decimals on the basis of the combined 100 pins found on four geoboards).

COMPASS

NEW✱✱
Learning at Home
Compass, $11.75. Shipping extra. Grades 4–12.

My husband Bill persuaded me to put this one in. Bill loves fine instruments, and you should have seen the gleam in his eye when he opened the case and took out this compass! (A compass is that thingummy with a point and a pencil-holder that you use for drawing circles and slicing angles in half in geometry class.) It's made in Bavaria, a province of Germany where they believe in old-world craftsmanship. Your kid needs a compass to do his geometry lessons, so why not get him the best?

3-D GEOMETRY: THEY DO IT WITH MIRRORS . . . AND FOAM!

Have you ever tried to find your way through a model home while using a floor layout that showed every room in the house backwards? We bought our house from a developer who, out of irrepressible hijinks, provided would-be buyers with mirror-image floor plans of every model. Bill was able to translate the plans easily, but to me they made no sense at all. This could be because women are generally worse off than men when it comes to spatial skills, or it could be because I never got any special training in spatial skills.

One great way to develop your spatial skills is to do it with mirrors. Manipulating mirror images is a tough mental operation that really helps you see shapes better. Below find a game, two courses, and a book that will help you learn to do it with mirrors.

NEW✱✱
Culsenaire Company of America
Mira, $5.95. *Mira Math Activities for Elementary School, Mira Math Activities for High School*, $6.95 each. *The Mirror Puzzle Book* (grades 1–8), $5.95. Mirror Game 1 (preK–2), Mirror Game 2 (grades 2–8), $10.95 each.

I always like to start with games, so let's look at the two Mirror Games from Europe. Each game contains four identical patterned cubes, two small square plastic mirrors, and a deck of 24 pattern design cards. Each player places two cubes and a mirror in a plastic holder. Pick a card and try to match the pattern on the card by turning your cubes around and observing the patterns in the mirror. Mirror Game 1 comes with red cards and cubes, and features easier patterns (or so they say—my sample copy arrived without cards!). Mirror Game 2 has blue cards and cubes and more complex patterns. The games really are fun—a gentle introduction to mirror skills.

The Mirror Puzzle Book is absolutely ingenious. This inexpensive little book has 144 colored puzzles for you to solve, using the included pieces of silvered plastic as mirrors. On each two-page spread is a "Mirror Master" and a number of designs. Place the mirror on the Mirror Master in such a way that the result matches one of the designs on the page. Keep going. Can you match all the designs on that page? Some of the puzzles are literally impossible—fill out the rows on the mystery chart as you work to find out which. Highly motivational, lots of fun.

The two *Mira Math* books use an ingenious device called a Mira. The Mira is a hunk of red plastic with two flaring sides that allow it to stand up. It's reflective *and* transparent, making it an ideal tool to teach such geometric concepts as symmetry and congruence.

Mira Math Activities for Elementary School first teaches the use of the Mira by making a cartoon plane take off and land, helping Jenny put on her hair ribbon, and making figures out of a curve. Kids then learn to use the Mira to draw reflection images, locating a line of symmetry, checking a wide variety of drawings and shapes for congruence, and constructing perpendiculars, parallels, and geometric figures. Activities are easy and often fun, but the black-and-white format and typewriter-style text marks it as a "school" book.

Mira Math Activities for High School pushes things a bit farther and eliminates most of the play. Gone are Jenny and her hair ribbon. Hello to angles, lines, and geometric figures. You'll be bisecting lines and building rhombi with your trusty Mira. Pretty dry, but still more interesting (and easier to manipulate) than standard protractor-and-compass work.

NEW**
Timberdoodle
DIME Geometry Build-Up Pack, $26, grades K–6. DIME Geometry 3-D Sketching Project, $26, grades 7–9. *3-D Build Up Book 1*, $6.50. *3-D Sketching Books 2* and *3*, $6.50 each. Prices are discounted. Shipping extra.

I can tell you one thing: any geometric program based on colorful foam blocks of interlocking shapes is guaranteed to appeal to kids. All you have to do is open the box.

OK, you've opened the box. The children, from the preteens on down, will immediately flock to the box and start building with the blocks. (The teenagers are watching out of the corner of their eyes and scheming to secretly play with the blocks in the privacy of their rooms after the little kids are in bed.)

Now you enter. "It's OK, kids—go ahead and have some fun with those blocks. When you're done, I've got some books here with diagrams of stuff you can build with the blocks." Nobody will be left out, since the DIME books start with two-dimensional puzzles even the preschoolers can work and progress to 3-D solids that will give you a challenge. In the process, children (and adults) discover mathematical patterns and relationships and develop amazing spatial skills.

The DIME 3-D Build-Up Pack comes with the blocks and a book, *3-D Build Up Book 1*. The book briefly explains the program and is mostly full of problems your kids can solve themselves. First they must learn the nomenclature. The large square is an F block. The L-shaped one is an L. The S-shaped one is an S. The small square is a 1, the rectangle twice that length is a 2, and the rectangle three times that length is a 3. The first page of the book is a set of labeled outlines, asking the children to fill the outline with the block of the right name. The next seven pages have more outline shapes for children to fill in with the prescribed combinations of blocks, e.g., "Fill the shape with LL," meaning "Use two L-shapes to fill in this outline." After this, kids make the jump to concocting increasingly complex shapes shown in isometric 3-D outlines.

The DIME program is a self-correcting activity, of the sort beloved by Montessori teachers. Children can see for themselves if they have found an answer, and can usually figure out new ways of attacking the problem if an answer is not immediately forthcoming. The teacher's role is simply to provide a supportive environment, observe the process, and *ooh* and *aah* over the results. No reading is required to solve the problems, an additional plus for parents of special-needs children, some of whom are brilliant at spatial tasks, though they may be slow with reading and writing.

DIME stands for Development of Ideas in Mathematical Education. Naturally, the program was invented by an Australian, pioneered in Scotland, and printed in Canada—Americans today are too strung out over basic skills to pioneer something this fun and effective. The DIME Build-Up program is good for grades K–6. Further DIME programs are available; see Volume 3.

CHAPTER TWENTY-SEVEN

MATH PROGRAMS

Kids are natural mathematicians. "Not true," you say? I can prove it! Here's a simple experiment:
Take four young children and eight cookies. Divide the cookies among them as follows: three to child A, three to child B, one each to children C and D. Immediately children C and D will begin to demonstrate their math abilities, as follows:

"That isn't fair! A and B got more than we did!"

Is this practical math or what? C and D can count and compare, and they're barely out of diapers! (A and B can count, too, but they're too smart to rock the boat while *they* have the extra cookies!)

For a more stringent test, take your classic blueberry pie. Divide it in unequal pieces and pass them out to a crowd of children. Every single child in that crowd will infallibly comment, in most uncomplimentary terms, on the intelligence of the person who cut the pie. When challenged as to how *they* would have divided the pie more fairly, they will prove they already have the rudiments of division "built in."

No, kids aren't confused about math. *Grownups* are confused. Our national confusion about arithmetic arose, you'll remember, with the introduction of the New Math. Hailed as a breakthrough in math instruction, the New Math taught kids mathematical principles in place of rote instruction. In this way, the math profs reasoned, children would be prepared for real math when they had mastered arithmetic. Unhappily, the New Math generation didn't ever learn their arithmetic!

Now that "math anxiety" and "math failure" are so widespread, what should we do about it? Debate rages. Some resort to flash cards and rote drill. Others believe children need to discover math for themselves with the use of colorful manipulatives. My personal belief is that this is yet another example of how grownups love to pit two truths against each other, instead of putting them *both* to work. (Blame Marx and Hegel. Those guys set the stage for all sorts of groups fighting each other who God intended to complement and bless each other: men and women, parents and children, rich and poor, black and white, artists and blue-collar guys. The key to endless strife and failure is to slice the tree in half and demand that it bear fruit.)

Kids learn *both* by repetition *and* by experimentation. Lean heavy on the one or the other, if you like, but try not to look down your nose at flash cards (if you are a hands-on type) or at manipulatives (if you are an egghead). End of sermon!

PRESCHOOL & KINDERGARTEN MATH

We learn best by first assembling raw data and then fitting it into a framework. So expose your kids to some real-world arithmetic first. Count things with the children. Add pennies. Subtract forks. Children don't have to be able to count or add themselves in order to benefit from simply seeing it done. This initial *number play* is essential to producing the raw arithmetic data that children's minds need to work on.

When a child learns to *count* (which he does by rote repetition) he is well on his way to learning *arithmetic*. Counting is adding by one. Subtraction is counting backwards. Multiplication is adding by groups (2 x 3 is the same as adding two three times, 2+2+2). Division is subtracting by groups. All of these concepts grow directly out of counting. If counting is an abstract series of noises, so is arithmetic. If counting is what you do to find out how many buttons are on your jacket, then arithmetic is much more likely to seem real to a child.

I personally believe in showing children the patterns ("principles") of arithmetic and, after they are comfortable with them, then drilling on the actual "facts." The "9s" pattern is that adding nine to a number is the same as adding ten and then counting backwards once. Whether a child discovers these patterns or you reveal them to him does not seem to me as important as making sure that he does become aware that arithmetic is full of patterns.

Whichever approach you choose, below you'll find an abundance of colorful, exciting programs for your littlest learner.

NEW**
A Beka Book
Teach-a-Coin Set, $5.95. Felt 5" Numerals, $3.95. Felt Objects for Counting, $8.95. *Learn about Numbers and Phonics I* and *II,* $4.80 each. *Sound and Count A* and *B,* $8.85 each. Add 10% shipping, minimum $3.25.

A Beka's early math instruction is combined with phonics instruction in books with titles like *Learn About Numbers and Phonics I* and *Sound and Count A.* Whether you want their early math, in other words, depends on whether you want their phonics.

A Beka also offers a wide variety of arithmetic teaching aids for this age level, such as their Teach-a-Coin Set or Number Charts and Games. They have felt sets for practicing counting or fractions, felt numerals, different kinds of flash cards, and so on, all originally designed for classroom use and described at length in their full-color catalog.

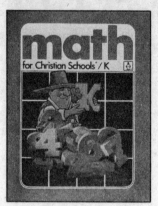

NEW**
Bob Jones University Press
Math for Christian Schools K5: student worktext, $5.95. Student Materials Packet, $1. Teacher's edition, $29.50. Optional supplementary *Math Kindergarten Activity Sheets,* $3.95. Shipping extra.

Here's my personal favorite kindergarten math program. Bob Jones kindergarten math not only is cute—featuring Farmer Brown and his pet mouse Cheddar as ongoing characters—but covers all beginning math so efficiently and in such an interesting way that I don't mind using it again and again with child after child (and I have *eight* children!).

The 165 lessons in this course only take about 15 minutes each. The first 85 lessons "are rather informal and require a minimum of written work—none of which is in the worktext." In other words, you need the teacher's manual, because without it you only get work for half the course. The teacher's manual also includes work center activities, calendar activities, time telling and all that manipulative pre-math to get kids ready for their first math workbook—*without* requiring that you purchase any manipulatives! You will need the inexpensive Materials Packet, which includes numeral, money, and dot flash cards for you to cut out. Other manipulatives, such as a demonstration clock, are built right into the workbook (see p. 31 for a really fun clockface with a real face in it!).

What makes this program really inspiring and great is that kids absolutely love it. They love the gentle pace. They love the colorful workbook pages, each new, fascinating, and doable. They love Farmer Brown. They love Cheddar. They love the comfortable, family-like activities. So I love it, too.

Cornerstone Curriculum Project
Kindergarten manual, $30. Grades 1-6 also available.

Making Math Meaningful, a math program based on manipulatives, is reviewed at length in the Arithmetic Programs section.

NEW
Cuisenaire Company of America
Mathematics Their Way, $32.95 (includes pad of blackline masters). Grades K–2.

This activity-centered program for early childhood math education is "the most popular activity-centered mathematics curriculum in use today." Over the years it keeps popping up in home-school magazines, especially those of the unschooling persuasion. So I finally begged a copy from Cuisenaire Company, expecting great things.

After working through the material, I have to honestly say I don't like it for home use. For one thing, it's just too much work for too little content. This is the familiar curse left to us by John Dewey, the father of the "if you don't experience it you don't learn it" educational philosophy. In a classroom, where children's backgrounds differ so widely, there may be value in approaching each new concept from twenty different angles, thus ensuring that even the dullest child can't help but catch on, but at home this is just a lot of unnecessary work. Kids can learn patterning, for example, without having to make dot charts *and* Unifix cube patterns *and* pattern blocks *and* stand in lines *and* do rhythmic clapping *and* decipher letter patterns.

Secondly, the program requires gazillions of different math manipulatives. Cuisenaire offers a "bargain kit" of manipulatives for use with this program—only $175, and it includes its own seven-drawer storage unit. This doesn't even include all of the materials you will need for the program. You'll still have to make your own counting audiocassettes, dot pattern cards, dot chart, dot to dot templates, egg carton graphing boards, geoboard sequence charts, graphing plastic, magic box and magic box numbers, milk carton graphing boxes, milk carton scale, junk box, number flips, numeral sequence cards, etc. 'Nuff said.

Thirdly, the author for some reason has seen fit to use the ugly and ungrammatical constructions *hisorher* and *sheorhe* throughout the book. Like mosquitoes, these minor annoyances become more aggravating each time you see one. They also betray the fundamental insecurity and sterility informing this program. John is a *he*. Mary is a *she*. But we never meet John and Mary: only *hesandshes*. One comes away with a feeling that the curriculum considers children as objects to be manipulated, just as all the manipulatives called for in the program are not enjoyed for their beauty of color and shape but only pressed into service for detached scientific explorations. Kids are allowed to use the manipulatives for "free play" before getting down to real work with them, but it's only because this free play time is "the foundation for later development," not because we enjoy watching happy children at play. The atmosphere is tense: kids have to *deduce* things and *explore* things under the guidance of a watchful adult, who makes sure things stay on track. This I don't object to in a straightforward 1 + 1 = 2 program, where we're all here to work, and no funny business, but it does seem a bit unfair to lead kids to chocolate pudding and fingerpainting and not let them play.

Part of the problem is that, as is the nature of early childhood education, the teachers are wearing themselves to a frazzle trying to explain concepts that come almost automatically to children a few years older. Problems raised in the book, such as, "What do I do for the child who thinks there are more windows in the room than pencils because the windows are bigger?" disappear once kids reach age 7 or 8. Home teachers have a great advantage over school teachers here, since we don't have to justify an early childhood education program by pushing concepts on kids who aren't ready for them.

Another advantage of home education is that many of the lessons in *Mathematics Their Way* come quite naturally as part of everyday living: measuring recipe ingredients with Mom in the kitchen, sorting the laundry, counting plates to set around the table. In fact, it is possible to think of *Mathematics Their Way* as a partly effective attempt at recreating in the classroom the rich mathematics possibilities inherent in the home. This probably explains why unschoolers are always talking about it. The program justifies their own approach to education.

If you want a really good course on basic mathematical thinking, the Miquon Math program is much better suited to home use. It covers lots more ground in lots less time, uses a more coherent set of manipulatives (love those Cuisenaire rods!), treats kids like kids, and is structured beautifully for home use. See review below.

NEW★★
Eagle's Wings Educational Materials

Kinder-Math, $20. Letterland Kindergarten (includes *Kinder-Math* and *Letterland Phonics*), $85. Add $4 shipping per program.

You remember the Letterland people from the phonics chapters of this book. Their Kinder-Math program includes far more sheets of cut-em-out flash cards than you really need, along with Kinder-Math "Count-By" cards and board and a clock board. All of this material is tucked into a printed vinyl organizer. Extra workbooks are available.

Want to make your life easier? The Flower, Penny, and Coin cards could easily be replaced by real money and real objects to count. Then you won't have to spend hours cutting them out!

Kinder-Math is well-designed sequentially. The best part of this program is the excellent teaching sequence, activities, and instructions in the teacher's manual. The workbook is a bit bare-bones (to be fair, the authors say each page is only meant to be used *after* the student has demonstrated mastery of the concept). You might want to supplement with some Frank Schaffer or other workbooks from your friendly teachers' store.

NEW★★
Frank Schaffer

Kindergarten Math, Beginning Math, Numbers, Beginning Activities with Numbers, Getting Ready for Math, $3.98 each. *My Number Book*, $4.98. *Kindergarten Math Activities*, $9.95. Add $3 shipping (orders under $20) or 15% (orders over $20).

Frank Schaffer has about the cutest, most fun, easy to use workbooks for young children around. The simple activities in his books are a great way to introduce kids to math, handwriting, and a host of other subjects.

Right now we're looking at math, so I pulled a few of the most applicable workbooks out of the current Frank Schaffer catalog. All the $3.98 workbooks are 24 pages of simple activities, such as counting and coloring a certain number of objects, writing numbers, counting objects and circling the correct number, and so on. *My Number Book* concentrates solely on writing numbers and numerals, counting, and coloring. *Kindergarten Math Activities*, a more ambitious 80-page workbook, covers number recognition 1–20, counting and sets 1–20, quantitative representation of numbers 1–20, basic shapes, patterns, one to one correspondence, ordinal and cardinal numbers. In this book kids color, match, trace, do dot-to-dots, and all the stuff in all the other books combined. These are great for keeping little ones happy and busy while you teach the older ones!

You can generally find these workbooks at your local teachers' store. Why not take a look at them the next time you pop in?

NEW★★
Individualized Education Systems

Beginning Math at Home, $10.95. Add $2 shipping.

This delightful little program for children ages 3–6 has the same format as *Beginning Reading at Home*, by the same author. You get four "kits," each designed to teach a different math concept. Each kit is a set of 3½ x 5" colored cards tied together with orange yarn. You also get a pre- and post-test, for checking how much your child has learned or needs to learn from this minicourse, and a very short program guidebook explaining what it's all about and how to use it.

Oh, I almost forgot—a game, Going to the Moon, and a chart showing the correct way to write the numerals are also included.

The kits are Shapes, Counting (0–12, plus more than, less than, and time telling to the hour), Addition 0–10, and Subtraction 0–10. No writing is needed, except tracing the numerals. All manipulatives and practice cards necessary are built in. You just cut out the little clock and its hands, the little number cards, less than, equal to, and the question cards for the Going to the Moon game.

This little program is the perfect example of a well-designed program for home use. It costs almost nothing, is ultra simple to use, has no unnecessary clutter, is charming to look at, involves the children right away, and includes everything except a brad for attaching the clock hands and a pair of scissors for cutting!

If author Elizabeth Peterson could only be persuaded to invent a *Beginning Math II* kit, with counting up past 100, skip counting, reverse counting from 20, money, and time to the quarter hour, with those two itty-bitty programs you'd be able to do everything it took the University of Chicago experts pages and pages of instructions and $300 of manipulatives to accomplish. Do it, Elizabeth!

NEW★★
Saxon Publishers
MathK: An Incremental Development, $34 postpaid includes teacher manual and student workbook. Preliminary version only: final version TBA, fall 1991.

I saw a preliminary version of this long-awaited Saxon program for kindergarten math. Let's talk about its more innovative aspects first. I love the idea of the teacher-made activities. Where another publisher might have come up with a $200 set of must-have classroom manipulatives, the Saxon program provides instructions at the beginning of each section of the teacher's manual for simple manipulatives the teacher can make herself, plus patterns in the back.

When the whole course is completed, your student will know:

Counting to 100 by 1s and 10s
Geometric shapes
Equivalence and one-to-one correspondence
Simple fractions, wholes, pairs, dozens
Measurement, weights
Ordinal numbers
Time to the half hour
Money (penny, nickel, dime)
Addition and subtraction 0—10
Patterning, sequencing, matching.

In *MathK*, the famous Saxon "incremental" approach is used, but not as obviously as in the upper-grades books. Skills and concepts, once introduced, are repeated in following lessons. However, in the manner of "regular" kindergarten books, the activities skip around a lot from day to day. You won't find children doing the same activities every day for a week.

This may be more interesting for the student, but is more work for the teacher and also is not as reinforcing as daily repetition. Some skills, such as counting, are repeated every day.

This might be as good a place as any to mention that you will not want to attempt this program without the teacher's manual. The student workbook, while pretty much self-explanatory and easy to use, does not contain the sequential lesson plans, teaching instructions, and manipulative activities. Those are all contained in the spiral-bound teacher's manual.

If I were revising this book, I'd perhaps cut the number of activities, repeat activities more, and include the following: skip counting by 2s and 5s, reverse counting from 20, addition and subtraction 10–20, and simple multiplication and division manipulation. Kindergarten children are definitely capable of this: as one publisher rightly points out, of children entering kindergarten,

> More than 80% can already count 14 dots on a card, above 30% can read and write the number 57, about 40% can read and write the number 100, and about 40% can count backward from ten. At the end of that kindergarten year, about 90% of the children can correctly share 12 things among 3 people, and 60% can respond correctly to, "Please give me half of these 12 blocks."

Children of this age could definitely enjoy some simple homemade division and multiplication activities and manipulatives, and once they have learned to write numbers to 100 there is no good reason not to take another two days and teach them how to write numbers up to the millions. Such achievements give little kids a real feeling of power, as opposed to the feeling they get when confined to numbers smaller than 10 until the end of kindergarten, and maybe even most of the way through first grade.

Because of the large number of homemade manipulatives, you should lay in a stock of tagboard, felt markers, tape, and various colors of thin cardboard stock if you are planning to use *MathK*. You will also need felt pieces and a flannelboard. Play coins and a play clock are provided. If you can, cover your manipulatives with clear contact paper, or visit your local teacher's store and get them laminated, as they will last much longer.

If this seems a lot of effort to go through to teach kindergarten math to one child, you're right. The Saxon kindergarten course is more strongly classroom oriented than any of his upper-grades courses.

TREND Enterprises, Inc.
Wipe-Off® Cards, $6.95/set. Wipe-Off® Books, $2.95 each. Wipe-Off® crayons, 79¢/pack of six assorted colors. Reusable Activity Books, $1.99 each. Flip Books, $1.99 each. Add $2 shipping. Minimum order $10. Ages 4 and up.

TREND's Wipe-Off Cards, Wipe-Off Books, and Reusable Activity Books are colorful early learning fun! Like Frank Schaffer materials, these are sold at your friendly local teacher's store.

Let's Count includes 12 full-color *large* write and wipe cards. Kids match numbers, count sets and circle the right number, and so on. Cards have activities on both sides. Use TREND's special Wipe-Off crayons, and use these cards again and again!

Alphabet and Number Fun, Count to 10!, and *I Can Add!* are TREND Wipe-Off Books. Each has 16 reusable, full-color pages. Even the covers are worksheets! They are really fun . . . and inexpensive!

Number Fun, a reusable activity book, is a smaller format, with 16 plastic-coated Wipe-Off pages. Kids match numbers to sets, write the numerals 0–10. Center pages in this series cut apart to make flash cards or other activities. The *Dot to Dot* reusable activity book includes upper and lowercase letters, numbers 0–36, and counting by twos. *Telling Time* and *Money Fun* obviously cover time and money.

ELEMENTARY MATH PROGRAMS

Schools make basic arithmetic drag on far longer then needed. In the 1800s, a child could go to school for three six-week sessions for four years and know more math than one of our high school graduates today. Great-great-grandpa put in less than one-fifth the time, yet he could solve tough compound-interest problems and figure the height of a pole by knowing the length of its shadow and the angle of the sun. To bring this more up to date, kids in Sweden, Germany, and Ireland all whop American kids on those international math tests. Coincidentally, in those countries they all complete basic arithmetic courses years earlier than we stop teaching it in the USA.

Arithmetic, after all, is logical. One step follows another. The key to success, in my opinion, is not interrupting this logical progression with all kinds of absurd classroom "activities" and unrelated topics. Measurement, for example, while it uses math, is really a *science* topic. The same goes for clocks, calendars, and even geometry. I know from experience it's possible to buzz along in arithmetic right up through algebra without having the foggiest idea of how to figure the circumference of a circle, given its diameter. All these other studies are worthwhile, but they do *not* belong in the basic arithmetic course, any more than the spelling class ought to be studying the geography of Mesopotamia. When arithmetic is mixed with any other subject, arithmetic (being abstract) is what loses out.

Your child won't necessarily fail to learn arithmetic by following the typical private- or public-school sequence, which mixes arithmetic with set theory, measurement, clocks, calendars, riddles, crossword puzzles, famous people of history, important dates, geometry, money, and so on. He just won't learn it as fast. With a little creativity, these "basic" courses can be (and have been) dragged on to last into high school and even college. The reason is that so much time is spent on everything *but* arithmetic.

Happily, homeschoolers are no longer confined to programs written for the current school scope and sequence. Some publishers have reprinted the math books our forefathers used. Others have developed their own streamlined programs. Maybe we can someday persuade the school publishers to catch up with us!

A Beka Book Publications

Drill, drill, drill. Pages and pages of problems. If you think this approach is character-building, A Beka has the math workbooks for you. Each day's work takes a single page and is easy to grade with the answer key. (I personally feel it's not necessary to do *that* much drill—how about assigning *part* of the problems on each page, like real schoolteachers often do?) Work progresses more or less sequentially, so if you understand basic math there's not all that much to helping your students use these books.

NEW**
Activities for Learning
A-L Abacus, $15.95. *Abacus Activities*, $16.95. *Worksheets for Abacus*, $24.95, grades K–6. Math Card Games, $16.95. Six decks of math cards for games, $16.95. Corners colored plastic tiles, set of 50, $5.95. Place Value Cards, $4.95. Base 10 Picture Cards, $1.95. Suffix Flow Charts, $4.95. Shipping 10%, minimum $1.50.

Joan A. Cotter, a lady with an impressive list of credentials, started developing math and language materials in 1975 to use with her son. In 1980 she formed a company, Activities for Learning, and started publishing some of them.

Today let's look at her nifty math manipulatives and card games.

First, here is a quite complete elementary math calculations curriculum that those who prefer kinesthetic learning styles would enjoy. In layman's language, we're talking about doing math with your fingers via an abacus and at the same time learning how all the math operations work. It's a nice abacus at a good price, and you can also purchase both an activities book with pre-K through grade 6 activities and two volumes of worksheets designed for use with the abacus and book.

More about *Activities for the Abacus.* This is the second edition (a good sign, since loser books never have second editions!). Like the worksheet books, it has an oversized spiral-bound format. This book is *very* complete. For example, in Unit Five, Introducing Subtraction, you get Simple Subtraction (oral subtraction, written subtraction, subtracting from 10, subtracting 1), Subtractions < 10 (subtracting tens, subtracting single-digit numbers, subtracting double-digit numbers), Subtraction Results (greater than, equal to, or less than; remainders and differences; subtraction twins; equations; checking), and Special Effects (minuend decreased by 1, subtrahend decreased by 1, counting up, and the complement method). This is just one of the 11 units, which cover everything from how to read the abacus and basic math concepts to fancy stuff like squares and percentages, millions on the abacus, and how to use both the Japanese and Chinese abacus. The associated worksheet volumes contain correlated exercises on both paper and the abacus.

Joan's *Math Card Games*, an oversized spiral-bound book with games for every math concept from numeration (we know this as "counting"!) through all four basic arithmetic operations, clocks, money, and fractions, and her card games and flashcard sets for place

value and base ten are described in detail in Chapter 25. It's the closest thing to a complete math games curriculum I've seen.

All the Activities for Learning materials I've seen (and I've seen most of them) were *very* professionally done, nice to look at, durable, easy to follow, and even fun! Another great resource for kinesthetic learners.

Alpha Omega Publications

Another drill-based program. Alpha Omega worktexts are not printed on the sturdiest paper—this can be a problem if your child needs to erase a lot. On the up side, like all Alpha Omega materials, their worktexts are inexpensive and ultra easy to use and grade.

On the down side, Alpha Omega's own studies have shown that children using their math worktexts lag behind students using other publishers' materials. This should be corrected in their revised edition. They are presently revising grades K–2 of their math program to include the curriculum goals in *Typical Course of Study* and other standard public-school scope and sequences. The revised versions should be ready in October 1991. Meanwhile, you can fill the gaps with Alpha Omega's *Bible-Based Math* LIFEPACS for grades 2–7 (two units for each grade level).

NEW**
Bob Jones University Press
Student worktexts: K, $5.95; 1 and 2, $7.95 each; 3–6, $13.95 each. Teacher's editions, $29.50 each grade K–6. Wide variety of supplementary materials available. Grades K–12.

If you're looking for an excellent school-style basic math program, here it is. We've seen and/or used them all—A Beka, Rod and Staff, Holt, Laidlaw . . . In my opinion, the BJUP math program towers over the competition.

Unlike other series, BJUP math combines a variety of drills with "thinking" exercises. Concepts are introduced first, and then cemented with practice and applications. New kinds of exercises on every page of the colorful texts give fresh insights into the particular area being studied. These include math tricks, games, and riddles; geometry play; charts, graphs, and so on. Basic arithmetic is always kept in view, though you don't move as swiftly as you would in a strict calculation-skills course.

Everything about this series is first class, including the art and even the bindings. The earlier grades' books are workbooks with quality kivar bindings. Starting with third grade, BJUP's math books are quality hardbound textbooks. You will be able to use these books for years. Downside: your student has to do his work in a separate notebook. This means extra work for both student and teacher. It is easier to comment upon work done right under a problem. The only alternative is requiring the student to copy the entire problem, which gets wearisome when working with charts and word problems.

While not as devotional as a series like Rod and Staff, BJUP does incorporate Biblical principles into their math program. This is done in a very natural, unforced manner.

Because BJUP is so thorough, you might want to get the text from your child's last grade level instead of his present one. Although our Ted had finished grade 3 of another publisher's series, I found that the BJUP grade 3 text was just right for him. The same went for Joseph, who had finished grade 1 of another series and started over with grade 1 of BJUP.

The series continues into junior-high and high-school math, including algebra and geometry. See Volume 3 for details.

NEW**
Contemporary Books, Inc.
Number Sense series, complete set, $53.26. Includes one copy of each student workbook, one copy of each diagnostic test, one answer key, and one teacher's resource guide. Individual workbooks, $3.93 each. Answer key, $3.93. Teacher's resource guide, $9.26. Pack of 10 diagnostic/mastery tests for a single topic, $13.26. Shipping extra. Grades 4–adult.

This brand-new program was especially designed for students "where traditional methods have failed." It consists of ten 64-page worktexts, diagnostic placement and mastery tests, separate answer key, and a teacher's resource guide.

Number Sense is a revision of the original program, *Programmed Learning*, which attracted some favorable

attention in home-school circles, as well as in classroom situations. The original program had more workbooks, fewer graphics, and a less sizable teacher's resource guide. In its present form, Contemporary Books is touting it as the ideal introduction for their best-selling *Number Power* adult math program for GED preparation.

Number Sense was originally designed for use by school teachers who need individualized math help for lots of students, especially those who were already having trouble with math. The "adult" format of the program makes it usable for all ages (each booklet of the original program had "Grades 4–12" printed on its cover), even though the entire program is designed at an easy reading level. Word problems focus on questions like figuring out how many pounds of roast beef you can afford, making change, or reading a thermometer.

Areas covered by *Number Sense* are:

- Whole Numbers—with one workbook for *Addition & Subtraction* and one for *Multiplication & Division*

- Decimals—with one workbook for *Addition & Subtraction* and one for *Multiplication & Division*

- Fractions—with one workbook for *The Meaning of Fractions*, one for *Addition & Subtraction*, and one for *Multiplication & Division*

- *Ratio & Proportion*

- Percent: *Meaning of Percent* and *Percent Applications* are the two workbooks.

The teacher's resource guide has simple, sensible activities for each skill area (e.g., practicing place value by playing a game with straws for "points" and bundling the straws by tens when you have enough) and an "Item Analysis Chart," which helps you find the exact lesson to assign for extra help in a given area. It also includes some basic math pedagogy (e.g., the necessity of moving students through the concrete, semiconcrete, semiabstract, and abstract levels of thinking, and what this means), and some good common teaching sense (e.g., don't overdo the praise—praise only genuine success, no matter how small).

Number Sense does not teach the arithmetic facts. You should spend some time working on those before beginning this program. What it does offer is:

• clear, easy-to-follow explanations of each math skill, broken down into bite-sized bits (one skill per page)

• a logical sequence of skills

• highly visual page design, with plenty of white space

• minimal reading load (grade 3–5 reading level)

• and plenty of practice.

You start by giving the student a simple diagnostic test in a particular area (Whole Numbers, Decimals, Fractions, or Ratio/Proportion/Percent). The results of this test show you where to start in the *Number Sense* series, or which particular "gaps" to fill by assigning specific pages. You work your way through the workbook, checking work against the answer key. After all assigned pages have been completed, the student takes a mastery test, to see if he really has mastered it all.

Everything is spelled out and every possible difficulty is anticipated; you don't have to know how to teach math to use this program.

The main strength of this program is its excellent explanations. Allan Suter, the program's author, has a real gift for making the complex simple. Problem areas, such as subtracting from a number that contains lots of zeros, or solving multi-step problems, are separated out and attended to separately. Nobody has to fail at math with this kind of material.

If your student is having trouble in any particular area—say, fractions—you might find it well worth your while to get the workbooks for fractions, along with the answer key and teacher's guide. It's too bad that Contemporary only sells single copies of the tests as part of a complete set—if you want the tests (an integral part of the *Number Sense* system) you have to buy a set of 10 fractions tests or 10 decimals tests, for example. In the long run, you may find it simpler just to get a complete set of *Number Sense* materials, or to skip the tests (the workbooks aren't all that long anyway, and it won't hurt for your student to do a few extra pages).

I could wish that along with the excellent explanations and step-by-step skill building came a continuous review of skills already learned. Home schoolers would be wise to provide some homemade "incremental" review problems from previous lessons along with the new skill of the day, to ensure that our students not

only understand, but can't forget what they've already learned. Alternatively, if your child is having special trouble with math, you could try using *Number Sense* in tandem with one of the Saxon basic-math courses (*Math 54* or *Math 65*). *Number Sense* has better explanations, and Saxon provides the review!

Cornerstone Curriculum Project
Kindergarten manual, $30. Manuals for grades 1–6, $35 each. Manipulatives for K–3, $15. Add 10% shipping.

A concept-based program designed specifically for home use, *Making Math Meaningful* is meant to lead children from observation to interpretation to application. Example: your child observes you sorting forks into a set of long forks and a set of short forks. When he understands what you are doing, you sort some other objects into "long" and "short" piles. The words "sort" and "long" and "short" arise naturally out of this activity. Finally the child does some sorting into "long" and "short" piles himself.

I just shared the first activity in the first module, "Equal and Unequal." As you go through the curriculum, activities move *slowly* from real objects to manipulatives to pictorial representations to, finally, the math symbols themselves: the numerals and operands.

Topics in the kindergarten book include: Equal and Unequal, Equalizing, Serial Ordering, Comparing and Ordering, and Representing. The latter includes graphing. Children also learn to write the numerals.

Each separate activity lists materials needed and tells what concepts the activity will develop. The lesson plan tells parents exactly what to do and say. All necessary student activity sheets are included, and the whole thing is packaged in a three-ring binder for easy accessibility. The Manipulatives Kit includes 50 Unifix cubes, 100 colorful plastic links, and 100 checker-style variously colored counting chips in a ziplock bag.

Making Math Meaningful looked better when it had less competition. Now that so much more is available for home schoolers, I must say this is not the easiest-to-use primary math material, because you spend so much time gathering and playing with actual objects. It also doesn't move ahead very rapidly. As one dissatisfied mom wrote me, "The repetition for the most simple concepts is incredible."

The edition I saw of CCP's *Making Math Meaningful* included no clocks, no measuring, no money, and no skip counting. In other words, don't count on this for your child's entire math curriculum.

Creative Teaching Associates
Creative Math Concepts K–4, $4 postpaid.

If you'd like to develop your own math program for the elementary years based largely on games and manipulatives, Creative Teaching Associates, a publisher of math games and manipulatives, can accommodate you. *Creative Math Concepts K-4* contains (1) a step-by-step review of each math concept your child must learn, (2) suggested activities you can do around the house, and (3) brief lists, where appropriate, of CTA games that help with a particular concept. The slim booklet makes it really easy to figure out where your child is mathematically and what should come next. Pre-math teaching steps are generally spelled out; for higher levels, you need to either know how to teach the concept, or buy the suggested games.

Education Services
Basics Packet, $10, includes *Easy Start in Arithmetic*, *Home Start in Reading*, and *Strong Start in Language*.

As usual, Ruth Beechick manages to take a subject that gives other people fits—teaching arithmetic to preschool and early elementary children—and to make it simple and obvious in less than 30 pages. *An Easy Start in Arithmetic* presents the different modes of learning arithmetic (manipulative, mental image, and symbolic) and outlines a K–3 program for teaching all the arithmetic curriculum without tears. Included are games and suggestions for a few homemade manipulatives. This booklet is definitely more for less, and worth buying no matter what math program you use.

NEW**
Equals
Family Math, $15. Add $4 shipping. Grades K–8.

From a letter by reader Dani Gellatly:

I have discovered a math book I am so thrilled with . . . It's called *Family Math* and it's published by the Lawrence Hall of Science at University of California, Berkeley. Other than drill (we like CalcuLadders), it's just about all you'd need for K–8 general math. . . . at last a family, multi-level math option!

Some of the units included are:

- Word Problems & Logical Reasoning
- Measurement
- Probability & Statistics
- Time & Money
- Geometry & Spatial Thinking
- Patterns & Number Charts

Each unit has several chapters and is so well laid out and easy to understand. There are many games and projects—the kind I can actually envision doing, since on most of them we can all be included!

Family Math is a collection of activities originally invented for community family-math classes. The book, however, is definitely meant for use at home. Activities require only common household objects (beans, toothpicks, paper, pencils, etc.), although you may want to photocopy some of the gameboards. Sample pages of graph paper are included for the activities requiring it.

The activities in *Family Math* were chosen because they allow parents and children to play with, discover, and experience math together. An icon at the top of each page indicates which age groups can do the activity.

The activities in *Family Math* are really satisfying. My only complaint about this book is that the illustrations are so grotesque. Many feature children in threatening situations—e.g. measuring an enormous, ugly snake with a huge bulge in his middle (he has evidently just eaten something or somebody). Tongues, claws, and overwhelming size are recurring features in the illustrations. There's a sense of alienation and of the universe being out of joint. For a book meant to empower kids to stress the themes of children's tininess and powerlessness seems odd, to say the least.

The motive behind *Family Math* was to make math accessible to those who otherwise might fear and fail it, notably girls and minorities. This explains why *housewife* and *mother* are not in the list of careers that use math at the back, but not why businessmen and executives (some of the world's biggest math users) are left off the list.

On balance, this is an excellent math (as opposed to arithmetic) course fully of ugly pictures. The first math exercise I'd do with this book is calculate how many stickers it will take to cover up the unappealing portions of the pictures!

NEW**
Golden Educational Center
Story Problems Made Easy, $5.95 each book. Add 10% shipping, $2 minimum. Grades K–3.

From the people who brought you Creating Line Designs and those handy outline maps comes an innovative new product: *Story Problems Made Easy*. Each book in the series is reproducible, has 29 different lessons with both teacher and student answer keys in the back (some people prefer to let the kids check their own work), a master grid for making up your own story problems, and optional enrichment activities at the bottom of each lesson page.

Book 1 covers sums to 20; book 2, sums to 99 without carrying or borrowing; and book 3, sums to 122 using carrying and borrowing.

What makes these books unique is the layout of the story problems. Each page presents a scenario at the top.—e.g., "I went to a garage sale and I saw two great bikes. There was a red one that cost twenty-four dollars and a blue bike that cost seventeen dollars." The page has a grid on it. Now, going down the page on the left-hand side of the grid, come the problems:

> How much more is the red one?
> How much less is the blue one?
> How much are both bikes?
> What is the total for the two bikes?
> If the red bike cost eight dollars less, how much would it cost?
> If the blue bike cost eight dollars less, how much would it cost?

In the middle column, students must decide whether to add or subtract. In the right column they must write and solve the problem, labeling each answer. Problems are different on different pages, allowing the student to work with all the different story problem types. The enrichment activities at the bottom are just for fun. Example:

> After we started the art project we used all of the paper. We also used 9 more pieces of red paper and 16 more pieces of white. How many pieces of paper did we use for this art project altogether?____ On the back of this paper, draw a picture of what you think we might have been making with all of this red and white paper. (HINT: It was February.)

Nifty!

NEW**
Hayes School Publishing Co., Inc.
Modern Mastery Drills in Arithmetic, grades 1–8, $3.50 each. Add $1.50 postage for first item, 35¢ each additional item.

Rule of thumb: Nothing with "modern" in its name really is. Modern, that is! Hayes' *Modern Mastery Drills in Arithmetic* is no exception. It's a reprint of math drill books originally published decades ago by the Benton Company of Fowler, Indiana. Your parents may have used these books—they are only slightly revised from the original old-timey edition. Nostalgic typography and simple exercises like, "On her way to school this morning, Mary Lou saw 5 robins, 1 kingbird, and 3 song sparrows. How many birds did Mary Lou see?"

To give you an idea of the era in which Hayes' *Modern Mastery Drills in Arithmetic* was published, consider this question: "Betty mailed two letters for her mother. On one there was a 4-cent stamp and on the other there was a 7-cent stamp. What was the total amount of postage?" Raise your hand if you remember 7-cent first-class stamps! How refreshing to see problem sets that evoke an America that really was kinder and gentler, in which membership in the local Pig Club (for owners of pigs) loomed large in a child's life, when movie tickets cost 45¢, when every boy owned a whittling knife and nobody ever knifed anybody.

As you might recall, in the old days kids really were expected to learn some serious *math*. Thus, although the first-grade book starts charmingly with apples to color in and large numerals to copy, by the time you hit grade 8 you're looking at how to figure percents, commissions, and bank interest, among other things.

These books cover *everything*: geometry, graphing, fundamental operations, exponents (called "powers"), units of measure, etc. And they do it all in the old-fashioned terms of Mrs. Smith's dress-goods yardage and the capacity of Mr. Jones' cistern. Refreshing!

No effort is required to use these books at all. No teacher's guides; answer keys are built in. Everything is step-by-step and logically arranged. Each new skill is explained in a little box at the top of the page. Problems are well designed for practicing new and old skills. Calm common sense throughout.

NEW**
Key Curriculum Press
Orange Book, Red Book, Blue Book, Green Book, Yellow Book, Purple Book, $4.85 each. *Miquon Lab Sheet Annotations,* $11.65. *Miquon Notes to Teachers,* $2.95. *Miquon First Grade Diary,* $4.95. Add 10% shipping ($4 minimum, $15 maximum).

I love Miquon Math. OK, so what *is* Miquon Math? First, it's a laboratory approach to math, so called because children are encouraged to demonstrate and discover how and why math principles work. It's called "Miquon" Math because it's based on clever lab sheet activities, some teacher-invented, some student-invented, pioneered 27 years ago at the Miquon School in Miquon, Pennsylvania.

Miquon Math is *math,* not a gussied-up arithmetic course. Lots of abstract thinking here. Children using this program do work with the real world mathematically, but the worksheets themselves are heavy on numerals and symbols. In other words, Miquon sets are

more likely to include circles and squares than frogs and mittens.

More unusual features: In a world of "Dress for Success" and hyped packaging, Miquon Math makes no attempt to dazzle the children with gorgeous color graphics—although the sheets do have a certain gracefulness of design.

Most unusual of all, often the same sheet can be used for a number of quite different activities. For example, on the very first sheet of the very first book you find a number of sets of circles. In anyone else's program, you'd find instructions asking the student to perhaps count the circles or find all sets of 3 circles. The Miquon approach, instead, is to take the teacher through a discussion of all the topics to be taught under the broad heading of counting. For that particular sheet, here are a few of the suggestions:

1. Pupils match each element in each set (picture group) with an object such as a rod or a bead.

2. Pupils check off each element in a set with a tally mark. [An illustration shows how this might be done.]

3. Pupils match each element in a set with a white [Cuisenaire] rod to get a model set. Then they arrange the rods in a row and exchange the row of white rods for a single rod of that length. [An illustrate demonstrates this process.]

4. Pupils count the elements in each set and match each set with a numeral card.

5. Sample questions appropriate for all three [first lab sheets]:
   Which collection (group, set)
   . . . is the smallest (the least?)
   . . . is the largest (most)?
   . . . has one more than three things?
   . . . . has twice as many as two things?

The list goes on and on with even cleverer suggestions. This is real math *teaching,* not cookbook arithmetic.

Miquon Math Lab materials include a set of six workbooks (the *Orange Book, Red Book, Blue Book, Green Book, Yellow Book,* and *Purple Book,* designed to be used in that order), a hefty volume entitled *Lab Sheet Annotations and Mathematics for the Primary Teacher,* another slimmer book entitled *Notes to Teachers,* and the most intriguing book of all, the *First-Grade Diary.* The latter is a literal diary, following the experiences for one year of one first-grade class taught by Lore Rasmussen, author of the Miquon Math materials. You find out not only what the children were told to do, but how they responded to the activities, including activities they invented on their own. The diary is not intended as a teaching guide, but as an example of math teaching in action. If you're fascinated by learning and teaching math, you'll love the *Diary*. If not, skip it and stick with the straight curriculum.

In contrast to the practical emphasis of the *Diary*, the *Notes to Teachers* book is Lore Rasmussen's educational manifesto. Here you discover the philosophy behind the Miquon program (rather similar to that of John Holt—by the way, John Holt used a Miquon-style approach in his own teaching!), plus various appendices. The most essential of these, from the point of view of the home teacher, who already knows her pupils quite well, are Appendices B and E. Appendix B, "Beginning Play with Cuisenaire® Rods," shows free play activities with the rods and how these prepare the children for Miquon Math. Appendix E lists all materials and supplies you need for your entire math lab program, and gives instructions for making your own number lines, Hundred Board, square geoboard, meter sticks, and yard sticks.

The core of the Miquon Math program is the lab workbooks and *Lab Sheet Annotations*. There is no answer key: although the *Lab Sheet Annotations* book contains miniature copies of every page in the entire curriculum (several pages reduced to fit on one *Lab Sheet Annotations* page), answers are not filled in, as they usually are in math teachers' books. So how are you supposed to check your children's work? You are supposed to be right there with them, observing and guiding. (This is not the program for parents who like to set kids working and leave the room!) Mrs. Rasmussen expects you to go through an entire set of workbooks, solving each problem yourself. Your set of completed workbooks will then be your answer key.

This is indeed wonderful preparation for teaching this course, but you'll need to take extra preparation time *and* purchase an extra set of workbooks. A less costly and time-consuming idea would be to stay just a few lessons ahead and simply write in the answers, in cases where each problem has just one answer, on the scaled-down copies of the lab pages in the *Annotations* manual. Thus you can have your own personalized answer key without buying (or toting around) an extra set of workbooks.

Teaching suggestions are scattered where necessary among the copies of student workbook pages in the *Lab Sheet Annotations* book. There is nothing in the nature of formal lesson plans of the "Do this on day one" variety.

Another unusual twist is that the *Lab Sheet Annotations* books lists lab sheets, and comments on them, in the order of the concepts on the sheets, not the order in which they appear in the workbooks. The *Orange Book*, for example, has 24 pages on the subject of counting, followed by 12 on addition, four on subtraction alone, 25 on addition and subtraction combined, 12 on multiplication, and so on. In *Lab Sheet Annotations*, however, all the addition sheets for all six books are listed sequentially, with corresponding teaching philosophy and tips, followed by all the subtraction sheets for all six books, etc.

Let me explain this a little further. In the Miquon curriculum, concepts are broken down into 26 areas, each labeled with a letter. I might as well give you the whole series:

A. Counting (book 1 only)
B. Odd-Even (books 2 and 3)
C. Addition (books 1–5)
D. Subtraction (all books)
E. Addition and Subtraction (all books except book 4)
F. Multiplication (all books)
G. Addition, Subtraction, and Multiplication (first three books)
H. Fractions (all books except book 4)
I. Addition, Subtraction, Multiplication, and Fractions (books 2 and 3)
J. Division (books 2 and 4–6)
K. Addition, Subtraction, Multiplication, Fractions, and Division (2, 3, 5)
L. Equalities and Inequalities (all books except book 3)
M. Place Value (books 4–6)
N. Number Lines and Functions (1, 4, 5)
O. Factoring (2, 4, 5)
P. Squaring (4, 6)
Q. Simultaneous Equations (book 5 only)
R. Graphing Equations (book 6 only)
S. Geometric Recognition (1, 3, 5)
T. Length, Area, and Volume (1, 4, 5)
U. Series and Progressions (4, 5)
V. Grid and Arrow games (3, 5, 6)
W. Mapping (book 4 only)
X. Clock Arithmetic (1, 4–6)
Y. Sets (book 6 only)
Z. Word Problems (book 6 only)

Kids are supposed to finish two books a year, completing the entire program by the end of third grade. Here kids who attend most public or private schools will have a real problem—they will already know everything the schools plan to teach them for the next three years. Home-taught children using this program should probably go straight to John Saxon's *Math 65*, or possibly even *Math 76*. Alternatively, they could pick up the Key Curriculum Press *Key to . . .* series (see below), which covers decimals, fractions, geometry, pre-algebra, and all that other upper-elementary stuff.

Would I be giving away any secrets if I tell you that all three of Lore Rasmussen's sons are now working in the field of math education, and that the *Key to . . .* series is a second-generation Rasmussen product?

Miquon Math is not for everyone, not because all kids can't learn this way (they can), but because not all adults like to teach this way. It requires patience. You have to be willing to let children discover things themselves, instead of always telling them the answer and testing them on the answers. If all you want is for your kids to be fast with the math facts, then you need another program. If, however, you are excited by the sight of your children thinking, pondering, discovering, and inventing . . . if you want the best program around for developing mathematical thinking skills and accelerating your children's native intellectual ability . . . this just might be the one.

UPDATED★★
Key Curriculum Press
Key to Fractions, $7/set of 4 books. *Decimals*, $7.40/set of 4. *Percents*, $5.55/set of 3. *Algebra*, $12.25/set of 7. *Geometry*, $23.40/set of 8. *Geometry Starter Set*, $5.85/3 books. Circle Master compass, $2.45. Plastic straightedge, 25¢. Answer Books, $1.95 each subject, except geometry where there are separate answer books for books 1–3, 4–6, 7, and 8. Reproducible Tests, $9.95 for each series (algebra and geometry tests not available). Add 10% shipping ($3 minimum).

You won't beat this guarantee. Steven Rasmussen, the publisher, says, "I unconditionally guarantee that *Key to . . .* worktexts will substantially improve your students' math skills and enjoyment. If, for any reason, you are not satisfied, return your books—even if they're used—and I'll give you a 100% refund. No questions asked."

Why is Mr. Rasmussen so confident? Because these workbooks assume nothing. Each page contains only one concept. Sample problems are handwritten to

reduce student intimidation. Visual models are used wherever possible, such as shaded-in area when studying fractions. Examples are worked out step-by-step. New terms are explained and underlined. Students get plenty of workspace and lots of exercises which gradually increase in difficulty. *Everything* you need is in the inexpensive workbook.

Key to Fractions includes:

Book 1: Fraction Concepts
Book 2: Multiplying and Dividing Fractions
Book 3: Adding and Subtracting Fractions
Book 4: Mixed Numbers

Key to Decimals features real-world uses of decimals—such as pricing, sports, metrics, calculators, and science—and includes:

Book 1: Decimal Concepts
Book 2: Adding, Subtracting, and Multiplying Decimals
Book 3: Dividing Decimals
Book 4: Using Decimals

Key to Percents includes:

Book 1: Percent Concepts
Book 2: Percents and Fractions
Book 3: Percents and Decimals

Key to Geometry covers basic geometry, and includes no proofs. It covers:

Book 1: Lines and Segments
Book 2: Circles
Book 3: Constructions
Book 4: Perpendiculars
Book 5: Squares and Rectangles
Book 6: Angles
Book 7: Perpendiculars and Parallels, Chords and Tangents, Circles
Book 8: Triangles, Parallel Lines, Similar Polygons.

For the *Geometry* series, you will also need a Circle Master compass and straightedge, both also available from Key Curriculum Press.

For older children, *Key to Algebra* is an algebra introduction. See reviews in Volume 3.

I finally went ahead and used the *Key to . . .* series with our children, and now I'm recommending them to everyone. Our seven-year-old zipped through the books, and our five-year-old could do the geometry. Anyone who knows arithmetic can succeed with these books.

NEW✶✶
Learning at Home
First Grade Mathematics Teaching Guide, $11. Second Grade, $11.50. Third Grade, $12.75. Grades 4–6 available only as combined Resource Units of language arts, math, social studies, and science: $36 each.

With these books and a little effort, you can provide a complete computational and math enrichment course for your child. The guides outline all math subjects commonly taught in school, and provide suggested ways of teaching each of these topics. The only manipulative the authors suggest you buy are the relatively inexpensive Cuisenaire rods, and even they are not essential to the program. Other manipulatives mentioned in the program, such as a calendar or clock with movable hands, you can easily make yourself. You'll also need to make some flash cards and sets of math problems for your children to solve.

At the end of each book is a separate curriculum outline, listing all the learning objectives so dear to the hearts of education bureaucrats everywhere. These can be photocopied and handed in to your local educrats, if the law in your area requires this sort of thing.

These Guides are really thorough, and should fully satisfy the neighborhood bureaucrats, your Aunt Sally, and everyone else. Topics covered in each Guide are arithmetic, set theory, probability and statistics, algebra and geometry experiences (patterns in nature, geometric shapes, etc.), elementary logic, and strategies for problem solving. Each guide also has some excellent advice on how to encourage your child to identify and solve problems by himself.

I would add a few thoughts here. One, feel free to go further than the curriculum recommends. For example, if your child becomes comfortable with counting and adding coins, don't feel you have to limit your

practice with them to totals of less than 50 cents, as the first-grade guide recommends. Two, you *will* need some math worksheets sooner or later. Books of worksheets are available for a few dollars each at your local teachers' store. Despite what the curriculum authors say, it is very important for kids to be quick with their math facts. Process is not more important than results (a false dichotomy); in fact, without results, knowing the process of how math works is useless. I would suggest that you add a good set of drill sheets, such as CalcuLadder, to this program for maximum results.

The approach this program takes is excellent. Since you are given types of activities, you are empowered to invent or modify activities to meet your own family's abilities and needs. This is a lot better than a clutter of time-consuming projects you feel compelled to do. The amount of suggested activities is realistic and doable. Best of all, you can be sure you haven't forgotten anything!

Leonardo Press
Arithmetic Mastery Kit, complete program, $119.95. Masters for students' worksheets, $16.95 per category. Manual, $9.95 per category. Criterion-referenced tests, $4 per category. *Math Anxiety* manual, $6. Individual category, all materials, $29.95. Add 10% shipping. Grades 1–8.

This basic math program, developed by Raymond Laurita, Phillip Trembley, and two other contributors, covers six categories: addition, subtraction, multiplication, division, fractions, and decimals. In each category a series of "prescriptions" is laid out for the student to master. Unlike other programs, the student learns through copying a model. The method Professor Laurita and friends use has the student either orally copying the teacher's example or physically copying models that are provided on his worksheet. Models are provided in a pattern and the worksheet problems are written out, rather than typeset. This has been shown to reduce student anxiety, as it makes the exercises more human and doable. Everything the teacher does and says is also spelled out, eliminating teacher anxiety.

The program is designed to let you follow it at your own pace. The entire program is laid out on a single sheet of paper. Since each subject area is taught independently, you can teach addition along with subtraction if you wish, and get into multiplication and division and the rest at the earliest opportunity. Thanks to the program's excellent design, you can see at a glance how you are progressing in each area and how much remains to do.

Brief tests are included to insure that the student is actually learning. However, most of the stress is on providing input for the student rather than forcing him to come across with output. This feature alone makes the Arithmetic Mastery Kit unique, as most basic math programs demand far more output from far less actual teaching.

You get folders for each area (addition, subtraction, multiplication, division, fractions, and decimals) that include reproducible student worksheets, a teacher's manual, individual progress charts, and criterion-referenced tests. In addition you get a manual, *Dealing with Math Anxiety,* and a scope and sequence outline of the entire program. The Kit comes in a sturdy plastic box. All folders are color-coded, as are the tests, progress charts, and manuals within, for easy access.

This program has been classroom-tested with over 1,000 Title I students, with excellent results. Your student literally *cannot* fail, unless he refuses to even try or has an organic disorder that interferes with learning. For kids with math anxiety, this may be the answer.

NEW**
Mastery Publications
Mastering Mathematics, entire program $99.95. Anticipated price after September 1, 1991 when Fractions book available: $109.95. Six extra workbook set, sold with complete series only, $39.95. Individual program, $22.95 each. Add/Sub, Mult/Div, or Point/Fractions program combos, $44.95 each. Extra workbooks, $6.95 each, except for Perfecting the Point, $7.95. Add 5% shipping (minimum $2, maximum $5). Grades 1–6 and remedial.

Mastering Mathematics is not at all what I expected it to be. From the titles of its component programs—*Attacking Addition, Subduing Subtraction, Mastering Multiplication, Defeating Division*, and *Perfecting the Point*—I had expected a series of single-skill workbooks similar to those sold in teacher's stores. Instead, it's a complete elementary curriculum.

Mastering Mathematics has many unique features. First, this is a Christian program. The Christian content is not overly evident in the *Attacking Addition* workbook, apart from an occasional problem that mentions Sunday School. Many pages of *Subduing Subtraction,* though, are devoted to problems involving biblical time lines, and the curriculum repeatedly refers to Jesus, Creation, the Flood, and other Christian teachings.

Also noticeable is the rapid progression to problems using large numbers. Curriculum author Letz Farmer rightly notes that young children can do problems with many numbers as easily as problems with few. It is no harder, for example, to add 2543 + 5344 than to add 3 + 4, 4 + 4, 5 + 3, and 2 + 5 as individual problems.

Another special feature is the pretests. Unlike other programs, Mastering Mathematics allows your child to "test out" of any subject areas he has already mastered. Thus, after taking the tests, you might find your child needs to start at page 42 of the addition book, page 27 of the subtraction book, page 7 of the multiplication book, and right at the beginning of the division book. The pretests are very well designed to ensure that your child only is given work he really needs.

Still another special feature is that kids don't learn subtraction and division facts in this program. Mrs. Farmer figures that if you know your addition facts, and a few other basic math principles, you automatically know your subtraction facts. That's because 3 + 4 = 7 really describes the same concept as 7 - 4 = 3.

The teacher's manual includes separate instructions for how to teach time, money, weights and measures, etc., using oral and real-life examples and homemade manipulatives. Pretests are now included in the back of each student workbook, with an additional copy in the teacher's manual in case you want to post-test any facts and skills.

Kids can do most of the work on their own. You just check answers, read directions on the work sheets (for younger non-readers), and play occasional math games with the kids. Assignments are short, in large print, and have lots of white space for problem solving.

Mastering Mathematics comes with special flash cards, board games, and self-checking fact wheels. You have to cut and assemble these, then store them in the envelopes provided. Beyond these, you will need some coins or play money, a clock with movable hands, a demonstration thermometer, and a few other manipulatives you can make yourself. Directions for making these manipulatives are provided. These are used while teaching time, measurement, money, temperature, and other non-computational concepts.

Because of Mrs. Farmer's background in special education, she developed this program to work with special needs children as well as average and gifted children. Thus her program minimizes the need for memorization, and memory facts are reinforced with flash cards, board games, and self-checking fact wheels. For the severely disabled learner, she recommends that only multiplication facts be memorized, since they can always do addition and subtraction on their fingers, but not multiplication! With an attitude like this, it's not surprising that children with IQs as low as 45 have been able to learn with her program. Conversely, kids with IQs as high as 138 who used this program have placed five years above grade level in mathematics within months.

Attacking Addition teaches all addition facts through 9+9; adding up to six-place numbers (this is great fun for kids); reading graphs, calendars, and perimeter.

Subduing Subtraction teaches subtraction facts as the reverse of previously memorized addition facts; practicing regrouping, including work with time and measurement; checking addition and subtraction; time lines; Roman numerals; and graphs.

Mastering Multiplication teaches all multiplication facts through 9x9; teaches 1, 2, and 3-place multipliers; exponents; pre-algebra variables; finding the area of squares and rectangles.

Defeating Division teaches 1- and 2-place divisors; rounding off and estimating; finding the best buys; unit pricing; miles per gallon; equations; etc.

Two other books, *Perfecting the Point* (point value, decimals, and percent) and *Finishing Fractions* are due out by fall of 1991.

Purchasers are now allowed to make sufficient copies for immediate family use. However, you'll probably find it cheaper to buy extra bound workbooks.

It would be nice if the reproducible appendix worksheets came in drill packs, like CalcuLadder, of sets of 10 or more. As it is, you'd be smart to use the plastic page protector (included) along with erasable pens (not included) over each workbook page, to avoid having to photocopy pages or buy extra workbooks when your child merely needs to do the same page over several times.

This is a good program—I'm using it with my own daughter Sarah, until she's ready to switch over to Sax-on Math. Excellent explanations, easy to use for kids of all ability levels.

NEW**
Mathematics Programs Associates, Inc.
Developmental Math, $140 for a complete set of all 16 student books, 15 teacher books, and all diagnostic tests. Partial set, 3 student workbooks and teacher's editions, $37. Inquire about single workbook prices, as I'm not sure whether MPA is still offering individual workbooks. Shipping extra.

Developmental Math is a series of 16 workbooks. Now don't tune me out, you non-workbook types, because these are different from any other workbook series you have seen. Based on a 10-year research project, they are designed to follow what educators call a "four-step taxonomy." In real life this means that kids are first taught concepts with real objects. In step 2, the concepts are represented with symbols (e.g., circles). Step 3, once the concept is learned, drills for speed using numerals-only problems. Step 4 is application with word problems.

What you get is a really clean, efficient program covering all your child's basic math. Each workbook comes with a diagnostic test, so you can quickly slot your child into the right workbook or figure out which pages of the workbook he needs to work to catch up on concepts he might be shaky on. The series is both "sequential" and "incremental." This means concepts are introduced in logical order, and old concepts are reviewed periodically to make sure they aren't forgotten.

The series explains itself. Teacher's manuals are just student books with the answers in brown—no complicated explanations or projects necessary.

The series is called "Developmental Mathematics" because it *develops* math concepts, rather than presenting them as isolated skills. For example: Children are drilled on combinations of numbers that add up to 10, in preparation for teaching them "regrouping," which we used to know as "adding with carrying." They then learn that $7 + 8 = 7 + (3 + 5) = (7 + 3) + 5 = 10 + 5 = 15$. This sounds more complicated than it is, as the workbook presents base 10 addition first with pictures. When I say it's not complicated, I mean that my six-year-old daughter is already at Level 7 (a fourth-grade level), zooming along and really enjoying her math! My non-mathematical 9-year-old is also picking up new math skills more quickly than with any other program I have seen.

At the rate of two pages per day, your child would be through K–6 arithmetic in 3½ years. At the still-quite-reasonable rate of four pages a day, it will take less than two years! I *know* this is possible, because my father taught me math up through the eighth-grade level the summer I was six, using a series very much like this one. I grant that I had an aptitude for math, but even spotting me a couple of years, the average home-schooled child should be able to whiz through his arithmetic studies, using these workbooks, about two to four times as fast as the average public-schooled child—and know his math a *whole lot better* in the end!

The series includes:

Level 1. Ones: Concepts and Symbols.
Level 2. Ones: Addition Concepts and Basic Facts.
Level 3. Ones: Subtraction Concepts and Basic Facts.
Level 4. Tens: Concepts, Addition and Subtraction Facts.
Level 5. Tens and Ones: Concepts, Simple Additions and Subtractions.
Level 6. Tens and Ones: Adding with Grouping.
Level 7. Tens and Ones: Subtracting with Exchange.
Level 8. Multiplication: Concepts and Facts.
Level 9. Division: Concepts and Facts.
Level 10. Hundreds and 3-Unit Numbers: Concepts, Addition and Subtraction Skills.
Level 11. Three-Unit Numbers: Multiplication and Division Skills.
Level 12. Thousands and Large Numbers: Concepts and Skills.
Level 13. Decimals, Fractions and the Metric System.
Level 14. Fractions: Concepts and Basic Skills.
Level 15. Fractions: Advanced Skills.
Level 16. Special Topics: Ratio, Percents, Graphs, etc.

All you'll need to teach your child on your own is (1) how to tell time and temperature and (2) weights and measures. These have nothing to do with basic arithmetic, but are usually thrown into basic math courses, breaking up the systematic course of instruction and confusing the children. A systematic proceed-at-your-own-pace arithmetic course, with time-telling and so on taught separately, is the best way to teach children computational math, in my opinion.

The series was written by a math teacher with a Ph.D. from the University of Birmingham in England, where they still know how to teach math. It is based on his series of elementary math textbooks that for over 25 years has been the official math series in Egypt, with over 200 million copies in print. The English-language series is the culmination of a 10-year project involving several schools, hundreds of students, and many teachers. I'm not telling you this so you will automatically accept this series, since other ostensibly research-based math courses have been disasters (remember New Math?), but so you will know Developmental Mathematics is not a fly-by-night kitchen-table production. The proof, as always, is in the pudding, which tastes good enough to me that all my younger children are using this series.

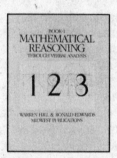

NEW★★
Midwest Publications
Mathematical Reasoning through Verbal Analysis, book $19.95, teacher's manual $9.95. Grades 2–4.

You will doubtless be gratified to learn that *Mathematical Reasoning through Verbal Analysis* "meets the new NCTM problem-solving and logical-thinking standards by asking students to analyze each problem, explore varied approach strategies, discover possible solutions, and verbalize analytic and problem-solving processes as they proceed." Don't go away just yet: the book is better than this paralytic prose indicates.

The NCTM is the National Council of Teachers of Mathematics. After several decades of basic skills slippage, these experts have in their wisdom decreed that kids should no longer concentrate on "mere" rote learning, but should instead master "problem-solving strategies." Since *all* of math involves problem-solving, the book we are currently examining is really a book of math problems, nicely organized by topic. These are (in plain language) counting and sequencing, geometry, arithmetic, measurement, comparing and ordering numbers, and tables and graphs. In turn, these topics are broken down into subtopics, such as Estimating Lengths or Sums Using Coins. You can thus open the table of contents and zip to a series of problems using a particular skill. The teacher's manual, as usual, provides teaching suggestions and answers for each exercise.

What it all boils down to is a big book of 282 pages that you can use to practice virtually every elementary math skill. Even topics like symmetry, of which you see very little in typical math texts, are covered.

For most exercises you only need a pencil; others require paper and scissors. A geoboard and set of place value materials (flats, rods, and unit cubes) also come in handy from time to time. Each section only has a few pages, in order to cover the maximum number of problem types, so it works better for reinforcement than for primary instruction.

Mortensen Math

Boxes-n-Stuff, Transportation-n-Stuff, Animals-n-Stuff, $6 each for book and manipulatives. Smiley face series, $3.50/set of 10 books. Algebra, Arithmetic, Problem Solving, Calculus, each 4 levels, each strand per level $3.50 (10 booklets). Teacher's manuals: Level 1, $10; level 2, $12; level 3, $14. Series A manuals, set of 10, $20. Many other manipulatives sets available; see reviews elsewhere in Math section. Add 10% shipping.

Putting math in a box. That's literally what Mortensen Math does. Creator Jerry Mortensen has developed a unique visual math analogy of boxes and squares to present not only the basic arithmetic operations, but such esoteric subjects as algebra and calculus.

For multiplication and division, the process is obvious. 3 x 4 is three rows of length four, or a square with surface area 12. Simple. In algebra, simply substitute x and y for any specific numbers. To present $(x + 1)(y + 2)$, you end up with a square of surface area xy flanked on one side by a bar length y and on the other by two bars length x, and two little squares (each val-

ued at 1) in the corner to make up the total square. Clear as mud, right? Maybe you'd better catch the demonstration.

For manipulatives, you get large squares, bars, and tiny unit-value squares. For counting practice, stack the lined bars in order of length . . . 1, 2, 3, and so on. For adding, add the bars. For subtraction, subtract. In multiplication and division life gets a bit more complicated. However, the workbooks creep along at a snail's pace repeating the same sort of problem over and over so your child is not likely to get lost.

The "-n-Stuff" and Smiley Face series introduce the manipulatives. Each "-n-Stuff" booklet asks children to fill in the bars and boxes in the pictures of boxes, animals, or vehicles with the correct manipulative. The Smiley Face series, which require you to purchase contact paper and smiley-face stickers, asks your child to either match a Mortensen Math symbol with the appropriate number (the *Counting* book) or do some simple multiplication (*Multiplication* book). Your child peels back the sticker of what he thinks is the right answer to see if the smiley face is underneath.

The Arithmetic series goes through the basic four operations: adding, subtracting, multiplying, dividing. Algebra goes a bit further with xs and ys. Due to the physical limitations of expressing all algebraic equations as squares, you are limited to equations with two factors. Consider this more as pre-algebra than as a substitute for a real algebra course. Ditto the calculus workbooks, which only in Book 5 get around to introducing the idea of taking delta x to zero. This is pre-calculus, not calculus.

At each level, there are arithmetic, algebra, problem-solving, and calculus workbooks. The teacher's manual for each level follows the workbooks. If you're just trying to understand how to introduce math concepts using Mortensen manipulatives, though, the Series A manuals (a set of 10 books) shows how to introduce addition, subtraction, multiplication, division, fractions, equations, functions and relationships, algebraic operations, and algebraic story problems. The set also includes a games and activities book.

The entire Mortensen series sticks firmly to the math-as-a-square vision. But math is not about making squares out of everything; it is about solving real-life problems. This entire reliance on an (admittedly helpful) abstract analogy makes it more helpful as a second chance for children with math troubles or an explanatory tool to accompany regular math lessons than as a complete or primary teaching tool. Personally, I find the Series A manuals (which explain how to use the manipulatives) much more useful than the workbooks.

New for fall 1991: a story problem/application series. I don't know anything about it yet; we'll wait and see!

Mott Media

Ray's Arithmetic, complete set with teacher's guide, $72.95. *Primary Arithmetic* (grades 1–3), $4.95. *Intellectual Arithmetic* (grades 3 and 4), $6.95. *Practical Arithmetic* (grades 5 and 6), $14.95. Key for those three books, $9.95. *Test Examples in Arithmetic*, $9.95. *Higher Arithmetic* (grades 7–12), $17.95. Key for *Higher Arithmetic,* $9.95. Parent/teacher guide for all books, $8.95. Shipping extra.

If you're into classics, you'll be glad to hear that Mott Media has resurrected a whole series of the texts America used in the days of Reverend McGuffey and Laura Ingalls. One of these selections is the Ray's Arithmetic series. The series goes from kindergarten to high school.

Primary Arithmetic starts with counting concrete objects and proceeds to counting, writing, and reading numerals. Word problems appear from the start. Mental arithmetic in this series precedes written, and some of it is tough (your kids will have to think!). Example: "If 3 lead pencils cost 18 cents, how many cents will 5 pencils cost?"

Intellectual Arithmetic, Practical Arithmetic, and *Higher Arithmetic* carry on with old-fashioned word problems and solid business math, right up to compound interest.

Ruth Beechick, author of *A Biblical Psychology of Learning,* has written the great parent/teacher guide.

NEW**
Rod and Staff Publications
Mathematics for Christian Living series. Grade 1, all materials, $19.95 (2 workbooks, 2 teacher books, set of reviews/tests). Grade 2 materials, $30.90 (4 workbooks, 4 teacher books). Grade 3, student book $10.95, teacher book $11.50. Grade 4, student book $12.35, teacher book $12.45. Grade 5, student book $11.95, teacher book $12.85, tests $1.40. Grade 6, student book $13.95, teacher book $14.90, texts, $1.65. Series continues to grade 7.

The Rod and Staff *Mathematics for Christian Living* series

- emphasizes Mennonite biblical values

- teaches number facts and skills

- present concepts, computation, and applications in a balanced mix

- enables the student to read instructions with only a minimum of help from the teacher

- includes reading or reasoning problems that involve a spiritual lesson, a Biblical principle, or other character-building emphasis.

Correlated with the *Bible Nurture and Reader* series (see the Bible chapter), there are multiple workbooks for grades 1–3. In grade 1, for example, there are two workbooks containing two units each, two teacher's books, and a set of reviews and tests. Individually, the books and workbooks aren't expensive; in fact, the whole grade 1 package only costs $19.95.

Grade 1 only covers the 1s to 5s facts, with more emphasis on skills mastery than memorizing. Subjects introduced are counting, time, place value, fractions, money, and skip counting. Grade 2 introduces the 6s to 9s facts, plus the 1s through 5s multiplication facts and addition and subtraction of two- and three-digit numbers. Lots of story problems. In grade 3, you switch from softcover workbooks to a hardcover textbook (which you can then use with all your subsequent children). Addition and subtraction of fractions, Roman numerals, and metric measure are introduced. The teacher's book for this grade has a reduced copy of the student's page on the left, the answers on the right, and teaching instructions at the bottom of the page. Grade 4 introduces the 7s through 12s multiplication facts, and one-digit multiplying of multi-digit numbers. Percent is also introduced. In grade 5, multi-digit multipliers and divisors are introduced, as well as tougher addition and subtraction problems. Banking is introduced in grade 6: deposits, withdrawals, and simple interest, as are graphs and tables. More advanced work in fractions, decimals, and percent is included, plus a review of all skills taught in previous grades. Story problems for this volume include two-step problems (which, as you recall, most public high-school graduates are unable to solve) with extraneous information thrown in, just as in real life, to make sure the student learns to pick out the information he needs to solve the problem.

Much emphasis is put on drilling the basic facts and skills. As always, the teacher's books were developed for classroom use, so in many home situations they may be most useful as answer keys. This is "farmer math," if you know what I mean—sober and sensible without any dazzling innovations, and lots of farm-oriented problems.

NEW✶✶
Saxon Publishers
Math 65, Math 76, $34 each postpaid for Home School Packet including student text, answer key, and tests.

Let's not be ambiguous here—I love these math courses! *Math 65* is for sixth graders of bright fifth graders. *Math 76* is for seventh graders or bright sixth graders. The series will eventually be extended backwards down through all the elementary grades.

These courses are superior in every way. First, the textbooks. They are hardbound (will stand up to use by all the children in a family) and printed in large type, for easy reading by the student. Lessons build "incrementally"; after a new problem type is introduced, it is repeated over and over in the following lesson sets.

Each book provides 140 daily lessons, each followed by a set of 25 problems. The student is expected to work all these problems, plus any practice problems that may be included in the lesson itself. To make your life much easier, purchase the Home School Packet, not just the textbook. Each Home School Packet includes a booklet with answers to practice questions and problem sets, answers to drill sets (sheets where students practice the basic math facts), a set of tests, and a test answer key. One test is provided for every five lessons.

When your child has finished *Math 76,* he is ready for Saxon's excellent *Algebra ½, Algebra I, Algebra II, Advanced Math (Geom-Trig-Alg II),* and *Calculus* courses, in that order. See reviews of these courses in Volume 3 of the *Big Book.*

Unless you and your child both have serious difficulty understanding basic math, I wouldn't use anything else for children at these grade levels.

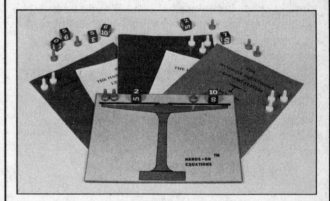

PRE-ALGEBRA FOR LITTLE KIDS

NEW✶✶
Borenson & Associates
Hands-On Equations® Learning System. Single student kit (comes with instruction manuals, game pieces, and worksheets), $34.95 plus $4.50 shipping. 19-minute video for teachers, $24.95. Classroom-sized kits also available. Grades 3–8.

Here's something *really* new—a hands-on approach to algebraic linear equations! You know what those are: fun stuff like $2x + (-x) + 3 + 2 (-x) + 15$. Most parents enjoy teaching this as much as visiting the dentist, and the kids feel likewise. But now, with Hands-On Equations from Borenson & Associates, learning pre-algebra and solving simple linear equations can be as fun and easy as playing a game. Kids aged eight and up simply set up any such equation using pawns and cubes. They then perform various "legal moves" (according to the simple instructions) and thus solve the equation.

Level I, seven lessons, is designed for third- or fourth-grade level. It takes students from setting up simple equations on a laminated representation of a balance scale through teaching them to solve equations as complicated as $2x + x + x + x + 2 = x + 10$ on paper. Level II gets into equations with negative variables (-x).

Level III introduces equations with negative whole numbers, including subtracting negative numbers. Again, the students learn to replicate the process on paper. Each level is supposed to take about two weeks of succeeding years in the average classroom.

The Hands-On Equations Learning System comes with manuals for Levels I, II, and II, a set of 26 worksheets plus answer keys, and one student kit of game pieces with a laminated picture of a balance. Game pieces included are eight blue pawns and four red number cubes (introduced in Level I), eight white pawns (to represent negative variables—Level II), and four green number cubes (to represent negative numbers—Level III). There is no dice-rolling or chance involved—the pieces are simply used to represent numbers and variables.

Henry Borenson, Ed.D., the gentleman who invented this system, suggests that you simply replace some class time spent on mental math or basic facts worksheets with his Hands-On Equations.

Why start so young? Four reasons:

1. It's *easy* for the kids.
2. It gives them "a tremendous sense of mathematical power and self-confidence."
3. It increases interest in math.
4. It lays a "concrete, intuitive foundation" for facing equations and thus improving future math performance.

Bottom line: Hands-On Equations is not a substitute for ninth-grade algebra (nor is it meant to be), but it is a wonderful, systematic, fun, empowering preparation for it!

NEW**
Cube-It
Mortensen Math

These two manipulative-based programs make teaching pre-algebra as easy as teaching arithmetic. In fact, you use the same manipulatives for both! See reviews in the Math Manipulatives chapter.

CHAPTER TWENTY-EIGHT

MATH PRACTICE

"Here's your math assignment, Sammy. I have to go make some bread, but I'll be back in a while to check on your progress."

Forty-five minutes later: "OK, Sammy, show Mommy what you did."

(Sound of rustling paper, followed by a loud groan.) "Sammy, I can't believe it! You've only done four problems out of fifty! And you had almost an hour to work on them!"

"Gee, Mom, I . . . uh . . ."

"What's the matter, Sammy? Why are you always so slow with your math? You know I explained how to do every one of those problems."

"Well . . . uh . . ."

Sound familiar? Then let's take a look at some materials designed to help parents whose kids suffer with or avoid math.

COUNTING & NUMERAL RECOGNITION

Educational Insights
Kitty Kat Number Bingo (includes 65 counters), Kitty Cat Counters, $16.95 each. Grades K–2.

Kitty Kat Number Bingo is supersimple hands-on practice for numeral recognition. You get eight full-color Bingo cards, spinner, instructions, and 65 cute little Kitty Kats in a variety of colors. Kitty Kats are also available separately, for use as counting and arithmetic manipulatives. (This is fancy language for "Count the kitty cats . . . add two kitty cats and two kitty cats . . . if you have six kitty cats and take away three, how many are left?")

NEW**
Timberdoodle
Wrap-Ups, $, $7.25 each, or three or more for $6.25 each. Shipping extra. Grades K–4.

Speaking of nifty ways to drill math, what about these self-correcting drill sticks? Each is about double the size of a butter knife blade and about as thick. You get 10 in a small cardboard can, each with different problems on it, plus 10 colorful strings. Pop the top off the cardboard tube, then attach a string to each Wrap-Up (this only has to be done once, thankfully). Simply wrap the string from the problem on the left to the answer on the right, going from top to bottom. Then turn the Wrap-Up around and see whether the string covers the embossed lines on the back of the Wrap-Up. If you did all the problems right, the string and the lines match up. If not, unwind the string and try, try again!

As you can see, this drill method is "self-correcting" because little learners can see for themselves whether they got the answers right. It does not require constant adult problem checking.

The math Wrap-Ups include one set each for addition, subtraction, multiplication, division, and fractions. For your preschooler, Timberdoodle has a Wrap-Ups set to drill numbers (matching, counting in sequence, etc.) and shapes & logic. Other Wrap-Up sets also available (e.g., preschool skills and geography).

NEW**
TREND Enterprises, Inc.
Numbers 0–25 Flash Cards, $3.99. Numbers Flip Book, $1.99. *Counting 0–10* Bull's-Eye Activity Cards, $3.49. Add $2 shipping. Minimum order $10. Ages 4 and up.

One inexpensive math tool you might want to invest in is the TREND Numbers 0–25 Flash Cards. Each card has a numeral on the front, along with the correct number of fun, colorful objects for counting practice. On the back you'll find both the numeral and the number spelled out. Motivational and fun for both mom and kid.

I really wonder how the people at TREND keep coming up with so many innovative, fun products! Here's another: their Numbers Flip Book. Flip the top halves of the pages until you find the number of objects that matches the numeral on the bottom half of the page. Look on the back of the page once you have the two halves together—it should make a picture! Spiral-bound, inexpensive early numbers fun.

Now, the *Counting 0–10* Bull's Eye Activity Cards. How many colorful objects are on the front of the card? Count them and poke your finger through the hole under the right answer. Check the back of the card and see if your finger is poking through the hole with the ring around it. Self-checking fun for budding mathematicians.

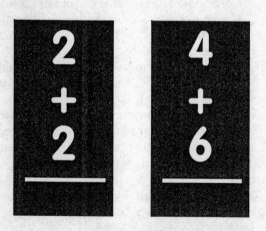

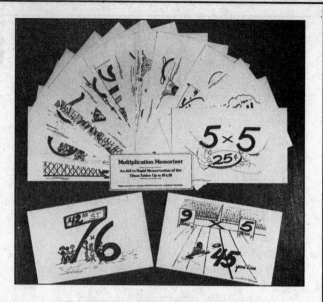

LEARNING THE MATH FACTS

Arthur Bornstein School of Memory Training
Addition and Subtraction Memorizer System: flash cards only $29.95, with instructional cassette tape $39.95. *Multiplication Memorizer System*: flash cards only $24.95; with teacher and student cassette tape, $39.95. Add 10% shipping.

Memory association technique flash cards to help children remember their math facts. Large, colorful flash cards use wacky associations like a tree (sounds like three) sitting in a shoe (sounds like two) on top of the sun (sounds like one). Thus, 3 - 2 = 1. Addition and subtraction set includes 110 flash cards; multiplication set has 40 cards. Patter and questions to ask students are on the card backs. This is not the method for training in mathematical thinking; however, it can help even the reluctant learner cement his math facts.

Educational Insights
Let's Learn to: ADD, SUBTRACT, MULTIPLY, DIVIDE, $17.95 each, records or casettes. *Mixed Math Drill,* $17.95, records or cassettes. Complete Math Facts course, $85, your choice of records or cassettes.

Using the same "Hear-See-Say" formula used in their basic phonics course, Educational Insights created a series of math drill records. Directions are recorded: this is a self-teaching program. The teacher on the record gives the problems, then your student tries to answer along with the Math Kids. Each set comes with three LP records or cassettes and a test pad.

NEW**
E-Z Grader Co.
Andy Addition, Milly Multiplication, $3.50 each postpaid. Grades K–4.

Talk about pocket calculators! From the folks who brought you the E-Z Grader itself, that peerless hunk of sturdy sliding cardboard with which you can calculate complex grades in a snidbit of time, here come Andy Addition and Milly Multiplication! These ingenious little devices are cardboard sleeves on which are printed math operations. Andy Addition, for example, has a cutout window through which peeks a number, a row of "+ 0 =, + 1 =, + 2 =" and so on going from top to bottom, and directly next to this row a cutout bar through which the answers can be seen. So if the number in the cutout window is 3, the numbers going down the cutout bar will be 3, 4, 5, 6, 7 etc. You operate it by pulling a cardboard tab in and out. Sally Subtraction appears on the back side of the Andy Addition card, and works in a very similar way. Andy Addition provides a whole row of 0 + problems at a time (also 1 +, 2 +, and all the way to 9 +). Answers appear to the right of the problem. On the reverse, Sally Subtraction shows a row of problems all having the same answer: 0—0, 1—1, etc. All basic operations

using the numbers 0–9 are covered between the two fact finders.

Danny Division and Milly Multiplication also share a card. Good little devices for teaching the regularity of math operations or for self-drilling, and amazingly durable, too.

These are, of course, neat toys for kids. Due to the patterned nature of the problem sets, they are not really good for self-testing; however, the patterns enable kids to see how arithmetic works.

UPDATED**
Hewitt Research Foundation
Pre-Math It (ages 4–6) and *Math It* (grades 2–6), $29 each. *Advanced Math It* (grades 4–8), $15. Math concepts book, $8, covers math learning for all three sets. Shipping extra.

Professor Elmer Brooks's *Math It* series leads kids through the basic math principles *and* drills them on arithmetic facts. Instead of memorizing tables, kids learn how to derive the answers (e.g., adding nine is the same as adding ten and subtracting one). Kids then practice adding nine (for example), until they can give all the plus-nine math facts instantly.

Pre-Math It involves exercises with dominoes (included). *Math It* tells you "How Stevie Learned His Math" and includes the Addit, Dubblit, and Timzit games. *Advanced Math It* has Percentit and Dividit. Each kit is nonconsumable and covers several years of arithmetic (no time telling or measurement, etc.).

With *Math It* and *Advanced Math It,* you get pre-perfed math facts cards for each game, color-coded as "facts families"—the +9 family, the +8 family, the doubles, the "neighbors," and the "leftovers" for Addit, for example. You also get game boards, facts sheets, envelopes for storing your cards and games, and an instruction book that covers not only the basic games, but extra math tricks, such as how to quickly "reduce" a complicated multiplication problem to check your answer, or how to add long columns of figures like a flash. The approach gets kids thinking mathematically, and is a lot more motivational than traditional memorization-only methods. (In plain English, it's *fun!*)

Packaging has improved a lot since the first edition of this product. It now comes in a fancy binder, like *Winston Grammar,* with professionally-printed books and materials. If you follow the directions, your child is bound to learn his math facts, and enjoy it, too!

NEW★★
Multiplication Teaching and Learning Made Easy

Multiplication Teaching and Learning Made Easy, Additional Teaching and Learning Made Easy, $6.95 each for home edition. Multiplication, addition flash cards, $2.95 each set. Computer disks for IBM, Commodore 64, and Apple, $29.95 each.

Multiplication Teaching and Learning Made Easy, a program originally designed for the classroom, now has been updated for the home. The complete program teaches kids all the multiplication facts in six weeks and includes:

- A simple, effective philosophy of how to teach multiplication

- Teacher's Manual with detailed instructions, daily lesson plans, six complete games, and two bulletin board ideas

- Coloring/Activity Book (bound together with the Teacher's Manual in the set I received). This includes 18 color-by-number pictures, 12 "just fun" coloring sheets, and activity sheets

- File folder games, bulletin board ideas, incidental learning suggestions, and other classroom-oriented extras

- Precoded flash cards for the weekly drills

- Three computer games for the computer: *Heart Chase* (basic), *Flash Fill* (intermediate), and *Math Invaders* (advanced).

This program was too pricey for the home market, so the publisher listened to us and came out with a very affordable home edition. Now you can get the teacher's instructions, lesson plans, games, coloring and activity pages, and so on all in one handy workbook, and for just a few bucks more get a set of flash cards as well. The computer games are also available separately now.

The formatting and layout of *Multiplication Teaching and Learning Made Easy* are excellent. The philosophy is easy to follow, also. You start by explaining that multiplication means adding the same number again and again, and showing students on a multiplication table that they do *not* need to memorize many of the facts (like 0 times, 1 times, and 10 times), since simple rules govern these multiplications. You also cross off the duplicate facts on the table (e.g., 3 x 4 = 4 x 3, so there is no need to memorize them separately). You then concentrate on a few facts each week in *random* order (to prevent guessing and counting), using color by number, flash cards, activities, tests, and games to reinforce the facts. If you have a computer, you can go one step farther and get the computer disk. Then use the three computer games on your disk for math fact drill.

Addition Teaching and Learning Made Easy is also now available, teaching the addition facts with a similar approach.

ARITHMETIC PRACTICE

Educational Insights
Primary Math Games, Intermediate Math Games, each $29.95/set of 3 included games. *Plus 'n Minus Games*, $14.95. *Thinkfast!, Gotcha!, Capture the Flags*, $6.95 each. *Presto Change-O*, $24.95. Available in teachers' stores and school supply catalogs.

Primary Math Games is a set of three games—*Sum Buddies* for basic addition, *Minus Maze* for subtraction, and *Time Out* for time telling—all colorful and actually fun to play. *Plus 'n Minus Games* is math drill made painless as students must add and subtract to find their way around the game board. The double-sided board (one for addition, one for subtraction) comes with a reproducible activity workbook.

Intermediate Math Games consists of *Prehistoric Times* (multiplication), *Dinosaur Division* (division), and *Ballpark Figures* (estimating skills).

Thinkfast!, Gotcha!, and *Capture the Flags* are high-speed math competition using all four basic arithmetic processes: addition, subtraction, multiplication, and division. *Thinkfast!* is for two players only, and can be played using addition only, or subtraction only, etc. In *Capture the Flags!* players roll dice and try to capture the cards laid down by finding one that equals any combination of the dice. If the numbers 2 and 3 are rolled, for instance, you can take a 5 (2 + 3), a 1 (3 - 2), or a 6 (2 x 3). But you have to be the first! *Gotcha!* players win by capturing the opponent's cards. If my 4 and 2 equal your 5 and 1, I can take them—if you don't figure it out first!

Presto Change-O helps kids learn to make change as they roam about the game board collecting an allowance, doing chores for cash, and blowing their stash on treats.

Golden Educational Center
Designs in Math: Addition, Subtraction, Multiplication, Division, $5.45 each. Shipping 10%, $2 minimum. Grades 2–8.

Right-brain math drill. Connect the dots from problems to solutions to create an intriguing design on each page. The correction key on each left-hand page tells you if you did it right. Once successful, color your design in, make it into string art, pound it into submission as a nail sculpture. Reproducible problem pages. A math drill kids will *ask* to do.

NEW**
Harlan Enterprises
Games, $3.50 each. Grades 1–6.

A bunch of card drill games, each packed in an attractive clear plastic box and sporting the same user interface, and each game printed a different color. You get a pack of sturdy 2¼ x 3½" cards. An answer card, so kids can play without calling on you constantly for the answers. All games are played in the same way, by matching an answer on one card to a question on another. Two to four players can play either by drawing cards from a stack á la Old Maid, or by laying them face down and turning over two at a time to try to make a match á la Concentration.

Each arithmetic operation is covered in several games. If you want to drill all the addition facts from 1 + 1 up to 12 + 12, for example, you will need to get six games. Game 1 is *Addition Fun: Numbers 1 & 2.* This covers 1 + 1 up to 2 + 12. Cards demonstrate the associative property, e.g., the 2 + 3 card also displays 3 + 2. The other Addition Fun games are *Numbers 3 & 4, Numbers 5 & 6, Numbers 7 & 8, Numbers 9 & 10,* and *Numbers 11 & 12.* The Subtraction Fun games are

Numbers 1, 2, 3, 4, & 5 (1 - 0 through 5 - 5); *Numbers 6, 7, & 8* (6 - 0 through 8 - 8); *Numbers 9 & 10;* and *Numbers 11 & 12.* Multiplication Fun games are *Numbers 1 & 2* (1 x 0 through 2 x 12); *Numbers 3 & 4; Numbers 5 & 6; Numbers 7 & 8; Numbers 9 & 10;* and *Numbers 11 & 12.* Division Fun includes *Numbers 1 & 2* (1 ÷ 1 through 12 ÷ 2; some pairs have remainders); *Numbers 3, 4, & 5;* and *Numbers 6, 7, 8, 9, 10, 11 & 12.* Other math games include *Money Fun* (matching a card with varying numbers of dollars and coins to an "amount" card) and *Telling Time* (match the clock face to the digital time).

Don't try to use these games to improve math calculation speed—the format does not lend itself to this. Do use them to help your kids learn the basic math facts in a fun, non-stressful way.

Home Run Enterprises
Math Mouse Games, $21.95 postpaid for 9 basic games plus variations. *Penny-Wise,* $3.50 postpaid (only $2.50 when ordered with Math Mouse Games). Grades K–6.

Christian math games? Who ever heard of such a thing! Well, you have now. This appealing set of games did start out as a kitchen table job, developed by a Christian home schooling family, but that just increases its charm. (The games are now professionally printed in full color.)

Cathy Duffy, a versatile lady whose *Curriculum Manuals* I have reviewed in Volume 1 and who contributed several of the reviews in Volume 3, is the inventor of the Math Mouse Games. Her only distinctively Christian game is the *Gardening* game, where Scripture references to sowing, weeding, watering, and reaping are included on the game board. The other games are math drill with a lot of soul. In *Grocery Store,* for example, you visit the four food groups and try to spend a total of $40 on your trip. But be careful:

you can't spend more than $10 in each category! *Grocery Store* is played with a game board, pawns, dice, and Math Mouse Money. The set as a whole contains six game boards, printed back to back on folding cardboard, a fraction/decimal card deck, four special dice, a number line, pawns, spinner, play money, round markers to cover up spaces in some games, and an instruction book. Games are *Gardening, Grocery Store, Blast Off, Space Race, Roll a Problem, Multiplication Board, Add Off, Fractions and Decimal War,* and *Gobbling Fractions.* All basic math concepts are practiced. The learner also gets an introduction to economics in the grocery store and the garden.

For those with young preschoolers, Home Run Enterprises offers *Penny-Wise,* an additional file folder game designed especially for young children just learning to count.

These games are really cute and kid-appealing. You get a lot for your money.

KNEXT Card Game Company
KNEXT game, $7 postpaid.

Less than 8; greater than 10; equal to 6; not equal to 12. Mix together 108 colorful playing cards, add some game rules, and what do you have? The *KNEXT* card game, for 2 to 8 players, ages 7 to adult. Each card has a condition (e.g., LT for less than), a number (0–16), and a special instruction in the center of the card. Each player is dealt a number of cards (varies with number of players). The rest of the cards are put in a neat pile, and the top card is turned over to start the discard pile. You then have to meet the condition(s) on that card in order to play a card. First to empty his hand wins. The rules, which include several semi-complicated rules for multiple condition cards (e.g. LT 3 and RED, or GT 4 and LT 9), take a while to master,

but then play is both fast and tricky. Professional-quality playing cards, and you get a *lot* of practice in mathematical logic.

Learning Systems Corporation
Seventy-nine-cent workbooks. Shipping 10%; $1 on orders under $10.

These professional two-color miniworkbooks are excellent for the home schooling family that needs to pinch pennies. Each skill is clearly presented in just a few pages along with exercises for practice. Because the workbooks are so small, there is no danger of boredom. Also, your learner gets an instant sense of accomplishment when he masters a new skill. Instead of just finishing a chapter, or section of a chapter, in a massive textbook, he finished a whole workbook! This sense of having completed a task is vital to keep a youngster's motivation strong.

Math miniworkbooks include Time, Money, Place Value, Addition with Regrouping, Subtraction with Regrouping, Fractions, Word Problems, English Measurements, Metric Measurements, and a number of workbooks on multiplication and division of whole numbers and fractions, materials on decimals, percent, graphing, and geometry. You can't beat the price and they cover the field.

Margwen Products
Match-A-Fact card games. *Addition, Subtraction, Multiplication, Division,* $9.95 each. Set of all four, $36. $3.50 shipping for first game, 50¢ each additional game.

Instead of dull, dreary flash cards, why don't you try *Match-A-Fact* for your math drill? Each set of cards comes with nine games: *Concentration, Winner Takes All*

(War), *Lucky Seven* (Old Maid), *Draw One* (Go Fish), *Solitaire* (two versions), *Match-A-Fact*, *Beat the Clock*, and *Flash Card Frustration*. You get a problem deck (cards with math problems like 2+5 on them), an answer deck (whole number cards—1, 2, 3 . . .), a self-checking answer key, instruction booklet, and progress chart. *Match-A-Fact* is no kitchen-produced job, either. The cards are real playing card quality, and the packaging would look quite at home in any school supply store.

How does it work? Some games use both decks, some just one. For *Winner Takes All*, children deal out the cards in the "problem" deck. The child whose answer is a higher number takes both cards. You remember the game from your youth. Thus 8-1 beats 5-4, for example. Children can resort to the answer key if they forget the answer. You can see how much drill they will get in math facts from just this one game! *Concentration* involves spreading all the cards in both decks face down, and turning over two at a time. If you match a problem with its answer, you get to keep the cards. This is an excellent memory drill as well as a math drill. Don't forget, each box has seven more games, plus you can make up games of your own.

Match-A-Fact has gone over big wherever it has been used. Children request it for birthday presents, and parents who see it used at school buy their own copies for home. It really is fun to use, and not much more expensive than a batch of commercial flash cards.

NEW★★
Old Fashioned Crafts
Muggins, $29.95 postpaid. Ages 7 to adult.

Muggins is an arithmetic drill and thinking skill game played with marbles on a beautiful wooden board. The board has a groove around it (for marble storage while playing), and 36 numbered holes.

The object of *Muggins* is to get your marbles in as many rows as possible, while blocking your opponent's attempts to do the same. You move by rolling three dice and (1) adding, subtracting, multiplying, or dividing the numbers on the first two, and then to that total doing the same with the third die. E.g., if your numbers are 2, 6, and 3, some possible moves are:

• Divide the 6 by the 2, add the 3. (Answer: 6)

• Multiply the 2 by the 3, multiply by six. (Answer: 36)

• Add the 2 and the 6, subtract the 3. (Answer: 5)

You move your marble into that slot on the board.
There are a few other rules, such as the automatic "bump," where anyone rolling triples gets to remove one of his opponent's marbles, but you get the general idea.
New variations now included in *Muggins*:

• *Muggins, Jr.* (for kids ages 7–9): add and subtract only, using the three included 12-face polyhedrons.

• *Super Muggins* (advanced skill level): add, subtract, multiply, and divide using the polyhedrons.

• *Dishes* (motivational version): dice is thrown only once. Players alternate making totals. First player unable to make a new total has to do the dishes!

• *Bluffing* (optional): encourages players to check each other's math for continual involvement.

Unlike all other math board games I have seen, *Muggins* is fast-paced, uses all the arithmetic operations, and involves a lot of mental math and strategy. Plus it's elegant, in a rustic, unstained kind of way. High-class math drill for families with brains who aren't afraid to use them.

Wff 'n Proof Learning Games Associates
Equations game, $17.50. *Real Numbers*, $5.50. *Wff 'n Proof*, $22.50. Imp Kits: 1 kit, $1.50; 5 kits, $6.50; 10 kits, $12.50; all 21 kits, $22.50. All prices postpaid. Ages 7 (smart kids) to adult.

Equations is the ultimate math game. You win by never winning, by never making it impossible to win, and by never letting your opponent win. Does this sound just a trifle confusing? *Equations can* be hard to figure out at first, but let's persevere in the knowledge that inner-city fourth graders have figured it out.

Briefly: The game comes with number cubes, symbol cubes, a game mat, an instruction manual, and an efficient and elegant carrying case. You roll the cubes. One player sets the "Goal" using the cubes. This will be a number, such as 2. On each following move, one cube must be put in the "Forbidden" or "Permitted" or "Required" area of the game mat. The remaining cubes are the "Resources." The idea is to make only moves that don't allow a solution to be built with the addition of only one more cube, and that don't prevent a solution from ever being built. You can challenge another player's previous move as violating these rules, or you can try to trap him by deliberately violating a rule yourself. It's actually not hard to follow, once you've worked through a couple of the sample matches in the manual.

The beauty of *Equations* is that it forces the players to continually make creative arithmetic calculations. You have to consider *all* the possible arithmetic combinations that can be built with the allowed cubes. In the classroom, students quickly develop math strategies in order to help their teams win *Equations* tournaments. At home, you can discover these strategies with Wff 'n Proof Imp Kits, instructional math play solitaire kits that each teach a specific mathematical lesson from the *Equations* game.

Real Numbers is a handy and very inexpensive introduction to *Equations*. You get colored number and symbol cubes cleverly clipped to a ballpoint pen, plus an instruction booklet that shows you how to play the game with real, rational, irrational, integer, and natural numbers. Smart and motivated kids six years old can play the easiest of the five games that come with it.

And don't let's forget *Wff 'n Proof*. It sounds like the name of a Saturday morning cartoon show, but actually Wff stands for Well Formed Formula and Proof means logical proof. It's a beautiful game for your family or to give as a gift—actually, 21 beautiful games, since the kit comes with an instruction manual listing 21 games of increasing complexity. Six-year-olds can play the first game (*Wff*), and from then on it gets steadily hairier. *Wff 'n Proof* is a game of logic: if this, then that. Physically, it is 36 colored cubes with letters and funny symbols on them and a one-minute timer with pink sand in it,. Mentally, it's a real workout that has been shown to *raise IQ by up to 20 points* in dedicated players.

It's only fair to warn you that these are *very* brain-intensive games. If you don't have at least two people in your family who enjoy math logic puzzles, you'll probably try these games for a bit, then put them aside. For those with a mathematical turn of mind, though, or for serious *assigned* math training in your home school, these games are an intellectual order of magnitude above the competition.

ARITHMETIC SPEED DRILLS

NEW*
Basic R's
Addition and Subtraction facts sets (4 drill boards), grades preK–4, $14. Multiplication, Time, Weight, Length & Measurement facts (3 drill boards), grades 4–12, $10.50. Facts Master set of all 7 drill boards, $21. Add $3 shipping.

Here's a new way to teach (not just drill) the basic math facts.

The Facts Master set comes with a drilling board for Addition Facts 1–10, Addition facts 11–20, Subtraction Facts 1–10, Subtraction Facts 11–20, Multiplication Facts 1–10, Multiplication Facts 11–20 (e.g., from 11 x 1 up to 20 x 10), and a board for drilling time, weight, length, and liquid measurements.

Each Facts Master board is really a pocket into which the child slides a sheet of paper. Math facts are listed in columns on the board, with windows next to each column of facts.

The child is supposed to copy the entire arithmetic expression next to its original. If, for example, the column is the six-times table, the child will copy 6 x 1 = 6, 6 x 2 = 12, and so on down the paper. He is then given ten minutes to copy every expression on the board. The number of columns he manages to complete is marked on the personal progress chart on the back of the Facts Master board.

Along with samples of the boards themselves I received numerous enthusiastic testimonials about how public-school children had increased in basic math skills while using these boards. Boring it might be, but the method seems to work.

You don't, of course, assign your child ten minutes of each board every day. This would take an hour a day! Instead, Facts Master inventor Jivan Patel recommends that a child continue with the same board until he is able to pass a timed test of math facts. (In other words, CalcuLadder works beautifully with this program.) He then gets to move on to the next board.

Since the activity only takes 10 minutes once or twice a day, it's an OK time filler for those dead minutes while waiting for the table to be set for supper, etc.

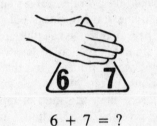

$6 + 7 = ?$

$13 - 6 = ?$ $13 - 7 = ?$

NEW**
Creative Teaching Associates
Triangle Flash Cards, $4.75 each for addition/subtraction set or multiplication/division set. Add 10% shipping ($3 minimum).

Four at one blow . . . four arithmetic facts, that is. Triangle Flash Cards are a new idea in math fact drill. The quickest way to explain them is to give you an example.

Let's say we have some traditional arithmetic flash cards. One card would say "2 + 3" on the front. Flip it over and you'd find the answer "5." Another would say "3 + 2." You would also have a set of subtraction facts cards, including "5 - 3" and "5 - 2." All these four math facts are shown on *one* Triangle Flash Card. In the top angle of the triangle is a red 5. In the bottom two angles are a black 3 and 2. To use these cards, tell the kids that you add together numbers of like color, and subtract different colors. Then cover one corner of the card to create an arithmetic problem. Let's say you cover the lower right-hand corner. Then the problem becomes 5 - 3 = ?. Move your hand to uncover the answer. In this way, 120 math facts can be covered on just 20 cards.

The multiplication/division set works in exactly the same way, except that the top number is blue instead of red. This makes it easy to keep from accidentally mixing the decks, or to even drill all four operations at the same time.

The Triangle Flash Card approach not only cuts down on the amount of memorizing by a factor of four, but introduces kids to mathematic principles right from the start.

NEW**
Dale Seymour Publications
Mental Math in the Primary Grades. Mental Math in the Middle Grades, $8.95 each.

Mental math is, quite simply, arithmetic calculations done in your head instead of with fingers, paper and pencil, or calculator. The *McGuffeys* generation used to do lots of mental math, in the belief that it increases both math speed and general mental abilities. *They* could cipher beautifully. Today, most kids can't. Case closed.

So, how do you do mental math with a workbook? *Mental Math in the Primary Grades* spends quite a bit of space teaching basic math concepts and practicing such examples as, "I'm thinking of two parts that total 7. One of them is a 2. What is the other part?" If I were you, I'd settle for simply orally giving "chain" problems (I'll explain what these are in a minute) and plan on starting with *Mental Math in the Middle Grades*. A chain problem is something like "1 + 4 - 3 + 2 + 5 - 7 . . ." and so on, its length and the size of the numbers used and the choice of operations geared to the skill level of the student. Chain problems can easily become games when you add the element of timing (how fast can I say it and have you get it right?) or competition (which of you can get the answer first?).

Mental Math in the Middle Grades, besides a bigger and brighter format and less teacher busywork, also includes more problem-solving strategies, good for quick solutions of mental math problems. For example, when adding, say, 35 + 48, turn 48 into 45 + 3. Then add 35 + 45 and tack on 3. Presto! 83. Or, if adding 98 to 65, change 98 into 100 - 2 first. Your answer then becomes 100 + 65 - 2 = 163.

Each book has 36 lessons, enough for one per week for a school year. Each lesson has two reproducible pages: a lesson page for introducing new math strategies and a Power Builder page with two sets of practice problems. You don't have to do all the exercises, but if you want to, the answers are in the back.

NEW★★
Kumon Mathematex
Monthly fee, around $50/student last time I checked.

Kumon Mathematex is a systematic set of worksheets invented by a Japanese math teacher named Mr. Toru Kumon. It all started when his own son got a bad grade on a second-grade worksheet. Investigating, Mr. Kumon discovered the same infection of "enrichment" clutter and New Math in his son's math text that has undermined math ed here in the good old USA. So he devised a series of worksheets, concentrating solely on calculation ability, with the ultimate goal of allowing his son to proceed step by step until he could solve all high school math problems (Japanese high-school math is like college math here in the dumbed-down

USA). The idea was to work through one sheet a day under trained adult supervision. The next day the student would self-correct any problems the adult had marked incorrect. This process is repeated until the student can do that worksheet perfectly in an allotted time period. He then goes on to the next worksheet. This takes about 20 minutes a day for young children, and 30-40 for older ones.

In Japan, Kumon Mathematex is used by about 1.3 million schoolchildren at present, all studying in classroom settings run by approved Kumon instructors (generally outside school hours). The sad and unfortunate thing is that Kumon is trying to sell the same approach here in America, charging a monthly fee to "tutors" who then are expected to hunt up students and sit with them every day. This means that home schoolers can't just buy the worksheets. Instead, they want you to attend a Kumon seminar and pay a rather steep monthly fee for each child enrolled. This entitles you to get the needed worksheets doled out in one-month-at-a-time batches. I couldn't get it through their heads that they would probably have 100 times as many people using it (of course, at less profit per child) if they would make the series available directly to parents.

Kumon *sounds* like a wonderful system. It starts with exercises in line drawing and use of puzzles, and progresses all the way through calculus and statistics (see what they do in high school in Japan)? You don't get geometry and word problems, but that's no big deal, as they should be taught in a different way anyway. Furthermore, I know this kind of approach works, because my father used a similar method with me when I was six years old that took me all the way to eighth-grade math (just short of algebra) in one summer. (Unhappily, I have not been able to find the math series he used with me, or I would recommend it to you!) However, the folks at Kumon are treating this series of theirs like it is gold and are *not* making it easy for home schoolers to obtain, or even to review. When I asked for a review set, I was told that I could only obtain scattered worksheets from different levels, which is no good at all for review purposes, since the value of the program depends almost entirely upon how good a job Mr. Kumon has done of systematically moving from one step to the next, not on how good any individual worksheet might be.

So I am frustrated—unable to recommend what sounds like it could be a great program because of the Kumon management's refusal to let me review it or let you have it except on what, to me, seem exorbitant terms.

NEW**
Providence Project

$15.95 per CalcuLadder unit (specify grade level: grades 1–6 available). It's a good idea to start *below* your child's grade level to build up confidence and make sure he *really* knows what he's doing. MasterPak 1 (guides, keys, and copy masters for ReadyWriter and CalcuLadders 1–3), $23.95. MasterPak 2 (guides, keys, and copy masters for AlphaBetter and CalcuLadders 4–6), $23.95. Shipping extra.

However, all is not lost. Before I ever heard of Kumon I and the kids had been having a wonderful time with Providence Project's CalcuLadder Series. Providence Project is not as fancy or hyped as Kumon—but then, it's $15.95 for a year's worth of math worksheets, as opposed to Kumon's $50 per child per month—and it uses the same exact approach. What you get is a set of calculation drill sheets, starting with numeral recognition in level one and winding up with fractions, percents, and all that other lovely pre-algebra stuff in level six. Each level consists of 12 copies of 16 different worksheets. Your child works a sheet once a day until he can get it all right in the allotted time (between 2-5 minutes). Then he gets to tackle the next sheet. Grading is super-simple with the QuicKeys™ grading key (just turn around the sheet, lining up the rows, and instantly see if your answer is correct). An Instructor's Guide is included for each set. Colored paper, cute visuals in the margins, and a Bible verse on the bottom of each page are freebie extras. The whole program only takes about five minutes a day, and let me tell you, it really does increase calculation ability and speed! Plus, each level now comes neatly spiral-bound, so you won't be chasing worksheets all over the house. The series doesn't go as far as Kumon, but I'm pestering Dr. Ed Meyers, the highly-credentialed American genius who invented CalcuLadder, to extend it farther. If he gets around to this, the Kumon people may find themselves wishing they had been a little freer with their materials from the start.

I recommend this supplemental program for all home schoolers whose children are anything short of supersonic in their math computation speed and understanding.

- CalcuLadder 1: Basic addition and subtraction for grades 1 and 2 or remedial. 2- and 3-minute drills.

- CalcuLadder 2: Advanced addition and subtraction and basic multiplication. Grades 2 or 3 or remedial, 3- and 4-minute drills.

- CalcuLadder 3: Intermediate and advanced multiplication and basic division. Grades 3 and 4 or remedial, 4- and 5-minute drills.

- CalcuLadder 4: Advanced multiplication review, intermediate and advanced division, place values, product estimation, basic fractions, and decimals. Grades 4 or 5 or remedial. 5-minute drills.

- CalcuLadder 5: Advanced division review, intermediate and advanced fractions. Grades 5–7 or remedial. 5-minute drills.

- CalcuLadder 6: Fractions review, percents, English & metric units, pre-geometry, more. Grades 6–8 or remedial. 5-minute drills.

NEW**
Shekinah Curriculum Cellar

Holey Cards, set of 4. Shipping extra. Grades 1–6.

Math facts drill can't be simpler or cheaper than this. You get four durable cards, each folded in the middle, each with 100 arithmetic problems printed on it. Under each problem is a literal hole in the card. When you close the card on the fold line, the white backside of the card shows through. The parent first solves all the problems in light pencil, writing them "inside the hole" (i.e., on the backside of the facing card). Then, the student places a half sheet of paper between the sides of the card and tries to solve all the problems in two minutes or less. Do it every day and keep a record to see how your student is speeding up!

With this type of repeated drill, there's a slight danger that some children will begin to memorize the first answers rather than working them. To avoid this, have them start the front of the card one time, the back another time, or have them work from the top one time and from the bottom another time, or vary working from right to left and left to right.

The Holey Cards set includes separate cards for addition, subtraction, multiplication, and division.

NEW✷✷
TREND Enterprises, Inc.
Spin 'n Learn Flash Cards, $3.99 a set. Add $2 shipping.
Minimum order $10. Grades 1–6.

TREND's *Spin 'n Learn* flash cards give math practice a new twist! Each self-checking flash card has a wheel in back. Turn the wheel to create a problem, check on the back for the answer! The multiplication set, for example, includes nine cards, one each for times 1, times 2, etc. For added fun, each flash card is shaped like a colorful electronic gizmo. For math practice, the series includes Addition (cards look like robots), Subtraction (space ships), Multiplication (computer), Fractions (video game), and Telling Time (video game).

PART VI

SCIENCE

CHAPTER TWENTY-NINE

NATURE STUDY

Did you ever lie on your back in a meadow watching the clouds go by? Did you ever sit on your front step, or on the sidewalk, or a patio, and watch ants carrying crumbs back to their home? Did you ever pick buttercups with your friends and hold them under your chins to see who liked butter? Did you ever make a daisy chain, or a wreath of dandelions? Did you ever chase a toad . . . and catch him . . . and let him go? Did you ever, shuddering with your bravery, hold a worm or daddy-long-legs in your hand? Did you ever call the family to the window to point out a beautiful sunset or the first robin of spring?

That, my friend, is Nature Study. In the years BTV (Before Television), it came naturally to kids everywhere. Some of us had greater opportunities than others, of course—but trees even grow in Brooklyn.

Every kid instinctively knows dandelions were created so kids can blow their fluffy white seeds all over the playground, and that the winged seeds of the maple tree, when thrown into the air, make very acceptable little helicopters, twirling around and around until they hit the ground. Acorns and chestnuts are a find always treasured in grubby little pockets, as are rocks of odd shapes and colors, beetles (traditionally kept in matchboxes), and autumn leaves of especially pretty colors.

In the great Nature Enthusiasm which swept the Victorian world, educators preached that children needed countless hours freely roaming in nature. This would, it was thought, develop their abilities to observe, as well as their spiritual and moral natures. Christian educators like Charlotte Mason pointed to the biblical examples of King David and Christ's frequent use of illustrations from nature in His sermons. Those of a more pagan bent waxed lyrical about "the great temple of the outdoors."

Today there is a revival both of the Charlotte Mason school of thought and the New Age pagan outlook. In a world of increasing bureaucratic complexity, it is not at all surprising that many people find comfort in simply sitting and contemplating a tree. Sharing such experiences with children has been a mini-industry ever since Robert Stephenson Smyth Baden-Powell founded the Boy Scouts in 1908 and the "camps" movement was firmly established in the 1940s. Nature study, many feel for various reasons, is an important corrective to the increasingly dehumanized, technical, confined life children lead.

NATURE STUDY

NEW★★
Carol Oppenheim
Science is Fun!, $9.50 postpaid. Ages 3–10.

This breezy, hand-lettered book of science discoveries for young kids and their moms covers nature walks, exploring, collecting, saving, trees, garden and house insects, windowsill gardening, recycling and conservation, fitness, and simple cooking experiments. Typical activity:

Earthworms!
Hold a cool, moist, wiggling earthworm in your hand. [Smiley face picture] Be gentle - - it can't hurt you. If you show the children that it is fun, they will try it, too!
[Picture of earthworm, identifying clitellum (band in the middle of the worm) and castings (earthworm droppings]
Earthworms are interesting and helpful.
• They work like plows mixing and loosening the soil.
• They don't have eyes or ears but they can tell light from dark and feel every vibration.
• They have no bones or lungs. Oxygen passes through their skin.
• They have 5 pairs of hearts.
• Their castings (elimination) enrich the soil.

Dig Up A Few Earthworms
Put them in a box with a thin layer of soil.
Watch how they move - - - examine them with a magnifying glass - - - look for the clitellum - - - let them go so they won't dry out!
• Earthworms must be moist or they will die.

All the book is on this simple, enthusiastic, direct level. No gross "Squirmy Science" activities—lots of respect for God's creation. None of the activities takes a lot of time or gets very complicated for either mom or child. Great backyard and kitchen science for this age group.

NEW★★
Children's Small Press Collection
Wintersigns in the Snow, Pond Life, Spring Signs, $5.95 each. Shipping extra. Grades 2 and up.

Years ago, when we were buying some used carpet, we met a man from Wisconsin and got to talking about his home state. When asked why he now was living in Missouri, he complained that Wisconsin was "too cold, too windy, winter lasts forever."

Well, count your blessings, you Northerners! Kids who live where it hardly ever snows can't use this book, *Wintersigns in the Snow,* to learn to track deer, rabbits, mice, mink, birds, and all sorts of critters.

Wintersigns tells you not only how to recognize tracks, with illustrations and even a special laminated card with the most popular animal tracks described, but how to recognize other signs of an animal's presence, such as nesting holes, broken bushes (from deer spurring with their antlers), droppings (how to tell which animal left it), and lots more. The book also is a condensed guide to Northern tree identification in winter, and details some winter wonders to watch for in the woods. Nothing else like it, especially at the price!

Pond Life, by the same author, helps you identify a wide variety of pond plants and animals, with a special section on easy-to-make gathering equipment. Also by the same author, *Spring Signs* helps you recognize the first, hidden signs of spring about you—the drumming of the ruffled grouse, stirrings of birds, mammals, and reptiles, the first woodland wildflowers to look for, and so on.

NEW★★
EDC Publishing
The Young Naturalist, $6.95 paperback. Ages 10 and up.

If any one book can introduce the entire field of nature studies to kids aged 10 and up, *The Young Naturalist* is the one. With the usual lively Usborne mix of text and illustration, facts and experiments, it covers

• Observing and recording—keeping a bird notebook, making a tree chart, and mapping mole hills, among other activities.

• Collecting natural objects and displaying them.

• Collecting and observing bugs.

• Breeding and observing the life cycles of tiny critters such as butterflies.

Projects include making nesting boxes and bird blinds, building an aquarium and formicarium (ant house), resurrecting an urban plot, pressing leaves, collecting and displaying spider webs, making plaster casts of animal tracks, and lots more.

The Young Naturalist is particularly strong on teaching nature observation skills. Simply reading through the book (not an easy task, with the wealth of information and illustration continually tempting you to browse!) will give you new eyes with which to view the natural world around you.

Don't underestimate this book. All the projects and activities, though worthwhile, require a fair degree of commitment. Country dwellers will also find it easier to do the activities, although the book includes indoor and urban activities as well.

NEW**
Fearon Teacher Aids
Nature Crafts Workshop, $8.95. Add $3.50 shipping. Grades 3–8.

Nature Crafts Workshop is a collection of more than 40 high-interest study and handicraft projects, all involving the student with living things. Projects span the whole field of nature: bugs, birds, animals, plants of various kinds, trees, reptiles, fish, amphibians, microscopic creatures, and animals. A number of the projects involve observing life processes (seeds and plants, caterpillars and moths, eggs and chicks). Some projects bring nature into your home (e.g., the aquarium and vivarium). Others get kids out in the field observing and collecting data (paw prints, field observations of birds, collecting and observing pond water). In the words of the introduction, "Each project is self-contained and fun, and each one yields a tangible item that kids can hang on the wall, give as a gift, or examine and study."

Teens can follow the illustrated project directions by themselves. Younger children will require more adult supervision.

Every project in the book is a classic. Your grandfather and grandmother probably did most of these things when they were young, from making applehead dolls and pressing wildflowers to making a nesting box and hatching chicks. Great stuff for rainy days and just plain celebrating life.

NATURE FACTS

NEW**
Christian Liberty Press
Nature Readers books 1, 3, 4, and 5, $2.95 each. Book 2, $2.50. Add 10% shipping ($1.50 minimum). Grades 1–5.

In Victorian times, adults wrote hundreds of books designed to spark children's interest in God's creation. Continuing in this tradition, the Christian Liberty Nature Reader Series "takes your children into the fascinating world of tiny creatures such as spiders, bees, hermit crabs, wasps, and turtles." One book each for grades 1–5.

EDC Publishing
Understanding Zoo Animals, $4.95 paperbound, $13.96 library bound. Mysteries and Marvels series (*Bird Life, Insect Life, Reptile World, Animal World, Ocean Life, Plant Life*), $5.95 each paperbound, $13.96 library bound. First Nature series (*Creepy Crawlies, Butterflies and Moths, Fishes, Birds, Flowers, Trees, Wild Animals*), $3.95 each paperbound or $11.96 each library bound, or combined into *The First Book of Nature*, $12.95. Shipping extra. Grades 1–8, or younger if you read to them.

As frequently mentioned elsewhere in this book, the Usborne series from England is the most colorful, exciting, educational line of "fact books" around. EDC publishes the series in the USA, and I hope they sell ten million or so.

The Usborne line covers just about every school subject—only these books are *interesting*. What you get is top-quality full-color artwork on every page, with text all around the artwork giving all kinds of fascinating details about the subject. Generally each book progresses beyond a mere collection of facts, with several sections introducing the subject and overviewing it. These books are so well organized that little children can actually remember much of the vast trove of information.

In the natural-science area, Usborne offers several series for different age levels. (My personal experience indicates that 32-year-olds should be included in these age levels!) *Understanding Zoo Animals* tells us how zoo animals are cared for and gives tips on animal behavior. Lots of lovely and amusing illustrations, lots of information. The Mysteries and Marvels series is a show stopper—as the catalog says, it's a "dramatic and detailed look at the amazing, the unexplained, and the mysterious in nature." *Mysteries and Marvels of Ocean*

Life, for example, has chapters on ocean giants, the miniature sea world, twilight and deep sea fish, lights and electricity, colorful characters, living together (symbiotes), mimics, marine hitchhikers, sea changes, the hunters' weapon, defence and escape, beware—poison!, unusual events, and record breakers. Throughout the book, true-or-false questions appear. These are finally answered in the back, just before the index. In theory, "these books will delight 8–11 year olds"; in practice, our two-year-old loves them as much as the rest of us do!

Moving along, the First Nature series has larger text and less detail, this being aimed at the six-and-up crowd. Get this series (either individually or in the durable combined volume) and you won't have to worry about what to do for science hour! Again, the illustrations are almost unbearably good and the text is filled with colorful details.

The price of these full-color books is, as you can see, unbelievably low. That's about the nastiest thing I can think of to say about these books. Bet you can't buy just one!

NEW★★
Educational Insights
Giant Step Picture Library, $9.95 each volume. Ages 4 and up.

I've heard it said that there really aren't many different kinds of dinosaurs. What happens is that a scientist, eager to make a name for himself, uncovers a variant of an already-known dinosaur type, and gives it a new name. Check the evidence for yourself with the *Dinosaurs* volume of the Giant Step Picture Library. These are *huge* picture books with 16 wipe-clean 16 x 20" pages each. *Dinosaurs* covers three hypothetical evolutionary time periods. See how few kinds you can break the 65 illustrated dinosaurs into. Then check out the *Wild Animals* book, with its nine different categories containing about 70 animals total, and the *Sea Life* book, with its 13 categories and 69 illustrations. Animals on each page are in no particular scale to each other.

Pages in the Giant Step Picture Library have a similar format to those in the Science Safari series (see below), with all illustrations labeled on a white background, but unlike the Science Safari books, these include no extra facts at the bottom of the page. Each book ends with a couple of activity pages in which children are exhorted to find and name the animals in the picture. Huge format is fun to look at while lying on the floor.

NEW★★
Educational Insights
Science Safari series, $3.95 each book or $29.95/set of eight. Ages 3–9.

Take the kids to the zoo without leaving your easy chair. Educational Insights' new *Science Safari* series has great full-color illustrations, each labeled with the name of the animal, plant, or whatever. At the bottom of the each page are fun facts about the animals (or whatever) shown on the page. At the end of the book are a few *very* simple activities of the find-the-critter-in-the-picture and match-this-part-to-the-right-critter sort.

Each 20-page book measures 8 x 11" jellyproof pages and includes over 100 full-color illustrations. They work best as first science books for pre-readers—lots to look at on each page. Older children will enjoy browsing through them, too. The illustrations, printed on shiny, wipe-clean pages, are really beautiful, with the exception of the *Birds* book, in which many birds unaccountably are pictured with snakes, spiders, and other yukkies dangling from their beaks. (OK—it might be good science, but if you want me to read a book to my kids, leave out the spider sandwiches!)

The *Science Safari* series includes *Sea Life, Birds, Fish, Dinosaurs, Wild Animals, Reptiles, Insects,* and *Exotic Animals.*

NEW★★
Frank Schaffer, Inc.
Floor puzzles, $12.95 each. Look and Learn series, $4.98 each workbook and poster combo.

I can't imagine a simpler, less-threatening way to introduce little kids to nature study than Frank Schaffer's Animal Life floor puzzles. Each 2 x 3' puzzle has 24 chunky, colorful pieces and fits neatly in a fairly sturdy storage box. *Animals and Their Babies* is a lush picture of a ewe and lamb, mare and colt, sow and piglets, cow and calf, hen and chicks, dog and puppies, duck and ducklings, goat and kid, and cat and kittens, all on country backgrounds. *Animals* highlights the giant panda, flamingo, blue whale, seal, tiger, blue jay, elephant, owl, lion, and more, on a white background. *Ocean Life* shows off unusual sea animals such as the octopus, starfish, manatee, and killer whale on an ocean background. Animals are not proportionately scaled to each other, as you probably realize, since there would be no way to picture a whale and a starfish on the same puzzle otherwise.

Frank Schaffer's new *Look and Learn* series is another way to involve your child in science while allowing him to practice basic readiness skills. Each page of each workbook has a large, captioned picture of an animal. Your child colors the animal and traces its name. That's all there is to it! According to the catalog, "This simple format teaches essential skills like fine motor and eye-hand coordination, vocabulary development, picture and word matching, reading, spelling, and categorizing." Each book includes a pull-out 17 x 22" full-color poster, which displays all animals in the workbook in their proper colors. The series includes *Dinosaurs, Ocean Life, Zoo Animals, Birds and Animals, Animals and Their Babies,* and *Reptiles.*

NEW**
Random House
Each Eyewitness volume, $12.95. Add $2 shipping first book, 50¢ each additional. Ages 10–adult.

The Eyewitness Books series is like a visual dictionary. Each oversized hardback book features a fantastic layout with hundreds of gorgeous full-color photographs and classic black-and-white engravings. Accompanying text provides background information; features of each illustrated item are pointed out with arrows and explanatory text.

Each double-page spread is a mini-chapter with maybe a dozen photographs, historical information, and lots of high-interest comments, plus a few classic engravings mixed in. Each book covers a lot of information in its 64 pages. Take, for example, the *Butterfly & Moth* volume. This book covers the butterfly's life cycle (with separate chapters devoted to such things as "The pupa stage" and "An emerging caterpillar"), butterflies and moths from different climate zones, migration and hibernation, camouflage and mimicry, endangered species, and how to raise butterflies and moths. The full-color photographs are absolutely exquisite, laid out so it appears the butterflies are actually sitting on the page. It's like a trip to the best butterfly and moth collection in the world, combined with an illustrated tour of a museum of lepidoptery! As in all the other volumes, there's an excellent, short index at the end.

These are gorgeous coffee-table books at one-fifth the price of a coffee-table book, and incredible educational resources as well. Kids *enjoy* browsing through the Eyewitness books, and can hardly help learning while so doing. Problem: the man-as-despoiler and state-as-solution viewpoint promoted in some of these volumes. In the *Butterfly & Moth* volume, for instance,

butterfly collecting is strongly discouraged while butterfly farms are not even mentioned as a possible method for reviving endangered species and maintaining existing ones. Such farms make it possible for collectors to keep on collecting, unlike the "greenie" approach which prefers to deny dominion over nature to people while allowing the animals to roam free. As the granddaughter of an accomplished butterfly collector (Cornell University now houses his collection), I also resent the book not even *telling* young people how to mount a butterfly. Come on, guys, the world is *full* of sulfur butterflies (the third stage of cabbage worms), and it won't hurt anything for Junior to have a couple in his room pinned to a piece of styrofoam. Practically *no* North American butterflies are endangered, anyway. A few kids in every suburb collecting butterflies won't make a dent in their population, compared to all the zillions of birds out there.

Those of us who still care about such things will also need to Magic Marker a naked goddess or mermaid or two in the old engravings (oh, those naughty Victorians!).

Science books in this series include *Butterfly & Moth, Pond & River, Tree, Bird, Rocks & Minerals, Shell, Seashore,* and *Plant.* Aggressively evolutionary offerings include *Skeleton* (which covers skeletons of both animals and humans), *Mammal, Early Humans* and *Dinosaur.* What I'd like to see for future volumes in this series: *Farm, Garden, Places* (i.e., a visual world tour) . . .

NEW**
Safari, Ltd.
Dinosaur Lotto, Ocean Lotto, Jungle Lotto, $8.90 each. *Ocean Pick-Up Pairs, Dino Pick-Up Pairs, Animal Pick-Up Pairs,* $8.90 each. Shipping extra. Ages 3 and up.

Learn nature identification painlessly with these cute card games from Safari, Ltd! First, the Lotto games. You know how to play Lotto. This version has lovely full-color photos for the versions featuring modern animals, and full-color pictures of the extinct beasties. You get four playing boards and 36 cards, all in a nice 8-inch-square box.

Second, the Pick-Up games. Here's how to play. Shuffle the cards and turn them over. (Actually, they are thick cardboard squares and you can't shuffle them, only kind of mush them around.) Turn them face down. Then pick two cards and turn them over. If they match, you get to keep them and pick another two cards to turn over. If not, you have to turn them face down again and the next player takes a turn. This game is wonderful for sharpening memory in even quite young children—and, as a bonus, you and your children will learn to identify dozens of critters. 96 cards per deck, 4 of each animal.

These games are commonly sold in museums and fancy gift shops. Now you can get them at home!

NEW★★
Safari, Ltd.
Dino Quiz, Ocean Quiz, Jungle Quiz, $5.90 each. Shipping extra. Ages 7 and up.

Here's a fun way to learn the answers to simple questions about wildlife past and present. Each of these quiz games consists of 36 different cards, each with eight questions and answers, packed in a 4¼ x 5¾" acrylic box. Sample questions:

1) Do LIONS hunts small animals?
2) LIONS live in groups called prides. A pride may consist of up to how many individuals?
     . . . .
8) Besides Africa, where else do LIONS come from?

The *Dino Quiz* game has evolutionary dating along with the full-color best-guess pictures and questions. The other games do not. Each quiz game comes with instructions for how to play, or you can just use them as fancy flash cards.

NEW★★
Safari, Ltd.
Animal Rummy games, $3 each. *Smithsonian Gem and Mineral Rummy,* $4. Shipping extra. Ages 6 and up.

Learn about nature with any of these acrylic-boxed rummy card games. Each includes 32 different animals. Each card has a beautiful color photo of the animal, plus its name and a fair chunk of interesting information about it. The *Savage Kingdom* animal rummy set, for example, tells you the length, weight, number of young, and lifespan of animals like panthers and gazelles, plus a mini-map showing where the animal lives and a brief paragraph describing its habits. Sets available are: *Undersea World, Mysteries of the Deep, Dinosaurs and Prehistoric Animals, Exotic Birds, Savage Kingdom, Vanishing Wild, North American Wildlife, Endangered Species, Animals of the Zoo, Snakes,* and *Hidden Kingdom.* Also available: *Smithsonian Gem and Mineral Rummy,* featuring items from treasures like the Hope diamond, to rose quartz, and copper in its natural form. Eight different categories from "Minerals Cut As Gems" to "Minerals in Fossils." Beautiful, durable, easy to keep neat—a fun way to learn.

Spizzirri Publishing
Activity/coloring books, 99¢ each. Educational coloring books, $1.95 each. Book/story cassettes, $4.98 each. Library albums (six educational coloring books and six cassettes), $34.95 each. Wall posters, $5.95 each. Floor puzzles, $14.95 each.

Your local natural history museum probably sells Spizzirri natural history coloring books and cassettes. But, just in case you don't toddle down to the museum every Tuesday, here's some more information.

Let's start with the little ones—your basic 99¢ activity/coloring books. These are actually *not* your normal basic coloring book, unless Hanna-Barbera decides to get into dot-to-dot whales and turtle mazes. (A turtle maze, in case you didn't know, is a turtle-shaped maze with the turtle pictured nearby and identified.) Next, the educational coloring books, a little matter of 63 titles covering such subjects as dinosaurs, prehistoric fish, state birds, animal giants, southeast Indians, and planets. These are, according to the publisher, "the only non-fiction coloring book/cassette packages available." Yes, you can get accompanying cassettes. These include sound, music, and professional narration.

NEW**
TREND Enterprises, Inc.
Each bulletin board set, $5.99, includes free Discovery Guide. Requires 4 x 6' bulletin board. Add 10% shipping. Minimum order $10. Ages 6–12.

Have I mentioned TREND's bulletin board sets before in this book? Sure I have. Well, here we go again with another neat line of sets—for nature study, this time.

I just hated to take the *Weather Elements* set down. This excellent visual aid teaches about air pressure, humidity, cloud formation, how to read a weather map, the water cycle, why we have seasons, and even weather folklore. Plus you get an activity guide with more ideas for teaching about weather! The design is incredibly clever, right down to the earth you can rotate on its axis to see how the distance of each part from the sun causes the seasons.

TREND's *Weather Around Us* set is not quite as detailed. Apparently designed for younger children, it shows the seasons, weather extremes, the water cycle, and other basic concepts. This set has more of an emphasis on understanding and being safe in extreme weather conditions than *Weather Elements*.

Solar System comes with 42 pieces. It's impossible to put the solar system in scale on a bulletin board (unless the planets are about the size of flea specks), but TREND tries to convey something of the size differences. The sun, for example, is not shown as a ball. Instead, you get a cutout with an edge-on view of the sun, illustrating just a small part of its outline—and

this cutout is four times as big as the earth cutout! Plus the inner-planets inset shows actual scale of these planets, along with Neptune and Uranus. Other solar system features, such as comets and the moons of the various planets, add some flash to this set. The accompanying guide provides lots of background information on the sun and each planet, plus some excellent study questions and activities.

How Plants Grow, a set for the stay-at-homes among us, packs a lot of information into a (relatively) small space. You get illustrations of the parts of a flower, how seeds and pollen are distributed, seasonal changes as they affect a tree, plants we eat, and lots of other stuff. The discovery guide makes this a complete plant science unit.

The *Wonders of Nature* set gives you colorful visuals illustrating wonders of animal life: migration, camouflage, hibernation, and so on. Cute basic nature science for little kids.

TREND also has two sets for sea dogs. *The Living Sea* presents over 40 marine animals. Punchouts include: sea animals shown at the ocean depth at which they live, their places in the food chain, their species, sea animals we eat, endangered sea life, and unusual sea critters. With *The Changing Sea* you get information about continental drift, an illustration of the ocean floor, fascinating facts about undersea volcanoes and tides, a picture of exploration equipment, and diagrams showing how men mine the sea. Again, the illustrations are superbly designed to communicate the content.

I can't figure out how TREND manages to produce such nifty visual aids for so little money. But that's not *our* problem, now is it? All we have to do is come up with the $5.99!

NEW**
Worldwide Slides
Most View-Master packets, $4.25 apiece. Battery-operated projector, $19.95. 3-D Viewer, $4.95. Slide sets, $2.50 each. Add 10% shipping. Ages 4 and up.

Do you remember that Christmas you got your first View-Master? Sure you do. Wasn't it fun to click the switch, advance the reel, and see the beautiful color display?

Most of us ended up with packs of cartoon reels as children. But View-Master also developed hundreds of packets of science and travel reels to go with their viewers. These are now available from Worldwide Slides.

The typical three-reel package includes 21 3-D images, all lovely pictures of famous or important sights. Some packages available: Los Angeles Zoo, Sea World Shows and Animals, Redwood Highway, Florida Everglades, Mammoth Cave (Kentucky), Glacier National Park (Montana), Animals in Our National Parks, Birds of the World, Sharks, Snakes, Wild Animals of the World (three sets), Wonders of the Deep. This is just the tip of the iceberg, as they offer dozens more nature-oriented View-Master reels.

For color slides, the Walt Disney Nature Series alone includes 34 sets (five slides in each set). Other nature and scenic slides are available.

With a View-Master projector, the whole family can go on a nature field trip from your living room. Or get the inexpensive standard viewers, point at a light source, and travel!

NATURE MAGAZINES FOR KIDS

National Geographic World
$12.95 U.S., $21.50 Canadian funds ($17.95 U.S. funds) per annum.

National Geographic World is a bright and beautiful kids' mag. Inside are stunning photos and interesting stories, some about nature and others about science, history, young achievers, and other subjects of interest to children. Mainstream editorial approach means I expect to see increasing "greenie" emphasis as time goes on.

World's adult counterpart, the *National Geographic* magazine itself, has some nature lore tucked in along with the sociology, politics, geography, and whatnot.

National Wildlife Federation
Ranger Rick (for kids 6–12); 12 issues $14. *Your Big Backyard* (for ages 3–5); 12 issues $10.

National Wildlife Federation's conservation agenda is strongly reflected in these two magazines for kids. Again, only time will tell whether the "greenie" anti-people approach or traditional conservation approach will predominate in this sort of magazine.

Ranger Rick is more like a "grown-up" magazine with feature articles, letters to the editor, and the like. *Your Big Backyard* comes wrapped in a "Parents' Letter" that has teaching suggestions for using the magazine. The photos are gorgeous and the activities are interesting. Both magazines have kid-appeal and are good value for money.

Nature Friend Magazine
$15/12 issues, $17 in U.S. funds for Canadian subscribers. Ages 4–14.

Aimed at readers from four to fourteen, this Christian magazine includes read-aloud stories, science articles, a readers' forum, child-submitted pictures and poems, "You Can Draw" pages that guide children to produce their own nature drawing, and activities, projects, and puzzles. With a creationist emphasis, and a smorgasbord of nature books and products offered for sale through the magazine, it sounds like everything a Christian family could wish for in a nature magazine.

Nature Friend's Nature's Workshop Catalog features tested nature-study products and books, plus some science equipment and art supplies. Books are either evolution-free or have "guideline sheets" included. Bird feeders, binoculars, ant farms, telescopes, microscopes, pocket knives, pocket compasses, nature study guides, nature coloring books, and lots more are all offered. Send $1 for catalog (refundable with first order).

DINOSAURS

Dinosaurs are a special subject. If you believe in frogs turning into princes, you will naturally want books and games that stress an evolutionary outlook. If not, you'll prefer creation science resources. If you haven't made up your mind one way or another, the unbiased truth is that the creation science materials are much more interesting . . . and now you'll know where to get them!

Aristoplay
Dinosaurs and Things, $22. *Paleo Pals*, $8.50. Shipping extra. Ages 4–7.

Dinosaurs and Things is an evolutionary board game for young dinosaur fans. You travel through the paleontological ages to the last gasp of the big reptiles.

The game ends when you reach the finish (symbolized by dinosaur skulls) and are the first to cover your side of the game board with Creature Cutouts. These last are jigsaw cutouts of dinosaurs that fit over pictures of the same dinos' skeletons. Littlest kids get to collect Creature Cutouts by simply landing on the right space during a roll of the die. Bigger kids have to answer a color-coded question pertaining to the reptile they hope to collect. Colorful four-piece game board, four fossil playing pieces, 36 Creature Cutouts, one die, nine Creature Question Cards, and a very thoroughly annotated bibliography and museum guide with extra questions for the game players. Fun to play for kids ages 4 and up, or anyone who needs to memorize evolutionary trivia to pass a test.

Paleo Pals, is a card game (36 full-color cards) with accompanying mini "Read-to-Me" book. Subject is, naturally, dinosaurs. You get instructions for four card games (Pairs, Memory, Dinosaur Hunt—like Go Fish, and Old Fossil—like Old Maid). Each card has its very own dinosaur. Book has some evolutionary content. Nice packaging fits manual and cards in same box.

Bible-Science Association
Membership: $22. Newsletter only, $12 student subscription, $15 others. Science Reader books, $6.95 each volume; add $1 shipping per book (minimum $2). Grades 1–12.

Series of creationist science readers designed to supplement the grades 1–12 curriculum. Seven volumes in all: doubled-up volumes for grades 9–10 and 11–12. The curriculum is spiral (that is, concepts and subjects are repeated in greater depth from grade to grade) and developmentally sequenced (e.g., coloring activities in the first-grade book, textbook-style articles in the senior high books). Topics repeated from grade to grade are:

- animals (various topics)
- birds (various topics)
- dinosaurs
- fossils
- Galapagos Islands
- insects (various topics)
- kinds (in the Biblical sense of separate animal groups that cannot cross-breed)
- life
- science and the scientific method
- space exploration.

To this, at different age levels, are added concepts of stewardship, reverence towards God and His creation, and arguments against evolutionary theory and evolutionary "proof texts," such as the Archaeopteryx and the famous Horse Series. Enjoyable activities in the lower grades, lots of interesting science facts (e.g., salamanders obtain moisture through their skin) at all ages. The proportion of creationist apologetics increases throughout the series. Young earth position. Small print and lower-quality reproduction in the eighth grade through senior high volumes. Well written. A good value.

NEW**
Christian Equippers
Unlocking the Mysteries of Creation, $18.95. Shipping extra. Grades 6–adult can read it on their own; read it aloud to younger children.

Incredible new creation science book. The engaging format combines illustrations, cartoons, text, and graphs; illuminating text unlocks the mysteries of the early earth and early civilizations. A wonderful book for reading aloud while your children look over your shoulder.

Unlocking the Mysteries of Creation grew out of author Dennis Petersen's creation science seminars, and thus has both lots of visual impact and an interactive, talk-to-the-reader style. Mr. Petersen evidently likes to keep his audience on the edge of its seat. Let's take a look at the "mysteries" he unlocks.

Section One, "Unlocking the Mysteries of the Early Earth," starts with an explanation of why it matters whether you believe in creation or evolution. It then proceeds to explain what really happened "In the Beginning" according to the Bible . . . why the early earth's climate could have been radically different . . . why volcanoes *weren't* present at the beginning, why radiometric dating methods aren't reliable (nor do they verify the approved Geologic Chart). "What Do Processes in Nature Tell Us About Earth's Age?" is an excellent section, showing the evidence from "geological clocks" such as interplanetary dust buildup, juvenile water, comets, oil deposit pressure, erosion, topsoil, coral reefs, the wearing away of the edge of Niagara Falls, stalactite growth in caves, igneous crust buildup, population studies, the magnetic field, dissolved minerals in the ocean, atmospheric helium, and so on. The section closes by giving evidence against the "Gap Theory" of creation.

Section Two, "Unlocking the Mysteries of Evolution," challenges the Big Bang theory, the idea that non-living matter produced life, the use of "Time" as the magic factor to make evolution plausible, the idea that random chance can produce increasing complexity, and the idea that simple forms develop into complex forms. In this section, he examines some famous "fossil links" such as the horse series, and the way geologists date rocks by the fossils while evolutionary biologists date fossils by the rocks. The section concludes with a look at three creatures—the bombardier beetle, and woodpecker, and the giraffe—each of which could not possibly have evolved, since they needed *all* their complex body systems to evolve at once in order to survive.

Section Three, "Unlocking the Mysteries of Original Man and the Missing Links," examines the famous "missing links" you learned about in school, and what's happened to this chart since. Why have some ancient human skeletons been ignored? What happened to the dinosaurs? Could man and dinosaurs live together? Were there really such things as dragons?

Section Four, "Unlocking the Mysteries of Ancient Civilizations," is my favorite part of the book. The "mystery" seems to keep cropping up: Why were ancient peoples *so advanced*—when in theory they should be just one step up from cave dwellers? This section includes amazing information on the technological achievements of ancient man, from the electric battery used by the Mesopotamians to 4,500-year-old examples of electroplating. How did ancient peoples like the race of giant dwellers in the Andes Mountains of Bolivia move 100-ton stones across rough terrain from a quarry 60 miles away? That, in turn, pales next to the building stones used in the temple at Baalbek, Lebanon, one of which weighs over 2,000 tons. Even with power equipment, modern engineers can't move anything that big! The list goes on and on, from the achievements of the Maya to those of China, Babylon, Egypt, Greece, and so on. Could it be that, instead of our modern doctrine of "continual progress," our ancestors actually knew more than we did about a lot of things? This section includes a time line showing how long the Biblical patriarchs lived, making it clear at a glance that the wisdom of previous generations was around for a *long* time!

None of the stuff in this book is weird "Chariots of the Gods" phoney baloney. Every fact is cited and sourced, often from sources as mainstream as *Reader's Digest* and *National Geographic*.

Unlocking the Mysteries of Creation will profoundly challenge your thinking, even if you already believe in creation science. If you *don't* already believe in creation science, it'll blow you away!

Institute for Creation Research
Dinosaurs: Those Terrible Lizards, $7.95 hardbound, full-color, illustrated. *Dry Bones,* $5.50. Two-model children's books, $3.95 each, Teacher's Guide for each $2.95. Shipping extra.

Major source of creation-science materials, all produced by scientists and writers associated with ICR. Large catalog, attractive and professional materials. ICR now has a strong line of creation science books for little kids. Some popular titles for younger children: *Dinosaurs: Those Terrible Lizards* (dinosaurs from a creationist viewpoint . . . including some mighty interesting speculations about what exactly were Leviathan and Behemoth), *Dry Bones . . . and Other Fossils* (find out all about fossils as you hunt 'em with the Parker family), and the two-model series designed for public schools that includes creation/evolution discussions on a kid's level (*Dinosaur ABC's, The Eye: A Light Receiver, Fossils: Hard Facts from the Earth,* and *Walk the Dinosaur Trail*).

NEW**
Institute for Creation Research
The Great Dinosaur Adventure Game, $24.95. Add 10% shipping.

The folks at Institute for Creation Research said they'd send me this game. They never did. However, I have the catalog copy in front of me, and this is what it says:

Most parents want to use their child's natural curiosity for dinosaurs as an effective teaching tool. Unfortunately, they find that a majority of popular dinosaur products being marketed to children promote the theory of evolution.

The Great Dinosaur Adventure Game takes you into a time before the Flood of Noah's day. It is a world filled with people, dinosaurs, and other strange animals. Make exciting discoveries as you find your way through the lands of Havilah, Assyria, Nod, and Cush on the path to Noah's Ark.

- 168 questions and answers on Creation Science and Bible history
- Play at two age levels (pre-school uses color matching)
- Rules for competitive and non-competitive play
- 2 to 8 players

NEW★★
Institute for Creation Research
Back to Genesis video series, $19.95 each video or $150 for all 11. Add 10% shipping.

I wouldn't want you to think that the folks at ICR never sent me *anything*. They did send me two of their Back to Genesis video seminar tapes.

What Really Happened to the Dinosaurs?, led by Ken Ham, is his presentation in front of a large group of elementary age children. Mr. Ham is an excellent speaker and teacher. Armed only with a craggy face and an Australian accent, he not only keeps the kids in line, but changes their minds about creation science before your very eyes! See the amazing Fossilized Hat (a miner's hat that fell into an Australian mine 70 years ago). Learn the one question an evolutionist hopes you'll never ask—"How do you know? Were you there?" Now everyone in our family can say Mr. Ham's definition of fossils,

> Billions of dead things
> Buried in rock lyers
> Lide down by wooter
> Owl ovah thee urth

just like an Australian!
Other videos in this series are addressed more to teens and adults. These include:

- *Ape-Men: Monkey Business Falsely Called Science*, debunking the ape-to-man sequence still taught in textbooks (by Michael Girouard)

- *Ayres Rock and Other Exciting Evidences for the Flood in Australia* (by Andrew Snelling)

- *Creation Evangelism* (Ken Ham)

- *The Dinosaur Mystery Solved* (John D. Morris)

- *Fascinating Design: Evidence for Creation* (Michael Girouard)

- *Genesis and the Decay of the Nation—The Relevance of Creation* (Ken Ham)

- *Genesis 1–11: An Overview—The Most-Asked Questions on Genesis Answered* (Ken Ham)

- *Is Life Just Chemistry?* (Michael Girouard)

- *The Long War Against God* (Henry M. Morris)

- *Why Death and Suffering?—and Six Other Questions Christians Must Answer* (Michael Girouard)

One of my friends attended the entire seminar, and thought it was wonderful. (You can see her smiling face in the audience on one of the tapes.) A good buy for your church or home school support group.

Kimbo Educational
Once Upon a Dinosaur, $10.95 plus $3.50 shipping. Ages 4–10.

Jumpin', jivin' tribute to the dinosaurs on an LP record or cassette. Songs include:

- Fossil Rock
- We Want to Learn About Dinosaurs
- The Stegosaurus
- My Pet Tyrannosaurus (fantasy song about a magician turning pet dog Bingo into a T. Rex)
- The Plant Eaters (description, list of names)
- Big Bad Al (allosaurus)
- Dinosaur Dance (movement exercises based on dinosaur movements)
- Brachiosaurus' Song
- Reptile Rap (dinosaur ABC's)
- Once Upon a Dinosaur (description of dinosaurs "a hundred million years ago")
- Ankylosaurus and Paleocincus
- The Meat Eaters
- Where Have They Gone?

Lyrics included. A Kimbo bestseller.

Master Books

A division of Creation Life Publishers, the world's largest producer of creation knowledge products. The

Master Books catalog contains every book in the ICR catalog, plus some more. Also, the CLP-Video listing contains a wide range of creationist films, videos, and filmstrips.

SPACE AND SKY

Ampersand Press
Good Heavens! $7.95 plus $2.75 shipping. Ages 10 and up.

Just what the world has been waiting for—an astronomy trivia game. Lots you never knew about comets, meteors, and other relatively small denizens of the sky. The 54 playing cards each include a question, answer, and informative paragraph as well as (aren't they tricky!) a list of *possible* answers to questions on other cards. You can guess and bluff, but you do better if you really know something. *Good Heavens* also includes a 24-page booklet with tips on celestial observation that introduces you to "the solar system's minor members." Evolutionary viewpoint.

NEW★★
Charlie Duke Enterprises
Moonwalk videos, $19.95 each. VHS only. Add $3.50 shipping.

The Russians wept as they watched the Apollo flight land on the moon. Now the Apollo flight is on video, starring Charlie Duke, one of the crew on that historic space mission. So what, you say? Well, aside from the fact that 1990 was the twentieth anniversary of the moon flight, what we have here is an educational space video. Charlie shows how an astronaut gets into his space suit, how he eats (with footage from the flight of astronauts chasing grapes around the capsule), and even explains what every kid wants to know, how they went to the bathroom when there were no bathrooms on the moon. He also shares a lot of behind-the-scenes details of things that went wrong and that *almost* went wrong. Plus you get some fantastic views of the flight itself, and the moonwalk.

Since going to the moon, Charlie has become a Christian. That's why Charlie Duke Enterprises has *two* videos available. *Walk on the Moon, Walk with the Son* includes his Christian testimony. *Charlie Duke, Moonwalker* lacks the testimony but in consequence spends more time covering an astronaut's work. We enjoyed them both.

The whole story is also available in book form. Entitled (what else?) *Moonwalker,* it is published by Thomas Nelson Publishers.

NEW★★
EDC Publishing
Young Scientist series: *Jets, Spaceflight, Stars & Planets,* $6.95 each paperbound or $13.96 each library-bound. Shipping extra. Ages 9–13.

The Young Scientist series introduces preteens to a wide variety of science topics. This was one of the first Usborne series, so some of the books feature "older" artwork and layouts (although the information is up-to-date in all of them). Practical projects and experiments are included wherever possible, along with the cut-away illustrations and fascinating facts.

Jets has an equipment checklist in the front, as does *Stars & Planets,* making it easy to gather materials for the experiments in these books. An older release, it includes photos as well as drawings. The history of jet flight and basic jet design are covered in a very readable way, making an excellent introduction to the *Spaceflight* volume, which takes us into the age of NASA.

Into the Wind
Kites and accessories for all ages. Kits recommended for children are marked in the catalog with a teddy-bear symbol; ages 8 and up. Octopus kites are good for younger children.

Personally, I'd rather play with the sky than study it. And now that we (oh, thank you Lord) have a backyard bigger than 20 square feet, any gust of air is excuse enough to whip out the Star Octopus or Rainbow Delta kite. These are two economy-but-still-fun kites we bought from Into the Wind (a ready-to-fly Star Octopus with 500 feet of line and a reel is less than $10). Into the Wind sells anything any kite flyer could reasonably want, including glow-in-the-dark gizmos so you can fly a kite at night and power stunt kites that take a real man (or Rosie the Riveter) to haul in. A great hobby—lots of fresh air, no stress, and, just like butterflies, the wind is free.

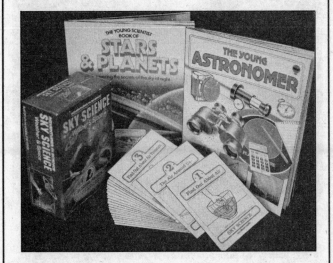

NEW★★
Learning at Home

This catalog for home schoolers has a good, but ever-changing, selection of space and sky science books and kits. Write for latest issue.

Multnomah Press
Destination: Moon, $9.95 hardback. Ages 8–12.

Moonwalking in words and pictures for 8–12 year olds. Yes, it's the story of yet another Christian astronaut, Jim Irwin. Jim is one of only twelve men to have walked on the moon. He was one of the crew members for the Apollo 15 mission, the first one to use a lunar car and the only one to visit the mountains of the moon.

This slim book (about one-fifth the size of Charlie Duke's book *Moonwalker*) is not really a science book, but a personal testimony for kids of what it was like to prepare for space and visit the moon. Did you know, for instance, that the astronauts had to be taken up hundreds of times in a plane high above the earth and the plane put into a temporary nose dive so they could experience 40–50 seconds of weightlessness each time? It's supposed to feel like going over the top on a roller coaster, only it lasts much longer. The book has a photo of the astronauts swimming in the air inside the plane. They look a lot happier than I would! Lots of other fascinating inside facts, good photos.

Nature Friend Magazine
Catalog, $1, refunded on first order.

Nature Friend's Nature's Workshop Catalog has a good selection of books about the stars, star locators, telescopes, binoculars, and microscopes, among many other things. All chosen for home use. We frequently shop from this catalog.

NEW★★
Rod & Staff Publishers
Discovering God's Stars, $2.95. *Star Guide*, $1.85. Blank Star Maps, pack of 25, $2.55. Star Packet (includes all above), $6.50.

Reader Mrs. Paul Steigerwald of La Pryor, Texas urged me to include Rod and Staff's star materials. *Discovering God's Stars* is a star locator booklet with a devotional air. The *Star Guide* is printed on heavy tyvek (a lightweight, untearable paper used sometimes in catalog envelopes). I don't really know what the Star Maps are. However, the whole packet is quite inexpensive, and coming from Rod and Staff is certain to be reverent and accurate.

NEW★★
Worldwide Slides

New space slides, $9/set. Pana-Vue Space slides, $2.50/set. Space videos (VHS only), $29.95 each. Add 10% shipping.

Comedians like to joke about people who go on trips and trap their neighbors into watching all the slides they took. I never thought those jokes were all that funny—I *love* to see other people's slides!

Here's a series of slides your neighbor didn't take on his last trip. The newer sets have 18 or 20 slides per set and include sets on the Apollo missions, Voyager I and II, Skylab, Space Shuttle missions (including the Challenger disaster), and so on. The original Pana-Vue Man in Space slides are five slides per set and include titles like "John Glenn's Historic 1961 Flight," "Space Walk," and "Moon Landing." Two videos are also available: *The Amazing Space Shuttle* (one hour, with highlights from all flights and lots of space views) and *America's Man in Space,* a 50-minute reprise of 25 years of space travel.

The Worldwide Slides catalog lists exactly what each individual slide is about. An easy way to pep up your space studies unit!

NATURE SUPPLIES

Carolina Biological Supply Company

Huge color catalog, $16.95 postpaid. Supplies for K–college.

From Carolina's Biology/Science Teaching Materials Catalog you can get rabbits, frogs, protozoa, and all sorts of other creepies and crawlies. Plus, of course, food, bedding, and "habitats" for same. Anyone for leeches? No? Tarantulas (not sexed)? Fiddler crabs? Venus Flytraps? How about unusual corn ears, for studying genetics?

Also of interest are Carolina's wide selection of biology and general science books, records, filmstrips, videos, software, and games. These are geared to public schools and reflect those values. Among the huge selection I found some items I liked: the bird-song records and hard science books and some of the science games.

NEW★★
Childshop

Bug Box Discovery Plans, $3.50. Hardware package, $6.50. Complete kit, $9.50. Wood glue, $1.75. Sandpaper pack, 75¢. Shipping extra. Ages 5 and up.

Get your kids outdoors with Childshop's Bug Box! This sturdy container, when finished, is shaped like a breadbox with three sides covered with fiberglass mesh, so captured critters can breathe easily. A large cork on a string can be pulled out when it's time to scoop in or release a bug. Every red-blooded child will be able to put the Bug Box to immediate use, prowling around house and neighborhood in search of six-legged friends. Kit is put together mostly with glue and tacks. Minimal nailing required. Our 10-year-old Ted made it all by himself, and I bet several of his younger siblings could have too, if we'd let them.

As with Childshop's other 30+ project kits, you can buy the Bug Box either as illustrated plans only, a hardware package (includes plans), or a complete kit (includes hardware, precut wood pieces, and plans). Kit looks really sharp, comes neatly packaged in a heavy-duty poly bag. The complete kit is the way to go, unless you're the macho type who just has to cut the wood yourself.

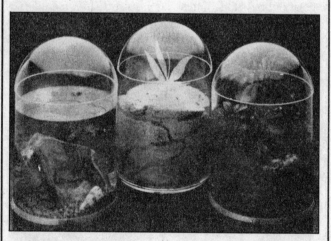

Educational Insights

Discovering Sea Life, Fossils, Rocks, $24.95 each, grades 1–8. *Discovering Nature,* $9.95, grades 3–8. BrainBoosters™: *Outer Space Adventures, Amazing Animals,* $5.95 each, grades 4–9; Decoder, $1.95. Critter Condo, ages 4 and up, $17.95. Nature Lab, $49.95.

Nothing is more frustrating than a natural science unit about the ocean when you live in Missouri. Your science text suggests, "Go to the beach and find a starfish, a sand dollar, and a barnacle." "Right," you think. "I'll just slide down to the ol' Mississippi and pick up some floating pop bottles instead." Now, thanks to Educational Insights, you can bring the great outdoors home without going outdoors. The Nature Collections are boxed sets of labeled specimens plus illustrated activity cards, a full-color illustration of the specimens, and a comprehensive teacher's guide with reproducible worksheets and answer key. *Discovering Sea Life* has 26 authentic sea life specimens (goodies like starfish, barnacles, sand dollars, coral, sea fan, conches, murex shells . . .) plus 16 activity cards. *Discovering Fossils* provides 12 authentic specimens (like trilobites, dinosaur bone, and petrified wood) from the supposed Paleozoic, Mesozoic, and Cenozoic eras in a sectioned plastic tray, plus 13 activity cards. *Discovering Rocks* lets you practice geological identification with 20 neatly packaged and numbered specimens (including the ever-popular quartz, pyrite—"fool's gold," and obsidian), four streak plates, 22 activity cards, and a rock identification game.

If all you really want is a box of suggested activities, EI's *Discovering Nature* activity box might do the trick. 135 activity cards for projects, observations, exhibits, field trips, and ecology study. No specimens included. If you *love* to get your hands on specimens, EI's Nature Lab has both activities (over 50 of 'em) and lots of fun specimens. Grow living Sea Monkeys® from eggs. Grow plants from seeds. Mess around with fossils. Identify rocks. Fiddle with seashells. Lots more included, plus a lovely full-color 32-page activity book.

In a completely different vein, EI's stunning new BrainBoosters series provides lots of fascinating facts and built-in review with the amazing Decoder. Colorful, spiral-bound 32 page books are jam-packed with information and extension activities, not to mention the ten topic-related questions on each two-page spread. Kids twiddle each of the ten dials on the Decoder to a circle, triangle, or square in order to answer the ten questions on the left-hand page. The right-hand page has clues in case you had trouble answering the questions, and also a panel of seemingly random circles, triangles, and squares. Place your Decoder over the panel and the correct answers appear in the Decoder's little see-through boxes. The series contains 10 books in all, two of which have to do with natural science. Hope they add more.

Finally, for you hardy hands-on hunters, EI's Critter Condo is the top-of-the-line home for whatever animal, insect, or whatever your little one brings home. It can be used as a terrarium when the hunting is bad, an ant theater, a butterfly hatchery, and even an aquarium.

NEW**
Hubbard Scientific Company
GrowLab Indoor Garden, includes indoor garden with lights, programmable timer, climate control tent and plastic tray, metal mobile stand with 26 x 50" storage shelf, and *Grow Lab: A Complete Guide to Gardening in the Classroom,* $469. Grow Lab Indoor Garden without mobile stand, $309. Grow Lab Starter Kit, $79. *Grow Lab* book only, $19.95.

Much more pleasant than Carolina's offerings, but not as complete, are the Hubbard Science catalogs. Hubbard's Biology Equipment catalog includes terraria, tanks, and other aids for studying real live beasties.

Hubbard asked me to mention their GrowLab, though I can't imagine why, as only schools have budgets big enough to buy it. Still, school teachers read this book too, so for your benefit, here goes.

The National Gardening Association's Grow Lab program includes a book—*Grow Lab: A Complete Guide to Gardening in the Classroom*—an indoor garden unit, and a mobile stand with shelves. The Indoor Garden unit is a fairly hefty 2 x 4 x 3 feet. It's made of welded tubular steel with a baked-on white enamel finish and a sturdy plastic planter tray, plus two four-foot, adjustable, fluorescent light fixtures and bulbs that provide more than twice the light intensity of a standard plant cart. This means your veggies and flowers can grow from seed to maturity in an average of just eight weeks.

The indoor garden's climate is completely controllable with the programmable timer and climate control tent. Thus, you can grow anything from cactuses to rain-forest plants in this garden (not at the same time, of course!).

The Grow Lab Starter Kit, again designed for classrooms, comes with enough supplies for two full growing seasons: nine different seed varieties, three 16-quart bags of potting soil, eight ounces of plant food, 24 ounces of insecticidal soap, 36 plant pots and markers, plus a capillary mat and plant mister. My opinion of this setup is that you can learn a lot more trying the various seed-starter kits from Park Seed, and it'll cost about the same.

I have not seen the Grow Lab or the *GrowLab* book. The catalog blurb, however, makes it clear that your little students are not supposed to be learning *just* gardening and botany. It's a "versatile interdisciplinary program." As the catalog goes on to warn us,

During field-tests, teachers had their students measure and predict plant growth rates for *math* assignments, grow cotton and peanuts to complement a *social studies* unit on the South, grow Japanese vegetables while studying Japanese *culture,* illustrate garden journals for *art* class, and research the *history* of vegetables.

My goodness!

NEW★★
Insect Lore Products
Butterfly Garden®, $19.95. Frog eggs, $11.95 (November–March only). Field Collector's kit, $19.95. Add 15% shipping. Hundreds of items available. All ages.

For the kid who likes what bugs him. It's not glamorous, but this thick, black-and-white catalog has tons of nature study books, kits, and accessories. Butterfly Garden for raising Painted Lady butterflies (more on this in a minute). Frog eggs. Silkworm eggs. Praying Mantis eggs. Ant farms. Caterpillars. Chick incubation supplies. Carnivorous plants. Hummingbird nectar and feeders. Field collector's kit (for butterfly collecting) includes everything you need to catch 'em and mount 'em. Nylon butterfly net available separately. Bird feeders. Rock tumbler. Owl pellet kit. Cheesemaking kit.

The Insect Lore catalog also includes lots of kits and books from suppliers reviewed in this volume of

Big Book. The Educational Insights *Adventures in Science* kits and Discovery collections. Mini Labs kits. Usborne nature and science books. Games from Ampersand Press. Plus videos, puzzles, and coloring books, all with a nature theme.

The company's slogan is, "Bring the magic of nature into your home or classroom." Let me tell you a little bit about that magic of nature. We bought the Butterfly Garden. It came with five small, black spiny caterpillars, in a jar with some green bug food. Instructions said not to open or clean the jar. So the little caterpiggles molted, spun small webs, and moved their bowels inside that jar for several weeks. During this time they got bigger and uglier. Then, one day, they finally spun their "beautiful" chrysalises. These were small, brown affairs, not at all the glorious green and gold of a Monarch chrysalis (for example). We carefully moved the jar top into the Butterfly Garden, as per instructions, and eagerly waited for them to hatch. Naturally, we missed the hatching of all five. However, we did get to see the first two thrashing about with broken wings, having fallen the short distance to the floor of the Butterfly Garden. The other three did better, wingwise, but I didn't find the sight of the long rivers of blood-like meconium oozing out of them and all over the uncleanable bottom of the Butterfly Garden to be all that inspiring. We learned something, all right—birth, even of butterflies, is a lot messier and more hazardous than the cute nature-study texts make out.

A few morals: Wait to buy the Butterfly Garden until it's springtime or summer, with flowers blossoming, so you can have the joy of releasing the butterflies rather than being forced to watch them spend their short lives in a cardboard box with plastic windows. I think it would also be a good idea to set the jar top *low* on the side of the Butterfly Garden, so when the critters hatch they will not fall too far and hurt themselves.

Nature Friend Magazine
Catalog, $1, refunded on first order.

Nature Friend's Nature's Workshop Catalog features tested nature-study products and books. Books are either evolution-free or have "guideline sheets" included. Bird feeders, binoculars, ant farms, telescopes, microscopes, pocket knives, pocket compasses, nature study guides, and nature coloring books, and lots more. Star locators, telescopes, binoculars, microscopes. Plus art supplies and "how to draw" books for budding nature artists.

ECOLOGY

Green is in right now. Hey, hey for Earth Day and all that. Let's get rid of styrofoam, so we can enjoy cold and soggy McBurgers. Save the spotted owls. Rescue the whales. Death to the tuna fleets and loggers!

Ecology, which started as a scientific attempt to determine the effects of living beings on each other, has become a religion. Here are its assumptions:

(1) Everything on Earth is interdependent on everything else. My sneeze in Missouri affects the monkeys in the rain forests.

(2) The Good Old Days theory: the best way for things to be is the way they were before people came along.

(3) All animals should be allowed to roam free (in their "natural habitat"). People, except for those approved by ecologists, should stay away from those habitats.

(4) Man is the only predator who should not be allowed to prey (e.g., political vegetarianism, "animal rights," paint-spraying attacks on ladies with fur coats, etc.).

(5) The Hansel and Gretel Theory: there's not enough food (and other resources) for all of us. Contrariwise, there are too many of us altogether. Thus, we should be sterilized and voluntarily choose to live as if we were poor.

(6) The End is Near Prophecy: the by-products of our civilization are about to wipe out all life on earth, unless we immediately repent and start using recycled shopping bags.

Most of us have accepted these assumptions. They have been dinned into us by educators and the media for years and years. They are in virtually every science textbook—*including* those published by Christian firms—every science magazine, and every science book. And they are *wrong*.

The Bible clearly teaches we are not as interdependent as all that. The sins of one nation do *not* affect the climate of the next. Furthermore, the sins that lay a land waste are *not* ecological sins (e.g., overpopulation and strip mining) but Ten Commandments sins like adultery and covetousness. Further than that, God is not a God of scarcity, but abundance. Even further than *that,* man is *supposed* to change the face of the earth, to till it and to build our cities.

So, what's ecology good for? Within a limited area, it is possible to study the effects of changes on animal and plant populations, including the effects of man-made changes. Even so, one of the elementary rules of logic holds that it is *very hard* to demonstrate that X causes Y. A decrease in the population of bullfrogs could be caused by excessive hunting of bullfrogs, an increase in the population of frog-eating birds, the effects of industrial pollution, or simply an especially cold spring. More fundamentally, the observer may not have noticed all the bullfrogs, or may have failed to note that they had migrated to a nearby marsh. Thus ecology, like sociology, is inexact. You can "prove" anything you like. Simply assert that X causes acid rain, or Y is about to destroy all the sea plankton. All the million *other* factors which might cause acid rain—or even proof that it exists—need not be examined; whether or not plankton are disappearing need not be proved. What matters is *belief*, not rigorous scientific proof.

Environmentalism, or ecological politics, is simply a bigger and greener type of communism, all of us one big happy interdependent family of organisms, none greater than the other, the cockroach lying down with the lad, in which an elite casts all the votes for the plants and animals. The doctrine of "the interdependence of all things" leads the way for global busybodies to meddle in the affairs of other people's countries. The doctrine that The End is Near justifies infringement on our basic rights (did you know all printing presses are now supposed to be registered with the government, according to the Clean Air Act?). All of this is overcast with religious terminology and expectations.

Home schoolers are about to be deluged by a flood of this material. I know, because the people who produce it send it to me, fully expecting a good word for their endeavors. Take, for instance, the letter I got yesterday, from the publisher of a book urging greenie principles on Christians:

> We feel - - - is a timely resource book that can be used by today's home schoolers. Please review our book and consider it for your next release. We are new publishers, but our editor has had extensive experience with promotion and we are in the process of sending our flyers to a variety of locations. We have had a local (northwest Ohio) book-signing event, articles in the newspapers, a radio interview in San Diego, and the book is available in Christian bookstores in various areas. . .

This particular book urges Christians to have "reverence" for the earth. It urges us not to wash our cars, to use the back sides of our white paper, and to wrap our kids' birthday presents in the Sunday funnies. Other books I have received range from the unabashedly antichild and evolutionary to the more typical "stewardship" tract asserting that we (not the Brazilians) are responsible for the future of the Brazilian rainforest and that we ought to buy our clothes at garage sales. In between are those that lightheartedly assume the necessity of regional land management programs (a euphemism for Washington bureaucrats telling you what you can do with your own property).

Christians are supposed to "revere" God (not the earth), and respect our neighbor's private property ("Thou shalt not steal . . . Thou shalt not covet."). Christians are also supposed to *admire* God's handiwork and *garden* the part of it we own, freely enjoying its good blessings. While we are not supposed to heap up great riches for ourselves, we certainly can wash the car and use birthday wrapping paper without guilt. We've got to turn our thinking around in this area—the Earth Goddess is a harsh mistress.

Ampersand Press
Predator, Krill, Pollination, $7.95 each. *Predator* available in Spanish and French. Games packaged in durable, attractive paperboard boxes. Add $2.50 shipping.

If you want to understand how food webs work (that is, who eats who and how it agrees with them), try playing some of Ampersand Press's inexpensive and classy games. *Predator* is a deck of 40 nice-looking playing cards based on a forest food web. Each card show a plant or animal, tells who eats it and what it eats, and assigns it Energy Points. *Krill* is simi-

lar, but it uses an Antarctic Ocean food chain card deck. Both decks have the usual levels in their food webs: producers, three or four consumer levels, and decomposers. Many games can be played with the cards: classification games, *Concentration, Solitaire, Rummy*, and of course the *Predator* and *Krill* food web games.

Pollination is about the birds and the bees, following a similar format.

These games furnish a great introduction to *real* ecology at a very manageable price.

EDC Publishing
Deserts, Jungles, Mountains, $3.95 each paperbound, $11.96 library bound, or combined volume *The Children's Book of Wild Places*, $11.95 hardbound. Ages 7–12.

Ecosystems are in right now. An ecosystem is a whole bunch of living things and the place they live (New York City should qualify, but I've never seen it called an ecosystem). We turn, then, from the ecology of Times Square to the ecology of deserts, jungles, and mountains. Here we are blessed with some everlovely Usborne books that happen to deal with who and what lives in which ecosphere. Interestingly enough, these Usborne books also mention the *humans* who live in the desert, the jungle, and the mountains. Thus, the kneeling camel on the cover of *Deserts* carries a stately Arabian saddle on his back. You also get to find out about fun things (to a kid) like volcanoes and avalanches along with much useful info about the flora and fauna that inhabit each region.

NEW★★
Home Life
The Greenie, Too Many Chickens, $9.95 each postpaid.

The Greenie and *Too Many Chickens* are two cartoon children's books by yours truly that point the reader to a more accurate view of ecology. In *The Greenie*, a lovable activist character discovers that personal stewardship is the most fruitful form of environmentalism. In *Too Many Chickens*, barnyard animals learn that resources aren't as scarce as they think and that a large family has its advantages. Both are illustrated by a well-known professional cartoonist, published by Wolgemuth & Hyatt Publishers, and available (we hope) at your local Christian bookstore.

NEW★★
Klutz Press
KidsGardening, $12.95. Shipping extra. Ages 8–adult (or younger if you read to them).

How can anyone not like a book with a title like *KidsGardening: A Kids' Guide to Messing Around in the Dirt?* Gardening is ecology in the useful sense, and this is *the* gardening book to get your urchins, folks. For one thing, it comes with five packets of kid-friendly seeds: good strong growers that also are annual favorites. Irresistible illustrations on the seed packets make even a blister-conscious adult anxious to plunge that old hoe into the dirt! The seed packets are bound right onto the outside of the book, so they stay where you want them until it's time to plant.

Like other Klutz Press books, this one has wire spirals, so it will stay conveniently open on your table, workbench, or grass, and sturdy, jellyproof pages. The usual colorful, goofy, accessible illustrations lead you right into the mostly hand-lettered text. This is brilliantly organized, starting with info on what plants need to grow and how to prepare your soil, moving on to the wonders of composting and transplanting, and how to battle the bugs organically. Separate sections are devoted to veggies, flowers and herbs, and indoor gardening. You even get recipes for yummies like garlic bread and guacamole (made with your homegrown garlic and avocados, of course!). *KidsGardening* closes triumphantly with directions for worm farming in a box and how to make a scarecrow.

I just have to give you a taste of the book's memorable style. How about this one: "Mulch is like a blanket that covers your garden and keeps weeds from growing and keeps your garden soil moist and soft." Next to this sentence is a picture of a flower snuggled in bed under a blanket of leaves. You can bet any kid reading this will remember what mulch is and what it's good for! Or how about this definition of weeds: "Weeds are any plants that grow where you don't want them." I've seen people write for *pages* about which plants are weeds and which aren't without saying it this well! And who could ignore the picture of two vicious-looking weeds in prisoner's clothes chained together with an innocent sunflower, next to the advice, "It can be hard to tell a weed from a plant you want to keep when they are just sprouting. Get your grown-up assistant to help you if you aren't sure."

The gardening directions in *KidsGardening* are as clear as the definitions. Example:

You can use leaves, straw or grass clippings to mulch your garden or you can buy bags of it at a gardening store. If you use grass, be sure you dry it in thin layers first. One kind of grass, called "bermuda grass," isn't good for mulching. Ask if you're not sure what kind you have.

Spread the mulch 2–3 inches deep over your garden. If you are planting big seeds—like corn—or if you're planting seedlings, you can spread the mulch right after planting. For small seeds like lettuce, don't mulch until after the seeds sprout.

When you're watering, be sure you use enough water to soak through the layer of mulch and into the ground.

Ruth Stout couldn't have said it any better!

CHAPTER THIRTY

SCIENCE CURRICULUM

Plato once pointed out (not exactly in these words) that all kids are born scientists. Show a two-year-old on separate occasions a wicker rocker, a Queen Anne armchair, and a La-Z-Boy rocker and tell him they are chairs. Sometime later, squirming on a hard folding chair in the storefront church you just started attending, Johnny will whisper, "Mom, this chair hurts!"

Now, Johnny never saw such a chair before in his life. How did he know that this peculiar torture contraption with the hollow metal legs was a chair? Because Johnny was blessed from birth with the ability to *take in data*, *categorize* it, and arrive at *conclusions*.

Here we are looking at a field of knowledge that covers the whole universe. How do we come to grips with it? Just like Johnny—we take in the data, categorize it, and arrive at conclusions. This is called "Science."

GETTING YOUR HANDS ON DATA

The first category of science resources is Raw Bits. Raw bits of data, that is. You have to observe it (see it, touch it, smell it, hear it, taste it) before you can do anything with it. Here we find the time-hallowed nature walk and trip to the zoo. Museums of Natural History, Museums of Science, planetariums (planetaria?), and so on all provide lots and lots of raw bits of data for us to chew over.

This is also why early grades curricula typically urge children to start a garden or get a pet. When those little nippers dig into the soil and sprinkle in the seeds they are observing plants in action! Science! When they feed and water Frisky and Friska, groom them, chase them around the house, and help dispose of their twelve lovable offspring, they are collecting data on animal life. Science!

You may, of course, not be content with all the free raw bits out there. Is money burning a hole in your pocket? Do you feel your children need more hands-on exposure than they can get in your backyard? (I can't believe I am writing this to home schoolers!) Well then, there *are* things you can send away for—see the Equipment section at the end of this chapter.

WHO LEARNS WHAT WHEN?

I just know you've been wondering when we would get to talk about textbooks. Textbooks really only become useful when your student has enough information to begin seriously categorizing it. They are no substitute for hands-on experience. For this reason, I personally don't get too excited about textbooks in the earliest grades. I've seen a lot of them, and frankly the average K–2 science textbook contains no more information than you'd find in some of the Berenstain Bears nature books available free at your public library.

Around the third grade level, when children begin to enter the Age of Reason and categorizing suddenly becomes important, a good science textbook can provide lots of handy mental file folders for children to stuff with the facts they have already learned. Typically, a good science text will break creation down into Plants, Animals, Minerals, Energy—a format well suited for great family games of Twenty Questions! Children will begin to learn some basic scientific rules, like the Law of Gravity, and perform some simple experiments, thus familiarizing themselves with the approach of the scientific method.

PROCESS SKILLS—FAD OF THE NINETIES

Process Skills science is big this year. "Process Skills" means that kids don't sit in lectures, work through textbooks, or memorize pages of facts. Instead they practice doing scientific things: observing, classifying, inferring, predicting, measuring, communicating, interpreting, questioning, experimenting, defining, and inventing models.

Process Skills are just Thinking Skills leached into the science classroom—with the important difference that hands-on science experiments are generally more fun than logic puzzles. The whole thing goes back to John Dewey, who, like Aristotle, thought children needed to be taught to think and that "mere facts" are simply the afterthoughts one strings on the educational necklace.

As usual, whenever a new educational fad comes along, all sorts of products are marketed under that brand name. To some people, Process Skills simply means including a lot of neat experiments along with traditional scientific explanations of what was happening in the experiments. To others, it means what audio-lingual French meant to me in eighth grade: a lot of things happening with no translation (and no progress in French).

Dewey believed that kids couldn't learn something without experiencing it, which is self-evident nonsense. I'll prove it. Think of Moscow. Now tell me . . . *were you ever there?* Your mental picture of Moscow (except for a few rare travelers) was based entirely on secondhand information. You have never experienced Moscow, or the American Revolution, or life as a professional football player. Yet you know something about all these things.

As always, this not-really-new theory (around which hover the shades of Dewey and Aristotle) is out of balance. You can learn many things quite efficiently by being told them, and simply trusting the people telling you. There is nothing wrong with memorizing the features of plants, animals, stars, and planets.

SQUIRMY SCIENCE

The secular version of "process skills," which appears to have been swallowed wholesale by Christian curriculum developers, is heavy on clinical terminology and what I call Squirmy Science. Kids studying Squirmy Science don't get to raise and make friends with hamsters, guinea pigs, rabbits, and chickens like kids used to do. Instead, they study jars of squirming mealworms and load up terrariums with crickets and cockroaches, which will subsequently become food for the frogs or chameleons they intend to introduce.

What goes on in a kid's mind when he realizes that he is god over those mealworms, crickets, and frogs? That he can feed them, starve them, or dissect them at his pleasure? It wouldn't be so bad if the kids would be allowed to do what normal kids do—kill the mealworms and cockroaches, let the crickets go outdoors, and play with the frogs a while before bringing them back to the pond. No. Instead Squirmy Science students are supposed to learn important lessons about "populations" and "systems" by nurturing the vermin and watching them eat each other.

It's not that Squirmy Science lessons aren't instructive. Dear me, no. The children learn a *great* deal. They learn to handle creation disrespectfully, to both magnify life and death (by focusing endlessly on them and filling out graphs and charts) and ignore it (by not caring in the slightest how many daphnia got eaten today). They learn to be uninvolved. They learn not to celebrate or mourn. Plants grow or die in the laboratory to no purpose. Animals give birth and are eaten.

The grownups say we should watch this happen and write it down, and that's all there is to it. The wheel of life rolls on. Death begets life begets death. And other Hindu doctrines.

I wonder how many people busily creating science programs for Christians have noticed that "food web," "food chain," and "ecosystem" all have pantheistic underpinnings? Always man is just one among many "organisms" in the "system," both eating and eaten. To have an unbroken food chain, for instance, you must eat the meat of the cow that ate the grass fed by the decaying body of dear dead Uncle Henry. (In real life, animals are not grazed in cemeteries.)

Try describing the "food chain" in biblical terminology. It's impossible! Why? Because man holds a *special position* in creation. We are not just one of the gang made up of flies, snakes, bluebirds, and great white whales. The Bible continually reminds us of our special position and responsibilities. Modern scientific jargon, on the other hand, is bent on making us nothing more than a trousered ape.

Scientific jargon is bloodless, loveless, uninvolved, irresponsible. You can do anything you want to with "organisms" and "objects," or even (if you are a social scientist) "clients" and "populations." Who cares what happens to an "organism"?

But God did not create "organisms." He created birds and fishes and "creeping things" and cattle and wild beasts. People in the Bible do not "observe objects." They burst into tears at the raising of the second temple in Jerusalem, or work with cunning craftsmanship on stones and silver, or select five smooth stones from the brook, or breathe out raptures of awe at the sight of the starry sky.

The dispassionate observer was invented by humanistic scientists—a role for Vulcans like Mr. Spock (who doesn't exist), not for humans. Science is at least as much poetry and worship as it is logic. Without poetry and worship, it becomes obscene manipulation of other people and the earth—quite commonly under pretense of saving both.

God in the Garden of Eden told the man to "dress the earth and *keep* it." It's this long-term view, this *involvement* with the creation, I have in mind when I think of science. It's an attitude of concern (not worship) towards plants, animals, and the soil. It's knowing Someone is going to check whether you really did remove all the trash from your campsite and put out the fire. It's realizing that another Artist created the painting, and it's your job to bring out the highlights, not to paint over it.

Can I share with you a brief illustration of the difference between Squirmy Science and biblical science? How about the classic grow-or-die experiment. In the Squirmy Science model, kids are asked to pot up pea seeds, one per styrofoam cup. One cup gets water and fertilizer, but is placed under a box so it gets no light. Another gets water and light but no fertilizer. Still another gets fertilizer and light but no water. The fourth gets water, light, and fertilizer. Children are supposed to observe these plants as three of them miserably expire and deduce that, yes indeedy, plants need water *and* light *and* food. They will also learn, contrary to all common sense going back to the Garden of Eden, that it's OK to let plants in your care die of neglect simply to prove a trivial point.

Now, the alternative. Kids would be given the same number of seeds and cups (probably not styrofoam!) and exhorted to grow as many stocky little plants as they can. Some plants will inevitably succumb to factors not considered in the Squirmy Science books—damping-off disease has slain its thousands and ten thousands—and those cases will be analyzed to determine the causes of death. Kids *will* experiment with water, light, and fertilizer, but to determine *which combination is best for the plant,* not to observe all the ways people can destroy plants. I can imagine some really great experiments in which a row of identical plants is each fed a different vitamin or soil amendment, and the most successful ingredients applied then to all of them. This is science with a *purpose.*

PROCESS SCIENCE PROGRAMS

NEW**
Cornerstone Curriculum Project
Science: The Search, Volume 1 and 2, $50 each. Add 10% shipping.

Science: The Search should now be out in two volumes. I saw *Volume 1: Properties • Interactions • Systems*. This is a process skills and terminology program, not a facts program. Kids learn by observation and experimentation, not by lecture and memorization.

Each volume is packaged quite nicely in a handsome three-ring binder, and includes a Materials Kit. The Materials Kit for Volume 1 includes a magnifier, horseshoe magnet, assorted small wooden pieces, container of BTB, brine shrimp eggs, and a gear set including a base, cover, handle, and pointer plus two each of small, medium, and large plastic gears. If you want more gears for the three lessons on this topic, the optional Extra Gear Set includes two bases and nine each of small, medium, and large gears.

Volume 1 is broken into two sections—Property and Interaction & Systems—each divided into three subsections: Physical Sciences, Life Sciences, and Spiritual Application. A total of 68 activities are covered.

Each activity begins with a list of materials needed, a lesson topic, and a step-by-step lesson plan that tells you exactly what to do and say. The brochure claims that most of the materials and supplies can be found in the home, grocery store, or pet supply store. The list of supplies needed for the volume takes five index columns, and includes such items as color chips from a paint store, different colors and grits of sandpaper, a circuit tester, fabric pieces, and red yarn. As you can see, you will have to visit quite a few places to pick up the materials.

The first 19 lessons are all typical sorting, classifying, and observing activities found in the better preschool programs. Life Sciences activities are most of the environmental type, involving life cycles, food webs and chains, groups of organisms, and habitat. A few kitchen science activities are thrown in, plus a goodish chunk of engineering (gears, electricity, magnetism) in the last half of the book.

The program stresses clinical terminology. Example:

Give your child a pair of shoes that need polishing, shoe polish, brush, and cloth.

"WHAT CAN YOU DO TO MAKE THESE OBJECTS INTERACT?" [Your speaking part is always capitalized and enclosed in quotes.]

After they polish the shoes . . .

"WHAT EVIDENCE IS THERE THAT THESE OBJECTS HAVE INTERACTED?"

The life cycle and populations activities are not for those with squirmy stomachs. You'll be growing mealworms in the privacy of your home and graphing how many aphids your crickets ate and how many live crickets your chameleon ate. Beverly Cleary's fictional Ramona threw up observing the classic mealworm experiment, and I'm with her.

The gears lessons are the best. You make a "black box" system by putting gears together and closing the

plastic case provided. The children have to duplicate the gear setup without seeing it. Clever!

Lessons are supposed to be completed at the rate of one a week, but you should know that some of these lessons take a month or even a year to finish. You'll be watching little bugs grow, die, and eat each other for a long time.

Although its author considers it a Christian program, *Science: The Search* is not very spiritual in its observations of nature, weather, aquarium animals, and so on. You won't find any "Praise the Lord!" excitement here. It's a dispassionate, clinical approach—students are not encouraged to relate to or enjoy the animals and plants observed, and reverence for life and death is not taught. Instead, the spiritual emphasis consists of four separate Spiritual Application activities: studying the names of God, writing down the attributes of natural/spiritual/carnal men, studying a dispensational seven-interactions-of-God-in-history, and a look at the church as "God's supernatural system."

NEW★★
Dale Seymour Publications
Everyday Science Sourcebook: Ideas for Teachers in Elementary and Middle School, $19.95.

We're all hearing a lot about "process skills" these days. In science, this means the ability to tackle and solve a scientific problem, as opposed to encyclopedic knowledge of scientific facts. *Everyday Science Sourcebook* is a great tool to help you develop science process skills in your children.

First, what the book is not. It is not a science program. It is not a "how to teach science" book. What you get are lots and lots of hands-on activities, organized in ways that make this book really easy to use.

Activities are in developmental order, first of all. That means that activities for teeny kids come before activities for teens. The theory subscribed to by this book is that kids start learning science by *observing* (ages 1 and 2), *communicating* (ages 2–4), *comparing* (ages 4–6), *organizing* (ages 6–8), *relating* (ages 8–12), *inferring* (ages 12–15), and *applying* (ages 15–adult). Activities are therefore provided in that order. Activities are also arranged numerically by categories: inorganic matter, organic matter, energy, inference models, and technology. These are further subdivided into topics. For example, the category "inorganic matter" breaks down into solids, liquids, gases, geology, oceanography, and meteorology. Each activity has a letter code that tells you exactly which skills and age level it is designed for.

So, need a science activity to correlate with your unit study or textbook? Look no farther . . . it's all here.

NEW**
Fearon Teacher Aids
The Big Fearon Book of Doing Science, $24.95. Add $3.50 shipping. Grades 1–6.

"Exploration and Adventures in Life, Earth, and Physical Science for Grades 1–6," as the subtitle has it. *The Big Fearon Book of Doing Science* focuses on "process skills" in its over 250 pages—observing, comparing, measuring, classifying and grouping, sequencing, collecting data, organizing data, and drawing conclusions. Each activity page covers one scientific topic and exercises one or more of the process skills.

The six book sections explore life science, physical science, and earth science on two different levels, with separate units for grades 1–3 and 4–6. Each book section starts with teacher pages, each of which includes a scaled-down version of the activity page, a lesson purpose, list of process skills used in the lesson, list of materials needed, step by step lesson procedures, and discovery questions. After the teacher pages come the activity pages. These unfortunately are printed on both sides of the paper, meaning you can't do the activities that involve scissors work without chopping up the activity page on the other side of the sheet. Activities get more complicated as you progress through the book.

The activities are excellent—interesting and doable—and cover a wide range of subjects, from distinguishing textures of objects to magnetism and optics. All activities require "common" materials—common for your neighborhood teachers' store, but not necessarily on hand in your house. Take my advice and collect all the materials for each full unit before beginning it, and put them all in one place. Even better would be to organize the materials by lesson in which they are used. This will make it possible for you to get right into your science studies every day, without wasting time on frustrating searches for items you may or may not have at home.

The Big Fearon Book of Doing Science covers every scientific area and skill, making it an excellent value if you're willing to take the time to collect and organize the materials you'll need to carry out the activities. This is probably all the process science your child will need for the first six grades, all in one book.

NEW**
Master Books
Good Science for Home Schools, Volumes 1 (preK–3) and 2 (grades 4–6), $49.95 each. Add $6 shipping.

Good Science for Home Schools is a K–6 "process skills" program. Like *Science: The Search* it teaches clinical vocabulary and concentrates on the discovery process more than individual facts.

The Institute for Creation Research originally developed the *Good Science* program for Christian schools. Their Good Science Seminars began to attract home schoolers, hence this targeted curriculum. Although the ICR staff still feels you will be best introduced to the program by attending a seminar in your area, they have provided a set of audiocassettes (in nice binder) recorded at a seminar to accompany each volume of this program. The cassettes provide how-tos and program philosophy for each of the topics studied.

The program's author, Dr. Richard Bliss, has worked 25 years in the public school system, and it shows throughout this course, from the terminology of "learning objectives" and "cognitive domain" in the introduction to the author's stated dependence on secular learning theories. His Christian convictions show in the occasional devotional thoughts incorporated into the activities and the attempt to "study science under the attributes of God." This means that, for each lesson, the pupil is supposed to think of an attribute of God that relates to the topic studied. When observing and classifying different kinds of buttons, for example, the pupil might think about God's *creativity* in making a world with such a variety of materials, or how He created man in His own image to be creative in designing buttons!

Surprisingly, there is not much mention of creation v. evolution after the introduction (which is written to parents). The program also uses the dispassionate vocabulary of food webs, organisms, objects, ecosystems, etc., rather than Biblical vocabulary.

You'll find almost 80 lessons in Volume 1 and about 50 in Volume 2. Volume 1, for the K–3 crowd, starts off with the typical smell-taste-touch-observe-sort-classify exercises found in preschool programs.

Kids also do some simple chemical, electrical, and machines experiments (no magnetism), grow and kill plants, and grow and kill small vermin. Great stress is placed on learning the terminology of "objects," "systems," "interaction," and the like.

Volume 2, for kids in grades 4–6, starts out with "relativity," which in this course has nothing to do with Dr. Einstein. Kids will be determining relative motion and position and graphing these in various ways. Next on the list is habitat and environment. "Environment" is defined in the text as "the total of all the living and non-living beings affecting an organism." Oddly, although the book keeps urging students to "state an attribute of God" in connection with each exercise, God Himself is not ever mentioned as an environmental factor. The unconscious assumption taught is that the spiritual and natural world are closed systems, not affecting each other. I'm sure this is not what the curriculum designer had in mind—just as he didn't intend to convey that God's Word has no rules regarding how people should handle plants and animals—but *Good Science* teaches absolutely nothing about these subjects.

Moving along in Volume 2, we come to a series of simple physics experiments. Although many of these resemble experiments I remember from high school, the kids aren't taught any of the underlying principles and formulae. In the next Life Science level, kids grow and stunt plants and grow critters and watch them eat each other. The Physical Science level following has some work on electricity and magnetism. Finally, the pinnacle of the program comes in the last Life Science level, where kids get to study ecosystems (e.g., a stocked aquarium and terrarium).

A materials kit is included with each volume. Volume 1 comes with BTB (a chemical you stick in water and bubble gases through to watch the color change), copper chloride, a hand magnifier, a battery holder, a few wires and alligator clips, and some teeny bulbs and teeny bulb holders. The materials kit for Volume 2 is much the same, except that this one has a mini ¼" lamp with two wires connected and a thin strip of metal instead of the poisonous copper chloride for Volume 1. You get to round up the rest of the materials: the aquarium, terrarium, mealworms, crickets, daphnia, guppies, chlamydomonas, hydra, euglena, brine shrimp eggs, duckweed, snails, amoebae, paramecia, chameleon, aphids, frogs, grass seed, clover seed, bean seed, cockroaches, and sowbugs (for the Life Sciences units), and styrofoam cups, magnets of various types, compasses, rivets, batteries, circuit

tester, switches, bleach, batteries, vinegar, vials, bags, straws, and so on for everything else.

NEW✶✶
Teacher's Laboratory, Inc.
Learning Through Science series, $27/unit. Teacher's guide and index, $9.75. Add 10% shipping ($2 minimum).

I like activity-card-based science. It's generally less stuffy and cluttered that textbook- or workbook-based programs—partly because the uniform card design with its small space forces authors to get to the point, and partly because doing activities is more motivational and memorable than filling out workbook pages. Thus with great expectations I requested a review sample of the Learning Through Science program from England.

This program is the result of over 20 years of research, and is used widely in British schools. After reading the teacher's guide and index, though, I believe the complete program, with its 12 units, is too unwieldy for home use. Getting together the materials required is a semester's work by itself for a mom or dad at home. At school, where people are paid to put together science materials, and where the teacher usually inherits piles of materials the district has already purchased, the program would doubtless work better. To make matters worse, the teacher's guide lists only *British* sources for the materials!

Another matter for concern is that, by its very design, the program gives as much weight to the study of color as it does to electricity. Some subjects just don't require a full-blown treatment, however well they may lend themselves to oodles of process-skill projects.

Each unit includes two complete sets of 24 activity cards and a teacher's guide. Again, for home use they should be repackaged less expensively with only one set of the cards. It's also regrettable that the cards are not numbered, since although this makes a statement about the equal merit of each activity, it also makes it a lot harder to keep the cards in order and thus to find the card you want.

Some of the individual units in this approach may well be worth the money (especially if repackaged for the home). I am thinking particularly of the *Electricity, Materials, On the Move, Moving Around,* and *Time, Growth, & Change* units, none of which I have had the opportunity to see. These topics work well as activities. Others, such as the *Sky and Space* unit (which I did see), include labored activities with little educational value, such as observing the moon's shape and location in the sky at different times of the night and day for a month or researching the origins of the names of the days of the week. Such projects provide little sense of accomplishment (unlike model building or real experiments). Although many projects in this unit were good, at the price *all* should be good.

SCIENCE BOOKS & TEXTBOOKS

UPDATED**
A Beka Book Publications

Discovering God's World (grade 1), $6.75. *Enjoying God's World* (grade 2), $6.85. *Exploring God's World* (grade 3), $7.65. *Understanding God's World* (grade 4), $11.95. *Investigating God's World* (grade 5), $11.95. *Observing God's World* (grade 6), $10.55. Teacher's editions available for all grades, from $10–$20. Student tests and teacher keys available for upper grades. Shipping extra.

A Beka's economically-priced science textbooks cover the gamut from K–12. As with all other science series I have seen, I'd skip the first few grades. You start getting some serious information in third grade. A Beka follows the encyclopedic format—lots and lots of facts and terminology. These are great books for browsing, but hard work to study through.

I wish I had a review copy of the new fourth- and fifth-grade books in this series, *Investigating God's World* and *Observing God's World*. From the catalog pictures and descriptions they look like hot stuff. A Beka has been justly criticized in the past for the pedestrian artwork in its books, but the new edition of *Understanding God's World* looks like it's following the winning visual format of the Usborne series. The catalog says that the book shows students "how to make an insect zoo, how to recognize the plants they see every day, how to attract birds to their own back yards, how

to use field guides, how to interpret cloud formations, and how to identify rocks." Seed germination, the causes of weather, God's design of the heavens, ecology of the ocean depths, and "many other aspects of God's creative genius" are also covered. One presumes that the new *Observing God's World* will be similarly enhanced to include exciting, doable experiments and visual explanations of science facts.

These new books are only 27-week courses, intended to be followed by the A Beka nine-week health courses for those grades. The books for grades 1–3 and grade 6 are regular 36-week science courses.

NEW**
Addison-Wesley Publishing Company, Inc.
Foodworks, $8.95 plus $2.50 shipping.

Addison-Wesley publishes this wonderful book written by the people at the Ontario Science Centre in Toronto, Canada. The Science Centre has three connected buildings filled with more than 500 hands-on exhibits for children to explore, experience, and enjoy science. This book (and others in the series) helps to make hands-on science available to everyone.

Foodworks is subtitled "Over 100 Science Activities and Fascinating Facts That Explore the Magic of Food." The facts are skillfully interwoven in story form. For instance, many of us know that the tomato once was thought to be poisonous, but do you know why people changed their minds? The book introduces us to Colonel Robert G. Johnson of Salem, Oregon who stood on the courthouse steps and ate an entire basket of tomatoes without becoming ill. We also read about Dr. Mile's Compound Extract of Tomato which was *then* sold as a quack cure-all, but *today* is better known and loved as ketchup. Along with the information are plenty of activities in "Try this" form such as the "Big Eater" experiment: "How much do you eat each day in relation to your weight? Weigh yourself and weigh your meals. Don't forget the snacks. Divide your weight by the amount of food you eat to find out." Many of the activities are more involved than this example, but you can easily find the necessary materials around your home or pick them up elsewhere.

While *Foodworks* is written for children, it will appeal to anyone who has reached the age of reason. Humor is generously scattered throughout the writing, and the black-and-white drawings and activities have that light touch that makes learning more enjoyable.
—Cathy Duffy

NEW★★
Alpha Omega Publications
LIFEPACS, $2.25–$2.45 each, 10 LIFEPACS per grade. Set of 10 LIFEPACS, $19.95–$21.95. Answer keys, teacher handbooks available. Shipping extra. Grades 1–12.

Alpha Omega has science courses based on work-texts. Kids read the text inside the workbook, answer the questions, write any essay answers, and do the experiments. Everything is right there in one booklet (called a LIFEPAC), with 10 booklets in all per course. The last LIFEPAC is always a course review.

With an answer key, these courses are very easy to use at home. With the teacher's handbooks, you get more teaching and enrichment ideas added in.

The curriculum is "spiral." This means you study the same topic again and again and again in succeeding grades, with greater depth each time. It's also greener than other Christian curriculum, with the exception of Christian Schools International, but more balanced than CSI. We hear a lot about the "web of life" and other environmental doctrines and terminology, but along with the knocking of man-as-polluter some attempt is made to point out how man has managed his environment for the better.

All Alpha Omega science courses include lots of simple step-by-step experiments and investigations. The first LIFEPAC of grade 6, for example, included seven experiments, from a setup involving a leaf, boiling water, a test tube, alcohol, and iodine solution, to the famous celery-stick-and-food-coloring osmosis experiment. Kids also work with microscopes, magnifying glasses, scalpels (dissecting beef hearts from the butcher shop), and so on. As you can see, a certain amount of basic lab equipment is needed. Kids also work with the encyclopedia, draw pictures of scientific phenomenon, and write simple reports. All this is excellent training for upper-grades science.

Grade 1 starts with three rinky-dink units on senses (You Learn with Your Eyes, You Learn with Your Ears, More About Your Senses), followed by one unit each on types of animals, types of plants, health, God's Beautiful World, energy, and simple machines.

Grade 2 units are: Living and Nonliving, Plants, Animals (classifying and defining), You (anatomy, self-esteem, family, health), Pet and Plant Care, Your Five Senses, Physical Properties (colors, shapes, sizes, textures), Our Neighborhood Environment (pollution and ecology), and Changes in Our World (seasons and growth contrasted to the unchangeableness of God).

Grade 3 units: Your Body and Change (respiratory system, digestive system, exercise, differences between people and animals), Plants (parts and growth), Animals (parts, growth, and environment), You are What You Eat (nutrition and hygiene, including junk food and mental hygiene), Properties of Matter, Sounds and You, Times and Seasons, Rocks and Their Change, and Heat Energy.

LIFEPACS in the first three grades often include science principles in story form, e.g., "The class was excited. Mrs. Farmer, the teacher, explained they were going to talk about food." Mrs. Farmer then lectures on food, with the children in the story interjecting questions. Some of us would consider this cute and appealing, while others find it silly.

Grade 4 starts the spiral again with plants, animals, man and his environment, and machines. New topics include electricity and magnetism, properties of water, weather types and causes, solar system and universe, and a layered view of earth as atmosphere, hydrosphere, and lithosphere. Rick and Mary visit Uncle George and learn about how plants are used for food. Mrs. Turner's class at Good Hope School recycle cans and learn about ecology. Pastor Miller explains simple machines. Kids learn about the "web of life" ("Life here on earth is like a spider web. Each thread depends on the other thread to hold the web together. Ecology is the study of the web of life.") and are pressured to take personal responsibility for instituting greenie reforms.

Grade 5 is the first serious science course. We kiss Uncle George and Mrs. Turner goodbye in favor of straight scientific explanations. The course has smaller print, a more balanced ecological viewpoint ("The big decision is whether to be careful or to be careless. Plants and animals are here to be used—*carefully*."), including a pro-hunting outlook ("Hunters can be helpful in keeping a balance, especially when other predators are scarce.") Serious microscope work is also introduced, beginning with staining your own slides. Units cover cells, life cycles of animals and plants, "The Web of Life," energy and work (physics, not manual labor), a three-unit study of fossils and geology that takes a look at the Biblical account of Noah's Flood, and a final unit on cycles in nature. Since grade

5 reviews most of what was covered in the first four grades, you might want to consider starting with this course.

Grade 6 looks at plant and animal systems (e.g., roots, stems, and leaves) and plant and animal behavior (animal nervous systems, responses, and intelligence, how plants react to their environment, and plant-animal interaction in nature). Sixth-graders also take a whack at biology with a unit on molecular genetics, a whack at chemistry with a unit on chemical structure and change (including a look at the periodic table, atoms, and acids and bases), and a double whack at physics with one unit on light and sound and another on motion and its measurement. The unit entitled "Spaceship Earth" has nothing to do with population issues; it's about earth's behavior in the solar system. The last unit, "The Sun and Other Stars," naturally follows. The sixth-grade course is an excellent "basic science" course, especially for those who have thus far managed to resist textbook science courses.

UPDATED★★
Bob Jones University Press
Student Worktexts: grades 1–6 (hardbound), $11.95 each. Teacher's editions: $29.50 each grade. TestBanks, Notebook Packets, and various supplemental teaching aids also available. Home-school teacher's editions for grades 1–4, due out fall 1991, prices TBA (expected to be between $12.95 and $14.95).

Bob Jones has a textbook science series for Christian schools that has met with a great deal of approval in home schooling circles. The first few grades, as usual with science series, are rather lightweight, but start-ing in grade 3 you get an excellent, lean, presentation of science. Topics range widely in any given volume, just as they do in the public school science curriculum (and just about everyone else's, too).

Grade 3 topics include classification of animals, the solar system, skin, photosynthesis, birds, mass, and weight. Grade 4 "presents God as the Author of order." Beginning with a study of the moon, in which the theories of creation and evolution are compared according to the evidence, it continues to the topics of insects, light, electricity, area and volume, simple machines, digestion, animal defenses, trees, erosion, and simple insect classifications. The grade 5 book presents the limits of science (compared to the infinite knowledge of God). Topics are fossils, airplanes, thermal energy, atomic theory, weather, plant and animal reproduction, oceans, forces causing wind, and animal tracks. The new grade 6 book explores earthquakes, volcanoes, the stars, nuclear energy, chemistry, circulation, space exploration, laws of motion, respiration, animal behavior, and the balance of nature (basic ecology).

BJUP attempts to combine factual learning with process skills and experimentation. Each chapter in each book has experiments or activities based on its topic; students are taught to observe and record their experiments. The teacher's manuals add considerably to the cost of this program, but for a full-scale science program you will find them worth it. Note: special home-school science teacher's editions for grades 1–4 will be released in fall 1991. These will cost considerably less and be designed especially for home use.

BJUP also carries most of the lab apparatus you are ever likely to need and chemicals in classroom-sized portions.

UPDATED★★
Christian Schools International
Grades 3–6 student books, $15.75–$16.75/grade. Teacher's guides, $33.45–$34.70/grade.

Christian Schools International's line of grades 3–6 science textbooks is hardbound (a plus for penny-pinching parents of large families). It is extremely well laid out, with material presented in an easy-to-learn-and-remember format. Inexpensive, too. Spiral-bound teacher's guides include assignments, experiments, enrichment activities, and tests.

At this point I must add some discouraging words. Since I hate to be discouraging, I'm going to quote from a letter sent by a reader:

I just ordered two science texts from Christian Schools International, for third and fourth grade. They were, as you said, very well laid out with good articles and well-done experiments. I could not bring myself to keep them, however, and this is why I am writing to you. . . .

I believe it was under the section entitled "Food" that there was a page on World Hunger. The question was basically, "What are we as RICH AMERICANS going to do about all those mass millions in the POOR countries of the world?" No mention was made of the fact that many of these countries are poor and unable to raise much food because of their governmental structure (Communism). Should we send them our grain to have it rot in warehouses or so that those governments can sell it to others for weapons?

In another section talking about ecosystems, men were portrayed as damaging different ecosystems and their organisms, as in the example of cutting down the trees around the edge of a pond and what that would do to the inhabitants thereof.

[Note from Mary—To be consistent, any textbook writer who complains about men cutting down trees near a pond should be against *beavers,* who do this for a living! But we continue . . .]

In another section talking about food webs and food chains, the authors were trying to talk us into being vegetarians, because it uses less energy. In other words, don't eat the pig which eats the corn, just eat the corn. I still haven't figured out how we would ship either the "saved energy" or the uneaten pig to all those hungry people.

There was an article in these books about Jacques Cousteau (whose documentaries are flavored with the depressing theme of overpopulation). Some Christian scientists were discussed, but I don't remember reading much about their faith.

There was also much talk about nonrenewable resources. Should we "as Christians" use wood or gas or solar heat? The flavor of some of the chapters in these two books really bothered me.

Don't get me wrong. My husband and I both support two children through World Vision in Kenya. And we just had our fifth child two months ago. I am concerned about our environment. I try to recycle. But I don't like being subtly indoctrinated in "Christian" socialism or radical ecology when all I wanted was a science text.

You get the idea. If you like the Greenpeace view of people and nature, you'll love these books.

EDC Publishing
Introductions series: *Introduction to Chemistry, Biology, Physics, Electronics,* $6.95 each. Combined volume *The Usborne Book of Science* $14.95 hardbound, includes intros to chemistry, biology, and physics. New Technology series: *Satellites and Space Stations, Robotics, Lasers, Information Revolution,* $6.95 each paperback or $13.96 library-bound. Electronic World series: *Films & Special Effects, Audio and Radio, TV & Video,* $5.95 each or $13.96 each library-bound. *Simple Science, How Things Work,* $10.95 each (hardbound).

All the science textbook suppliers offer courses in at least some particular disciplines—biology, chemistry, and physics being among the most popular. These are usually geared to the high school years. But why wait until then? Younger children can pick up a *lot* of science from the colorful, engrossing Usborne Science Series. These books, produced in England, offer full-color, cartoon-style explanations on every page. Titles include not only such standard offerings as *Introduction to Physics* and *Introduction to Chemistry,* but fascinating applications like *Robotics, Lasers,* and *Films and Special Effects.* The technology books are easier going than the science books, but all can be read with profit by an alert preteen.

NEW✶✶
KONOS Character Curriculum

One of the best ways to learn the scientific method is to *study the history of science.* Instead of dull lectures about Rule A and Hypothesis B, why not find out why and how someone bothered to invent the rule or the hypothesis in the first place? For anyone interested in this approach, Volume II of the KONOS curriculum is hard (maybe impossible) to beat. See review of KONOS in Volume 1 for more details.

Learning at Home

Science Teaching Guides, $13.75/grade, grades 1–3. Grades 4–6 available only as combined resource units of language arts, science, math, and social studies—about $36 each.

Truly excellent teaching guides with reasonable experiments, good outlines, and teaching tips. Many experiments use household objects. For those that don't, a supplier and address is given. You may find some of the experiments a bit elaborate—like keeping guppies and watching them have babies—but since the outline format explains what you are trying to teach, you can readily substitute a similar, simpler activity.

Like all Learning at Home products, their science teaching guides encourage a lot of questioning and thinking—the scientific process—along with the accumulation of facts and terminology.

SCIENCE "FACT" BOOKS

NEW**
EDC Publishing

Facts and Lists series: *Ocean Facts, Bird Facts, Animals Facts, Weather Facts, Space Facts*, $5.95 each. Shipping extra. Ages 8–12.

Hey, betcha didn't know . . . that a long time ago people in Madagascar used the shells of elephant birds to carry water . . . a giant albatross can fly up to 600 miles per day . . . Mauna Kea in the Pacific Ocean is the highest mountain on earth, when measured from its base . . . the plough snail of southern Africa "surfs" its way in to shore? These, and hundreds more records, lists, facts, and comparisons, all illustrated in a vibrant cartoon style, are found in the Usborne "facts" books.

Each book in this series is organized in double-page spreads, each devoted to a single topic such as "Birds of prey" or "Eggs and young." Fascinating browsing. Evolutionary outlook.

NEW**
TREND Enterprises, Inc.

Each bulletin board set, $5.99, includes free Discovery Guide. Requires 4 x 6' bulletin board. Shipping $2. Minimum order $10. Grades 3–8.

I get jealous sometimes when I look at all the neat stuff available today for science-minded kids. Back when *I* was a kid . . . in the days when we had to walk to school for miles through waist-high snowdrifts (OK, so I'm exaggerating) . . . when 25¢ was a week's allowance, and the town square didn't even have a Radio Shack . . . I had never even *heard* of an electricity study unit. Come high school days, I did manage to put together a crystal radio. Big deal: it could only pick up one station!

Times have changed. Here are *three* excellent bulletin-board science kits to jump-start your young children's engineering and physics knowledge. First, *Magnets and Electricity*. Its bulletin-board visuals provide colorful introductory information illustrated in a memorable fashion. For example, the "Kinds of Electricity" visual shows the difference between static and current electricity by the familiar examples of a kid generating static electricity combing his hair and then getting a shock on a doorknob, contrasted with a picture of a light connected to a bulb. As with other TREND bulletin-board sets, the visuals are only the beginning. The four-page discovery guide provides excellent background information and discovery activities.

By the way, let me mention right here that I'm really impressed with TREND's Discovery Guides. It's not easy to pack the most important information about a topic into four pages *and* explain it clearly as well—not to mention adding in just the right amount of suggested activities! Someone at TREND evidently understands that brevity is the soul of wit.

Back to the bulletin board. TREND's *Heat, Light, and Sound* kit includes visuals explaining the basic nature of heat, light, and sound, their characteristics, how they are used in daily life, and how we measure all three. You can hold the included pinwheel cutout over a lit light bulb to demonstrate convection currents (the pinwheel will spin as the heated air moves up past it), or spin the color wheel cutout to see how colors blend to form white. The discovery guide contains lots more simple experiments you can do as well.

Simple Machines is another example of basic scientific knowledge I never discovered until college. Cutouts illustrate everyday examples of an inclined plane, wheel and axle, screw, pulley, lever, and wedge.

This particular discovery guide gets really into it, with a list of 18 suggested materials so you can set up your own Simple Machines Science Center, plus several interesting experiments using the materials. Oh, yes—the discovery guide also explains the six simple machines in detail, and includes a reproducible match-up page for children to identify the simple machines used in everyday objects. A boon to non-mechanically-minded moms!

CHAPTER THIRTY-ONE

SCIENCE EXPERIMENTS AND ACTIVITIES

Short and sweet: you're doing a science *experiment* when you actually measure, observe, and/or combine things together. When you model a natural object, or color a picture of it, or observe a model of it, that's a science *activity*. The difference is whether you are actually getting your hands on the "real" items you are studying, or simply working with copies of them. Got it? Great! Then let's look at some . . .

But first, a word from our sponsor. I thought it would be a good idea to separate the simple machines experiments from the regular science experiments, since wheels and gears have rather little to do with baking soda volcanoes and other traditional science experiments. Since many of you are entering science fairs, there's also a small section on this topic. Now you know what's in this chapter . . . so let's get into it!

SCIENCE EXPERIMENTS

UPDATED✶✶
Backyard Scientists
Original book $9.50. *Backyard Scientist, Series 1* (ages 4–12) , *Series 2* (ages 9–14), and *Series 3* (ages 4–12), $9.50 each. Videotape, $6 to cover shipping and duplication. Free shipping on books.

The Original Backyard Scientist is a book that gives children a "fun hands-on introduction to science," with thirty step-by-step science experiments that four- to twelve-year-olds can perform using things found around the house. Unlike many books that make this claim, you probably actually do already possess most of the experiment ingredients. The experiments range from fun to spectacular (lots of visual effects), and are laid out like easy-to-follow recipes.

The author, Jane Hoffman, has received national attention for her Backyard Science program, now in its tenth year. Mrs. Hoffman now works as a consultant to school systems. Her book is highly recommended by the National Science Foundation.

Backyard Scientist, Series 1 is a sequel to *The Original Backyard Scientist* and the first in a projected new series. Fully illustrated, it has a larger and easier-to-read format. Like the original, the Series 1 book is a hit with home schoolers and imaginative elementary teachers. Try it—your kids will like it!

Backyard Scientist, Series 2, is a bit more advanced. While the first two books are for children ages 4–12, this one is for preteen ages 9–14. Like the others, it includes simple, illustrated instructions and common household materials. The format: (1) Step-by-step instructions. (2) A section, "Can you answer the following questions from your observations?" follows each experiment. (3) The "Backyard Scientist Solution to Experiment" answers the questions and provides further background information about the topic studied. Designed for home schoolers, extensively used by same.

New: *Backyard Scientist, Series 3* concentrates on the life sciences. Same easy-to-use format, designed for ages 4–12. Also new: a short videotape of assorted Backyard Scientist experiments, taken from Jane Hoffman's TV appearances. These are neat experiments, featuring Jane's bouncy enthusiasm and a lot of foaming, surging, color-changing stuff.

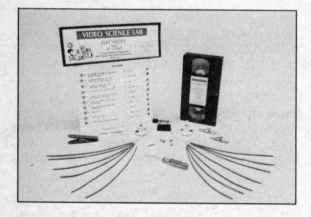

NEW★★
BG Science
Video Electricity Lab, Video Chemistry Lab, $39.95 each. Grades 3–7.

A neat new concept in science education—videos! Mr. Wizard may have invented the medium on TV, but he didn't provide material kits for viewers. BG Science, sensing a market niche, is doing just that. Both its Video Electricity Lab and its Video Chemistry Lab include *all* materials (except ingredients like water, which are available everywhere).

BG, the lady scientist on the video, leads you through the experiments step by step. I appreciate her professional style; too many video teachers come across like gushing phonies.

First, the Video Electricity Lab. BG and the kids build circuits, test conductors and insulators, make a

telegraph, and investigate fuses. The hit of the kit is the quiz board, which kids construct themselves. Using the board, they test themselves on the electricity concepts they just learned! Seven experiments in all, in a kid-appealing package.

The Video Chemistry Lab didn't interest my kids quite as much. Included along with the video in the clear plastic carrying case are are safety goggles, two 100-ml graduated beakers, a screwtop 100-ml graduated container, a 50-ml graduated cylinder with a stand, two long-handled measuring spoons, a funnel, filter paper, two marking pens, a balloon, a special paper strip, and labeled containers of litmus paper, sucrose (otherwise known as white sugar), starch, and baking soda. It demonstrates the Periodic Table of the Elements (hard to get kids excited about this), a chemical reaction, suspensions, solutions, paper chromatography, acids and bases, and speed of solution. Nothing blows up or zaps a fuse, and all the ingredients are non-toxic; hence my young ruffians' disinterest! (They did wake up for the experiment in which you combine baking soda and vinegar to inflate a balloon. Baking soda and vinegar make a nice fizz.) Nonetheless, this kit is very professional and educational, you get a lot of quality science equipment (which is good for other experiments you might do in future), and I enjoyed the experiments!

Each kit is good for at least several hours of hands-on science, with *no* preparation or teaching time needed! Teacher's guide included with each kit, with teaching tips, lab worksheets for each experiment, and an answer key for questions. Great for home teachers who need a break. These kits also make great gifts.

NEW★★
Creative Teaching Associates
Discover the Wonders of Water, $6.95. Add 10% shipping ($3 minimum). Grades 4–12.

A book of 20 simple, fun experiments using water and normal household objects. Activities are designed to teach kids about the properties of water in its solid, liquid, and gaseous forms. Kids try to float oranges, with and without peels, in water; make paper clip boats; observe evaporation and melting; and find out why popcorn pops, among other things. All experiments are easy to set up and require no onerous written work. If you do your science experiments once a week, like we do, it's almost a half-year's easygoing science for very little money.

NEW★★
EDC Publishing
Science with Water, Science with Light and Mirrors, Science with Magnets, $3.95 each. Shipping extra. Ages 6–11.

I've just seen the first book in the new Usborne Science Activities series for young children. It's *Science with Water,* and it's excellent! Its 24 pages are a series of simple step-by-step illustrated experiments, capped by notes for parents and teachers explaining the scientific topics covered and a complete index. Topics include surface tension, volume, boat design, evaporation and condensation, solutions, water power, air and water tricks, absorption, and ice. These technical terms aren't used in the book: instead it talks about water's "skin," floating, fun with boats, and other nonthreatening terms. The experiments are all doable, requiring no fancy equipment nor much preparation time. This kid-pleasing series is great for injecting a dose of science into even the heaviest home schedule.

NEW★★
EDC Publishing
Where Does Electricity Come from?, What Makes a Flower Grow?, What Makes it Rain?, What's Under the Ground?, Why is Night Dark?, What's Inside You?, What's Out in Space?, $3.95 each. Shipping extra. Ages 3–8.

The new Usborne Starting Point Science series for young children features simple text and lively explanatory cartoon illustrations. The question in each title is answered step by step. Each book also includes simple experiments.

Unlike some Usborne books, whose pages are so loaded with sidebars and graphics that your eye just has to jump from thrill to thrill, you can actually read the Starting Point Science books to your children from start to finish. Older children can read them by themselves. Lots to look at and discuss on every page. Evolutionary content in *What's Under the Ground*, *Why is Night Dark?*, and *What's Out in Space*.

UPDATED★★
EDC Publishing
Pocket Scientist series: *Fun with Electronics, Chemistry Experiments, Flight and Floating,* $4.95 each paperbound or $11.96 each library-bound. Shipping extra. Ages 10 and up.

The Usborne Pocket Scientist series includes experiments, projects, and puzzles that explain basic sci-

entific principles. Lots of things to make, using readily-available components. The chemistry book only uses household materials, for safe experiments. Full-color, fully-illustrated, 64-page books, with the famous Usborne visual layout.

Educational Design, Inc.
Mini-Labs, individual prices, $7.99 to $35.95, most around $8. These are school prices. Grades 3–7.

For all-in-one colorful, inexpensive, hands-on science, Educational Design's Mini-Labs look hard to beat. Electronics, solar energy, chemistry, physics, even paper airplanes—it's all here. If you're a school you're entitled to the special school price and can order directly from the manufacturer. If not, you can send in a prepaid order, or order them from Insect Lore Products.

Educational Design also has Comprehensive Science Labs—*Power-Tech Electricity, Physics Lab, Chemistry Lab, Electronics 60, World of Radio and Electronics,* and *Solar Energy*.

NEW★★
Educational Insights
Adventures in Science series, $12.95 each from Learning at Home. Shipping extra. Ages 8 and up.

The good folks at Learning at Home sent me some samples of these Educational Insights kits. (You might as well buy these kits from Learning at Home, since Educational Insights doesn't sell directly to the public.)

What we have here is the perfect drop-of-a-hat science program. Each kit comes with a few ingredients not normally found around your house and a set of 35 mini Project Booklets. Each Project Booklet is a single greeting-card-shaped sheet of heavy paper folded in half, numbered in sequence, and illustrated on the front with a picture of the experiment inside. The scientific topic explored is the title of the booklet: e.g., *Find Out About Air* or *Build a Hygrometer*.

Inside each booklet are some introductory thought questions, a list of materials needed, and step-by-step instructions for one or more discovery experiments. Often you will be observing strange things, like paper inside an underwater glass remaining dry or a balloon full of air weighing more than an uninflated balloon. The scientific processes causing these phenomena are explained on the last page of each booklet.

The Adventures in Science format is super handy for quickie experiments. Just grab the first little booklet you haven't yet completed, round up the materials, and do the experiments! Or, if you prefer, browse through the booklets until you find one that meets your fancy.

The scientific equipment included in each kit is not terribly deluxe. The Sky Science kit includes a teeny-tiny compass, a test tube, a packet of balloons, and a thermometer. The Light kit includes a small prism, several sheets of colored cellophane (the "colored and polarized filters"), a piece of silver plastic (that's the "reflective surface"), and a small piece of clear plastic with zillions of teeny, invisible lines (the "diffraction grating"). Hey, at the price of these kits, we can't expect them to throw in a stereo microscope!

The Adventures in Science series includes:

- *Light*—Build a periscope, shadow clock, kaleidoscope, spectroscope, water magnifier, model of the human eye. Explore color illusions and the effect of light on plants. Play with mirrors.

- *Sky Science*—Build a barometer, anemometer, weather vane, salad dressing bottle thermometer, rain gauge, hygrometer, and weather map, and put them together to make a complete weather station. Make a sundial, lunar eclipse model, model solar system, moon craters, refracting telescope, bearing dial, constellarium, model galaxy, balloon space ship. Perform magic tricks, like turning a glass full of water upside down without spilling it. Learn about air, weather, the solar system, spaceships. A terrific kit!

- *Electricity*—comes with light bulbs, insulated wire, light sockets, and battery clips. Build an electronic quiz game, parallel and series circuits, galvanometer, telegraph, and rheostat. Learn principles of electrical safety, battery handling. Split water molecules with electricity.

- *Backyard Science*—magnifying bug viewer, copper wire, beads, metal washer. Build bird feeder, butterfly model, tetrahedral kite, astrolabe. Print with leaves. Collect and observe bugs. Learn to recognize the constellations.

- *Magnetism*—includes horseshoe magnet, disk and bar magnets, nails, insulated wire, iron filings. Build electromagnets, other magnets, floating polygons. Go on a magnetism treasure hunt.

- *How Things Work*—nontoxic stamp pad, magnifying glass, medicine cups, cup hook. Build a balloon-powered "rocket boat," pin piano, and more. Learn about inertia, friction, simple machines, levers and pulleys, sound and sonar.

- *Kitchen Science*—four peat pots (the kind that expand to full size when you pour water on them), radish seeds, candlewicks. Make play dough, paint with tissue paper, grow your own salad, etc.

Between these seven kits, you get more hands-on science and *memorable* exposure to more science topics than most schoolkids get in grades K–12. No miserable workbook pages or opaque directions—just lots and lots of *fun!*

NEW**
Exploratorium Publications
Exploratorium Science Snackbook, $19.95. Add $4 shipping for first copy, $2 each additional copy. Grades K–12.

I know you're dying to ask, so here are the answers to your questions:

First, the Exploratorium is a hands-on science museum in San Francisco.

Second, they once published a book for science museums explaining how to put together some of their most popular exhibits. That book was called the *Cookbook.*

This book, written for classroom teachers, explains how to make kiddie versions of the exhibits—hence the term *Snackbook.* (Get it? Cookbook? Snackbook?) Each project takes somewhere between a minute and an hour to put together, and often kids can do it themselves with just a bit of adult help.

The *Snackbook* is arranged alphabetically, starting with "After Image," a perception and light experiment, and ending with "Whirling Watcher," whatever that is. (I'm reviewing the book in manuscript form, and the last few pages were left off my photocopy.) An index helps you find individual experiments more quickly, as does a cross-reference by subject and phenomenon. Another index, "Sources and Suppliers of Materials," should make it easier for you to come up with the few nonstandard supplies needed. About the "Cross-reference to California State Science Framework" I couldn't care less, and neither will most parents.

The *Snackbook* has a really nice layout. At the beginning of each "snack" is a picture of the Exploratorium exhibit, and a drawing or picture of what your project should look like when finished. The main difference between the two is that the Exploratorium builds its exhibits to be beaten on by thousands of kids and incorporates fancy stuff like buttons and electronic gear. Your version simply demonstrates the scientific principle without a lot of fuss.

Beneath the pictures is a sidebar with a list of materials needed, most of which you have lying around the house. A very short introduction explains what scientific principles your project will demonstrate. Illustrated assembly instructions make it easy to put the "snack" together, and a "What's Going On?" section at the end explains how it works. An "Etc." sidebar shares project extensions and follow-up activities.

The *Snackbook* is heavy on perception and light experiments, as they are flashy and fun and many of them can be done using only a flashlight, index card, paper, and/or mirror. It also includes some simple chemistry, electricity, magnetism, mechanics, sound, heat, and other projects. I would have liked to see a more even spread of projects—when you've seen one optical illusion, you've seen 'em all. All the same, it's a good resource for simple and satisfying Friday afternoon science experiments.

NEW**
Fearon Teacher Aids
Science Cookbook, $8.95 plus $3.50 shipping. Grades 4–8.

We home schoolers keep telling ourselves that we can teach kids almost anything in our kitchens. Measurement—yeah. Adding and subtracting—no problem. Fractions—piece of cake (pause here to laugh at the joke). Phonics—fingerpainting letters with vanilla pudding. Etiquette—never fingerpainting with vanilla pudding. Social studies—observing the reaction of the guests to Junior's fingerpainting in the vanilla pudding. And so it goes.

We like to talk about kitchen science, too. Nutrition. Observation. Classification. But how about dissolution . . . oxidation . . . evaporation and absorption . . . coagulation . . . softening . . . thickening . . . separation . . . leavening? All this, and more, gallops right into your kitchen with *The Science Cookbook* by Julia B. Waxter.

Let me hasten to inform you that the kitchen science experiments in this book are *not* cutesy rainy-day time-wasters. Nor are they beat-it-and-eat-it home ec. The terminology is scientific, the methods are scientific, and the goal is scientific.

Gourmets beware: you will have to ruin some good food to carry out these experiments! Overcooking a bit of an omelet teaches kids about what heat does to protein. On the other hand, the kids will get to discover which procedures make the omelet fluffier—and why.

Every chapter tackles a different topic (e.g., coagulation) and begins with an explanation of the topic, learning objectives, applied skills used in the experiments, and key ideas to teach. Each experiment likewise includes explanation and teaching tips, scientific vocabulary, materials needed, discussion questions, and related activities. All vocabulary words are indexed, and the book closes with 28 pages of reproducible cookbook experiments. Typical experiment: learn about coagulation by preparing hard-boiled eggs. Bonus knowledge from this experiment: learn about chicken metabolism and life cycle, osmosis, digestion of cooked and raw protein, and why eggs cook better if punctured on the proper side with a pin.

The program was developed for a class of kids with "learning disabilities," and rapidly became one of the most popular courses in that school. This "real" approach to science held the kids' attention, too (keep in mind that we're talking classes of 90 percent boys, many of them labeled hyper).

NEW★★
Ladybird Books, Inc.
Junior Science series, $3.50 each. Ages 8 and up.

From England, the Ladybird Junior Science series
has basic introductions and simple, safe experiments
with light, air, simple machines, simple chemistry,
botany, zoology, and weather. I haven't actually seen
any of these books, but if they're up to the standard of
other Ladybird books, they're a lot of information for a
very low price.

NEW★★
Midwest Publications
Developing Critical Thinking through Science, $19.95.
Grades 4–6.

So you don't know nuttin' about science. So you
don't have a lot of time to do science. So you don't
have a lot of fancy equipment. "So what?" say the folks
at Midwest Publications. Schools are full of teachers
just like you. With the help of their *Developing Critical
Thinking through Science* (a hot title if I've ever seen
one) you'll have 80 step-by-step science experiments
covering 17 science areas.

Each activity in this book is presented as a dialog
between teacher and student. Example:

3. What is in the cup?
Nothing. It's empty. Air.

4. How do we know?
Air is all around us, so there must be some in the cup.

5. Now watch as I put the plastic bag in the cup.
Put the bag in the cup, fold the edges of the open end over
the rim of the cup, and wrap the rubber bands around the
mouth as shown in the drawing.

6. What has happened to most of the air in the cup?
It was pushed out by the bag when you put the bag
into the cup.

7. Now . . . come up and pull the bag out of the cup.

8. What happened?
I can't pull the bag out. . . . [and so on]

Obviously, your kids aren't going to be in the picture enough to figure out all the answers, but that's
OK, since *you* know the answers.

The catalog copy for this book burbles about how
"the study of science works best in a cooperative, open
learning environment where there are no 'wrong' answers, but many possible right ones." The book itself,
as you have seen, happily recognizes that science consists of finding the right answers. The kids are not free,
for example, to tell you that the cup is full of mustard
when it is empty, or that the cup is still full of air when
you've eliminated most of the air with a plastic bag.

Each lesson begins with a goal, list of skills, list of
materials, and step-by-step preparation guide. The
time needed to prepare for a lesson (generally 2–5
minutes) and to teach the lesson (generally 15–30
minutes) is also given right up front. The preparation
time figures do *not* include time spent gathering the
materials. Some of these are common household objects but others, like different types of magnets, need
to be purchased from commercial venders. You'd be
smart to plan ahead and gather materials for several
lessons at a time.

After the first five lessons on science process skills,
the book covers:

- Force, movement, work, systems, and weight
- States of matter
- Mass, volume, and density
- Air pressure—the pressure of the atmosphere
- Heat, expansion, and molecular movement
- Energy transfer
- Flight and aerodynamics
- The speed of falling bodies
- Graphing, the flight of helicopters, and
  controlling variables
- Rocket flight and action-reaction
- Inertia and satellite flight
- Surface tension
- Bubbles

- Sounds
- Light: reflection and refraction
- Magnetism and electricity

The experiments are the usual classics like balloon rockets and getting eggs into bottles. Easy to use, lots of good "thinking" questions, and lots of good answers.

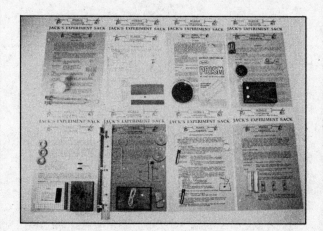

NEW★★
Norris Science Kits
Jack's Experiment Sacks, $3.25–$12.50 each. Catalog, $2, refunded on first order. Shipping extra. Grades 3–7.

Jack's Experiment Sacks are just the thing for a rainy day. Each includes everything you need for investigating one scientific topic: for example, constructing a wooden helicopter (and learning how a real helicopter flies), or using litmus paper to test for acids and bases. You get an experiment sheet on colorful, durable cardstock, ready to slip into the student's notebook or science journal, also. These very simple experiments don't take long to set up or complete. The series includes:

- Paper Clip Float (magnetism)
- The Tuning Fork (sounds)
- Hand Lens (observation skills)
- The Prism ("An en-light-ening experiment")
- Testing for Acids and Bases
- Galvanometer/Compass (detecting electric current)
- Floating Magnets ("Opposites attract")
- Wood Helicopter ("Watch it fly")
- Growing Bacteria
- The Pulley.

NEW★★
Teacher's Laboratory, Inc.
Genecon Kit, $48. Generator only (no wires, bulb holders, etc.), $25. Notes/Skill Cards only, $15. Add 10% shipping.

The minute my boys laid eyes on Teacher's Laboratory's Produce Your Own Electricity Kit, also listed in their catalog as their Genecon Kit, their eyes lit up just like the little bulbs included in the kit. "Are you going to review that one now? When are you going to review it? Can we have it when you're done?"

The heart of this kit, and the main attraction to my science-minded lads, is the attractive handheld generator. This cute little gizmo, which rather resembles a small pencil sharpener, is really a surprisingly durable tool. Plug something in to the "sharpener" end, crank the handle, and it produces electric power—up to 12 volts if you crank really fast. This is a *lot* more exciting than batteries, and safer, too, for many experiments.

Also included in the kit are a plug with two color-coded wires ending separately in alligator clips, two additional wires with alligator clips on each end, two light sockets with bulbs included, and one solid-state buzzer. The *Notes to Teachers* explain how to use the kit, and the 17 skill cards explain how to build and test everything from simple series and parallel circuits to fancier combinations with lights and buzzers. A few of the skill cards require extra ingredients, such as a nail, piece of wood, or slice of potato, but most of the discovery experiments can be done just with what's included in the kit. A terrific, high-interest introduction to electricity. (By the way, you can use the handheld generator as a power source for the electric motor included in LEGO's Technic Kit II, if you like.)

UPDATED★★
Things of Science
$36/year for 12 science kits (one mailed each month). Ages 8–14.

The gift that keeps giving all year long. Every month the subscriber gets a science kit in the mail, filled with safe, simple materials and easy instructions for as many as 30 experiments. Each month the topic changes. Recent kits have covered such topics as gravity, magnetism, friction, static electricity, heat, light, sound, surface tension, lever and pulley, and seed growth.

In the past, the kits were designed for older children, but the new kits have been revised and repackaged for preteens. Most of the club members are 10–12 years old.

$3 a month is not a lot to spend for enough Friday science experiments to last that month! I also like the topic-by-topic approach, which helps kids learn more than a scattershot "let's do an experiment and who cares what it's about" approach.

Things of Science has been around for over 50 years, so you can be fairly confident they know what they're doing. Many *Big Book* readers have subscribed to this series in the past, and I haven't heard any complaints.

NEW★★
Timberdoodle
TOPS Structured Worksheets, $13–$14 each subject. Shipping extra.

The TOPS company is revising its popular task-card science modules. The new version comes in a bound workbook complete with an introduction to the TOPS philosophy, teaching notes for every task card, a set of review/test questions with answer key, and two-up sheets of reproducible task cards in the back. This new format is a dream for the home teacher. Every single concept and activity is explained in full in the teacher notes, which consist of a copy of the task card at the top of the page and all answers, materials needed, and teaching tips at the bottom of the page.

OK. So we like the new format. Now what is TOPS? First, it's an attempt to combine both the "process" approach and the "traditional knowledge" approach to science. Kids learn facts *and* do open-ended experiments. Just about the entire field of science is covered, as a series of separate topics. Second, TOPS is science with simple things. No need for expensive kits of chemicals, miles of glass tubing, Bunsen burners, and so on.

Timberdoodle presently offers the TOPS modules for probability, electricity, solutions (stuff dissolved in liquid), cohesion/adhesion, electricity, magnetism, animal survival, and the brand new *Rocks and Minerals* module. No evolutionary preaching in any of these modules. All mostly use simple materials found around the house. For example, the *Electricity* TOPS module has your child building bulb holders, battery holders, and switches out of paper clips, rubber bands, clothespins, aluminum foil, and pennies. Any additional materials are clearly listed at the beginning of each book.

What this all means is that for around $15 you can have 4–5 weeks of real science experiments with easy-to-gather materials like paper clips, string, test tubes, and candles.

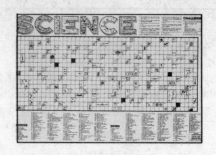

SIMPLE MACHINES & ENGINEERING

UPDATED★★
Ampersand Press
AC/DC game, $7.95. *Science Participoster*, $9.95. Shipping $2.75. Items shipped UPS. Ages 8 and up.

The neatest introduction to the study of electricity that I've seen, Ampersand's *AC/DC Electric Circuit Game* is played with a deck of special cards. Cards depict energy sources, wires, switches, energy users, and fuses. The object of the game is to construct workable circuits. Players may get "shocked" or "shorted," so watch out! You can't help but learn the rudiments of electricity playing the game. I wish someone had given me this game before I went to engineering school (but then, it probably hadn't been invented way back then!)

The *Participoster* is a huge crossword puzzle loaded with science questions. It's been updated since the last edition of *Big Book*: now it comes laminated, with four write-and-wipe crayons included.

Ampersand Press also has some nifty ecology games, reviewed under Nature Study.

Burt Harrison & Company, Inc.
Batteries and Bulbs Mini Kit, with activity book, $29.95. Book alone, $6.50. Add $3 shipping. Grades 3–7.

Science books, games, equipment for hands-on experiments, and "things." "Kitchen physics." Equipment for measuring and looking. Fantastic prices (example: 30x/100x microscope for $7).

Burt's niftiest science kit is the *Batteries and Bulbs Mini Kit* (a larger size is available for schools). Suggested for children aged eight to twelve, but also usable for impatient four- to seven-year-olds, the kit is a whole pile of materials for investigating magnetism and electricity, including (believe it or not) four batteries! Now when's the last time you ever saw a supplier include batteries with anything? Kids not only "perform experiments," but come to understand the basic principles of electricity and magnetism while making a flashlight, galvanometer, electromagnet, telegraph key, and buzzer. The activity book reveals all, and if our children's reaction means anything, your red-blooded American tyke would love it, too. Small-fry need adult help, of course.

If you love widgets and whatzits, don't miss this catalog.

NEW**
Cuisenaire Company of America

Two-Student Baufix set, $28.95, grades preK–4. Baufix Cog Wheels and Propulsion Parts set, $14.95, grades 1–4. Shipping extra.

This Baufix stuff is really neat. It's a construction kit for kids ages three through 10, with large, chunky pieces cleverly designed to introduce young kids to simple mechanical and technical skills.

The Two-Student Baufix set includes an assortment of 34 wooden bolts of different lengths, all color-coded; six wooden block nuts; a collection of three-hole, four-hole, five-hole, and seven-hole connecting bars; four wheels with tires you can stretch over them; several sizes of base plates; nine wooden diamond nuts; spacers and washers galore; and a wooden wrench. The included wordless manual has visual instructions for nine projects, but of course your children can make hundreds of models with these open-ended materials.

The Baufix Cog Wheels and Propulsion Parts set comes with two large (3.75") gears and six small (1.25") gears, along with two hooks, cranks, lots of spacers, and a goodish number of shafts and locknuts. Unhappily, you can't make any of the projects in the included wordless manual, because they all require a wooden baseplate or three-hole threaded blocks, neither of which are included in either Baufix set from Cuisenaire Company.

Even little kids can handle the Baufix materials, screwing bolts into block nuts and sliding spacers on bolts. My son built the first project—a rather complicated vehicle—on his fourth birthday!

Baufix is a great toy that beats Duplos, Erector sets, and Lincoln Logs hollow. Now what we need for full educational value are (1) wooden baseplates and threaded blocks, (2) pulleys, and (3) a separate project manual or set of task cards along the lines of the LEGO Dacta Technic materials. Even without these goodies, Baufix is a lot of creative fun. With them, it would be a deserving candidate for Educational Product of the Year.

NEW**
EDC Publishing

Young Machines series: *Diggers and Cranes, Tractors, Trucks,* $5.95 each, or combined volume, *Machines That Work,* TBA. Beginner's Knowledge series: *Trains, Tracks & Railways; Castles, Pyramids, & Palaces; Ships, Sailors, & the Sea;* $7.95 each paperbound or $13.96 each library-bound, ages 7 and up. *How Things Work,* $10.95 (hardbound), ages 7–11. *How Things are Built, How Things are Made,* $3.95 each (ages 7–9). New Technology series: *Satellites and Space Stations, Robotics, Lasers, Information Revolution,* $6.95 each paperback or $13.96 library-bound (ages 9–adult).

Let's start with the little kids. The brand-new Young Machines series looks extremely promising. Each book explains how a class of large vehicles works (with large, bright pictures), what jobs they do, and even a history of some of the machines. Parts are named, and you get to see many different types of that machine. A visual index in the back of each book has smaller pictures and facts about each individual machine. *Diggers and Cranes* is already out at the time I write this, and it's a hit! We're looking forward to *Tractors* and *Trucks,* both due out in fall 1991.

On to the Beginner's Knowledge series. This, too, is brand-new. Find out how trains, tracks, and railways were invented and improved through time. See how castles, pyramids, and palaces were built. And what about those sailing boats, from Egyptian reed boats and clipper ships to ocean liners? A visual time line in the back of each book shows how each artefact developed over time. (A neat feature in the *Castles* book: an illustration showing many famous buildings in the same picture, so you can see their relative sizes.) *Castles, Pyramids, and Palaces* and *Ships, Sailors, and the Sea* are both here. *Trains, Tracks, and Railways* is due to be released in fall 1991.

How Things Work explains . . . how things work. Basic physics for the preteen set from the Simple Science series.

From the Explainers series, *How Things are Built* and *How Things are Made* take a different tack. *How Things Work* is more scientific; the Explainers books get into the nitty-gritty of engineering, construction, and assembly lines. Lots of terrific illustrations make it all clear.

In theory, the New Technology series is for teens and adults. In real life, I've found our six-year-old browsing these books. (She started reading when she was four.) Any seven- or eight-year-old who is a good reader should find these how-things-work books fascinating. They go into greater detail than the Explainers series, and cover more futuristic technology.

NEW★★
LEGO Dacta

Technic I, $49, ages 7 and up. *Technic II*, $66.50, ages 10 and up. Teacher's guide for each set, $10 each. Add 5% shipping.

I love 'em, I love 'em, I love 'em, I love 'em. After years of wishing for a systematic hands-on engineering curriculum, my wish has been granted. The new *Technic I* and *II* kits from LEGO Dacta are everything I wished for, and more!

First of all, the kits are beautiful. Pieces are constructed of colorful, sturdy plastic and beautifully engineered. Second, the brilliant designers of this program (God bless 'em!) have put the pieces together in a compartmentalized molded-plastic storage case. This means *no* little Technic pieces crunching underfoot or getting eaten by the vacuum cleaner. In fact, the first exercise in each kit is taking the pieces out of the little plastic bags and learning to put them away neatly in their proper places! Third, the 20 step-by-step Activity Cards included in each kit are *wonderful*. Full-color illustrations show real-life examples of the principles you are learning right along with drawings of the models you are constructing. The accompanying teacher's guide to each kit explains the assignments, gives in-depth instruction in the engineering principles, and provides numerous follow-up activities. *You need the teacher's guide for each kit*, since there are no words on the cards, just illustrations of the project steps.

Here's how it works. You open the kit. You take out an activity card. You do the activities on the card. After you've finished one card, move on to the next. Can it get any simpler than this? Not only that, individual activities can be completed within 20 minutes!

The *Technic I* "Simple Machines" set for children ages 7 and up starts with simple frames and how to make frames rigid. Further activities teach principles of levers, moving objects by sliding and rolling, gears, rotation, transference of energy from one form to another, ways of lifting, steering, and wind and water power. No complicated terminology—you *do* things and then discuss them in everyday language. Each model can be built within 20 minutes using some of the 179 pieces!

Technic II, "Transmission Systems," includes a 4.5 volt motor, worm and differential gears and chain links among its 278 pieces. This set includes more challeng-

ing projects, like models of kitchen mixers, cars, and robots and is intended for children ages 9 and up. Like the *Technic I* kit, the first cards teach how to put away the kit pieces and the difference between movable and rigid frames. Both kits also include the same theme studies (on different levels): Green Fingers, a theme about garden tools and gardening; Away We Go, a transportation theme; and Home Sweet Home, a theme centered on household utensils and equipment. From here on it gets quite different, as the Technic II kit dives into using the provided motor. You'll investigate belt transmissions, build and use a vibrating machine (to study the need for balance and symmetry in machinery), work with chain/gear/worm transmissions, set up drives that use transmission through a right angle, practice translating rotary motion to up-and-down motion, build simple vehicles and a differential, and build cranes, conveyor belts, and robots.

Many of the follow-up activities suggested in the teacher's guides will be a lot easier if you get Bernie Zubrowski's *Drinking Straw Construction* and *Wheels* books from Teacher's Laboratory. These give the principles and steps for building many of the suggested non-kit projects.

Until fishertechnik decides to produce simple, sequential activities *in English* and inexpensive compartmentalized boxes for its kit pieces, these new LEGO Dacta kits will remain, in my opinion, the best engineering education buy. Combine with the *Drinking Straw Construction* and *Wheels* books from Teachers' Laboratory for a full-orbed engineering education!

NEW★★
Teachers' Laboratory, Inc.

Wheels at Work, Bubbles, Messing Around with Water Pumps and Siphons, Messing Around with Baking Chemistry, $6.95 each. *Messing Around with Drinking Straw Construction*, $7.95. Add 10% shipping. Ages 8 and up.

I like Bernie Zubrowski. I haven't the faintest idea whether he is a male or she is a female, but this I know—he or she writes great science books for kids!

Take *Messing Around with Drinking Straw Construction*. In anyone else's hands, a book with that title would have featured some cute patterns for kids to make using drinking straws. Since Bernie wrote it, the book is about using and testing frames made of drinking straws to learn the basic rules of how to design strong structures. First kids learn how to make frames that don't wiggle. Then they experiment with small and large drinking-straw houses and bridges, eventually graduating to serious-looking structures made out of wooden dowels and large rubber bands. The book is profusely illustrated with drawings illustrating design principles and photographs of kids making these structures. Thanks to the clear directions and drawings, any kid eight and up (better yet, several kids eight and up) can make everything in the book. Don't underestimate them, though. If you're a typical adult, you probably don't know one-tenth of the engineering principles effortlessly taught in *Messing About with Drinking Straw Construction.* After reading it, you'll never look at a bridge or skyscraper the same way again!

Bubbles, also by Bernie, solved a problem at my house. We had bought my daughter Sarah a "Bubble Thing" for her birthday. This gizmo, advertised as making the world's hugest bubbles, got busted before Sarah had any real fun with it. We don't have to get her a new one, though, since *Bubbles* explains how to make huge bubbles using a couple of tin cans or two drinking straws and about three feet of light string. The book gets into bubble sculpture, soap-film curves, bubble machines, tabletop dome houses made of bubbles, bubble building blocks, bubble sandwiches (picture blowing bubbles between the two layers of a thermal window), measuring bubbles, shrinking bubbles, and observing bubbles. Along the way kids can't help but learn some science and architectural principles. I know this book will be a hit—my kids, bubble fiends all, had invented several of its activities before we ever saw it.

Wheels at Work is perhaps the most obviously "educational" of the trio of Bernie books Teachers' Laboratory sent me. You will get to build your very own gears, water wheel, windmill, windlass, and paddle wheel. You will use store-bought pulleys to experiment with, discovering which pulley setups work best. All the other gizmos can be manufactured at home out of nothing more complicated than tin cans, paper cups, broomsticks, wire coat hangers, and masking tape. Once you get good at building water wheels, you can build a mechanical music maker and a bubble-blowing machine. Or how about a rubber-band powered paddle boat for the bathtub?

Your kids will learn buckets of real engineering skills from these books

Bernie Zubrowski has also written science activity books entitled *Messing Around with Baking Chemistry, Messing Around with Water Pumps and Siphons,* and *Milk Carton Blocks.* These I haven't seen, but I can just imagine the skull-popping surprises they must hide.

NEW**
Timberdoodle
BRIO-MEC student set, $50. Apprentice set, $100. Contractor set, $200. Extra 4-piece tool set, $6.50. These are discount prices. Ages 4 and up. Shipping extra.

BRIO-MEC is the competition for Baufix (see the Cuisenaire Company review). Compared to Baufix, the BRIO-MEC pieces are thicker, and each set comes with working tools—a claw hammer, spring-action pliers, wrench, and screwdriver—all made of tough, colorful plastic. The blocks are beams are made of beechwood, while the axles, wheels, pulleys, and tires, and the nails, plugs, nuts, and bolts that hold it all together are plastic.

To my mind, BRIO-MEC easier for very young children to work with. Although you must be certain that your child is past the stage of putting small objects in his or her mouth, that's the only real age restraint. Young children especially love the tools, with their satisfyingly chunky shapes and workmanlike capabilities. Another nice touch is the "people parts" included with each kit. These allow your child to install little people in the cabs of his tractors, on the seats of his cranes, and so on, thus adding an extra play dimension. The packaging is also nicer, for those of us who care about keeping our houses neat. Although Baufix is comparable in many ways to BRIO-MEC, and is a good product, the only area in which Baufix clearly beats BRIO-MEC is price.

The BRIO-MEC Student kit comes with 147 pieces, including tools, in a small duffel bag—great for getting the kids to put it away neatly! The included wordless booklet shows how to put together 17 projects, but of course your child can invent hundreds more. The BRIO-MEC Apprentice kit has 339 pieces, including 4 large gears and a set of tools, and a wordless booklet with 30 projects. The Contractor, the most deluxe set, has 560 pieces, two complete sets of tools, and eight gears, plus a booklet with over 40 projects, all packed into a wooden box with a bright blue cover. This last has to be considered an heirloom set, because of its cost. (This means Dad gets to play with it for a week before the kids are allowed to touch it.)

NEW**
Timberdoodle

Fishertechnik Basic Sets: Start 200 set, $70 (needed with all other sets); Start 200/1 set, $29; Motors & Gears set, $55; Statiks set, $54; all for ages 6 and up. Advanced Sets: Electromechanics set, $105; Pneumatics+ set, $110; Electronics set, $160; all for ages 10 or 12 and up. Robotics, computing, and Geometrics kit prices TBA. Shipping extra.

Quality engineering construction kits are a serious investment. Most of us can't afford to spend $50, $100 or more on a modeling set that doesn't work out. So I have spent hours pondering the characteristics of fishertechnik v. LEGO Dacta v. Capsela, etc., while my husband and children spent hundreds of hours playing with them!

Hearing back from our team of experts, plus what I could glean from the folks at Timberdoodle, who have also spent years looking into this, here's what we find.

Fischertechnik invented their engineering modeling kits 40 years ago, not for kiddie use, but for engineering professionals. Today engineers use these components to put together models of new installations, to debug them, and to train the professionals who will operate them. We're talking heavy-duty, quality, realistic design here, good enough for real industrial engineers to use. When you put the pieces together, they *stay* together until you take them apart. This is important when making motorized or moving models, where cheaper components tend to fly apart.

For home use, fischertechnik's advantage is an ability to model authentic, real-world items both in look and action. Components slide together and interlock in uncomplicated ways. Gears, pulleys, wheels, universal joints, winches, cams, motors, struts, connectors, rivets, gussets, and many other real-world-type goodies are available for your budding inventor.

You don't need to know a whole lot to use fischertechnik, either. Basic sets come with wordless drawings that illustrate how to put together a variety of projects, which get more complex as you proceed through the manual. If you want to be educational about it, you can work through the projects in order, picking up quite a bit about design principles along the way. You can also bag the manual and just play with the kit, putting together whatever creations you feel like inventing. I have personally seen four- and five-year-olds enjoying their fischertechnik kits!

Fischertechnik's "basic" sets are designed for the elementary child who is not yet ready for the detailed explanations in fischertechnik's advanced sets, but is anxious to begin building working models of the things he sees around him (e.g., cars, trucks, and cranes). The wordless manuals in each set mean you don't have to be able to read to do the projects. These basic sets help your child get familiar with real-world hardware, and set him on the road to really understanding how things work.

The Start 200 set is the basis of all fischertechnik sets. You need to buy this one first, no matter which other kits you're interested in, because the items in this one are needed *along with* the items in the other ones to do the projects in the more advanced sets. You can build up to 200 different models with the Start 200 set, which includes nearly 400 pieces ranging from base plates to 100 chain links. Wordless plans for 17 models include a road grader, mobile crane, tractor, catapult, helicopter, and more.

The Start 200/1 is the recommended second step. (You need the Start 200 first, as I said above.) It adds additional pieces, like a universal joint, disc-cams, and bevel gear wheels, plus extra pieces of types already included in the Start 200. With it you can build more working models, like a giant forklift, conveyor, and chute.

Motors & Gears, another basic set, also builds on the Start 200. It includes loads of different gears, a six-volt motor, a reduction gear box, a conveyor belt, and much more. Projects include a vertical lift, fan, gearbox, lathe, and more.

The Statik set is for the child who loves to build working models of large cranes, towers, runabouts, bridges, merry-go-rounds, and Ferris wheels. It contains hundreds of struts in various lengths and all the connectors you'll need to build the projects above.

Now, let's look at the Advanced sets. Meant for teens or advanced preteens on up to 90-year-olds, these include manuals with instructions in theory and "schematic skills" (e.g., how to read the project diagrams), as well as information on how to control motors through electrical, electronic, or air-control (pneumatic) systems. They include clear demonstrations of technical processes and principles and step-by-step directions that logically progress through these more advanced topics. The final step? Controlling your project from your home computer! The fischertechnik robotics kits, for those who can afford them, are a great way to introduce robotics just as it is actually used in real-world applications.

The Electromechanics set includes a key, switch, slip ring, magnets, electromagnet, vibratory spring, thermal bimetallic strip, lamps, contacts, leads, and more—everything you need to study circuits and electrical models. Projects range from rotating searchlights to motor control and overload protection for a model crane . . . from thermostats to a Morse code transmitter that also receives code on a paper tape recorder! Lots more.

The Pneumatics+ kit has the special parts you need for air circuits: single and double cylinders, diaphragm cylinders, directional and flow control valves, and tubing and connectors. It even includes a small fischertechnik compressor to supply compressed air to your projects. Projects include an air engine, a pneumatic excavator, and more.

The Electronics kit includes parts for steering and controlling models. You can put together working models of a photoconductive cell, an alarm system, a handclap switch, an automatic flashing light, and more.

Fischertechnik presently has three robotics kits, each available for IBM compatibles, Apple II series (except IIc), and Commodore 64/128 computers. Kits come with software and detailed instructions. The Computing Experimental kit includes experiments using turtle graphic orders, photoresistor light measurement, hot conductor temperature measurement, and more. The Robotics Computing Kit enables you to build 10 projects, from a basic traffic light with pedestrian button to a solar cell tracking platform that will maintain a constant angle to the sun. This one is popular for beginners. The Training Robot Three-Axis Arm kit goes a step farther. You can program this robot arm (which works like those on factory assembly lines) by stepping it through the desired activity or by computer programming in BASIC.

The brand-new fischertechnik Geometrix kits are the fanciest, yet simplest, engineering construction kits I've seen. Not to be confused with fischertechnik's other engineering construction toys, these have no moving parts. No pulleys, no wheels, no gears. Instead, you get beautifully engineered chunky grey blocks of various intriguing shapes, which you connect with little red strips that slide into slots in the blocks. When put

together, they make professional-looking buildings. You can make walls with holes of any shape . . . turrets with pointy cones on the top . . . almost anything you want. Anything you make with these sets looks wonderful. Some of the sets have curved and conical pieces; others have more rectangular-shaped blocks. All come with idea books showing various constructions for your child to model. You really have to see and handle these building pieces to appreciate the beauty and ingenuity of their design.

Timberdoodle is the sole importer of these kits for the home market.

NEW✶✶
Timberdoodle
LEGO™ *Technic I* Activity Center, $75. LEGO *Technic I* Set, $44. Shipping extra. Grades 3–12.

What comes in a plastic case that looks like a huge red LEGO brick, includes 110 activity cards, 7 index cards, a 144-page teacher's guide plus a 24-page teacher's supplement, and teaches thinking skills by having kids create and build working models to solve real-world engineering problems? It's the brand-new LEGO *Technic 1* Activity Center!

For some reason, the folks at LEGO disbelieve that home schoolers and parents in general would be interested in this program. Timberdoodle thinks they are wrong, so they put the Activity Center in their catalog and sent me a review sample. (They sell the Activity Center and Technic kits at *discount,* by the way, and since LEGO doesn't sell directly to consumers, you might as well buy your Technic stuff from Timberdoodle.)

Let me explain how the plastic case works first. This is itself an intriguing engineering exercise. When shut, the grey plastic straps hold it firmly closed. When opened, you can swivel the two side straps around to lock into holes that keep it just as firmly open, turning it into a display case for the cards and manuals. (It only took me five minutes to figure this out!) Nothing in the teacher's manuals, or anywhere else, explains how to set up the display case, by the way!

You will need a LEGO *Technic 1* set to use with the Activity Center, since you can't build working models without any components out of which to build them. As you already know, the *Technic 1* set includes 20 step-by-step project cards. So what does the Activity Center add to this? It includes the same 20 cards, so there is some overlap. However, the teacher's manual for the Activity Center gives many additional teaching tips and helps for these cards, and goes much, *much* farther than the Technic 1 set in teaching kids how things work.

The teacher's manual explains how to use the Activity Center. The best way is to start by locating the cards for the different topics (e.g., gears) and rubber-band those together. Topics covered in this Center are forces and structures, levers, pulleys, gears, wheels and axles, and energy. The teacher's manual includes a simple description of each topic. For a more in-depth explanation of how, say, gears work, turn to the teacher's supplement. This has excellent, concise descriptions of a gear's function and how gears work together, plus several illustrated projects for demonstrating these ideas.

Each topic is covered in many different ways, and the tops of the cards are color-coded to reflect this.

The green Exploration cards introduce kids to the building materials. Kids play with many different variations of the same device, for example, building lots of different wheeled vehicles or spinning tops. The extension suggestions on these cards often include imaginative writing assignments or add-on features you can build onto your project.

The cards with a blue band across the top are the Guided Investigation cards (same as those in the *Technic 1* kit), with step-by-step instructions for building specific models.

Those with a yellow band are Simulation Activity cards. Kids design and build working models of specific items, but the card doesn't show them how. (The teacher's manual lists extra materials to be used, questions to be asked, and has a photo of a finished model, so you can give wise adult guidance as needed.)

The red Invention Activity cards simply give a problem, e.g., "The castle kitchen has a mouse . . . The cook wants to catch it and release it outside." Your child then is supposed to invent and build a device to solve the problem, e.g., a better mousetrap! Since there are hundreds of possible solutions to each invention question, the teacher's manual supplies, along with ways to test each invention, only a rough sketch of some of the main ideas usually built into the inventions.

To make life more interesting, activity cards are grouped around themes like The Medieval Castle (build a movable covered ladder so the invading knights can scale the castle walls), The Farm (build a working model of a wheelbarrow), The Harbor (invent a machine to help clean up the dock), The Amusement Park (build a working model of a gear box to open and close the curtains for the puppet show), Getting Around (build working models of a baby stroller and skateboard), and The Big Race (build your own land yacht and rubber band-powered racing car). I've listed only one or two of the activities under each theme, just to give you a taste of them. All cards have bright graphics, and some have humorous pictures as well, to draw kids into eagerly solving the problems.

Timberdoodle is pushing the Activity Center as a thinking skills course. I think it's really a Good Old American Know-How course. Any kid who works through the Activity Center could probably sit down and design an assembly line for a chocolate factory . . . or a better wheelchair . . . or a burglar-alarm system. Technical literacy, in other words. The ability to understand mechanical things, take them apart, and build new things of your own. Isn't that worth slightly over $100 per family? (Just think, if we got rid of NASA, we could give every family in the country a LEGO *Technic 1* Activity Center and *Technic 1* kit! I think we'd come out ahead . . .)

SCIENCE ACTIVITIES

These differ from experiments in that you are observing models or pictures of objects, or constructing models or pictures.

NEW***
National Teaching Aids, Inc.
Human Skeleton Construction Kit, $29.95.

It's only a paper man . . . I am intrigued by the catalog pictures of what National Teaching Aids assures me is a full-size articulated human skeleton made entirely of paper. The invention of a British professor with the twin hobbies of anatomy and origami, your skeleton comes packaged in a flat box containing 10 die-cut cardboard sheets scored and printed with the name of each bone. Full illustrated instructions show you how to put Bonzo together—*without* glue or scissors. When completed, your paper man can be moved into every position taken by a real skeleton. Bonzo is supposed to be durable, and he's certainly less ethically upsetting than the real article and less expensive than plastic.

NEW**
National Teaching Aids, Inc.
Micromounts™, $18/pkg of 150. Includes instruction sheet.

Do glass microscope slides tend to slip and slide out of your fingers and go crash on the floor? Dislike spending big bucks for them? National Teaching Aids has a new alternative: Micromounts. These are made of paper and plastic. Insert your specimen on the clear plastic part of the mount, peel off the protective tape, fold the mount onto itself, and label. Micromounts include space to indicate specimen number, name, date found, where found, how prepared, main observations, and who prepared the slide. You can use it for both wet and dry mounts.

Let me warn you about one possible pitfall. The peel-off backing is the exact same color as the paper itself: white. I discovered the peel-off portion on the top of the mount by trial and error, but didn't discover the other part at all—which keeps the slide stuck together—until I read the instructions in the catalog and experimented awhile. Just make sure to *read the instructions first* and you'll be fine!

NEW**
Shekinah Curriculum Cellar
Wall Projects for Students, $2.50 each. Shipping extra. Grades 4–8.

It comes in a pouch, like a baby kangaroo. It goes on your wall when it's done. What is it? (You can tell I've been reviewing too many preschool programs!)

Not to torture you any longer, we're talking about the Wall Projects series carried by Shekinah Curriculum Cellar. You get a long, thin plastic pouch with a folded black-and-white poster inside, plus a teacher's guide and a few extra info sheets. Using the information on the back of the poster and elsewhere, you fill in the blanks on the poster and color it. For example, the *Solar System* poster project requires you to fill in the diameter, distance from sun, revolution time, and rotation time for each planet in the solar system. This information is on the enclosed Planet Information Sheet, and the colors you should use are given in the teacher's guide.

The teacher's guides, as usual, overdo things a bit. Don't feel you must burden your child with writing a

report on Halley's Comet just become some frenzied teacher stuck this in!

The Wall Projects series includes *U.S. Space Travel and Exploration, The Solar System and Universe, Wonders of the Human Body, Simple Machines,* and *Weather.* The *Weather* project is an especially good deal: it includes eight weather projects, the making of three weather instruments, temperature reading and conversion from Fahrenheit to Celsius, weather forecasting and map reading, and of course the wall poster project itself. (For Social Studies Wall Projects, see the Social Studies section.) An inexpensive, organized way to learn a lot of information.

Tin Man Press
Discover! series, $2.10 each package. Shipping extra.

Your children can improve their observation skills can by a continual diet of Sherlock Holmes mysteries and Dr. Doolittle books. Sherlock Holmes and Dr. Doolittle, in their various fields, are excellent models of keen observers, and kids just naturally want to imitate them. Or you could just get the Discover! series from Tin Man Press. These really neat little card packs each feature 20 observation and thinking activities centering on common household items. In *Discover Aluminum Foil,* for example, one card asks the child to look carefully at both sides of the foil and write about what he notices. Another card asks him to drop a square of foil and a ball of foil at the same time and see which falls faster. Each card pack covers all learning styles (visual, conceptual, tactile, etc.) and is really FUN! The Discover! series covers 24 items such as pencils, spoons, popcorn, egg cartons, and crayons. Inexpensive.

SCIENCE FAIRS

NEW★★
Teacher Created Materials
All About Science Fairs, $9.95. Grades 3–8.

All About Science Fairs is the best workbook I have seen for actually getting home-taught kids rolling with a science fair project. The book was written for school classes, not home schools, and is full of busywork. So what makes it so good?

- The bound-in comic book, in which a goofy alien explains to the earth kids what science fairs are all about and how to design a project. Simple, memorable explanations.

- The Science Project Checklist. Follow the steps for success!

- The list of 120 science project ideas—divided into three ability levels.

- The teacher's guide in the front, which goes through the whole project development process step by step. The guide also neatly explains how to use graphs, data charts, and so on effectively in your science project.

The worksheets, designed to provide practice in scientific procedures, are not the high point of this book. No need to actually fill them out—just read 'em and you'll get the idea.

CHAPTER THIRTY-TWO

SCIENCE EQUIPMENT

When purchasing science equipment or courses, it's not necessary to copy the schools. A Sears microscope or chemistry kit may do your kid (or you) just as much good as a fancy course with workbooks—perhaps more.

In science, learning is supremely by doing, and those who *do* will beat out those who memorize and fill out workbook pages every time. I had a sad experience of this in engineering school, where the fellows who had spent their high school years putting together Radio Shack kits breezed about enjoying their electrical courses, while I, who had never even seen a transistor before, had to struggle out my grades through sheer rote memory, and afterward promptly forgot most of what I had "learned."

Hacking about in the basement is a great way to get into science. If every schoolkid were allowed to read novels during science period, but given a chemistry kit and a microscope with prepared slides to play with at home, would we see those articles in the paper about how superior Russian children are to Americans scientifically? As Gollum said, "We wonders, aye, we wonders."

UPDATED**
American Science & Surplus (formerly Jerryco)

Wonderful widgets from the world of surplus. Only the American Science & Surplus catalog can make a petri dish sound enticing. The man who writes the catalog description has a wry sense of humor and a lot of imagination. Catch this description of a humble petri dish:

CULTURE DISHES
Caviar is of course a culture dish. So is Foie Gras. These are neither. Rather, they are round plastic dishes just under 2" in dia. with tight fitting lids. The notion is to put nutrient agar or another life-sustaining medium into the dish, to add some microbiological life form, and to watch nature produce mold, vaccine, fungus, and other unappetizing life forms. Ralph Petri, or one of his cousins, must have had a hand in the process, as the Becton, Dickinson package insists these are 50 x 9 mm Petri dishes, their style 1006. Packaged in sterile sleeves of (20). You may share the biologist's notion that a swarm of microbes constitute a culture, or you may simply want to understate your

Beluga at a plush picnic. Either way, they are culture dishes.

AS&S not only sells motors and sprockets and gears and everything else, but generously shares ideas about what to do with all these gizmos, as per this ad:

URINOMETER
So much for the bad news. Looking through that, we have a nice unmarked glass cylinder 1¼" in diameter by 5¾" high. It has a crude and handmade look to it, which is good news. Nice accessory item for flowers and other high tech houseware applications. Assuming that you really wanted a hydrometer that also comes with the deal. It's about ⅝" in diameter by 5" long and is calibrated from 1.0 to 1.06 times the specific gravity of distilled water. That likely enabled one to determine particulate or dissolved solid content, but whatever the intent, the ten-year old catalog price was about $7. Working with normal kitchen solubles (salt, vinegar, cornstarch, etc.) one might have the makings of a nifty science project here. Just be sure to toss out the plainly marked carton before inviting the science fair judges for lunch.

Constantly changing inventory as industrial America makes new mistakes. Many items are military surplus, as you may have guessed, but a lot are components of mass-produced items that bombed in the market. Clever folks can make something with them. Unclever folk can just get their bellylaughs reading the catalog.

NEW★★
Bob Jones University Press

Good selection of basic science equipment and supplies, coordinated to BJUP science textbooks, offered at attractive prices. Great service, too: BJUP is ultra-friendly to home schoolers.

Christian Light Publications

It's not cheap, but if you want science equipment to perform all your science experiments, CLP has it. CLP's lab materials are available in complete sets or as individual components. If your children are serious about science, I'd look upon this as an investment. All the lab materials to set up all your kids with real experiments costs less than a good stereo system or a fancy racing bike.

NEW★★
Crane's Select Educational Materials

Excellent selection of low-cost science lab equipment specifically chosen for home schoolers. Alcohol burners, beakers, test tube brushes, capillary tubes, clamps and clamp holders, crucibles, graduated cylinders, dissecting sets, funnels, filter paper, Erlenmeyer flasks, glass tubing cutter, goggles for children and adults, scalpels, scoops, stoppers, pipettes, test tubes, glass tubing, you name it. Plus a *wide* variety of lab chemicals, sold by the individual chemical, and microbiological cultures and supplies.

Crane also *rents* microscope slides of uncommon objects often examined in university courses. These slides do *not* include common material such as human hair, fabrics, etc. We're talking sets of algae, bacteria, protozoa, and so on.

Edmund Scientific Company

Every neat scientific widget under the sun. Microscopes, telescopes, stethoscopes, orotoscopes, binoculars, and the ever-popular sextant (don't leave home without one!). Crazy gifts for the child who has everything, from quarters that "blast off" when you tip the waiter to your personal robot. For serious tinkerers and investigators. Plus a pile of science kits with kid appeal.

Now tell me honestly, where else can you get a giant gyroscope ($8.95) or a fossil collection ($23.95) or a paper clock kit ($10.95)? Sea monkeys! Butterfly collecting! Make your own perfume! Stargaze! Much, much more! Plus survival gear, tools, photography supplies, and everything else far out and technological.

Educational Insights
Science equipment kits: Primary $160, Intermediate $189. Shipping extra.

Now *this* is convenience, for those of you who need classroom-sized kits! Educational Insights has packaged everything you need for early- or intermediate-grades science experiments in a reusable storage container and included 100 tab-divided activity cards and a four-page teacher's guide. Surprisingly, the activity cards focus mostly on supplemental activities using (often readily available) items *not* found in the kits, such as fresh celery, potting soil, gummed stars, and so on. Most of the items other science programs' experiments require is right here in these kits.

In either kit you get an alcohol burner, balloons (25), batteries, 250 ml beaker, candle, clay (one pound of plasticine), cork, craft sticks (75), measuring cups, eyedropper, flask with stopper, food coloring, funnel, iron filings, light bulbs, litmus paper, magnets, magnifiers, mirrors, nails, one pound of plaster of Paris, 20 plastic cups, metric ruler, four sheets of sandpaper, 10 seashells, spring scale, 150 straws (red, white, and blue!), 50 feet of string, test tube with holder, tongs, trays, two feet of plastic tubing, tweezers, and six feet of insulated wire—more than 300 items in each kit. The Primary kit also contains buttons, cellophane in the three primary colors, comb, 20 plastic bags with ties, and a thermometer. The Intermediate kit does not have these last items. Instead, you get a glass tube, glass plates, marbles, net, pencil compasses, pipe cleaners, protractor, steel wool, tape measure, washers, and six feet of copper wire. These are good, durable, classroom-quality items. Everything in my two kits arrived in excellent condition except the large jars of food coloring, which leaked slightly (not affecting the other items, which are mostly sealed in plastic).The included teacher's guides list the activity cards and their topics, give safety directions, and list the contents.

These kits are a *lot* more than your typical tubes-of-chemicals-and-alcohol-burner science kits sold in department store catalogs. Any family serious about science—especially those with lots of children—ought to be able to cook up several award-winning science fair presentations with this batch of ingredients.

UPDATED**
Learning Things, Inc.

This is the place for all your electrical and science lab needs: microscopes, gyroscopes, scales, mineral collections, scales, laboratory equipment like flexible tubing and funnels, electrical equipment like alligator clips and switches, fiber optics, etc. Anatomical models. Photography supplies. Math manipulatives. Pages and pages and pages of biology equipment, electrical equipment, chemistry equipment, magnetism supplies. Now, how about a deck prism—a replica of a special prism laid flush in the wooden decks of old-time sailing vessels to transmit sunlight between decks? Or a periscope for $5? Or a solar system mobile that spans 3½ feet? Then there are kits for building molecular models, crystal growing, or a DNA model. What about the papermaking kit and book? A complete set of cardboard carpentry tools and accessories? Now, the topper, a technological breakthrough in the science of mi-

croscopy: an optical light guide (lightpipe) that collects, condenses, and transmits ambient light to the specimen, eliminating the need for a mirror and all the headaches of making constant adjustments. Would you believe it—a 30x model for $11! If you like hands-on learning and experiments, you owe it to yourself to get this catalog.

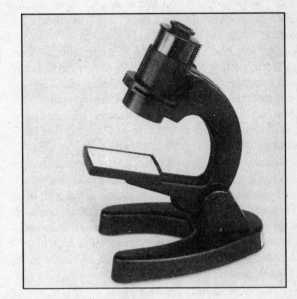

National Teaching Aids
$7.25 per viewer, $4.45 per title. Five year guarantee. Grades 3–12.

Here is a nifty idea! Since most schools can't afford high-powered microscopes for every student, why not take pictures of slides as they would appear under ideal viewing conditions and then let children look at those in lieu of expensive specimens? National has a wide range of "photomicrographs" (spell *that* and go to the head of the class!) plus explanatory text folders. You need a viewer, of course, and National also sells those. The viewers are rugged, coming with a five-year guarantee against breakage. These materials have been used by over one hundred and seventy *million* students.

Norris Science Labs and Kits
Mini-Lab $90. Primary Lab I $195. Intermediate Lab II $225. Items may be purchased separately, including the manuals. *Science is Fun* video (VHS or Beta) $50 purchase price. Video rental available. Inquire about discounts for home schoolers.

The ad says, "Now for the first time! ONE SCIENCE LAB equipped for all experiments in any standard science textbook or teacher's guide . . . for elementary and junior high school physical science programs. Ideal For Both Public and Private Schools. Grades K through 8." You have a choice of three lab kits. The Mini-Lab has basic supplies for 50 or so included experiments. Kids can make a thermometer, a friction scale, a steam turbine engine, glass, and a fuse. The Primary Lab I (for grades K–3) lets you find acids and bases, see how light and temperature affect plants and how materials conduct electricity, make a "realistic volcano," work with seed growth, and so on—about 50 more projects. You get seeds, potting soil, sprouting jar, thermometer, magnetic compass, balance and spring scales, test tubes with rack, radiometer, burner column, motor, prepared slides, critter collector, and much more. Intermediate Lab II contains a formidable array of little labeled bottles holding "safe to use chemicals" (sulfur, starch, soda, white sand, rosin, lime, litmus paper, copper sulfate, borax, acetic acid, and ammonium dichromate for your adult-supervised homemade volcano), along with over 100 items such as a compass, funnel, thermometer, test tubes, flask, battery, measuring cups, beaker, magnets, prism, and test tube rack and clamp. With each of these kits comes a spiral-bound teacher's manual with "easy-to-follow instructions and diagrams."

For those hungry for hands-on demonstrations by a real live science teacher, Norris Science Labs and Kits presents the *Science is Fun* video starring Jack Norris, a man with more than 40 years' experience as a science teacher. Mr. Norris, who has also served as a superintendent of schools and science and math coordinator, demonstrates 19 crowd-pleasing experiments, some

correlated with experiments in the various lab kit Teacher's Manuals. These include:

- Introduction to Science
- The Mysterious Black Box
- The Envelope
- Tools of Science (cutting glass)
- Balance Scale
- Friction Scale
- Casts and Molds
- Making a Fossil
- Fuses
- Making a Galvanometer
- Electric Circuits
- Ions
- Magnetism (Paper Clip Float and Attraction & Repulsion)
- Chemical Replacement Exchange
- Steam Turbine Engine
- Stretching Glass
- Making the Steam Engine's Tube
- and, last but not least, the ever-popular Volcano.

Norris Science Labs and Kits is a family-owned business willing to answer your questions. Their Mini-Lab "was designed especially for home schoolers—as they do not need a lot of equipment to start, are resourceful enough to make their own, and can add to their science lab apparatus as their interest dictates." Norris Labs will let you purchase items separately. Their catalog contains many fascinating things (live butterfly culture, anyone?) not included in the kits.

SOCIAL STUDIES

CHAPTER THIRTY-THREE

CITIZENSHIP

Little kids don't vote. There is, therefore, no great rush to teach them about the great democratic principles of our glorious republic, or (if you prefer), the materialistic principles of our corrupt statist/capitalist/bourgeois/elitist (pick one) nation. For that reason, I seriously considered saving all the Government resources for the Teen & Adult volume, since teens and adults are more capable of understanding political gymnastics and have more hope of using that knowledge in a positive way.

After more thought, though, we discover that little kids can easily understand the basic competing systems of government. These are The State is Great theory, the State's Dead Weight theory, and The State I Hate theory.

Most Americans fall into category one or two. We either expect the government to solve all our problems ("There oughta be a law!") or admit massive government is here to stay, without particularly rejoicing in the fact ("You can't fight City Hall!"). Only a few idealistic souls, of whom I am proud to be one, consider that the State often *is* the problem, *and* that it might be possible someday to do something about it. Not abolish the State altogether, à la Count Tolstoy, but give it a haircut. Trim it down to size. Institute checks and balances. Give the people back their inalienable rights. Stuff like that.

Oddly enough, it turns out that the gentlemen who put together the Declaration of Independence and Constitution had similar thoughts on their minds. Which is, perhaps, why kids get such a garbled version of the Constitution presented in school—when it is presented at all! The current line is that since society is facing such grave problems, little things like the freedom of assembly, the freedom of the press, the right to bear arms, freedom of religion, the right to protection against warrantless search and seizure, the right to due process of law, and so on need "reinterpretation" in the light of the current situation. Often the textbooks reinterpret them right on the spot, without bothering kids with the original meaning of the Constitutional text.

School textbooks view our political history through the rosy lens of "progress." Each new bureaucracy is hailed as a step forward for mankind. Those who crusaded to establish the bureaucracies are celebrated as "reformers." Some books and teaching aids go even farther, promoting the cause of bureaucracies yet to be formed. Example: there's a lot of enthusiasm bubbling around for "regional land management" programs—e.g., statewide, nationwide, and worldwide zoning administered by central bureaucrats unaccountable to the voters. I can hardly wait.

You've seen that bumper sticker, "I'm Spending My Children's Inheritance." Well, at least those who spend an inheritance get some good out of it. How about *this* bumper sticker—"I'm Throwing Away My Children's Inheritance"? Let's not do it, folks. Let's at least give the kids a chance to find out what ol' Tom Jefferson, Ben Franklin, and George Washington had in mind before we decide we've improved on it.

EDC Publishing
Politics and Governments, $6.95 paperbound. Ages 10 and up.

Although somehow I missed receiving my review copy of *The Usborne Introduction to Politics and Governments*, I can tell you something about this book. Like the rest of the Usborne series published in England, it relies on lots of colorful, captioned illustrations and a clever organizational scheme to present you with masses of information in a possible-to-remember format. According to the cover photo in the catalog, you will find out about such things as dictators, summits, senates, republics, fascism, Marxism, apartheid, diplomacy, democracy, and elections.

NEW★★
Educational Insights
American Archives set, $9.95. Minimum order $25. Shipping extra. Ages 9–adult.

Yes, you too can have your very own set of the Declaration of Independence, Constitution, Bill of Rights, and Gettysburg Address. The American Archives collection provides these documents, reproduced on authentically antiqued parchment, all rolled neatly in a plastic tube. The largest document is 12 x 19", if you're thinking of putting them up on the wall.

Educational Products (formerly CBN Publishing)
Songs of America's Freedoms, $19.95. Grades 3–6.

In theory, we in America have certain rights. Find out what they were with this kit. Kit includes placemats/posters to color that illustrate our constitutional freedoms, sing-along cassette, teaching guide with complete text of cassette, booklet with Constitution, Bill of Rights, and some very interesting info about which amendment was passed by whom and what it all means. On the cassette you'll find "We the People . . . The Preamble Song," "Introduction Song . . . What is the Constitution?" (an ode to "the best laws ever by the mind of man"), "The Song of America's Freedoms" (16 freedoms—count 'em), "A Founding Father Speaks to Us Across the Centuries" (fades out with the refrain, "We the People . . . Limited Government . . . We the People . . . Limited Government"), "A Challenge for

Us," and "America" ("My country, 'tis of thee . . .).

For the record, the freedoms we are supposed to enjoy are: worship, speech, the press, assembly, elections, movement, ownership of property, choice of work, ownership of a business, petition, contracts, trial by jury, privacy (no search and seizure without a warrant), bargaining, no heavy controls, innocent until found guilty. How interesting, then, that judges now forbid pro-life protestors to assemble together with or speak to other pro-lifers or to move about anywhere near an abortion clinic on the public sidewalk. How interesting that social workers can invade your home under threat of taking your children if you refuse to open the door to them, on the basis of someone phoning in an *anonymous* hotline call that does not even necessarily accuse you of anything criminal. How interesting that judges force people not accused of any crime to obtain psychological evaluations and/or counseling . . . at their own cost, yet . . . under threat of an indeterminate sentence for contempt of court. To paraphrase Simon and Garfunkel's "Mrs. Robinson"—"Where have you gone, Thomas Jefferson? Our nation lifts its lonely eyes to you . . . "

Foundation for American Christian Education
Christian History, Teaching and Learning, $15 each. *Rudiments*, $7. *Christian Self-Government with Union*, $18. *Consider and Ponder*, $23. Add 10% regular mail, 15% UPS. Adults read the books, present the information to children.

FACE is trying to revive the "Principle Approach" to government, an approach based on Biblical law, on which they say the U.S.A. was founded. Their material traces America's roots through source documents. Political freedom begins with self-government, FACE says, and self-government begins in the home.

Before we proceed any farther, let me make it clear that these are *not* workbooks for young children. The theory is that you are going to work through this information yourself and then present it according to a set of complicated teaching suggestions that require you continually to flip back and forth between books.

The Christian History of the Constitution documents that America is a Christian nation (that is, it *was* dedicated to Christ once upon a time) with a Christian Constitution (that is, one based on Christian principles). The "Chain of Christianity" is traced westward to America, as the gospel spread from Israel to the Roman Empire and thence to the uncouth white tribespeople who, once Christianized, spread it over the world. A large book, 8½ x 11, hardbound in red cloth, beautifully gold-stamped, almost 500 pages, consisting almost entirely of quotes from source documents.

Teaching and Learning America's Christian History is the original how-to manual of the Principle Approach. Each principle is spelled out, precept on precept, line on line. Likewise beautifully bound and gold-stamped, likewise large, likewise red. Under 400 pages.

Rudiments of America's Christian History and Government is a workbook for students filled with source quotes from distinguished American Christian leaders of the past and questions designed to develop both Christian thinking and an awareness of our Christian heritage. For teens and adults.

Christian Self-Government with Union is red vellum, gold-stamped, eagle-embossed, illustrated, indexed, and 640 pages. More history from source documents, emphasizing the colonist's voluntary union that led to self-government.

Consider and Ponder is the first volume of a projected series on the Christian history of the American Revolution. Covering the Constitutional Debate period of 1765–1775, its 736 pages nestle between blue vellum covers.

Foundation for Economic Education
The Law, $3.95 cloth, $2.95 paper. Shipping extra. Grades 5–adult.

Books from a free-enterprise position. Classics no educated person should miss. Most are written for teens and adults. For the elementary age group, start with *The Law* by Frederic Bastiat. Bastiat explains how, under democracy, special interests can use the vote to "plunder" (his word) others . . . and why the redistribution of income via taxes and government aid (as opposed to private charity) is always wrong. Bastiat, a Frenchman writing in the early 1800s, also predicts the

Civil War as an outgrowth of tariffs and slavery, two anti-freedom positions respectively adopted by the North and the South. Very easy to read and understand.

God's World Publications
Weekly papers, $15.95 per year. Any two editions to same address: $9.95 each. Specify paper: *God's Big World* (kindergarten), *Sharing God's Word* (grade 1), *Exploring God's World* (2–3), *It's God's World* (4–6), *God's World Today* (7–9). Free samples available.

While you're at it, you might consider signing up for subscriptions to God's World weekly-reader newspapers for your children at the same address. Each age group has its own newspaper during the school year. These great little papers feature news stories, editorials, zany Foto Files and cartoons, and letters to the editor. I'm probably not the only mother who races her kids to read them! Even kids who HATE regular newspapers love these! Very highly recommended.

NEW**
Intrepid Books
Level A–H books, $10.95 each. Add 10% shipping ($2.50 minimum). Grades 1–8.

Those of you who have felt overwhelmed by the sheer volume of cross-referenced information included in the Foundation for American Christian Education materials (see above) will be glad to know there's now a series of study guides for elementary and preteen kids based on their most popular books, *The Christian History of the Constitution* and *Teaching and Learning America's Christian History*. The Level A book is for first-graders, Level B is for second-graders, and so on.

To quote from the brochure:

Does Your Child Know . . .
* What his inalienable rights are?
* How our Founding Fathers felt about taxes?
* Why the Boston Tea Party could only have happened in Boston?
* Who John Locke or William Blackstone were?
* Why America is a Christian nation?
* How the Bible came to be translated into English and thus began the American nation?
* How to contrast the Pagan Idea of Man with the Christian Idea of Man?
* That before Christianity, women were regarded as only property to be dealt with as one saw fit?
* What it means to be self-governed?
* That conscience is the most sacred of all property?
* That our Founding Fathers believed God's providence ruled their lives and guided this country?

Each Study Guide is broken into the following sections:

1. God's Principle of Individuality
2. The Christian Principle of Self-Government
3. America's Heritage of Christian Character
4. Conscience is the Most Sacred of All Property
5. The Christian Form of Our Government
6. How the Seed of Local Self-Government is Planted
7. The Christian Principle of American Political Union

Here's how it works. You (the adult) read the recommended portions from FACE's *Teaching and Learning America's Christian History* and *Christian History of the Constitution* listed at the beginning of each section. You also read the Bible portions, definitions, and statements of purpose. Sample, from the Christian Self-Government section:

> A man cannot rule our country
> Unless he can manage a state,
> But . . . A man cannot manage a state
> Unless he can lead a county, But . . .
> A man cannot lead a county,
> Unless he can head a city, But . . .
> A man cannot head a city,
> Unless he can guide a family, But . . .
> A man cannot guide a family,
> Unless he can govern himself, But . . .
> A man cannot govern himself,
> Unless he has reason, But . . .
> A man cannot have reason,
> Unless he is ruled by and obedient to God!

Each section then speaks right to the student, with historical excerpts and character and Bible lessons designed to teach them about individuality, self-government, America's principled heritage, conscience, Christian form of government, local self-government, and proper political union. The historical events covered differ from level to level, as does the depth of the teaching. In level A, for example, most pages have large illustrations and little text. History covered is the story of John Wycliffe, the "Miracle of 1623" when the Plymouth Colony survived, the First Charter of Virginia, how Washington's army was providentially saved from the British at Long Island, and how the colonists united to defeat the Stamp Act. The Level F book, in contrast, has fairly small print, long extracts from historical source documents, and looks at the role geography has played in history, representative government

in Virginia and Plymouth colonies, representation and separation of powers, Sam Adams and the Committees of Correspondence, and how the colonists reacted to the closing of Boston Port—among other things! As you can see, the upper-grades books contain proportionately more colonial political philosophy.

Each book includes writing and discussion exercises following each historical reading, and ends with a glossary. Lower-level books also include simple art activities and feature more illustrations and graphics.

These books are very pro-Protestant, pro-reasoning, and pro-Founding Fathers style patriotism. The only obviously modern note is the (somewhat misguided, I feel) emphasis on self-esteem in the Individuality sections. Aside from that, you could have taken these books into any 1800s public-school classroom, no questions asked.

NEW**
Shekinah Curriculum Cellar
United States Constitution, United States Government, Bill of Rights wall projects, $2.50 each. Shipping extra. Ages 10–16.

Pull the folded poster out of the plastic sleeve. *Read* the extensive historical background information. *Use* the enclosed teacher's guide for additional information, projects, vocabulary, and directions on how to complete the wall poster. *Fill in* the requested information on the poster. *Color* it, using colored pencils. *Hang it* on a wall, file it away, or whatever . . . your kids will have learned more than they would have from a textbook unit on the topic!

Shekinah carries ten different history/geography wall projects, of which I have seen three. *United States Constitution* gives historical events leading up to the signing of the Constitution, introduces the signers, and provides an outline of the Constitution. The wall poster shows the famous signing scene, surrounded with state flags to color in and lines for your child to write the names of the signers from each state.

The Bill of Rights follows the same format, with the entire text of the Bill of Rights included. The wall poster is an illustrated outline of the Bill of Rights, with spaces for children to fill in the topics under each amendment. On the bottom is a historical outline section, with more blanks to fill in.

United States Government describes the three branches of government. The wall poster shows past U. S. flags at the top, a fill-in-the-blanks outline of the three branches of government below, a list of U.S.

presidents, and the flags of the military agencies. The executive departments included in the President's Cabinet are described on a separate sheet of paper.

All these wall projects include a crossword-puzzle quiz, further research projects, and teaching suggestions.

Others in the series include *United States Map, World Map, Holy Land Map, State Flags and Symbols, California State Map, Christopher Columbus and the Age of Exploration,* and *Presidents and Presidential Elections.* Shekinah has science Wall Projects too: see the Science Activities chapter for details.

Because of the involved nature of these projects, they are best suited to kids with ages in the double digits.

NEW★★
TREND Enterprises, Inc.
Each bulletin board set, $5.99, includes free Discovery Guide. Requires 4 x 6' bulletin board. Add $2 shipping. Minimum order $10.

TREND's *U.S. Government* bulletin board set demonstrates difficult civics concepts in easy-to-understand visuals. Children can learn about the system of checks and balances, the three government branches, the Constitution and Bill of Rights, voting, and how a bill becomes law through these visuals. Also included is a useful discovery guide which summarizes how U.S. government works and provides interesting thought and research questions and activities.

I did notice one mistake in the guide. It says, "The Constitution may be changed through statutes, amendments, or court decisions." Actually, the Constitution may only be changed *legally* through the amendment process, although today legislators and courts routinely ignore this! Discussing why this is so and how it happened would make a fruitful—and long-lasting!—unit study. (Hint: Start with Frederick Bastiat's book, *The Law,* available from the Foundation for Economic Education.)

NEW★★
Vic Lockman
Patriotracts sample pack, $5.

Talented cartoonist Vic Lockman is also prolific cartoonist Vic Lockman. Besides free-lance cartooning for major firms, book cartooning, and so on, he's produced dozens of books and tracts of his own, mostly illustrating basic Christian doctrine and classic liberal (as in Founding Fathers constitutionalism, which now is called conservative or libertarian!) principles of government.

Vic's Patriotracts series takes on bureaucracy, unconstitutional paper money, the New World Order, inflationary politics, the unfunded Social Security system, and power-grabbing judges. He promotes local government, the free-enterprise system (including the right to make a profit), reduced government, gun-owner rights, an end to the income tax (did you know we didn't even *have* an income tax until 1913?), private property rights, and limiting the jurisdiction of the courts.

Vic has a genius for taking complex issues and making them simple enough for kids, and even adults, to understand. While I haven't seen most of these tracts, they ought to be zippy, thought-provoking reading.

CHAPTER THIRTY-FOUR

ECONOMICS

E conomics for kids in one lesson: in theory, "the economy" is the sum of individual people's transactions. Smith wants Sullivan's product. He pays Sullivan some money for it. Now Smith has the product and Sullivan has the money. That's "free market" economics. In "socialist" economics, the government owns all the products and the people buy them from the government with the wages the government pays them. In "mixed" economies, some people and products belong (in a manner of speaking) to the government, and others to the "private sector." The "private sector," however, is constantly being told by the government how to conduct business. When the government completely regulates all aspects of the private sector, while still allowing private ownership of the means of production, the technical term for this is "fascism."

Got all that? Great! Now if you can explain it to your kids, they'll know more about economics than some folks who write economics columns for major magazines. Add to that the resources below on how the stock market works and how the economy works (or *ought* to work, if Uncle Sam would leave it alone), and they'll understand economics better than many of the people we keep re-electing to Congress!

NEW★★
Academy for Economic Education
Ump's Fwat: An Annual Report for Young People, 1 copy free, more than 1 copy 50¢ each. Teacher's Kit—Instructor's Guide and 30 copies of *Ump's Fwat*—$15. Instructor's Guide alone, $2. 8-minute animated VHS video, $24.95. *The Economic Baseball Game,* $7. Ages 10–adult.

What's a "fwat"? It's the product of Ump's business. Ump is a caveman who excelled with the fwat in the game of fwap, and *Ump's Fwat* is the story of how he made his fortune manufacturing fwats for other cavemen. This fanciful tale is used to illustrate many of the concepts and terms used in business—savings, marketable product, invest, employed, etc.

If I were to criticize anything about this thoroughly winsome booklet, it would be the constant emphasis on how Ump's fwat business is so great at creating jobs. I believe that the ideal is for every man to sit under his own vine and fig tree, i.e., to have his own business and not have to work for someone else's. Since *Ump's Fwat* is written from the entrepreneur's perspective, this is not a major problem.

Also available: an instructor's guide, an eight-minute animated video retelling Ump's success story, and *The Economic Baseball Game*. The latter is a supply-and-demand simulation in which players buy and sell baseballs, and is designed for ages 10 to adult.

I have not seen the instructor's guide, the video, or the *Economic Baseball Game*. Myself, I can get a lot out of the free *Ump's Fwat* book, but if you are not already knowledgeable about free-market economics the instructor's guide and game might be helpful. The video is too pricey for single-family viewing.

Aristoplay, Ltd.
Made for Trade, $22. Add $4.75 shipping. Ages 8–adult.

Made for Trade is a historical board game that teaches economics lessons. See full review in the History chapter.

NEW**
Bluestocking Press
Whatever Happened to Penny Candy,? $6.45 postpaid. New teacher's materials, 75¢. Ages 10–adult.

So, whatever *did* happen to penny candy? Inflation, that's what! And where does inflation come from? From governments inflating the money supply. And how do governments inflate the money supply? By "legal tender" laws that force people to treat pieces of paper that can't be redeemed for precious metals as if the pieces of paper were worth something, and by a few other little tricks and quirks that you will fully understand after reading this book.

Whatever Happened to Penny Candy, a new book from Bluestocking Press, is written as a series of letters from an economist uncle to his teen nephew (or niece)

Chris. The origin and history of money, the origin and history of the dollar, the business cycle, inflation, recession, depression, foreign currencies, why and how governments meddle with the value of our money, and so on, are all covered in an easy-to-read style. The author, Richard J. Maybury, has drawn on years of experience explaining these things to his own students and colleagues. What you get is not witty, but it *is* clear and understandable, which is more than you can say for 99% of economics books!

Advantages for home schoolers: the book has a glossary, and words in the glossary are in boldface in the text. It also has an excellent Bibliography and Recommended Reading list, with mini-reviews of the books on the list. This will come in extremely handy if you want to pursue further study in economics. Most of the books recommended are available from LibertyTree. You also get a fine Resources list; a list of cassettes, games, and software; and a list of financial newsletters recommended by the author.

The author follows the "monetarist" or "Austrian" school of economics, popularized by writers such as Milton Friedman and Friedrich A. Hayek. If you never heard of monetarism or Hayek, don't worry—this is just the book for you! An excellent introduction to economics for teens and adults that will change the way you read the paper (both the newspaper and the fine print on your dollar bills). Highly recommended.

The new teacher's support material is a little brochure with some suggestions, a reproducible quiz with answers printed separately, a set of short reproducible essay questions, and discussion questions.

NEW**
Bluestocking Press
It Doesn't Grow on Trees, $5.95 plus $1.75 shipping. Adults read the book, use the information to train their children.

It Doesn't Grow on Trees is a thought-provoking course on financial responsibility for kids disguised as a slim book with a dollar sign and tree on the cover. Getting right to the point, author Jean Ross Peterson hits you hard with several all-too-familiar tales of kids whose financial training (or lack of it) left them totally unprepared for reality. She then gets into the psychology of money—how parents manipulate kids with money and how kids manipulate us right back—and how to get out of these emotional traps. Chapters on chores, allowances, comparison shopping (with the kids' own money!), saving, investing, and giving to those less financially blessed take your thinking a lot farther in this area than it's probably ever gone before.

The author favors no-strings allowances and children doing chores for free, while earning extra cash on special projects and outside jobs. I don't agree with this approach entirely, but let's not hassle over this. I'm also a little uneasy about the "let's invest!" advice. All the world needs is a bunch more people who want to live off interest (usury), who do no work except to loan their money to other people, who take no risks and yet expect dividends. Isn't this a perfect description of all those yuppie Wall Street investment bankers, so many of whom are helpless outside that cushy environment, as we saw when they lost their jobs after Black Monday? All the same, here's a lot of realistic advice worth reading.

NEW**
Teaching Home
February/March 1989 issue, $3.75. Complete six-issue set for 1989, $17.50, includes free set of 6 plastic magazine holders for your ring binder.

Teaching Home magazine as its usual policy devotes each issue of the magazine to one educational theme. Articles treat the topic in depth, suggesting ideas and profiling methods and resources. It's like a minicourse in teaching that topic! February/March 1989 was the issue on teaching political science and economics. Articles covered principles of political science, how to make economics and government fun, teaching the Biblical philosophy of government, basic economics, and economics for little kids.

UPDATED**
Vic Lockman
Biblical Economics in Comics, $6.95. Add $1 shipping. Ages 8–adult.

Our kids have just about worn the covers off our one and only copy of Vic Lockman's *Biblical Economics in Comics*. This is undoubtedly partly a tribute to Mr. Lockman's cartooning skill—after all, the man has put

in more than 30 years in the comic book industry, authoring over 7,000 comic book stories and publishing more than 100 cartoon booklets. The rest of our youngsters' fascination with this 100-plus page small paperback stems from the intriguing storyline. In Mr. Lockman's hands, economics is transformed from the "dismal science" into a series of cartoon vignettes featuring mice, rats (Bureau-Rats!), and cats.

Episode One, "The Market," starts with Adam Mouse shipwrecked on an island. There he is joined by a lady mouse, and bingo! the division of labor. They next have a family, which works as a mini-marketplace (more division of labor). When Junior gathers so much fish it begins to spoil, Pop diverts Junior's efforts to wood chopping . . . "and so, production is diverted to fill a greater demand!" The principles of exchange, competition, supply and demand, medium of exchange, capital and savings, loans and interest, profit and productivity, taxes, and even international trade are all explained so clearly a six-year-old can understand them. (I know. I asked him.)

Next, Mr. Lockman starts explaining some of our economic woes. Enter the Bureau-Rats, who, taking their lead from Karl Marx, inflict a graduated income tax on Mouseland. (I say this as someone who most of her life has honestly qualified for one of the bottom tax levels!) This is swiftly followed by a central bank, fiat money, inflation through expansion of printed money, checkbook money (the money printer got tired), tariffs, immigration quotas, public works, government aid to farms and industry, minimum wage laws, price fixing, rent control, public housing, welfare, monopolies, and that eternal favorite of Keynesian economists for stirring up sluggish economies, war. The rest of the book is devoted (still in cartoon form, but without story plots) to an exposition of the proper roles of government, law, money, and taxes, all from a specifically Biblical viewpoint.

The revised edition of *Biblical Economics in Comics* includes a new 12-page cartoon section on usury: what it is, what the Bible says about it, and how to live without it. Excellent teaching on this complex subject, simple enough for a child to follow.

CHAPTER THIRTY-FIVE

GEOGRAPHY

If it's true that finding all the wrong answers is one of the best ways to discover a solution, I should be a geography expert. Geography was my very worst, absolutely lousiest subject in school. This may be partly due to my very low level of natural navigational ability. I can get lost crossing the street! Still, looking back on my school experience, I see that I was taught by some pretty poor methods.

We had units on Tundra and Plains and Mountains. We memorized (and promptly forgot) Famous Rivers and Famous Forests. We studied Large Bodies of Water. We memorized State Capitals and State Flowers. After years of this sort of training, I still thought Missouri was somewhere in the Far West! The only geographical fact I retain from those days is the shape of Italy, because of a homework assignment that required us to make an outline map of that country.

Out of all this emerges two grave errors common when teaching geography, and one sound method of instruction. The grave errors are (1) to present facts in a meaningless way and (2) to make learning passive. Who cares about tundra and plains and mountains, anyway? These geographical features are extremely important in understanding the *people* who live on or near them, and for the history of wars and commerce: but none of my teachers emphasized this. Eskimos are interesting; tundra is not.

Geography is one of those subjects that needs a peg to hang on. Otherwise it is stored in short-term memory and quickly lost. You can memorize the map and its geographical features, but unless this is related to the needs and history of the people (and to a lesser extent, animals) who live there, geography is not only forgettable but valueless.

Passive learning means that kids are supposed to sit there and soak up geography. But if there ever was a subject meant for discovery learning, geography is it. Everything that any person has ever done was done somewhere. Look up that "somewhere" on a map or globe, and the map and globe come to life.

It's boring to watch a hockey game if you don't know anything about the teams or players. It's just as boring to look at places on a map and not know what happened there. Also, when studying shapes (the outlines of nations, states, and continents and the course of rivers, etc.), the best way to get these into the brain is to copy the shapes. I am not a particularly kinesthetic learner, but I will forever remember that Italy looks like a boot because I had to copy its coastline.

Drill has its place, in my opinion, and as far as geography is concerned that place is supplying simple facts and shapes again and again until we are comfortable with them. It then is easier to fill that data with content. When the Sudan comes up in dinner conversation, you'll at least have a vague idea that it's on the other side of the world. You won't think it's one of the fifty states or a province of Mexico!

We are now blessed with a superabundance of colorful and fun geography products. There are books to introduce geographic concepts, hands-on projects, drill products, and maps and atlases and globes. All of these (1) help you get from point A to point B in your personal travels or (2) provide the "where" of "Who did what where?" If these points are kept firmly in mind, geography study can be a thrilling discovery—as it is now for me!

MAPS, ATLASES, & GLOBES

NEW★★
Educational Insights
3-D Landform Maps, $14.95. Minimum order $25. Shipping extra. Grades 3–8.

This really is hands-on learning! *3-D Landform Maps* is a set of (1) three full-color raised-relief maps of an imaginary land, showing the 44 most popular geographic features, (2) a teacher's guide bound together with (3) six reproducible worksheets. Your students literally get their hands on the map and *feel* the shape of a mountain range, peninsula, or delta. You start to feel eerily like a giant looming over the earth after you've used this ingenious educational tool for a while. A fun way to learn about geographic features, with no sermonizing about how the features may have gotten there.

NEW★★
Educational Insights
Project: Earth, $29.95. Minimum order $25. Shipping extra. Grades 2–7.

Ever want to take over the world? Do it now with the *Project: Earth* kit. There's a catch; you have to make the world first. Yes, it's a do-it-yourself globe kit.

Banish from your mind all thoughts of blowing up balloons, covering them with sloppy papier mâché, waiting what seems like weeks for the goop to dry, and painting continents on the lumpy result. Educational Insights, being a trendsetter, has done away with this Dark Age technology. Instead, you get:

- Eight styrofoam globe sections
- A large bottle of blue acrylic paint (the Earth is mostly covered by water, which is blue)
- Smaller flip-top pots of other needed paint colors, all on one handy strip
- A brush
- A cardboard base on which to set your globe
- 112 labeled peel 'n stick country flags
- 11 famous places flags
- 25 resource and manufacturing flags
- 10 numbered but otherwise blank flags
- A set of continent outlines to help you locate and trace these landforms on your globe, and
- An activity guide with a full-color world map on the cover.

Everything is included but the masking tape, flour paste, and papier-mâché strips (yes, you still need these, unfortunately). However, since you are covering sturdy styrofoam, attaching the papier maché shouldn't be as much of a chore. The excellent step-by-step instructions in the activity guide explain exactly how to attach the styrofoam pieces together, how to cover the globe with papier mâché, how to draw the continents where they should go (a reference map keyed to the continent outlines makes this easy), how to paint the finished product or add extra geographical features, and last but not least, how to add the flags. Simply peel them off their backings, fold in half around a toothpick so the flag back and front stick together, and push into the styrofoam globe wherever the flags go!

I've looked at globe kits from both sides now—the goop-covered balloon and *Project: Earth*—and believe me, *Project: Earth* wins hands down. With this kit, your kids can make a globe they'll be proud of—and with the flags, they can learn (and be tested on) what goes where on the globe. A great motivational teaching tool.

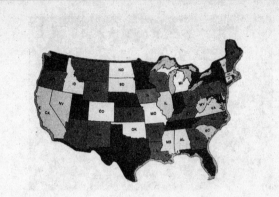

NEW**
Frank Schaffer

U.S. Map Floor Puzzle, $12.95, ages 3–8. U.S. Map bulletin board set, World Map bulletin board set, $5.95 each, grades 3–8. Bulletin board sets require 4 x 6' bulletin board.

For littlest learners, the U.S. Map Floor Puzzle is 51 large, chunky pieces. State capitals are shown. When completed, the puzzle is two feet by three feet.

For slightly older children, the U.S. Map bulletin board set includes labels for regions, like the Rocky Mountain States and South Central States, a label for the two oceans and the Gulf of Mexico, a map scale and compass rose, and separate state pieces, so you can study states or regions individually or put it all together as one map. Fifty-four pieces in all. In the World Map bulletin board set, continents and oceans are color-coded individual punch-outs with countries outlined in black. Set includes labels, compass rose, area chart, and banner. Twenty-six pieces in all.

Golden Educational Center

Forty-eight 11 x 17" maps (2 each of 24), $11.95. Set of 50 of the same map, $5.50. Add $2 shipping. Grades 2–adult.

From the publishers of the *Creating Line Designs* and *Designs in Math* series, yet another tool for integrating your artistic side with your intellectual one. We're talking about a package of black-and-white outline maps for your students to label and/or color in themselves. The size is a comfortable 11 x 17"—easy for children to work with. Price is right, too.

Set includes World (outline, political boundaries, political with lakes), United States (outline, waterways, state boundaries), Africa, Asia, Australia, Europe, North America, and South America (separate maps for outline, waterways, and political boundaries of each).

By looking up and labeling states, countries, rivers, and so on, your student will really learn where these things are. The open-ended format of white spaces to fill in also means you or he can add notes of interest—historical, cultural, or whatever. I haven't found a package like this anywhere else.

UPDATED**
Hammond

Discovering Maps: A Child's World Atlas, $10.95 plus $3 shipping. Ages 8 and up.

Maps and atlases are Hammond's strong suit. They have great prices for some really fine geography material. *Discovering Maps: A Child's World Atlas* now replaces their previous *The Wonderful World of Maps* as an introductory atlas for young readers. The first part of the book teaches map skills (symbols, direction, distance, scale, different types of maps, latitude and longitude, time zones, etc.). The second part presents simplified, easy-to-read, full-color political, physical, and special maps of the world, continents, Canada, and the U.S.A. Part three is 16 pages of fun facts and trivia (Why is the ocean blue? What is the world's northernmost piece of land?) plus a glossary of important geographic terms and a digest of world statistics.

Hammond's World Atlases (which come in models from economy to deluxe) feature an index right next to each map (where you need it the most) as well as a separate master index in the back (in some versions). Hammond also has all sorts of atlases, color relief maps, and hundreds of specialized travel maps (great for unit studies).

An unusual offering is *Hammond's Antique Map Reproductions*. These are full-color repros of the original old-time (mostly before 1700) maps.

Hammond has a separate Education catalog, which I recommend. Hammond's Map Skills program will interest some home schoolers, particularly since it is so inexpensive and well laid out. Student atlases start as low as $4.65. Hammond also has reference maps for less than $3 and a wide selection of other maps.

NEW**
Hayes School Publishing Co., Inc.

Outline Maps of the U.S.A., Outline Maps of the World, $4.95 each. Specify blackline masters. Add $1.50 shipping for first item, 35¢ each additional item. Grades 2–8.

Here's a wonderful resource for learning and testing geographical facts: Hayes' *Outline Maps* series.

These workbooks are just what the name implies: outline maps of various regions. The student can fill in country names, label geographical features, and so on. Although each book includes a teacher's key," you will need an atlas or globe to check your work. The teacher's key gives teaching suggestions and lists the names of countries, states, etc. to be filled in on each map.

Both workbooks have maps of the U.S.A. *Outline Maps of the U.S.A. and Other Parts of the World* presents the U.S.A. in more depth, with separate maps for each geographical region. It also covers Europe, South America, and just about everywhere else except Africa and Australia. *Outline Maps of the World* covers the entire world. Maps are drawn rather broadly; not much fine detail. Forty-eight pages of outline maps in each workbook.

Hubbard
Relief maps start at $15.95. Map Reading Model, $31.

Hubbard is the place for raised relief maps. You can get regional maps (West of the Rockies and some eastern areas), National Park maps, U.S.A., and World maps, all framed or unframed.

For geography study, Hubbard has a map reading model packet that includes a plastic terrain model with five stacking contour sheets, five unprinted stacking contour sheets, a wall map, 50 student project sheets, and even a grease pencil.

Hubbard's catalogs are free, and the map catalog is well worth sending for.

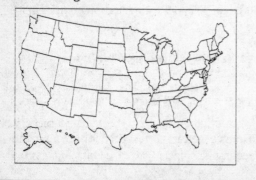

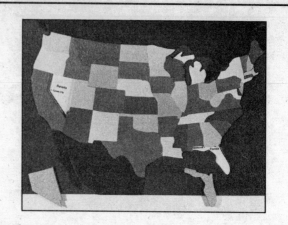

Lauri
Fit-A-State, $18.95. *Fit-A-World*, $19.95. Shipping extra. Ages 8–10.

I went out and *paid money* for Lauri's crepe rubber maps. If you knew how stuffed my storage cabinet already is with things geographical, you'd realize how great I think these Lauri maps are! First, they are beautiful. Nations (in the World map) and states (in the U.S. map) are different colors of crepe rubber. Second, they have texture and heft. The pieces are ¼ inch thick and feel great. Third, they are puzzles. You *have* to learn something about geography just by putting the puzzles back together! Novices quickly learn to look for clues: the funny-shaped, tiny states come from New England, and the big blocks from out West. State names are shown on the underlay, so you can see what you are looking for. And if you lose Rhode Island, Lauri will replace it for 50¢.

NEW**
Learning at Home
Geographical Terms Charts, $1.80 for a set of 2. Shipping extra.

Learning at Home says that their pair of Geographical Terms Charts is "the best land-water forms learning aid we've ever seen." It ranks right up there with the landforms section of GeoSafari (though not with the *3-D Landforms Kit*), and costs less than $2. Chart 1 is a full-color composite landscape with each geographic term printed right on its corresponding feature (e.g., *butte, island, delta*). Chart 2 is a blue and white reproduction of this same landscape, but without the printed terms. Kids can use this to test themselves on how well they know the terms. I found it a little fuzzy to work with, and of course, being blue, it is not reproducible.

National Geographic Society

Membership, $15, includes the magazine. Most maps: $3/paper, $4/plastic.

You know all about *National Geographic* magazine. As befits an originally geographical society, NGS has maps, maps, and more maps. Lands of the Bible today. Bird migration in the Americas. Mural maps to cover your wall. Ocean floor relief maps. Space maps. U.S. regional maps. Canadian provinces. Antarctica (plan in advance for your trip!)

NGS also has a couple of fancy atlases and a quint of fancy globes.

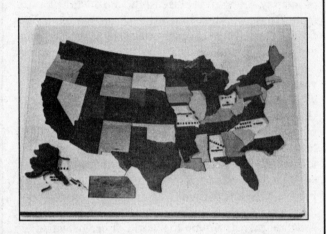

NEW**
Pacific Puzzle Company

Set of five hardwood continents puzzles, $80. Large World Political/Physical puzzle, $84. U.S. puzzles: small $23, medium $40, large $65, beginner's $40. Dymaxion™ World puzzle, $22. Add $3 shipping for first puzzle, $1 each additional. Shipping for Continent Set is $7. Add an additional 50% shipping for Canada, AK, HI. Replacement puzzle pieces are available at $5 per piece postpaid, or $7 per piece for large U.S. and World puzzles.

Pacific Puzzle Company has an excellent collection of wood geography puzzles. These utterly gorgeous puzzles are crafted of birch plywood with the best maps available laminated on and cut along political boundaries. Let me tell you about my personal picks from their collection.

The Continent puzzles are a set of five gorgeous puzzles covering all the inhabited continents of the world. These are great for country studies; see the writeup below under Country Studies!

Pacific Puzzle Company's new World Map puzzle, again, is utterly gorgeous. It requires some large, flat area where you can store them. The Large World-Physical/Political puzzle is a huge 19 x 28" and contains about 106 pieces. Some small countries are doubled up with other small countries, but otherwise the pieces are cut along country borders. Bill says, "This puzzle is absolutely unbelievable. Every time I look at it I am flabbergasted at how beautiful it is." This also is a heirloom quality puzzle, with top-quality detailed maps laminated onto birch plywood. The puzzle assembles in its own frame—you just pop the countries in where they go. The Physical map also shows longitude and latitude. (This map should not be confused with Pacific Puzzle Company's small Political World and Physical World puzzles, which have only 15 and 11 pieces, respectively, and which are not nearly as useful.) I really recommend the world puzzle highly!

Pacific Puzzle Company offers a wide variety of United States puzzles: small (8½ x 11"), medium (14 x 19"), and large (19 x 25") United States puzzles with, respectively, 51, 51, and 45 pieces, or the Beginner's United States, a 51-piece puzzle of stained wood pieces. Lift each piece to see the state name, capital, and outline underneath. The Beginner's U.S. puzzle is a fine testing tool; the other three all use the well-known political map of the U.S. These are PPC's most popular puzzles.

And then there's the Dymaxion puzzle. Based on a Buckminster Fuller design, these 20 triangular shapes fit together to present one of the most accurate flat representations of the earth around. However, unlike other map puzzles, you can put it together correctly dozens of different ways, depending on which viewing angle you choose to highlight. Look at the earth from the viewpoint of an Australian or a polar bear! See how the oceans and landmasses connect! There's very little distortion of the shapes and sizes of the continents. Short of using a globe, this puzzle is the best way to gain understanding of the continents and oceans. Its 3½" triangles don't take up much storage space, nor does it take too much room to construct. And since it's manipulative, it has some educational advantages over a globe.

Pacific Puzzle Company also has fun (and relatively inexpensive) puzzles for young children, alphabet and number puzzles, geometric shape puzzles, and their newest entry, the Apple Puzzle. This 3-D puzzle looks like a real apple, but is actually 35 pieces you put together around the wooden "core." Our kids *love* these puzzles!

Rand McNally
Family World Atlas, $12.95. Grades 4–adult.

No listing of geography materials would be complete without Rand McNally, the people whose maps help America navigate on summer vacations. Rand McNally has bunches of atlases for the incurably curious, including a number of astronomical atlases. Does anyone you know need a map of Jupiter? Of more interest to the average family is Rand McNally's *Family World Atlas*, so called because it has information of interest to any age bracket. This atlas has 60 pages of tables, charts, intriguing facts, and comparisons. It's always fun to get down the *Family Atlas* and browse with the kids, and it makes a great resource for discovery projects. What is the largest island in the world? How much of Australia gets by on less than 10 inches of rain a year? Kids will like the "Today's World in Maps" section consisting of colorful regional maps devoted to different attributes, such as landforms, natural hazards, minerals, etc.

GEOGRAPHY CURRICULUM & DRILL

NEW✶✶
A Beka Book Publications
The History of Our United States (grade 4), $10.15. *Old World History and Geography* (grade 5), $11.30. *New World History and Geography* (grade 6), $12.05. Teacher's editions available for all books, include complete text of student book. Grades 1–12.

The colorful A Beka texts include American customs, songs, and other vital parts of our cultural heritage, as well as general history. The entire curriculum includes an emphasis on geography mastery—you get 22 pages of map skills and a mini-atlas in the *Old World History and Geography in Christian Perspective* book for fifth graders, for instance. Grade 5 covers Old

World history and geography, while grade 6 covers New World history and geography. These two grades do a more thorough job than all the previous four combined. If you also want a U.S. history course, add the new grade 4 book, *History of Our United States*. See writeup in History chapter.

NEW✶✶
Alpha Omega Publications
LIFEPACS, $22.5–$2.45 each, 10 LIFEPACS per grade. Set of 10 LIFEPACS, $19.95–$21.95. Answer keys, teacher handbooks available. Shipping extra. Grades 1–12.

Alpha Omega's social studies courses cover history, geography, economics, citizenship, and a whole lot more. These worktext-based courses are written up in detail in the History chapter. Here's the scoop on their geography content:

Grades 1 and 2: almost none. Grade 3 is a whole year spent on American cultural anthropology. In other words, it's a simplified field trip around the country. Units are: A Fishing Community, A Farming Community (Kansas), A Fruit-Growing Community (Washington), Oregon: Land of Forests, A Golden Land (California), Cattle Raising in Texas, Coal Mining and Pennsylvania, Manufacturing Community (Michigan), and Florida: Gateway to Space.

Grade 4 examines the geography and cultures of geographic areas around the world. It begins with a touch of world geography, then looks at two island countries (Japan and Hawaii), two mountain contries (Peru and Switzerland), the polar pegions, tropical jungles (Amazon and Congo), grassland regions (Kenya, Argentine, U.S.A.), desert lands, seaport cities (San Francisco, Hong Kong, and Sydney), and The United States: Your State (basic U.S. history, geography, and government, plus activities for doing your own state report). Each unit on a country or area includes information on its history, geography, culture, and industries, from a Christian perspective. For example, the unit on Hawaii tells how the missionaries came to Hawaii and what effect they had (Hawaii was once a Christian country!).

Special note: The unit on the United States and Your State (LIFEPAC #9 of the fourth-grade course) also includes really good activities to help children generate their own state reports.

Grade 5 mostly focuses on U.S. history. LIFEPACS 7–9 of this course cover geographic regions of the U.S., "Our Southern Neighbors" (Mexico, Central America, and Caribbean), and Canada.

Grade 6 tackles world history. First there's a very good unit on world geography, then we move from the Cradle of Civilization (excellent background for your Bible studies) to The Civilizations of Greece and Rome, Life in the Middle Ages, and one unit each on Western Europe (from the Renaissance on) and Eastern Europe (from Byzantium to the Space Age). This sequence is interrupted by two mostly-geographic units on South American countries and one on Africa (tucked in right before we move to Europe). Each history unit includes information about the geography of the time and place being studied, along with information on daily life in that time period, plus its social institutions, and economics. The units on geographic regions (South America and Africa) include history, geography, types of people who live in each country, industries, major cities, and holidays.

All Alpha Omega levels are very easy to use, as long as you keep up with your grading of workbook exercises and writing assignments. The tests are right in the workbooks, as are pre-tests and teacher checkpoints.

Arthur Bornstein School of Memory Training
States and Capitals Kit, $39.95. Add 10% shipping. Ages 7–adult.

How can a set of 56 8½ x 11 illustrated flash cards help your youngsters memorize the capital of every U.S. state, and each state's general location? What if I told you that one flash card has a picture of a big ARK on top of a LITTLE ROCK and another shows the BOYS watching while IDA HOES potatoes? Yes, Arthur Bornstein has struck again. The outrageous associations and goofy scenes in his States and Capitals Kit make it easy to remember which capital goes with which state. More: the back of each card shows the state's outline and relative size, its abbreviation, nickname, flower, tree, bird, and date of entrance into the Union, plus teaching tips. Accompanying booklet and cassette tape explain whatever else you need to know about using this kit. Then, when your students have finished giggling their way through all fifty states, cards 51–56 feature a map of states and their capitals, and memory associations for the 13 original states, Western states, Midwestern states, Southern states, and Northeastern states. Exaggerated cartoon-style, busty females in low-cut dresses, quite a few Catholic and Christian allusions (Mass for Massachusetts, Ark for Arkansas, St. Paul's Cathedral for St. Paul). Very easy to use.

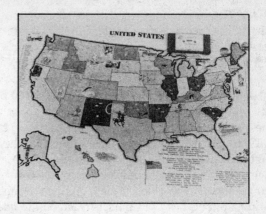

NEW★★
Audio Memory Publishing
Sing Around the World Geography Kit, $24.95. *Sing Around the World* book, $6.95. Coloring map of world, U.S.A., $3 each. States and Capitals song kit, $9.95. Add $2 shipping. All ages.

Learn what's where by singing along with tapes! Audio Memory Publishing's new *Sing Around the World* kit has two cassettes with 18 songs, a 25 x 26" map of the world to label and color, and a 96-page songbook with all the lyrics plus regional maps to color, crossword puzzles, and several pages with pictures of landmarks to match to their names. Answer keys to the puzzles are in the back of the book. To make things more lively, the book also features many pictures of the people, pastimes, landmarks, and cultural detritus of each area. Song lyrics are also printed on the world map, each near the region it describes. Sample lyrics:

The central plains are called the "outback"
with the sheep and cattle stations.
The aborigines were the first
people in this nation. . . . (from the song "Australia")

Afghanistan, Sri Lanka
Nepal and Bangladesh
Bhutan and India
Maldives and Pakistan
are the countries of South Asia. (the entire song "South Asia")

The French have French Guiana
The British have the Falkland Islands
Brazil is the biggest country
and Chile is the longest. (From "South America")

The two cassettes with 18 upbeat, folksy songs cover the world. Song topics include Southeast Asia, the Middle East, Europe, Australia, New Zealand,

Canada, Central America, South Asia, Mexico, Asia, Greenland, Oceania, South America, Africa, West Indies, United States, Continents and Oceans, and the Solar System.

How helpful will these cassettes be? It's all up to you. If you and your kids are the type who like to have music playing, sooner or later you will pick up the lyrics to all of these songs almost unconsciously. They won't *mean* anything, though, until you get out the songbook and start locating the countries you are singing about. They are numbered in the same order as they are sung on the 18 book maps and on the large world map. This has 171 numbers listed on the side, corresponding to numerals on the map.

If you'd like to focus on the United States, Audio Memory Publishing's *States and Capitals Song Kit* comes with a cassette and 25 x 36" map of the U.S.A. with 172 items to label. You can pick a location from the list and find out where it is on the map. "I'll be! So *that's* where the Okefenokee Swamp is!" The songs teach the names and locations of the 50 states and their capitals. The Capitals songs are sung in echo fashion and repeated for self-testing.

NEW★★
Bob Jones University Press
Teacher's edition, each grade, $28.50 (include complete text of student book). Student text, each grade, from $9.95–$17.95. Tests and additional activity sheets available for some grades. Shipping extra. Grades 1–12.

History, geography, and cultural studies combined, from an conservative evangelical Protestant point of view. Grades 5 and 6 are the most geography-oriented of the elementary curriculum. In grade 5, the emphasis turns from history to the geography and cultures of nations in the Western Hemisphere. Grade 6 does the same for the Eastern Hemisphere. Economics and politics are also handled more formally in the latter two volumes.

NEW★★
Crane's Select Educational Materials
Geography Flipper, $5.95. Add $1.50 shipping. Ages 10–adult.

Ever confuse latitude with longitude? Can you tell me whether the Prime Meridian is the same thing as the Greenwich Time Line? Quick, now: spell and define isthmus. How about estuary? Viaduct?

Unlike the *3-D Landforms* and other geography-at-a-glance teaching tools, the *Geography Flipper* is designed as a ready reference. You don't have to spend long minutes searching for the geographic feature you are trying to define. It's all laid out in overlapping clear pockets filled with 49 handy illustrated reference cards. Starting with maps and globes, rotation, latitude, longitude, circles and topics, degrees, mapping, earth's relationship to the sun, and so on, the cards proceed to describe every type of geographic feature, from islands to highlands. These are laid out very logically, with such categories as "Landforms—Steep Places" and "Water—Inland." If you know the name of what you're looking for, a short index at the end helps you find it quickly. If you don't, just find the right category and flip until you find what you're looking for.

Not all geographic features are visually illustrated, just those that need it. Definitions are very simple, e.g., "Source: The beginning of a river or stream . . . Bayou: A slow-moving waterway which is a lake's outlet or a river's path through its delta." The whole thing is mounted on a sturdy , reinforced, three-hole-punched piece of cardboard, the better to fit into your binder, my dear. A really neat, well-organized condensation of a lot of geographical information.

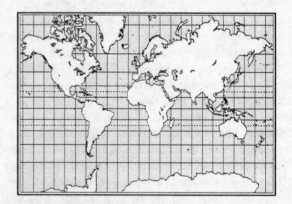

EDC Publishing
Usborne Book of World Geography, $17.95 hardbound. Ages 8–adult.

More colorful facts than you can imagine about the earth, the seas, people and houses of the world, and maps of the world. Heavily illustrated, with many captioned pictures and mini-story sequences. Geography is placed in the context of the people who live in each place and the ways they live. Slightly evolutionary in a few spots. Like all Usborne books, the *Book of World Geography* makes fascinating browsing.

NEW★★
Educational Insights
GeoSafari, $99, GeoSafari Map Packs, $14.95 each. GeoSafari AC Adaptor, $9.95. Minimum order $25. Shipping extra. Grades 2–adult.

Geography drill is boring. You know this. I know this. But someone at Educational Insights didn't know this. So they invented the GeoSafari teaching machine. This super resource comes equipped with 20 double-sided large (9½ x 13¼") and colorful laminated sheets. Place a sheet on the "screen" area, type in the code on the upper-right-hand corner, tell the computer whether you are playing with a friend or alone and how long you want to be given to answer each question, and go! The computer will flash lights randomly and then flash a light by the question it wants to ask you. You have to quickly look on the sheet for the answer and type it in. If you miss the answer, it will flash a light by the right answer. Sheets are such things as a U.S. map with states and capitals and a picture map of geographical terms (island, butte, volcano, delta, etc.). You will learn to identify continents and countries, natural resources, bodies of water, world landmarks, and lots more with just the sheets included in your GeoSafari purchase.

GeoSafari is (I'm warning you) addictive. Reluctant geography students will happily spend hours testing themselves on geography with GeoSafari and learning the facts they missed. Two kids can even learn together, thanks to the feature that allows two kids to compete!

Additional GeoPacks now available include: U.S. Geography (natural resources and industry, U.S. territorial acquisitions, special points of interest, etc.), World Geography (religions, currencies, cultures, ancient civilizations, literature, natural resources and in-dustries, etc.), Animals of the World, and Puzzles, Thinking Games, and Make Your Own. As you can see, this teaching machine is not necessarily limited to teaching geography. Educational Insights plans to keep bringing out more GeoPacks on a regular basis.

Bottom line: GeoSafari is absolutely the best geographic home-teaching resource for anyone who has—or can scrape up— that kind of money to spend. (Other people think so too: GeoSafari was rated the number one toy in the Great American Toy Test of 1990.) Very highly recommended.

NEW★★
The Learning Works
United States Geography Journey, $24.95 plus $3 shipping. Grades 4–8.

United States Geography Journey is a workbook and game rolled into one. First, the workbook. It's divided into six sections. The first section, "General Geographic Facts," teaches kids how to read maps of all kinds. Each of the next four sections focuses on one particular region—southern, northeastern, central, and western—of the U.S.A. Activities include matching states to their outlines, matching states to their geographic features and locations, and a detective story that the reader can follow on his map. The sixth section, "Just for Fun," has quiz questions covering all states and regions.

Included with the workbook are six 8½ x 11" Colorprint™ U.S. maps, a large U.S. outline map, and 128 U.S. Geography Grab Bag game cards (printed in sheets of eight questions per sheet). Using the maps, a whole group of students and their teacher can solve the quiz problems at once.

U.S. Geography Grab Bag is a look-it-up game. Categories for the question cards include Using a Map Scale of Miles, Which is Farther?, Rivers-Lakes-and-Seas, Latitude and Longitude, North-South-East-or-West, Borders and Boundaries, Comparing Size, and The Name's the Same. Each category includes 16 cards, color-coded to the category. These are not "knowledge" questions, but look-it-up questions, such as "The distance between Columbia and Sumter, South Carolina, is about 50 miles—true or false?"

When you get a card, use your U.S. map to determine whether the information on the card is true or false. If true, place your card in the True box on the game sheet (or in a box labeled "True" on any old plain sheet of paper). If false, place it in the False box. Game variations include moving markers across individual U.S. maps, or claiming states with different-colored markers for each student on a large U.S. map. Answer key is in the back of the workbook.

U.S. Geography Journey has more map work than any other single program I have seen. Good for larger families (who can use more of the maps!) and as a unit to train kids in map work.

NEW**
McDougal, Littell & Co.
Daily Geography program, $12 each teacher's manual. Grades 2–11 available. Add $4 shipping.

Can your child answer these questions:

1. What two oceans do not touch Australia?

2. The Prime Meridian passes through which three continents?

3. Two countries in South America are totally land-locked. Bolivia is one; what is the name of the other country?

Dollars to doughnuts he can't. The amount most kids today know about geography is pitiful. You know that. I know that. So what are we going to do about it?

How about a geography program that takes five or ten minutes a day, and teaches kids not just the simple stuff like, "Find Florida on this labeled U.S. map," but how to answer toughies like the questions above? *Daily Geography* from McDougal, Littel & Company is a set of teacher's manuals with geography questions and answers for every week of the school year, plus a scope and sequence, glossary of geography terms, and simple teaching suggestions. The teacher's manuals for grades 2 and 3 have six geography questions a week. The manuals for grades 4–11 have eight questions a week. If you use the entire program, your child will have worked through nearly 2,500 sequenced geography questions.

Here's how it works. You write two geography questions on the chalkboard. (Every home teacher needs a chalkboard, anyway.) Your child then copies the questions into his geography notebook and looks up the answers using maps, globes, and atlases. He then reports his answer orally and/or shows you the answer on the map. Correct answers are recorded in the geography notebook. You can either do one or two

geography questions every day, or have a single, longer geography session once a week.

The questions for each week fit on a single page of the manual, and are divided according to concept. These are *not* multiple choice—the student has to figure out the answers himself. Concepts taught run the gamut from states and capitals to map reading, relative positions of geographic features (e.g, "Which of the Great Lakes is farthest east?" and "If you were in the Gulf of Bothnia, between what two countries would you be located?"), and "thinking questions" like, "Look at a map of Asia. Why would you find little farming in Northern Asia?" (answer: It's very far north and very cold). The Grade 2 work starts off slowly with questions like, "Is the United States a city, a state, or a country?" and by grade 10 you are finding your way about the Gulf of Bothnia.

The *Daily Geography* program builds on itself. Your average eighth-grader would have trouble jumping right in with the eighth-grade book, in my opinion. The solution is to order all the levels up to and including your student's grade level, and doing extra questions in each geography session until he is caught up. All the school-age children in a family can learn their geography at once, although you may need to write separate questions for each grade level.

NEW**
Milliken Publishing Co.
Map Skills transparency/duplicating series, $12.95 each. Grades 4–9.

Milliken's *United States Map Skills* transparency/duplicating workbook is a complete course in U.S. geography. With the aid of 12 colorful full-page transparencies, kids learn about time zones, climate, states and capitals, postal abbreviations, population density, state mottoes, major geographic features, and how to use city, state, and interstate road maps. 28 workbook pages and a teacher's guide with answer key round out the book.

This book is much easier to use than a traditional geography textbook, partly because of its highly visual approach. Some of the transparencies are fascinating, like the cutaway view of the heights of the waterways included in the St. Lawrence Seaway. Regions of the U.S.A. are briefly introduced, but covered in more detail in the other books in this series: *Eastern U.S.A.*, *Southern U.S.A.*, *Central U.S.A.*, and *Western U.S.A.*. The series also includes a book on Canada.

NEW**
Teacher Created Materials
Writing a State Report, $5.95. Grades 3–6.

This really should be titled *How to Write a BOOK About Your State*! After the initial workbook pages on the mechanics of report writing, the rest of this workbook consists of idea-prodding outlines and checklists designed to help you find out *everything* about your state. Example: under the heading "Resources," page 35 says: "Listed below are the many natural resources of _____." Then comes this list, each item followed by several blank lines: Water, Soil, Minerals, Plant Life, Animal Life. On some pages you draw pictures of the state flower and state bird. On a U.S. outline map (included) you color your state blue and label all of its neighbors. You fill in a population density map, write a few directed paragraphs of state history, research its political and geographic features, and a whole lot more!

Writing a State Report was obviously designed for school classes in grades 3–6 where each child picks a different state and reports back to the class. It has no actual info about any of the states; kids have to look this up themselves. As with other Teacher Created Materials, no page requires very much writing to complete. This is a perfect example of a project where a little bit of work, faithfully done every day or week, can result in a satisfying project. Since most states *require* a course in state history for graduation, it's also about the simplest way I've seen to organize a state course and prove that the work has been done. (Older students might find the workbook pages too childish; they can use it as a takeoff point for their own research and writing.)

The only other resource I have found as helpful for writing a state report is LIFEPAC unit 9 of the fourth-grade Alpha Omega social-studies course (see review above).

NEW**
Teacher Created Materials
United States Geography, World Geography, $5.95 each. Grades 3–6.

You need access to a photocopier to use these books. There! I put it up front, so you can't miss it. Now, we can talk about the workbooks themselves.

United States Geography and *World Geography* are two reproducible, activity-laden workbooks for kids in grades 3–6. Both share the same format. The "Windows to the World" section in *World Geography* is similar to the "Windows to the Capitals" in *U.S. Geography*, for instance. Each has a Geography Pocket Book, Treasure Hunt game, Where Am I? puzzles, Landform Identification page, and systematic coverage of (respectively) world continents and United States regions. Now hold your horses, 'cuz I'm going to tell you what all those doodads are.

• The Geography Pocket Book. This is several reproducible pages of world or U.S. facts, subdivided into four pages each. You photocopy the pages, kids slice them up to make their own pocket books of facts. Facts included: areas, sizes and locations of seas or lakes, facts about rivers, climate extremes, elevation extremes, and other fun things to know. Turns out these facts are also handy for answering some of the workbook questions: remember that, before you send Junior to the encyclopedia searching for answers.

• The Treasure Hunt game. Photocopy the cards. Label and color each card back according to its category. (Laminate 'em, too, if you're smart.) Photocopy and color the gameboard. Move around the gameboard, following directions and answering questions. 32 questions included: add more if you like. It's like a mini version of *Know It All* that you make yourself.

• "Where Am I?" puzzle questions. Many clues help you identify a state or country. Only two puzzles per book, unfortunately.

Let's just skip through the rest of the goodies, OK? I like the way continents and regions are broken up into individual countries or states for the student to label. Lots of other find-and-fill-in-the-answer questions, all relatively easy to do (not too much work per worksheet, some clues included to make the job easier). All answers are given in the back. The "Windows" section is a set of pages for you to photocopy and lay on top of each other. Cut out the windows, then lift a labeled window to see the capital and continent for each country, or the capital of each state. Great drill tool!

These are the two best workbooks Teacher Created Materials has produced, in my opinion. I'd like to see more Where Am I? puzzles (How about a separate book of these, folks?), but aside from that, there's nothing to complain about. Where else can you get a mini book of facts, board game, manipulative drill tool, and all these high-interest geography worksheets for such a low price?

NEW**
Teaching Home
August/September 1988 back issue, $3.75 postpaid. Complete six-issue set of 1988 back issues, $17.50, includes free set of 6 plastic magazine holders for your ring binder.

Want a quick, yet deep minicourse in how to teach geography? Then grab the August/September 1988 issue of *Teaching Home* magazine. *Teaching Home* keeps its back issues continually in print, since each is just crammed with useful information on how to teach the topic-of-the-issue at home. In this issue we find out why modern American schoolkids can't find Florida on a map even when they *live* there (because geography was deep-sixed by "social studies," a totally nebulous substitute), how to have fun with geography, how to learn geography through planning and taking imaginary trips, map literacy, and lots more! This issue also has a missions emphasis, with several articles on how to make missions support a part of your child's life.

COUNTRY STUDIES

UPDATED**
Asia Society
Video Letter from Japan (grades 1–6), *Video Letter from Japan II* (grades 7–college), $22.95 each package or $130 for series of 6 prepaid. *Discover Korea* (grades 1–6), $22.95 each package, or $65 for series of 3 prepaid. VHS only. Shipping extra on non-prepaid orders.

I had only slight expectations when writing away for a review copy of the *Video Letter from Japan* series (produced by The Asia Society in cooperation with

TDK Corporation). After all, I've seen enough half-baked classroom lectures on video to know that most educational video ain't exactly United Artists quality.

Well, I was really impressed. Beautiful photography, excellent script, state-of-the-art effects (used sparingly where helpful), and a warm understanding of both Japanese culture and the video's intended American audience all combine to make this the *best* educational video I have ever seen, bar none.

A different Japanese child is your host for the 25-minute "letter" on each video. You see Japan through the eyes of this child, as he or she attends school, swims in a river, shares a holiday meal with the family, and so on. Each letter illustrates some aspect of Japanese culture. Programs include *My Day, Tohoku Diary, My Family, Making Things, Living Arts,* and *Our School* (this was the one we saw). Each package also includes a teacher's manual and a classroom poster. Beyond this first *Video Letter* series designed for elementary school children, another series of six video packages, entitled *Video Letter from Japan II,* is available for high school and early college.

The Asia Society has also produced a similar series on Korea, entitled *Discover Korea.* The first video in this series, *Family and Home,* was just as engaging as the *Video Letter from Japan.* The program is 21 minutes long and comes with a teacher's manual and a double-sided, full-sized instructional poster. Other titles in the series are *School and Community* and *Geography and Industry.*

EDC Publishing
Peoples of the World, Houses and Homes, $6.95 each paper or $13.96 library-bound. Combined volume, *People and Homes,* $10.95 hardbound. Ages 8 and up.

Like all of the Usborne series from England, which EDC publishes in the United States, *Peoples of the World* and *Houses and Homes* are filled with fascinating facts and colorful illustrations. Think of these as prep sheets for playing the nonexistent game of Cultural Trivia. Lots of lowdown on the way other people live.

NEW★★
Golden Educational Center

Continent Maps & Studies, $6.95. *South America Country Studies*, *North America Country Studies*, $6.95 each. *California—Early History*, $9.95. *California—Geography*, $7.95. Add $2 shipping. Grades 4–8.

From the creators of the clever *Creating Line Designs* series, here are some easy-learn, high-interest basic geography and history workbooks. *Continent Maps & Studies* is 48 pages of maps, questions, and additional activities. Recognizing that children have trouble finding information on a map when the map is too loaded with text, Golden has provided separate outline, waterway, and political boundary maps for each continent except (for obvious reasons) Antarctica. The book also includes a World Outline, World Political Boundary map, and World Pacific-View map. Each continent also has a completed political boundary and waterway map. Designed as a supplement for any geography, history, social studies, or world literature course.

The activities are simple, fun, and each can be accomplished in a reasonable amount of time. Example: "Write a paragraph describing the food and clothing of the people" in that country, state, or continent. Other questions and activities can similarly be used for every geographical region studied. The book also provides basic facts about each continent: the number and names of independent countries on that continent; its area; greatest distances north-south and east-west; population; highest and lowest elevations; physical features; waterways; main religions; and other interesting facts. You then can photocopy as many copies of the maps as you need for your own family or classroom and write in the countries, waterways, etc. for a number of great learning activities. Really nice, clean, nonthreatening format makes this workbook and the others in the series (*South America Country Studies* and *North America Country Studies*) a good choice.

NEW★★
Ladybird Books, Inc.
Each book, $3.50. Grades 5–9.

Places to go . . . Ladybird's fully-illustrated Discovering series of little hardcover books takes you on guided tours of famous places. The series includes *London*, *Scotland*, *Tower of London*, *Shakespeare Country*, *Castles*, *Cathedrals*, and *Natural History Museum*. The series also has a book apiece on the Vikings and the Spanish Armada. Text is designed for a preteen reading level.

NEW★★
Pacific Puzzle Company

Set of five hardwood Continents puzzles, $80. Shipping for Continent Set is $7. Add an additional 50% shipping for Canada, AK, HI. Replacement puzzle pieces are available at $5 per piece postpaid, or $7 per piece for large U.S. and World puzzles.

The Continent puzzles are a set of five birch plywood puzzles with full-color maps laminted on them and cut along political boundaries for (gasp!) $80. Sounds like a lot? It's really, really worth it. If you want your family to have a real grasp of what is where in the world, this is the best resource I have ever found to teach them. Puzzles are ideal for the purpose, since geography is based on shapes. Pacific Puzzle Company's puzzles are heirloom-quality works of art, making geography study not only fun but also nurturing a sense of beauty. And if all this doesn't convince you, let me just say that I have found these puzzles to be a great starting point for developing a Christian worldview. You can study all the countries on one continent one by one, or have a number of children working several different puzzles at once. They are a size that fits well on a shelf, but big enough to really see the countries and the map details. Pick a country of the day, have the children trace its shape (use the puzzle piece like a stencil), and look it up in the encyclopedia. (Don't have an encyclopedia? Get a cheap one at a yard sale, or invest $10 in a newspaper ad asking for an inexpensive used encyclopedia, e.g., "I'll pay $50 for a used World Book Encyclopedia.") Have one child read the encyclopedia entry aloud. Then look up the country in Send the Light's *Operation World* set. *Operation World* provides general information on every country from a Christian and missionary point of view, plus lots and lots of statistics, historical background information, ethnic information, and prayer needs. At the rate of one country a day, in just a few months your children will know their way around the world!

One caveat: PPC uses two-sided maps for the Continents series. Some very slight show-through of the map from the other side is unavoidable. I didn't personally notice any show-through until it was drawn to my attention.

NEW★★
Quantum Communications
Traveloguer videos, $29.95 each. Quantity prices: 3–11 tapes, $24.95 each; 12+ tapes, $19.95 each. Shipping extra. All ages.

Part of a real education includes learning what life is *really* like in other countries. Wealthy parents, understanding this, used to send their sons on the Grand Tour, a worldwide tour lasting up to two years after they graduated from the university. Few of us can afford the Grand Tour, but now there's an affordable alterative!

I am really excited about Quantum Communications' fabulous Traveloguer Collection of travel videos. Now, I know what you're thinking. "*Travel videos?!?* What's so great about those?" Too many travel videos are the updated equivalent of Uncle Harry's slide show of Europe, long on tourist attractions and short on descriptions of the real countries and their people.

Not so with the Traveloguer Collection! These 60-minute videos are adapted from films produced by real "traveloguers." Traveloguers are independent film producers who spend years studying what makes a country unique, as well as spotting the best film shots. They then present their films to live audiences of thousands throughout North America. The best of these films of European countries have been brought together into the Traveloguer Collection.

I know that videos can be a risky business, not to mention a risqué business. Makers of travel videos sometimes like to linger on the seamy, nightclub side of a country, and heaven knows we don't need to bring any more of this into our homes. So I asked the people at Quantum Communications to allow me to review their entire 18-video series. I was really impressed! Not only is this some of the most spectacular film footage I have ever seen, narrated by people who obviously know what they're talking about, but these videos have

tremendous educational value (again setting them apart from other travel videos series).

The videos teach you *geography,* as every visit to a new part of the country is introduced by highlighting the parts you are about to visit on a video map, and the videos each make a point of showing you each country's distinctive terrain. The *culture* and *history* are introduced, through visits to dozens of important cultural events and historic sites. The traveloguers also make a point of introducing us to interesting craftsmen and businesses in each country, and showing us in detail how several local crafts are made (e.g. Swedish wooden horses, Irish porcelain baskets).

You find out about the day-to-day life of both urban and rural inhabitants, and what they do for sport and entertainment. The traveloguer narrator gives you a verbal picture of the social and political structure of the country while showing you examples of government buildings and state institutions.

You are also treated to a trip down the major waterway of each country, and taken to the home of a typical inhabitant.

Lest all this sound dull and dry, let me hasten to assure you that these are tremendously entertaining videos, put together with a lot of intelligence and wit. I won't soon forget the spectacle of the kilt-clad Scotsman doing his best to hurl a 300-pound telephone pole end over end! (That's a national sporting event, believe it or not!) You get a real "feel" for countries that previously were just names on a map.

The videos come in impressive, durable gold-stamped cases that will look lovely on your shelf. And on top of all this, you get a free companion reference guide with each videotape purchased directly from Quantum Communications. It's a gold-imprinted pocket-sized booklet with a map locating the places visited on the video, a representative recipe of the country, a brief history of the country, cultural pointers for visitors, and a recommended reading list for further study of that country.

I can heartily recommend 16 out of the 19 Traveloguer videos. The remaining three require more serious consideration, for the following reasons. *Eternal Greece* starts with a squirrelly sequence featuring a girl posing as Gaia, the earth goddess, and presents paganism throughout in rather too glowing terms to make Christians comfortable. (This is not at all true of the other videos in the series, by the way—they mention each country's Christian heritage in very positive terms.) The *Americans in Paris* video also has a brief nightclub sequence (the only one in all 17 videos), and if you know anything about Paris nightclubs, this is not something you want the children watching. ¡Si Spain! also has a brief shot of a portrait of the nude wife of a Spanish nobleman. Said portrait created a scandal at the time it was painted, and it doesn't really belong on a family video. I'm telling you about this only so you are forewarned. I don't want you getting the impression that the rest of the videos suffer from these problems. Even in the case of the Paris and Spain videos, these are only lapses in what are otherwise fine videos. In general, the traveloguers have done a commendable example of showing us what is worth showing and depicting a society honestly, without dragging us through its seamy side or pushing any propaganda.These are videos you can watch again and again, learning more and enjoying them more each time.

Tapes available: *Song of Ireland*, *The Romance of Vienna*, *Austrian Odyssey*, *¡Si Spain!*, *A Russian Journey*, *Treasures of Italy*, *Bonny Scotland*, *Byways of Britain*, *Bonjour France*, *The Spirit of Sweden*, *Discovering Denmark*, *The Glory of England*, *Romantic Germany*, *This is Switzerland*, *The Wonders of Norway*, *Americans in Paris*, *Eternal Greece*, *The Charm of Holland*, and *Portugal and the Azores*. The Germany video has been recently revised, by the way, and is even better than the original. Great footage of those kids taking down the Berlin Wall!

NEW**
Rand McNally
World Atlas of Nations, $34.95. Shipping extra. Grades 4–adult.

One of the very best ways to study geography and world cultures is to focus on a country-of-the-week or month. Rand McNally's *World Atlas of Nations* presents 216 countries in alphabetical order, from Afghanistan to Zimbabwe. Each country has a map locating it in relation to its neighbors . . . a fact box or two giving key facts and figures . . . a more detailed map of the country itself showing cities, mountains, lakes, and rivers . . . a concise country profile . . . and (usually) a photo or two showing interesting sights.

NEW**
Send the Light (a ministry of Operation Mobilization)
Operation World, $12 for complete set. Book alone, $8.95. Prayer cards alone, $2. World map alone, $4.95. All prices postpaid.

Operation World began in 1963 as a sheaf of facts, country by country, for use during a week of prayer for the world. Since then, author Patrick Johnstone fell prey to the same syndrome as your humble *Big Book* writer—he kept adding *more* and *more* facts and updating the information while his book got bigger and bigger!

In its present form, *Operation World* provides over 500 pages of densely packed information on every country in the world from a Christian and missionary point of view, plus lots and lots of statistics, historical background information, ethnic information, and prayer needs. This is information you can't find in your *World Book of Facts* or encyclopedia: stuff like, "What is the ratio of missionaries to the number of people in that country?" "How many languages are spoken in the country, and into how many of them is the Bible translated?" "How are Christians treated in that country?" and "What is the history of Christian missionary activity in that country?" Along with this are geographical, social, population, and other facts. The reader is given specific prayer requests arising from the recent history of each country, plus names and addresses of mission groups operating in that countryand a section on "special ministries" such as medical missions and student ministries.

I didn't find it easy to follow the suggested prayer calendar format (which assigns you a country or ministry to pray for each day of the year), mainly because it takes more than one day to digest all the information about a country or mission! A more promising format for home school use might be to concentrate on one country per week, or even a country of the month. For behind-the-scenes information on that country from a Christian perspective, *Operation World* is unsurpassed.

A complete *Operation World* kit includes not just the book, but also a set of 70 "World Prayer Cards," each with facts and prayer requests about a foreign country, and a world map, for locating your country of the day (or week, or month!). It's a really good deal, and I hope a lot of you take advantage of it!

NEW**
TREND Enterprises, Inc.
Famous Places Fun-To-Know Flash Cards, *States and Capitals* Fun-To-Know Flash Cards, $3.99 each. Add $2 shipping. Minimum order $10. Ages 8–14.

Visit 26 exciting landmarks from around the world with *Famous Places* Fun-to-Know Flash Cards. Each landmark is illustrated in color on the front, while on the back it's located on a mini-world map and its history is described. A "Think About It!" section provides fun facts about the landmark and asks "thinking" questions about it, e.g., why did the Eiffel Tower take less time to construct than St. Peter's Basilica or the Great Pyramid when it's twice as tall as each of them? The illustrations aren't all that detailed, but then, look at the price!

TREND has also packed an awful lot of information on the *States and Capitals* Fun-to-Know Flash Cards, while keeping all that information accessible. On the front of each card: state outline, location on a U.S. map, capital location, year of statehood. On the back: the state's capital, nickname, date and number of statehood, flower, bird, industries, attractions, fun facts about the state, and a couple of quiz questions, plus a mini regional map with the state highlighted. Fifty cards in all (if New York State ever gets smart and secedes from New York City, that'll be 51).

Worldwide Slides

Most View-Master packets, $4.25 apiece. Battery-operated projector, $19.95. 3-D Viewer, $4.95. Add 10% shipping.

Do you remember that Christmas you got your first View-Master? Sure you do. Wasn't it fun to click the switch, advance the reel, and see the beautiful color display?

Most of us ended up with packs of cartoon reels as children. But View-Master also developed hundreds of packets of travel reels to go with their viewers. These are now available from Worldwide Slides.

The typical three-reel package includes 21 3-D images, all lovely pictures of famous or important sights. Some packages available: Scenic U.S.A., Alaska, Eskimos of Alaska, Alabama, Grand Canyon , Tour of Canada, Maritime Provinces, Library of Congress, Paris, France, Castles in Europe, Puerto Rico, Luxembourg, Athens, Norway , Disneyland. This is just the tip of the iceberg, as you can find slides or reels for just about every state and every country.

With a View-Master projector, the whole family can travel from your living room. Or get the inexpensive standard viewers, point at a light source, and travel!

GEOGRAPHY GAMES

Aristoplay, Ltd.
Where in the World?, $35. Add $6 shipping.

You can really learn some rote geography—what is where and what goes on there—with this colorful set of four games in one. Starting with the simple *Crazy Countries* card game, played like Crazy Eights, you progress to the *Statesman, Diplomat,* and *Ambassador* board games.

First, *Crazy Countries*. As in Crazy Eights, you try to follow suit (region, in this case) or put down a card with the same number. In level 2, you follow suit by putting down a country with the same religion, literacy rate, population level, or whatever. It's doubtful that kids will really bother to stop and memorize much about countries at this level, but they are getting familiar with the idea of different countries, each with its own characteristics.

In level 3, the *Statesman* game, you learn the location and relative sizes of countries. Select the color-coded cards for a particular region and pass them out. Then pull out the Region Board for that region. Each country on the board is colored differently than its neighbors and numbered according to size—largest with the lowest number, smallest with the highest number. Now, draw a card and read the name to the player on your left. He must locate the country by either locating its size number on the Region Board or spinning the Spinner and giving the right answer for the category selected. Each correct answer wins you a country. Add up the country numbers at the end. Highest score wins. Since the smaller the country the higher its number, you have much incentive to learn the location of the hard-to-remember little countries.

Diplomat is played the same way, except that you have to provide the answer to a preselected category.

The *Ambassador* game takes this to a new level of challenge by making you guess the name of the country from clues, instead of answering questions about a known country. At the Junior level, clues are taken from categories on the cards themselves. At the Senior level, players are supposed to invent their own clues. A clue for U.S.A., for instance, might be "Blue jeans and cowboys."

The categories provided are useful, but somewhat sterile. It would be great if Aristoplay could give us bigger cards with categories like culture, racial composition, art, musical instruments and music styles, governmental form (totalitarian, democracy, republic, canton republic . . .), major lifestyles (urban, rural, jungle . . .). I'd gladly trade some of these for Literacy Rate and Imports and Exports.

You get a lot for your money: six durable, colorful Region Boards; 174 playing-card quality Country Cards, each listing capital, population, monetary unit, literacy rate, major languages, major religions, major export, major import, and major seacoasts; five Wild Cards; a Category Spinner; 120 playing pieces in six different colors (for placing on countries you identified); game instructions; neat, durable box.

NEW**
Crane's Select Educational Materials
U.S. Geography Game, $9.95. Add $2 shipping. Grades 3–adult.

If you'd like your family to learn a *lot* about U.S. geography and you'd like to only spend a *little* money, the *U.S. Geography Game* is a great resource. Packed in an attractively illustrated box you get five color-coded sets of cards (200 question cards total), five U.S. maps color-coded to the cards, and a set of instructions and answers. The blue State Question cards, for example, go with a map on blue paper showing state political boundaries, with the states numbered in random order. In all there are 50 blue States cards, 50 yellow State Capitals cards, 40 green Geographical Features cards, 30 ivory Large U.S. Cities cards, and 30 pink U.S. Historical Sites cards.

Each card has the same format: three regular questions and a multiple-choice question. If you can figure out the answer from question 1, you get five points. If you figure it out after being asked both question 1 and question 2, you get four points. If you need all three questions to get the answer, you get three points. Finally, after all this, if you pick the right one of the three multiple-choice possibilities, you get one point. The answer key on the back of the directions gives the answer. The map gives the location. The card's number corresponds to the correct location on the map. To get the answer right, you have to both answer the question and point to the proper location on the map.

Here's a sample question set from the Historical Sites deck:

(1) It is the site of the first permanent English settlement in America. (5 points)
(2) Williamsburg is to the northwest. (4 points)
(3) It is located on the James River. (3 points)
     Three Choices: (1 point)
a. Plymouth b. Jamestown c. Charleston

Notice how the less you know in this game, the more you learn. By the time the geography novice figures out the answer is Jamestown, he has learned that Jamestown was the first permanent English settlement in America, it's to the southeast of Williamsburg, and it's located on the James River. Also notice the breadth of this game, and how it seamlessly integrates history and geography.

You can play *U.S. Geography Game* many ways. The way I like best (not included in the directions) is to pick one category of cards. Take out the map of that color. Shuffle the cards. Players take turns answering the questions, as in a spelling bee. Mom or Dad holds the Answer Key and exudes curiosity and excitement. Kids try to beat *their own* previous best scores for that deck. This works a whole lot better than the anxiety of competing with siblings or parents, and the intimidating task of facing all 200 question cards at once.

NEW**
Educational Insights
Worldwide Pen Pals, $19.95. Minimum order $25. Shipping extra. Ages 9 to adult.

Worldwide Pen Pals is a board game that drills kids on the locations of 60 countries. Players travel around the board by spinning a spinner and locating the country on which the spinner stops on the small world political map on the gameboard. Countries are numbered, so a referee looks at the Answer Key to see if you picked the right number. Then you can move the number of spaces indicated by the spinner.

If you land on a Worldwide Postcards space, someone reads the top postcard to you. Typical postcard:

Dear Pen Pal,
Ni Hao! My country is the most populated in the world and we're doing a lot to protect our giant pandas. Name my country!
Zei Gian,
Bao

If you can figure out that Bao lives in China, move two spaces ahead.

Some spaces on the board have special directions, e.g., "MAIL STRIKE! Move back one space."

The pen-pal theme is cute, and so is the idea of giving kids some extra info about the countries through "postcards." It's a pity that so many world countries are left out, due to the board design. The spinner is built into the board, and since it's only a single-fold board, that didn't leave much space for the world map. Thus most of Eastern Europe, half of Africa, most countries to the east of India, and all the less well-known countries of South America are left out. Even the countries that are included are so tiny it's not easy to pick some of them out.

If I were redesigning this game, I'd use a duofold board (thus adding an extra 12" of width to the unfolded board), double the size of the world map, and increase the size of the spinner circle to accommodate *all* the countries (this could also be done through a two-tier arrangement). The spinner idea is cute, keeps the game moving along—and it *could* be taken all the way to cover the whole world.

Educational Insights
Name That State, $19.95. Minimum order $25. Shipping extra. Grades 3–adult.

Name That State is a board game correlated with a U.S. map. Name the state that corresponds to the number you spin before you can move your marker further on the board. Two to four players. It's painless geography drill, slightly overpriced.

NEW★★
Educational Insights
Windows of Learning, U.S. Geography or World Geography, $6.95 each. Minimum order $25. Shipping extra. Ages 7–adult.

"Build your knowledge of geography with fun, self-checking quiz wheels!" Here's how it works. Slip one of the compact 7" question-and-answer disks into

the circular case. A question will appear in the cutout window at the top. Look in the window on the other side for the answer. Then rotate the disk for the next question! Keep track of how you're doing with the handy scorekeeper. Practice by yourself or with a friend. Each set contains scorekeeper, map case, and five two-sided disks with 10 questions on each side, for 100 questions in all.

The geography sets ask questions about country or state locations and capitals, and other facts usually drilled in geography class. Each circular map case has a full-color political map on the front: a world map for the World Geography *Windows of Learning*, a U.S. map for the U.S. Geography version. A nice update of the old-fashioned geography drill disks we used to play with when we were children.

NEW★★
Harlan Enterprises
Games, $3.50 each. Grades 3–8.

Your basic match-the-states-to-their-capitals game. *State Capital Fun* is actually *two* games. The first matches states with beginning letters A–M to their capitals; the latter covers states with beginning letters N–W. Each game can be played as a memory game (turn over two cards and if they match you keep them and take another turn) or as a pick-from-the-stack style game. For more detailed description, see the Math Drill chapter.

NEW★★
Know It All
Know It All, $29.95 plus $3 shipping. Ages 6–adult.

Know It All is a U.S. geography and history board game designed to teach players the states, capitals, state slogans, general U.S. geography, and U.S. history in a fun, systematic way. Drive your car around a colorful playing board with a U.S. map in the middle. Along the way you may help a fellow motorist, get caught in a speed trap, take your car in for repairs, or even get elected Governor!

As in all geography games, you need to learn the answers before you can really play the game. The instruction manual provides lots of help with this. The State Fact and Clue Sheets include helpful hints like COW and CAN (California-Oregon-Washington, going north, California-Arizona-New Mexico going east), clues for remembering state capitals like "Nebraska is the 'Linc' between east and west," plus state nicknames and reasons for the nicknames. For learning general geographic facts (landform descriptions and major geographic features of the U.S.), author Beth Kimmich suggests students research the answers to three Geography Quiz cards a day until they have studied them all (this takes about a month).

After learning about the states and some basic geography, you can move up to the U.S. History questions. Here you will learn U.S. history—including black and Indian history—in manageable sections from before the white man came through the Reagan administration. Since the U.S. History questions are divided up by time period, a similar approach can be used for mastering these. Going through these cards is a wonderful way to spark mini unit studies through the entire field of U.S. history and geography, which you can then drill by playing the game itself.

Know It All is designed so the whole family can play together, each at his own level. Each person can be playing a different game. Since you move around the board by answering questions correctly, there is no need for each person to answer questions from the same card deck. Thus, Dad could be using the entire U.S. History Quiz deck, while Sammy is only tangling with the first 27 cards of that deck, and Suzy is working on Name and Find the State.

Know it All includes:

- Colorful duofold game board with road on the outside and U.S. map with each state outlined, capitals shown as stars, and colored by region in the middle.

- Six sports car playing pieces of different colors.

- One die.

- 72 clear plastic chips, 12 of each color.

- 50 state quiz cards.

- 72 U.S. geography quiz cards.

- 287 U.S. history quiz cards.

- Instruction manual with answer keys.

What we need now, of course, is a *European Know It All, South American Know It All, Arab World Know It All, African Know It All,* and *Asian Know It All.* (Australia and New Zealand should count as part of Europe for historical reasons, no matter how you Aussies and Kiwis might jibe at this!) While we're at it, how about a *Bible Lands Know It All*? This would give lucky *Know It All*-ers more in-depth understanding of world affairs past and present than most (maybe *all*) Presidential candidates!

Know It All, despite its fun appearance, is a serious teaching tool that covers more history and geography than many elementary textbook curricula. It presents and drills the facts in a memorable way. I bet many families end up using *Know It All* as the centerpiece of their social studies program.

NEW★★
Timberdoodle
Take-Off!, $26.95. Shipping extra. Ages 6 to adult (they say); ages 8 to adult (I say).

Take-Off! from Resource Games, Inc. (sold by Timberdoodle at discount) is more absorbing and educational than many other geography games I've seen. For one thing, it's a real game, not just flash cards with a game board. Here's how it works:

(1) Uncork the navy blue tube and pull out the contents. These turn out to be a full-color, laminated 56 x 24" map, two decks of capital city/flag cards, two weird-looking eight-sided dice, and a rules sheet with a pronunciation guide for all those "furrin" places.

(2) Unroll the 56 x 24" map. Notice it is about as long as your ten-year-old. You're going to have to clear either the table or the floor to play this game!

(3) Scrap the crummy little plastic bag you ripped apart to get the playing pieces. Replace it with a ziplock bag.

(4) Pick a color . . . any color. You have six fleets of jets to choose from: red, orange, blue, green brown, and yellow. (Incidentally, when will games manufacturers realize that red and orange look very much alike in dim indoor lighting?)

(5) Pick a number from one to four. That's how many jets you will be using per player. (Yeah, the game directions say you have to use at least two jets, but no lightning bolts will zap you if you use only one jet when playing with your four-year-old.)

(6) Roll the dice. If a color comes up, move one of your jets from its present location along a line of that color to the next location. (Some people let you go backwards, if that's the only way you can follow a line of that color. Some prefer to just skip a turn.) If a jet symbol comes up, move along any color route to another city. If a TakeOff! facet comes up, pick a TakeOff! card.

(7) What's this? The TakeOff! card has a city name on it and a flag. But you haven't the faintest idea where "Ouagadougou" is. Here's where the intellectual stimulation comes in. Around the edges of the map are flags of the countries. Flags of North America are together, as are flags of Central America, South America, Africa, etc. It is merely child's play to match the flag on the card to the right flag on the map. Literally child's play, since this is exactly the sort of matching activity they do in preschool. The country's name is under the flag. So now you know Ougadougou is in—where else?—

Burkina Faso. And, since the flag was with the other Africa flags, Burkina Faso is in Africa. A bit of staring at the countries and capitals on the Africa portion of the map, and voila! You can now move your jet to Burkina Faso.

(8) But there's already a jet in Ougadougou. Too bad for him. He has to go back to start.

(9) All jets start in Honolulu. You win by getting your jets around the world and back to Honolulu.

(10) To make your life slightly less complicated, the board is divided into East and West. A line smack down the middle of Africa separates the two. The 169 capitals cards are also divided into two color-coded decks, so you only have 85 (at most) possible flags to check out before you find Burkina Faso.

(11) You will notice there is no well-meant teacherly rubbish about "Tell me how many people live in Burkina Faso and what its chief exports are before you can fly to the next city." Play is fast-paced, and the educational value comes directly through playing the game. The game gives its players a need to know where all these places are and satisfies the need, all at once.

Timberdoodle tells us, "Students who played this game only 14 times improved their test scores on the average of 340 percent!"

New: *Take-Off North America* includes Canada and Central America. Less to learn than the full *Take-Off!* game. Ask Timberdoodle for details.

CHAPTER THIRTY SIX

HISTORY

History happens. Yes, it do. It can even happen to *you* . . .

The most painless way to teach history to young children is through stories. Our kids love to hear their birth stories, and stories about the funny things Mom, Dad, Grandma, and Grandpa did when we were younger. Such simple stories give kids a sense of *past, present,* and *future,* and show them where they fit into the general scheme of things. You can then follow this up with simple historical tales, either from your own memory or from the library. Once a child learns to read well, the library is full of historical biographies he will enjoy (the old Bobbs-Merrill *Lives of Famous Americans* series is particularly good—look for it at your library). Good historical fiction serves much the same purpose in giving kids a taste of life in different time periods. Then wrap it all together with a time line, and your preteens will know as much about history as you can decently expect!

HISTORY CURRICULUM

In deference to the opinions of those of you who don't believe kids can learn history without units, tests, and suchlike, here are some of the most popular history programs for elementary-age children. I also threw in some bulletin boards and flash cards, just to make things really educational—even a book of poems, for those of you who aren't all *that* serious!

NEW**
A Beka Book Publications
My America (grade 1), $6.75. *Our America* (grade 2), $7.40. *Our American Heritage* (grade 3), $8.80. *The History of Our United States* (grade 4), $10.15. *Old World History and Geography* (grade 5), $11.30. *New World History and Geography* (grade 6), $12.05. Teacher's editions available for all books, include complete text of student book. Grades 1–12.

As is generally true with history textbooks, those in this strongly evangelical Protestant series for the first three grades are skippable. Things pick up in grade 4, with the new *History of Our United States* textbook, and go on swimmingly to cover Old World history and geography and New World history and geography. These volumes have a semi-encyclopedic format, with tantalizing bits of information tucked away under pictures and in sidebars.

The colorful A Beka texts include American customs, songs, and other vital parts of our cultural heritage, as well as general history. The entire curriculum includes an emphasis on geography mastery (you get 22 pages of map skills and a mini atlas in the *Old World History and Geography in Christian Perspective* book for fifth graders, for instance).

The new *History of Our United States* has an emphasis on sung and unsung American heroes, including inventors, evangelists, missionaries, and entrepreneurs (*much* more interesting than just memorizing dates!). It is a fresh, readable, beautifully illustrated and laid-out book, with good coverage of all the important historic events. Some of the historic interpretations are open to question (e.g., that the Aztecs were merely innocent victims of the greedy Spaniards, that Lincoln was justified in committing the Union to war and Sherman was justified in destroying Georgia, and that John D. Rockefeller Sr. greatly benefited American civilization). Others are a little hard to understand, such as the consistently pro-public school tone taken by this textbook written for Christian schools and home schools! Otherwise, the book is, as expected, conservative and pro-free market. I'm probably going to use it myself, taking care to give "the other side of the story" where necessary (did you know Cortez preached to the Aztecs that they should give up human sacrifice, and that the other Indian tribes gladly cooperated with him to rid themselves of the hated Aztecs?). It's worth going to a little trouble of this nature, because *History of Our United States* really is about the easiest-to-use, most thorough, elementary-school history text I've seen.

NEW**
Alpha Omega Publications
LIFEPACS, $2.25–$2.45 each, 10 LIFEPACS per grade. Set of 10 LIFEPACS, $19.95–$21.95. Answer keys, teacher handbooks available. Shipping extra. Grades 1–12.

Alpha Omega's social studies courses are based on worktexts. Kids read the text inside the workbook, answer the questions, write any essay answers, and do any required activities. Everything is right there in one booklet (called a LIFEPAC), with 10 booklets in all per course. The last LIFEPAC is always a course review.

With an answer key, these courses are very easy to use at home. With the teacher's handbooks, you get more teaching and enrichment ideas added in.

The curriculum is spiral. This means you study the same topic again and again and again in succeeding grades, with greater depth each time.

Elementary-grades social studies courses follow the public school formula of "widening circles" from the student to his family, his community, his nation, and the world. History and geography are also included, as is a certain amount of "cultural studies," e.g., what life is like in Japan or on a Kansas farm. The whole elementary-grades program is integrated with language arts instruction, meaning that you get exercises on vocabulary, spelling, and so on in your social studies workbooks.

Here's what you get. In grade 1: I Am a Special Person, Communicating with Sound, I Have Feelings, I Live in a Family, You Belong to God's Family, Places People Live (farm, city, seaside), Community Helpers (fireman, policeman, two doctors, minister, teacher, librarian), I Love My Country (three-week overview of early American history, the flag, songs, and holidays), and I Live in the World (with two subunits on Friends in Japan and Friends in Mexico).

In grade 2: Families and Neighbors, more Community Helpers (including the church community), Neighborhood Stores (intro to free-market business), Farms and Cities (of yesterday and today), A World of Neighbors, A Japanese Family, How We Travel (your basic unit on transportation, including Bible-times transportation), Messages from Neat and Far (communication), and Caring for Our Neighbors (intro to green thinking with Carl the Cleanup Raccoon and Paul the Pollution Pig).

Grade 3 is a whole year spent on American cultural anthropology. In other words, it's a simplified field trip around the country. Units are: A Fishing Community, A Farming Community (Kansas), A Fruit-Growing Community (Washington), Oregon: Land of Forests, A Golden Land (California), Cattle Raising in Texas, Coal Mining and Pennsylvania, Manufacturing Community (Michigan), and Florida: Gateway to Space.

Grade 4 is the world tour. Units are: The Planet Earth (world geography, historic explorations, and modern space and underseas exploration), Living in Island Countries (Japan and Hawaii), Living in Mountain Countries (Peru and Switzerland), The Polar Regions, Tropical Jungles (Amazon and Congo), Grassland Regions (Kenya, Argentina, U.S.A.), Desert Lands (including A Nomad Family of the Sahara), Seaport Cities (San Francisco, Hong Kong, and Sydney), and The United States: Your State (basic U.S. history, geography, and government, plus activities for doing your own state report). Each unit on a country or area includes information on its history, geography, culture, and industries, from a Christian perspective. For example, the unit on Hawaii tells how the missionaries came to Hawaii and what effect they had (Hawaii was once a Christian country!). The unit on the United States and Your State also includes really good activities to help children generate their own state reports.

Grade 5 covers U.S. history in five units, starting with the explorers and the colonies, then turns to a unit each on transportation and communication in U.S. history, geographic regions of the U.S., "Our Southern Neighbors" (Mexico, Central America, and Caribbean), and Canada. The units on U.S. history include quite a bit of information on life during each time period, national symbols and holidays, inventions and industries, and forms of government in each time period. It also is better balanced in its presentation of the Civil War than most texts I have seen on this subject, giving four major differences between the North and the South that led to the war, rather than the standard—and mistaken—view that slavery was the sole issue. The LIFEPACS on Mexico and Canada are also excellent, pithy presentations of the history, geography, and culture of our southern and northern neighbors.

Grade 6 tackles world history. First there's a very good unit on world geography, then we move from the Cradle of Civilization (excellent background for your Bible studies) to The Civilizations of Greece and Rome, Life in the Middle Ages, and one unit each on Western Europe (from the Renaissance on) and Eastern Europe (from Byzantium to the Space Age). Unaccountably, this sequence is interrupted by two units on South American countries and one on Africa (tucked in right before we move to Europe). Each history unit includes information about daily life in that time period, plus its social institutions, and economics. The units on geographic regions (South America and Africa) include history, geography, types of people who live in each country, industries, major cities, and holidays.

My feeling about this program is that, as usual, the first three grades can easily be skipped. Grade 1 *ought* to be skipped, as should the community-helpers, transportation, and Carl-the-Cleanup-Raccoon units in grade 2. (Keep in mind that grade 2 also comes with *ten* separate answer keys, not including the test answer key—a definite minus.) Grade 3 is fun but inessential. Grade 4 is likewise fun, but only the first and ninth LIFEPACS are really essential. Between them these contain a basic introduction to world geography and

U.S. history, geography, and government, plus a step-by-step plan for producing a report on your state—which is legally required of homeschoolers in many states. Grades 5 and 6 cover a lot of important material. I would straighten out the sequence of unit studies in grade 6 by putting South America and Africa *after* the unbroken sequence of European history.

All Alpha Omega levels are very easy to use, as long as you keep up with your grading of workbook exercises and writing assignments. The tests are right in the workbooks, as are pre-tests and teacher checkpoints.

NEW**
Bellerophon Books
Most coloring books, $3–$9 each. Ages 8 and up.

"Art Books for Children?" Yes, but with a historical emphasis. These coloring books are full of line-drawing reproductions of art from the past, usually accompanied by text describing the period. Examples: *A Coloring Book of Ancient Egypt. A Coloring Book of Rome. Alexander the Great. California Missions. Cowboys. Pirates. Viking Ships. A Coloring Book of the New Testament* (from St. Albans' Psalter and other early medieval manuscripts). *A Coloring Book of the Old Testament* (from 13th and 14th century manuscripts). *A Coloring Book of the Middle Ages. Infamous Women. Civil War Flags to Color. A Shakespeare Coloring Book. A Coloring Book of American Indians.* Tons more, from ancient Ireland to Amelia Earhart.

The artwork in these books is irregular, and some of it needs more clothes. The catalog itself, for example, features an armless, bare-breasted Indian goddess right on the order form. Magic Markers unfortunately show right through the other side of the paper, making it difficult to solve the clothes problem in the normal way!

These are not coloring books for *young* children, as the pictures are too detailed for that. Colored pencils work better than crayons on these books—thinline markers would work even better, if they didn't show through—so that should give you an idea of the proper age level.

Bellerophon also has cut-out kits (e.g., *Magnificent Helmets* with silver and gold helmets made in ancient styles, *Great Trains* with four cut-out locomotives) and paper dolls (e.g., *Henry VIII and His Wives Paper Dolls to Color, Paper Soldiers of the Middle Ages*). These are not at all expensive, and come with historical text, so they are educational as well.

NEW★★
Bob Jones University Press
Teacher's edition, each grade, $28.50 (include complete text of student book). Student text, each grade, from $9.95–$17.95. Tests and additional activity sheets available for some grades. Shipping extra. Grades 1–12.

History, geography, and cultural studies combined, from an conservative evangelical Protestant point of view. The Bob Jones Heritage Studies series follows the public-school approach of "widening circles." In grade 1, the focus is on "God's Plan for the Family," plus an introduction to American patriotism, symbols, and holidays. Grade 2 broadens outward into "Life in a Community." Like public-school texts for this age group, it introduces transportation, communication, and industry. Grade 3 takes a more traditional approach, studying American Indian culture and early European exploration and settlement, up to the signing of the Constitution. Grade 4 carries on from there, right up to the present day. In grade 5, the emphasis turns from history to the geography and cultures of nations in the Western Hemisphere. Grade 6 does the same for the Eastern Hemisphere. Economics and politics are handled more formally in the latter two volumes.

NEW★★
Bob Jones University Press
American History in Verse, $7.15. Shipping extra. Grades 5–adult.

It's just what the name says: poems about every major incident and personage in American history by a hodgepodge of bards, many contemporaries of the persons or events. You get some queer gems here, as well as many poems rollicking, tender, tragic, and even ludicrous. Find out what the Man in the Street used to think about American history, back when he used to know enough to think something about it.

NEW★★
Christian Liberty Press
History Book B, *A Child's Story of America,* History Book E, $4.95 each. Add 10% shipping ($1.50 minimum).

America *über alles* in these patriotic history books. *Christian Liberty History Book B* is a 96-page two-color workbook designed for use at the first or second grade level. In huge print and easy language, it introduces American history from Pilgrim days through the Industrial Revolution, plus a smidgin about the three branches of government and a speck of geography (continents and oceans). The book is pro-industrial capitalism and favors traditional American freedoms.

A Child's Story of America, for third and fourth graders, reviews the history of America from Columbus to the 1990s. Each chapter ends with review questions. The book's tone makes it evident that it is adapted from an older work, with more recent history added later, but no information about the original edition is given. Like American history books of a bygone era, it tells kids right from wrong, according to the lights of that period. America is great and wonderful, and there are good guys and bad guys. George Washington is brave and gallant; the Indians are cruel fighters; Daniel Boone is an admirable woodsman. You find out some surprising facts of colonial life and some stories you may not have heard, such as the sad fate of the Acadians, French-Canadian settlers in what is now Nova Scotia, who were deported by the British on just a few hours' notice. You also find out about the explorers, different ways of life in each colony, pre-revolutionary life, Revolutionary War adventures and heroism, the founding of the republic, American inventiveness (and the fate of several inventors), and our subsequent wars, winding up with the Cold War.

Christian Liberty History Book E, for fourth and fifth grades, takes a biographical approach. You follow the life of one famous man and what was happening during the time he lived. It covers each of the major characters and events of American history from Columbus to Theodore Roosevelt. A special supplement covers the major events and personalities of the 20th century.

Christian Liberty Press has a number of miscellaneous patriotic biographies (Robert E. Lee, George Washington, Stonewall Jackson, the Mayflower Pilgrims, *Stories of the Pilgrims, Boys and Girls of Colonial Days*). Just released: a biography of J. E. B. Stuart, and a new third-grade reader entitled *History Stories for Children*. All are quaint, inexpensive, and old-timey in flavor, strongly preaching the importance of hard work, selflessness, courage, and godliness.

NEW**
Christian Light Publications
God's World—His Story, $16.80 plus $2.50 shipping. Grades 6–8.

The Creation and Flood. Sumeria. Egypt. Greece. Rome. Israel and Judah. The Church. Middle Ages. The Reformation. The Inquisition. Age of Exploration. Age of Colonialism. Age of Missions. Russia. China. India. World Wars. Cold War. This one book, *God's World—His Story*, covers the entire history of the Western world. Written from a staunchly Mennonite viewpoint, it makes very interesting reading, as the trials and tribulations of that group are thrown into relief against the background of the great movements of the time.

History is not only presented, but analyzed from a conservative Mennonite perspective—including the mistakes of Mennonites and Anabaptists of the past. Topics are covered in reasonable depth, with many intriguing sidelights on how people lived in each age. Each chapter ends with review questions and Bible exercises, in which you either read about the history of the time period or study passages and apply them to the situations people faced at that time. Good, readable writing, presented with both sobriety and feeling. Lots of character-building emphasis on the frequent necessity of suffering for Christ in this world. No uncritical American patriotism, as in many other Christian textbooks, nor yet any uncritical America-bashing, as in many secular texts.

With all this in mind, I believe *God's World—His Story* provides a good overview of Western world history for this age group while it adds a wholesome balance to the home schooler's history bookshelf, even for those of us who aren't Mennonites. Warning: lots of religious denominations persecuted the Mennonites (e.g., Lutherans, Anglicans, Catholics . . .), so if you're a member of one of these groups and it bothers you to have the failings of your forebears pointed out, don't say I didn't warn you!

NEW**
Greenleaf Press
Famous Men of Greece, Famous Men of Rome, Famous Men of the Middle Ages, $15.95 each. Study guides, $7.95 each. *Greenleaf Guide to Ancient Egypt*, $7.95. Ancient Egypt Study Package (includes *Greenleaf Guide*), $36.95. Add $1 shipping per book ($2 minimum). Grades 3 and up (if you read to them, or they are good readers). Public-school reading level: grade 6 and up.

The *Famous Men* series is an attempt "to spread world history over the elementary school years and proceed at a leisurely pace that would allow the child to live with the material for a period of months." The publishers recommend that you begin the study of each book by having the child make a salt relief map—mountains, rivers, and valleys—of the areas covered in the book. Then you can plunge into the biographies, printed in more-or-less chronological order.

The spiral-bound *Famous Men of Greece* and *Famous Men of Rome* are reprints of two works originally published in 1904. Something called "The Committee of Ten" had recommended "that the study of Greek, Roman, and modern European history in the form of biography should precede the study of detailed American history in our elementary schools," and another group called "The Committee of Fifteen" had ardently seconded the motion. Written in response to this urgent educational cry, *Famous Men of Greece* and *Famous Men of Rome* present Greek and Roman mythology along with short biographies of famous men from each area. Mythology and biography are written in the exact same style: "Pericles did this" and "Zeus did that." (The study guides give suggestions on how to point out the difference between history and mythology!)

Those who know enough about Greek and Roman history to notice will observe that statism is exalted in these books. Lycurgus, for example, who persuaded the Spartan citizens to divide their property and slaves equally, kill their feeble and deformed babies, and live on only the simplest food served in a communal dining hall, is called "one of the wisest and best men that ever lived in Greece." Such were the views common in the early 1900s, proving that yesterday isn't always wiser than today. Questions in the study guides highlight some of these problems in Greek and Roman culture and encourage readers to judge ancient customs by Biblical attitudes.

Aside from such *faux pas*, the books are fairly easy and entertaining reading. Example:

Besides great philosophers, Athens had some famous painters. Two of the most celebrated were Zeux'is and Par-rha'si-us, who lived about 400 B.C.. They were rivals. Once they gave an exhibition of their paintings. Zeuxis exhibited a bunch of grapes which had such a natural look that the birds came and pecked at them. The people exclaimed, "Astonishing! What can be finer than Zeuxis' grapes?"

Zeuxis proudly turned to his rival's picture. A purple curtain hung before it. "Draw aside your curtain, Parrhasius," he said, "and let us look at your picture."

The artist smiled, but did not move. Someone else stepped toward the curtain to draw it aside, and it was then discovered that the curtain was part of the painting.

"I yield," said Zeuxis. "It is easy to see who is the better artist. I have deceived birds. Parrhasius has deceived an artist."

It is said that Zeuxis died of laughing at a funny picture that he had painted of an old woman.

As you can see from the vocabulary level of the excerpt above, the young children who are supposed to profit from these books either must be above-average readers, or you must read the books to them.

My opinion of this series changed dramatically when I read the Greenleaf study guides for Greece and Rome. These books are really well-organized and thorough. Each chapter of the *Famous Men* books is covered separately, with vocabulary words called out and discussion questions. Background information is provided where necessary. The guide for Greece includes supplementary reading assignments from Homer's *Iliad* and *Odyssey* and selections from Plato. The guide for Rome assigns supplementary readings from *Foxe's Book of Martyrs*, Virgil's *Æneid*, Macaulay's *City*, and more. Geography is covered (via salt-dough maps), and story characters are analyzed in terms of Bible standards of righteousness. Not only that, but Greenleaf Press's catalog lists supplementary books for each time period, so your children can cut out historically-accurate models, see how cities and towns were built, and read the history of each time period both as straight history and historical fiction.

Here's the Greenleaf philosophy:

In general, high school level history material is written in a way that assumes some prior knowledge of the stories. If you already know the basic facts about, say, Charlemagne when you study him in high school,

you have less to memorize about him. You can simply add the additional information to what you already know. (One of the things that makes history classes so boring is that very few students come to them with such a background. Because *everything* is new, *everything* must be memorized.)

The Greenleaf way, then, is to get elementary-age kids familiar with the basic setting and people from each historical time period. Perhaps the best example of how this works is the Ancient Egypt Study Package. The *Greenleaf Guide to Ancient Egypt* stands alone, not having a *Famous Men* book to accompany it. To make up for this, the people at Greenleaf have put together several Usborne books (*Time-Traveler Book of Pharaohs and Pyramids* and *Deserts* from the First Travelers series), a book on King Tut's mummy, David Macaulay's great book *Pyramid* that shows the construction of the pyramids, a history book entitled *Pharaohs of Ancient Egypt* written at a fourth-grade reading level, and an illustrated book on Egyptian boats that second-graders can read by themselves. Using these as the basic texts, the *Greenleaf Guide* pulls it all together with reading assignments, salt dough maps, modeling activities, and discussion questions. It's an absolutely enthralling introduction to this time period for preteens and younger, designed so the whole family can study the same lessons at once.

Though guides are not yet available for these time periods, the Greenleaf catalog includes good selections of activity, history, and story books for Middle Ages and Renaissance and Reformation. *Famous Men of the Middle Ages,* another book in the series, should be out by the time you read this.

NEW★★
Ladybird Books, Inc.
Each book, $3.50. Kings and Queens Wall Chart, $9.50.
Grades 5 and up.

Ladybird used to have a series of three dozen small, hardcover history books covering British and ancient history. The old series is almost completely out of print, except for *Kings and Queens of England Book 1* and *Kings and Queens of England Book 2*. These should stay around for awhile.

The new Ladybird History of Britain series is much more up-to-date, with a lavishly-illustrated visual format like Usborne books. This series includes *The Romans, The Saxons and the Normans, The Middle Ages, The Tudors, The Stuarts,* and *The Georgians.* Lots of fascinating, condensed history.

The *Kings and Queens Wall Chart* is an illustrated genealogy of the kings and queens of England. It's approximately 24 x 16" in size, all of which is needed to cover the complex story of who was related to whom!

Although the Ladybird history books are designed for a fifth-grade and up reading level, you and I know that any seven-year-old who has been taught to read properly with the phonics method can read these books. And enjoy them, too!

Our Christian Heritage
Complete set of 5 books, $23. Books A-C, $4.75 each. Books D and E, $4.95 each. Add 10% shipping (minimum $1).

Workbooks based on the Principle Approach for grades 1 to 6 with a Scriptural approach to the studies of geography, history, and government. History is the biggest component of the three. These workbooks are well liked by Reconstructionists. Christian Liberty Academy uses some of the volumes. Inexpensive.

NEW★★
Teaching Home
Complete six-issue set of 1985 back issues, $12.50, includes free set of 6 plastic magazine holders for your ring binder.

As I've said before, each *Teaching Home* magazine back issue on a given topic is like a minicourse in teaching that topic. August/September 1985 was the issue on teaching history. How about an article on using family storytelling to teach Bible, personal, and national history? Find out about the Principle Approach and the providential view of history. How can old books help your children learn history *painlessly*? Delve into the controversy over how secular texts present history, or find out how to make history relevant to today. Lots more! This back issue is not available separately, but don't let that bother you, since it's really fun to read all those old back issues and see how useful all those articles still are today. Home schoolers are not what you'd call *faddy*. I mean, several issues in '85 carried articles on the Trivium, the classical course of study used in

medieval schools and pre-university training, including a reprint of Dorothy Sayers's timeless essay, "The Lost Tools of Learning." (You may remember Miss Sayers as the author of the Lord Peter Wimsey mystery series, and a friend of J. R. R. Tolkien and C. S. Lewis.)

NEW★★
TREND Enterprises, Inc.
Each bulletin board set, $5.99, includes free Discovery Guide. Requires 4 x 6' bulletin board. Add $2 shipping. Minimum order $10. Grades 3–8.

History instruction via the bulletin board? What will they think of next?

TREND has quite a few history-teaching bulletin board kits. *Early Explorers* starts things off, with a world map showing the explorers' routes and punchouts for Leif Ericsson, Christopher Columbus, Amerigo Vespucci, Vascó de Balboa, Ponce de Leon, John Cabot, Bartholomew Diaz, Vasco da Gama, and Ferdinand Magellan. You may have noticed that WASPs aren't big on this list—even John Cabot was really an Italian (his birth name was Giovanni Caboto). Another thought for my fellow Americans—did you ever consider how lucky we were to have our country named after Amerigo Vespucci's *first* name? Think of the alternative: "Vespucci-land, Vespucci-land, God shed His grace on thee . . ."

On to the *U.S. Presidents* kit. Here you get a pin-up punchout for each president, including his signature, the number of states in the Union during his term, his order in office, and the years he served as president. Each pin-up is 8½" tall. The accompanying discovery guide has info about every president except George Bush, with whom I presume you are sufficiently acquainted. For example, did you know that Gerald Ford was christened Leslie Lynch King, Jr.? No kidding!

Outstanding Black Americans features prominent people from the areas of scientists and inventors, reformers and leaders, drama and music, athletics, education and scholarship, and speaking and writing—39 in all. The discovery guide highlights each famous person's accomplishments.

RELIVING HISTORY

Creation's Child
Stories of the Pilgrims, $4.95. *Boys and Girls of Colonial Days*, $3.95. Shipping extra. Ages 8–12.

Facsimile reprints of old-timey history stories. Original art, paperbound. A point of view increasingly hard to find at the public library. *Stories of the Pilgrims* tells the history of the Pilgrims from the beginning at Scrooby Inn to the death of the Indian chief Massassoit and the adventures of some Pilgrim children with unfriendly Indians. A good read-aloud book for younger children, or for preteens to read on their own. Lots of stories on these 240 pages! *Boys and Girls of Colonial Days* tells stories about children from the times of the Puritans onward to Betsy Ross, Benjamin Franklin, and George Washington.

NEW**
EDC Publishing
First History series, $4.50 each paperbound. Ages 7–9. Time Traveler Series, $6.95 each paperbound. Combined volume *The Traveler's Omnibus* $17.95 hardbound. Ages 8–11. Children's Picture World History series, $6.95 each paperbound or $13.96 each library-bound. Combined volume *The Usborne Book of World History*, $19.95 hardbound. Ages 8–12. Explainers series Living Long Ago books, $3.95 each paperbound or $11.96 each library-bound; ages 7–9.

The most fascinating, child-appealing "history books" I have ever seen. The First History series books each follow one boy's daily life and family through town and country. Emphasis is on everyday life, but because of the superb full-color illustrations you can't help noticing the architecture, furniture, clothing, and artefacts of each time period. The series includes *Pre-*

historic Times (the "caveman" viewpoint is followed), *Roman Times*, and *Castle Times*.

For slightly older children, the Time Traveler series takes a child back in time to see how life really was for the high and lowly in ancient Egypt (the *Pharaohs and Pyramids* book), Rome (*Rome and Romans*), Norseland (*Viking Raiders*), and medieval Europe (*Knights and Castles*).

The Children's Picture World History series does the same for *First Civilizations* (strong evolutionary outlook); *Empires and Barbarians; Warriors and Seafarers; Crusaders, Aztecs, and Samurai; Exploration and Discovery;* and *The Age of Revolutions.* All are full-color throughout, 8½ x 11 inch, in quality cartoon style on glossy paper, with plenty of descriptive text. See how Baron Godfrey's castle defenses were designed, or how the Egyptians turned papyrus into paper! Watch the Vikings build their ship, or the Romans prepare a feast! Kids can't put them down (and neither could I). Slight Magic Marker-ing needed in a few places (Cretan ladies dressed like Playboy models).

The new Living Long Ago books from the Explainers series includes *Food and Eating, Homes and Houses, Clothes and Fashion,* and *Travel and Transport.* Each book chronologically follows its theme through the following sequence: primitive times (mostly speculation), ancient Egypt, Rome, Vikings, medieval period, European, early American, and modern times. The book on transport also takes up to China. You find out how things were made and used (again, with great illustrations). Activities in each book include such things as making your own medieval fish pasties, model coracle, or model teepee. Nice open page layout.

NEW**
EDC Publishing
Cut-Out Models series, $8.95 each. Shipping extra. Ages 9–adult.

If you have a pair of scissors and a glue stick, you can put together wonderful accurate historic models of an Egyptian temple, Viking settlement, Roman villa, Roman fort, medieval town, cathedral, castle, and Old English village. Each Cut-Out Models book includes full-color buildings, people, and a baseboard. Bonus: the baseboards of the village, town, castle, and cathedral can be combined to make one *large* medieval setting! Models are compatible with 00/HO scale, so you can add extra figures and scenery pieces from a model shop, if desired. Great fun for those with sufficient shelf or table space to display the finished products!

LibertyTree

Jean Fritz American Revolution series, 6 paperbacks, $49.95. Childhood of Famous Americans series: Set I (Great Patriots), Set II (Great Innovators), $22.95 each set of 5 paperbacks. Cornerstones of Freedom series, $16.95 each set of 5 paperbacks. Adventures in Early America, $21.95 each set of 7 paperbacks. Great American Indians series, $21.95/7 paperbacks. Liberty Jigsaw puzzles, $7.95 each. *1776* game, $24.95. Shipping extra. Grades 1–8. New: $25 annual LibertyTree membership fee entitles you to an unlimited 10% discount on orders plus a 1-year subscription to *LibertyTree* and free poster of either the Bill of Rights or the Fall of the Berlin Wall.

If you are anxious to raise well-informed, liberty-minded kids, LibertyTree can accommodate you. This foundation, besides books for adults on economics, history, politics, and self-improvement (including home schooling), and books for kids on economics, reading, writing, and 'rithmetic, also carries more than four (count 'em!) different series of history books for kids. Taking them one by one . . . Jean Fritz has won all kinds of awards for her children's biographies of Revolutionary War figures. Kids aged five to 12 will enjoy the down-to-earth incidents and humor in *And Then What Happened, Paul Revere?, Why Don't You Get a Horse, Sam Adams?, Where Was Patrick Henry on the 29th of May?, Can't You Make Them Behave, King George?, What's the Big Idea, Ben Franklin?*, and *Will You Sign Here, John Hancock?* Personally, I think Mrs. Fritz was a bit too hard on John Hancock, and the book on Ben Franklin didn't need an illustration of his little brother drowning while the family sits there looking like stuffed stooges, but the latter was the artist's fault. Moving along, the Childhood of Famous Americans Great Patriots series for children aged seven to 12 covers Benjamin Franklin, Molly Pitcher, Davy Crockett, Crispus Attacks (I thought his last name was spelled Attucks, but perhaps the catalog is right and I'm wrong), and Paul Revere. Great Innovators include, Thomas Edison, Clara Barton, Albert Einstein, Wilbur and Orville Wright, and Henry Ford. I will get worn out if I try to list all the books in all four sets of the Cornerstones of Freedom series for preteens, so let's just say this includes a Documents of Freedom set (five books from *Mayflower Compact* to *The Nineteenth Amendment*), a Defending Freedom set (*Alamo, Boston Tea Party, Old Glory, Lexington and Concord, Liberty Bell*), Freedom and Tyranny (*Ellis Island, Homestead Act, Salem Witch Trials, Trail of Tears, Underground Railroad*), and Frontiers of Freedom (*Gold Rush, Lewis and Clark Expeditions, Oregon Trail, Charles Lindbergh's flights, Mississippi steamboats*). Also for ages 8 to 12, Adven-

tures in Early America includes the Colonial America and Frontier America series of seven volumes each. Great American Indians series includes Chief Joseph, Pocahontas, Black Hawk, Sacajawea, Sequoyah, Sitting Bull, and Squanto. Also games, dioramas, coloring books, and lots more.

NEW**
Mantle Ministries

Tape series, 12 volumes, $16 each, workbooks $4 each. "Little Bear's" Resource Guide, $4. Shipping extra.

Those of you who attend home school conventions have heard of, or even seen, Richard "Little Bear" Wheeler doing his historical reenactments wearing period costumes and carrying period artifacts. So have those of you with camp ministries.

Mr. Wheeler has a particular burden for the revival of true history. Towards this end he has prepared a series of audiocassettes in which he reads and reenacts historical accounts from the 1300s to the 1800s. Each volume of this series has twenty 3–15 minute long historical accounts with Biblical application, narrated by Mr. Wheeler, with music and sound effects. Each volume also has an accompanying reproducible workbook, with spaces for students to fill in answers to the questions, plus selected color illustrations and/or projects. Here they are:

- Volume 1: 1300s–1620. Wycliffe, Tyndale, Columbus to the Pilgrims.

- Volume 2: 1607–1775. Jamestown to Paul Revere's ride.

- Volume 3: 1775–1781. God's providence during the American Revolution.

- Volume 4: 1775–1781. Heroes of the American Revolution.

- Volume 5: 1803–1806. Highlights of the Lewis and Clark Expedition.

- Volume 6: 1806–1861. Davy Crockett, Kit Carson, Oregon Trail, and Westward Movement.

- Volume 7: 1861–1865. The Civil War.

- Volume 8: 1865–1890. Cowboys, Indians, soldiers, and gunfighters of the Old West.

- Volume 9: 1620–1880s. Twenty stories from the book *American History and Home Life*.

- Volume 10: 1700s–1900s. Ten godly presidents and ten valiant women of God.

- Volume 11: The Holiday Series. Twenty of our national holidays from a Biblical perspective.

- Volume 12: Highlights of previous volumes.

Mantle Ministries has republished a number of historic books suitable for teens and adults, and is in the process of producing several videos featuring "Little Bear" in his period roles.

"Little Bear" also has a resource catalog, called "Little Bear's" Resource Guide, for those of you who'd like to have access to his sources of period clothing and personal effects, instruments, and weaponry.

NEW★★
Pleasant Company
Doll and book, $82. Doll with hardcover book, $88. Doll with Keepsake Edition paperback set (6 books), $108. Doll with Keepsake Edition hardcover, $148. Books, $5.95 each paperback, $12.95 each hardcover. Basic accessories, $20. Other accessories, mostly $16–$20 each. Twelve Months of Traditional Pastimes, $16/month. Six-Month Activity Book Subscription, $14/month or $85 one-time payment. Six-Month Craft Kit Subscription, $18/month or $108 one-time payment. Shipping extra on everything except kit subscriptions. For girls ages 7–12.

The best new history resource I have seen is the wonderful line of books, dolls, and historically-accurate accessories and activities from Pleasant Company.

These are role-play dolls for girls ages 7–12. Each has tons of delightful accessories and an entire six-book series introducing her character.

The books are beautiful, entertaining, and also serious tools for history education. Embellished with many color drawings and authentic historical photos and engravings, they include both stories about their subject American Girl but also a "Peek into the Past" section with even more pictures and descriptions of social conditions at the time the story takes place. These vignettes cover subjects of interest to young girls: clothing styles, how people did their laundry, what it was like to be a factory girl or a debutante. The pictures in the text are often of artifacts from the period. Doll-sized copies of many of these artifacts can be purchased from Pleasant Company, adding an entirely new dimension to history study!

Each American Girls book series follows the same format. The first book is *Meet Kirsten* (or Samantha, or Molly). The next book is *Kirsten (Samantha, Molly) Learns a Lesson: A School Story*. In this volume you find out about how children were educated during that particular time period. Next comes *Kirsten's (Samantha's, Molly's) Surprise: A Christmas Story*; *Happy Birthday, Kirsten!* (Samantha, Molly): *A Springtime Story*; *Kirsten (Samantha, Molly) Saves the Day: A Summer Story*; and *Changes for Kirsten* (Samantha, Molly): *A Winter Story*. Following each girl through the year, you discover how people prepared for and survived winter, the major social events in a girl's life back then, and how the world was changing around them. The stories are extremely well-written and realistic without being depressing. A girl can easily relive these time periods through the books, without anyone nagging her to study her history.

Please note that you do not need to buy a doll or any accessories in order to purchase the books. Pleasant Company does give you a "deal" on the doll and a set of books purchased together, though, and if you can possibly afford it, it's a wonderful, once-in-a-lifetime gift any normal girl will cherish. They also sell a doll/one book combination, in which the doll comes dressed in the outfit pictured on the book cover.

The American Girls Collection books are also available at bookstores, as are the Portfolio Activity books. All other American Girls products are available through the Pleasant Company catalog only.

Meet the dolls: Kirsten is a Swedish pioneer girl who comes to America with her family in the mid-1800s. Samantha is a rich nine-year-old Victorian orphan, living with her grandmother in turn-of-the-century New York. Molly is from a more modest, but not poor, background. Her story centers around life in America during the Second World War.

The 18" dolls are absolutely beautiful, as befits their price! They have cuddly cloth bodies and posable vinyl arms, legs, and head. (You can send your doll back to get the head replaced if your little one mangles the hair—I found this out the hard way! Much better to buy the special doll-wig brush when you get the doll!) Each comes fully dressed in historically-accurate garments (except for the Velcro closures!), and with at least one book. The Keepsake Editions are worth getting, if you can manage it, as the boxed set is not only much more attractive and a good way to keep the books nice, but it comes with a built-in bow and gold-tone bookmark clip. Romantic!

Once you have a doll and at least one book about her character the fun *really* begins! First, you can get a basic accessories kit, featuring items mentioned in the books. In Kirsten's case, that included an embroidered *hankie* to tuck into her apron pocket, a wooden *spoon* and *spoon bag,* a *sunbonnet,* and an *amber heart* on a cord to hang around her neck. Then, for each book in the six-book series, there are special accessories. Here are some examples: A slate bag with chalk (it really works!) and other supplies, all in a calico bag (Kirsten). A Summer Amusements kit with a tuffet, paint set with palette, brush, and six tiny tubes of watercolor paint, and a doll-sized sketchbook for you to paint in (Samantha). Capture the Flag gear kit includes whistle, armband, flag, canoe paddle, letter, picture, and a bean can full of creepy crawlers (Molly). These are just a few of the dozens of accessory kits available.

These are not cheap, crummy items, like the kind of doll accessories you find in too many stores, but solid props with accompanying historical information. Your girls can really get into *learning* about the historical periods while imagining themselves into the lives of these dolls. The girl-sized outfits now available from Pleasant Company (e.g., Saint Lucia Dress in sizes 6X, 7, 8, 10, 12, 14, and 16) let them playact the part as well.

To take the process even further, Pleasant Company now has a Twelve Months of Traditional Pastimes subscription program. It starts with a paper dolls kit—Kirsten, Samantha, and Molly paper dolls plus old-fashioned paper clothes and accessories and historical information. Other months' offerings include a theatre kit (star in three plays, one for each girl, all packed in a lovely ribbon-tied box), family album, old-fashioned games, a cookbook, a diary, embroidery

sampler, Victorian valentines, Knitting Nellie, weaving loom, lanyard kit, and straw ornaments. If ordered separately, items vary in price. Or you can order six-month subscriptions of just the crafts kits or just the activity book kits. We've ordered a single kit or two, and found they were very enjoyable and included high-quality ingredients.

Given the extreme distortion of the past in so many modern textbooks and histories, how does it fare in the American Girls books? As far as I could tell, the Kirsten series mostly avoids the temptation to preach modern values, though there is, I regret to inform you, a smidgin of subtle propaganda spread throughout the Samantha and Molly series. In the Samantha stories, feminism is introduced as Samantha's favorite New York aunt becomes a crusader for The Cause. The suffragettes' opponents' views are not presented at all (except as a mindless resistance to change). I also regret the anti-boy tone of the Molly books. Her brothers are described on the inside covers as "a five-year-old pest" and "a 12-year-old pest." This series also presents the emerging Youth Culture as a good thing. ("During the 1940s, people began to see that the teenage years were a special stage of life and that teenagers had their own special interests.") The disappearance of many women from the work force when the soldiers returned evidently arouses the disapproval of the series editors. In other places, people are said to "know" or "think" certain things, but the text here implies that women did not *really* choose to stop working—rather, patriotic posters and women's magazines "told them it was patriotic to give their jobs back to the men" and "said that women's most important work was caring for children, cooking, and keeping clean houses." (Silly females, to be thus misled!) The last of the Molly books closes in a blast of liberal optimism with this dorky paean to the United Nations:

> The real lesson of World War Two was that all people in every country on earth must learn to live together in peace. In 1945, right after the war ended, the United Nations was born. It is a place where countries still come together to work out their differences, so that the world will never have to go to war again.

As I write this American soldiers are at war under U.N. auspices. Maybe Saddam Hussein should read the Molly books . . . .

Don't get me wrong. The historical notes at the end of each book are full of useful information. These are good stories that give you the flavor of the times, only minimally distorted.

My children's only negative criticism of this series was, "Why don't they have an American *Boys* collection? Like a Daniel Boone doll, or Jim Bowie doll?" I think it would be a great idea!

TIME LINES

You can make your own time line by gluing or stapling strips of paper together, or by recycling the back side of a long strip of computer paper. Mark off the years, write down some names and dates, and you're in business!

Time lines can be as simple or complicated as you want. The simplest time line consists of a single line with only a few major events. More elaborate time lines incorporate color, pictures or stickers to highlight particular types of data, and may include fairly complete histories of several nations. You can make parallel time lines for the history of politics, music, art, and inventions; fashion time lines; or family time lines. It's a great way to organize and get a grip on data that otherwise would overwhelm you, as well as graphically demonstrating the relationships between events that otherwise would have been missed. See how art influences philosophy, or theology politics.

Since making your own time line from scratch can be such a massive chore, I've included reviews of several different time line products. All look nice on your wall. All contain information you very likely would never find yourself, and one employs your children in cutting out the already-printed pieces.

NEW★★
Creation's Child
Simplified U.S. Time Line, $5.95. *U.S. Activity Time Line,* $7.95. Junior version *U.S.Time Line,* $14.95, or $21 for laminated version. *Large U.S. Time Line,* $18.95 or $31 for laminated version. *World History Chart,* write for price. Prices include 1991 shipping. Grades 4 and up.

Education writer Ruth Beechick recommends that young children study history with a simplified time line. The idea is to start with big chunks of history—say Middle Ages and The Age of Exploration. Then, as your child matures, you divide these up into smaller chunks and add more information. That way he has a complete world history framework from the beginning.

Now Creation's Child has a set of two time lines based on this philosophy. The *Simplified U.S. Time Line* covers the highlights of U.S. history from the 1400s to 1989. Events such as Gutenberg's invention of modern printing and Columbus's first voyage are shown, sometimes accompanied with old-timey engravings. Printed on heavy brown paper stock.

The Activity Time Line provides a guided way for your child to get personally involved in making his own time line. You get a ruled time line and sheets of events and people for him to cut out. A typical event will be enclosed in a ruled box and described with both words and a picture. Your child cuts out the box and pastes or staples it to the time line in an appropriate place. In the coming edition of this time line, author Paula Carlson intends to provide "period" dates for the event boxes, so your child will know exactly where on the time line to place them. Until then, a one-page reference sheet explains what goes where.

Also from Creation's Child: *The United States Time Line 1400–1900* is organized in general horizontal bands. The top row pertains to England and Europe. The areas of religion, education, publications, presidents, government, economy, industry, arts, science, and health are presented from top to bottom on each panel. The time line is printed in black on heavy white paper, with many line art illustrations and engravings of people and events. You get six 17 x 22" panels, each covering 50 years, plus an extra panel for 1775–1800, which has been expanded to include more details of this interesting period in our history, plus the 1400s and 1500s panels originally developed for the Junior version, which are half as tall as the other panels. You also get six lined pages half as long and tall as the time line panels, for adding your own family and state history to the bottom of the time line.

The *Junior Version U.S. Time Line* includes many of the same pictures and the most important information from the larger *U.S. Time Line*. Again, blank lined student panels are included, for adding extra information. One century per 8½ x 22" panel.

If you have young children around, the laminated version is a definitely better buy, as it takes little fingers no time to rip and dog-ear your carefully tacked-up time lines.

The *Chronological World History Chart* covers all history for all important civilizations from Creation to 1900 A.D. Originally produced in 1871 by S. C. Adams, it was over 50 feet long and five feet high and depicted world history in words, graphs, and colored engravings. Mr. Adams made his living for a while traveling around and displaying this monster achievement! Since then, other hands have added some extra years, bringing it up to 1989. The history of nations and their rulers are shown as colored streams, sometimes converging, sometimes disappearing, as one civilization is conquered or superseded by another. As with most Victorian productions, a few naked ladies appear here and there (e.g., Eve in the Garden of Eden). Creation's Child suggests you clothe the naked with crayon or erase the problem areas with fine sandpaper.

The *World History Chart* comes in book form. It comes in accordian-fold style full-color 12 x 17" cardstock panels, which unfold to one continuous 15-foot panel. The chart may easily be removed from the book binding for use on a wall, or you can do as I do and keep it in the book, where it is easier to store (who has 15 feet of clear wall space?!).

The *World History Chart* is a highly complex work, more suitable for reference in my opinion than for primary instruction. Find out what was going on all over the world at the same time, or follow the fortunes of the Chinese or Assyrians, not to mention the kings of Israel and Judah. Who was king of England while Christopher Columbus was sailing the ocean blue? The answers are all here!

NEW★★
Frank Schaffer Publications
Each time line set, $5.95, requires 4 x 6' bulletin board. Add $3 shipping (orders under $20) or 15% (orders over $20). Ages 7–12.

Frank Schaffer Publications offers *three* separate time line sets. *Columbus to Washington* has 21 pieces, each illustrating an important event in history, such as Betsy Ross designing the first U.S. flag. *Washington to Civil War* has 21 more visuals, such as Lincoln signing the Emancipation Proclamation and a map showing how America grew through land purchases and otherwise, each with dates and explanatory text. *Civil War to Present* completes the set with another 21 pieces, including a map of Vietnam and a visual for the space program. You'll need a lot of room to put up the complete set, but if you've got the room, this set will certainly spark some interest in historical studies.

KONOS
Volume 1 Time Line and 176 Figures, Volume 2 (190 figures), Volume 3 (122 figures), $59.95 each. Save $10 if you buy either volume of the time line with corresponding curriculum volume. *Time Line of Bible Characters* (about 190 figures), $59.95. *Artists and Composers* (about 90 artist figures), $20.90. Laminated display lines alone, $9.95. Add 10% shipping. Grades K–8.

The KONOS Time Line and Figures: sturdy, laminated, colored sheets with time lines printed on some pages and little cutout figures on others. The time line covers 2099 B.C. to 1999 A.D., with three lines each for the 1400s on (so much was happening!). You get the laminated display lines plus 176 people in Volume 1, with dates, some carrying insignia of their profession, others with little colorful stickers to identify them. Prophets carry staffs, mountain men wear coonskin caps, humanitarians have a red heart, preachers and missionaries carry a Bible, and so on. The people in Volume 1 are those studied in Volume 1 of the KONOS Character Curriculum, reviewed in the Curriculum Buyers' Guide. This time line contains a preponderance of Biblical figures, along with major cultural leaders like Michelangelo and Martin Luther King, Jr. Volume 2, corresponding to Volume 2 of the KONOS curriculum, emphasizes American historical figures and scientists with less Bible-times people. Volume 3 contains a cross-section: Bible-times characters, inventors, singers, Olympic champions, doctors, etc. Volumes 2 and 3 do *not* come with the laminated display lines, since the publishers figure you most likely got Volume 1 first, which *does* include the display lines.

The price reflects the extra cost of providing laminated time strips and figures, which render the product much more attractive and durable. KONOS suggests you mount the time line in ascending and descending steps around a doorway, with B.C. on one side and A.D. on the other. Their time line looks nice enough so your children's room will look decorated rather than defaced.

I should also mention that the kit contains a number of "free" figures, so you can add the people of your choice: family members, for example.

Additional packets and lines are also available: *Bible Characters* and *Artists and Composers*.

Cutting out and setting up the time lines is fun and relatively easy. Cutting out the elaborate figures is neither. Partial solution: instead of cutting out each figure on its outline, why not cut around it in a circle? This speeds the project up considerably. It also works better to take a few days at the beginning of the school year to cut out *all* the figures and separate them into envelopes, ready for use when needed.

NEW★★
Rand McNally
Histomap of World History, $6.95. Shipping extra.

What in the blue blazes is a "histomap"? You're gonna love it when you find out! It's a full-color, vertical time line showing the story of civilization. Unlike other time lines, though, the *Histomap of World History* shows the balance of power at each point in time by the width of the culture's "band" on the chart. See the rise and fall of Egypt's fortunes merely by observing how wide or narrow the pink "Egypt" band is at any time period. Important events in Egypt during that time are printed on its band, too. Civilizations are presented side by side, so you can easily tell who was more powerful than whom, and what events occurred at the same time but in different places.

The *Histomap* opens to 11½ x 70" for wall display, and folds to 11½ x 9½" if you haven't got that much wall to spare.

NEW★★
TREND Enterprises, Inc.
Presidents of the United States Fun-To-Know Flash Cards, $3.99. Shipping $2. Minimum order $10. Ages 9 and up.

A colorful portrait of each president on the front, with his dates in office and the number of his presidency. Biographical details, noteworthy events of his presidency, and fun facts on the back. Forty cards in all. Inexpensive, worth it. Get an extra set for stapling on your time line.

HISTORY MAGAZINES

NEW★★
Calliope
$17.95/year (5 issues). Back issues, $3.95 each. Foreign subscribers add $6. Grades 5–10.

This magazine used to be called *Classical Calliope* and focus on the ancient classical world. Now it has been rechristened "World History for Young People." With this wider and more updated focus, it looks like a better bet.

From the blurb:

By showing students that world history is a continuation of events rather than a series of isolated, unrelated occurrences, *Calliope* helps young readers understand how and why those events took place.

Carefully selected themes explore in-depth circumstances leading up to and following specific events —from ancient times through the Middle Ages and into the Renaissance. Maps and time lines broaden readers' concepts of times and places.

In coming issues, readers can travel from Byzantium to Constantinople to Istanbul, follow the ancient Egyptian mariners on their trade routes, meet with epic heroes, and relive major naval and land battles. Complementary articles, activities, puzzles and illustrations—plus recommendations on further reading —involve young readers in the excitement of past events.

I've looked at a few issues of this magazine, and they've done a good job of putting it together. It's readable, well laid out, and interesting. Relativistic flavor, with equal time and acceptance given to Western, African, and Eastern civilizations and all historic world religions. This means, of necessity, that some uncomfortable facts about ancient pagan civilizations are understated or passed over, since all civilizations and religions are *not* equal (and you think so, too, or we'd have Aztec temples featuring daily human sacrifice in every major city, and you'd have gone back to your ancestors' native countries).

Future issue themes for 1991 and 1992: Major Naval Battles, Lost Cities, Foreign Invasions, Queens of Egypt, Great Explorers to the West, Defenders of France, and Vanished Civilizations.

Cobblestone

$22.95/year (12 issues). $39.95/2 years. Back issues, $3.95 each. Over 135 back issues available. Back issue annual sets, $44.95, include 12 issues, slipcase, and cumulative index. Bulk rate subscriptions available. Foreign subscribers add $8. Grades 4–9.

Would you believe a history magazine for kids? This very professionally-done magazine has lots of kid appeal, being loaded with pictures, puzzles, cartoons, and lots of short, zippy stories. Whoever locates the pictures does a terrific job, as they include a lot of rare and apt photos, woodcuts, engravings, and whatnot that truly add to the depth of the stories.

Each issue of *Cobblestone* is organized around one theme. Upcoming issue themes: Andrew Jackson, Jewish Americans, African American Inventors, First Ladies of the White House, the Cold War, and the Sioux. Recent issues: Harlem Renaissance of the '20s and '30s, Chinese Americans, North Pole Exploration. (You can see the melting pot is coming unmelted just from looking at the issue titles.) All are loaded with interesting facts and graphics. An issue on the theme of Newspapers, for example, featured a two-page time line beginning with Roman slaves sweating out newsletters by hand and ending with the Columbus, Ohio *Dispatch* whipping off the first totally electronic newspaper. Articles took off on tangents: Newspaper illustration, war correspondence, rural papers, and specialty presses were some of the unusual subjects covered. The whole issue was held together by several major articles on the history of printing and the freedom of the press. I've described half of that one issue; if it whets your interest, why not send away for a back issue, perhaps choosing one of the themes above?

Back issues, of which there are over 135, are available in boxed annual sets as well as individual copies. The *Cobblestone* brochure thoughtfully lists them in alphabetic order by topic, rather than in order of publishing. So if you're interested in Civil War Reconstruction or Children Who Shaped History, you can quickly

find what you're looking for. Baseball? American Theater? The Amish? Cherokee Indians? Great Depression? Jazz? Laura Ingalls Wilder? As you can see, topics can be cultural, famous people, time periods, or groups of people.

All back issue annual sets include the cumulative index to all previously published issues.

HISTORY GAMES & DRILL

Aristoplay, Ltd.
Made for Trade, $22. Add $4.75 shipping. Ages 8–adult.

Historical board game that teaches economics lessons. In *Made for Trade*, you play the part of a character like Makepeace Middleton, a continental soldier or Eliza Oglethorpe, tavern maid. After escaping indentured service, you try to earn shillings and barter for goods in the town shops while avoiding taxes. Find out what a free-market economy was like, and how taxation without representation messes things up. Work your way up from indentured service to colonial prosperity. Historical events crop up now and then, to which you must respond. Congress, for example, might authorize the establishment of a navy and you, as shipowner Christian Fairhill, collect 4 shillings in increased profits. Some fun touches: if you visit the tavern you lose a turn for self-indulgence, and you have to pay a church tithe every time you pass the meeting house.

Like other Aristoplay games, *Made for Trade* is a work of art as well as educational. You get a lot for your money: the colorful game board (laid out like a colonial town for atmosphere), eight character cards with stands, eight inventory lists, 48 object cards (things you can buy or barter), 30 Event I cards, 30 Event II cards, 60 plastic shillings, and one pair of dice. In addition, *Made for Trade* includes a special information sheet compiled by the staff of the Winterthur Museum. This sheet describes all 48 objects and adds extra historical interest to the game. Two to four characters can play at any of the four play levels.

NEW**
Educational Insights
Windows of Learning, U.S. History or World History, $6.95 each. Minimum order $25. Shipping extra. Ages 7–adult.

"Build your knowledge of history with fun, self-checking quiz wheels!" Here's how it works. Slip one of the compact 7" question-and-answer disks into the circular case. A question will appear in the cutout window at the top. Look in the window on the other side for the answer. Then rotate the disk for the next question! Keep track of how you're doing with the handy scorekeeper. Practice by yourself or with a friend. Each set contains scorekeeper, map case, and five two-sided disks with 10 questions on each side, for 100 questions in all.

NEW**
Know It All
Know It All, $29.95 plus $3 shipping. Ages 6–adult.

Know It All is a U.S. geography and history board game designed to teach players the states, capitals, state slogans, general U.S. geography, and U.S. history in a fun, systematic way. See detailed writeup in Geography chapter.

PART VIII

LIFE SKILLS

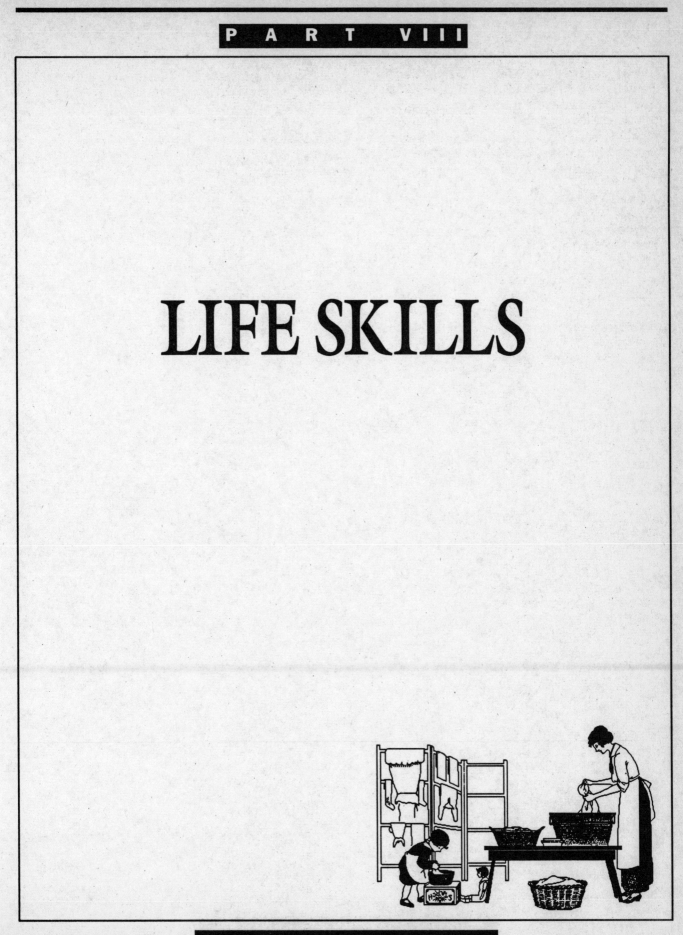

CHAPTER THIRTY-SEVEN

BUSINESS

Many kids today are out of touch when it comes to work and money. I mean *really* out of touch. In outer space somewhere, slowly circling the planet Saturn.

A year ago Focus on the Family's *Clubhouse* magazine asked kids to write in with their answers to the question, "Should kids have to do chores?" Here are some of the answers, published in the June 1990 edition:

"I don't think kids should have to do chores because they might get dirty." Jennifer, age 11, from Oregon.

"I think kids shouldn't have to do chores, because you don't want to wear out a kid." Matthew, age 8, from Montana.

"I think the only reason God made parents is to clean my room, and I should get my allowance for nothing." Sam, age 9½, from Alaska.

This neatly parallels what author Jean Ross Peterson observed when interviewing children for her book on money management. In her own words,

My eyes were opened when I interviewed children whose ages ranged from six to fourteen:

Susan, age thirteen, "I'm going to be a model and a fashion designer."

Dave, also thirteen: "I'll be a world class swimmer and a Supreme Court judge."

Eric, age twelve: "I'm going to own hotels and travel on my boat."

Beth, age seven: "Someday I'll be like a famous person on TV, or a model."

Steve, age eleven: "I want to be a private eye."

Rick, age nine: "I'm going to have my own business, be on a SWAT team, and live on a horse ranch."

This is a random sample from over one hundred children who told me what they intended to do when they grew up. It's interesting to note that when I asked each child if he or she knew how to become whatever occupation was selected, the unanimous answer was, "Go to college."

We'll have more to say about the College Thing in Volume 3. Right now all I can say is, "Good luck, kids," because as Mrs. Peterson notes, no less an authority than the *Wall Street Journal* has discovered that today's typical kid expects "to make a lot more money than my folks do, but I won't have to work as hard to get it."

Bringing up kids with financial and career expectations like this amounts to financial abuse. The real world doesn't work like this. Never has. Never will. The kids will find this out, too, when their VISA bill rises up and eats their new car or their spouse divorces them because they financially ruined the family.

That's why, although I originally intended to only include Business in Volume 3, I have changed my mind. If we want to build responsible thinking about money into our children, we'd better start now!

UPDATED★★
Achievement Basics
Junior Business Set, $18.95 plus $1.50 shipping. Grades 3–10.

Achievement Basics offers something unique: a Junior Business Basics series designed to teach entrepreneurial skills to kids from fourth grade on up. The series is correlated with an optional Junior Business newsletter for inspiration. It comes with a parent/teacher guide with cartoon pages.

The cassettes for younger children are dramatized stories of lovable Uncle Hersh and his nephew Dow and niece Joan. *There's No Such Thing as a Free Ice Cream Cone* teaches kids about productivity and setting standards. In *The ABC's of the Stock Market,* Dow and Joan go to the stock exchange. *You Can Lead a Horse to Water, But . . .* is about incentive, profit, and loss. Along with these three cassettes comes the Simple Sample Bookkeeping Notebook that teaches bookkeeping and budgeting.

The cassettes are done by professional actors or announcers and designed for home use. A parent/teacher guide is included free.

Bluestocking Press
Capitalism for Kids, $9.95 plus $2 shipping. Grades 4–12, plus a chapter for adults.

Capitalism for Kids by libertarian Karl Hess is definitely the best book I have ever seen directed to children on the *theory* of how to go into business for yourself. In fact, it is the *only* book I have ever seen on this subject!

Capitalism for Kids was written to teach kids aged 9 to 19 the following: Determine your level of enterprise with a self-test. How parents can help you succeed. What you need to know about working for yourself. How to make your product or service stand out. How to manage money and time. Risk taking. Getting the most from your education. Setting up a family company. What type of college education is most useful (I'm interested in that section!). Making the most of your home education. Computers and your business. How to find a high school entrepreneur club. Starting your business career as a volunteer. Practical review of laws, licenses, and liability. Contracts you can legally make as a minor. Three common types of business liability. Best fields with greatest opportunities for young entrepreneurs.

Mr. Hess provides a lot of how-tos, testimonies from business leaders on what in their upbringing prepared them for success, and resources your child can track down for more help in getting started. This is not a list of One Hundred Good Businesses for Kids, but more of a worldview. As such, you will want to discuss the sections which Mr. Hess makes his case for modified personal autonomy ("doing your own thing as long as it doesn't harm anyone else") with your child, and point out that God's way works better. To Mr. Hess's credit, he does recognize the need for philanthropy and voluntarism, and urges youngsters to get started now helping others as well as working for themselves. This book really is absorbing reading.

NEW**
Busines$ Kids
The Busines$ Kit, $49.95 plus $8.50 shipping. Teacher's guide, $39.95. Ages 10–adult.

Ever wish there were an easy way to start a business? Coming up with the business *idea* is not the problem. It's getting organized . . . getting financed . . . finding out what forms you need to fill out to keep the bureaucrats happy . . . advertising . . . management . . . record-keeping . . . hiring and firing (and whether you *should* hire help) . . . and all those other imponderables that keep would-be entrepreneurs biting their fingernails with frustration. They don't teach this stuff in school!

Nasir M. Ashemimry, a Saudi Arabian airline pilot turned businessman, became aware of this problem when his nine-year-old son Ibrahim asked him for a business card. Little Ibrahim wanted a business card of *his own*, you see, so he could start his own business. Mr. Ashemimry, naturally very proud of his enterprising offspring, felt duty-bound to explain that it takes more than a business card to start a business.

"Like what?" Ibrahim wanted to know.

The answer to Ibrahim's question took a few years to put together, and you'll know why when you see it. From the fancy lacquer-finished cardboard case in which the Busines$ Kit is packaged, to the glossy booklets, to the complete line of Busines$ Kids accessories, this product is first-class. The objective is twofold:

(1) Teach American teens that, although we may live in a country where 98 percent of the people work for two percent of the people, they can beat the percentages, and

(2) Set up Busines$ Kids clubs throughout the U.S.A. and (why not?) the world.

Following his empowerment philosophy down the line, Mr. Ashemimry enlisted the aid of a multiethnic teenage board to help finalize the design of his how-to-go-into-business-for-yourself kit. The result has a certain McBiz look about it. Swank. Hip (at least as hip as 90s kids manage to be). The kind of yuppie puppies who would buy a Busines$ Kids "I'M THE BOSS" T-shirt ought to love it.

(Depressing aside: Did you know that sales of California Raisins accessories are larger, dollar-wise, than sales of California raisins? No wonder so many people need Ex-Lax! This definitely proves the smart money should ride on accessories rather than the real thing, or to put it another way, more kids are likely to buy T-shirts announcing their willingness to go into business than are likely to seriously go into business. Even more likely: Mom and Dad will buy the T-shirts, hoping Junior will thus subliminally be motivated to become Bill Gates.)

While hip, there's substance behind the hype. The Busines$ Kit is endorsed by Future Business Leaders of America, Phi Beta Lambda, the Technological Students Association, the National Foundation for Teaching Entrepreneurship, and the editors of *Success* magazine. The kit is already the accepted curriculum for dozens of school, community, and institutional educational programs as well as agencies of the U.S. Federal Government. The Busines$ Kit was recently used to teach entrepreneurship to young Soviet students at the invitation of the Central Committee of the Young Communist League and the Ministry of Education of Russia . . . now *there's* "going into the red" for you!

Now you have an idea of the user interface. What's in the kit?

1. A Business Plan Packet containing: Business plan and product/service research worksheets, Going into Business Checklist, Monthly Bookkeeping record, Monthly Profit/Loss Statement, Official Business Kids IOU, Job Application Form, SS-4 Application for Employer Identification Number, and W-4 Employee's Withholding Allowance Certificate.

2. Template Packet containing: A Very Short Course in Advertising and four sample templates for ads.

3. Appointment calendar.

4. Instruction Booklets: The World of Business—Introduction, The President's Message, The Business of Business, Business Heroes, Looking Inside a Large Corporation, Small Business Opportunities; 1. Getting Started—Getting Started, Some Businesses to Consider, and Some Help with Choosing YOUR Business; 2. Organizing—Researching Your Business, Planning Your Business, and Finding Cash; 3. Mastering Management—Introduction: The Importance of Management, Setting Up Shop, Hiring People, Managing Your Money, and Taxes; 4. Marketing—Marketing Your Business and Satisfying Your Customers; and Super Index—Table of Contents, Glossary of Terms, and Index.

5. Stationery and business cards printed with the Busines$ Kids logo.

6. A catalog of everything from cuff links to backpacks emblazoned with the Busines$ Kids logo.

7. A teenybopper motivational audio tape.

As you may have guessed, the booklets are the heart of the program—and they are really good. Everything you need to start up and run a growing company is spelled out, right down to such details as the benefits of renting expensive equipment rather than rushing out to buy it, the child labor laws, how to advertise your business, where to get the money to start your business, and even what kind of business to start. While the Kit is fun, it's not a game or a cookie-cutter approach—you're told about the different types of businesses and given brief descriptions of 76 businesses well suited to teens. Things kids might not realize are covered, like the importance of dressing properly for the job (even kids who mow lawns should keep their shirts on!) and how to find out the pay scale in your area.

Even though the information is well presented, with lively graphics and explanations, a kid will do better to walk through the material with an adult, preferably one with some business experience.

I hear the question you're asking. "Can adults use this kit, too?" Sure! Skip the accessories and try to ignore the teenage success stories. You have enough trouble getting up your nerve to start a business without knowing that some infant has already succeeded more than you ever will! Concentrate on the business plan, product research worksheets, and booklets. As much information is packed in there as

you could pick up at hundreds of dollars' worth of seminars.

If Mr. Ashemimry is smart, he'll tweak the Busines$ Kit, add some overheads, and put together his own seminar for grownups. (We adults need these things spelled out, not to mention the support of seeing other people in the room who want to start their own business.)

Did I mention that, included in the purchase of the kit, you get a year's membership, entitling you to participate in the club and get monthly issues of the newsletter? This, again, is a slick production, given to hyping the successes of sundry teen businessfolk, and definitely worldly in its outlook (peace, ecology, money, teenage rebellion, and the American Way). I have hopes it will improve to offer more in-depth coverage of *why* certain kids have succeeded, à la *Inc.* magazine's articles. Mr. Ashemimry could hire an *Inc.* writer, perhaps, to do a feature article each issue; it would be a start.

Bottom line: The Busines$ Kit is a good place to start, if you hope to start a business. Even its packaging is a call to excellence. Keep your head screwed on straight, remember that success is not making big bucks but doing what is right, work through the kit, and we'll see what happens!

NEW**
Children's Small Press Collection
Fast Cash for Kids, $9.95 plus $1.50 shipping. Ages 10–14.

How to develop your money-making goals and plans. Salesmanship and marketing. How to set prices properly. How to get organized. 10 helping jobs. 12 service jobs. 10 ideas for employment. 13 cleaning jobs. 9 yard and garden jobs. 11 holiday projects. 19 sales projects. 17 recycling ideas. For each project, there's a brief description and instructions on how to start the business or do the job. Some have bonus ideas, such as (under Window Washing)

- Work with a partner and do twice as many jobs!
- Keep a list of all your customers and call them again in 6–12 months.

Some chapters provide addresses where you can write away for more information concerning the businesses or jobs covered in that chapter. Generous use of line art throughout (mostly clip art) adds to the book's warmth and eye appeal. The instructions are not terribly detailed; the authors do presume the reader is able to take an idea and go with it. Doable projects, nothing flaky. You're not likely to get rich on any of them, but you can make some fast cash, as the book title promises.

Home Life
Extra Cash for Kids, $9.95 plus $1 shipping. Ages 8–adult.

Extra Cash for Kids is the most useful and most entertaining job-ideas-and-how-tos book I have seen. One hundred mini chapters on kid-sized jobs. Some unusual but workable ideas are tucked in with the usual car wash, snow removal, and party for little kids lineup. The authors not only suggest business ideas and explain why each one is a possible moneymaker, but provide How to Do It and Special Notes sections. The Special Notes tips include ideas on how to expand some of the businesses into other areas. SuperIdeas, a mini menu of general business tips like how to keep records or how to clean up on school fads, are scattered throughout the book, along with inviting cartoons and graphics. Published by Wolgemuth & Hyatt Publishers, also available in bookstores.

CHAPTER THIRTY-EIGHT

HEALTH & SAFETY

Early to bed, and early to rise
Makes a man healthy, and wealthy, and wise.
—Benjamin Franklin

Life has become just a bit more complicated since old Ben penned those famous words. Today we worry about what we eat and how we exercise more than about when we go to sleep. "Are my deltoids in shape? Ooh, my thighs are getting fat!" That's why health education in the schools focuses on fitness, nutrition, and simple anatomy lessons.

Schools also teach lessons on hygiene, toothbrushing, and other topics I'm sure you cover at home (which is why you won't find them in this chapter). Put away that dental floss—we're about to discover why greaseburgers are bad for you and how to find your liver when you need to! We'll also look at a few wholesome sex education resources, some important safety skills, and simple first aid.

NUTRITION

Jack Sprat could eat no fat.
His wife could eat no lean.
And so, between them both, you see,
They licked the platter clean.
—Mother Goose

For kids in this age range, nutrition education doesn't have to be a big deal. They can probably live without knowing the health benefits of vitamin B6 or how to find the alimentary canal. I assume we all know that greasy fried food is worse for you than carrot sticks, and that megadoses of sugar make kids fat, grouchy, and prone to develop diabetes. Since most home schoolers seem to be keenly conscious of such health issues, and we have so many basic subjects to cover, nutrition might well be relegated to dinner-table discussion (as in answering the perennial question, "Mom, why can't I just have ice cream for supper?").

For these reasons, and also because most big-time nutrition education material is written for kids in junior high, you'll find it in Volume 3. Below, however, are a few nutrition-'n-fitness resources for preteens.

NEW**
Center for Science in the Public Interest
 Membership includes *Nutrition Action Healthletter*,
$19.95/year (10 issues). Posters $4.95 each, quantity
discounts available. Grades 5–adult.

Are you ready for . . . the Food Police? Yes, Jane
Greer's worst nightmare has come true. It's . . . the Anti-
Twinkie Squad!

The Center for Science in the Public Interest cru-
sades relentlessly for full disclosure of ingredients on
packaged and restaurant food, and more healthful ingredients therein. The main thrust is educational, in
hopes an aroused electorate will arise and demand
Food Reform. Towards this end, they publish a number of amusing and educational materials.

Let's look at their wall posters. These are full color
on glossy paper and packed with useful and educational information.

First, the poster you've all been waiting for: CSPI's
Fast Food Eating Guide! My, it's fun to see the competitors line up to get their GLOOM ratings. The GLOOM
index "reflects a food's overall fat, sodium, sugar, and
calorie content." And the losers are . . . Arby's Fish Fil-
let sandwich . . . Arby's cheddar fries . . . Arby's Bac'n
Cheddar Deluxe . . . Arby's Steak Deluxe . . . Well, Arby's doesn't lose in *every* category, but they're sure in
there pitching! Jack in the Box, Wendy's, Taco Bell, and
Dairy Queen manage to pick a few last places and sec-
ond-to-last, and even meek and mild Burger King wins
the booby prize for their scrambled egg platters with
bacon or sausage. In fact, one of those feasts provides
all the GLOOM points you can get away with in a day!
Fat, sodium, and calories per serving are included in
every listing, so you can figure out for yourself that a
McDonald's Quarter Pounder with cheese is only about

half the calories of a Jack-in-the-Box Ultimate Cheese-
burger (the loser in that category). A great argument
for staying home.

The *Nutrition Scoreboard* rates categories of foods
in terms of nutritional value. Fresh spinach is the big
winner in the veggie category (see, Popeye knew what
he was doing!) and cucumber the relative loser, with
avocado hanging in there as the only high-fat veggie.
President Bush can relax: broccoli is only #7 on the
list, surpassed by spinach, fresh collard greens, sweet
potato, potato, fresh kale, and winter squash. Watermelon is the #1 fruit, out of a field of 21 contenders,
in which grapes finished last. Raisins, not on the list,
would presumably fare even worse. Take that, you California guys! No surprise to find Coca-Cola and "other
sodas" in last place on the beverages list, while carrot
juice barely beats out unsweetened orange juice for the
top spot. This *Scoreboard* is such fascinating reading I
am tempted to go on and on. Can you imagine that
they found three snacks worse for you than Twinkies?
I'll just hint that if you like hominy grits, American
cheese, and Sugar Smacks you lose out in three categories. Also covered are condiments, breakfast cereals,
dairy, grain foods, and poultry-fish-meat-eggs (a single
category). Grading is done, of course, in harmony with
CSPI's ideas about what's good for you and what ain't.
Unreconstructed Southerners lose big everywhere except in the watermelon and collards categories.

The *Sodium Scoreboard* poster tells you, by food
category and brand name, how much sodium is in
each, from least to greatest. Wheat Bran has the least
sodium of cold cereals listed, while Cheerios packs a
walloping 330 mg/serving. That's nothing, though,
compared to the 1,700 mg in one serving of Armour
Sloppy Joe Beef or the 4,778 mg in one serving of Ban-
quet Cheese Enchilada Dinner. I hate American cheese,
and Velveeta even more, so am not dismayed to find
that these two are the biggest sodium carriers under
Cheeses. Categories included are Beverages, Condiments, Potpourri, Crackers & Chips, Soups, Natural
Foods, Fish, Frozen Foods, Processed Meats, Canned
Entrées, Canned Vegetables, Packaged Dishes, Dairy
Products, Breads, Cereals, Sweet Baked Goods, Sweets,
and Fast Foods (in which you will be gratified to learn
that McDonald's french fries come in lowest).

Like the other *Scoreboards*, *Sugar Scoreboard* tells
you by category and brand name how much of the
goodie is in a serving. Lots of other interesting info, including a graph showing the per-person consumption
of sugar in the U.S.A. from 1840 to now and descriptions of the different types of sugars found in food.

Fiber Scoreboard shows Granny offering you a salad ("It's good for you, Sonny! Lots of roughage!") Cereals, nuts & seeds, cakes-pastries-muffins, breads, crackers, fast foods, grains & pasta, frozen dinners and entrees, soups, veggies, fruits & juices, cookies-candies-chips, and beans-peas-tofu are all listed from greatest fiber content per serving to least. Brand name products form the bulk (pardon the pun) of these lists. Unsurprisingly, revolting Kellogg's All Bran with Extra Fiber, a cereal I can barely choke down thanks to its strong resemblance to cardboard shreds, is the high-fiber winner for cereals, while something called Kellogg's Nut & Honey Crunch has absolutely zip (none, zero) fiber per serving unless you eat part of the box. You'll also be delighted to learn that poor Arby's, the big GLOOM factor loser, comes in high in fiber for their baked potato with broccoli and cheese. Granola bars are a fiber joke compared to air-popped popcorn, the poster also shows. As a bonus, the chart also tells you how much fat is in each serving.

CSPI's *Cholesterol Scoreboard* scores brand-name and regular foods on their cholesterol content. Some foods get negative scores, indicating that they lower blood cholesterol. However, CSPI warns, "Don't gorge yourself on them. Diets high in *any* kind of fat may promote obesity and colon and breast cancer." That's why fat content is also shown for each food. Sometimes foods that are big losers on other scoreboards (for sugar content, for example) turn up as cholesterol winners: marshmallows and jellybeans each have zero cholesterol, for instance! It turns out that Ben and Jerry, the popular ice-cream makers, are Public Enemy Number Two for their superfatted vanilla ice cream. Light 'n Lively Ice Milk has only *one-seventh* the bad cholesterol of Ben & Jerry's offering! It's even worse than gargling eggs—twice as much cholesterol in one serving as an egg, and more than four times the fat. You can also find out the dope on yogurt brands, cereals, and lots more with this handy poster.

The CSPI *Chemical Cuisine* poster has food additives listed in alphabetical order, with a description of each. Each entry is color-coded as "Avoid" (blue), "Caution" (yellow), or "Safe" (green). Lots of interesting info all in one place. Handy for use in home kitchen science research.

The *Anti-Cancer Eating Guide* breaks down current cancer research into easy-to-follow graphs. The Fiber chart, for example, shows grams of fiber for each product, from least to greatest, while telling you current recommendations for dietary fiber. The Fat chart works similarly, as do the Vitamin C and Vitamin A

charts. Other categories covered on this poster include Selenium, Contaminants, Vegetables, Food Preparation, Alcohol, Food Additives, Coffee, and Facts to Ponder. The research certainty of each eating suggestion is marked in red, so you can tell whether it is very certain that an eating suggestion prevents cancer or only somewhat certain. Cancer protectors are shown in green, and cancer promoters in red. All together, an excellent job of visualizing and organizing a tremendous amount of data.

The CSPI *Exer-Guide* gives information about the health benefits of exercise, exposes various myths, and lists activities in terms of calories per hour from least (sleeping) to greatest (ice hockey and lacrosse). Juggling, our favorite family exercise, unfortunately is not on the list.

Busy little bees that they are, the people at CSPI gain about 15 percent of their income from selling books, posters, and so on. The rest comes from membership dues, contributions, and non-government and non-food industry grants. Members get the *Nutrition Action Healthletter*, a zippy, colorful 'zine with good graphics and energetic articles written in unpretentious language. At the back are a slew of cookbooks, kiddie toys, and kitchen devices for sale to the members, who presumably want to increase their personal health as much as they want to increase everyone else's.

Do you want to join? It all depends on your religious views about salt, grease, and liquor advertising (CSPI takes a dim view of all three). CSPI's newsletter is very bouncy and earnest, and as long as they don't interfere with Jane Greer's First Amendment to nosh on Twinkies, it's fun as well. Good posters, anyway!

NEW✶✶
Concerned Communications
Bodywise. Three editions: *Secrets to Wellness* and *Exercise and Fitness* (grades 5–8) and *Foods and Nutrition* (grades 4–6). $7.95 each. Teacher's guide for each edition, $3 each. Add $3.50 shipping for up to 4 items, or 10% of total for over 5 items.

"The Student Workbook of Puzzles, Games, & Stories That Makes Health Fun For Christian Kids!" These large perfect-bound workbooks with full-color covers each include over 100 health-related activities. Lots of background info, too, like the story of the Greek mom who trained her son to box in the Olympics (the ancient Greek Olympics). In those days it was a capital crime for any woman to see the Olympics, but Mom just couldn't resist watching her boy win the big one. He won it, her robe slipped when she rushed out to congratulate him, she was caught—but escaped the sentence because her family was so famous for athletics, on condition she never, ever try to see the Olympics again.

There's more teaching (through fascinating stories and articles) than testing in these books, which is just fine with me. The puzzles and games are, well, there. You can do them or not do them, as the fit takes you. You only need the teacher's manual if you can't figure out the answers.

Educational Insights
The Nutrition Box, $9.95. Shipping extra. Grades 4–8.

Perhaps the best introduction to public-school nutrition ideas is Educational Insight's *Nutrition Box.* "A complete self-contained kit on nutrition," this low-priced kit consists of 50 cards, each with background info and suggested follow-up activities, neatly stored in a handsome box. Topics include vitamins, minerals, and proteins (a more sensible approach than solely concentrating on the Four Food Groups), nutrition around the world, and proper food preparation. The *Nutrition Box* is suggested for grades four and up, but at home could be used to some extent even with preschoolers.

Kimbo Educational
Slim Goodbody's Nutrition Edition, $10.95 plus $3.50 shipping. Grades preK–5.

Slim Goodbody is an actor/singer in a body suit. A real body suit: all the inner organs and veins and such printed in living color on a jumpsuit. Yuk. Naturally, kids love him.

Slim (real name: John Burstein) likes to sing, and what Slim likes to sing about is health. *Slim Goodbody's Nutrition Edition* has Slim going to town with inspira-

tional songs about how neat it is to eat natural foods, along with some educational ditties about Protein Power, the Vitamin ABC's, how food gets digested, and the virtues of water-glugging. Easy to remember, upbeat.

NEW**
Teaching Home
October/November 1988 back issue, $3.75. Complete six-issue set of 1988 back issues, $17.50, includes free set of 6 plastic magazine holders for your ring binder.

Once again, *Teaching Home* magazine is your best source for info on how and what to teach on a particular topic. This time it's the October/November 1988 issue, and the subject is Health Education. Find out about Biblical principles of health, ten topics generally covered in health education, how to teach safety and first aid, a Biblical approach to informing kids about human sexuality, lots more!

ANATOMY

There was a young lady from Lynn
Who was so excessively thin
That when she essayed
To drink lemonade
She slipped through the straw and fell in.
            —Anonymous

Now that we know what Jack Sprat and his wife should eat, we can study what their peculiar lifestyle actually does to them. Anatomy uncovers the systems digestive, endocrine, muscular, skeletal, and reproductive, among others. Part of the required Health subject is the study of all these layers of anatomy.

NEW★★
Aristoplay
Some Body, $22. Add $4.75 shipping. Ages 6–10 (they say), but fun for all ages.

The new *Some Body* game from Aristoplay is the simplest, most fun, hands-on body parts instruction I have yet seen. You can play it right out of the box, after a little time spent parting the peelable vinyl body parts from their storage sheets. Basically, the idea is to place body parts in the correct places and the correct order (from back to front) on the game board, an outline drawing of a child's body. You get four *Some Body* game boards with outlines showing where body parts go, four Body Part sheets of labeled vinyl body part peel 'n stick cutouts, one reference chart showing you where's what in the human body (inside the box top), 40 each illustrated Body Part identification cards and Body Part question cards, four wild cards, and the indispensable instruction sheet.

Savvy home schoolers will immediately think of all kinds of ways to teach anatomy using the peel 'n stick body parts and the game board. Or you can just play the games suggested. Draw cards to find which body part you can place on your Body Board. More difficult version: answer questions about body part functions before you get to place an item on the body board. Cards-only version: match questions and answers about body part functions.

NEW★★
Cuisenaire Company of America
Your Amazing Senses Discovery Book, $9.95. Shipping extra. Grades K–6.

Planning a unit on the senses: sight, hearing, touch, smell, taste? *Your Amazing Senses Discovery Book* is the name of a really neat $9.95 book that will teach your children what they need to know (and more!) while entertaining the whole family. This extraordinary full-color book has things that pop up, things to pull, trick eyeglasses to look through, optical illusions,

scratch 'n sniff, a reflex-testing experiment—over 30 activities in all, and all built into the book! Nothing for you to do but leave it out where Junior can find it.

NEW★★
EDC Publishing, Inc.
How Your Body Works, $6.95. Shipping extra. Ages 7–adult.

Take a trip through the Body Machine with this incredibly visual kids' introduction to the human body and how it works. See the white blood cell "police" chase down germs. Learn how the bones and muscles and reproductive organs function. Terrific cartoon-style illustrations make the concepts vivid. One of our kids' favorite science books.

Educational Insights
Human Body Kit, Pumping Heart Kit, Human Lung Kit, Human Skull, Brain Kit, Heart Kit (non-pumping), Human Ear Kit, Human Tooth Kit, Human Eye Kit, $29.95 each. Models come disassembled. Anatomy Apron, $19.95. The Human Body Box, $9.95. Shipping extra. Grades 4–8.

Others must agree that these kits are a good value, since Educational Insights now has twice as many to offer as last year. Each kit contains 25 activity cards, reproducible worksheets, games, student and teacher record sheets, and quizzes. The Human Body kit includes not only a transparent human form with muscles molded inside, but also a small plastic skeleton with some abdominal organs exposed. The new Human Tooth model stands on an easel and is hinged to show interior detailing. The Pumping Heart, a rather yukky concept sure to be beloved by preteen boys, is a working model of the heart and circulatory system. Squeeze the bulb and red "blood" wends its ways through veins, arteries, atria, and ventricles. The regular Heart Model is your normal take-apart plastic model. All models look quite attractive, at least as attractive as this sort of thing can. Color is used where appropriate.

A brand-new, fun idea beloved by schoolteachers is Educational Insight's Anatomy Apron. The teacher puts on this washable vinyl apron pre-printed with outlines of the internal body organs. No big deal so far, you say? What about colorful cutout body organs that attach to the apron with Velcro? Put 'em on, peel 'em off, again and again! The Anatomy Apron is one-size-fits-all, so kiddies can proudly wear it, too.

Lastly, just as Educational Insight's Nutrition Box is the best deal for public school nutrition, their Human Body Box is the most interesting, least expensive substitute for ye boring anatomy text. Fifty durable cards grouped by body parts give info and suggest practical activities.

NEW★★
Educational Insights
3-D Human Body Charts, $29.95. Grades 5–8.

You've seen 3-D maps; the mountain peaks literally stand out. This set of eight Human Body Charts works the same way. You can *see* the body parts in full color, and *feel* them, too, getting an idea of their volume and shape as well as of their outlines. Each chart has exploded views of important features. The Circulatory Systems chart, for example, shows the inside and outside of the heart, as well as a full-body view of the circulatory system. All parts are clearly labeled.

The set includes charts of the circulatory, digestive, muscular, nervous, respiratory, and skeletal systems, plus one each for eye-ear-skin and smell-and-taste. If you purchase it, you'll have hands-on access to more anatomical information than Leonardo da Vinci possessed in his pre-grave-robbing days.

Frank Schaffer
Human Body bulletin board set, $5.95. Requires 4 x 6' bulletin board. Add $3 shipping (orders under $20) or 15% (orders over $20). Grades 3–6.

See the amazing Mr. Bones! *Observe* how blood travels through the heart! *Read* the labels and learn to recognize the muscle groups! *Know* where your food goes! This 80-piece bulletin board set presents labeled, full-color drawings of the skeletal, digestive, circulatory, and muscular systems. Some pieces are enlarged for more detail.

NEW★★
National Teaching Aids, Inc.
Human Skeleton Construction Kit, $29.95. Grades 5–adult.

It's only a paper man . . . I am intrigued by the catalog pictures of what National Teaching Aids assures me is a full-size articulated human skeleton made entirely of paper. The invention of a British professor with the twin hobbies of anatomy and origami, your skeleton comes packaged in a flat box containing 10 die-cut cardboard sheets scored and printed with the name of each bone. Fully illustrated instructions show you how

to put Bonzo together—without glue or scissors. When completed, your paper man can be moved into every position taken by a real skeleton. Bonzo is supposed to be durable, and he's certainly less ethically upsetting than the real article and less expensive than plastic.

Sycamore Tree
Anatomy coloring book, $13.95. Dover anatomy coloring book, $2.50. Human Body felt set, $25.95.

Sycamore Tree has a great selection of health and anatomy materials for home study. Their anatomy coloring book is meant for high school students. Descriptive text accompanies each drawing. Far cheaper and more suitable for elementary kids is the Dover anatomy coloring book (don't confuse the two!). Sycamore Tree has several other books on the body and health. Skipping over all these, let me tell you about the Betty Lukens felt Human Body Set. When I saw the picture in the brochure I knew this was the teaching tool to get! It is an incredibly beautiful set of felts, containing all the innards and muscle layers, etc. that you'd ever hope to see—even a womb with a little baby inside! Ten talks accompany this set, plus the "I Am Joe's Body" series from *Reader's Digest*, the most popular series ever printed in their history. The Human Body Set is not overly expensive, and with care it will last almost forever. Where else can you get a life-sized *overlayable* model?

NEW★★
Teacher Created Materials
My Body, $5.95. Spanish version also available. Grades preK–6 (adult help needed).

My Body is an anatomy book with a difference! Along with handwritten explanations of body parts, you get patterns for making your own life-sized illustrated person. You start by tracing your child's body on tagboard or other sturdy paper. Then photocopy the pattern pages and color as directed. Place as directed on the paper body. Some organs will "lift up" to expose others beneath when finished. A neat project for hands-on (lungs-on, heart-on . . .) learning!

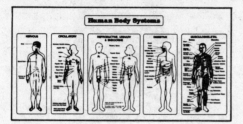

NEW★★
TREND Enterprises, Inc.
Each bulletin board set, $5.99, includes free Discovery Guide. Requires 4 x 6' bulletin board. Add $2 shipping. Minimum order $10. Grades 4–9.

Searching for inexpensive ways to teach human anatomy has become something of a hobby with me. So far I've turned up a game, a felt kit, a slew of build-it-yourself models, and now a bulletin board set!

TREND's *Human Body Systems* is a set of six colorful visuals and a text header. Visuals cover: reproductive, urinary, and endocrine systems, with both male and female figures; digestive system (male figure); respiratory (female); musculoskeletal (male); nervous (male); and circulatory (female). Each tasteful visual features outline figure(s) with body parts clearly labeled. For easier reading, the body part names run around the outside of the figure. Each name has a line connecting it to its corresponding body part. Reproductive organs are shown.

As usual , the accompanying discovery guide packs a lot of useful information into a small space. In this case, you get information about how each body system and part works, plus a smattering of fascinating facts and ten suggested hands-on health activities (e.g., pulse measurement activities). A good value.

SEX EDUCATION FOR CHRISTIAN KIDS

Mommy and Daddy, sitting in a tree
K-I-S-S-I-N-G
First comes love
Then comes marriage
Then comes baby in the baby carriage!
 —Children's rhyme

First comes love. Then comes *marriage. Then* comes baby in the baby carriage! Simple, isn't it?

UPDATED★★
Master Books
Life Before Birth book, $9.95; cassette, $5.95; video, $9.95. All three, $24.95. 15% shipping: minimum $2. Grades 3–8.

You will adore this cute, colorful hardcover book from Master Books. *Life Before Birth: A Christian Family Book* is written as a series of dialogs between Dr. Gary Parker and his children. Crammed with colorful cartoon illustrations, it not only gives the facts of life, but a Christian pro-life and creationist outlook as well. Topics like abortion and birth defects are presented to your children in a way that will make them want to stand for life and love. All is done in good taste: nothing gruesome. You can get it three ways: the book alone, the book and a read-along cassette in a plastic pouch, the book and cassette and a six-minute VHS video that capsulizes the book's message. Nicest looking book on the subject I have ever seen. Highly recommended.

Wolgemuth & Hyatt Publishers
Decent Exposure, hardbound $14.95. Adults read it, use information with children.

Best book ever written on how to teach kids about sex. Very little emphasis on the how-tos of reproduction (hey, you know all that—you *had* the kids, after all!). Author Connie Marshner devotes her energy to explaining the psychology of why kids rebel sexually in the first place. Her analysis of the Youth Culture is alone worth the price of the book. Then she gets to the root of things with some compelling insights on how to teach kids self-control, piety, and independent (non-peer-pressured) thinking. Excellent!

FIRST AID FOR KIDS

Jack and Jill went up the hill
To fetch a pail of water
Jack fell down, and broke his crown,
And Jill came tumbling after.

Up Jack got, and home did trot
As fast as he could caper.
Went to bed, and wrapped his head,
In vinegar and brown paper.
—Mother Goose

Isn't it about time we taught our kids some *real* medical skills? There's plenty of space in the school curriculum for such esoteric subjects as the ecology of freshwater marshes and the nomenclature of plants' reproductive systems. This knowledge is hardly ever used in the students' real lives, but almost everyone needs to use first aid and practical medicine at some time!

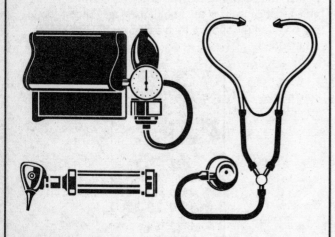

Parenting Press
A Kid's Guide to First Aid: What Would You Do If . . . ?, $4.95 plus $2.95 shipping. Ages 4–12.

What do you do if . . . Your clothes catch on fire—Your best friend is bitten by a snake while you are hiking together—Your little sister sticks her scissors in the electric socket—Someone eating with you begins to choke? Parenting Press's *A Kid's Guide to First Aid: What Do You Do If . . . ?* book presents children with these, and dozens more, real-life medical emergencies and gives them simple, illustrated rules to follow. A pictorial index helps children quickly find what to do in an emergency. It's a small investment in preparedness that could really pay off.

VISION SCREENING

NEW**
Blackbird Preschool Vision Screening System
Blackbird Story Book Home Eye Test, $9.95. Preschool Vision Screening Kit, $94.95. Ages 3–7, special needs children.

This vision screening kit is a real breakthrough! No longer do pre-readers have to learn the Snellen E or the vocabulary of the picture chart in order to have their eyes examined. You can check all your young kids with this kit in the privacy of your home.

The Blackbird Story Book Home Eye Test starts with the story of a blackbird who flies in different directions, trying to find out what kind of bird he'd like to be. Kids follow the story with hand motions, meanwhile learning "up" from "down" and "left" from "right." When they have these down, you detach the included set of screening specs. Each lens has a pop-out circle, so you can cover either the left or right eye while testing. You then measure off 10 feet away from the child (you can use the included one-foot ruler), and hold up the Blackbird cards. Turn the card of the large blackbird and ask the child which direction the blackbird is flying. Do the same for the two smaller blackbirds. The included report sheet allows you to record the results for both eyes. If your 3–5-year-old child has difficulty seeing the second blackbird with each eye, or if your 6-year or older child has trouble seeing the smallest blackbird, he needs a full eye examination. Similarly, if your child can see well but tilts his head, squints his eye, moves closer in order to see, has crossed or wandering eyes, or if your family has a history of "lazy-eye" disease, you are urged to consult an eye doctor.

For schools, the Preschool Vision Screening Kit includes instructions, guidelines, and 50 pairs of screening specs. Extra packs of screening specs are also available separately, as is a Blackbird Wall Chart, with blackbirds of various sizes in various positions. The latter is recommended for older non-English speaking or non-reading students or adults.

Teachers everywhere are raving about how simple this kit is to use and how the kids now love having their eyes tested. Kudos to Blackbird for making it available for parents at home as well!

HOUSE SAFETY

NEW★★
Perfectly Safe
Catalog, $1.

"The Catalog for Parents Who Care," with 32 pages of products for child safety. Electrical outlet protection. Appliance latches. Stove protection. Bathroom protection. Portable monitors for baby's room. First aid kits. Pool safety (alarms, life vests). Bike safety (helmets, pads). Safety skates and trikes. Car seats, baby shades. Escape ladders, fire alarms. Choke tube (to check size of child's toys). Books on kid-proofing your house and house-proofing your kids! Simple one-stop shopping.

DOG SAFETY

NEW★★
M R K Publishing
Jellybean, $19.95 plus $4 shipping. Adults read the book, apply info to protect their children.

Every year, hundreds of children are bitten seriously by dogs—sometimes even their very own pets. Yet "dog safety" and "proper dog handling" are not subjects commonly taught in safety courses. Dog psychologist C. W. Meisterfeld, a man with lots of experience reclaiming dogs that have been turned vicious through the foolish mistraining provided by their own-

ers, has written a book on this subject. This is it: *Jelly Bean versus Dr. Jekyll & Mr. Hyde: Written for the Safety of Our Children and the Welfare of Our Dogs*. The strange title refers to an actual case (described in the book) of a dog with excellent breeding and loving owners who turned into a menace, but was reclaimed by Dr. Meisterfeld. The book itself, besides the story of Jelly Bean, explains how dog personality and dog behavior work, why dogs "go around the bend" and start attacking their own owners, and Dr. Meisterfeld's own "totally positive" system of dog training, as contrasted with the jerk-em-around school of thought. The book includes numerous other case histories (with photos) along with Jelly Bean's. One photo shows a child whose dog bit him in the face, and it'll cure you instantly of the idea that dog safety is some trivial little thing we can easily ignore.

I recently received a partial list of fatalities from dog bites in 1990. Half the victims on the list were babies ages 18 months or less, right down to 5 and 6 days old. All but four of the 22 fatalities were inflicted by huskies, German shepherds, wolf hybrids, chows, malamutes, pit bulls, or dogs with one parent from those breeds. If you own one of these dogs, it is especially important for you to read this book. Also note that, for every dog-bite fatality, there are hundreds or even thousands of non-fatal dog bites, many of which are disfiguring and painful. Dog-bite *deaths* occur mostly to toddlers-and-under and senior citizens. Dog-bite *injuries* can happen to anyone.

One warning: in some short sections of the book a California child psychiatrist makes some analogies between dog psychology to the training of human children. This sounds very plausible, and some of his ideas are good, but human beings are not mere animals acting on instinct. The point of child training, for Christians, is not just to get the child to behave, but to teach him how to relate to God, who does not rely totally on positive incentives alone in His relationship with His wayward children. Otherwise, recommended.

GENERAL SAFETY SKILLS

A Beka Book Publications

I'm only going to recommend one series on health and safety. Here it is: A Beka's bright, cheery, colorful *Health, Safety, and Manners* series for grades 1–6.

The books cost around $6 and follow the typical A Beka "programmed" format, where the text talks to the

VIII

child in the first person (e.g., "I will take care of my body"). I was impressed by the thoroughness of this series, and enjoy the emphasis on manners.

NEW**
TREND Enterprises, Inc.
Personal Safety Fun-To-Know Flash Cards, $3.99. *Signs and Symbols* Fun-To-Know Flash Cards, $3.99. Add $2 shipping. Minimum order $10. Ages 4–10.

Personal Safety, from TREND's popular Fun-To-Know series, teaches kids how to handle possibly life-threatening situations. Each card gives an illustrated safety rule on the front. "Be safe in stormy weather," for example, shows a child sitting safely indoors reading a book while lightning flashes outside. The back of the card contains more information about safety in that situation, plus a "What If?" exercise that presents a safety dilemma plus three possible solutions. The best choice is given and explained.

Swimming safety, fire safety, street safety, car safety, and personal safety are among the topics covered.

I especially appreciate the way these cards give kids the *reasons* behind the rules. The "What If?" scenarios only take a few seconds to introduce and read, and can be quite involving.

Another entry in TREND's Fun-To-Know series, *Signs and Symbols* is a set of 26 flash cards. Each has a symbol on the front, e.g., a STOP sign or the international handicapped symbol of a person in a wheelchair. On the back are questions designed to teach the social rules and laws pertaining to the sign. For example, on the back of the Phone card, question 4 asks,

> What is your home phone number? The Police? The Fire Department? A Poison Control Center? Hospital Emergency? Why is it important to know these numbers and post them near telephones whenever possible?

Ages 4 and up will enjoy learning to spot these signs, while older children will benefit from learning to apply these simple survival skills.

CHAPTER THIRTY-NINE

HOME ECONOMICS

Home economics has fallen on hard times. You remember our junior high school courses on housecleaning, nutrition, cooking, and sewing. Well, some people have decided that children should not be "forced" to perform "distasteful chores" such as taking out the trash or doing the dishes. To them, life at home until age 18 should be an idyllic time to lounge on the furniture while Dad does 100 percent of the cooking and cleaning and picks up all the toys and lugs out 100 percent of the trash—since Mom shouldn't be "forced" to do those "distasteful chores" either. If Junior gets a sweaty job in the supermarket hauling boxes that's OK, but at home nobody should expect him to lift a finger.

This attitude that household work is *bad* for children is ultimately both unrealistic and unhelpful. Unrealistic, because children, just like adults, truly enjoy the feeling of success that can only be obtained from a job well done that needed doing, and nothing needs doing as much as fixing up one's daily environment. Unhelpful, because sooner or later these children will be "forced" by life itself to take care of a home of their own.

The character and skills gained by children who know how to cook, clean, and sew will not only make the home a more pleasant place, but enrich their future homes as well.

MAKING CHORES PLEASANT

If you want your children to actually enjoy and become expert at their home duties, it helps to:

1) Carefully explain each step of the job. Then let your youngster try it with you helping on the tough spots.

2) Repeat step one again.

3) And again.

4) In short, don't expect a one-time lecture to do it all.

5) Count on inspecting their work forever. Everyone loves praise for a job well done, and everyone profits from immediate feedback and suggestions on how to improve a less-than-perfect job.

6) Also count on helping out every now and then, just to show that you're not dumping an unwanted job on the child.

7) Some people give allowances regardless of what the child does. We consider it smarter to pay a child for his work at a reasonable rate (assuming the family can afford it). As the Bible says, "The worker is worthy of his hire." What would it cost you to hire an outsider to do the floors weekly, or wash the dishes, or mow the lawn? Pay less than market wage at first (after all, you are training your youngster for free) and try to work up to market rate. This allows the child to take pride in his work, since you value it highly yourself.

8) Important Tip: *Give a bonus for work done with a cheerful attitude.* I promise you, this will make a real difference!

Children pick up their parents' attitudes towards work. It really pays to avoid negative comments and grumbling about your own chores. Instead, try to concentrate on the results. Take time to enjoy the clean floor, the scent of the freshly-baked bread, the line of clean damp sheets snapping in the breeze. Share with your children this artistic way of looking at the domestic arts. It worked for Tom Sawyer and it can work for you!

HOUSEWORK FOR KIDS

UPDATED✶✶
Don Aslett's Cleaning Center
Who Says It's a Woman's Job to Clean?, $5 for a personally-autographed copy. *Is There Life After Housework* video, $19.95 plus $2 shipping. Don Aslett's *Clean Report* newsletter plus catalog, free.

You want your kids excited about cleaning and doing a professional job? Think it can never happen? Think again! Don Aslett, "America's Number One Cleaning Expert," has produced a series of books on housecleaning that both educate and motivate. Of these, the most suitable for children is *Who Says It's a Woman's Job to Clean:* not because of the title but because this book, designed to ease recalcitrant hubbies into the cleaning force, is so simple and so well illustrated with

clever cartoons that even a child can understand it. Believe it: we frequently find our son Joseph reading it.

Good news: Don Aslett's Cleaning Center has purchased all rights to Don Aslett's wonderful *Is There Life After Housework* video, in which he combines comic patter with classy cleaning skills. My advice: snap it up. Our kids love the toilet humor (really, it's *clean* toilet humor), and they can't wait to clean windows, vacuum, and wash walls just like Don.

More good news: now you can get all the professional cleaning tools and supplies you need from Don Aslett's Cleaning Center! Everything from squeegees for your windows and floors to concentrated cleaning supplies (you only need four kinds to do everything in your house). Mops, buckets, sponges, lambswool dusters, dusting cloths, and even the stuff you need to seal your concrete basement floor are all covered in this catalog. Save time and aggravation—get what you need to do it right. Speedy service, good prices.

NEW✶✶
Whirlpool Appliance Information Service
Laundry Tips for Beginners, single copy free. Quantity orders, 15¢/copy.

Laundry Tips for Beginners is an oversized fold-out brochure, completely illustrated, that shows kids exactly how to do the family laundry! Kids are warned against possible mishaps (e.g., don't put plastics in to dry on a heat setting or they might melt or burn), and the reasons for sorting laundry, cleaning lint traps, and so on are all explained. No ads for Whirlpool washers or dryers, just excellent step-by-step laundering instructions. Need I say more?

NEATNESS COUNTS

Montessori Services

I read somewhere that boys who grew up doing chores had more success in business, happier marriages, and a sunnier outlook on life as adults than boys whose parents did all the picking up. (Don't you just love studies like this?) Extrapolating from the data, I surmise that the same would be true of girls. The problem is, *how* to get the kids to help?

If you start while the children are young enough, and if you don't make the fatal mistakes of grouching about your own chores and trying to shove off all the worst jobs on the kids, you are halfway there. But only halfway. No matter how willing a little child may be to help, he just won't be strong enough to shove around an adult-sized broom or use the other standard-sized cleaning implements we all take for granted.

Decades ago Maria Montessori, an Italian physician, discovered the amazing fact that kids do a *much* better job of helping out if they are given tools their own size. There is, of course, a lot more to the Montessori philosophy than this. However, since we're being practical at the moment, let's focus on the large array of kid-sized tools available from Montessori Services, a company founded to produce and distribute products necessary to Montessori education. For the two- to seven-year-old set, Montessori Services carries kid-sized household tools. Would you believe a kid-sized scrubbing board (you can't even find adult-sized scrubbing boards nowadays!). Child-sized clothespins? Vinyl and cloth aprons for all ages of children? Kid-sized apple corers and brooms and washbasins? Mops, brooms, dustpans, baking equipment, and so on, all sized for little hands? Good quality, not like that discount store stuff. Montessori schools shop from this catalog, so if it will hold up for their classes of kids, it should hold up for yours.

Not a lot of high-tech stuff here, you'll notice—no kiddie vacuum cleaners—but everything your child needs to take care of the house the way Grandma used to.

COOKING FOR KIDS

Children's Small Press Collection
Come and Get It: family/library/school edition, $13.95; paperback, $8.95. Shipping extra. Grades preK–9.

Spiral-bound natural foods cookbook for kids. Printed in lovely, readable calligraphy. Yellow pages, for beginners, have no-cook recipes; green pages are easy-to-cook recipes; orange, intermediate recipes. Red pages, for the advanced, have dishes like tacos and pizza. Nice normal recipes, occasional lighthearted illustrations, no refined sugars, closing section on what vitamins come from what food and what each is good for. Your choice of two editions: a hardcover family/library/school edition, or the handy paperback edition.

NEW**
Klutz Press
KidsCooking, $11.95. *KidsCooking* with muffin tin, $16. Shipping extra. Ages 6 and up.

I love it! This is great! It's *KidsCooking: A Very Slightly Messy Manual* from the geniuses at Klutz Press. Like other Klutz books, it's bound with wire spirals, printed on wipe-clean heavy-duty cardstock, heavily illustrated with cute and corny full-color drawings, loaded with sensible instructions, and packaged with a "goodie." This time the goodie is a set of colored plastic measuring spoons, or (your choice) a mini muffin tin.

All this nifty packaging wouldn't count unless the recipes were good. They are. Basics like four ways to cook eggs and three recipes for popcorn. Fudge brownies from scratch. Burritos. Spaghetti. Fruit salad. Chocolate chip cookies. Not-so-basics like homemade applesauce and carrot-raisin salad. Something for every meal course and time of day, from early morning breakfast to party desserts. Plus inedibles like play dough, face paint, finger paints, giant soap bubbles, and puppy crackers.

I could swear I've seen every recipe in this book (except the play dough and puppy crackers) at some potluck supper or other over the last 10 years, testifying to the all-American canniness of the recipe choosers. Sixty-eight parent-approved and taste-tested recipes in all, each explained so simply that the average preteen can make 'em. The best kids' cookbook; the bestseller.

NEW**
Montessori Services
Small World Cookbook, $9 plus $3 shipping. Ages 2–6, adult help needed for some recipes.

Is this a cookbook or a course in world cultures? Here's a bunch of recipes that children ages 2-6 can either help with or cook entirely by themselves, all coded to show the amount of involvement you should expect. *Small World Cookbook* has recipes from every continent, color-coded to match the world puzzle maps used in Montessori schools. Each section includes cultural information, simple games and craft activities (e.g., how to make a no-fuss piñata), and very nice, simple, basic recipes. You like Belgian waffles? Irish soda bread? Chicken teriyaki? Fruit and veggie curry? Chicken Kiev? (It's torture to write this just before dinner time!) A marvelous resource for adding to unit studies on countries.

R & E Publishers
Learning with Cooking, $7.95 plus $2 shipping.

If you really want to get fancy with *educational* cooking—*Learning With Cooking: A Cooking Program for Children Two to Ten* is for you. This large, spiral-bound book covers how to teach concepts through cooking, four different approaches to a cooking program, how to organize and finance a cooking program (no problem for you at home!), recipes for different age groups, "parent-initiated cooking experiences," and all sorts of recipes. The book is salted with humor and experience:

> Try to overcome your own feelings of personal likes and dislikes and present the food in a matter-of-fact way. If a child says, "I don't want to eat it," or, "I don't like that," you can say, "You don't have to eat it, just help us fix it for someone else. I like it." . . . You might be amazed when a child who has already committed himself to, "I can't stand it!" will then eat the repulsive food as he sits at the eating table watching other children and the adult eat this "awful stuff." He might taste, even eat three helpings of this terrible food *when he has the choice.*

You might call *Learning Through Cooking* a child psychology of cooking mixed with teaching techniques

and a lot of info. With six (count 'em) indexes and a bibliography, there's a whole lot of bakin' going on.

Sycamore Tree

Sycamore Tree's catalog has a decent little section on Cooking and Nutrition, emphasizing sugarless and meatless cooking as well as simple recipes. Get their catalog for the latest listings.

Warren Publishing Company/Totline Press
Super Snacks, $3.95 plus $2 shipping.

A compendium of seasonal, sugarless snacks that also contain no honey or sweeteners of any kind. Designed primarily for day-care centers, the book is laid out month-by-month, with easy recipes and inviting graphics on each page. Fruit is the stand-in for other sweeteners in the sweet recipes like Egg Nog and Rice Pudding. You get almost 60 pages of popular recipes and an index. No spiral binding, unfortunately. Title in its present form is slated to go out of print in July 1992.

NEW**
Whirlpool Appliance Information Service
Adventures in Basic Cooking, single copy free. Quantity orders, 25¢/copy.

This excellent booklet with 24 illustrated jelly-proof pages belongs in every home. *Adventures in Basic Cooking* explains basic safety and economy rules for each appliance covered in the book: stovetop, oven, microwave, refrigerator, dishwasher, and trash compacter. It defines basic food-preparation terms such as *slice, chop,* and *roast.* It explains how each appliance works and which pots and pans to use with each. It even includes simple recipes for stovetop, oven, microwave, and refrigerator! A basic home economics course for beginning cooks, and it's *free!*

DRESSMAKING AND SEWING

EDC Publishing

Knitting, Making Clothes, $5.95 each, ages 11–adult. Beginner's Guide to Sewing and Knitting, $2.95, ages 8–adult.

The Usborne series from England, published in the U.S.A. by EDC, has recently added a guide to knitting and a guide to making clothes. Like other Usborne books, these colorful, large (but not thick) glossy paperbacks teach technical terms and techniques in an inventive cartoon style. Each book contains several projects so the novice sewer or knitter can put theory into practice. The *Guide to Knitting* and *Guide to Making Clothes* are designed for young teens on up.

Even more simply, the *Beginner's Guide to Sewing and Knitting* presents the basics for 10-year-olds and above.

NEW**
Right at Home Productions

The Dorcas Series, $35. Creative Sewing Kits, $2–$6 each. Add 10% shipping ($2 minimum). Grades K–12.

Teach your kids basic sewing skills and Christian character traits with *non-clothes* sewing projects. That's the purpose of *The Dorcas Series,* a set of 60 sewing projects that includes patterns and instructions for both older and younger children, but not fabrics or notions.

The idea behind non-clothes sewing is that

(1) Sewing clothes is expensive . . .
(2) And traumatic, if the clothes don't turn out perfectly the first time . . .
(3) And complicated, if the clothes are to look halfway decent.

Instead, *The Dorcas Series* provides 15 projects in each of these categories:

- "The Growing Disciple"—items like prayer pillows, memory verse treasure chest, a church shoe box (special place to keep shoes ready for churchgoing), tithe purse, Bible book cover, and Scripture banner.

- "The Loving Sibling"—gifts and baby needs like a mini diaper bag, receiving blanket, hooded towel and washcloth set, stroller bag, and crib mobile.

- "The Family Helper"—organizers and gifts like a bread basket, fabric lunch sack, teddy-bear pillow for storing pajamas, quilted wallet, and four-sided cleaning cloth.

- "The Playful Learner"—homemade games and toys like a numbered quilt, checkerboard made of glued-on felt squares, magnetic fishing game, fuzzy football for indoor play, juggler's beanbag set, car town play mat, and playhouse table cover.

The entire 60 projects, plus a glossary of fabric terms and another glossary of sewing terms, comes in a tabbed three-ring binder. The introduction explains the program philosophy, plus how to organize and keep records for your home school. A reproducible monthly planning sheet is included, so you can plan your excursions to the fabric store and coordinate projects your child might like to give as gifts with upcoming birthdays and holidays. Each pattern is numbered and color-coded, so you can keep it organized after cutting it out and using it the first time. (Program author Ellen Lyman suggest storing pattern pieces for each project in a ziplock bag, which could be three-hole-punched to keep in the binder with its instructions.)

Each project begins with a character or function objective, e.g., "Designed to encourage your children to spend time each day in prayer with God," or "Designed to encourage your children to store their pajamas where they'll be sure to find them each night!" Next are illustrations of the finished project as completed according to the instructions for younger and older children. Next, skills learned are listed separately for both younger and older children, as are supplies required and patterns to cut out. Illustrated directions for younger children are next, followed by illustrated directions for older children, and additional ideas and variations for each project. Color-coded pattern sheets are last (generally, only older children's projects use patterns).

What do kids learn with *The Dorcas Series*? Little kids learn to use a measuring tape, pin and cut out patterns, glue, stitch, decorate, and use pinking shears. Some of the "Playful Learner" projects are also designed to help teach younger kids regular academic skills like counting, time telling, and numbers, colors, letters, and shapes. Older children can use a sewing machine for straight seams, finish edges, appliqué, and perform more complicated maneuvers such as turning stuffed pieces inside out before stuffing and then whip-

stitching the last edge. Older children also use buttons, bias tape, lace, zippers, velcro, batting, fabric paint pens, and other popular sewing notions. They also are supposed to learn to have a pious devotional life, serve their family, love their baby brothers and sisters, and have fun!

Right at Home Productions also sells a number of projects from *The Dorcas Series* as kits. These kits do include pre-cut fabrics and notions, and are just the thing for a quick rainy-day project. Also available: over 50 books on sewing, knitting, crochet, quilting, patchwork, appliqué, embroidery, cross-stitch, and other crafts.

CHAPTER FORTY

PHYSICAL EDUCATION

For physical education, you need both a program that takes you through all the different stretching, strengthening, and coordination skills and a daily (or at least thrice-weekly) program of actual aerobic exercise—preferably exercise that increases your coordination while it tones your heart, lungs, and body. A *home* physical education program needs to be all this, plus not require gym facilities or expensive equipment, plus be doable by individuals or small groups (no large team sports), plus be interesting enough for your children to want to keep with it.

Happily, I have been able to locate two programs that together meet all these tests. See below!

NEW★★
Christian Life Workshops
Fun Physical Education for the Home School, $15.95 plus $2.50 shipping.
Ages 0–10.

Some of us are beautiful and lithe. Others are not. Sono Harris, wife of well-known home schooling speaker Gregg Harris, falls into the beautiful and lithe category. (Where *I* fall is nobody's business!) Sono's agility is no accident, though; it's based on her personal fitness program. Her interest in fitness inspired Sono to develop a fitness program for her home schooled

sons, to develop their coordination, strength, flexibility, and stamina. Son Joshua at the age of 10 was already an award-winning gymnast, indicating that Sono must be doing something right.

Sono's home program, refined and tested, is now available for other home schooling families. What you get is two cassette tapes and a very nice booklet with an outline of the cassette presentation, detailed explanations of the movements, and room in the margins for your notes. You listen to the cassettes and follow along in the booklet. The combination of listening, reading, and taking notes will help you remember what you're learning much better.

Sono starts out by explaining the need for physical education, what a good phys ed program should provide, and why a home phys ed program can be superior to classroom or institutional (e.g., YMCA) physical education. She then gives a complete phys ed program for all preteen age groups from infants on up. Fun exercises for strengthening come first, separated by age group and body section exercised. Shoulder and thorax exercises for each age group come first, then leg exercises, then abdominal exercises. Sono doesn't forget to list games and play equipment that have physical education benefits, either. Next are fun exercises for stretching feet and ankles, flexing and pointing games, leg stretching activities, and activities for stretching hips and back.

These really are "fun" exercises. Consider the following example for one-leg balance:

> Marionette Puppet: Mother acts as puppeteer and gives commands to puppet (e.g., "I just pulled the string attached to your left elbow up high; I dropped it. I pulled the string on your right knee. I pulled the string on your left hand up high.")

After all this, we move on to locomotor movement. Sono includes a helpful chart showing the definitions of various movement terms, how you would use the movement in everyday life, and how you would use it in dance. She then provides simple locomotion exercises (some straight from the Monty Python Ministry of Silly Walks), basic tumbling exercises, and eye-hand coordination skill exercises. For every one of these activities, Sono describes the exact movements needed to perform it correctly. Finally, as a bonus, she has an extended section on how to incorporate academic training into your phys ed program. This can be quite simple, such as stressing "right" and "left" movements, or more sophisticated, such as reviewing long and short vowel sounds by switching between different physical positions when you hear each type of sound. How about "dancing" your punctuation lesson, with a different movement for every punctuation symbol that should be inserted in the sentence? Sono tells you how to do it!

Sono's program covers all the basic physical skills, with specific exercises for each age level from babies on up! It's pre-ballet, pre-gymnastics, and pre-team sports, all rolled into one inexpensive, easy package. If you faithfully follow her program, your kids will have a well-rounded physical education (not to mention well-rounded biceps, triceps, and quadriceps!).

NEW**
Home Life
Juggling Step by Step video (VHS only): $25 for the half-hour video, $49.95 for the two-hour video. *The Complete Juggler* book, $14.95. Flutterflies scarves (three nylon scarves with complete directions in self-mailer), $9.95. Round beanbags (set of 3), $15. Tough beanbags (lifetime guarantee, set of 3, cubes), $13. Ribbed balls set, $7.50. Bouncy solid rubber balls set, $15. Clubs set, $29. Rings set, $19. Devil Stick set (includes two handsticks), $19. Junior Juggling Kit (3 each of child-sized scarves, ribbed balls, clubs, and rings plus instructions), $35. More kits, new equipment frequently added. Add 10% shipping USA/Canada, 25% overseas ground, 60% overseas air mail. Ages 4 and up (scarves), 6 and up (beanbags and balls), 7 and up (clubs, rings, devil sticks).

Physical education can be a difficult subject in the home school. Not all of us live on farms; many families lack enough outside space to play most sports. It's also difficult to find activities suitable for all ages to play together, and then there's all those rainy days with everyone trapped inside!

Calisthenics are one answer, but let's face it, they're not much fun. Aerobic exercises to Christian music are another possibility, but many of us lack the motivation to really work up a sweat when we're at home with just the family.

Our family has finally discovered the perfect solution to these problems. It's called "juggling." Now before you tell me that juggling is just for those with special talent, and that you tried to learn once but failed, let me explain that I know *exactly* where you're coming from. I, too, tried to learn to juggle with *Juggling for the Complete Klutz*. I, too, failed miserably. (Bill did learn to juggle a little with that book, so it does work for *some* people.) But, in the providence of the Lord, we discovered a wonderful wholesale source of juggling equipment and how-to videos that really make it possible for a Total Klutz like myself to learn to juggle, and got so excited we now sell it through Home Life, our home business.

Why juggling? Because it's • great aerobic exercise • tremendously motivating exercise • takes little room • takes little money (you can get our most deluxe juggling kit for less than the price of two good tennis rackets) • develops coordination and the catching and throwing skills needed in most games • promotes family togetherness • and can even become a profitable hobby or career! All members of the family can practice juggling at their own level, all having fun and getting lots of good exercise at the same time. You don't have to set aside any "school time" for juggling, since all your kids will consider it play and do it during recess! Nor does it necessarily take a long time before you can impress your friends and neighbors. The day we saw the video, I was able to juggle three scarves briefly. A week later I was just starting to juggle three balls. Now, a year later, I can juggle three balls almost forever (including fancy tricks like "clawing" and "Mill's Mess"), juggle four balls for 10 or more catches, juggle three clubs or rings, and Bill and I can pass-juggle six beanbags back and forth. Pretty soon we'll be able to team-juggle six clubs. Every child of ours over the age of four can now juggle three scarves, and the older ones can handle balls and rings as well. For more inspiration, consider this: *the two 15-year-old boys on the video who demonstrate team club juggling had only been juggling for three years.* Compare that to a sport like baseball or figure skating, where you have to start practically in the cradle to become a professional!

Believe me, you'll look on juggling in an entirely different light after watching the tremendously entertaining and educational *Juggling Step-by-Step* video! In *Juggling Step-by-Step* you meet Professor Confidence (a smooth fellow in tophat and tails who introduces the lessons and performs many of the moves), Won Israel (a colorful little clown), Amy (a beautiful Filipino girl), Andrew (an incredibly talented young juggler), John (a great club juggler), and Robert (a Huck Finn-type kid). Each of these has a particular speciality: balls, clubs, rings, scarves, devil sticks, diabolo, and team juggling are some of the topics covered. Again, after the first lessons on basic moves, you are expected to pick up more advanced moves from simply watching the tape. The lessons and illustrative performances are set to music, and are as much fun to watch as a stage show.

The *Juggling Step-by-Step* video is available in both a less-expensive ½ hour version and the full two-hour version. The ½ hour version gives you a basic introduction to juggling scarves, beanbags, balls, rings, and clubs. The full two-hour version includes everything on the ½ hour version, and then goes on to more advanced routines with clubs, balls, unusual equipment like cigar boxes and hats, and even flaming torches! You'll also be introduced to team juggling, juggling with many objects, multiplex juggling, two-in-one-hand, and lots more. Each instruction sequence includes a routine by some really great jugglers. These videos are a quantum leap in juggling education.

Since not every single move on the video is explained in detail, I recommend you also get the *Complete Juggler* book. It includes detailed illustrated directions for all the moves on the two-hour video.

Here's why none of your friends can juggle—they started out with beanbags (or balls, or oranges). Here's what you should do; pitch the beanbags and try our juggling scarves. These "training wheels of the juggling world" can repair your sagging confidence, and as an added benefit they won't knock over vases. Once you have mastered scarves, *then* move on to beanbags, but *only after watching the video several times.* Juggling is just too hard to learn from a book for most of us; we need to *see* how it works. Even a juggling friend can't show you the moves in slow motion, but the video can (and does)!

One final word on juggling as the ultimate family sport: When's the last time you saw two guys throwing a football, baseball, soccer ball, or hockey puck back and forth on a street corner, with a hat beside them on the ground, and people throwing money into the hat? Now if they'd been passing *juggling clubs* instead . . . Get in on the ground floor while you can!

NEW**
Teaching Home
October/November 1988 back issue, $3.75. Complete six-issue set of 1988 back issues, $17.50, includes free set of 6 plastic magazine holders for your ring binder.

The October/November 1988 issue of *Teaching Home* magazine was a twofer: two for the price of one. It covered both health *and* physical education! Issues like that one, frankly, depress me. For one thing, I found out I'd *never* get the President's Physical Fitness Award, even if I weren't too old already to compete for it. (My chances are good, however, for the Physical Fatness Award.) I also found out I knew even less on the subject than I thought I did. The good news is that now I've read the issue, and so am much wiser than before! The even better news is that for less than $4 all this wisdom can also be yours. Topics include how to teach phys ed, walking for fitness, indoor P.E., how support groups can fill P.E. needs, and exactly what it takes to win the President's Physical Fitness Award. Plus, as I said, all that good info on teaching health ed as well!

PLAY AND EXERCISE EQUIPMENT

If you're thinking of making a major investment in play equipment, you might first want to send for Community Plaything's free illustrated booklet, *Criteria for Selecting Play Equipment for Early Childhood Education.*

The booklet is more interesting than it sounds, containing numerous candid pix of children playing with (naturally) Community Playthings equipment. The booklet is both philosophical (stressing cooperative play) and a handy guide to what equipment is best for what age, and what features make for superior equipment. There is also a section on the special play needs of handicapped children. You don't have to take all the suggestions as gospel—if you do, you will end up spending your year's wages!

Childcraft Educational Corporation
Constructive Playthings

These companies both offer standard playground equipment, plus exercise equipment for indoors such as balance beams and mats.

Child Life Play Specialties
Sample prices: Jungle End Swing Set, $585. Complete Fireman's Gym, $465. Kinder climber, with platform, knotted rope, and climbing pole, $205. Knotted rope alone, $20 (it's manilla, with large knots). Doorway Gym, $40. Kits are about 20% less. Shipping is extra.

Play equipment is this Massachusetts company's only product. It's durable and distinctive, too, painted with lead-free forest green enamel. Products are all made from Northern hardwoods except for chains and ropes and suchlike. The prices are quite acceptable

considering the quality, and you can start with a basic frame and add on accessories, such as swings and ladders. Some products are also available in kit form.

Child Life has quite a few small items, such as their Doorway Gym, their Knotted Rope, a Tree Hanger that attaches a swing to any tree of at least sixteen inches diameter, etc. Many items are clever and innovative. The Doorway Gym, for example, includes a flexible belt swing, a trapeze bar, steel trapeze rings with comfort-grips, and a blocked climbing rope. You just hitch the contraption to your doorframe and let 'er rip. Kids can adjust the height of the paraphernalia themselves.

Do we have a Child Life swing set in our back yard? Yes, we finally do. When we moved into our house, I finally had an excuse to leave the old budget Sears T-Gym behind. After all, it was mired in about three hundred pounds of concrete! So we saved up until we could get a really BIG set from Child Life, and boy, do the kids and their friends love it!

Community Playthings
Sample prices: Variplay Triangle Set, $175. Kiddie Car, $54.50. Scooter, $87.50. Mini Scooter, $62.50. Free shipping. Grades preK–6, special needs.

Good solid play equipment, originally designed for schools and day-care centers. The Hutterite community makes its living assembling and selling these items. Many are made of solid wood and most have exceptional play value. Example: the five-piece Variplay Triangle Set. It can be a seesaw, a balance beam, a ride-a-plane, a go-cart, a wheelbarrow, a slide with steps, a steering wagon . . .

I should mention that Community Playthings equipment is quite attractive, in a sensible, solid sort of way. The maple is clear-finished, wheel hubs are painted red, and some wood is stenciled. The catalog is adorned with pictures of Hutterite children enjoying play on the equipment.

All this equipment is designed to *last*. Community Playthings has testimonials from schools that have been using the same piece of equipment for 20 years. This explains why their products cost more—over $100 for a tricycle, for example. The machine in question has a solid wheel (no spokes), and a frame that Superman would get a workout trying to bend. Prices are significantly less than the other institutional suppliers, like Childcraft. It's a real alternative to the tinny, mass-produced items available in standard mail-order catalogs and department stores.

Rifton: for People with Disabilities

The Hutterites also manufacture very sturdy and useful exercise items for children and adults who need extra help in these areas. It all is quite attractive, as much as this type of equipment can be, and the prices are not any more outrageous than anyone else's.

MOVEMENT EDUCATION

What *did* kids do for exercise before grown-ups invented Little League, anyway? Girls played hopscotch and jumped rope. Boys shinned up trees and played pick-up games of football, baseball, stickball, and street hockey. Everyone played catch and "It" and "Blind Man's Bluff" and dodgeball. Everyone did somersaults and handstands and drove their parents crazy on rainy days running around the house.

Modern kids are fat and soft compared to their old-time counterparts, thanks to TV and adult-sponsored game leagues which force most children to spend hours waiting for a turn to play. The schools try to remedy this by providing "physical education" classes a few hours a week. These classes often provide very little exercise for the ones who need it most: just more standing around in line watching the athletes perform. We are almost at the point upper-class Americans had arrived at in 1920, not believing children will exercise unless some adult stands around and *makes* them.

There are, then, two kinds of exercise products on the home market. One is exercise furniture, like the stuff we were looking at above. There it sits, the Jungle Gym or climbing rope, trusting that children will hop on it and use it. The other is programmed "movement learning." Children are put through a series of movements and exercises in time to music. The second approach can result in a useful physical skill, such as folk dancing or ballet. But if movement education is used as an compulsory exercise program, it is a waste of time and insulting to children, besides. Just because we adults are obsessed with the shape of our bodies is no reason to dump this trip on a five-year-old!

Bright Baby Books

Homegrown Babies, $3, ages 0–8 months.*Homegrown Infants*, $3, ages 8–12 months. *Easy Going Games*, $8, ages 5–12. Add $1.50 shipping first book, 50¢ each additional. Other toys, books available.

I mentioned this company in the Baby and Toddler Education chapter, but it also belongs here. Founded by occupational therapist Barbara Sher, a lady with a lot of experience in movement and exercise training for children, Bright Baby Books publishes a whole series of physical development books with easy activities and games for different age groups.

Homegrown Infants, for babies 0–8 months, has a slightly risqué cover (crude pen sketch of undressed mom holding baby in such a way that he covers her torso). Its interior graphics are also on the amateurish side. The text contents, however, have good suggestions for stimulating and developing each muscle area, as well as general balance and mental stimulation.

Homegrown Babies, for ages 8–12 months, has better graphics. Like the first book, this is nicely arranged in logical topics, such as Movement, Self Care, Exploring and Experimenting, and Social Awareness. *Caution:* Suggested toys for baby in both these books include some that are *not* safe for him to be left alone with, since he might choke on them. The author intends for you to be there with your child as he plays with these items.

Easy Going Games, for kids 5–12, shows you how to turn mateless socks, hula hoops, and carpet squares into instant games. These are really good, doable activities that don't involve a lot of fuss. Just reading these books awakens you to new possibilities for physical development.

Kimbo Educational

Kimbo's colorful catalog has more exercise and movement albums for children than any other I've seen. Kids can mess around with folk dancing, bean bags, parachutes, Hawaiian rhythm sticks, and so on. Page after page after page of gymnastic routines (with ribbons or without), pre-ballet and ballet, tap dancing, stunts and tumbling, plus the usual leap-and-stretch stuff we all have seen for years on Romper Room. Many of the recordings feature simple, folk-style music. Some thump about with disco. Georgiana Stewart's popular *Good Morning Exercises for Kids* gets sleepy-heads moving with first gentle, then more vigorous exercises, followed by a cool-down exercise. This secular album asks children to make a good morning wish that will "last the whole day long." More vigorous stuff is available for older kids and adults, like gymnastics and various types of dance.

Kimbo has movement and exercise albums for adults, too: square dancing, slimnastics, jumpnastics, ethnic dancing, and of course the unavoidable Jackie Sorensen. Kimbo has not forgotten senior citizens, either; the elder set can work out in their chairs, if desired, with Kimbo's exercise albums for senior citizens.

Montessori Services

Perceptual-Motor Lesson Plans, Levels 1 and 2, $9.95 each. *Step By Step*, $17.95. Shipping extra. Ages 3–9.

Montessori Services devotes the entire next-to-last page of their catalog to Movement Education of a "non-competitive, non-threatening" sort. Besides parachute activities, parachutes ($66 and up), and kits with rhythm sticks and bean bags, Montessori Services offers several sets of movement education lesson plans.

Perceptual-Motor Lesson Plans is 25 weeks of activities for gross motor skills, plus equipment construction diagrams for such things as a balance beam and a jump box. Level 1 is for ages two and a half to six; Level 2 is for ages seven to nine.

Step By Step is the output of one Sheila Kogan, a Montessori teacher, dancer, and movement consultant. It has eighty flexible lesson plans and a comprehensive index. The lessons use movement to teach physical concepts and reinforce academic concepts. Most activities require little or no equipment. The rest describe "innovative uses for balls, balloons, scarves, ropes and other inexpensive props." Example: "Throw the scarf in the air and catch it. Catch it with your elbow, head, shoulder, tummy, seat, hip, knee, foot, anything but your hands." Just like the rules for that ol' competitive soccer!

SUGGESTED COURSE OF STUDY

What should your child study when?

Until this point, most of us have been more-or-less following the typical course of study devised by the public-school curriculum designers. (For those of you who are interested, it is outlined in *Typical Course of Study,* a booklet published by World Book, Inc., and available from them for a nominal price.) Most published curriculum, whether Christian or secular, uses *Typical Course of Study* or some similar guide as a rule for what should be taught when.

Looking at *Typical Course of Study,* the first thing that strikes you is the large number of skills taught in each subject at each grade level. The second thing that strikes you is the totally arbitrary nature of where many of these skills are placed. The third thing that strikes you is how often many of these skill and content areas are repeated from grade to grade.

Let's look at some examples. "Presenting original plays" is listed as a grade 5 language arts skill. "Introduction to mythology" is listed as a grade 6 learning area. The two could easily be reversed, presented at lower grades, presented at later grades, or skipped altogether (especially since the mythology presented in public schools is no longer just classic Greek and Roman mythology). Under Health and Safety, "sewage disposal" makes its one and only appearance in grade 5 (why grade 5?), while "dental health" or "dental hy-giene" is presented and re-presented eight years in a row (does it take that long to learn to floss and brush your teeth?). Sentence grammar is first presented in grade 3 (simple punctuation), skipped altogether in grade 4, and then spread out over grades 5–8, only to pop up once again in grades 10 and 11. As one girl complained to me, "They keep teaching us this stuff again and again, and I *learned* it three years ago!" Science topics appear in an equally capricious fashion, with a dozen or more topics presented each year, some of which are repeated almost every year while others are not. The solar system, in various forms, is studied every year in grades K–5. Simple machines, on the other hand, pop up only in grades 1 and 3.

Another thing worth noting about the typical course of study is that *each skill and topic is given equal emphasis.* Learning to read and write are just *part* of the language-arts program, which before children can even read already includes "simple pantomimes and dramatic play" and 15 other topics, including "development of class newspaper." "Dressing for weather and activity" and "neighborhood helpers" are not shown in any obvious way to be lower priority than "establishing sight vocabulary." This undoubtedly accounts for the huge number of cluttered projects teachers are always publishing in teachers' magazines, where first-grade kids spend a whole week making a cardboard box village in order to learn about "me and my neighborhood" rather than working on reading, writing, and arithmetic.

Our children need more than better educational resources. They need a better educational schedule. Here are what I see as the basic steps in that schedule:

1. First give kids the tools of learning (Bible, reading, writing, and arithmetic).

2. Second, present them informally with lots of data in all the subject areas.

3. Third, tie it together with organizing devices like time lines.

4. Once steps 1–3 have been accomplished, *then* introduce formal study of science, history, geography, art, and so on, while continuing to read voraciously and *discuss* what is read.

STEP ONE: THE TOOLS OF LEARNING (GRADES 1–3)

No matter how young or old your child is, here's where he needs to start once you begin taking an active part in his education and once he's passed the "readiness" stage (can use crayons, scissors, hold a pencil properly, knows left from right, etc.).

1. Bible
   A. Memorize books of the Bible in order by name.
   B. Read through the entire Bible, with explanations of the difficult parts (many times).
   C. Memorize the Ten Commandments.
2. Learn to read *well*.
3. Learn printing and handwriting.
4. Learn to write *well* (creative writing), including proper grammar and spelling.
5. Learn summarizing and narrating (child is able to recount a story well).
6. Learn basic arithmetic, from numeral recognition up to decimals and fractions.

These are the *real* basics, to be studied together until mastered. Don't assume just because he's in fifth grade that he's on top of all these areas. Check him out with Step One skills first.

If your child can't read or write well, *don't worry* about teaching him Civil War history or cell biology.

Get the reading and writing under control *first*, without distracting him with hours of studies in areas he can't handle due to his lack of language-arts skills.

STEP TWO: THE FACTS (GRADES 1–3)

You don't have to let the science and social studies vanish during the time your children are mastering the basics. Here's some simple ways to provide social studies and science facts and experiences during the first three grades of school:

1. History
   A. Read historical biographies and fiction aloud. Good readers can read them to themselves. Try to focus on explorers, inventors, entrepreneurs, scientists, artists, musicians, preachers and evangelists, mothers, writers, and so on, not just on political figures. "Daily life" books that give a feel for the cultural setting of each time period are also good.
   B. Rent historical videos.
   C. Discuss the history of each holiday as it comes up.
2. Geography
   A. Look up locations on the map or globe as they come up in family conversation.
   B. Teach the kids to use a map and globe.
   C. U. S. and world puzzles.
   D. Geography games (optional, if you have the time) .
3. Science
   A. Read science books aloud, or have the child read them alone. Topics to cover: plants, animals, farming, rocks, weather, seasons, solar system and universe, measurement, human anatomy and senses, dinosaurs, magnetism, electricity, and simple machines.
   B. Nature walks and field trips (as time permits).
   C. Pet care (if desired).
   D. Simple experiments (if time permits).
   E. Basic personal hygiene (washing, brushing, flossing, putting dirty clothes in the hamper, etc.).

Here's what *not* to bother with:

• Any K–3 formal social studies or science courses. Without exception, these are all rinky-dink.

• Units on transportation. You could with equal justification study clothing, food preparation, architecture, or cosmetics (none of which I recommend bothering with). As your child studies history and drives in your car, he is bound to pick up transportation information without any special effort.

• Units on "community helpers," "interdependence of people," "basic human needs and wants," and other code words for statism. Community helpers units teach careerism (only paid jobs are represented, never volunteers or people who serve their families and neighborhoods) and subservience (self-employment and leadership positions are rarely presented). Units on interdependence and human needs invariably present gigantic institutional structures as *the* way to live.

• All collective-guilt studies, whether the guilt be racial, ecological, religious, economic, or whatever. These sometimes come disguised as "cultural appreciation" or "conservation" studies.

• Complicated, cluttered projects that "integrate skill areas" (e.g., handwriting assignments that include spelling words). It's safer to keep those skill areas separate until you're sure your child has actually mastered the skills!

If you want to integrate Bible with social studies and science, you can use Christian books or take the time to discuss what your children are reading (a good idea anyway!). It's always interesting to look up what the Bible has to say on a subject, too. Just pick your topic (e.g., "ear" or "liberty") and look up the references found under that topic in your concordance. You can pursue such studies further by adding cross-references. Example: "hearing" and "listening" fit naturally with a study of what the Bible says about ears, just as "freedom," "slave," "slavery," and "subjection" go along with a study of liberty. This can be done on Sundays or during family devotions time, if your regular home-school time is too short. You can also draw on the Bible for reading, literature, history, handwriting, drama, narrating, science (developing a proper attitude toward creation and the Creator), and even grammar assignments—McGuffey did!

The first three grades are also a good time to introduce the rudiments of baking, sewing, housecleaning, child care, and other daily-life skills. Again, with the exception of personal cleanliness and picking up after oneself, these can be fit in as time allows.

STEP THREE: PUTTING IT ALL TOGETHER WITH FORMAL STUDIES (GRADES 4–6)

We're only in the fourth grade at this point, so there is no reason to panic just because your son or daughter isn't sure whether Columbus discovered America in 1492 or 1776. (Let's keep this in perspective: a hefty minority of high-school graduates aren't sure about the dates either!) Up to this point we've been working on stories, not dates. Does your child know Columbus discovered America? Good: that's the first step! Now's the time to start your history time line, if you haven't already, and to perhaps work through a beginning history textbook. Now is also the time to get a bit more systematic about science (if desired), although serious science studies can really wait until junior high or even high school without major educational consequences.

I am not suggesting "dumbing down" the curriculum. I am suggesting that it's dumb to suffocate kids with more information than they are able to remember. Keep in mind also that the public schools teach kids all the information from this age onwards at least *twice*. The assumption is that they will *not* learn or remember most of it the first time around. My position is that we shouldn't teach them material we don't expect them to remember in the first place. Thus, it makes more sense to present the excellent fourth- through sixth-grade history and geography texts to seventh- through ninth-graders, who will actually be able to retain all that information, than to the age group for which they were written.

Therefore, here's what I suggest for grades 4–6:

1. Bible studies
   A. Time line.
   B. Maps (Middle Eastern geography).
   C. Memorizing the theme and a key verse for each book of the Bible.
   D. Knowing how to quickly look up any given Bible verse.
   E. Hebrew and Greek alphabets.
   F. Use of the basic Bible tools (dictionary, concordance).
2. Reading: a lot. Include good classic literature. Some Nancy Drew and Hardy Boys won't hurt, but don't let that level of book be *all* they read. If a child reads a lot, you can almost get away with skipping everything else except math. (I am *not* suggesting that you do this!)
3. Handwriting: developing a beautiful hand. Typing can be taught now, but is optional (do only if time permits).

4. Creative writing: all literary types (letters, journals, poems, stories, essays, plays, memos, reports, newspaper articles). Pen pals are great, as is writing for one of the homemade homeschool-kids newsletters.

5. Oral presentation skills.

6. Grammar: formal study. It should only take a year or so to cover *all* of it at this age level.

7. Spelling: formal study if necessary (some children are naturally almost-perfect spellers). Rule-based program and child's own misspelled words, not canned "word lists."

8. Arithmetic: continue. If finished, proceed on to pre-algebra, etc.

9. Geometry.

10. History.
    A. Time line of U.S. history.
    B. Time line of world history.
    C. First history textbook (if desired: semi-formal study; read it as a book and *discuss* it).
    D. More mature history-oriented books from the library or EDC Publishing, etc.

11. Geography: continue as above. Add geography quizzes and drills, if desired.

12. Science.
    A. Engineering with construction kits (e.g., LEGO Dacta, fishertechnik).
    B. Simple experiments every now and then (child has more responsibility for setting up experiments on his own, calls you over to see the results).
    C. First science textbook (if desired; semi-formal study; do exercises, but don't worry about keeping up a standard classroom pace).
    D. History of science (through biographies or as a separate study). Can also be done later.

13. Health and safety: totally informal, as family situations arise (e.g., washing wound and putting on bandage, using Desitin on diaper rash, pointing pot handle to the back of the stove, etc.).

14. Physical education: pick a lifetime sport and get good at it.

15. Home economics: assign chores, let kids bake using simple recipe books. Weaving, knitting, and woodworking kits are also popular with this age group.

Of the above list, only Bible, grammar, and math actually need formal preparation time. Handwriting, creative writing, oral presentation, spelling, and engineering and science experiments require adult feedback, but not necessarily a lot of up-front teaching. If your child reads well and you get him good resources, he is able at this age to follow the instructions by himself.

FOR THOSE WHO WANT MORE

I personally feel that the elementary grades are also a fine time to introduce art, music, and foreign languages (all covered in Volume 4). Other subjects worth introducing in grades 4–6 are business, economics, and citizenship (covered in this volume). Consider adding those subjects if any of the following apply:

- Your family considers such studies part of family play time, so they don't take any extra time from your day.

- Your family has a history of being musical (or artistic, or good at languages, or owning your own business) and you feel one of these subjects is likely to become your child's vocation.

- You are using resources that don't require you to prepare for the lessons.

- You are willing to take several weeks at a time off from your normal studies to really get into these new areas and get comfortable with them, or you have the basic studies under control and can afford the extra time for regular instruction in these areas.

Remember, the more time you spend on the basics, the more time you'll have later on to spend on everything else!

INDEXES

INDEX OF AMERICAN SUPPLIERS

A Beka Book Publications
Box 18000
Pensacola, FL 32523-9160
1-800-874-BEKA (2352) M–F 8–4:30
VISA,MC. FL: (904) 478-8480
Fax: (904) 478-8558
Free catalog, order form, and brochures. Returns: In resalable condition, in original packaging, within 120 days.
Christian texts and supplies, preK–12.

Academic Therapy Publications
20 Commercial Boulevard
Novato, CA 94949-6191
1-800-422-7249 for location of nearest distributor.
Check or M.O., AmEx.
(415) 883-3314
Fax: (415) 883-3720
Free catalog. Returns: With permission, in resalable condition.
Remedial educational materials.

Academy for Economic Education
125 Sovran Center
Richmond, VA 23277
(804) 643-0071 Check or M.O.
Economics education programs.

Accent Publications
P.O. Box 15337
Denver, CO 80215-0337
Free examination packet. Specify department.
Bible program.

Achievement Basics
800 South Fenton Street
Denver, CO 80226
(303) 935-6343 Check or M.O.
Free brochures. Returns: In resalable condition, within 15 days.
Junior Business and speaking.

Activities for Learning
21161 York Road
Hutchinson, MN 55350

(612) 587-9146 Check or M.O.
Free brochure for SASE. Returns: I resalable condition, within 30 days.
Abacus-based math curriculum.

Addison-Wesley Publishing Co.
Jacob Way
Reading, MA 01867
1-800-447-2226 VISA, MC, C.O.D.
(617) 944-3700
Fax: (617) 942-1117
Free catalog.
Textbook and trade publisher.

Advanced Training Institute of America
see Institute in Basic Life Principles

Alpha Omega Publications
P.O. Box 3153
Tempe, AZ 85280
1-800-622-3070 (orders)
VISA, MC, C.O.D.
1-800-821-4443 (information)

AZ: (602) 438-2717
Fax: (602) 438-2702
Free catalog. Returns: Unconditional
guarantee, within 30 days.
Christian curriculum.
Home school program.

Alphagator AI
P.O. Box 1325
Taylors, SC 29687
(803) 292-1990 Check or M.O.
Free brochure/catalog.
Add $2 shipping on orders less
than $25, or 5% on orders over
$25.
Returns by permission only.
Pre-reading curriculum.

American Science & Surplus
601 Linden Place
Evanston, IL 60202
(708) 475-8440 VISA, MC.
Fax: (708) 864-1589
$12.50 minimum. Flat $4 ship-
ping/order.
Catalog $1 first class, free
otherwise.
Returns: Unconditional, within 15
days, except shipping and handling.
Surplus stuff described with wit.

Ampersand Press
691 26th St.
Oakland, CA 94612
(415) 832-6669
Check or M.O., C.O.D.
Fax: (415) 832-3918
Free brochure. Returns: In original
packaging.
Educational games publisher.

Aristoplay, Ltd.
P.O. Box 7028
Ann Arbor, MI 48107
1-800-634-7738 VISA, MC.
School P.O.'s net 30.
(313) 995-4353
Fax: (313) 995-4611
Free color catalog.
Refund or exchange of damaged or
defective games.
Educational games publisher.

Arthur Bornstein School of Memory Training
11693 San Vicente Blvd.
Los Angeles, CA 90049
1-800-468-2058 VISA, MC, AmEx
(213) 478-2056
Fax: (213) 207-2433
Free brochures.
Returns: With permission, in resal-
able condition, within 14 days.
Memory training materials.

Asia Society
725 Park Avenue
New York, NY 10021
(212) 288-6400
Check or M.O., or school P.O.
Fax: (212) 517-7246
Free brochure and materials list.
Educational videos about Japan
and Korea.

Audio Memory Publishing
1433 E. 9th St.
Long Beach, CA 90813
1-800-365-SING VISA, MC.
(213) 591-1548
Free catalog with SASE. Returns:
Within 30 days.
Audio cassettes and related
educational materials.

Backyard Scientists
P.O. Box 16966
Irvine, CA 92713
(714) 551-2392 Check or M.O.
Brochure with long SASE.
Returns: In resalable condition,
within 15 days.
Books of science experiments in
physics, chemistry and life science.

Baker Book House
P.O. Box 6287
Grand Rapids, MI 49516-6287
(616) 957-3110 VISA, MC
Fax: (616) 676-9573
Christian book publisher.

Ball-Stick-Bird Publications, Inc.
P.O. Box 592
Stony Brook, NY 11790
(516) 331-9164 Check or M.O.
Free color brochure. No returns.
Reading system that even works for
labeled children.

Basic R's
731 W. Center Street
Duncanville, TX 75116
(214) 780-5615 or (214) 580-8485
Check or M.O.
Returns: In resalable condition, in
original packaging, within 21 days.
Math drill materials.

BCM Publications
237 Fairfield Ave.
Upper Darby, PA 19082
(215) 352-7177 Check or M.O.
Free catalogs.
Returns: With permission.
Bible centered lesson materials
and visuals.

Bear Creek Publications
2507 Minor Ave E.
Seattle, WA 98102
1-800-326-6566 VISA, MC.
(206) 322-7604
Free brochure with long SASE.
Returns: In resalable condition with
sales receipt.
Publishes *No Bored Babies* book.

Bellerophon Books
36 Anacapa St.
Santa Barbara, CA 93101
(805) 965-7034 Check or M.O.
Fax: (805) 965-8286
Free catalog with SASE. Returns:
For credit, within a year, in
resalable condition.
Educational coloring books and
cutout books.

Betty Lukens, Inc.
P.O. Box 1007
Rohnert Park, CA 94928
Check or M.O.
Free catalog.
Bible felts manufacturer.

BG Science, Inc.
13725 Drake Dr.
Rockville, MD 20853
(301) 460-1275 VISA, MC.
Free brochure. Returns: No
questions asked within 30 days.
Video science labs.

Bible Memory Association
P.O. Box 12000
Ringgold, LA 71068-2000
(318) 894-9154
Bible memorization course.

Bible Talk Times
P.O. Box 2503
Columbus, MS 39704
(601) 328-4879 Check or M.O.
Free brochure.
Bible-teaching newsletter.

Bible Visuals
Box 153
Akron, PA 17501-0153
(717) 859-1131 Check or M.O.
Free catalog.
Returns: With permission, in
resalable condition, within 30 days.
Bible lessons with visuals.

Bible-Science Association
P.O. Box 32457
Minneapolis, MN 55432
1-800-422-4253 VISA, MC.
(612) 755-8606
No returns on Science Readers.
Publishes creation-science series.

Bio-Alpha, Inc.
Box 7190
Fairfax Station, VA 22039-7190
Check or M.O.
Preschool activity book.

Blackbird Vision Screening System
P.O. Box 277424
Sacramento, CA 95827
(916) 363-6884 Check or M.O., or
school P.O.
Free brochure.
Returns in resalable condition
within 30 days.

Bluestocking Press
P.O. Box 1014
Placerville, CA 95667-1014
(916) 621-1123
VISA, MC. U.S. funds only.
Free info with large SASE and 2
first-class stamps. Returns: In
resalable condition, within 30 days.
Free-market economics and business
books for children and adults.

Bob Books Publications
P.O. Box 633
West Linn, OR 97068
(503) 657-1883
Primers.

Bob Jones University Press
Customer Services
Greenville, SC 29614
1-800-845-5731 EST weekdays.
VISA, MC.Free catalog. Orders and
info on toll-free line.
Returns: Resalable condition, with
permission, within 30 days.
Christian textbook publisher.

Bookstuff
4B S.W. Monroe, Box 200
Suite 139
Lake Oswego, OR 97034
(503) 288-3805 Check or M.O.
Free catalog with long SASE. Free
poster with each order. Returns:
With permission.
Pre-reading and early reading
materials.

Borenson and Associates
P.O. Box 3328
Allentown, PA 18106
(215) 820-5575 VISA, MC.
Fax: (215) 820-9993
Free brochure.
Satisfaction guaranteed.
Publishes Hands-On Equations®.

Bright Baby Books and Videos
101 Star Lane
Whitethorn, CA 95489
(707) 986-7693
Check or M.O., purchase order.
Free catalog.
Returns: Unconditional guarantee.
Physical development books.

Burt Harrison & Co., Inc.
P.O. Box 732
Weston, MA 02193-0732
(617) 647-1001 Check or M.O.
Fax: (617) 647-0675
Catalog $2, refunded with first order.
Math/science manipulatives and
publications.

Busines$ Kids
301 Almeria Ave., Suite 330
Coral Gables, FL 33134
1-800-852-4544 VISA, MC, AmEx.
Fax: (305) 445-8869
Free catalog. No returns.
The Busines$ Kit.

Calliope
30 Grove St.
Peterborough, NH 03458
(603) 924-7209
VISA, MC. $10 minimum.
Fax: (603) 924-7380
Free catalog.
Children's world history magazine.

Carden Educational Foundation
P.O. Box 659
Brookfield, CT 06804
(203) 740-9200
Free catalog. Returns: 30 days, re-
salable condition, call first.
Complete private school curriculum.

Carol Oppenheim
2214 Park Ridge Ave.
Brentwood, MO 63144
(314) 962-2884 Check or M.O.
Science book.

Carolina Biological Supply Company
2700 York Rd.
Burlington, NC 27215
1-800-334-5551
VISA, MC, Discover, AmEx. NC:
(919) 584-0381
Fax: (919) 584-3399
Catalog $16.95, free to science
teachers.
Returns: Unconditional, within 30
days.
Huge K–12 math/science catalog.

**Center for Science in the Public
Interest**
Suite 300
1875 Connecticut Ave. N.W.
Washington, DC 20009-5728
(202) 332-9110 VISA, MC.
Fax: (202) 265-4954
Free catalog.
Returns: Within 30 days.
Nutrition Action Health letter.
Membership $19.95.

Chalen Edu-Systems
412 Laurel Ave.
Brielle, NJ 08730
(908) 528-6335 VISA, MC.
Reading Step-by-Step program.

Char-L, Inc.
570 S. Church, Apt. 2E
Decatur, IL 62522
(217) 422-0077
Phonics course.

Charlie Duke Enterprises
P.O. Box 310345
New Braunfels, TX 78131-0345
(512) 629-1223 VISA, MC
Fax: (512) 620-1255
Moonwalk videos.

Cheryl Morris
"Teach America to Read"
1150 Fairview
Fruitland, ID 83619
Check or M.O.
Free brochure with SASE.
Phonics program.

Child Evangelism Fellowship Press
Box 348
Warrenton, MO 63383
1-800-748-7710 VISA, MC, C.O.D.
(314) 456-4321
Fax: (314) 456-2078
Free catalog. Returns: With permission, in resalable condition, within 270 days.
Multimedia evangelism, teaching.

Child Life Play Specialties
55 Whitney St.
Holliston, MA 01746
1-800-462-4445 VISA, MC.
(508) 429-4639
Free catalog.
Replace transit-damaged parts.
10 year warranty.
Wood outdoor playground equipment.

Childcraft Education Corp.
20 Kilmer Rd.
Edison, NJ 08818
1-800-631-5657 9–6 M–F EST.
VISA, MC, AmEx.
NJ: 1-800-624-0840
Free color catalog.
Returns: With permission, within

30 days, unused.
Educational furniture, toys, and games.

Children's Bible Hour
Box 1
Grand Rapids, MI 49501
(616) 451-2009 VISA, MC.
Free catalog.
Returns: Unconditional.
Radio programs, Christian tapes, audio-visual materials for kids.

Children's Small Press Collection
719 North Fourth Avenue
Ann Arbor, MI 48104
1-800-221-8056 VISA, MC.
MI: (313) 668-8056
Free catalog.
Returns: In resalable condition.
Children's books, records, and games from more than 100 small publishers.

Childshop
P.O. Box 597
Burton, OH 44021-0597
VISA, MC, Discover.
Catalog $1.
Unconditional guarantee.
Children's woodcraft plans and kits.

Christ Centered Publications, Inc.
2101 North Partin Drive
Niceville, FL 32578
(904) 678-9621 VISA, MC, C.O.D.
Free information.
Phonics, reading, and math materials for ages 3–7.

Christian Book Distributors
Box 3687
Peabody, MA 01961-3687
(617) 532-5300 VISA, MC.
Free sample catalog. Returns: Shipping mistakes, defective products.
Membership $3/year. You don't have to be a member to order.
Discount Christian books/Bibles.

Christian Equippers
P.O. Box 16100
South Lake Tahoe, CA 95706
(916) 542-1509
Fax: (916) 541-7980
Publisher of creationist books.

Christian Liberty Academy
see Christian Liberty Press

Christian Liberty Press
502 W. Euclid Ave.
Arlington Heights, IL 60004
(708) 259-8736 Check or M.O.
Free catalog and brochure.
Returns: Within 30 days, 10% restocking charge.
Christian textbooks/home-school program.

Christian Life Workshops
P.O. Box 2250
Gresham, OR 97030
(503) 667-3942 VISA, MC.
Catalog and brochure $1.
Returns: 100% refund, except shipping and handling, in resalable condition, within 30 days.
Home-school workshops, rescources.

Christian Light Education
see Christian Light Publications

Christian Light Publications
1066 Chicago Ave.
P.O. Box 1126
Harrisonburg, VA 22801-1126
(703) 434-0750 VISA, MC, C.O.D.
Free catalog, brochure, and samples. Returns: With permission, in resalable condition, within 30 days.
Science equipment, curriculum, and school supplies, Mennonite-approved books.

Christian Schools International
3350 E. Paris Ave., S.E.
Grand Rapids, MI 49512
1-800-635-8288 VISA, MC.
Canada: 1-800-637-8288
(616) 957-1070
Fax: (616) 957-5022
Free catalog.
Returns: Within 60 days, in resalable condition, with authorization.
60-day examination privilege for pre-paid and credit card orders.
Christian textbooks.

Returns: In resalable condition.
MEMLOK Bible memory system.

Cobblestone Publishing
30 Grove St.
Peterborough, NH 03458
(603) 924-7209
VISA, MC. $10 minimum.
Fax: (603) 924-7380. Free catalog.
Children's magazines.

Community Playthings
Route 213
Rifton, NY 12471
(914) 658-3141 Check or M.O.
Fax: (914) 658-8065
Free catalog. Returns: With permission, in resalable condition.
Toys and equipment for infants through five years.

Concerned Communications
Highway 59 North
Siloam Springs, AR 72761
1-800-447-4332 Check or M.O.
Free catalog.
Returns: With permission, in resalable condition, within 30 days.
Christian handwriting course.

Constructive Playthings
1227 E. 119th St.
Grandview, MO 64030
1-800-255-6124 VISA, MC
MO: (816) 761-5900
Fax: (816) 761-9295
Free home catalog. Free catalog of Jewish educational materials. Play furniture, toys, school supplies preK–3.

Contemporary Books
Attn: Wendy Harris
180 N. Michigan Ave.
Chicago, IL 60601
1-800-621-1918
(312) 782-9181
Fax: (312) 782-2157
Number Sense math program.

Cornerstone Curriculum Project
2006 Flat Creek
Richardson, TX 75080
(214) 235-5149 Check or M.O.
Free brochure. Returns: In resalable condition, within 30 days.
Home-school curriculum publisher.

Crane's Select Educational Materials
P.O. Box 124
Bedford, IN 47421
(812) 279-3434
Check or M.O., C.O.D.
Catalog $1, refunded with first order. Returns: Unconditional, in resalable condition, within 30 days.
Supplemental teaching materials catalog.

Creation's Child
P.O. Box 3004 #44
Corvallis, OR 97339
(503) 758-3413 Check or M.O.
Free brochure with SASE.
Returns: In resalable condtion, within 30 days.
Home-school supplies.

Creative Teaching Associates
Attention: Laurie Long
P.O. Box 7766
Fresno, CA 93747
(209) 291-6626
Fax: (209) 291-2953
Catalog $1.
Returns: With permission, in resalable condition, in original packaging.
Educational games preK–12.

Crossway Books
1300 Crescent St.
Wheaton, IL 60187
(708) 682-4300 Check or M.O.
Fax: (708) 682-4785
Free brochure.
Publisher.

CUBE-IT! Manipulative Math
P.O. Box 141411
Spokane, WA 99214
(509) 928-6843 8-5 M-Sat PST.
VISA, MC, budget plan available (for Series 1, 2 or 3).
Free catalog. Returns: With permission, in resalable condition, in original packaging, within 5 days.
Publishers of Cube-It! Manipulative Math, Counting House.

Cuisenaire Company of America
12 Church Street, Box D
New Rochelle, NY 10802
1-800-237-3142 VISA, MC, C.O.D.

(914) 235-0900
Fax: (914) 576-3480
Free catalog and brochure with SASE.
Manufacturer of math manipulatives.

Cumberland Missionary Society, Inc.
Rt 2, Box 446
Evensville, TN 37332
(615) 775-3796 Check or M.O.
Catalog $1. Returns: Negotiable. In resalable condition only.
Publisher, *Pictorial Tract Primer*.

Dale Seymour Publications
P.O. Box 10888
Palo Alto, CA 94303
1-800-872-1100 VISA, MC. (orders)
(415) 324-2800
Fax: (415) 324-3424
Free catalog. Returns: In resalable condition, within 30 days, call first.
Publisher of supplemental teaching materials K–12.

DIDAX, Inc.
One Centennial Drive
Peabody, MA 01960
1-800-458-0024 VISA, MC.
(508) 532-9060
Fax: (508) 532-9277
Free catalog.
School supplies.

Don Aslett's Cleaning Center
P.O. Box 39
311 S. 5th
Pocatello, ID 83204
1-800-451-2402 (orders) VISA, MC, Discover, C.O.D.
ID: (208) 232-6212 (inquiries)
Free catalog and brochure.
Returns: Unconditional, within 60 days.
House cleaning supplies and books.

Donald and Mary Baker
37 Delsie Street
Clarksville, AR 72830
(501) 754-2223 or 754-3309
Check or M.O.
Free brochure with SASE. Returns: Satisfaction guaranteed.
Bible Study Guide for All Ages.

Donut Records
4518 Ensenada Dr.
Woodland Hills, CA 91364
(818) 884-3447 Check or M.O.
Sampler cassette, catalog, and $2
coupon, $2.
Bibletoons musical Bible stories.

Doorposts
P.O. Box 1610
Clackamas, OR 97015
Check or M.O.
Free brochure with long SASE.
Returns: In resalable condition,
within 10 days.
Character education materials..

Dove Christian Books
order through Christian bookstores

E-Z Grader Co.
P.O. Box 24040
Cleveland, OH 44124
(216) 831-1661 collect.
Check or M.O.
Fax: (216) 831-1667
Samples. Free brochure. Returns:
Resalable condition, within 30 days.
Grading help tools, phonics slide
rule, math aids.

Eagle Forum Education Fund
Box 618
Alton, IL 62002
(618) 462-5415 VISA, MC.
Fax: (618) 462-8909
Free brochure lists items, prices.
Phonics kits.

**Eagle's Wings Educational
Materials**
P.O. Box 502
Duncan, OK 73534
(405) 252-1555 Check or M.O.
Free brochure. Returns: Resalable
condition within 10 days.
Letterland phonics.

Easy Reading Kit
c/o Home Teachers
P.O. Box 8724
Stockton, CA 95208-0724
Check or M.O.
Free brochure.
Satisfaction guaranteed.
Beginning reading program.

EDC Publishing
Division of Educational Development
Corporation
P.O. Box 470663
Tulsa, OK 74147
(918) 622-4522 VISA, MC, C.O.D.
Fax: (918) 663-4509
Catalog $2.00 ($2.00 rebate on
first order). Returns: With
permission in resalable condition,
after 60 days, before 360 days.
10% shipping, $2.50 minimum.
Usborne books.

Edmund Scientific Company
101 East Gloucester Pike
Barrington, NJ 08007
(609) 573-6250 VISA, MC, AmEx,
Discover, and OPTIMA.
Fax: (609) 573-6295
Free catalog. Returns:
Unconditional, within 45 days.
Science supplies, optics, kits for
all ages.

Education Services
6410 Raleigh St.
Arvada, CO 80003
Books by Ruth Beechick.

Educational Design, Inc.
47 W. 13th St.
New York, NY 10011
1-800-221-9372 Check or M.O.
(212) 255-7900
Free catalog.
Returns: Within 30 days.
Skillbooks, various subjects.

Educational Insights
19560 S. Rancho Way
Dominguez Hills, CA 90220
1-800-933-3277 VISA, MC.
(213) 637-2131 or 979-1955
Fax: (213) 605-5048
Free catalog.
Returns: With permission.
10% shipping, $2 minimum.
Producer of innovative, hands-on
materials for grades K–12.

Educational Products
CBN Center
CSB336
Virginia Beach, VA 23463
1-800-288-4769 VISA, MC.

Free color brochure. Returns: Within
30 days, in resalable condition.
Total language arts K–3.

Educators Publishing Service, Inc.
75 Moulton St.
Cambridge, MA 02138-1104
1-800-225-5750 VISA, MC,
Discover, AmEx.
MA: (617) 547-6706
Fax: (617) 547-0412
Free catalogs and brochures.
Indicate grade level you need.
Returns: In resalable condition,
within 30 days.
Language arts, math, college prep,
and parent helps.

Elijah Company
P.O. Box 12483
Knoxville, TN 37912-0483
(615) 691-1310
Check or M.O.
Catalog $1, refunded with first
order. Returns: In resalable
condition, within 30 days.
Shipping 10%, $2.50 minimum.
Home school catalog.

Equals
Lawrence Hall of Science
University of California
Berkeley, CA 94720
(415) 642-1823
Check or M.O., or purchase order
for amounts over $25.00.
Fax: (415) 642-1055
Free brochure. Non-returnable.
Publishes *Family Math* book.

Essential Learning Products Co.
2300 W. Fifth Ave.
P.O. Box 2607
Columbus, OH 43216-2607
(614) 486-0631 VISA, MC, Discover.
Fax: (614) 486-0762
Free catalog. Returns: With permis-
sion, in resalable condition.
Math and language arts practice
books.

Exploratorium Mail Order
3601 Lyon St.
San Francisco, CA 94123
1-800-359-9899 VISA, MC.
Science museum and publisher.

F & W Publications
see Writer's Digest Books

Family Learning Center
Rt. 2, Box 264
Hawthorne, FL 32640
(904) 475-5869 Check or M.O.
Free catalog. Returns: Resalable
condition, within 30 days.
Home-school curriculum and
widgets.

Fearon Teacher Aids
P.O. Box 280
Carthage, IL 62321
1-800-242-7272 VISA, MC.
(217) 357-3900
Fax: (217) 357-3908
Free catalog.
Publisher.

**Foundation for American Christian
Education**
Box 27035
San Francisco, CA 94127
(415) 661-1775 VISA, MC.
Free catalog and brochure. Re-
turns: In resalable condition.
Principle Approach to America's
Christian history and education.

Foundation for Economic Education
Irvington-on-Hudson, NY 10533
(914) 591-7230 Check or M.O.
Fax: (914) 591-8910
Some free material.
Free enterprise literature.

Frank Schaffer Publications, Inc.
23740 Hawthorne Blvd.
Torrance, CA 90505
1-800-421-5565 VISA, MC.
Fax: (213) 375-5090
Free catalog.
Sold in educational supply stores
and catalogs.
Preschool & elementary materials.

Gazelle Publications
5580 Stanley Drive
Auburn, CA 95603
(916) 878-1223 Check or M.O.
Free brochure (long SASE appreciated). Returns: 100 percent satisfaction guaranteed.
Home-school books.

Global Visuals
Box 281-B
Wadsworth, OH 44281
(216) 336-5450 VISA, MC.
Free catalog. Returns: Within 30
days, in resalable condition, in original packaging.
Christian visualized application
lessons and songs.

God's World Publications
P.O. Box 2330
Asheville, NC 28802-2330
1-800-476-8924
VISA, MC, Discover.
Fax: (704) 253-1556
Free catalog, brochure, and sam-
ples. Returns: In resalable condi-
tion, within 30 days.
Weekly Christian current event
newspapers for K–12. Book Club.

Golden Educational Center
P.O. Box 12
Bothell, WA 98041-0012
(206) 481-1395 Check or M.O.
Free catalog. Returns: Damaged
merchandise only.
Products completely guaranteed.
Line design, supplemental math,
geography books and maps.

Good Things Company
Drawer 'N'
Norman, OK 73070-70130
(405) 329-7797 Check or M.O.
Free brochure.
"Adam and Eve Family Tree."

Great Christian Books, Inc.
229 S. Bridge St.
P.O. Box 8000
Elkton, MD 21922-8000
(301) 392-0800
VISA, MC, Discover, C.O.D. (U.P.S.)
Fax: (301) 392-3103
No returns unless defective. Mem-
bership $5/year U.S.,
$8 Canada, $12 overseas.
Discount Christian books, music
and home-schooling supplies.

Greenleaf Press
1570 Old Laguardo Rd.
Lebanon, TN 37087
(615) 449-1617 Check or M.O.

Catalog $1 (refunded with first order).
Returns: With permission, in resal-
able condition.
"History for the thoughtful child."

Hammond Inc.
515 Valley St.
Maplewood, NJ 07040
1-800-526-4953 Check or M.O.
NJ: (201) 763-6000. Free catalog.
Returns with permission.
Geography and other school
supplies.

Handwriting Without Tears
8802 Quiet Stream Ct.
Potomac, MD 20854
(301) 983-8409 Check or M.O.
Returns: In resalable condition,
within 30 days.
Handwriting system.

Harlan Enterprises
United Educational Services
P.O. Box 1099
Buffalo, NY 14224
1-800-458-7900
VISA, MC, school P.O.
(716) 668-7691
Fax: (716) 668-7875
Free catalog.
Returns: With permission, in
resalable condition, within 30 days.
Simple drill games.

Harvest House Publishers
1075 Arrowsmith
Eugene, OR 97402-9197
1-800-547-8979 (including Oregon)
VISA, MC.
OR: (503) 343-0123
Fax: (503) 342-6410
Free catalog and brochure.
Returns: With permission, in resal-
able condition, within 365 days.
Christian publisher.

Hayes School Publishing Co., Inc.
321 Pennwood Ave.
Wilkinsburg, PA 15221-3398
1-800-245-6234 VISA, MC.
PA: (412) 371-2370
Fax: (412) 371-6408
Free full-color catalog.
Minimum phone order $15.
Supplemental materials.

Hear An' Tell Adventures
320 Bunker Hill
Houston, TX 77024
Check or M.O.
Fax: (713) 784-7689
Free brochure.
Returns: Resalable condition.
Foreign language programs.

Heritage Products, Inc.
P.O. Box 246
Glencoe, IL 60022
Check or M.O.
Free flyer with SASE.
Bible overview chart.

Hewitt Child Development Center
P.O. Box 9
Washougal, WA 98671-0009
1-800-348-1750 for catalog
requests only.
(206) 835-8708 VISA, MC.
Fax: (206) 835-8697
Free catalog.
Returns: With permission, within
10 days, in resalable condition.
Home-school curriculum supplier.

Hewitt Research Foundation
see Hewitt Child Development Center

Hide the Word in Your Heart Club
Star Family
P.O. Box 6424
Katy, TX 77491
Check or M.O.
Bible memory program.

High Noon Books
20 Commercial Blvd.
Novato, CA 94949-6191
1-800-422-7249 VISA, MC, AmEx
(415) 883-3314
Fax: (415) 883-3720
Free catalog.
Returns: With permission, in
resalable condition, with 6 months.
Hi-lo mystery novels and language
arts teaching aids.

Home Educator
R.R. 1 Box 41
Martinsville, IL 62442
(217) 382-4236 Check or M.O.
Free flyer with SASE.
Bible memory program.

Home Life
P.O. Box 1250
Fenton, MO 63026
Fax: (314) 225-0743
Free catalog.
Returns: In resalable condition,
within 30 days.
Our home business.
HELP newsletter ($15/4 issues):
tips, reviews, resources for growing
families. Juggling equipment. Books.
Organizers. TV-free video systems.

Home Run Enterprises
12531 Aristocrat Ave.
Garden Grove, CA 92641
No phone orders.
Brochure w/SASE. Returns: In
resalable condition, within 10 days.
Math Mouse games.

Homeschool Instructional Services
423 Maplewood
San Antonio, TX 78216
(512) 828-5179 Check or M.O.
Free flyer.
Phonics helps.

HoneyWord
P.O. Box 18035
Tampa, FL 33679-8035
(813) 832-1234 Check or M.O.
Free brochure.
Returns: Within 30 days.
Bible program.

**Hubbard Scientific Division of
Spectrum Industries**
P.O. Box 104
Northbrook, IL 60065-9976
1-800-323-8368 VISA, MC, AmEx.
IL: (312) 272-7810
Fax: (312) 272-9894
Free catalogs.
Maps. Science supplies.

**Human Resource Development
Press**
22 Amherst Rd.
Amherst, MA 01002
1-800-822-2801 MC, VISA, AmEx.
Fax: (413) 253-3490
Free catalog. Returns: In resalable
condition, within 30 days.
Books about peer pressure.

Individualized Education Systems
P.O. Box 5136
Fresno, CA 93755
(209) 299-4639 8–10 AM PST
Check or M.O.
Free brochure. Returns: In resalable
condition, within 10 days.
Beginning reading program.

Innovation Station
P.O. Box 620
LaVerkin, UT 84745
(801) 635-2986 Check or M.O.
Free flyer with SASE. Returns: In
resalable condition, within 10 days.
Creative Play Areas book.

Insect Lore Products
P.O. Box 1535
132 S. Beech
Shafter, CA 93263
1-800-Live Bug (548-3284) VISA, MC.
School P.O. by mail or fax only.
(805) 746-6047
Fax: (805) 746-0334
Free catalog. Returns: In resalable
condition, in original packaging,
within 10 days.

Institute for Creation Research
10946 Woodside Ave. N.
Santee, CA 92071
(619) 448-0900
Creation science resources.

Institute in Basic Life Principles
Box One
Oak Brook, IL 60522-3001
(708) 323-9800
Check or M.O.
Fax: (708) 323-6394
General public may purchase
Sentence Analysis course.
Seminars. Supplier of ATIA curriculum.

Into the Wind Kites
1408 Pearl
Boulder, CO 80302
(303) 449-5356 M–Sat 10–6 MT,
credit card orders only. VISA, MC,
AmEx, Discover, JCB, C.O.D.
Fax: (303) 449-7315
Free catalog. Complete refund or
exchange. You return prepaid and
insured.
Kites and wind-play supplies.

Intrepid Books
P.O. Box 179
Rough and Ready, CA 95975
(916) 432-3197
Check or M.O, C.O.D.
Free brochure.
Returns: In resalable condition.
Principle-Approach history
workbooks.

Isha Enterprises
5503 East Beck Lane
Scottsdale, AZ 85254
(602) 482-1346 VISA, MC.
Free brochure with SASE.
Returns: In resalable condition.
Grammar materials.

Janzen Specialties
1381 S.E. Godsey Rd.
Dallas, OR 97338
(503) 623-4144 Check or M.O.
Free catalog. Returns: With
permission, in resalable condition.
Flannel backgrounds for Bible
stories.

Jonson Specialties
Box 357
Cedarhurst, NY 11516-0357
1-800-221-6714
(entire U.S. & possessions)
VISA, MC, AmEx.
(800) 221-6714
Fax: (718) 868-1202
Free catalog.
Satisfaction guaranteed.
Toys and rewards.

JTG of Nashville
1024C Avenue South
Nashville, TN 37212
(615) 329-3036 VISA, MC.
Fax: (615) 324-4028
Free catalog. 90-day guarantee.
Play a Tune™ Books series.

Judah Bible Curriculum
P. O. Box 122
Urbana, IL 61801
(217) 344-5672 VISA, MC.
Free brochure. Returns: Resalable
condition only, within 60 days.
Bible curriculum.

Judy Rogers
P.O. Box 888442
Atlanta, GA 30338
(404) 339-3898 Check or M.O.
Free brochure for long SASE.
Catechism questions and proverbs
in song.

Kanos Enterprises
P.O. Box 1976
Vancouver, WA 98668
(206) 256-2853 or 694-4895
Fax: (503) 279-5615
Check or M.O.
Satisfaction guaranteed.
Will ship internationally.
Phonics Adventure game.

Key Curriculum Press
P.O. Box 2304
Berkeley, CA 94702
1-800-338-7638 VISA, MC.
CA, AK, HI: (415) 548-2304
Fax: (415) 548-0755
Free catalog. Orders under $25
from individuals must be prepaid.
Math workbooks.

Kimbo Educational
P.O. Box 477
Long Branch, NJ 07740
1-800-631-2187
VISA, MC. Free color catalog.
NJ: (908) 229-4949
Fax: (908) 870-3340
Returns: Within 10 days.
Records, cassettes, filmstrips,
read-alongs, and videos, especially
early childhood and movement.

Klutz Press
2121 Staunton Ct.
Palo Alto, CA 94306
(415) 857-0888
VISA, MC, C.O.D.
Fax: (415) 857-9110
Free catalog.
How-to books for juggling, yo-yo,
marbles, etc.

KNEXT, Inc.
P.O. Box 368
Englewood, OH 45322
Check or M.O.
Math game.

Know It All
733 West Naomi Ave.
Unit I, Suite 165
Arcadia, CA 91007
1-800-I-KNOW-IT (456-6948)
Check, M.O., or C.O.D.
(818) 287-0158
Fax: (818) 447-5667
Free brochure with SASE.
Returns: Within 30 days in
resalable condition.
Geography game.

KONOS
P.O. Box 1534
Richardson, TX 75083
(214) 669-8337
Fax: (214) 699-7922
Check or M.O.
U. S. funds only. No phone orders.
Free brochure. Catalog $1.
Returns: Within 21 days, in resal-
able condition, 10% restocking fee.
Home-school curriculum, seminars.

Kregel Publications
P.O. Box 2607
Grand Rapids, MI 49501-2607
(616) 451-4775
Fax: (616) 459-6049
Christian publisher.

Kumon Mathematex
1900 W. Loop South
Suite 1234
Houston TX 77027
(713) 622-8880
Math program.

Ladybird Books, Inc.
49 Omni Circle
P.O. Box 1690
Auburn, ME 04210
1-800-523-9247
(207) 783-6329
Fax: (207) 783-6130
VISA, MC, C.O.D.
Open account for established
businesses.
Free catalog. Returns: With permis-
sion, in resalable condition, for ac-
count holders only.
Educational books, readers.

Landmark Company
1580 Raven Hill
Wheaton, IL 60187
(312) 690-9978 VISA, MC.
Returns: Within 15 days, in
resalable condition.
Lighthouse Adventures tape series.

**Landmark's Freedom Baptist
Curriculum**
2222 E. Hinson Ave.
Haines City, FL 33844-4902
(813) 421-2937.
VISA, MC, Discover.
Free brochure.
Curriculum supplier.

Lauri, Inc.
P.O. Box F
Phillips-Avon, ME 04966
(207) 639-2000 Check or M.O.
Fax: (207) 639-3555
Free brochure.
Crepe foam rubber education prod-
ucts and developmental toys.

Learn to Look
Box 1340
Eau Claire, WI 54702
Preschool book.

Learning at Home
P.O. Box 270bb
Honaunau, HI 96726
(808) 328-9669 VISA, MC.
Free catalog. Returns: Within 15
days, in resalable condition.
Home-school catalog.

Learning Systems Corporation
P.O. Box 201
Wyncote, PA 19095
(215) 855-4948 Check or M.O.
Catalog $1. All sales are final.
Mini workbooks, skillforms.

Learning Things, Inc.
P.O. Box 436
Arlington, MA 02174
(617) 646-0093 Check or M.O.
Fax: (617) 646-0135
Minimum order, $15. Free catalog.
Returns: In resalable condition.
Science apparatus, math aids,
cardboard carpentry, tools and con-
struction kits for kids K–12.

Learning Works
P.O. Box 6187
Santa Barbara, CA 93160
(805) 964-4220 Check or M.O.
Fax: (805) 964-1466
Free catalog. Returns: Resalable
condition within 10 days.
Supplemental materials.

LEGO Dacta, Inc.
555 Taylor Rd.
P.O. Box 1600
Enfield, CT 06083-1600
1-800-527-8339
CT: (203) 749-2291
Fax: (203) 763-2466
Hands-on engineering kits, activities.
Sold only through educational
distributors and teacher stores.
Available directly from LEGO Dacta
in certain states. Call for details.

Leonardo Press
Box 1326
Camden, ME 04843
(207) 236-8649 Check or M.O.
Free catalog.
Spelling and math programs.

Letter-Match Co.
215 Oak Tree Rd.
Norristown, PA 19401
(215) 275-5915
Alphabet flash cards.

LibertyTree
The Independent Institute
134 - 98th Ave.
Oakland, CA 94603
1-800-872-4866 VISA, MC, AmEx.
24 hrs 7 days. Credit card orders only.
Inquiries: (415) 568-6047
Fax: (415) 568-6040
Free catalog. Returns: In resalable
condition, in original packaging,
within 10 days of receipt.
Libertarian books 'n gifts.

Libraries Unlimited
P.O. Box 3988
Englewood, CO 80155-3988
1-800-237-6124 VISA, MC.
(303) 770-1220
Fax: (303) 220-8843
Free catalog. Returns: In resalable
condition, within 30 days.

Publisher of resource books for
teachers.

**LifeWay Christian School
Curriculum**
Scripture Press Publishers
1825 College Ave.
Wheaton, IL 60187
1-800-323-9409 VISA, MC.
IL: (708) 668-6000
Fax: (708) 668-3806
Free catalog. Returns: Within 90
days, in resalable condition.
Bible curriculum.

Literacy Press, Inc.
Eunice S. Coleman
24 Lake Drive
DeBary, FL 32713
(407) 668-1232
Check or M.O.
Free brochure with long SASE.
Returns: Unconditional guarantee.
Phonics, math programs.

Living Heritage Academy
P.O. Box 1438
Lewisville, TX 75067-1438
1-800-873-3435
(214) 462-1776
Fax: (214) 462-8681
Installment plan.
No refunds once program opened.
Home school program.

Lynn's Bookshelf
P.O. Box 2224
Boise, ID 83701-2224
Proverbs for Parenting.

MacMillan Publishing Company
Front and Brown Streets
Riverside, NJ 08075-1197
1-800-323-9563
Handwriting supplies and courses.

Majesty Music
P.O. Box 6524
Greenville, SC 29606
1-800-334-1071 M–F 8:30–5 EST.
VISA, MC, school or church P.O.
(803) 242-6722
Free brochure.
Returns: Unconditional.
Patch the Pirate cassettes, books,
scripts.

Mantle Ministries
140 Grand Oak Drive
San Antonio, TX 78232
(512) 490-BEAR Check or M.O.,
Account for businesses.
Free catalog.
Returns: Within 30 days.
History resources by "Little Bear."

Margwen Products
382 34th St. SE
Cedar Rapids, IA 52403
(319) 365-6398 No phone orders.
Check or M.O.
Free brochure with SASE.
Returns: In resalable condition,
within 10 days.
Match-A-Fact math games.

Marketplace 29 A.D.
P.O. Box 29
Stevensville, MI 49127
1-800-345-29AD (2923) VISA, MC
(616) 429-6442 or (616) 429-9863
Free brochure. Returns: Resalable
condition, within 15 days.
Bible-times simulation.

Master Books
P.O. Box 1606
El Cajon, CA 92022
1-800-999-3777 VISA, MC.
CA: (619) 448-1121
Free brochure.
Creation Science books, videos.

Mastery Publications
90 Hillside Lane
Arden, NC 28704
(704) 684-0429 Check or M.O.
Free brochure with SASE.
Returns: In resalable condition,
within 30 days.
Mastering Mathematics program.

Mathematics Programs Associates, Inc.
P.O. Box 118
Halesite, NY 11743
(516) 588-4391 or 549-9061
Check or M.O.
Free catalog and brochure.
Developmental Mathematics
program.

Maupin House Publishing
P.O. Box 90148
Gainesville, FL 32607
(904) 336-9290
VISA, MC, school purchase order.
Returns: In resalable condition,
within 30 days.
Publisher of *Caught'Ya!: Grammar
with a Giggle.*

McDougal, Littell & Co.
P.O. Box 8000
St. Charles, IL 60174
1-800-225-3809 Check or M.O.
(312) 869-2300
Public school textbook publisher.

Merrill Publishers
1300 Alum Creek Dr.
P.O. Box 508
Columbus, OH 43216-9886
1-800-848-6205
OH: 1-800-445-6409
Require some sort of evidence that
you are a legitimate school or certified teacher (e.g, copy of affidavit
or teacher credential) for purchase
of teacher materials.
Public school textbook publisher.

Message of Life Publications
58607 Rd. 601
Ahwahnee, CA 93601
(209) 683-7028
Fax: (209) 683-7028
Check or M.O. Phone orders
accepted. No collect calls.
Free brochure. Returns: With
permission, in resalable condition.
"Krata-Kraft" visualized Bible
lessons.

Midwest Publications
Critical Thinking Press and Software
P. O. Box 448
Pacific Grove, CA 93950
1-800-458-4849 VISA, MC.
(408) 375-2455
Fax: (408) 372-3230
Free catalog.
Returns: Unconditional.
Thinking-skill materials.

Milliken Publishing Company
1100 Research Blvd.
St. Louis, MO 63132-0579

1-800-333-READ
VISA,MC, C.O.D., school P.O.
(314) 991-4220
Fax: (314) 991-4807
Free catalog. Available catalogs:
K–8, 7–12, computer software,
Reading, Early Childhood.
Educational publisher preK–12.

Montessori Services
228 South "A" St.
Santa Rosa, CA 95401
(707) 579-3003
VISA, MC, C.O.D.
Free catalog.
Returns: Unconditional.
Early childhood supplies..

Mortensen Math
see V. J. Mortensen Co.

Mott Media
1000 E. Huron St.
Milford, MI 48042
1-800-348-6688 VISA, MC.
MI: (313) 685-8773
Free catalog.
Classic texts, McGuffeys.

MRK Publishing
448 Seavey
Petaluma, CA 94952
(707) 763-0056
Fax: (707) 763-1539
Check or M.O. Free brochure with
long SASE. No returns.

Multiplication Teaching & Learning Made Easy
P.O. Box 1482
Conway, AR 72032
(501) 327-1968
Math program publisher.

Multnomah Press
10209 SE Division St.
Portland, OR 97266
1-800-547-5890
OR: 1-800-452-6994 VISA, MC.
(503) 257-0526
Fax: (503) 255-7690
Returns: In resalable condition.
Books sold in Christian bookstores
and inspirational sections of
secular bookstores.

National Geographic Society
P.O. Box 2895
Washington, DC 20013
(202) 857-7000 or 857-7589
(301) 948-8970: 8971 for books
and globes
Geography supplies.

National Geographic World
P.O. Box 2330
Washington, DC 20077-9955
1-800-368-2728 Check or M.O.
(301) 921-1330
Fax: (301) 921-1380
Returns: Within 30 days.
Picture mag for kids.

National Teaching Aids, Inc.
1845 Highland Ave.
New Hyde Park, NY 11040
(516) 326-2555 Check or M.O.
Fax: (516) 326-2560
Catalog $1.
Returns: 60 days with permission.
Teaching aids for science/ health.

National Wildlife Federation
1400 16th St. NW
Washington, DC 20036
1-800-432-6564
(202) 797-6800
Publishes *Ranger Rick* and *Your Big Backyard* magazines.

Nature Friend Magazine
P.O. Box 73
Goshen, IN 46526
(219) 534-2245 Check or M.O.
Christian nature/science magazine.

NavPress/The Navigators
P.O. Box 6000
Colorado Springs, CO 80934
1-800-366-7788 ext. 681
(703) 552-3263
Bible memory/discipleship program.

Norris Science Labs and Kits
P.O. Box 61281
Las Vegas, NV 89160
(702) 458-6427
Check or M.O. or school P.O.
Catalog $2.00. Refunded on first
order. Returns: In resalable
condition, within 30 days.
Science lab equipment, supplies.

Northstar Learning Systems
19519 38th Ave., N.E.
Seattle, WA 98155
(206) 365-4338 Check or M.O.
Fax: (206) 362-9413
Lookshelf.

Old Fashioned Crafts
Route 2 Box 2091
Ellijay, GA 30540
1-800-962-8849 VISA, MC.
(404) 635-7612
Free brochure.
Returns: With permission.
Wooden board games for the whole family.

Ornament Publications
2301 Country Club Road
Garland, TX 75041
Check or M.O.
Free brochure. Returns: In
resalable condition, within 30 days.
Publishes *Richest Christian* game.

Orton Dyslexia Society, The
724 York Rd.
Baltimore, MD 21204
1-800-ABC-D123
(301) 296-0232
Help for dyslexics. Information and
referrals.

Our Christian Heritage
7923 W. 62nd Way
Arvada, CO 80004
(303) 421-0444 Check or M.O.
Free brochure.
Christian textbooks/workbooks.

Pacific Puzzle Company
378B Guemes Island Rd.
Anacortes, WA 98221
(206) 293-7034
VISA, MC. U.S. funds only.
Free catalog.
Refund or exchange if dissatisfied.
Beautiful hardwood puzzles.

Paradigm Company
P.O. Box 45161
Boise, ID 83711
(208) 322-4440 VISA, MC.
SASE for free price list.
Publishes Sam Blumenfeld's
books, *Blumenfeld Education Letter*.

Parent-Child Press
P.O. Box 767
Altoona, PA 16603
(814) 946-5213 Check or M.O.
Fax: (814) 941-3415
Free catalog.
Montessori philosophy, art materials.

Parenting Press
11065 5th Avenue, N.E., #F
Seattle, WA 98125
1-800-992-6657 VISA, MC, C.O.D.
(206) 364-2900
Free brochure. Returns: In resalable
condition, within 30 days.
Kids' first aid book.

Pathway Publishers
2530N 250W
La Grange, IN 46761
Check or M.O.
Free price list.
Returns: In resalable condition.
Amish publisher.

Pecci Educational Publishers
440 Davis Court #405
San Francisco, CA 94111
(415) 391-8579 Check or M.O.
Free brochure.
Returns: In resalable condition.
Reading program and Super
Seatwork.

Pennsylvania Homeschoolers
RD 2 Box 117
Kittanning, PA 16201
(412) 783-6512 Check or M.O.
Brochure with SASE. Returns:
Resalable condition, within 30 days.

Perception Publications, Inc.
10801 E. Happy Valley Rd., #138
Scottsdale, AZ 85255
(602) 946-6454 VISA, MC.
Fax: (602) 946-6624
Readiness workbook series.
IQ-building workbooks, parent
training.

Perfectly Safe
7245 Whipple Ave., N.W.
North Canton, OH 44720
1-800-837-KIDS
VISA, MC, minimum $10.
(216) 494-2323

Fax: (216) 494-0265
Free catalog. Returns: Within 30 days.
Children's safety products.

Plain Path Publishers
P.O. Box 654
New Freedom, PA 17349
(717) 235-3349 Check or M.O.
Free brochure. Returns: In
resalable condition, within 10 days.
Christian character and manhood
training for young people.

Play 'N Talk
7105 Manzanita St.
Carlsbad, CA 92009
(619) 438-4330 7 AM–10 PM M-
Sat PST VISA, MC, or post dated
checks for total price.
Total language arts program.

Pleasant Company
P.O. Box 497
Dept. 8388
Middleton, WI 53562-0497
1-800-845-0005
VISA, MC, Discover, AmEx.
(608) 836-4848
Fax: (608) 836-4403
Free catalog.
Returns: Satisfaction guaranteed.
American history books, dolls,
accessories, girls' clothing.

Plough Publishing House
Spring Valley
Route 381 North
Farmington, PA 15437-9506
(412) 329-1100 Check or M.O.
Fax: (412) 329-0942
Free catalog. Returns: With
permission, in resalable condition,
within 365 days.
Hutterite books, songs.

Portland State University
Continuing Education Press
Box 1394
Portland, OR 97207
1-800-547-8887 X 4891 VISA, MC.
(503) 725-4891
Free brochure. Returns: With
permission, in resalable condition,
within 90 days.
Italic handwriting series.

Providence Project
P.O. Box 1760
Wichita, KS 67201
(316) 265-0321 VISA, MC.
Catalog $2, refunded with first order.
Returns: Unconditional, within 1 year.
Learning Vitamins: CalcuLadder,
ReadyWriter, AlphaBetter.

Quantum Communications
3301 West Hampden Ave., Suite N
Englewood, CO 80110
(303) 781-0679 Check or M.O.
(Made payable to Traveloguer
Collection) VISA, MC, AmEx.
Fax: (303) 761-8556
Returns: Within 15 days.
Traveloguer videos.

Questar Publishers, Inc.
P.O. Box 1720
Sisters, OR 97759
(503) 549-1144 Check or M.O.
Fax: (503) 549-2044
Publishes *The Beginner's Bible*.

R & E Publishers
P.O. Box 2008
Saratoga, CA 95070
(408) 866-6303 VISA, MC.
Fax: (408) 866-0825. Free catalog.
Returns: Satisfaction guaranteed.
Publisher.

Rainfall Inc.
1534 College Ave., S.E.
Grand Rapids, MI 49507
1-800-437-4337 VISA, MC.
(616) 245-5985
Fax: (616) 245-2127
Free brochure for large SASE.
Returns: With permission.
Bible games, toys, gifts, and
videos.

Rand McNally & Company
P.O. Box 7600
Chicago, IL 60680
West/West Coast: 1-800-323-1887
East and Midwest: 1-800-245-1647
Atlas and map publisher.

Random House, Inc.
400 Hahn Road
Westminster, MD 21157
1-800-733-3000 VISA, MC, AmEx.

Orders only.
1-800-725-0600 Inquiries and
customer service
Fax: (301) 848-2436
Shipping: $2 first book, 50¢ each
additional book.
Returns: Resalable condition.
Publisher.

Rapids Christian Press
Box 487
Wisconsin Rapids, WI 54495
(715) 423-4670
Bible tools.

Reading Reform Foundation
P.O. Box 98785
Tacoma, WA 98498-0785
(206) 588-3436
NY chapter: (212) 307-7320
Check or M.O.
Fax: (206) 582-7877
Catalog $2.
Membership $25/year, includes
newsletter.
Resources on reading debate and
phonics materials.

**Reformed Free Publishing
Association**
Box 2006
Grand Rapids, MI 49501
(616) 534-1927
Bible helps.

**Reformed Presbyterian Board of
Publications**
Board of Education and Publication
7408 Penn Avenue
Pittsburgh, PA 15208-2531
(412) 241-0436 Check or M.O. or
they bill you.
Fax: (412) 731-8861 5 PM–8 AM EST.
Free catalog. Returns: Within 30
days, in resalable condition.
Quantity discounts for bookstores
and churches.
Psalm books, cassettes.

Resource Publications
9403 Winding Ridge
Dallas, TX 75238
(214) 341-1157 Check or M.O.
Free brochure with SASE.
Grammar book.

Rifton: For People with Disabilities
Rt 213
Rifton, NY 12471
(914) 658-3141 or 658-3143
Fax: (914) 658-8065
Physical therapy equipment.

Right at Home Productions
6628 - 193rd Street, S.W.
Lynnwood, WA 98036
Check or M.O.
Free brochure. Returns: Uncondi-
tional, within 10 days.
Non-clothing sewing projects.

Rod and Staff Publishers
Crockett, KY 41413
(606) 522-4348 Check or M.O.
Fax: (606) 522-4896
Free catalog listing texts. Returns:
With permission, 10 percent re-
stocking charge.
Christian schoolbooks. Mennonite.

Safari Ltd.
P.O. Box 630685
Miami, FL 33163
1-800-554-5414 VISA, MC, C.O.D.
(305) 621-1000
Fax: (305) 621-6894
Free catalog.
Returns: With permission, in
resalable condition, within 10 days.
Educational games.

Saxon Publishers, Inc.
1300 McGee, Suite 100
Norman, OK 73072
(405) 329-7071
Fax: (405) 360-4205
Call or write for free brochure.
Math and algebra texts.

Send the Light
P.O. Box 28
Waynesboro, GA 30830
(new name: Operation Mobilization
Literature)
(404) 554-5827
Fax: (404) 554-7444 VISA, MC.
Open account for churches or schools.
Make check out to "O.M. LIT."
Free brochure and catalog.
Returns: Resalable condition, with
permission, within 90 days.
Publishes *Operation World.*

Shekinah Curriculum Cellar
967 Junipero Drive
Costa Mesa, CA 92626
(714) 751-7767 Check or M.O.
Catalog $1.
Refunds: Resalable condition, with-
in 15 days.
Co-op buying plan.
"Quality books and teaching aids
for home educators."

Shining Star
Division of Good Apple
Box 299
Carthage, IL 62321
1-800-435-7234 VISA, MC.
Free catalog.
Returns: Permission required.
Christian educational materials.

Sign Talk
P.O. Box 141411
Spokane, WA 99214
(509) 928-6843 8–5 M–Sat PST.
VISA, MC.
Free brochure.
Returns: In resalable condition, in
original packaging, within 5 days.
Publishers of *Sign Talk.*

Sing, Spell, Read and Write
see Educational Products

Small Ventures
11023 Watterson Drive
Dallas, TX 75228
(214) 681-1728 Check or M.O.
Free catalog. Returns: Resalable
condition, within 30 days.
Phonogram cards.

Smiling Heart Press
P.O. Box 229
Corbett, OR 97019
(503) 695-2740 Check or M.O.
made out to Ann Ward.
One-book preschool curriculum.

Spizzirri Publishing Company, Inc.
P.O. Box 9397
Rapid City, SD 57709
1-800-322-9819 VISA, MC, C.O.D.
SD: (605) 348-2749
Fax: (605) 348-6251
Free catalog. Non-returnable.
Educational coloring books.

St. Ursula Academy, S.U.A.
Phonics Department
1339 E. McMillan St.
Cincinnatti, OH 45206-2180
(513) 961-4877 or 961-3410
Check or M.O.
Free brochure. Returns: In resalable
condition, within 30 days.
Professor Phonics program.

Standard Publishing
8121 Hamilton Ave.
Cincinnati, OH 54231
1-800-543-1353 VISA, MC.
OH: 1-800-582-1385
Free catalog.
Bible-centered everything.

Stone Soup
P.O. Box 83
Santa Cruz, CA 95063
1-800-447-4569 VISA, MC.
(408) 426-5557
Free brochure.
Satisfaction guaranteed.
Secular literary mag by/for kids.

Success House
1025 Balboa St.
San Francisco, CA 94118
(415) 668-4121 Check or M.O.
payable to Siva Tardos.
Free brochure with long SASE.
Returns: In resalable condition,
within 30 days.
Math manipulatives.

Sycamore Tree
2179 Meyer Place
Costa Mesa, CA 92627
(714) 650-4466 (info) (714) 642-
6750 (orders) VISA, MC.
Fax: (714) 642-6750
Catalog $3. Includes $3 rebate
good toward first purchase.
Returns: In resalable condition,
within 15 days.
Full-service home-school supplier.

Teach America to Read and Spell
PO Box 44093
Tacoma, WA 98444
(206) 531-0312 Check or M.O.
Free brochure. Returns: Within 30
days, call first.
Phonics program.

Teacher Created Materials
5445 Oceanus Drive, #106
Huntington Beach, CA 92649
1-800-662-4321 VISA, MC.
(714) 891-7895
Fax: (714) 892-0283
Supplementary materials for public schools.

Teachers' Laboratory, Inc.
104 Canal Street
P.O. Box 6480
Brattleboro, VT 05302-6480
(802) 254-3457 VISA, MC.
Fax: (802) 254-5233
Free catalog. Returns: With permission, in resalable condition.
Math and science supplies.

Teaching Home
P.O. Box 20219
Portland, OR 97220-0219
(503) 253-9633
Fax: (503) 253-7345
Free brochure.
Satisfaction guaranteed.
Christian home-schooling magazine.

Ten Commandments
P.O. Box 577
Marlborough, NH 03455
(603) 876-4685 or 876-4505
Fax: (603) 876-4128
Contribution appreciated but not required.
Free brochure.
Ten Commandments packet.

Things of Science
P.O. Box 579
Sarasota, FL 34230-0579
(813) 951-1688 Check or M.O.
Free brochure. 100% guarantee.
Monthy science kits.
Secular.

Thoburn Press
Fairfax Christian Bookstore
P.O. Box 6941
Tyler, TX 75711
1-800-962-5432
TX: (903) 581-0677
Check or M.O. or they'll bill you.
Free catalog.
Returns: discouraged. With permission, resalable condition.

10% returns charge plus postage, return UPS, no returns over $35.
Christian books, texts, McGuffeys.

Timberdoodle
E. 1610 Spencer Lake Road
Shelton, WA 98584
(206) 426-0672
Check or M.O., or COD.
Fax: (206) 427-5625
Free catalog. Returns: In resalable condition, in original packaging, within 60 days.
Educational materials.
Fischertechnik kits.

Tin Man Press
P.O. Box 219
Stanwood, WA 98292
1-800-676-0459 VISA, MC, or C.O.D.
(206) 387-0459
Free brochure. Returns: With permission, within 60 days.
Discover, Nifty Fifty, and Brain Stations card series.

Total Reading
P.O. Box 54465
Los Angeles, CA 90054-0465
(213) 545-7015
A comprehensive language arts program.

Toys To Grow On
P.O. Box 17
Long Beach, CA 90801
1-800-542-8338 24 hrs, 7 days.
VISA, MC, AmEx. $10 minimum.
(213) 603-8890
Fax: (213) 603-2991
Free catalog.
Returns: Within 30 days.
Mail-order toy catalog.

TREND Enterprises, Inc.
P.O. Box 64073
St. Paul, MN 55164-0073
1-800-328-5540 Check or M.O.
$10 minimum order.
MN: (612) 631-2850
Fax: (612) 631-2861
Free catalog.
Satisfaction guaranteed.
Stickers, wipe-off books, bulletin board cut-outs, flash cards, more.

Triangle Press
23 Fifth Ave. S.E.
Conrad, MT 59425
(406) 278-5664 VISA, MC.
18th/19th century children's books.

V.J. Mortensen Co.
P.O. Box 98
Hayden Lake, ID 83835-0098
(208) 667-1580 or 772-4074 VISA, MC, Discover, AmEx
Fax: (208) 667-4787
Free catalog and brochure. Returns: Within 30 days, with authorization.
Math manipulatives and program.

Vic Lockman
P.O. Box 1916
Ramona, CA 92065
Check or M.O. Minimum order $5.
Fax: (619) 739-0537 (files)
Free brochure. Returns: Wholesale buyers only, with permission, in resalable condition.
Cartoon illustrated booklets.

Victory Drill Book
P.O. Box 2114
La Habra, CA 90632-2114
(213) 947-6933 Check or M.O.
Free brochure. Returns: With permission, in resalable condition, within 30 days, 15% handling.
Speed drill, phonics.

Vision Video
2030 Wentz Church Rd.
Worcester, PA 19490
1-800-523-0226 VISA, MC, C.O.D.
(215) 584-1893
Fax: (215) 584-4610
Free catalog and brochure.
Returns: In resalable condition, within 30 days.
Church history, Bible story videos.

Warren Publishing House, Inc.
Totline Books and Newsletter
P.O. Box 2250
Everett, WA 98203
1-800-334-4769 VISA, MC.
(206) 353-3100
Fax: (206) 355-7007
Free catalog. Refunds: 30 days, in resalable condition.
Early learning materials.

Weaver Curriculum Series
2752 Scarborough
Riverside, CA 92503
(714) 688-3126 Check or M.O.
Free catalog.
Integrated curriculum K–6.

Wff 'n Proof Learning Games
1490-FS South Blvd
Ann Arbor, MI 48104-4699
(313) 665-2269 VISA, MC, C.O.D.
Free catalog.
Games for school subjects.

Whirlpool Redemption Center
P.O. Box 85
St. Joseph, MI 49085
Check or M.O.
Free pamphlets (single copy).
No returns.

World Book, Inc.
Educational Services Department
Merchandise Mart Plaza
Chicago, IL 60654
(312) 245-3456 Check or M.O.
Orders over $25 may be billed.

Encyclopedia. Workbooks. Learning aids. Posters.

World's Greatest Stories
P.O. Box 2021
South Hamilton, MA 01982
(508) 468-1556 Check or M.O.
Free flyer with SASE. Satisfaction guaranteed.
Dramatized Bible cassettes.

Worldwide Slides
7427 Washburn Avenue South
Minneapolis, MN 55423
(612) 869-6482 Check or M.O.
Pana-Vue catalog $1, refunded on first order. Minimum 5-packet order.
Free View-Master™ catalog.
Travel slides, videos, books.

Writer's Digest Books
1507 Dana Ave
Cincinnati, OH 45207
1-800-289-0963 VISA, MC
Fax: (513) 531-4744. Free catalog.
Returns: 30 days, resalable condition. Publisher.

You Can Read
10015 Armstrong Plaza
Omaha, NE 68134
(402) 572-1471
Check or M.O.
Free flyer with SASE.
Phonics drill materials.

Young Companion
Pathway Publishers
Route 4
Aylmer, Ontario, CANADA N5H 2R3
Check or M.O. in U.S. funds, except Canadians.
Magazine for Amish teens.

Zondervan Publishing House
1415 Lake Drive, S.E.
Grand Rapids, MI 49506
1-800-253-1309
MI: 1-800-253-4475
Zondervan prefers that you buy their books in Christian bookstores.
Christian publisher.

INDEX OF FOREIGN SUPPLIERS

Realizing that you overseas and Canadian readers prefer to shop in your own countries, I asked every distributor listed in this book for a list of their non-USA distributors. The results, while scanty, might be of help to some of you. The American company is listed first, with its distributor's name (and where available, address) second.

As you can see, any of you who are interested in starting an importing business featuring American home-education materials have a wide-open market. Most other countries do not have as well-developed home-schooling movements as the U.S.A., and consequently Americans are blessed with more than our fair share of innovative products designed for home use. Why not even things out a bit? And when you start your business, let me know so I can put you in the next edition!

Australia

Baker Book House
S. John Bacon
P.O. Box 223
9 Kingston Town Close
Oakleigh, Victoria, 3166
(03) 563-1044

Bible Visuals
Evangelistic Literature Enterprise
P.O. Box 10
Strathpine, Queensland 4500

Child Evangelism Fellowship Press
CEF
P.O. Box 222
Parramatta, N.S.W. 2124

Children's Small Press Collection
The Book Garden
Unit E3 Cnr. Windsor Rd.
Castle Hill N.S.W. 2154
02-634-2558

Harvest House Publishers
Hodder and Stoughton
10-16 South St.
Rydalmere, N.S.W. 2116

Human Resource Development Press
Power Human Resource Development
443 Victoria Ave. 1st Floor
Chatswood, NSW 2067
02-411-4811

Kregel Publications
S. John Bacon Pty., Ltd.
9 Kingston Town Close
P.O. Box 223
Oakleigh, Victoria 3166

Midwest Publications
Hawker Brownlow Education Pty. Ltd.
235 Bay Road
Cheltenham, Victoria 3192
Fax: (03) 553-4538

Milliken Publishing Company
Encyclopaedia Britannica (Australia) Inc.
Britannica Center 12 Anella Ave.
Castke Hill, N.S.W. 2154
02-680-5607 Fax: 02-899-3231

Multnomah Press
Bookhouse Australia
P.O. Box 115
Fleminton Markets, N.S.W. 2124
(02) 763-1211

Rainfall Inc.
Care and Share
44B Harley Crescent
Condell Park, N.S.W., Bankstown 2200
(02) 707-3111

Teacher Created Materials
Southern Cross Educational
348 Orrong Road, P.O. Box 161
Caulfield, Victoria 3161

Vic Lockman
Light Educational Ministries
P.O. Box 101
Booleroo Centre 5482

Vic Lockman
Reformation Book Centre
119 Adelaide Arcade
Adelaide, S.A. 5000

Vision Video
Australian Religious Film
Society/Esdras Giddy
Blenheim Road and Warwick Street
(02) 888-2511
Fax (02) 958-2812

Australia/New Zealand

Learning Works
Hawker Brownlow Educational Pty. Ltd.
235 Bay Road
Cheltenham, Victoria 3192
(03) -555-1344
Branch Office

Canada

Alpha Omega Publications
Academic Distribution Services
528 Carnarvon St.
New Westminster, B.C. V3L 1C4
(604) 524-9758

Baker Book House
G. R. Welch Co. Ltd.
960 Gateway
Burlington, Ontario L7L 5K7
(416) 681-2760

BCM Publications
BCM Publications
798 Main St. E.
Hamilton, Ontario L8M 1L4
(416) 549-9810

Bible Visuals
Evangel of Canada
P.O. Box 294
Brantford, Ontario N3T 5M8

Bible-Science Association
Creation-Science Association
P.O. Box 367
Surrey, British Columbia V3T 5B6

Child Evangelism Fellowship Press
Beacon
Box 2000
55 Woodslee Avenue
Paris, Ontario N3L-3X5

Children's Small Press Collection
Books and Toys to Learn On
1745 Golfview Drive
Windsor, Ontario
(519) 978-0999

Educators Publishing Service, Inc.
Educators Publishing Service
1100 Birchmount Road
Scarborough, Ontario M1K 5H9
(416) 755-0591

Harvest House Publishers
R. G. Mitchell Family Books, Ltd.
565 Gordon Baker Rd.
North York, Ontario M2H 2W2

Home Run Enterprises
Window Tree Learning Project
9862 - 156 A Street
Surrey, British Columbia V3R 7X7
(604) 583-2882

Human Resource Development Press
Pride Canada
2220 College Ave.
Regina, Saskatchewan
(306) 975-3755

Kimbo Educational
Monarch Books of Canada
500 Dufferin St.
Downsville, Ontario M3H 5T5
(416) 663-8231

Kregel Publications
R. G. Mitchell Family Books, Ltd.
565 Gordon Baker Road
North York, Ontario M2H 2W2

Midwest Publications
Western Ed. Activities, Ltd.
10929-101 St.
Edmonton, Alberta T5H 2S7

Midwest Publications
Educational Resources, Ltd.
109-8475 Ontario St.
Vancouver, British Columbia V5X 3E8

Midwest Publications
Kahl's, Inc.
Box 126
Kitchener, Ontario N2G 3W9

Milliken Publishing Company
Encyclopedia Britannica Publications
175 Holiday Drive
Cambridge, Ontario N3C 3N4
(519) 658-4621

Multnomah Press
Beacon Distributing
55 Woodslea N.E.
Paris, Ontario N3L 3X5
(519) 442-7853

National Teaching Aids, Inc.
Concepts in Learning
302 Broadway Avenue
Toronto, Ontario M4P 1W3
(416) 486-3331

Pathway Publishers
Pathway Publishers
Route 4
Aylmer, Ontario N5H 2R3

Plough Publishing House
Plough Publishing
Crystal Spring
Ste. Agathe, Manitoba R0G 1Y0
(204) 433-7634

Rainfall Inc.
Main Roads Productions
55 Woodslee Avenue
Paris, Ontario N3L 3X5
(519) 442-1303

Roper Press
Rainbow House Enterprises, Inc.
205 Hilda Ave.
Willowdale, Ontario M2M 4B1

Shining Star
Beacon Distributors, Ltd.
104 Consumers Drive
Whitby, Ontario L1N 5T3
(416) 668-8884

Teacher Created Materials
Educator Supplies Limited
2323 Trafalgar Street
London, Ontario N5W 5H2

Triangle Press
Valley Gospel Mission
Box 412
Sardis, B.C. V2R 1A7

Vic Lockman
Discount Christian Books
12719 126th St.
Edmonton, Alberta T5L 0X9

Vic Lockman
Still Waters Revival Books
12810 - 126 Street
Edmonton, Alberta T5L 0Y1

Writer's Digest Books
Prentice-Hall Canada
1870 Birchmont Rd.
Scarborough, Ontario M1P 2J7
(416) 293-3621

England

Bible Visuals
Child Evangelism Fellowship
64 Osborne Rd., Levenshulme
Manchester M19 2DY

Harvest House Publishers
Nova Distributors
29 Milber Industrial Estate
Newton Abbott, Devon TQ12 43G

Milliken Publishing Company
Gemini Teaching Aids
19 Kirkgate
Sherburn-in-Elmet
Leeds, LS25 6BH
0977-684524

Multnomah Press
Scripture Press Found.
Raans Rd., Amersham-on-the-Hill
Bucks HP6 6J0
0494-722151

Plough Publishing House
Plough Publishing
Darvell
Robertsbridge, E. Sussex TN32 5DR
0580-880626

Rainfall Inc.
New Wine Ministries
Unit 22, Arun Business Park
Bognor Regis
Chichester, West Sussex PO22 95X
0243-683000

Reading Reform Foundation
Reading Reform of England
2 The Crescent, Toftwood
East Dereham
Norfolk NR19 1NR

Teacher Created Materials
Gemini Teaching Aids
19 Kirkgate
Sherburn-in-Elmet
Leeds LS25 6BH

Triangle Press
Evangelical Press
Wooler Street
Darlington County
Durham DL1 -1RQ

Triangle Press
Gospel Standard Trust
7 Brackendale Grove
Harpenden, Herts AL5 3EL

Vision Video
Bagster Video/West Brooke House
76 High Street
Alton, Hampshire, GU34 1EN
0-420-89141 Fax 0-420-541160

Writer's Digest Books
Freelance Press
5/9 Bexley Square
Salford, Wanshester M3 6DB

Germany

Plough Publishing House
Plough Publishing
Michaelshof
5231 Birnbach
49-2681-6250

Ireland

Bible Visuals
Anchor Distributors
7 Fair St.
Drogheda, County Louth

New Zealand

Baker Book House
Omega Distributors, Inc.
Box 26-222
69 Great South Road
Remuera, Auckland
548-283

Harvest House Publishers
Omega Distributors
P.O. 26-222 Epsom
Auckland 3

Kregel Publications
Omega Distributors, Ltd.
69 Great South Road
P.O. Box 26-222
Remuera, Epcom, Auckland

Multnomah Press
Omega Distributors
P.O. Box 26-222
Epsom, Auckland
09-524-8283

Rainfall Inc.
Heyes Enterprises
P. O. Box 24-086
Royal Oak, Auckland
64-665-5951

Scotland

Kregel Publications
John Ritchie, Ltd.
40 Beansburn
Kilmarnock KA3 1RH
Ayeshire

Singapore

Midwest Publications
Global Educational Services
3 Irving Road
#03-06 Irving Industrial Building
Singapore 1336

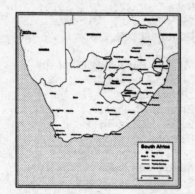

South Africa

Baker Book House
Harvest House Publishers
Kregel Publications
Christian Arts Wholesalers
20 Smuts Avenue, Laan 20
P.O. Box/Postbus 1599
Vereeniging, 1930
(016) 21-4781/5

Multnomah Press
ACLA
Box 332
Roodeport 1725
763-3471

Vic Lockman
Signposts
PO Box 26148
0007 Arcadia

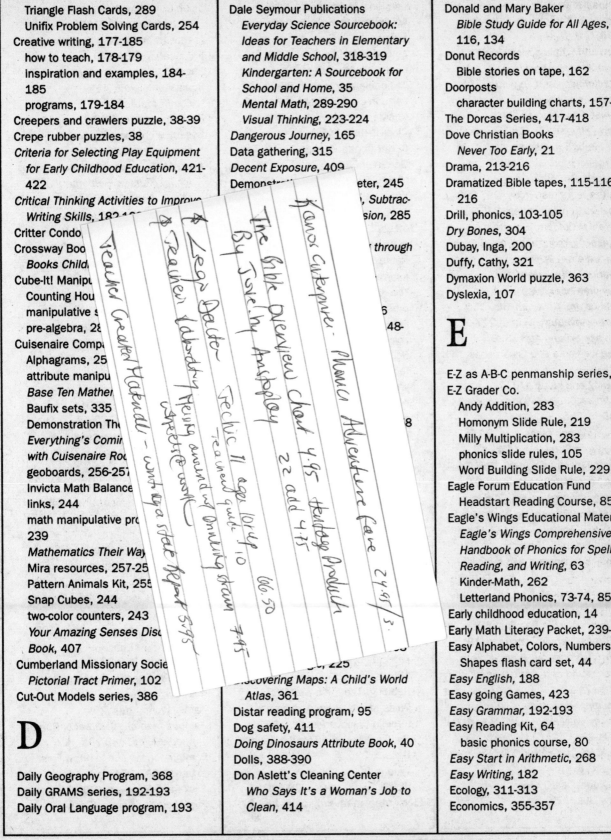